FAILURE. RUSSIA UNDER PUTIN

FAILURE.
RUSSIA UNDER PUTIN

EDITED BY
HARLEY D. BALZER
AND
STEVEN A. FISHER

"National prosperity is created, not inherited."
The Competitive Advantage of Nations
Michael Porter

Brookings Institution Press
Washington, D.C.

Published by Brookings Institution Press®
1775 Massachusetts Avenue, NW
Washington, DC 20036
www.brookings.edu/bipress

Co-published by Bloomsbury Academic
Bloomsbury Publishing Inc, 1385 Broadway, New York, NY 10018, USA
Bloomsbury Publishing Plc, 50 Bedford Square, London, WC1B 3DP, UK
Bloomsbury Publishing Ireland, 29 Earlsfort Terrace, Dublin 2, D02 AY28, Ireland
https://www.bloomsbury.com/us/

Copyright © 2025 by Brookings Institution Press®

Typeset in Janson Text
Composition by Circle Graphics
Printed and bound in the United States of America

All rights reserved. No part of this publication may be: i) reproduced or transmitted in any form, electronic or mechanical, including photocopying, recording or by means of any information storage or retrieval system without prior permission in writing from the publishers; or ii) used or reproduced in any way for the training, development or operation of artificial intelligence (AI) technologies, including generative AI technologies. The rights holders expressly reserve this publication from the text and data mining exception as per Article 4(3) of the Digital Single Market Directive (EU) 2019/790.

The Brookings Institution is a nonprofit organization devoted to research, education, and publication on important issues of domestic and foreign policy. Its principal purpose is to bring the highest quality independent research and analysis to bear on current and emerging policy problems. Brookings' publications represent the sole views of their author(s).

Library of Congress Control Number: 2025935427

ISBN: 978-0-8157-4082-7 (hbk. : alk. paper)
ISBN: 978-0-8157-4083-4 (pbk. : alk. paper)
ISBN: 978-0-8157-4084-1 (ebook)
ISBN: 978-0-8157-4107-7 (ePDF)

For product safety related questions contact productsafety@bloomsbury.com.

∞™ The paper used in this publication meets the minimum requirements of American National Standard for Information Sciences—Permanence of Paper for Printed Library Materials, ANSI/NISO Z39.48-1992.

Contents

Acknowledgments vii
In Memoriam, Alfred B. Evans Jr. ix

Introduction 1
HARLEY D. BALZER AND STEVEN A. FISHER

PART I
Economy

1 The Failure of Putinomics 23
SERGEI GURIEV

2 Foreign Direct Investment and International Capital:
Lost in a Russian Abyss 43
STEVEN A. FISHER

3 Russian Energy: From Leading Supplier to Purveyor
of Discounted Goods 79
AGNIA GRIGAS

4 Counterpoint: The Rationalization of Russian Agriculture 103
ALLAN MUSTARD

PART II
Society

5 Who Are We? Post-Soviet Russia's Identity-Building Failure 143
MARIA SNEGOVAYA

6 Protests in Civil Society in Russia 169
ALFRED B. EVANS JR.

7 Russian Human Capital: Decline or Demise? 193
HARLEY D. BALZER

8 Ethnic Diversity 277
GUZEL YUSUPOVA

9 How Putin's Sexism and LGBTQ-Phobia Endanger Russia's and the World's Future 299
JANET ELISE JOHNSON

PART III
Governance and Security

10 The Siloviki 327
BRIAN D. TAYLOR

11 "Dictatorship of Law" or Just Dictatorship? 353
IVAN PAVLOV

12 Russia's Military Failures in Ukraine: Causes and Consequences 377
ALEKSANDR GOLTS

13 How Putin Turned Foreign Policy Success into Strategic Defeat 405
PETER CLEMENT

Afterword 445
HARLEY D. BALZER AND STEVEN A. FISHER

Contributors 463

Index 469

Acknowledgments

This book is the result of collaboration among thirteen diverse, globally dispersed scholars, united in their effort to critically assess Russia's trajectory under twenty-five years of Vladimir Putin. As it is often said, books are not made by one hand or one mind; they are mosaics of talent and effort, crafted by many. It has been a most rewarding experience to produce this volume. The editors take pride in this achievement and are grateful for the outcome.

The contributors have benefited from constructive advice and input from colleagues, some of whom are acknowledged in the endnotes of individual chapters. While it may not be possible to mention everyone who provided valuable feedback, their contributions are deeply appreciated.

We are grateful to the team at Brookings Institution Press, which provided essential support during a period of transition. The manuscript was initially accepted while Brookings was partnering with Rowman & Littlefield for printing and distribution. Subsequently Rowman & Littlefield was acquired by Bloomsbury Publishing, necessitating adjustments during the production process.

We wish to thank our editor at Brookings, Yelba Quinn, who skillfully managed communications with editors and authors throughout this transition. Her professionalism and focus ensured that the review process and production proceeded smoothly. Katie Merris delivered superbly in the cover design process, offering a range of options and responding with a high-quality final product. Marjorie Pannell undertook the challenging task of copy editing a multi-author volume with diligence and expertise. The index was prepared with care by Ezra Freeman of Twin Oaks Indexing Collective.

The Brookings Institution deserves acknowledgment for its commitment to maintaining a publishing program that bridges academic analysis and practical policy applications. This volume aspires to serve both academic and policy-oriented audiences effectively, as well as a broader readership.

Finally, a big thank you to our families and friends for their constant support throughout the two years of our work.

Any royalties from the book will be donated to RAZOM for Ukraine.

Harley D. Balzer and Steven A. Fisher
Cabin John, Maryland, and Chicago
November 2024

In Memoriam, Alfred B. Evans Jr.

As this book was going to press, Alfred B. Evans Jr., or Al, as many of us knew him, passed away. He was much more than what it says in his bio. He was a lifelong scholar who brought deep knowledge and astute insight to the study of Russia both before and after the end of the Soviet Union. His curiosity continued to grow after he retired in 2007, as he went on traveling to Russia to do fieldwork and expanded the range of his scholarship by drawing comparisons with China. He also continued to inspire undergraduates to be interested in Russian politics as an emeritus instructor at his home institution, the University of California, Fresno.

Al was also a lifelong mentor, not just to us but to many others. He was always organizing panels on civil society at AAASS/ASEEES conventions and coediting books or special issues of journals with junior colleagues. Al was attentive to balancing gender and rank on panels and in publications long before it was considered a best practice. He was also open to and engaged with feminist analysis of Russia's politics, a relatively uncommon interest among male political scientists, especially of his generation.

Last but not least, Al represented a rare combination of personality traits in the academy. A keen and thoughtful intellect who unstintingly offered analytical insights that got to the root of any paper's argument, Al was also thoroughly unassuming, kind, and generous to the core. We have all witnessed and benefited from the collegiality and warmth he demonstrated toward contemporaries and junior colleagues alike, and have enjoyed the big-hearted friendship he offered in tandem with his unerring professionalism.

Laura Henry
Janet Elise Johnson
Valerie Sperling
Lisa McIntosh Sundstrom

Introduction

HARLEY D. BALZER AND STEVEN A. FISHER

Russia's trajectory in the twenty-first century has been defined largely by the leadership of one man: Vladimir Vladimirovich Putin. Since assuming the presidency at the beginning of 2000, Vladimir Putin has exerted a forceful influence over the political, social, and economic landscape of Russia. With his firm grip on power, he has promised stability, prosperity, and a return to greatness. He has sought to regain Russia's status as a global superpower. He has also bent his nation in a manner that is unsettling and unstable. It may take more time to render an ultimate judgment on Vladimir Putin and compile his final scorecard. His legacy's scale, however, tips decidedly toward failure, in terms of what he sought to achieve and his impact on Europe and the world.

This volume presents a critical analysis of Putin's rule through the lens of failures that have come to define his regime. The scholars and global practitioners contributing to the thirteen chapters herein navigate the complex landscape of contemporary Russia, defining and demarcating its detritus: an unresolved natural resource curse, a stagnant economy, rampant corruption, eviscerated foreign direct investment, a shrinking and aging population, ethnic and gender tensions, a resentment-driven national identity crisis, severe dependence on imported technology, and smothering domination by state-controlled monopolies. Putin's failure to implement structural reforms has aggravated economic inequality, concentrated Russia's wealth in the hands of an elite few, and snuffed out much of Russia's entrepreneurial spirit.

The contributors to this volume do not represent a single academic school or approach to the study of Russia. Their contributions cover a range of important topics and do not conform to a single orientation. Nevertheless, all are inclined to believe that Putin's leadership of Russia has been detrimental to the country's long-term development. Putin's failure is evident, though each author's precise characterization varies across distinct policy domains.

Putin has not failed at everything he has sought to accomplish. His "sovereign democracy" program has succeeded in de-institutionalizing Russia's government and replaced constitutional checks and balances with presidential rule constrained only by bureaucratic rivalries, inertia, and malfeasance. This story has been well documented by political analysts, including many who question whether it has resulted in effective policy.

The authors focus on failures in policy areas where Putin has decreed programs with specific goals. Most of these goals have been reiterated each of the five times he has delivered an inaugural address. Official documents now criticize lack of achievements in these realms as if someone else had been in charge since 2000. These failures are self-inflicted, not the work of unfriendly powers.

Organization of the Book

Part I begins with Russia's economy. The scope, however, extends far beyond economics. The authors analyze Putin's approach to governance, focusing on his curtailing of press freedom, dismantling of independent institutions, systematic crackdown on dissent, stifling of civil society, suppression of LGBTQ rights, dissipation of Soviet scientific achievements, and manipulation and falsification of historical narratives. The volume explores issues surrounding Russia's national identity, civil society, demographics and human capital, the moribund state of Russian science and technology, failures in diversity management, gender inequality, the perversion of law, and the power machinations of Chekists and the *siloviki*. The book concludes by examining Putin's foreign policy failures, especially Russia's bloody military invasion of Ukraine and its long-term consequences.

The timing and extent of the damage Putin leaves behind vary across the range of topics covered here. Many observers perceived promise in the economic reforms implemented during Putin's first term as president. There were also warning signs, beginning with the restoration of Cheka founder Felix Dzerzhinsky's bust in FSB Lubyanka headquarters. The destruction of Yukos, once Russia's largest private company, presaged a more state-controlled economy. Curtailing civil society was a classic case of Soviet-style "salami" tactics that reached its apex only with the Ukraine war.[1]

Policies in some realms initially embraced international collaboration and welcomed foreign advice and funding. Cooperation, including joint funding, developed in health care, education, science, and in a range of civil society efforts. Cooperative projects took place in the sphere of environmental protection, continued joint space projects, and much else. Putin's most significant failure may be his reversal of his own genuine accomplishments in a vainglorious effort to restore Russia's "greatness." The "normal country" that some scholars welcomed at the beginning of Putin's second presidential term no longer exists.

Success or failure is invariably assessed against a benchmark. One such criterion is Putin's stated ambition for Russia: to attain a status akin to that of major powers such as the United States, China, and the EU. In recent years, Russia has made no headway toward achieving this objective. Another gauge of Putin's effectiveness lies in his track record of implementing the priorities he sets during each presidential inauguration. The frequent recurrence of these proposals implies failure. Putin himself acknowledged that many of his decrees were not implemented.

In chapter 1, Sergei Guriev describes the failure of "Putinomics," debunking the myth of Putin's economic competence. Putin was lucky that oil prices rose almost continually from 1999 until the end of his second presidential term in May 2008. Nonetheless, Putin's political model stifled Russia's economic growth potential. Guriev explains how corruption, the centralization of political power, and increased state domination collectively undermined economic diversification, innovation, the development of small and medium-size enterprises, and the effective utilization of foreign direct investment (FDI) to catalyze domestic investment. Guriev posits that Putin's primary goal was neither economic success per se nor the political popularity it would provide but instead the centralization of political and economic power. Russia's disastrous war in Ukraine has created new, serious challenges, generating an even more uncertain future for the Russian economy. Guriev concludes that Putin now faces an unresolvable contradiction: economic reform is necessary to restore his social contract with the Russian people, but that would go against his preferred political economy model and the need for full wartime mobilization.

In chapter 2, Steven Fisher details how Russia squandered approximately $3 trillion in FDI and international capital since Putin assumed power. Numerous negative endogenous and exogenous factors, many self-inflicted, impeded Russia from leveraging this unparalleled opportunity to facilitate necessary economic structural changes and tackle its natural resources curse—an overreliance on oil and gas sector revenues. Drawing on twenty years of capital markets transactional data, Fisher sheds light on how entities aligned with Putin's power vertical have dominated both international and domestic fundraising endeavors, crowding out capital that could otherwise have been directed to other sectors of the economy.

Widespread rent-seeking, pervasive corruption, and weak rule of law made Russia relatively unattractive as an investment destination. Simultaneously, Russia experienced astounding capital flight. Severe sanctions imposed by the West following Russia's second invasion of Ukraine in 2022 severed access to global capital, leading to the departure of many prominent international corporations and the evisceration of inward FDI stock. Fisher concludes that rubles and yuan cannot supplant dollars and euros, and the prospects for future foreign investment in Russia remain bleak.

No analysis of Russia's economy is possible without looking at Russia's natural resources sector. In chapter 3, Agnia Grigas concludes that much of Vladimir Putin's ephemeral success domestically resulted from the hydrocarbon boom of the 2000s when the rise in oil prices, compared to the 1990s, fueled economic recovery. Grigas argues that despite the extended period of high oil prices, the Russian energy sector demonstrated multifold failure: Russia failed to leverage an oil price windfall to transform and diversify the economy. It lost dominance over Central Asian energy markets, failed to timely develop Asian markets to diversify away from Europe, missed the shale revolution, and failed to become a market leader in liquefied natural gas despite having been a leading gas exporter. Grigas concludes that Russia's energy sector is no longer an attractive destination for FDI, the "pivot to Asia" since 2022 is not replacing sales to Europe, and, overall, the Russian energy sector faces an increasingly challenging future.

While Russia's oil and gas industry failed to free itself from its own natural resources curse, the Russian agricultural sector achieved rather better results. In chapter 4, Allan Mustard analyzes why agriculture performed more successfully than other sectors of the Russian economy. Prior to 1917, Russia was in some years a major grain exporter and competitor to the United States. In the Soviet Union, collectivization, flawed science, and centralized control resulted in generally low agricultural productivity. During the Brezhnev era, the USSR needed to import massive amounts of wheat and corn.

Mustard finds that Russian agriculture during the Putin administration has not failed and likely will continue to be able to feed the nation. He cautions that much of the progress since 1991 has been based on imported technologies, and international sanctions threaten to cut Russian agriculture off from the foreign inputs it depends on for efficiency and productivity. Corruption impedes innovation, investment, and entrepreneurship in the agricultural sector. Climate change and labor shortages pose significant challenges. Mustard concludes that Russian agriculture will eventually stagnate and fall further behind the West.

Part II examines issues facing Russian society. In chapter 5, Maria Snegovaya addresses the question of national identity and suggests that one of the reasons for Russia's transformation failure is rooted in the struggle to create a cohesive post-Soviet identity substantively different from its Soviet predecessor. Can Russia's current (or future) leadership ever conceive of Russia having its rightful place as a great power without being an empire? Snegovaya explains how during Soviet times, the sense of being a citizen of a respected superpower that controlled other countries and competed directly with the United States compensated somewhat for the continuous state of humiliation and poverty ordinary Russians experienced.

Yeltsin-era attempts to find a "national idea" to substitute for Russia's historical imperialistic orientation were short-lived and unsuccessful. Snegovaya recounts how Vladimir Putin restored many Soviet symbols and tried to reconquer formerly Soviet territories, and why the Crimea annexation accelerated the process of resurrecting Soviet myths. Craving recognition as a community and a great power, many in Russian society focused more intensely on this mythologized past and on hunting down enemies who allowed the empire's collapse. Emphasis on a national "enemy" allowed Russian society to reexperience a sense of national unity and belonging while avoiding tough questions about the country's future and, in particular, the real reasons for the Ukraine war. Snegovaya concludes that no unified vision of a future direction exists and that the failure to develop alternative visions has led to societal susceptibility to the backward-looking narratives pushed by Vladimir Putin and his elites.

In chapter 6, Alfred Evans focuses on three trends in Russians' protest activity that reveal shifts in the relationship between the state and civil society since 2012. First, protest activity in Russia has decentralized; Moscow is no longer the main center of protests. Second, the types of demands presented by most protest movements have changed. Rather than calling for democratic principles and the protection of human rights, most protesters now voice indignation over disruptions to their everyday lives and call for remedies requiring specific and limited changes. Third, support for protests focused on problems at a practical level comes from wider circles in Russian society, including citizens who have not identified with the political opposition.

Evans states that while the opportunity structure for political opposition protests has been severely constrained, other forms of protest have not faced similar limitations. These trends have been affected by changes after Russia's invasion of Ukraine as Putin increasingly fears any open expression of discontent among the Russian population. Evans concludes that the dilemma the Russian state faces in dealing with narrowly focused protests has become more acute because of those changes, and repression only increases. Evans believes that from Vladimir Putin's point of view, it probably is good that Russia's political regime has become ever more authoritarian and dominating of society. However, he questions how this trend has brought Russia closer to Putin's goal of regaining great power status and believes that in many ways, it has detracted from progress toward that goal.

The magnitude of Russia's accumulating demographic and human capital problems clearly emerges in Harley Balzer's analysis in chapter 7. Balzer believes that Putin's failure to continue Yeltsin-era reforms suited to globalized education systems and increasingly internationalized production processes is one of the most important geostrategic phenomena of the twenty-first century. It has profound long-term consequences for the Russian economy and the balance of military power. Russia's population will be smaller, older, and less Slavic. Russia's diminished capacity in education and the sciences represents a tragic loss to the international scientific community. Within Russia, a shrinking and less well-educated population limits the potential for economic improvement. Russia's knowledge economy has declined because of inadequate yet wasteful funding, exacerbating problems stemming from bureaucratic tutelage by competing agencies, aging personnel who resist change, limited involvement of business in research and development, and declining ethical standards.

Balzer summarizes ways the war in Ukraine has intensified these already daunting challenges by disrupting educational institutions still recovering from COVID-19 and causing many leading specialists and hundreds of thousands of talented young people to exit Russia. Import substitution has failed in the crucial high-technology sectors. The heavily publicized partnership with China provides a massive influx of Chinese goods that threatens Russian manufacturers without generating visible scientific collaboration or technological innovation.

In chapter 8, Guzel Yusupova describes how Vladimir Putin transformed Russia from a multicultural federation to a nationalizing unitary state. Putin built his vertical of power, stripping the regions of their autonomy. He implemented changes in fiscal relations, merged regions, altered the titles of regional heads, and modified other aspects of federalism. These actions undermined the checks and balances necessary for a robust democracy by concentrating power in the executive branch (i.e., Putin himself), putting control of the judiciary in the Kremlin's hands, and simplifying the manipulation of elections. Yusupova argues that transforming nationalities policies resulted in failed multiculturalism.[2] Instead, the goal became the cultural homogenization of the population, using tools such as unifying educational curricula, diminishing regional components in education, and eliminating second official languages in ethnic republics. Perceived threats of Islamization, migration, and separatism helped legitimize the police state in Russia.

Problematic policies have included changes to the rules governing naturalization and citizenship, failed programs aimed at returning compatriots from abroad, and policies encouraging xenophobia in Russian media, police profiling, and overt racism in everyday life. The transformation of migration policies failed.

Yusupova concludes that Putin views diversity as a threat rather than a value. Instead of building on the rich experience and advantages won through some aspects of Soviet nationalities policy, as well as the federalization trends that flourished in the 1990s, diversity management under Putin's rule has led the country to become increasingly nationalistic. By emphasizing the core Slav ethnicity, Putin has created systemic incentives for xenophobia and racism.

Janet Elise Johnson in chapter 9 demonstrates that Putin's Russia has failed women and LGBTQ people. Russia's regression on women's rights can be traced back at least to the increased restrictions on abortion that began in 2011. This was followed by the repression of feminist groups and activists starting with Pussy Riot in 2012, and the partial decriminalization of domestic violence in 2017. Putin and socialist feminists might highlight as progress the 2006 "maternity capital" program offering financial incentives for more births. As Johnson points out, however, this program is marred by widespread fraud and is only a Band-Aid on the problems faced by poor mothers. Any progress on this issue is belied by increasing gendered violence inflicted in the North Caucasus and neighboring Ukraine that Putin's regime has either committed or condoned.

The conservative turn on women's rights in 2011–2012, followed by an ultraconservative conversion in the year before the 2022 invasion of Ukraine, has had more severe consequences for LGBTQ people. Their rights have been severely curtailed, including their right to life, as evidenced by the so-called "gay propaganda" ban in 2013 and an extension in 2022 authorizing judicial and extrajudicial violence, including "gay purges" in Chechnya. Other limitations include formal and informal constraints on LGBTQ marriages and parenting, and laws banning document changes, surgery, and hormone treatments for transgender people (2023). Johnson concludes that the regime is now unquestionably sexist, homophobic, and transphobic, and that these policies endanger Russia's (and the world's) future.

Part III examines governance and security issues.

In chapter 10, Brian Taylor asserts that one of Putin's shortcomings is reflected in his decision to rely on Chekists and *siloviki* (strongmen in positions of power) while pursuing his self-proclaimed objectives of rejuvenating the Russian state and elevating its status to that of a "respected great power." Taylor contends that a regime grounded in siloviki leadership engendered autocracy and adherence to Soviet-era ideologies. Putin's imperialistic conflict with Ukraine, the culmination of this trend, stands as the most profound and lamentable illustration of the repercussions following more than two decades of Putin's rule alongside his siloviki associates.

Taylor differentiates among approaches that treat the siloviki as a cohort of people with power ministry backgrounds, approaches that focus on the different power ministries as organizations, and approaches that treat the siloviki as a clan or clans competing with other clans. He takes issue with arguments that Putinism and the Chekists/siloviki had the singular goal of enriching themselves and that Putin followed a long-standing KGB plan to do this. He sees a fundamental incompatibility between turning Russia into a kleptocracy and another key Putin policy direction of pursuing a confrontational and aggressive foreign policy that challenges core Western interests and principles. Taylor outlines the role of the Chekists and siloviki in Putin's decision to invade Ukraine in 2022, and how the military and the security services contributed to Putin's disastrous decision. Scholars have demonstrated that personalist autocracies are more internationally belligerent than other regimes, a pattern that certainly applies to Vladimir Putin.

Ivan Pavlov in chapter 11 relates how the abuse of the criminal justice system for political and economic goals is a dominant feature of the failure of the Russian legal system under Putin. The author traces significant milestones in the evolution of manipulating national security concerns to achieve legal counterreforms. The Soviet roots of the abuse of the justice system, including the Soviet doctrine of law as an instrument of political control, presaged post-Soviet abuse of the justice system. The disappearance of Soviet ideology resulted in the expanded use of political tools as instruments of ordinary criminality. More recently, Putin has manipulated the system during wartime by rapidly enacting new laws against criticism of the military or the war effort, along with initiating new political persecutions. Pavlov concludes that criminal justice always reflects the broader political system. Criminal justice under Putin is a failure for the same reasons that other aspects of the Putin system are failures: weak institutionalization, the lack of independence, and manipulation by elites for their own interests. Putin sees these measures as essential for maintaining order and control.

Chapter 12 addresses Russia's failed military reforms. Aleksandr Golts explains how Russia's war in Ukraine developed naturally out of the domestic and foreign policies in Putin's militaristic state. Golts argues that Russia's initial failures in Ukraine are grounded in the way the Russian army changed after the collapse of the Soviet Union. The Russian armed forces were assigned tasks they could not fulfill. Golts describes how the inherent contradictions of Vladimir Putin's regime thwarted two decades of incomplete military reforms undertaken by Defense Ministers Anatoly Serdyukov and Sergei Shoigu. The weaknesses in Russia's armed forces have forced the Kremlin to abandon modernization of the military and to rely instead on the older concept of mass mobilization. Mass mobilization in the context of the archaic structure of the Russian state will fail because of Russia's worsening demographic and economic situation. Golts concludes that any drastic attempt at military rebuilding will only result in chaos and that Russia's inability to win its war in Ukraine will sooner or later create a crisis in Russia.

The final chapter addresses Russian foreign policy. Peter Clement assesses Putin's foreign policy using the core criterion for evaluation: does it advance or diminish the state's national security? Clement employs a classic chronological approach, reviewing key Putin statements, decisions, and events. Putin achieved some success in restoring Russia's role as a major international actor up to Russia's February 2022 invasion of Ukraine, and has failed disastrously since. Prior to 2022, Putin had been a prudent risk-taker in three prior foreign interventions: in Georgia in 2008, in Crimea and eastern Ukraine in 2014, and in Syria in 2015. In Georgia and Crimea, Russian forces overpowered a surprised and overmatched adversary; in Syria, Russia provided matériel plus air and naval support while Iran and Hezbollah did the heavy lifting on the ground.

The question that must be examined in rendering judgment on Putin's foreign policy performance is why Putin eschewed the pragmatism that earlier brought success in favor of a high-risk, full-scale invasion of Ukraine. The strategic consequences of Putin's second attack on Ukraine extend well beyond current-day battlefield losses—Putin's miscalculation has significantly diminished Russia's national security. Some have argued that Putin invaded Ukraine to halt NATO enlargement, yet ironically, Putin's war not only has strengthened NATO cohesiveness but has pushed Finland and Sweden into NATO's arms and made future Ukrainian membership plausible. Putin's war in Ukraine and his oft-articulated divorce from the West have tightened Putin's embrace of Xi Jinping. Yet expanded political and trade ties have clearly rendered Moscow the junior partner in the relationship, securing it a position as China's vassal. Clement concludes that Putin's fierce desire to secure his place in Russian history will be realized, but not in ways he imagined.

Briefly Noted

The topics covered in this book focus on economics, Russian society, governance, and international affairs. Striving to be comprehensive is laudable but unachievable, and the recent lack of updated statistics from

Russian governmental authorities, including Rosstat, makes analysis of certain topics more challenging. While we have sought to address as many important subjects as possible, some significant areas must be left to others. Domestic politics has been studied in depth by many scholars, and it is a dubious exercise to attempt to add to the existing literature when access to the country is severely limited. The literature on Putin himself is vast, but few recent studies have emphasized his failures. Culture has been covered well by others and deserves far more than a single chapter.[3]

Religious freedom, social and economic dislocation among Russian youth, regional disparities and income inequality, and a precarious environmental outlook also are topics that are not addressed in dedicated chapters. However, we summarize some key issues below.

Religion

In the context of Vladimir Putin's war actions and his perceived failures, religion has played a complex and multifaceted role in shaping public opinion, propaganda, and national identity in Russia. A poll by the independent Levada Center in 2020 found that 63 percent of the Russian population identified as Orthodox Christian, 7 percent as Muslim, and 26 percent reported having no religious preference. (However, according to Mufti Ravil Gaynutdin, chairman of the Religious Board of Muslims of the Russian Federation, in 2018 there were 25 million Muslims in the Russian Federation, or approximately 18 percent of the population.) The USCIRF (United States Commission on International Religious Freedom) *2023 Annual Report* identifies other religious groups, each representing roughly 1 percent or less of the Russian populace. These small-numbered groups include Russian Orthodox sects, Buddhists, adherents of traditional indigenous religions, Protestants, Roman Catholics, Jews, adherents of the Church of Jesus Christ of Latter-day Saints, Jehovah's Witnesses, Hindus, Baháʼís, members of the International Society for Krishna Consciousness, Tengrists, followers of the Church of Scientology, and practitioners of Falun Gong.

The Russian Orthodox Church enjoys a privileged but complicated status, as Johnson notes in chapter 9. Church leadership has welded itself to Putin's political agenda to the degree that the Church publicly supports Russia's war in Ukraine, blessing Russian military weaponry and declaring that war is tragic but inevitable. Putin's government has increasingly emphasized the role of religion, particularly Russian Orthodox Christianity, in shaping national identity to counter perceived Western influences and strengthen Russian cultural and social cohesion. State authorities utilize narratives rooted in a perceived fight between "traditionalism" and foreign influence.[4] The state in return provides the Church financial support and grants legal privileges.

Religious freedom is increasingly under attack in Russia. The war in Ukraine has exacerbated religious tensions. Russian state propaganda justifies the war and frequently resorts to rhetoric demonizing Jews, distorting the Holocaust, denigrating "nontraditional" religious groups, and characterizing Russia's war in Ukraine as justified based on religion.[5] Incidents of antisemitism have notably increased. Foreign Minister Sergei Lavrov's May 1, 2022, antisemitic remarks on the Italian TV program *Zona Bianca* provoked a wave of international indignation when he bizarrely tried to justify Russia's portrayal of Ukraine as a "Nazi" state. The chief rabbi of Moscow, Pinchas Goldschmidt, fled Russia in July 2022 after refusing to support the war. He later warned that Jews should leave Russia while they still can, before they are made scapegoats for the hardship caused by the war. A growing number of religious groups, such as Jehovah's Witnesses and Evangelicals, have been labeled extremist organizations and face legal restrictions.

The U.S. Department of State Office of International Religious Freedom in its report for 2021 describes how recent Russian laws and regulations impose various constraints on the free expression of religion.[6] These constraints include requirements that religious organizations conform to specific counterterrorism measures, limitations on places where prayer and public religious observance may be conducted without prior approval, and onerous ongoing reporting requirements on financial and economic activity, funding sources, and compliance with antiterrorist and anti-extremist legislation. Pavlov in chapter 11 explains how multiple recently enacted laws and regulations specifically facilitate implementation of these constraints.

Russian missile and drone attacks have damaged a growing number of Ukrainian places of worship. Russia's 2014 aggression against Ukraine had already spurred the split of the Ukrainian Orthodox Church from the Moscow Patriarchate. On January 5, 2019, Bartholomew I, the Ecumenical Patriarch of Constantinople, signed an official decree (*tomos*) granting autocephaly and officially establishing the Orthodox Church of Ukraine. Russia-installed authorities in Crimea and in Donbas have enforced repressive Russian laws that severely curtail religious freedom and target religious minorities. Crimean Tatars, one of the "punished peoples" who were deported from their homeland during World War II, oppose the Russian occupation of Crimea, and many have been imprisoned.

Russia's demography, as Balzer explains in chapter 7, points to an increase in the share of Islamic and other non-Slavic populations in Russia in the coming decades. This will change the dynamics of religion and politics in Russia, as will the outcome of the war. What impact will changes to Russia's religious landscape have on the Russian Federation? What will be the impact of a growing share of draft-age males coming from predominantly Muslim regions?

Russia's Youth

Youth in Putin's Russia face challenges that some argue exceed those caused by the economic and social dislocations of the 1990s. The growing specter of state fascist-leaning political indoctrination, particularly since the invasion of Ukraine, has subverted prospects for productive social and civic participation. Personnel shortages now mean that food delivery workers earn more than doctors. Balzer in chapter 7 illustrates how Russia's educational system does not adequately prepare young people for the demands of the modern job market and global economy but does require that even young children learn to assemble assault rifles. Access to quality education increasingly bifurcates between urban and rural areas, while special quotas favor veterans, magnifying inequality.

Higher military conscription rates in poorer rural and non-Russian regions provide a telling example. Restrictions on freedom of expression and a tightly controlled political environment have discouraged political activism among Russia's youth but increasingly require demonstrations of patriotic fervor. Maria Snegovaya in chapter 5 highlights ways the Russian blogosphere and social media channels reflect increasing proto-fascist trends and zealous patriotism. Vladimir Putin's war agenda enthusiastically immerses Russia's youth in state-encouraged "Z" movements to the degree that young children must endure political and military indoctrination in public schools and participate in child soldier parades on the streets.

As the regime insists on traditional gender roles and conservative values, young Russians debate these issues at least as much as previously, particularly in matters of career choices, relationships, and family expectations. Long-unresolved problems such as substance abuse, including alcohol and drug addiction, and HIV/AIDS reduce productivity and aggravate existing social challenges. The number of homeless children in Russia, rarely mentioned in the political or public agenda, is estimated to be between three and four million.[7] Hundreds of thousands of talented and ambitious young Russians have sought opportunities abroad because of the war, a tumultuous domestic job market, and the other problems described above. Today young (and not so young) Russians face the prospect of military mobilization and death in Ukraine. Chapter 7 provides analysis of the resulting brain drain.

How do Russian youth view Russia today and their place in the world? How will youth navigate the future Putin promises even as they face today's harsher realities? And, as the brain drain continues, how will the Russian economy and Russia's federal budget cope with a worsening dependency ratio (the ratio of children, disabled, and pension-aged Russians to the employed population)?

Regional Disparities and Income Inequality

According to the IMF, regional disparities have fallen over the past two decades in Russia but remain relatively high.[8] The World Bank in 2018 estimated Russia's richest region to be seventeen times richer than its poorest one, and assigned blame to the Soviet legacy and Russia's unique geography of a large, sparsely populated country with pockets of abundant natural resources.[9] Another crucial factor was legislation making the main office of a corporation the basis for where it pays taxes, rather than where it conducts its main business activities. This law took large sums away from regions where natural resources are extracted. Even Nigeria pays the oil-producing regions something extra for the environmental costs of resource extraction.

Russia's regional income disparities are greater than in most other countries. A small percentage of the population controls a significant portion of Russia's wealth. This not only amplifies income inequality but also limits opportunities for social mobility. Economic stagnation, military conscription, and demographic decline intensify these problems. Access to resources, including quality education, health care, and public services, has become increasingly unbalanced.

Although Russia's richer regions, including big cities such as Moscow and St. Petersburg as well as oil-rich regions, were hit harder by the twin shocks of COVID-19 and lower oil prices, income inequality between major cities and rural areas, as well as across different regions in Russia, has worsened in recent years. Underdeveloped regions, including Soviet legacy "monotowns," face limited job prospects, inadequate infrastructure, and reduced access to essential services. Increased defense industry spending may temporarily ameliorate this morass but will make the problem worse when the war ends and the funding stops. Socioeconomic disparities limit opportunities for disadvantaged individuals and communities and are closely linked to poverty rates and social exclusion. Vulnerable groups, such as single-parent families, the elderly, and disabled individuals, are disproportionately affected by poverty and have limited access to resources and opportunities.

Endemic corruption and cronyism allow the privileged and empowered to exploit their positions for personal gain, perpetuating wealth concentration and reducing opportunities for others. Wage gaps, including a large gender pay gap of 23.7 percent, exist across different sectors and industries.[10] The presence of a significant informal economy, moreover, can limit the earning potential and social protection of workers since under-the-table pay or self-employment in unregulated sectors often (but not always) provides lower wages and fewer benefits. The social safety net in Russia, while providing some support, is often insufficient to sustainably address the needs of those facing income inequality and poverty. Gaps in social assistance programs can perpetuate social exclusion and hinder upward mobility. In recent years, the Russian government has failed to implement comprehensive policy measures, such as progressive taxation, investment in quality education and skills development, promotion of equal access to opportunities, improvement in social safety nets, and a reduction in corruption. The war in Ukraine has led to a rise in military and security spending in Russia's federal budget, reducing funds available for social and economic infrastructure, regional development, and programs that could promote inclusive growth. No immediate reversal of this trend is expected.

Environment

Like nearly all communist regimes, the Soviet Union created multiple environmental disasters.[11] Russia inherited some of the planet's most daunting environmental challenges, now exacerbated by climate change. Vladimir Putin remains in denial. Russia's government is unfocused, unprepared, and unfunded to cope.[12] Necessary robust policies, investments in sustainable infrastructure, improved waste management, strengthened environmental regulations, and international cooperation are lacking. Russia's Arctic regions are warming two and a half times faster than the rest of the globe.[13] Air and water pollution from industrial activities, including mining, manufacturing, and energy production, have deleterious effects in Russia and beyond. Approximately 60 percent of Russia's energy is derived from fossil fuels.[14] Aging power plants lack modern pollution control equipment. Approximately 56 million Russians in 143 cities breathe bad air, according to the Russian state weather and environment service.[15] Excessive and wasteful logging (up to 40 percent of harvested trees are lost owing to inefficiency) has caused widespread deforestation and poses a threat to Russia's vast forests, leading to habitat loss, reduced biodiversity, and increased carbon emissions.[16]

Insufficient recycling infrastructure, improper disposal practices, and illegal dumping contribute to environmental degradation. Water scarcity, inadequate water treatment facilities, and pollution from industrial and agricultural sources threaten future supply. About one-quarter of Russians have no access to clean water.[17] The extraction and transportation of oil and gas in Russia's vast territories pose risks of oil spills, which have had devastating consequences for ecosystems and marine life. Russia has a significant nuclear legacy, including aging nuclear power plants, radioactive waste storage sites, and the environmental impact of past nuclear accidents. Safe disposal and management of radioactive materials remain ongoing concerns. Climate change will make fixing these problems more challenging.

Russia received a low score of 46.5 (on a scale where 100 is the highest score) on the Global Environmental Performance Index, or EPI, in 2024.[18] By comparison, Estonia secured the highest spot, with a score of 75.3; the United States was at 57.3, China at 35.5, and Vietnam at the bottom, with a score of 24.5.

Russia is committing environmental crimes in Ukraine. It has destroyed industrial facilities, causing heavy air, water, and soil pollution and exposure to toxic chemicals and contaminated water. The horrific possibility of Russian sabotage of the occupied Ukrainian Zaporizhzhia Nuclear Power Plant, the largest such plant in Europe, remains a concern. Russia destroyed Ukraine's Kakhovka Dam, causing massive environmental damage. Russia has made Ukraine the most heavily mined country in the world.

State oppression of religious freedom, social and economic dislocation among Russian youth, worsening regional disparities and income inequality across a diverse and expansive nation, and a precarious environmental outlook all contribute to the myriad challenges confronting Russia.

The chapters that follow shed light on the defining failures of Vladimir Putin's regime, presenting a nuanced analysis of the economic stagnation, corruption, democratic erosion, geopolitical confrontations, and societal transformations and traumas during his tenure. By exploring these themes, the contributors seek to foster a deeper understanding of contemporary Russia and its future trajectory.

No single narrative can encapsulate the complexities of a nation as diverse and multifaceted as Russia. This book thus aims to contribute to an ongoing discourse by encouraging readers to question, reflect, and engage in a thoughtful exploration of the mostly ephemeral successes and overwhelmingly self-inflicted failures that have shaped Russia under Vladimir Putin's leadership.

* * *

Preparing a work of this sort faced challenges from fast-moving events in Russia and Eastern Europe, especially developments in Russia's war in Ukraine. The contributors brought their analyses forward to the degree possible before the manuscript was submitted to the press. Inevitably, the complexion of several issues has changed to a lesser or greater degree since then: Russia's crackdown on human rights has hardened and expanded, the country's economic trajectory has altered, and Russia has increased its support from a small bloc of nations, despite some reluctance. As it is difficult to stay current in a large printed volume, we encourage readers to follow the individual authors, who frequently publish both in academic journals and in popular media, for their insights into further developments in Russia.

NOTES

1. The term "salami tactics" was coined by Hungarian Communist leader Mátyás Rákosi, who described the process as slicing away opposition as one would slice salami.

2. The "Soviet transforming nationalities policy," also known as the Soviet nationalities policy, was a complex and multifaceted approach to manage the diverse ethnic and national groups within the Soviet Union's borders. The goal was to create a unified Soviet identity while simultaneously addressing and managing the distinct ethnic identities of various groups.

3. For a model of how culture may be covered even in the midst of war, see Ruble (2023).

4. Oliker (2018).
5. USCIRF (2023).
6. U.S. Department of State (2022).
7. Khvostunova (2012); Agronina et al. (2020).
8. Dynnikova, Kyobe, and Slavov (2021).
9. World Bank (2018).
10. Data for 2021 are from Statista.com (https://Notes.statista.com/statistics/1261581/gender-pay-gap-russia/).
11. Feshbach and Friendly (1992); Feshbach (1995).
12. For an excellent analysis of Russia's environmental challenges, see Gustafson (2021).
13. Vladimir Kattsov, a climate expert at the Voeikov Main Geophysical Observatory, quoted in *Novye izvestiia*. Browne (2022).
14. BP (2021); EIA (2024).
15. *Moscow Times* (2019).
16. Curtis (1998); Yorke (2020).
17. Macrotrends, "Russian Clean Water Access 1960-2024" (Macrotrends .net), last accessed November 1, 2024.
18. The Global Environmental Performance Index (EPI) is compiled by the Yale Center for Environmental Law and Policy (YCELP) and the Columbia University Center for International Earth Science Informational Network (CIESIN). The 2024 EPI combines fifty-eight indicators across eleven issue categories, ranging from climate change mitigation and air pollution to waste management, sustainability of fisheries and agriculture, deforestation, and biodiversity protection. The top five performance criteria in the index are health impacts, water resources, climate change impacts, habitat diversity, and ecosystem vitality. For details, see the website at https://epi.yale.edu/measure/2024/EPI (last accessed June 29, 2024).

REFERENCES

Agronina, N. I., T. B. Belozerova, S. A. Gorbatenko, N. P. Krasnova, I. N. Medvedev, and A. P. Savchenko. 2020. "Homelessness and Neglect of Children in Modern Russia: Literature Based Analysis." *Bioscience Biotechnology Research Communications* 13 (2): 475–81.

BP. 2021. "Statistical Review of World Energy—2021: Russia's Energy Market in 2020." BP.com.

Browne, Ed. 2022. "Russia's Climate Is Heating Up Faster Than the Rest of the World." *Newsweek*, October 11.

Curtis, Glenn E., ed. 1998. *Russia: A Country Study*. Washington, DC: Library of Congress, Federal Research Division.

Dynnikova, Oksana, Annette J. Kyobe, and Slavi T. Slavov. 2021. "Regional Disparities and Fiscal Federalism in Russia." IMF Working Paper, May 20.

EIA (U.S. Energy Information Administration). 2024. *Country Analysis Brief: Russia*. Washington, DC, April 29.

Feshbach, Murray. 1995. *Ecological Disaster: Cleaning Up the Hidden Legacy of the Soviet Regime*. New York: Twentieth Century Fund Press.

Feshbach, Murray, and Alfred Friendly Jr. 1992. *Ecocide in the USSR: Health and Nature Under Siege*. New York: Basic Books.

Gustafson, Thane. 2021. *Klimat: Russia in the Age of Climate Change*. Cambridge, MA: Harvard University Press.

Khvostunova, Olga. 2012. "Russia's Invisible Children." New York: Institute of Modern Russia, May 31.

Moscow Times. 2019. "56M Russians Breathe Polluted Air—Weather Service." November 8.

Oliker, Olga, ed. 2018. "Religion and Violence in Russia." Washington, DC: Center for Strategic and International Studies, June.

Ruble, Blair A. 2023. *The Arts of War: Ukrainian Artists Confront Russia, Year One*. Stuttgart: ibidem-Verlag.

U.S. Department of State. 2022. *2021 Report on International Religious Freedom*. Washington, DC: Office of International Religious Freedom, June 2.

USCIRF (U.S. Commission on International Religious Freedom). 2023. *2023 Annual Report*. Washington, DC.

World Bank Group. 2018. *Rolling Back Russia's Spatial Disparities: Re-assembling the Soviet Jigsaw under a Market Economy*. Washington, DC, May.

Yorke, Oliver. 2020. "Deforestation in Russia: Depleting the Lungs of the World." Earth.Org, November 19.

PART I

Economy

ONE

The Failure of Putinomics

SERGEI GURIEV

What is Putinomics? Does Vladimir Putin have—or has he ever had—a consistent set of views on economic policy? How should we evaluate the success of his economic policies, and how would he himself determine it? The answers to these questions lie in Putinomics' unbalanced scorecard and inevitably lead us to the reasoning behind Putin's fateful decisions to invade Ukraine in 2014 and in 2022.

Unbalanced Scorecard

Early Successes

International Monetary Fund (IMF) data portray Russia's economic performance under Putin in terms of a most important economic metric, gross domestic product (GDP) per capita. Putin came to power at a very low point in Russia's economic development. When Boris Yeltsin appointed Putin prime minister and thus his heir apparent in August 1999, the Russian

FIGURE 1.1. Russia's and China's GDP Per Capita as a Share of U.S. GDP Per Capita, 1990–2024

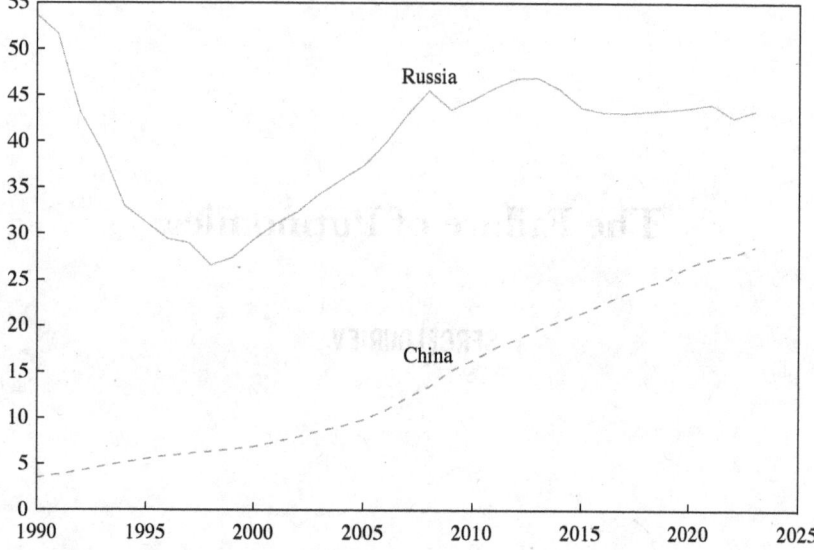

Source: IMF (2024).

economy was still suffering from the aftermath of the 1998 financial crisis. However, drastic ruble devaluation had already provided an impetus for economic recovery that coincided with Putin's arrival on the scene. The Russian public associated the subsequent fast economic growth with the younger, more energetic leader taking the helm.

Russia's economic growth during Putin's early years was spectacular, especially relative to the decline of the 1990s. In 1990 the Russian Federation's GDP per capita adjusted for purchasing power was 53 percent of the U.S. level (figure 1.1). By 1999 this ratio had declined to 26 percent, its lowest point in Russia's post-Soviet history. By 2008 it had increased to 45 percent. In absolute terms, economic growth was even more impressive: in 1999 Russian GDP per capita was less than $1,400, but by 2008 it had increased ninefold, reaching $12,500. When adjusted for the change in purchasing power, it was still an amazing increase: from $13,000 to $25,000, a virtual doubling in just nine years.[1]

Putin's first decade in power, 1999–2008, was one of the most successful periods in Russian economic history. Even Stalin's rapid industrialization in the 1930s, despite its enormous human cost, produced lower average annual GDP growth.[2] Only the period of the New Economic Policy (NEP) of 1921–1928 delivered faster growth: Soviet GDP per capita tripled in just seven years.[3] This result was partly due to a low base effect: in 1921, Russia was coming off a bloody civil war, but nevertheless, the sensible NEP warranted credit. The NEP success, however, proved short-lived: in order to cement his political control, Stalin renationalized much of the economy, introduced full central planning, and brutally collectivized agriculture, which led to catastrophic famines throughout the Soviet Union, including the Holodomor famine in Ukraine and the Asharshylyk famine in Kazakhstan.

The fast economic growth that Russia achieved in Putin's first decade of power benefited from several factors: a rapid increase in global oil prices, the effect of a low 1998 base, and the impact of pro-market reforms implemented in the 1990s and early 2000s. Guriev and Tsyvinski explore these factors and show that the growth in oil prices accounted for about half of Russia's economic growth during 1999–2008.[4] Putin started his tenure at the lowest point of post-Soviet Russia's economic history, and this fact helped: oil prices were very low, unemployment and poverty rates were high, Russian labor and the ruble were cheap, and spare productive capacity was abundant. Russian and foreign entrepreneurs saw opportunity but needed a supportive and stable business and investment climate.

Putin grasped the need for immediate economic reforms. After being appointed Russia's prime minister, he commissioned his colleague from St. Petersburg, Herman Gref, then vice-governor of Saint Petersburg, to prepare a pro-market reform program. Gref proposed a ten-year program that included a major tax reform, land reform, deregulation, the introduction of deposit insurance, reform of federalism and central government, pension reform, reform of energy markets, and many other reforms. In his first three years in office, Putin enacted many major proposals of Gref's program. But, as the program's own authors admitted ten years later, only a third of Gref's proposed reforms were actually implemented,[5] although the reforms that were implemented contributed substantially to Russian economic growth. Land reform, for example, enabled private ownership of land and boosted investment and productivity in Russian agriculture (see chapter 4). Tax reform, which entailed lowering and simplifying household and corporate taxes, and deregulation improved entrepreneurial incentives and encouraged many businesses to come out of the shadows. Deposit insurance created a level playing field between state-owned and private banks. Previously, only the state-owned banks benefited from a de facto deposit guarantee; the reform extended deposit insurance to private banks, hence strengthening competition and innovation in the financial system. This move eventually created consumer lending and mortgage markets in Russia. If in 2000, total household debt accounted for 1 percent of GDP, by 2008 it had exceeded 10 percent—similar to today's levels in Turkey or Uruguay.[6]

Macroeconomic stabilization also helped the investment climate. Several years of robust global oil prices enabled Russia to repay almost all of its sovereign debt and to begin setting aside financial reserves to cushion against possible future economic shocks. Russia obtained an investment-grade sovereign rating for the first time in 2005, which helped bring down borrowing costs and further encouraged an influx of foreign investments.[7] The Russian stock market capitalization soared. By 2008 the dollar-denominated RTS stock price index had increased by twenty times relative to its level in August 1999.[8]

The striking economic success of Putin's first decade in power brought substantial political benefits as well. Treisman shows that the correlation between Russian economic performance and presidential popularity is very strong.[9] Putin's approval rating was much higher than Yeltsin's and remained high throughout these years (figure 1.2).

Putin's primary goal, however, was neither economic success per se nor the political popularity it would provide. He instead aimed to centralize political and economic power. Putin proceeded methodically and quickly. In 2001, he cracked down on independent media by instructing the state (via Gazprom) to take over the main independent TV channel, NTV.[10] This helped reduce political transparency and competition.

Putin also understood that state monopolies were economic instruments for political power. In 2002 he reversed his views on the reform of Gazprom, the state natural gas monopoly, although he initially had acceded to the reformers around him and allowed some pro-competitive reforms. The next year Putin imprisoned Mikhail Khodorkovsky, his main critic among Russia's oligarchs, and directed the state oil company, Rosneft, to take over Khodorkovsky's company, Yukos. Rosneft then became Russia's largest oil company.

Putin also undid Russian federalism by canceling gubernatorial elections in 2004. In 2007, he shelved all plans for large-scale privatization. Instead, he created a special legal structure, the "state corporation"

FIGURE 1.2. Putin's Approval Rating, August 1999–June 2024 (Percent)

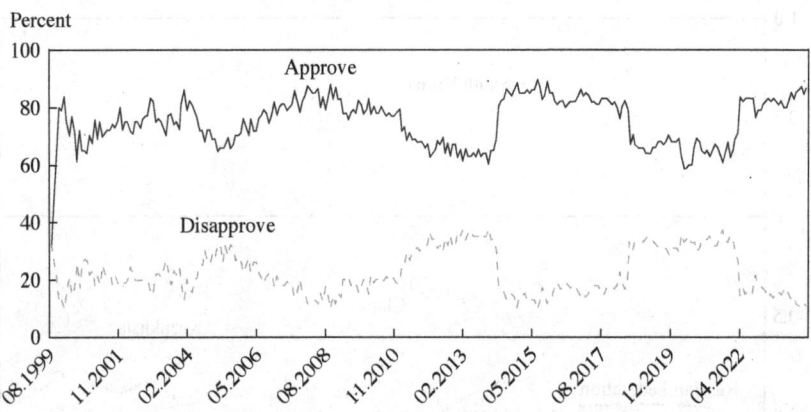

Source: Levada Center, "Putin's Approval Rating" (https://www.levada.ru/en/ratings/).

Note: The jumps in Putin's approval rating correspond to the Orange Revolution in Ukraine and the reform of social benefits (late 2004–early 2005), the annexation of Crimea (early 2014), pension reform (summer 2018), and the incompetent handling of the COVID-19 pandemic (spring–summer 2020).

(*goskorporatsiia*), an opaque organizational entity acting on behalf of the state. Several newly established state corporations (such as Rostec, VEB, Fond ZhKKh, Olimpstroi, and Rosatom) secured major ownership positions in the industrial, finance, real estate, and construction sectors of the economy.

Putin reversed anticorruption policies that were in effect during his first years in office. The increasing curtailment of public oversight emboldened huge economic rent-taking and endemic graft. Putin and his cronies particularly benefited as state domination of the economy grew. Many journalistic investigations have revealed that from his very first day in office, Putin started to amass financial assets for himself and his friends, who may have acted as his proxies.[11] As a result, Russia is now as corrupt as it was when Putin arrived in power, and much more corrupt than China or Kazakhstan, according to the World Bank's Control of Corruption Index (figure 1.3).

The aforementioned negative developments, however, did not immediately inhibit economic growth. Up until the 2007–2008 global financial crisis, the Russian public enjoyed unprecedented income growth and, in return, expressed strong support for Putin. Essentially, throughout this period each side stuck to its part of an implicit social contract the Putin

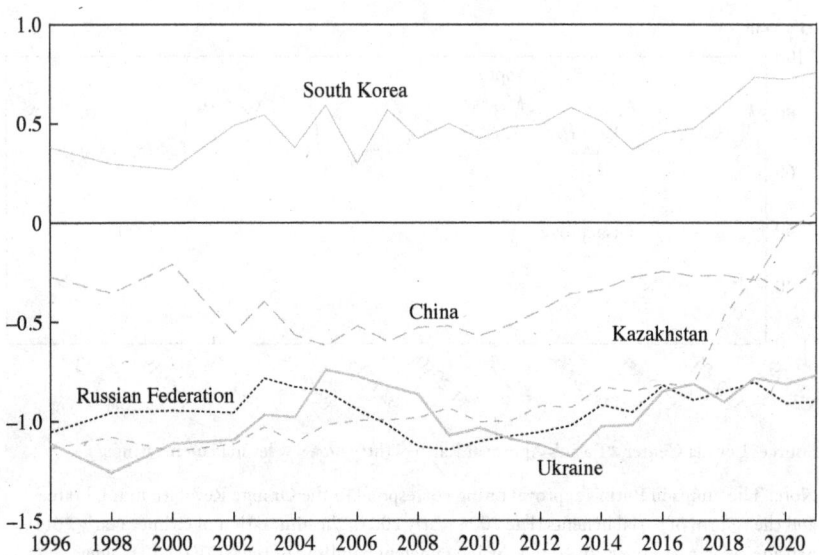

FIGURE 1.3. **Control of Corruption Index**

Source: Worldwide Governance Indicators, World Bank.[12]

regime embodied. Putin provided prosperity, and the Russian public (and the oligarch class) did not interfere in the way Putin ran the economy and politics.

Challenges and Failures

Like the NEP, Putin's early growth model proved short-lived. The global financial crisis hit Russia particularly hard. Russia's GDP declined a stunning 8 percent in 2009—the largest fall among the G20 countries. Afterward, Russia embarked on a recovery trajectory, but its GDP growth rate significantly lagged behind that of Putin's first decade in power. By 2021, Russian GDP was only 10 percent above its 2008 level. Russia began to fall further behind the West. Russia's GDP per capita in purchasing power terms remained below 45 percent of the U.S. level. Meanwhile, for an average emerging and developing country, this gap reduced substantially, going from 14 percent of the U.S. level in 2008 to 18 percent in 2021. China narrowed its gap even more dramatically, with the ratio of China to U.S. GDP per capita increasing from 13 percent to 27 percent (see figure 1.1).

The global financial crisis sounded an important wake-up call for Putinomics. It brought about a substantial decline in oil prices; for the first time since Putin ascended to power, Russia suffered a major recession. The Russian government made several policy mistakes which aggravated the impact of the crisis. First, the Russian Central Bank's gradual ruble devaluation policy only convinced the global markets to further bet on the unsustainability of the ruble exchange rate. This cost the Russian economy its liquidity as buying dollars became a highly profitable short-term alternative to lending to Russian firms in rubles. Second, unlike other G20 countries, fiscal support for the economy came too late as the Russian government produced its first anticrisis plan only in June 2009.

On the other hand, the Russian government effected other steps that actually reinforced Putin's hold on power. Putin benefited from the precrisis conservative fiscal policy of his finance minister, Alexei Kudrin. Kudrin had directed the accumulation of oil and gas revenues obtained during the previous prosperous years to create two sovereign wealth funds, the Reserve Fund and the National Welfare Fund. These two funds amounted to approximately 20 percent of Russia's GDP in 2008, and Kudrin allocated money from these funds to cushion the impact of the financial crisis on Russian households. Second, Russian state banks distributed billions of dollars to bail out overleveraged private businesses hurt by the crisis. The ability of the state to support faltering private firms reinforced Putin's conviction that it was the state, not the private sector, that should occupy the economy's driver's seat. Third, the global financial crisis distracted the West, and Putin took advantage of this. Russia launched its 2008 war with Georgia, saw to and then recognized the breakaway of two Georgian provinces—and suffered no sanctions. This outcome likely contributed to Putin's sense of impunity in the realm of foreign policy adventures.

Russia's "short, victorious war" against Georgia further increased Putin's approval ratings (see figure 1.2). He likely believed that the worst was behind him, but this was not exactly true. As global oil prices rebounded, the Russian economy started to recover. However, Putin's preferred political-economic model of expanding state and crony capitalism had already begun to take its toll on the Russian economy. In 2010–2012, Russian GDP returned to its precrisis level, but thereafter Russia's economic recovery ran out of steam. In 2013 the Russian economy grew by less than 2 percent compared to an average annual growth rate of between 6 percent and 8 percent in the several years before 2008–2009 (figure 1.4).

FIGURE 1.4. Putin's Slowdown: Real Disposable Household Income and Real GDP, 2007–2021

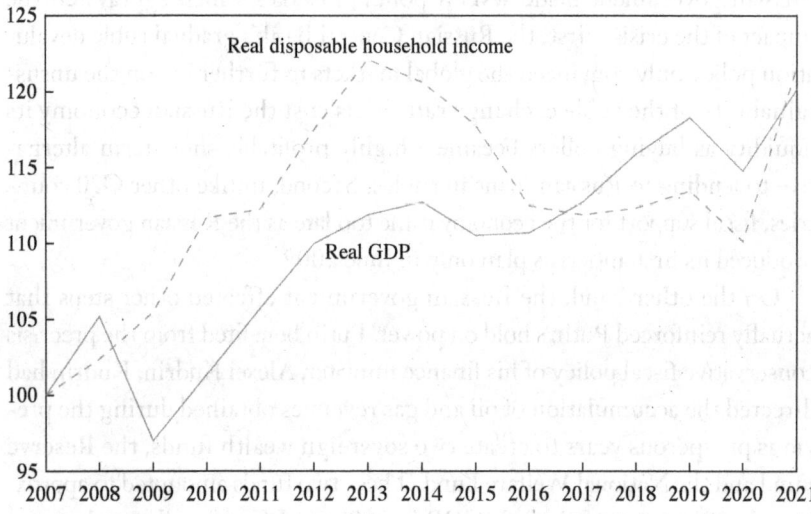

Source: Rosstat. 2007 = 100.

This was not surprising. Guriev and Tsyvinski warned that Russia needed to relaunch pro-market reforms or Putin's model would lead Russia into a long period of stagnation.[13] They described this risk as a "Scenario 70–80"—with oil prices at $70–$80 per barrel and the sclerotic economic growth rates similar to those in the Soviet Union of the 1970s and 1980s. This was exactly what happened.

Economic slowdown led to a steady decline in Putin's approval ratings. In November 2013, only 61 percent of Russians approved of his work, substantially lower than his 88 percent approval rating in September 2008 (see figure 1.2).

Putin's centralization of power and corruption eventually destroyed economic growth. This meant that Putin could no longer fulfill his part of the social contract with the Russian public: "I run the country, you don't interfere in politics but enjoy economic prosperity." He was in a bind: the only way to increase his popularity was to restore economic growth, but this necessitated economic reforms that would go against his preferred political-economic model. To accelerate economic growth, that is, to attract new investments, he would need to privatize, deregulate, reform the judiciary to make it truly independent and efficient, and prosecute corruption at all levels, including among his own friends. Such actions, however, would empower independent economic agents and break the loyalty of his own entourage. His political control would weaken; Putinomics would be upended.

Putin instead opted for another foreign military adventure in the form of a quick, victorious war: the annexation of Crimea. Taking the whole world by surprise, Russia invaded Ukraine in 2014. This military action, however, while temporarily providing Putin a badly needed boost in his popularity ratings, only aggravated Russia's economic problems. The West imposed sanctions to isolate Russia, which further inhibited Russia's GDP growth.

Putin's uptick in popularity ratings lasted probably longer than Putin himself expected, yet it faded away eventually. Economic stagnation continued. Putin realized that he could not relaunch Russian economic growth or offer Russians a convincing vision of the country's future. In 2022, he again pursued the "short, victorious war" solution, hoping that a replay of 2014 would once again substitute for absent economic success.[14] Putin's invasion of Ukraine in February 2022, however, proved to be his greatest, and potentially fatal, blunder.

Putinomics and Its Discontents

The brief history of Putinomics recounted above provides the necessary context to answer the main questions posed in this chapter. What is Putin's preferred economic policy model? How did it emerge, and how does it work and not work?

Up until 2022, Putin's governance system was a typical "spin dictatorship" based on manipulation of information, pretension to a democracy, and lack of a coherent ideology.[15] Putin has essentially never presented a consistent set of beliefs that we could identify as his own. In some speeches he would support the United States, in others harshly criticize it. In some speeches he would criticize the Soviet model, in others praise it. We therefore need to look not at what Putin says but at what he does, analyzing what economists would call his "revealed preferences."

As discussed above, initially Russia faced low oil prices, and Putin needed economic growth for his political survival. Once he understood that Russia's fiscal stance was secure, he started building a model of what we can call "Putinomics." The model is straightforward: rely on the state; manipulate big business to control the media and politics; and use state coffers (and petrodollars) to enrich himself and his cronies, bribe media and politicians both inside and outside Russia, and prevent the advancement of independent actors, whether they are domestic or foreign entrepreneurs, professionals, or other possible challengers.

This model is not very original. Putin may have learned it from his Italian friend, Silvio Berlusconi, who controlled media to reinforce his political power, relied on his political power to protect his businesses from competition, and used profits from his businesses to buy and subsidize his media. The model is actually much older than that. Luigi Zingales dates it back at least to Cosimo de' Medici in the early fifteenth century.[16] He calls this model "Medici vicious circle" as Medici's motto allegedly was "Money to get power. Power to protect money."

Putinomics protects Putin's hold on power but does so at the cost of economic growth. It provides Putin with control of both economics and politics but inherently stifles competition and innovation. Putinomics exists to protect the rents of incumbent businesses, shielding them from potential domestic and foreign competitors, and to extract rents to reinforce political power.

Putin had been fortunate to run an oil-rich country during a period of high oil prices. On the other hand, raw natural resource exports cannot sustain long-term growth for a country as vast as Russia. This is why Putin from the very beginning emphasized the need to diversify the Russian economy. Nevertheless, diversification has never happened, and for an obvious reason. Large oil and gas companies can survive and even prosper for extended periods without good economic and political institutions.[17] They can import technology, capital, and high-skilled labor. They can use foreign legal and financial systems.[18] In a high-middle-income country like Russia, however, diversification and innovation necessitate growth in knowledge-intensive services.[19] These industries require protection of property rights, constant application of the rule of law, competitive financial and education systems, antitrust policies, removal of entry barriers for new businesses, and the empowerment of subnational and local governments to develop their economies.[20] Putinomics resists pro-diversification reforms that would create and reinforce independent economic actors and, consequently, independent political actors.

Once we understand that the main goal of Putinomics is to centralize and preserve political power, it becomes clear why it cannot support innovation and the growth of small and medium-size enterprises. Nor is it surprising why the Russian financial system remains dominated by state actors. State banks, which opaquely give loans to loyal players and withhold finance from potential political challengers, command large market shares in retail banks that provide access to huge funding from household deposits. These banks increasingly crowd out the remaining viable private banks.

The failure of Russia to innovate and compete is especially sad in light of earlier indications that Russia could have succeeded. The Russian IT sector once produced notable companies that successfully competed with American big tech in Russia and abroad.[21] Russia's deteriorated investment environment hampered their growth and prospects.

Putinomics has a particular approach to Russia's human capital situation and brain drain (see chapter 7). The Soviet Union was founded to promote global domination by a particular ideology, and it needed talent in order to win that Cold War. All other things being equal, Putin favors economic growth, but he also believes that, with respect to investment in human capital, all other things are not equal: highly educated Russians are likely to be critical of his regime.[22] Putin unsurprisingly has tolerated, if not even encouraged, Russia's brain drain. Russia's investments in higher education and research under his leadership have been half-hearted at best. While the Soviet Union and Russia once laid claim to global competitiveness, Russian science has lagged behind its Western peers' and China's during Putin's years. This is especially striking given Russia's continuous (until recently) fiscal surpluses.

Russia failed to keep up with advanced economies and missed the boat taken by other emerging market countries (figure 1.5). China and India have fundamentally transformed their economies and become more open, competitive, and innovative. Additionally, Central and Eastern European countries, which have implemented pro-European reforms, serve as even more pertinent examples. Presently, these nations enjoy greater freedom, reduced corruption, and consequently increased prosperity.

South Korea serves as another important point of comparison. South Korea emerged from a dictatorship precisely at the moment when it needed to transition to a new economic development model. Until the 1990s, South Korea's fast economic growth was driven by its industrial investment and government-backed financial-industrial groups (chaebols). South Korea

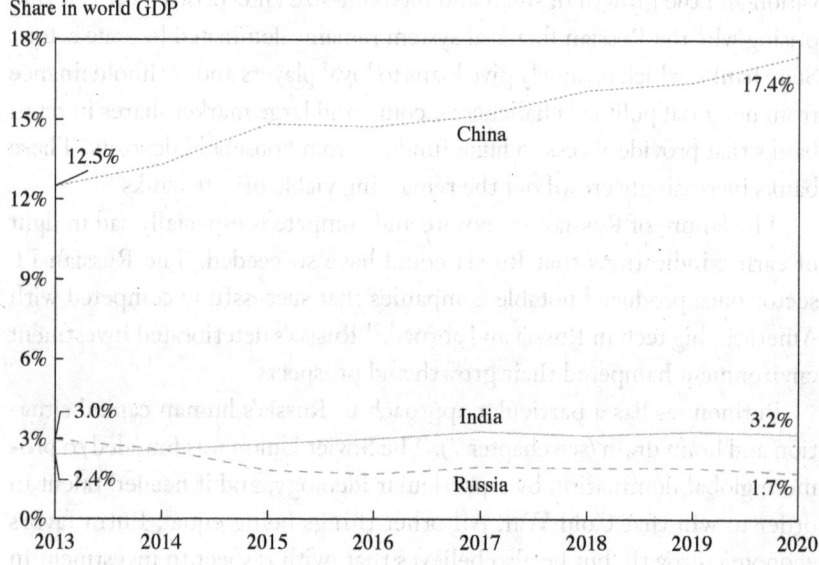

FIGURE 1.5. Russia's Share in World GDP Falling behind India's and China's, 2013–2020

Source: IMF (2024).

had limited the entry of new businesses and foreign investors, and its antitrust policy was weak. This resulted in inefficient investment, productivity growth slowed down, and South Korea risked falling into a middle-income trap. However, the democratic transition and the Asian currency crisis of 1997–1998 created an opportunity for reform. Acemoglu points out how South Korea switched from an oligarchic model (where power is concentrated in the hands of a small number of major economic actors who erect entry barriers) to a democratic one (where political power is more widely spread, thus leading to more redistribution but also reduced barriers to entry).[23] South Korea restructured or closed chaebols, removed barriers for foreign investment, and substantially strengthened competition policy. Innovation and productivity growth accordingly accelerated.[24]

Eleven years after the Asian crisis, Russia faced the global financial crisis of 2007–2008. Russia's GDP per capita then was similar to that of South Korea eleven years earlier. Russia could have escaped the middle-income trap as South Korea did but Putin's governance model rejected pro-competition reforms. Russia instead entered a "lost decade" of protracted growth slowdown (figure 1.6), which was completely predictable.[25]

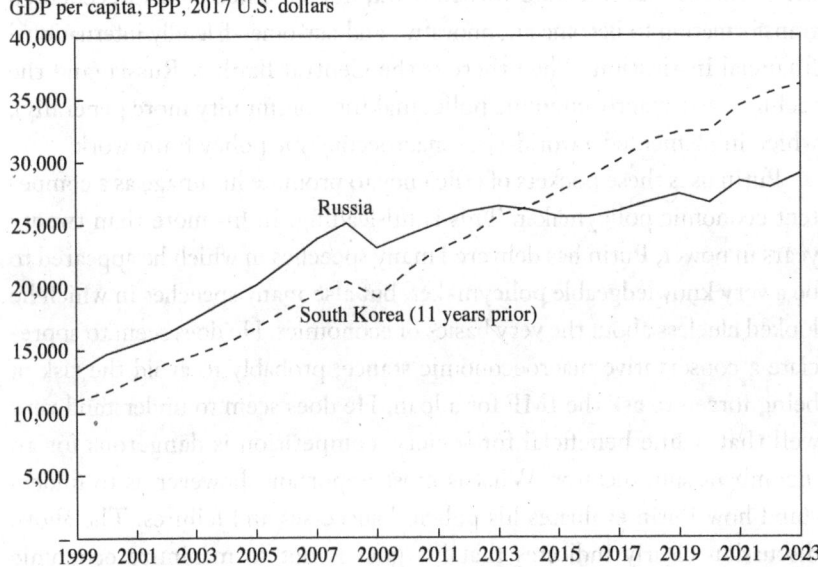

FIGURE 1.6. Middle-Income Trap: Russia Is Not South Korea

Source: IMF (2024).

Note: At the time of the 2007–2008 global financial crisis, Russia's GDP per capita was similar to that of South Korea eleven years earlier, during the Asian currency crisis of 1997–1998.

Fighting against oligarchs and launching pro-competition reforms—the path that South Korea has taken—is the path that Putin occasionally mentioned in his first years in power. This path, however, would require a different political-economic model. Putin consciously chose to centralize and preserve power, at a cost to the Russian economy.

Pockets of Efficiency

As a "spin dictator," Putin does not have a consistent ideology. He does not object to competition, meritocracy, or efficiency as a matter of principle, so long as these do not represent an immediate threat to his rule. Putinomics therefore may feature "pockets of efficiency."[26] Information manipulation plays a prominent role in Putin's governance model and presents examples of success as proof that Putinomics works. These examples are few and everybody agrees on what they are. There is Yandex, a world-class IT company that has successfully competed with Google in Russia and, before 2014, in international markets. Sberbank, for example, although being Russia's largest state-owned bank, implemented an unprecedented transformation to become an innovative and customer-friendly international financial institution. Then there is the Central Bank of Russia (and the technocratic macroeconomic policymaking community more generally), which implemented a world-class macroeconomic policy framework.

Putin uses these pockets of efficiency to promote his image as a competent economic policymaker. This is misleading. In his more than twenty years in power, Putin has delivered many speeches in which he appeared to be a very knowledgeable policymaker, but also many speeches in which he looked clueless about the very basics of economics. He does seem to appreciate a conservative macroeconomic stance, probably to avoid the risk of being forced to ask the IMF for a loan. He does seem to understand very well that, while beneficial for society, competition is dangerous for an incumbent spin dictator. What is most important, however, is to understand how Putin evaluates his policies' successes and failures. The above discussion clearly indicates that his goal is not to maximize economic growth but to prolong his time in power. (Judging by his very long tenure, he is very competent at playing this game.) In some, very few, cases, his goals are compatible with pro-growth policies. In these cases, he tolerates competition and meritocracy.

The War: The Present and the Future of the Russian Economy

Russia's 2022 full-scale invasion of Ukraine has changed many things, including Putin's economic policies. Putin quickly understood that the invasion was a mistake, but he also understood that he could not afford to lose the war. He accordingly raised production of war matériel and spent substantial resources on recruiting and paying soldiers. Military expenditures and sanctions have imposed a major burden on the Russian economy, but the economy has not collapsed. Russia's GDP declined by 1.2 percent in 2022 and grew by 3.6 percent in 2023 as a result of increased military expenditures. According to the IMF forecast, it is expected to grow in 2024 by 3 percent.

One could argue that from Putin's point of view, the previous failures of Putinomics were not important as long as his pre-2022 policies prepared the Russian economy for the 2022 war. This is a misleading argument. First, Putinomics did not deliver what Putin wanted. Second, the Russian economy avoided collapse in 2022 not thanks to Putinomics but despite it.

The Russian economy is doing much worse than it would in a counterfactual scenario without the war. Before the war, the Russian economy experienced a post-COVID-19 recovery; 2022 prewar IMF forecasts suggested that Russian GDP would grow about 3 percent in 2022.[27] Russia ultimately recorded negative 1 percent growth that year. The 3 − (−1) = 4 percent difference between the actual and the counterfactual is substantial. It would be even larger if we took into account the fact that global oil prices in 2022 were much higher than expected.

Second, the small decline in GDP in 2022 and recovery in 2023 certainly overestimate Russia's true economic performance. Because of the war, Putin has significantly increased production of military equipment and munitions. These expenditures directly contribute to measured GDP but do not affect the Russian population's quality of life. In wartime, it is therefore misleading to use GDP numbers. Instead, retail turnover, a measure of consumer spending on goods, provides a better indicator. According to official estimates, this measure fell by 6.5 percent in 2022, which is a much larger impact.

The fact that the post-2022 GDP growth has been explained purely by government spending and military production has been documented by Simola and by Gorodnichenko and others.[28] In 2021, Russia's official defense budget accounted for 2.7 percent of its GDP. However, by 2023 the defense budget had risen to 3.9 percent of GDP, and in 2024 it reached 6 percent of GDP. This has created significant inflationary pressure. When the Russian government spends trillions of rubles on missiles that attack Ukrainian cities, tanks that are destroyed in Ukrainian fields, or compensation for families of Russian soldiers killed in Ukraine, it injects a significant amount of money into the Russian economy. However, this spending doesn't correspond to an equivalent increase in the production of goods and services in the country. As a result, it drives up domestic aggregate demand without a corresponding boost in aggregate supply, leading to inflation. In the latter half of 2023, the Russian Central Bank raised its policy rate from 7.5 percent (annual) to 16 percent, with no intention of lowering it in 2024. This move significantly affected the nonmilitary sector of the Russian economy. Civilian firms already grapple with labor shortages and substantial wage growth, driven by competition from both army recruiters and military producers with generous procurement orders. Additionally, the emigration of hundreds of thousands of antiwar Russians compounds the challenges. Now these civilian firms also face the burden of high capital costs. Given the official inflation rate of 7–8 percent, the 16 percent policy rate translates to an unprecedentedly high real interest rate of 8–9 percent.

Despite its focus on defense production, Putinomics has failed to build a self-sufficient military-industrial complex. Once Western export controls were introduced, Russia faced a shortage of many important components to produce modern weapons and even artillery shells. Russia resorted to buying drones from Iran and munitions from North Korea. Still, once Russia's initial stocks were depleted, Putin could not supply enough munitions to his army. This led to public complaints from military officers and especially from private mercenary groups such as the now-deceased Yevgeny Prigozhin's private military company Wagner. Russia continues to rely on third countries for importing Western military and dual-purpose technology.[29] Tightening sanctions make such imports more difficult and costlier, thus adding further financial strain to Putin's regime.

The failure to diversify the Russian economy has exacerbated Putin's war problems. When Europe introduced oil sanctions in December 2022 for crude oil and in February 2023 for refined oil products, and together with the United States installed a $60 per barrel oil price cap, the Russian government budget suffered a severe blow. In the first months of 2023, the oil and gas revenues of the Russian federal budget declined by about half year-over-year. Later in 2023, Putin managed to build a shadow tanker fleet that helped him circumvent oil sanctions. Still, by the end of 2023, the liquid part of Russia's sovereign wealth fund (held in gold and Chinese yuan) had shrunk to $55 billion—roughly equivalent to one year's budget deficit. In late 2023 and early 2024 the West intensified enforcement, warning of secondary sanctions against companies aiding Putin's sanctions evasion. Faced with mounting budget constraints, in early 2024 Putin announced a significant tax increase.

Given the performance of Putinomics since 2022, what should we expect in the future? Can Putin drastically change the system? One option is to liberalize. Another option is to move to a wartime economy. It is safe to assume that Putin will choose to maintain the status quo of crony capitalism that supports his control of domestic politics. He will pursue this course, and as long as he is in power, sanctions will not be removed, and the Russian economy will continue to stagnate.

Yet even with the unprecedented sanctions and substantial increase in military spending, it is not likely that Putinomics will collapse. In economic terms, Russia is very different from the late Soviet Union. First, the Russian economy is a market-based economy; there are no regulated prices, which led to shortages of consumer goods in the late 1980s. Second, Russia is still not a military economy. Since 2022, Russia has classified a lot of economic statistics, making it challenging to ascertain the exact amount spent on the war. However, there are no estimates that suggest that Russia is currently spending as much as the late Soviet Union, where the defense sector accounted for 12–17 percent of GDP. Finally, Russia has a sound macroeconomic policy framework that protects the economy from a financial crisis and fiscal bankruptcy. Putinomics does not provide economic growth but up to now has helped avoid a meltdown.

Does this analysis imply that Putin's system will endure indefinitely? No. It suggests that the end of the regime will be driven more by political factors than by economic ones. Sanctions intensify the pressure on both elites and ordinary citizens. At some point, this will result in political change.

NOTES

1. All GDP data from IMF (2024).
2. Cheremukhin et al. (2017).
3. Markevich and Harrison (2011).
4. Guriev and Tsyvinski (2010).
5. Dmitriev and Yurtaev (2010).
6. CEIC Data (2024).
7. FDI increased greatly starting 2003, and further accelerated starting in 2005. See chapter 2.
8. In July 2024 the RTS index was at 44 percent of its 2008 peak.
9. Treisman (2011).
10. Enikolopov, Petrova, and Zhuravskaya (2011).
11. See Belton (2020), Dawisha (2015), and Ignatius (2010).
12. The Control of Corruption scores are calculated annually and are constructed in such a way that the global mean equals zero and the cross-country standard deviation equals one. The higher the Control of Corruption score, the less corruption there is in the country. Thus Russia's –1 score implies that Russia is one standard deviation more corrupt than an average country in the world.
13. Guriev and Tsyvinski (2010).
14. The choice of Ukraine in both 2014 and 2022 was not random. Given ethnolinguistic proximity, a democratic and European Ukraine presented an especially important challenge to Putin by demonstrating to Russian citizens that their country could also become a member of the European family.
15. Guriev and Treisman (2022).
16. Zingales (2017).
17. Incompetent autocratic leaders can undermine the oil sector's performance even during periods of high global oil prices, as shown by the example

of Venezuela. However, Putin's management of the oil sector has been much better than that of Chávez or Maduro.
18. Of course, this was the case until the Western sanctions were imposed in 2022.
19. Guriev, Plekhanov, and Sonin (2009).
20. EBRD (2012).
21. Graham (2013).
22. Guriev and Treisman (2019).
23. Acemoglu (2008).
24. Aghion, Guriev, and Jo (2021).
25. Guriev and Zhuravskaya (2010).
26. Gel'man (2022).
27. See IMF (2022).
28. Simola (2023, 2024); Gorodnichenko, Korhonen, and Ribakova (2024).
29. Bilousova et al. (2024).

REFERENCES

Acemoglu, Daron. 2008. "Oligarchic versus Democratic Societies." *Journal of the European Economic Association* 6 (1): 1–44.

Aghion, Philippe, Sergei Guriev, and Kangchul Jo. 2021. "Chaebols and Firm Dynamics in Korea." *Economic Policy* 36 (108): 593–626.

Belton, Catherine. 2020. *Putin's People: How the KGB Took Back Russia and Then Took On the West.* Glasgow: William Collins.

Bilousova, Olena, Benjamin Hilgenstock, Elina Ribakova, Nataliia Shapoval, Anna Vlasyuk, and Vladyslav Vlasiuk. 2024. *Challenges of Export Controls Enforcement: How Russia Continues to Import Components for Its Military Production.* Kyiv: Yermak-McFaul International Working Group on Russian Sanctions and KSE Institute.

CEIC Data. 2024. "Russian Household Debt: % of GDP" (database), as of March 24.

Cheremukhin, Anton, Mikhail Golosov, Sergei Guriev, and Aleh Tsyvinski. 2017. "The Industrialization and Economic Development of Russia through the Lens of a Neoclassical Growth Model." *Review of Economic Studies* 84 (2): 613–49.

Dawisha, Karen. 2015. *Putin's Kleptocracy: Who Owns Russia?* New York: Simon and Schuster.

Dmitriev, Mikhail, and Alexei Yurtaev. 2010. "Strategy 2010: Taking Stock. 10 Years After" [in Russian]. *Ekonomicheskaia politika* 3:107–14.

EBRD (European Bank for Reconstruction and Development). 2012. *Diversifying Russia: Harnessing Regional Diversity*, ed. Erik Berglöf. London: EBRD.

Enikolopov, Ruben, Maria Petrova, and Ekaterina Zhuravskaya. 2011. "Media and Political Persuasion: Evidence from Russia." *American Economic Review* 101 (7): 3253–85.

Gel'man, Vladimir. 2022. *The Politics of Bad Governance in Contemporary Russia*. Ann Arbor: University of Michigan Press.

Gorodnichenko, Yuriy, Iikka Korhonen, and Elina Ribakova. 2024. "Russian Economy on War Footing: A New Reality Financed by Commodity Exports." CEPR Policy Insight 131. Paris: CEPR Press.

Graham, Loren. 2013. *Lonely Ideas: Can Russia Compete?* Cambridge, MA: MIT Press.

Guriev, Sergei, Alexander Plekhanov, and Konstantin Sonin. 2009. "Development Based on Commodity Revenues." European Bank for Reconstruction and Development Working Paper no. 108. London: EBRD, December 8.

Guriev, Sergei, and Daniel Treisman. 2022. *Spin Dictators: The Changing Face of Tyranny in the 21st Century*. Princeton, NJ: Princeton University Press.

———. 2019. "Informational Autocrats." *Journal of Economic Perspectives* 33 (4): 100–27.

Guriev, Sergei, and Aleh Tsyvinski. 2010. "Challenges Facing the Russian Economy after the Crisis." In *Russia after the Global Economic Crisis*, ed. Anders Åslund, Sergei Guriev, and Andrew Kuchins. Washington, DC: Peterson Institute for International Economics.

Guriev, Sergei, and Ekaterina Zhuravskaya. 2010. "Why Russia Is Not South Korea." *Journal of International Affairs* 63 (2): 125–39.

Ignatius, David. 2010. "Sergey Kolesnikov's Tale of Palatial Corruption, Russian Style." *Washington Post*, December 23.

IMF (International Monetary Fund). 2024. *World Economic Outlook*. April.

———. 2022. *World Economic Outlook Update*. January. Last accessed September 12, 2023.

Markevich, Andrei, and Mark Harrison. 2011. "Great War, Civil War, and Recovery: Russia's National Income, 1913 to 1928." *Journal of Economic History* 71 (3): 672–703.

Simola, Heli, 2024. "Russia's Wartime Investment Boom." BOFIT Policy Brief 4/2024. Helsinki: Bank of Finland Institute for Emerging Economies.

———. 2023. "The Role of War-Related Industries in Russia's Recent Economic Recovery." BOFIT Policy Brief 16/2023. Helsinki: Bank of Finland Institute for Emerging Economies.

Treisman, Daniel. 2011. "Presidential Popularity in a Hybrid Regime: Russia under Yeltsin and Putin." *American Journal of Political Science* 55 (3): 590–609.

Zingales, Luigi. 2017. "Towards a Political Theory of the Firm." *Journal of Economic Perspectives* 31 (3): 113–30.

TWO

Foreign Direct Investment and International Capital

Lost in a Russian Abyss

STEVEN A. FISHER

Russia's great asset, which would allow it to escape the fatal dilemma of underdevelopment, was a vast external pool of entrepreneurship, knowledge and capital waiting to be tapped.

—John P. McKay, *Pioneers for Profit: Foreign Entrepreneurship and Russian Industrialization, 1885–1913*

Between 2000 and 2022, Russia attracted more than $3 trillion in foreign direct investment (FDI) and international capital. FDI can stimulate essential innovation and foster structural transformation, but it requires an enabling environment to thrive. This chapter explains why this was not the case in Vladimir Putin's Russia. Numerous adverse factors—many of which were self-inflicted by Putin's rule—hindered Russia from capitalizing on this unparalleled opportunity to modernize and diversify its economy.

The chapter begins by analyzing the macroeconomic relationship among FDI activity, the price of oil, and specific endogenous and exogenous factors that have had an impact on Russia since 2000. Before the global financial crisis of 2007–2008, oil prices and FDI inflows to Russia strongly correlated. However, post-2008, especially in the aftermath of Russia's invasion of Ukraine in 2014, the nation grappled with new economic and geopolitical challenges that overshadowed the influence of oil price fluctuations. As a result, inward FDI growth came to a standstill, leading to economic stagnation. Russia's economic performance progressively lagged behind that of its emerging market peers.

The following section delves into self-inflicted challenges and their wide-ranging consequences. First, it explains how large corporate entities, controlled in one form or another by the Kremlin, dominated international and domestic fundraising, crowding out other sectors in the economy from raising capital. Next, the chapter examines the impact of Russia's renewed invasion of Ukraine in February 2022 on its equity market, considering that market's major dependence on Western financial centers prior to the event. Finally, it describes how numerous prominent international companies swiftly exited Russia after Western nations imposed extensive sanctions, resulting in a severe depletion of Russia's accumulated FDI stock.

Russia, unsurprisingly, failed to address its "natural resources curse," characterized by an excessive reliance on inherently fluctuating oil and gas sector earnings. Remarkably, the percentage of oil and gas revenues in the Russian federal budget has actually increased over the last two decades.[1] Instead of addressing this issue head-on, Russia acquiesced to unabated rent-seeking behavior, widespread corruption, and selective law enforcement. These factors contributed to massive capital flight amounting to upward of $1.5 trillion.

The chapter concludes that what remains, Russian domestic finance, is ill-equipped to substitute for the FDI and international finance that the West once supplied.

Foreign Direct Investment in Russia

FDI can play a crucial role in enhancing a country's economic growth. By attracting new investment capital, advanced technology, and valuable management expertise, FDI contributes significantly to the host nation's development. Elitza Mileva points out that, similar to other forms of capital inflow, "FDI can also increase the total supply of savings to finance investment and, as a foreign currency inflow, it can help strengthen the exchange rate, making investment goods cheaper." Mileva concludes that FDI acts "correspondingly to foreign loans and portfolio inflows" and can "crowd in" domestic investment because "relatively underdeveloped financial markets and weak institutions tend to depend more on FDI compared to countries with bigger financial markets and better institutions."[2]

Over a century ago, Sergei Witte, the Russian imperial finance minister, recognized that FDI was crucial for accelerating Russia's economic growth. During the period from 1893 to 1914, inward FDI accounted for approximately 50 percent of new capital formation in Russian industrial corporations.[3] In the first decade of Vladimir Putin's leadership, it seemed that Russia had repeated Witte's success. American, Belgian, British, French, and German investments made up more than 90 percent of FDI into Russia. In certain years, these countries' FDI even constituted as much as one-third of Russia's total annual investment.

Figure 2.1 summarizes by industry category cumulative FDI inflow totaling $2,021 billion for 2010–2021. FDI included huge Western oil and gas sector investments such as British Petroleum's venture with Rosneft, ExxonMobil's in the Sakhalin-1 project, Shell's in Sakhalin-2, and other large investments pursued by Equinor, Total, ENI, and Chevron, among other global petroleum sector giants. In the decade prior (2000–2009), the weight of foreign investments in fuel and energy in total foreign investments roughly matched the weight of that sector in the Russian GDP.[4]

An Unsustainable Feat. Why?

Russia's fiscal and economic management boasts notable "pockets of efficiency," including substantial foreign exchange reserves, positive current account balances, and a low government debt-to-GDP ratio.[5] These factors played a pivotal role in Russia achieving investment-grade sovereign credit ratings between 2005 and 2014 (and again from 2018 to 2021). Credit is due to the Central Bank of Russia for its prudent policies. However, despite these achievements, net FDI as a percentage of GDP started to decline after the global financial crisis of 2007–2008 and worsened significantly from 2014 onward. It became evident that relying solely on an investment-grade credit rating was insufficient to attract foreign capital (table 2.1).

Several phenomena explain this failure.

First, a multitude of adverse endogenous and exogenous factors, many of which were self-inflicted or triggered by Russia, impeded investment or undermined its efficacy.

FIGURE 2.1. Cumulative FDI Inflow, 2010–2021 (Billions of USD)

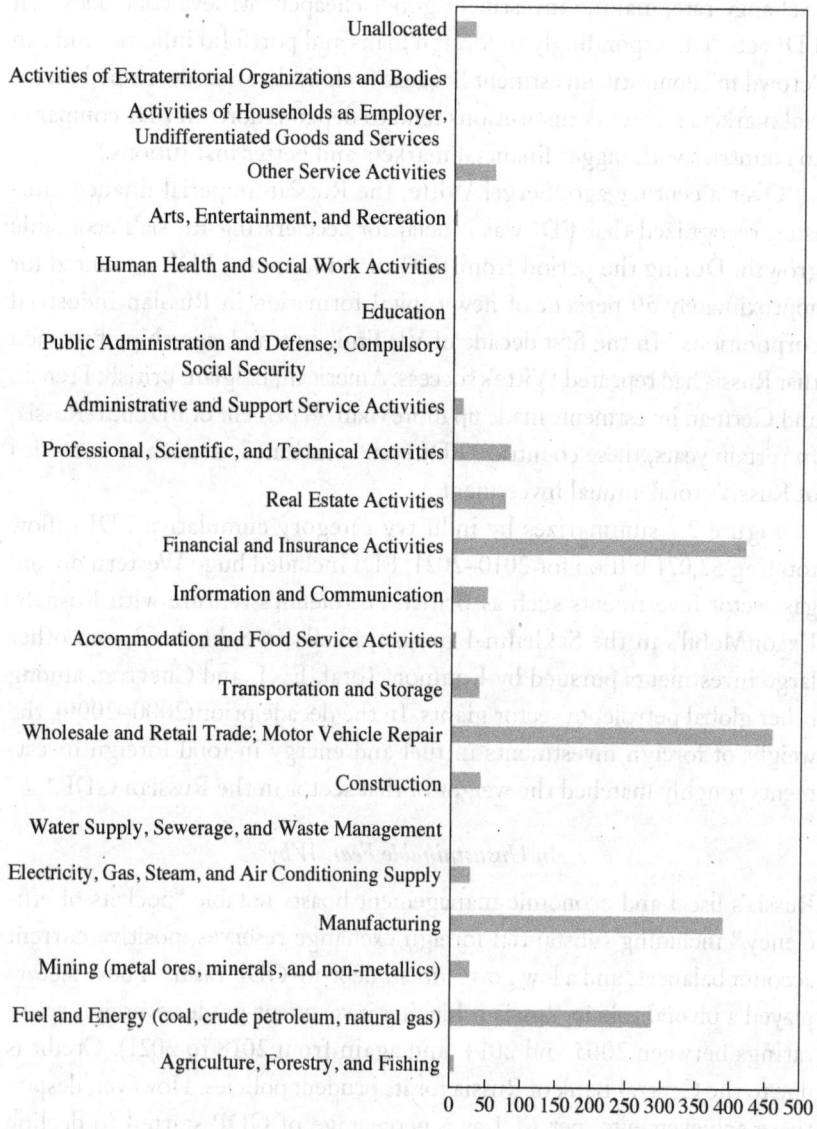

Source: Central Bank of Russia: Foreign Direct Investment in the Russia Federation: Flows by Industry (https://www.cbr.ru/eng/statistics/macro_itm/svs/, 08e-dir inv).

Table 2.1. Financial Indicators, 2000–2024

Year	Sovereign S&P rating*	Year-end Europe Brent spot FOB ($bbl)†	International foreign exchange reserves, incl. gold ($bln)‡	Ruble/ euro†	Constant 2015 GDP ($trn)§	Year-over-year GDP %¶	Current account balance, % of GDP‖	Government debt, of GDP**	Net FDI inflow % of GDP††
2024 (Nov.)	NR	81.09	628.5	106.1					
2023	NR	76.24	599.3	98.2	1.53	4.1%	2.1%	14.9%	-1.3%
2022	NR	93.33	567.7	75.7	1.47	-2.0%	12.0%	13.4%	-1.8%
2021	BBB-	74.17	630.6	84.1	1.50	5.6%	6.9%	18.2%	2.2%
2020	BBB-	49.97	595.8	90.7	1.42	-2.7%	2.4%	23.0%	0.6%
2019	BBB-	67.31	554.4	69.3	1.46	2.1%	3.9%	17.3%	1.9%
2018	BBB-	57.36	468.5	79.5	1.43	2.9%	7.0%	16.2%	0.5%
2017	BB+	64.37	432.7	68.9	1.39	1.5%	2.0%	16.3%	1.8%
2016	BB+	53.31	377.7	63.8	1.37	0.7%	1.9%	14.2%	2.5%
2015	BB+	38.01	368.4	79.7	1.36	-2.2%	5.0%	13.5%	0.5%
2014	BBB-	62.34	385.5	68.3	1.39	0.7%	2.8%	11.2%	1.1%
2013	BBB	110.76	509.6	45.0	1.38	1.5%	1.5%	9.1%	3.0%
2012	BBB	139.49	537.6	40.2	1.36	4.6%	3.2%	8.6%	2.3%

(continued)

Table 2.1. (continued)

Year	Sovereign S&P rating*	Year-end Europe Brent spot FOB ($bbl)†	International foreign exchange reserves, incl. gold ($bln)‡	Ruble/ euro‡	Constant 2015 GDP ($trn)§	Year-over-year GDP %¶	Current account balance, % of GDP‖	Government debt, of GDP**	Net FDI inflow % of GDP††
2011	BBB	107.87	498.6	41.7	1.30	4.0%	4.8%	8.6%	2.7%
2010	BBB	91.45	478.4	40.3	1.25	4.2%	4.4%	9.1%	2.8%
2009	BBB	74.46	439.5	43.4	1.20	-7.7%	4.1%	8.7%	3.0%
2008	BBB	39.95	426.3	41.4	1.30	5.7%	6.3%	6.5%	4.5%
2007	BBB+	90.93	478.8	35.9	1.23	7.9%	5.6%	7.2%	4.3%
2006	BBB+	62.47	303.7	34.7	1.14	8.6%	9.3%	9.9%	3.8%
2005	BBB	56.86	182.2	34.2	1.05	6.3%	11.0%	16.7%	2.0%
2004	BB+	39.60	124.5	37.8	0.99	7.3%	9.9%		2.6%
2003	BB	28.33	47.8	36.8	0.92	7.2%	7.7%		1.8%
2002	BB	24.99	48.2	33.1	0.86	4.7%	8.0%	41.4%	1.0%
2001	B+	18.71	36.6	26.5	0.82	5.1%	10.5%	49.0%	0.9%
2000	B–	25.66	28	26.1	0.78		17.5%	62.2%	1.0%

Sources: *S&P; †U.S. Energy Information Administration (www.eia.gov); ‡Central Bank of Russia; §World Bank (Data.WorldBank.org); ¶2023 data from Bank of Finland Institute for Emerging Economies; ‖World Bank 2023; Q4 2023 (ceicdata.com); **World Bank, December 2023 (ceicdata.com); ††World Bank.

Note: Italic indicates years of major external shock ("Year" column) or noninvestment-grade sovereign credit rating ("Sovereign S&P rating" column).

Endogenous factors:

- Endemic corruption and rent-seeking
- Increased state control of key institutions and Kremlin power vertical expansion
- Escalating autocratic government repression
- Weak rule of law favoring insiders
- Exploitation of weak property rights by insiders and criminal elements
- Transparency deficit
- Foreign misadventures affecting exogenous relations
- Predatory behavior of the elite, stifling entrepreneurial dynamism and available resources
- Trade and customs impediments
- Human capital exodus aggravating labor and demographic challenges

Exogenous factors:

- Negative foreign image of Russia (as reflected in business sentiment indices such as the World Economic Forum *Global Competitiveness Report*)
- Oil and gas price volatility
- Foreign exchange rate volatility
- Changing nature of international commodity markets
- Relative attractiveness of other emerging and developed markets competing for investment funds
- Western sanctions and trade impediments (decoupling effect), including an oil export price cap and freezing of over one-half of Russia's international reserves after February 24, 2022
- Reputational risks for Western investors not leaving Russia
- Russia's sovereign rating downgrade to NR (No Rating, or insufficient information on which to base a rating)

The aforementioned challenges contributed to Russia losing its appeal as a prime investment destination. According to the World Economic Forum's *Global Competitiveness Report* for 2020, Russia ranked lowest globally among thirty-seven surveyed countries in two critical categories (table 2.2).

Table 2.2. Russia's Competitiveness Compared to China's, Brazil's, and India's, 2020

Ensure public institutions embed strong governance principles and a long-term vision to build trust by serving their citizens

China	64
Brazil	45
India	49
Russia	43

Rethink competitive and antitrust frameworks ensuring market access, both locally and internationally

China	72
Brazil	59
India	57
Russia	42

Source: World Economic Forum 2020 *Global Competitiveness Report*.
Note: Scale 0–100 (best).

Unfortunately, this time, the Central Bank of Russia could not come to the rescue.

Second, the two main episodes of declining FDI in Russia, in 2009 and 2014, coincided with oil price collapses.[6] The dominance of the oil and gas sector in the Russian economy made it the focus of a significant percentage of FDI inflow, a dynamic that did not necessarily help Russia.[7] Arshad Hayat argues that whereas FDI inflows generally accelerate economic growth of the host country, FDI-supported expansion of the natural resources sector actually *diminishes* FDI's overall effect on economic growth.[8] Specifically, FDI devoted to oil extraction rarely provides spillovers and thus has a lesser effect on growth and diversification. Wright and Czelusta state that the natural resources sector can be a driver of high technology development, as exemplified by the case of the United States, and potentially offers an escape from the natural resources curse. However, they caution that "many countries made poor use of their one-time gains" and that "there are no guarantees against corruption, rent-seeking and mismanagement."[9] Nonresource industries, on the other hand, less susceptible to changes in oil prices, more often promote diversification into value-added sectors that support a virtuous circle that attracts greater FDI.[10]

The pervasive impact of the natural resources curse is a phenomenon not unique to Russia. Few nations have successfully sidestepped this predicament, with Norway standing out as a remarkable exception. Russia's heavy reliance on oil and gas renders it acutely vulnerable to fluctuations in global commodity prices. These market swings can trigger substantial revenue shortfalls and strain the national budget. The overexploitation of natural resources, moreover, stifles diversification efforts. While oil and gas dominate, other sectors struggle to flourish, hindering long-term economic growth and limiting job prospects. The extraction of natural resources diverts attention and investment away from critical areas such as education, health care, and infrastructure. Consequently, overall social and economic progress faces impediments (see chapter 7). Beyond economic consequences, environmental degradation and sustainability issues pose significant concerns to Russia's ecology and, by extension, the global ecosystem.

Putin took advantage of fortuitously high oil prices before the global financial crisis of 2007–2008 to trickle down economic benefits to the general population. Now, bereft of an oil price windfall, his social contract with the Russian people has frayed.

The geography of FDI also matters. The regions of the Central Federal District of Russia account for more than 50 percent of direct FDI in the Russian economy. This lopsided geographic distribution hindered FDI's contribution to the overall national economy.[11]

Third, amid the global financial crisis, its aftermath, and Western sanctions triggered by Russia's invasion of Crimea and the Donbas in 2014, Russia faced significant economic challenges. The share of FDI in overall investment plummeted from a peak of 20 percent in 2007 to about 5 percent in 2018. Fixed capital investment growth in Russia began to lag industrial growth and GDP as the funding dynamics behind investment changed. Companies typically fund capital investments through internal funds (such as equity, cash flow, and profits) or from external sources, such as domestic and foreign capital markets, banks, or public funds. In Russia, external financing usually funded fixed capital investments, but during times of crisis, there was an exceptionally high demand on equity owing to reduced access to external capital.[12] Between 2009 and 2015, 51 percent of fixed capital investments in Russia relied on equity, compared to 37 percent in 2009.[13] Reduced capital expenditures hindered construction and industrial growth, perpetuating structural imbalances and technological gaps within the Russian economy.

The missed technology and entrepreneurship skills spillover effect has had immeasurable consequences.[14] For instance, the number of registered entrepreneurs in Russia, the cradle of private sector innovation, plunged from 8.3 million in 2008 to 2.8 million in 2015, a staggering drop of 66 percent. Notably, the largest one-year drop occurred following the West's imposition of sanctions in 2014.[15]

Fourth, capital flight from Russia significantly undermined the effectiveness of FDI. Experts provide astounding estimates of this capital hemorrhage. According to *Bloomberg Economics*, about $750 billion in Russian assets moved offshore between 1994 and 2019.[16] Timothy Ash of BlueBay Asset Management refers to Central Bank of Russia data for "other capital flows"—a reliable proxy for capital flight. He calculates an average annual capital outflow of $58 billion, which cumulatively amounts to over $1.5 trillion between 1994 and 2021.[17] Capital flight reached an annual size equivalent to 0.8 percent of GDP from 2015 to 2020.[18] A report published by the Central Bank of Russia's Center for Macroeconomic Analysis and Forecasting on July 24, 2023, revealed that a record $253 billion had been withdrawn from Russia since February 2022.[19]

Russian multinational enterprises play a significant role in capital flight.[20] Approximately 75 percent of FDI stock in Russia originates from jurisdictions such as Cyprus, Luxembourg, the Bahamas, the British Virgin Islands, Bermuda, Ireland, and the Netherlands. These countries are highly ranked for their international facilitation of tax and money flow management, which contributes to the round-tripping of capital.[21]

Fifth, Russia's nontariff barriers have discouraged investment. According to the World Bank's 2018 *Doing Business* report, Russia imposes export border compliance costs that are 6.7 times higher than the EU average and import costs that are a staggering seventeen times higher.[22] These trade impediments, coupled with Russia's reputation as a challenging investment environment, led potential investors to perceive Russia as an unattractive market for global manufacturing.[23]

In summary, the decline in FDI can be attributed to several factors:

- Unfavorable institutional conditions,
- Adverse macroeconomic conditions,
- Competition from other emerging market (EM) countries, and
- Geopolitical tensions and Western sanctions.

The cumulative stock of inward FDI in current U.S. dollars remained stagnant after external shocks, including the oil price decline from 2007

FIGURE 2.2. Russia: Inward FDI Stock, 2000–2022 (Millions of USD)

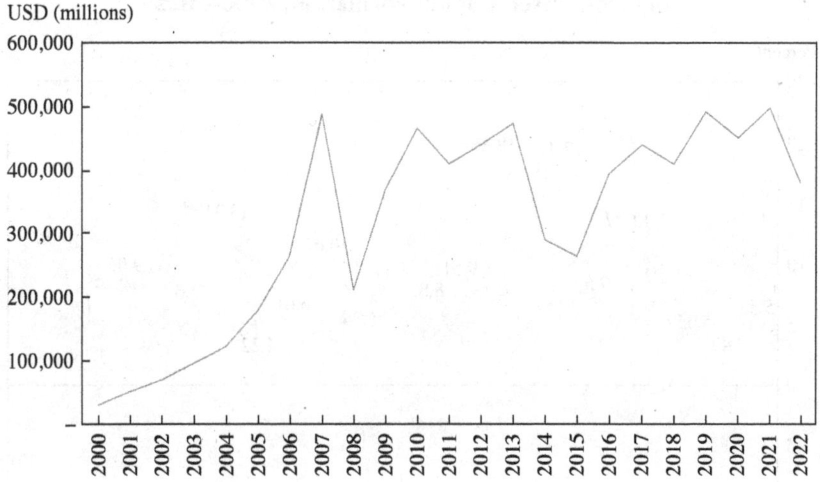

Source: Data from Unctadstat.unctad.org.

to 2009 and the global financial crisis of 2007–2008 and its aftermath (figure 2.2). Subsequently, the trend of inward FDI as a percentage of gross fixed capital formation deteriorated (figure 2.3). Likewise, FDI as a percentage of Russia's GDP declined (figure 2.4). By 2022 it had turned negative.

Russia Becomes Less Competitive

Russia fares unfavorably when compared to peer emerging market countries such as Brazil, China, India, and Mexico in terms of FDI flows, as indicated in table 2.3. The actual situation is likely even more concerning. Approximately half of the FDI inflow to Russia follows a convoluted path: it is initially invested by offshore-owned Russian entities and then "round-tripped" out of Russia. This practice primarily occurs for tax-related reasons and because of concerns about the safety of retaining wealth within Russia. This continuous money carousel distorts the true picture of Russian FDI.

From the data in table 2.3, we may conclude the following: (1) Russia's inward FDI is consistently less than that of its BRIC peers. (2) Russia's net FDI was consistently negative in the years cited. (3) Russia's negative net FDI as a percentage of GDP becomes increasingly larger over time.

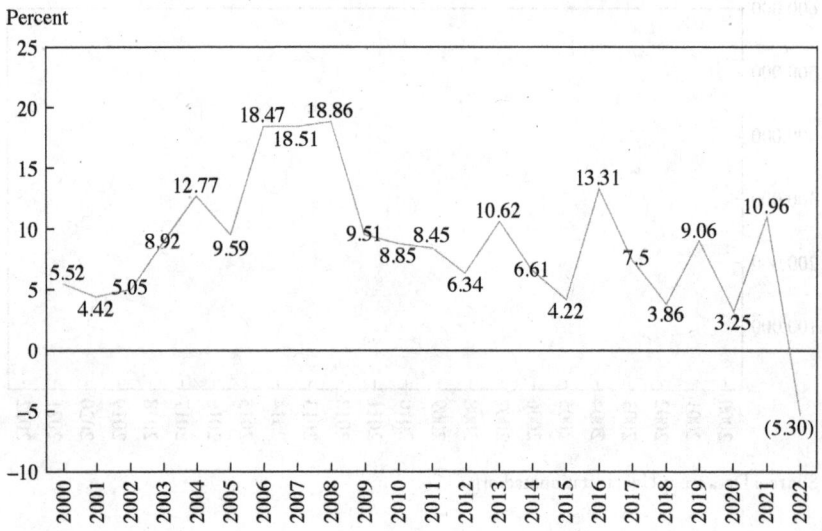

FIGURE 2.3. Russia: Inward FDI Flow as a Percentage of Gross Fixed Capital Formation, 2000–2022

Source: Data from Unctadstat.unctad.org.

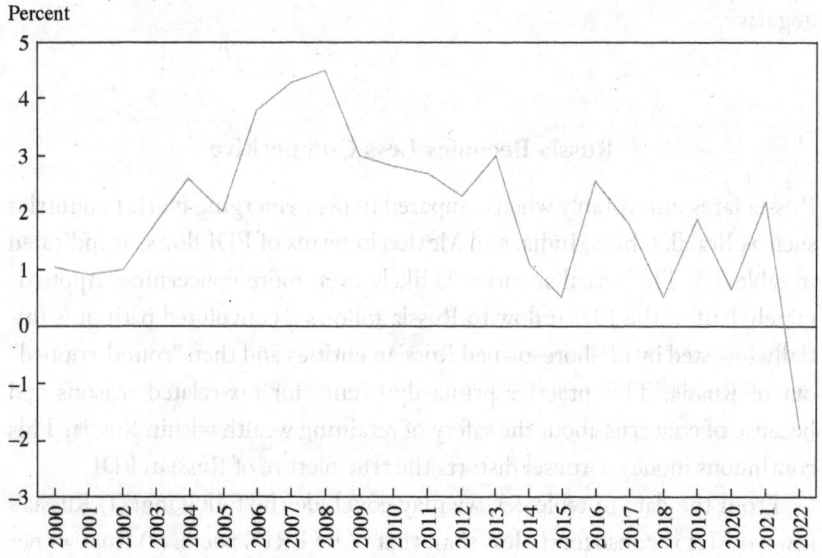

FIGURE 2.4. Russia: Net FDI Inflow as Percentage of GDP, 2000–2022

Source: Data from WorldBank.org.

Table 2.3. Foreign Direct Investment Flows (Billions of USD)

	2005	2010	2015	2021	2022
Russia					
Inflow	14.38	31.67	11.86	38.24	−18.68
Outflow	16.75	41.12	27.09	63.60	10.44
Net	−2.37	−9.45	−15.23	−25.36	−29.12
Net, % of GDP constant 2015 USD	−0.23%	−0.76%	−1.12%	−1.69%	−1.98%
GDP, constant 2015 USD	1,050	1,250	1,360	1,500	1,470
Brazil					
Inflow	15.07	77.69	49.96	50.37	86.05
Outflow	2.52	22.06	−11.64	23.08	25.24
Net	12.55	55.627	61.603	27.284	60.81
China					
Inflow	72.41	114.73	135.58	180.96	189.13
Outflow	12.26	68.81	145.67	145.19	146.50
Net	60.15	45.92	−10.09	35.77	42.63
Mexico					
Inflow	25.80	27.19	35.94	31.62	35.29
Outflow	6.47	14.56	10.67	−0.72	12.85
Net	19.33	12.63	25.27	32.34	22.44
India					
Inflow	7.62	27.42	44.06	44.74	49.35
Outflow	2.99	15.95	7.57	15.52	14.54
Net	4.64	11.47	36.49	29.21	34.81

2022 FDI Inflows as a ratio to 2022 GDP, current $:		2022 GDP, current $ millions	
Russia	−0.8%		2,240,422
Brazil	4.5%		1,920,095
China	1.1%		17,963,171
Mexico	2.4%		1,463,324
India	1.4%		3,465,541

Source: Data from UNCTAD (Unctadstat.unctad.org).

Note: UNCTAD definitions: Foreign direct investment (FDI) is defined as an investment reflecting a lasting interest and control by a foreign direct investor, resident in one economy, in an enterprise resident in another economy (foreign affiliate).

FDI inflows comprise capital provided by a foreign direct investor to a foreign affiliate, or capital received by a foreign direct investor from a foreign affiliate. FDI outflows represent the same flows from the perspective of the other country.

FDI flows are presented on a net basis, that is, as credits less debts. Thus, in cases of reverse investment or disinvestment, FDI may be negative.

Table 2.4. Selected World Development Indicators

	2000	2005	2010	2015	2021	2022
Domestic credit to private sector as % of GDP						
Russia	–	26	43	56	54	
Brazil	31	32	53	67	70	72
China	111	112	127	153	177	185
India	28	40	51	52	50	
Gross savings as a % of GDP						
Russia	36	31	26	26		34
Brazil	14	18	18	14		19
China	36	46	51	45		47
India	29	34	36	32		29
GDP per capita, current USD						
Russia	1,772	5,323	10,675	9,313		15,271
Brazil	3,750	4,790	11,286	8,814		8,918
China	959	1,753	4,550	8,016		12,720
India	443	715	1,358	1,606		2,411
Medium- and high-tech value added as % of GDP						
Russia	33	22	25	29	32	
Brazil	35	34	36	36	31	
China	43	42	41	41	42	
India	41	40	39	43	46	

Source: World Bank, World Development Indicators database (https://databank.worldbank.org/source/world-development-indicators).

The impact of FDI on innovation within the Russian economy is limited. Notably, the contribution of medium- and high-tech value-added components to total manufactured value added has stagnated since 2000. In this regard, Russia significantly trails its emerging market counterparts (table 2.4). For instance, China's innovation-driven value-added percentage surpasses Russia's by almost 50 percent, and China's economy is ten times larger. Remarkably, China's foreign-invested firms, alongside private enterprises, account for up to 99 percent of the country's high-tech exports (see chapter 7). Additionally, China's domestic credit to the private sector as a percentage of GDP and gross savings as a percentage of GDP far exceed Russia's. Repinskiy et al. offer a compelling example, highlighting that the creation of a high-tech industry in the production of measuring and analytical equipment in a highly competitive environment is impossible in Russia without developing and producing innovative products. They conclude that "the vast majority of Russian enterprises invest their funds in the purchase of imported innovations instead of investing in their own R&D (Research, Development and Engineering) and that such path of development by Russian enterprises is, or seems to be, a dead end."[24]

In November 2009, then president Dmitry Medvedev announced with great fanfare the establishment of the Skolkovo Innovation Center in Moscow oblast. Russia aspired to replicate the success of Silicon Valley in the United States. However, Russia has not demonstrated many high-tech achievements. CB Insights, a private business analytics platform and global database that follows venture capital investments, startups, patents, partnerships, and tech news, publishes a Unicorn List. As of May 2024, this list includes 1,248 unicorns (companies with valuations of $1 billion or more) globally, with a combined total valuation of $4.065 trillion. Conspicuously, no Russian company appeared on the list.[25]

Vladislav Inozemtsev offers a thought-provoking alternative frame of reference by calculating that the personal wealth of a single Russian émigré, Sergei Brin, a cofounder of Google, exceeds the total technology budget of the Russian federal government over an eight-year period.[26]

The annual U.S. patent issuance statistics, as depicted in figure 2.5, shed light on Russia's relatively modest impact on global innovation. Between 2000 and 2020, Russia's share of U.S. patents granted worldwide has oscillated between 0.10 percent and 0.18 percent of the total patents issued by the United States Patent and Trademark Office (USPTO). In contrast, China has significantly expanded its global share of U.S. patents during the same period, growing from 0.09 percent to an impressive 6.90 percent, while India's share increased from 0.07 percent to 1.54 percent.

Crowding Out in the International and Domestic Debt Markets

In addition to FDI, Russian companies and Russia as the sovereign borrower raised over $1 trillion in funding from international and domestic capital markets between 2000 and 2022. While this amount may seem substantial, only a portion was ultimately invested in fixed assets. Instead, the bulk of it was used to refinance previous loans and borrowings, pay dividends, build inventories, fulfill "working capital needs," or engage in various financial speculations that contributed to Russia's massive capital flight.[27] External financing, therefore, played a lesser role in supporting economic development when compared to FDI. Unlike FDI, which is typically more stable and long-term-oriented, international and domestic

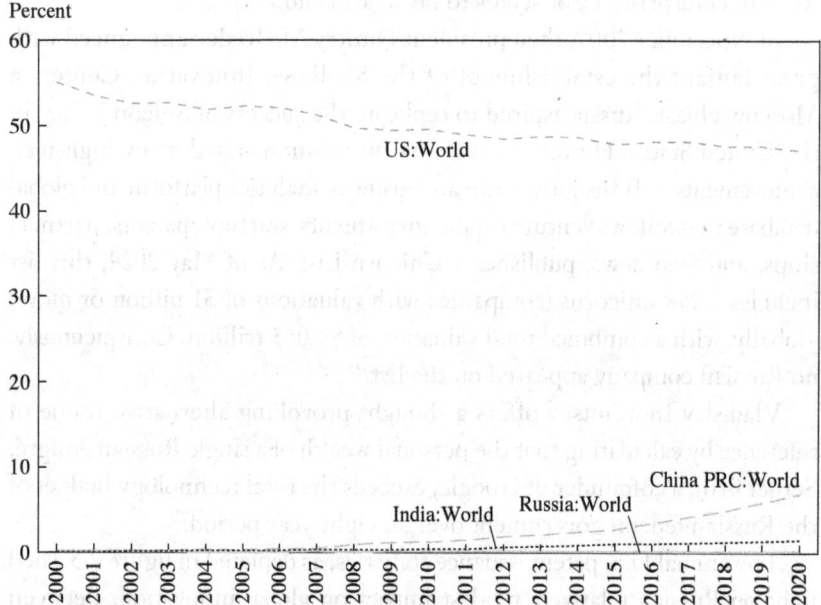

FIGURE 2.5. U.S. Patent Counts by Origin, 2000–2020 (Percent of Total U.S. Patents Worldwide)

Source: U.S. Patent and Trademark Office, "U.S. Patent Statistics Chart, Calendar Years 1963–2020" (https://www.uspto.gov/web/offices/ac/ido/oeip/taf/us_stat.htm).

capital markets have shorter-term perspectives and more rapidly reflect the ever-changing vagaries of markets.

Starting from 2014 onward, Russia's debt and equity fundraising activity closely mirrored FDI inflows. Russia's invasion of Crimea and the Donbas in 2014, the imposition of Western sanctions, and a substantial decline in oil prices prompted rating agencies to downgrade Russian sovereign debt ratings to non-investment-grade status (BB+) in 2015. Consequently, financing activities, including Russian equity issuance, decreased, and the net inflow of FDI declined.

Figures 2.6 and 2.7, in conjunction with tables 2.5, 2.6, and 2.7, vividly demonstrate the substantial impact of Kremlin-associated entities on external financing activities. In this specific case, Gazprom, Gazpromneft, GazFinance, VTB, VEB, Sberbank, Norilsk Nickel, Rosneft, Russian Railways, Rusal, and Russia as the sovereign borrower (here collectively referred to as "sovereign and power vertical–aligned" entities), accounted for an exceptionally high concentration of external financing activity.

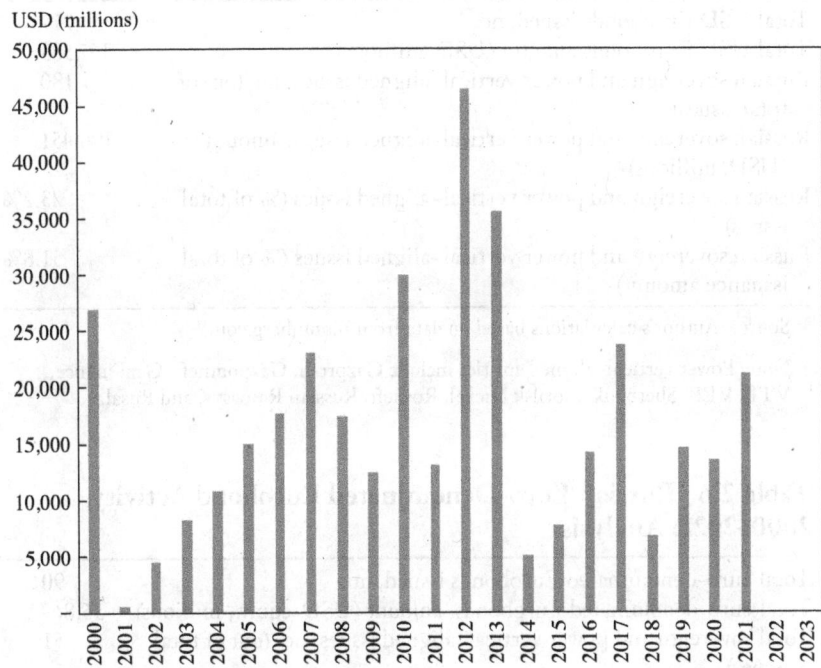

FIGURE 2.6. Russian USD-Denominated Eurobond Issuance, 2000–2023 (Millions of USD)

Source: Author's calculations based on data from Bloomberg.com.

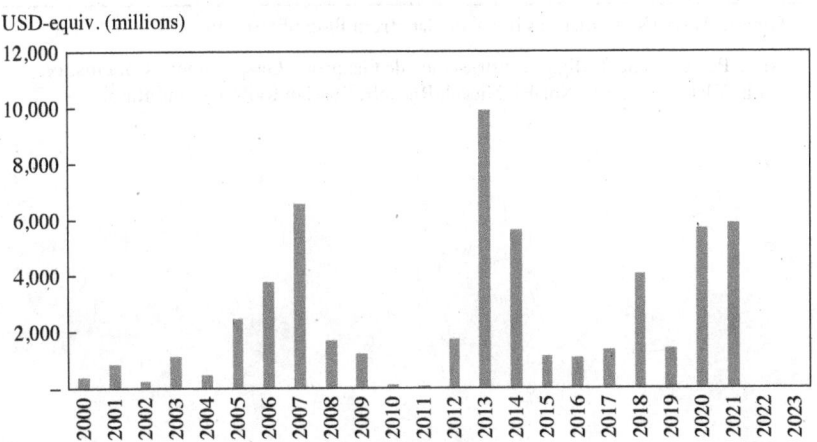

FIGURE 2.7. Russian Euro-Denominated Eurobond Issuance, 2000–2023 (Millions of USD-Equivalent)

Source: Author's calculations based on data from Bloomberg.com.

Table 2.5. Russian USD-Denominated Eurobond Activity, 2000–2022: Analysis

Total USD Eurobonds issued, no.	777
Total USD Eurobonds amount (USD, millions)	367,583
Russian sovereign and power vertical–aligned issues, no. (out of total issues)	180
Russian sovereign and power vertical–aligned issues, amount (USD, millions)	190,451
Russian sovereign and power vertical–aligned issues (% of total issues)	23.2%
Russian sovereign and power vertical–aligned issues (% of total issuance amount)	51.8%

Source: Author's calculations based on data from Bloomberg.com.

Note: Power vertical–aligned entities include Gazprom, Gazpomneft, GazFinance, VTB, VEB, Sberbank, Norilsk Nickel, Rosneft, Russian Railways, and Rusal.

Table 2.6. Russian Euro-Denominated Eurobond Activity, 2000–2022: Analysis

Total euro-denominated Eurobonds issued, no.	90
Total euro-denominated Eurobonds, amount (USD-equiv., millions)	56,867
Total sovereign and power vertical–aligned issues, no. (out of total issues)	51
Total sovereign and power vertical–aligned issues, amount (USD-equiv., millions)	47,278
Total sovereign and power vertical–aligned issues (% of total issues)	56.7%
Total sovereign and power vertical–aligned issues (% of total issuance amount)	83.1%

Source: Author's calculations based on data from Bloomberg.com.

Note: Power vertical–aligned entities include Gazprom, Gazpomneft, GazFinance, VTB, VEB, Sberbank, Norilsk Nickel, Rosneft, Russian Railways, and Rusal.

Table 2.7. Russian International Syndicated Loans, 2000–2020 (November) (USD and Euros)

Russian syndicated loans (USD)	
Funds raised (USD, millions)	631,750
No. of transactions	1,580
No. of transactions executed by power vertical–aligned entities*	271
As % of total transactions in USD syndications loan market	17.2%
Funds raised by power vertical–aligned entities (USD, millions)	211,475
As % of total funds raised in USD syndications loan market	33.5%
Russian syndicated loans (euro)	
Funds raised (USD equiv., millions)	76,343
No. of transactions	311
No. of transactions executed by power vertical–aligned entities†	67
As % of total transactions in euro syndications loan market	21.5%
Funds raised by power vertical–aligned entities (USD equiv., millions)	40,229
As % of total funds raised in euro syndications loan market	52.7%

Source: Author's calculations based on data from Bloomberg.com.

*Russian sovereign, Gazprom group, Lukoil, Norilsk Nickel, Rosneft, Russian Railways, Sberbank, VEB/VEB Leasing, VTB.

†Gazprom group, Lukoil, Rosneft, Russian Railways, Sberbank, VTB, VEB.

Specifically, in the USD-denominated Eurobond market, these entities raised over 50 percent of the total funds, while in the euro-denominated equivalent, they raised more than 83 percent. A similar concentration existed in the syndicated USD and euro loan markets, where they attracted 34–53 percent of the total funds raised between 2000 and 2020. Additionally, in the global equity markets, these entities were responsible for more than 40 percent of the total equity raised.

Such figures are likely conservative. In a 2012 *Forbes* investigation, it was revealed that a close group of Putin's long-term loyal friends and associates exerted control over large state corporations, key industries, strategically important public projects, and state contracts. The total revenue overseen by this group, which included such individuals as Alexei Miller of Gazprom and Arkady Rotenberg of Stroygazmontazh, reached 12.3 trillion rubles. This amount was equivalent to 22.6 percent of Russia's GDP in that year.[28]

In 2018, Russia regained its investment-grade rating, leading to a modest increase in fundraising. However, immediately after February 2022, the West closed its financial markets to Russia. Rating agencies such as S&P, Moody's, and Fitch downgraded Russia's rating to NR ("rating no longer

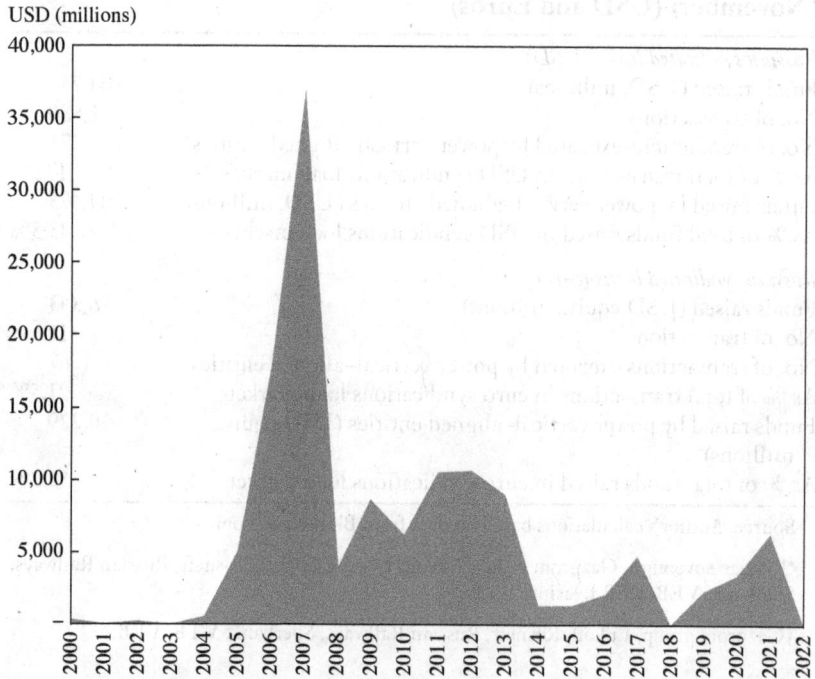

FIGURE 2.8. Russian Equities Issuance, 2000–2022 (Millions of USD)

Source: Author's calculations based on data from Preqveca.ru.

assigned") by April of that year. Russia defaulted on part of its foreign currency–denominated debt two months later. As a result, Russia could no longer raise any significant amount of capital.

The Russian Equity Market and Its Decreasing Relevance

Russian equity issuers have significantly relied on foreign stock exchanges, as highlighted in figure 2.8 and table 2.8. Only 20 percent of Russian equity issuance between 2000 and 2022 was exclusively carried out on Russian stock exchanges, specifically the Russian Trading System (RTS) and the Moscow Interbank Currency Exchange (MICEX), which merged in December 2011 to form the Moscow Exchange (commonly known as the MICEX-RTS or MOEX). The remaining 80 percent of issuers sought support through colistings on larger, well-established foreign stock exchanges. Under the existing Western sanctions regime, the world's largest stock

Table 2.8. Russian Equity Issuance Breakdown by Exchange, 2000–2022 (Millions of USD)

Total Russian equity issues (USD, millions)		131,368
On Russian RTS and Micex exchanges only	26,577	20%
RTS/Micex jointly with London LSE	43,557	33%
On London LSE only	22,658	17%
Power vertical–aligned large cap issuers as % of total issuances	54,257	41%

Source: Author's calculations based on data from Preqveca.ru.

Note: Power vertical–aligned issuers in the above calculation are Aeroflot, Sovcomflot, Evraz, Norilsk Nickel, EN+, Russneft, Alrosa, Mechel, VTB, Rusal, MMK, Sberbank, Severstal, and Rosneft.

exchanges, including the London Stock Exchange (LSE), the New York Stock Exchange (NYSE), and NASDAQ, remain effectively closed to Russian issuers.

Russian equity issuance data reveal that the stock market capitalization-to-GDP ratio in Russia significantly lags behind its emerging market counterparts. This ratio is grounded in the idea that the stock market's value reflects the present value of expected future economic activity. Given that GDP measures the most recent actual economic activity, the ratio of these two data series signifies the expected future returns relative to the current performance. In other words, a higher ratio suggests that investors anticipate more efficient returns from labor and capital due to technological advancements and innovation. Conversely, a lower ratio may indicate a lack of innovation and change, resulting in less efficient returns. Currently, Russia's ratio, 3 percent, ranks among the lowest in the world, closely aligning with that of such countries as Armenia and Serbia. For comparison with other large developing economies, Brazil's ratio is 45.2 percent, China's is 61.3 percent, and India's is 124 percent (the United States' ratio is 194.5 percent).[29]

Russian equity issuance falls significantly short when compared to that of Brazil, India, and China. This discrepancy is evident across various metrics, including the number of transactions executed, equity amounts raised, and amounts raised as a percentage of the country's GDP (table 2.9).

According to World Bank 2020 year-end data, the total market capitalization of Russian listed (domestic) companies amounted to $695 billion. This represented only 0.75 percent of the global stock market capitalization, which stood at $92.5 trillion during the same period. By the end of 2022,

Table 2.9. Comparative Equity Issuance: Russia, Brazil, China, India, 2021 (Millions of USD)

Country	2021 Total Deals	2021 Issuance Amount	2021 Country GDP	Issuance as % of GDP	GDP as % of world GDP
Russia	18	6,300	1,778,000	0.35	1.85
Brazil	54	16,400	1,600,000	1.03	1.66
China	645	131,500	17,730,000	0.74	18.45
India	125	18,000	3,173,000	0.57	3.30
2021 World Total	2,227	433,000	96,100,000		
Russia as % of	0.81%	1.45%			

Sources: Author's calculations based on data from Preqveca.ru, Bloomberg.com, and World Bank.

Note: Russia's largest equity transaction was Rosneft's initial public offering (IPO) in 2007 for $10,656 million (representing 8.1 percent of total Russian stock equity issuance in the last twenty-two years). Andrei Illarionov, Russian economist and former senior policy adviser to Vladimir Putin, called the Rosneft IPO transaction an "international legalization of ownership of assets previously illegally acquired."[31]

Russia's market capitalization had dwindled further to $530 billion. In contrast, the global stock market capitalization had increased to $93.7 trillion, resulting in Russia's share declining to 0.57 percent of the total global market capitalization.[30]

The current weighting of stock issues by shares on the MOEX exchange, as detailed in table 2.10, highlights a pronounced concentration of value and market power. Notably, 72 percent of this influence is wielded by twenty-one power vertical–aligned enterprises.

Innovation is mostly absent from the Russian equity story, although there are some notable exceptions, such as Yandex (discussed in chapter 1). Russian equities listed on the MOEX, shown in table 2.10, lack an equivalent to the American FAANG or "Magnificent Seven" tech stocks—companies that command remarkable market capitalizations compared to their humble origins two decades or just several years earlier. FAANG is an acronym that stands for five major technology companies listed on U.S. stock exchanges: Facebook (now Meta), Amazon, Apple, Netflix, and Google (now Alphabet); the Magnificent Seven grouping replaces Netflix with Nvidia and adds Tesla and Microsoft.

In addition to Eurobond, syndicated loans, and equity markets, international financial institutions, such as the International Finance Corporation (IFC) and the European Bank for Reconstruction and Development (EBRD), along with export credit agencies (ECAs), have also provided financing. However, the cumulative financial contributions of these agencies pale in comparison to the aforementioned markets. For instance, by 2014, the EBRD had cumulatively extended €27.1 billion in loans, undrawn loan commitments, and guarantees. It subsequently ceased investing in Russia and closed its offices that year. ECAs played a similarly visible but minor role, with at least ten of them stopping or limiting coverage for Russia since February 2022. ECA exposure to Russia ranged from a minuscule A$3 million from Export Finance Australia to €1.7 billion from Austria's OeKB, €1 billion from Finland's Finnvera, U.S. $453 million from Sweden's EKN, U.S. $428 million from the U.S. Export-Import Bank, and €170 million from Poland's Kuke. Both the U.S. Exim and Export Development Canada (EDC) halted business with Russia following its annexation of Crimea in 2014.[32]

Domestic Ruble Finance Sector

In 2022, international debt and equity markets closed their doors to Russia. However, Russia's ruble market continues to operate. Ruble financing relies on Russian banks and the domestic bond market. As of January 1, 2025, according to the Central Bank of Russia, there are 314 banks in Russia, 96 of which were thinly capitalized (with capital less than 1 billion rubles). Between 2000 and 2017, the Central Bank of Russia took decisive action, closing approximately 2,600 out of just over 3,000 registered banks. This extensive cleanup aimed to eliminate so-called banks that were systemically involved in destructive illegal practices, including money laundering, pyramid schemes, wholesale theft of depositors' funds by unscrupulous shareholders, tax evasion, and oligarch piggy-bank lending practices.

The Russian banking system is top-heavy, largely state-controlled, and heavily regulated by the Central Bank of Russia. The two largest banks in Russia, Sberbank and VTB, account for around 50 percent of the entire banking sector. State ownership of the banking sector has continuously grown under Putin and constituted 72 percent by November 2021 (see tables 2.11 and 2.12), and may further increase. The Central Bank of Russia

Table 2.10. Russian Companies Listed on the MOEX as of December 16, 2022

Code	Security name (English)	Number of issued shares	Free-float factor	Weight (30.11.2022)
GAZP	PJSC Gazprom, ordinary shares	23,673,512,900	50%	15.00%
SBER	PJSC Sberbank, ordinary shares	21,586,948,000	48%	11.81%
SBERP	PJSC Sberbank, preferred shares	1,000,000,000	100%	1.10%
LKOH	PJSC Lukoil, ordinary shares	692,865,762	55%	14.73%
GMKN	PJSC MMC Norilsk Nickel, ordinary shares	153,654,624	37%	6.83%
NVTK	JSC Novatek, ordinary shares	3,036,306,000	21%	5.53%
YNDX	Yandex NV, shares of a foreign issuer	326,016,891	97%	5.53%
ROSN	PJSC Rosneft, ordinary shares	10,598,177,817	11%	3.69%
MGNT	PJSC Magnit, ordinary shares	101,911,355	67%	3.09%
TCSG	TCS Group Holding PLC, DR (issuer of depository receipts, JP Morgan Chase Bank)	199,305,492	58%	2.96%
TATN	PJSC Tatneft, ordinary shares	2,178,690,700	32%	2.39%
PHOR	PJSC PhosAgro, ordinary shares	129,500,000	26%	2.04%
PLZL	PJSC Polyus, ordinary shares	136,069,400	22%	2.03%
SNGS	PJSC Surgutneftegas, ordinary shares	35,725,994,705	25%	1.82%
MTSS	PJSC MTS, ordinary shares	1,998,381,575	41%	1.82%
FIVE	X5 Retail Group NV (issuer, Bank of New York Mellon)	271,572,872	41%	1.61%
ALRS	PJSC Alrosa, ordinary shares	7,364,965,630	34%	1.53%
CHMF	PJSC Severstal, ordinary shares	837,718,660	23%	1.43%
SNGSP	PJSC Surgutneftegas, preferred shares	7,701,998,235	73%	1.32%
NLMK	PJSC NLMK, ordinary shares	5,993,227,240	21%	1.26%
MOEX	PJSC Moscow Exchange, ordinary shares	2,276,401,458	64%	1.19%
IRAO	PJSC Inter RAO, ordinary shares	104,400,000,000	35%	1.13%

Ticker	Company	Value	%	%
POLY	Polymetal International PLC, shares of a foreign issuer	473,626,239	71%	1.11%
OZON	Ozon Holdings PLC, DR (issuer of depository receipts, Bank of New York Mellon)	216,413,733	36%	1.04%
OZON	Ozon Holdings PLC, DR (the issuer of depository receipts - The Bank of New York Mellon)			
RUAL	United Company Rusal IPJSC, ordinary shares	15,193,014,862	18%	0.99%
PIKK	PJSC PIK Group, ordinary shares	660,497,344	22%	0.83%
VTBR	VTB Bank (PJSC), ordinary shares	12,960,541,337,338	36%	0.74%
MAGN	PJSC MMK, ordinary shares	11,174,330,000	20%	0.66%
VKCO	VK Company Ltd., DR, on shares of foreign issuer	226,136,827	53%	0.56%
RTKM	PJSC Rostelecom, ordinary shares	3,282,997,929	29%	0.51%
TATNP	PJSC Tatneft, preferred shares	147,508,500	100%	0.49%
TRNFP	PJSC Transneft, preferred shares	1,554,875	37%	0.48%
HYDR	PJSC RusHydro, ordinary shares	439,288,905,849	15%	0.47%
CBOM	PJSC Credit Bank of Moscow, ordinary shares	33,429,709,866	22%	0.43%
FIXP	Fix Price Group Ltd, DR	850,000,000	27%	0.38%
AFKS	Sistema PJSFC, ordinary shares	9,650,000,000	32%	0.36%
ENPG	EN+ GROUP IPJSC, ordinary shares	638,848,896	14%	0.34%
GLTR	Globaltrans Investment PLC, DR (issuer of depository receipts, Citiank NA—New York City)	178,740,916	57%	0.27%
DSKY	PJSC Detsky mir, ordinary shares	739,000,000	54%	0.26%
AFLT	PJSC Aeroflot, ordinary shares	3,975,771,215	25%	0.23%
	Power vertical–associated Russian corporations listed on the MOEX			100.00% 72.08%

*As of November 30, 2022.

Source: Moex.com.

Note: As of November 30, 2022. Entries in shaded boxes are power vertical–associated Russian corporations listed on the MOEX.

Table 2.11. Top Ten Banks in Russia as of November 2021

Bank	Assets (rubles, bln)	Russian state majority controlled
Sberbank	38,778	Yes
VTB	19,896	Yes
Gazprombank	8,267	Yes
Alfa-Bank	5,592	No
Rosselkhozbank	4,258	Yes
Credit Bank of Moscow	3,415	No
Otkritie FC	3,294	Yes
Promsvyazbank	4,334	Yes
Sovcombank	1,847	No
Rosbank	1,500	No
Total	91,181	
Total Russian banking sector assets	119,000	
Total number of banks in system	335	
Non-bank credit institutions	35	
Total	370	
% held by top ten banks	76.6%	
% held by top state controlled banks	66.2%	
% held by Sberbank and VTB	49.3%	
Total State-Owned banks as % of all banks	72.0%	
Not included: National Clearing Centre	5,852	

Source: Bank of Russia, Banking Sector 2021 (https://www.cbr.ru/eng/banking_sector/), last accessed April 2, 2023. Current data can be found at https://www.cbr.ru/eng/banking_sector/#:~:text=Russia%20also%20has%20a%20deposit,include%20loans%20to%20general%20government.

Note: Otkritie FC and Promsvyazbank are specially managed by the Central Bank of Russia under the bank resolution process.

also intervenes to rescue banks facing financial difficulties, as seen with the cases of Otkritie and Promsvyazbank in 2017. Otkritie was subsequently purchased by VTB in 2022.

Despite the Central Bank of Russia's cleanup efforts, Russia's financial sector is poorly ranked in the World Economic Forum's *Global Competitiveness Report* of 2019, which assessed 141 countries. Russia's rankings are as follows: 95th in financial system competitiveness, 115th in the soundness of banks, 132nd in the banks' regulatory credit ratio, 118th in financing of SMEs, and 107th in the level of nonperforming loans. The World Economic

Table 2.12. Russian Banking System "Balance Sheet" as of December 31, 2021 (Trillions of Rubles)

Assets	Amount	(% of total)	Liabilities	Amount	(% of total)
Corporate loans	52.7	(43.7)	Individual funds	34.7	(28.8)
Retail loans	25.1	(20.8)	Escrow accounts	3	(2.5)
Securities	16.9	(14.0)	Companies' funds	38.3	(31.8)
Deposits with Bank of Russia	2.8	(2.3)	General govt. funds	6.3	(5.2)
Cash and equivalents	6.8	(5.6)	Bank of Russia loans	3.1	(2.6)
Interbank loans	12.4	(10.3)	Bank funds	12.8	(10.6)
			Capital	12	(10.0)
Other assets	3.8	(3.2)	Other liabilities	10.3	(8.5)
Total	120.5	(100)	Total	120.5	(100)

Source: Bank of Russia.

Forum has not updated financial sector competitive rankings in its most recent, 2020 survey edition.

Before February 24, 2022, the Russian banking sector faced several challenges. The war introduced significant new ones:

- More severe sanctions, including the exclusion of most banks from SWIFT;
- Limited access to cheaper and efficient international capital markets;
- Changes (when negative) in natural resources prices, impacting cash flows;
- Ruble devaluation, adversely affecting depositors, funding, and liquidity;
- Increasing NPL (nonperforming loan) ratios and extended loan "grace periods" for domestic borrowers;
- Loss of liquidity, technology, and management skills as a result of foreign banks exiting the market, with no replacement by Chinese or other banks;
- Higher state ownership concentration and alignment with Putin's power vertical;

- Russian federal budget deficits, necessitating greater investment of available liquidity into OFZ securities (Облигации Федерального Займа, Obligatsyi Federal'novo Zaima [Federal Loan Obligations]—coupon-bearing federal loan bonds issued by the Russian government). Currently, OFZ securities occupy about 17 percent of the banking system's balance sheet;
- Rising state ownership of banks, potentially diverting liquidity to state-owned enterprises (SOEs) that already constitute 60 percent of Russia's economy and government revenue, at the expense of SMEs and the private sector;
- New levies related to the "special military operation" in Ukraine; and
- Persistent inefficiencies, including excessive and sometimes capricious reporting requirements.

Despite the Central Bank of Russia's clean-up efforts in recent years, some argue that "Russia's banking system will remain a bankrupt system that merely facilitates the enrichment of people who know how to game the system."[33]

Ruble Bonds

Ruble bonds play a crucial role in financing the Russian economy. Owing to inflation in Russia, they feature higher interest rates compared to dollar and euro equivalents. Between 2000 and 2022, a total of 5,935 ruble bond issues raised over $554 billion in USD-equivalent finance, as reported by Bloomberg. Notably, the Russian state and various municipalities and districts accounted for more than 50 percent of the total issuance.

Crowding Out in the OFZ Market

The Russian federal budget heavily relies on the OFZ market.

Nonresident participation in the OFZ market once played a significant role, particularly starting in 2013, driven by the following factors:

- The Russian government relaxed certain market regulations governing OFZ investment.
- OFZ transactions became euro clearable.
- As the global financial crisis receded, international investors returned, seeking higher yields in the emerging markets, making Russian OFZ more attractive.

Table 2.13. OFZ Issuance, 2011–February 2024

	Issued (rubles, bln)	Nonresident market share (%)
February 29, 2024	20,162	7.2
February 28, 2023	18,560	9.7
2022	15,534	17.6
2021	15,494	19.9
2020	13,699	23.3
2019	8,905	32.2
2018	7,333	24.4
2017	6,740	33.1
2016	5,633	26.9
2015	4,991	21.5
2014	4,693	18.7
2013	3,735	23.9
2012	3,297	19.9
2011	2,903	3.7

Sources: Bank of Russia, "Nonresidents Share in the Russian Federation Domestic Bonds (OFZ)" (https://www.cbr.ru/eng/search/?Text=ofz&Category=Any&Time=Any&DateFrom=&DateTo=.).

- Derivative instruments, such as cross-currency and interest rate swaps, enabled foreign investors to hedge risks.

OFZ issuance and Eurobonds were the primary sources of financing for Russia's budget deficit. However, this dynamic shifted in 2022 when the Eurobond market closed to Russia, and foreign purchases of OFZs steeply declined (table 2.13). Consequently, the domestic banking system redirected more assets to bridge the gap and support OFZ issuance. For instance, in 2020, Sberbank held over 2.4 trillion rubles and VTB over 900 billion rubles, accounting for approximately 25 percent of the total outstanding OFZs.[34]

Conclusion

Some $3 trillion later, Russia's economy still lacks significant modernization. Numerous sectors have stagnated, with some even experiencing regression.[35] Russia failed to capitalize on an unprecedented resource.

Beginning with the onset of the global financial crisis in 2007, Russia fell behind its emerging market peers, as depicted in figure 2.9 and measured by various performance metrics. These metrics include inward FDI

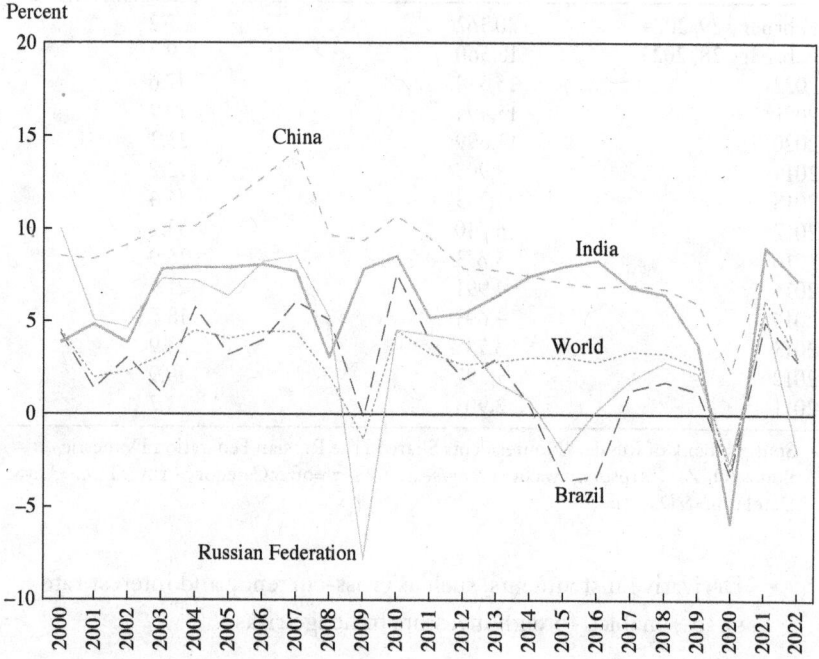

FIGURE 2.9. GDP Annual Growth Compared: Brazil, China, India, Russian Federation, World, 2000–2022 (Percent)

Source: World Bank (data.worldbank.org).

as a percentage of gross fixed capital formation, FDI as a percentage of GDP, annual net FDI inflows, medium- and high-tech value added as a percentage of manufacturing value-added, equity market capitalization as a percentage of GDP, and anemic or negative GDP growth. Overall, Russia's financial health has undeniably weakened. The West's freezing of over half of Russia's foreign exchange reserves in 2022 eroded the substantial buffer that the Central Bank of Russia had long used to safeguard against systemic shocks and a weakening ruble.

Russian economic policymakers struggled to establish an environment conducive to attracting consistent FDI for driving rapid economic growth, diversification, and innovation within the economy. Notably, the lion's share of FDI and international capital funneled into the natural resources sector, accounting for approximately 65 percent of Russia's total exports. This concentration of investment primarily benefited enterprises aligned with the Kremlin power structure. Despite these inflows, Russia witnessed extreme capital flight, reaching up to $1.5 trillion.

Russia remains ensnared in an enduring natural resources curse, a predicament that the Kremlin has shown little inclination to rectify. Vladimir Putin's priorities with regard to Russia's natural resources sector provide the rationale: state control and resource nationalism. Domestically, Putin "protected Russia from the liberal West," but in doing so, marginalized key foreign investors. Russia's "national resource champions," Gazprom and Rosneft, supported the Kremlin's foreign policy goals through numerous overseas investments, which only diminished corporate value. Putin may consider himself successful in pursuing what he believes is best for Russia, his regime, and himself, but this has come at a definitive cost to Russia's economy.

Perhaps Putin's greatest disappointment lies in Gazprom's failure to achieve a stock market capitalization of $1 trillion, a boast made by the company's CEO, Alexei Miller, back in 2008. As of November 1, 2024, Gazprom's market capitalization stood at a mere $30 billion. Rosneft's was $49 billion. To provide some context, consider that Uber, the asset-less ride-hailing company, commanded a market capitalization of $155 billion at that time.[36]

The West has significantly distanced itself from Russia. Investors such as BP, ExxonMobil, Shell, McDonalds, IKEA and other multinational enterprises—with substantial FDI holdings—have departed, writing off billions of dollars in shareholder value. Prominent players in the automotive sector, including Ford, Volvo, Volkswagen, BMW, Renault, Scania, Nissan, and Daimler Benz, have either halted production or divested their assets altogether. The valuable "spillovers" of technology and management/entrepreneurship skills have come to a halt. However, certain multinational entities, particularly in the consumer products domain, remain in a state of waiting, expressing concern about their Russian staff or claiming to "safeguard the ordinary consumer."[37] For instance, French retailer Auchan Retail Russia continues to operate 230 stores with 30,000 employees.[38] Meanwhile, Nestlé, Heineken, and Mondelez have suspended fresh investments, scaled back their existing presence, and now aim for an organized if improbable exit. We are told that "the situation is complex." Recent decrees signed by Putin have placed the operations of other companies—such as Germany's Uniper, Finland's Fortum, Denmark's Carlsberg, and France's Danone—under the management of the federal state property management agency, Rosimushchestvo, under the guise of "temporary management."

This action paves a disconcerting path leading to corruption and the potential for coercion.

Putin's ongoing war in Ukraine has significantly reshaped Russia's financial and investment landscape. The combination of escalating military and security expenditures, coupled with reduced revenues, is poised to exacerbate deficits within the Russian federal budget. This new reality clashes with allocations for critical areas such as human capital and welfare. Given Russia's grim demographic and labor forecast, particularly following the acceleration of talent emigration in 2022, this becomes a pressing concern.

The state-controlled banking sector will allocate a greater portion of liquidity toward OFZ, further limiting borrowing opportunities for the private sector. Ideally, banks should serve as primary catalysts for economic diversification, innovation, and increases in factor productivity. However, under these circumstances, they will become more restricted and less effective in their functions. As a consequence, Russia's global economic rankings and competitiveness are likely to continue declining.

Russia's vulnerability to paradigm shifts in the global energy industry has increased, exacerbated by Western sanctions. As a natural resources supplier in a "buyer's market," Russia is compelled to offer discounts and accept inferior terms dictated by buyers, including China and India. Despite these constraints, Russia continues to navigate the energy landscape, finding ways to sell its energy goods despite Western restrictions.

The limited investments from China cannot match the scale, caliber, and scope of the previous Western commitments that have been withdrawn. Furthermore, these investments are unlikely to secure significant financial support. It has become obvious that selling to Russia is more attractive than investing. For instance, Chinese automobile exports now dominate Russia's new automobile market, capturing an impressive 61 percent market share in 2023. Yet Chinese FDI in Russia's automotive sector remains at zero.[39]

The future outlook for Russia remains grim. The FDI and international finance that sustained Russia over two decades are now lost, with little chance of revival.

NOTES

1. In 2004, oil and gas revenues contributed 30.19 percent of the total Russian federal budget revenues, versus 36.9 percent in 2021. Data for 2004 from Sabitova and Shavaleyeva (2015). Data for 2021 from Gurevich et al. (2022).

2. Mileva (2008), 24–25.
3. Hirschman (1964), 37.
4. Vinhas de Souza (2008).
5. Russian political scientist Vladimir Gel'man introduced the term "pockets of efficiency" to Russian studies. See Vladimir Gel'man, *The Politics of Bad Governance in Contemporary Russia*, University of Michigan Press, 2022.
6. Domínguez-Jiménez and Poitiers (2020).
7. Domínguez-Jiménez and Poitiers (2020).
8. Arshad Hayat (2014, 2018). See also several follow-up studies by Hayat on this topic at https://scholar.google.com/citations?user=VtvuhjEAAAAJ&hl=en.
9. Wright and Czelusta (2004), 24.
10. Domínguez-Jiménez and Poitiers (2020), 158. See also the papers by Gavin Wright and Jesse Czelusta arguing that the way out of the natural resources curse is to use the resources sector as the place to begin developing domestic technology.
11. Galeeva and Kadeeva (2018).
12. Berezinskaya (2017).
13. Ibid., 71–82.
14. Becker (2019).
15. Krylova (2018), 1.
16. Johnson (2019).
17. Ash (2022).
18. Bulatov (2022).
19. *Moscow Times* (2023).
20. Bulatov (2022).
21. Galeeva and Kadeeva (2018), 2.
22. World Bank's 2018 Doing Business report.
23. Domínguez-Jiménez and Poitiers (2020).
24. Repinskiy et al. (2021). Another noteworthy analysis of Russia's lost innovation base is Satoshi Mizobata's "State-Led Innovation and Uneven Adaptation in Russia" (2021).
25. CB Insights (2024). It may also be mentioned that decades earlier, Igor Sikorsky (helicopters) and David Sarnoff (television) fled Russia for the United States and flourished there.
26. Vladislav Inozemtsev quoted in Wimbush and Portale (2017), 7. Inozemtsev refers to the years 2008–2015.
27. Galeeva and Kadeeva (2018), 6.
28. Krylova (2018), 28.
29. Moscow Exchange data and Brazil market cap data from CEICdata.com; U.S. data from Wikipedia; Brazil GDP data from brasildefato.com.br.
30. World Bank data from https://data.worldbank.org/indicator/cm.mkt.lcap.cd?locations=1W,=ru (last viewed July 5, 2024).

31. Andrei Illarionov, quoted in Cato Institute (2007).
32. Atkins and Thompson (2022).
33. Movchan (2018).
34. Sberbank Annual Report (2021), 40 (https://irpages2.eqs.com/Download/Companies/sberbank/Annual%20Reports/US80585Y3080-JA-2021-EQ-E-00.pdf. See also Bank of Russia Annual Report for 2022 at https://www.cbr.ru/collection/collection/file/46299/ar_2022_e.pdf, pp. 36, 49, and 54).
35. Kudrin and Gurvich (2014) provide valuable perspective on the debilitating dominance of state-owned and quasi-state companies in the Russian economy in "A New Growth Model for the Russian Economy."
36. Market capitalization data from https://companiesmarketcap.com (last accessed November 1, 2024). See also Åslund and Fisher (2020).
37. For a summary of foreign businesses' actions regarding exiting Russia (after February 2022), see Shapoval, Hribanovskyi, and Onoprieenko (2023).
38. Interfax (2024). See also Maria Shagina of the International Institute for Strategic Studies, quoted on CNN, July 26, 2023.
39. AutoNews (2024). See also Voronin and Khorunzhii (2024). This study of the role of Chinese FDI in Russian transport infrastructure cites Central Bank of Russia 2021 data that indicate that only approximately 1 percent of incoming FDI to Russia comes from China and only 5 percent of that amount is in the transport sector. The identified transport sector investments were for bridges and highway segments, tankers, customs and logistics terminals, a cross-border cable car, and agrologistic centers. There was no investment in the automotive sector. The study concludes that "the total volume of Chinese foreign direct investment in Russia does not align with the high level of political relations between the two countries."

REFERENCES

Ash, Timothy. 2022. "London Laundromat." Timothyash.substack.com, February 15.

Åslund, Anders, and Steven Fisher. 2020. "New Challenges and Dwindling Returns for Russia's National Champions, Gazprom and Rosneft." Atlantic Council, June 5.

Atkins, Jacob, and Felix Thompson. 2022. "Export Credit Agencies and Trade Credit Insurers Slam Door on Russia." *Global Trade Review*, March 9.

AutoNews. 2024. "Dolia kitaiskikh avtomobilei na rossiiskom rynke prevysila 60%" [The share of Chinese cars in the Russian market has exceeded 60%]. AutoNews.ru, January 10.

Becker, Torbjörn. 2019. "Russia's Macroeconomy—A Closer Look at Growth, Investment and Uncertainty." SITE Working Paper no. 49. Stockholm School of Economics, Stockholm Institute of Transition Economics (SITE), June.

Berezinskaya, Olga. 2017. "Investment Drought in the Russian Economy." *Russian Journal of Economics* 3 (1).
Bulatov, Alexander S. 2022. "MNES and Capital Flight: The Case of Russia." *Russian Journal of Economics* 8 (2).
Cato Institute. 2007. "Oil and Freedom in the New Russia." Policy report. Cato Institute, January/February.
CB Insights. 2024. "The Complete List of Unicorn Companies" (https://Notes.cbinsights.com/research-unicorn-companies). May 2024 data (last viewed November 1, 2024).
Domínguez-Jiménez, Marta, and Niclas Frederic Poitiers. 2020. "An Analysis of EU FDI Inflow into Russia." *Russian Journal of Economics* 6 (2).
Galeeva, G. M., and E. N. Kadeeva. 2018. "Problems of Attracting Foreign Direct Investment into the Regional Economy." *Journal of Physics*: Conference Series 1730, January 21.
Gel'man, Vladimir. 2022. *The Politics of Bad Governance in Contemporary Russia*. Ann Arbor: University of Michigan Press.
Gurevich, V., S. Drobyshevsky, V. Mau, and S. Sinelnikov-Murylev, eds. 2022. "Monitoring of Russia's Economic Outlook: Trends and Challenges of Socio-economic Development," no. 4 (148), March. Moscow: Gaidar Institute for Economic Policy, Russian Presidential Academy of National Economy and Public Administration.
Hayat, Arshad. 2018. "FDI and Economic Growth: The Role of Natural Resources?" *Journal of Economic Studies* 45 (2).
———. 2014. "FDI and Economic Growth: The Role of Natural Resources." Institute of Economic Studies (IES) Working Paper 36/2014. Prague: Charles University, IES.
Hirschman, Albert O. 1964. *The Strategy of Economic Development*. New Haven, CT: Yale University Press.
Interfax. 2024. "Auchan Not Planning to Change Strategy or Operations in Russia." April 16.
Johnson, Scott. 2019. "Capital Flight from Russia Carries $750 Billion Price Tag." Bloomberg, March 12.
Kudrin, Aleksei, and Evsei Gurvich. 2014. "Novaia model' rosta dlia rossiiskoi ekonomiki" [A new Russian economic growth model]. *Voprosy ekonomiki*, 12:4–36.
Krylova, Yulia. 2018. *Corruption and the Russian Economy*. London: Routledge.
McKay, John P. 2015. *Pioneers for Profit: Foreign Entrepreneurship and Russian Industrialization 1885–1913*. Chicago: University of Chicago Press.
Mileva, Elitza. 2008. "The Impact of Capital Flows on Domestic Investment in Transition Economies." European Central Bank Working Paper Series no. 871. Frankfurt am Main: ECB, February.
Mizobata, Satoshi. 2021. "State-Led Innovation and Uneven Adaptation in Russia." In *Putin's Russia: Economy, Defence and Foreign Policy*, ed. Steven Rosefielde. Singapore: World Scientific.

Moscow Times. 2023. "Russia Loses Record $253 Bln in Wartime Capital Flight." July 24.

Movchan, Andrey. 2018. "How to Fix Russia's Broken Banking System." *Financial Times*, January 14.

Repinskiy, O. D., et al. 2021. "Improving the Competitiveness of Russian Industry in the Production of Measuring and Analytical Equipment." *Journal of Physics*: Conference Series 1728 012032.

Reuters. 2021. "Update 1-VTB Ready to Buy More OFZ Bonds If Russia Raises State Debt, CEO Says." March 29.

Rosefielde, Steven, ed. 2021. *Putin's Russia: Economy, Defence and Foreign Policy.* Singapore: World Scientific.

Sabitova, Nadia, and Chulpan Shavaleyeva. 2015. "Oil and Gas Revenues of the Russian Federation: Trends and Prospects." Paper delivered at the 22nd International Economic Conference—IECS 2015, "Economic Prospects in the Context of Growing Global and Regional Interdependencies." *Procedia Economics and Finance* 27:423–28.

Shapoval, Nataliia, Oleksii Hribanovskyi, and Andrii Onoprieenko. 2023. "How the Income of Foreign Businesses in the Russian Federation Has Changed in 2022 and Why So Many Companies Still Do Not Leave." KSE Institute, May.

Vinhas de Souza, Lúcio. 2008. "Foreign Investment in Russia." *ECFIN Country Focus* 5, no. 1 (January 11).

Voronin, V., and A. Khorunzhii. 2024. "The Role of Chinese Foreign Direct Investments in the Russian Transport Infrastructure." Special issue, *Journal of Management & Technology (Revista Gestão & Tecnologia)* 24 (2): 159–73.

Wimbush, S. Enders, and Elizabeth M. Portale, eds. 2017. *Russia in Decline.* Washington, DC: Jamestown Foundation.

World Economic Forum, Klaus Schwab, and Saadia Zahidi. 2020. *The Global Competitiveness Report Special Edition 2020: How Countries Are Performing on the Road to Recovery.* December 16.

Wright, Gavin, and Jesse Czelusta. 2004. "Mineral Resources and Economic Development." Working Paper no. 209. Stanford Center for International Development, February.

THREE

Russian Energy

From Leading Supplier to Purveyor of Discounted Goods

AGNIA GRIGAS

In earlier decades, energy exports were the driver of the Russian economy, the backbone of the state budget, the main tool of the Kremlin's diplomacy and foreign policy, and a source of national pride. Much of Vladimir Putin's success domestically, as reflected in such popular comments as "Putin raised Russia from its knees since the 1990s," has been attributed to the economic recovery of the 2000s, which was largely driven by the rise in oil prices of that decade compared to prices in the difficult 1990s. This created the impression of growing wealth and economic development. Despite the rather long run of both high oil prices and Putin's regime, however, the Kremlin has failed to implement many of its official goals in the Russian energy sector, leaving Russia as dependent on the sale of its resources as ever, increasingly isolated in the global markets, and with a vulnerable economy.

Examining Russian decade-old energy policies and assessing what has been achieved can provide benchmarks for evaluating the successes and failures of the Kremlin's energy agenda. The *Russian Energy Strategy for the Period up to 2035* document, released in September 2015, already acknowledged that "the main external challenge for Russia's energy sector is increased competition on external energy markets." In light of these constraints, the document laid out a clear set of priorities that have largely failed: (1) "stable relationships with traditional consumers of Russian energy" (such as the European markets), (2) faster "access to the Asia-Pacific market," (3) "export diversification," including increasing volumes of liquefied natural gas (LNG) exports, (4) "integration of Russian companies into the international energy business," and (5) "formation of a common energy market for Eurasian Economic Union members."[1] The war in Ukraine since 2022, along with the resulting sanctions and isolation, has further exacerbated the situation if not downright thwarted the achievement of these intended goals.

Of the five goals the energy strategy document laid out, the only one that has been successful is expanding market share in the Chinese and Indian energy markets. While Russia has launched its LNG industry and has seen an increase in exports in absolute terms, it still significantly lags behind other countries, including newer players in the market. Some additional successes can be identified, including the growing global presence of state nuclear giant Rosatom and Russia's collaboration with OPEC regarding oil production.

Meanwhile, the failures are glaring. Russia is no longer perceived as a reliable supplier in the European energy markets. Russian energy companies are under sanctions and face various barriers in the global markets. The EEU has not expanded, and among its members, the only other significant energy producer, Kazakhstan, has gravitated toward China, as have other Central Asian states.

The energy sector is one Putin has personally highly involved himself in, from managing energy diplomacy to creating state champion energy companies and appointing key personal allies to run these companies. At the outset of his leadership in the 2000s, Putin focused his attention on the state energy giant, Gazprom, appointing his trusted allies, later president Dmitry Medvedev and Alexei Miller, to oversee the management of the company. Before he was elected president of Russia (2008–2012), Medvedev had served as Gazprom's chairman of the board in 2000 and then on the board of directors between 2000 and 2001 and again between 2002 and 2008. Putin's aim was to strengthen state energy companies such as Gazprom, the oil giant Rosneft, and the oil transportation leader Transneft in order to break the oligarchs' power in the Russian energy industry. As a result, the Russian economy transitioned from being one-third state-controlled to being two-thirds state-controlled in the 2000s. Under Putin's leadership, the so-called national champions sought not only to maximize revenues but also to advance Russia's national (and particularly foreign policy) interests. These dual goals have often proved contradictory. The strategic and economic importance of the Russian energy sector enables us to assess the successes and failures of this sector as a reflection of the broader successes and failures of the Putin regime.

Within the limited scope of this chapter, I examine the key failures of Russian energy policy of the past decade with a special focus on the gas markets since they were more important for political leverage and have experienced the greatest structural impact. Nonetheless, oil was and remains the main source of revenue for the state, especially during the war economy that has prevailed since 2022. Oil and gas played and will continue to play an important role in shaping relations with China and India. The most significant failures include, first and foremost, Russia losing its dominant position as an oil and gas supplier in the European energy markets. Specifically in the gas sector, the inability to launch Nord Stream 2 and the decline of Gazprom stand out as major setbacks. Additionally, there has been limited success in LNG markets, and Russia failed to participate in the technology and shale revolutions. Finally, instead of integrating into the global energy markets, Russia has become increasingly isolated. Before we examine these strategic failures of Russian energy policy, the next section looks at Russia's energy realities and position in the global markets.

Vast Reserves and Squandered Potential

Be it Russian state television programs or citizen street interviews, all point to the country's preoccupation with its vast energy resources. Of these resources, the most significant in the global markets and to geopolitics are Russian oil and gas. Russia ranks among the top six countries globally in terms of proven oil reserves and possesses the largest proven oil reserves in

Europe and Eurasia, surpassing Kazakhstan and Norway. In 2022, Russia was among the top crude oil exporters in the world, following Saudi Arabia and Canada. That year, Russia exported $119.5 billion or 8.9 percent of global export value.[2] Russia boasts the largest natural gas reserves in the world, totaling some 48 trillion cubic meters (tcm), or around a quarter of the world's proven reserves.[3] Russia remains the world's second largest gas producer after the United States, and, until it was overtaken by the United States in 2022, it was the leading gas-exporting country.

Given its vast reserves, Russia will maintain its role as an energy exporter irrespective of any shifts in the Kremlin or the arguments presented in this chapter. Some may argue that for these reasons alone, it is impossible to consider Russia's energy sector a failure. However, when examining Russia's energy sector, it is important to highlight the relative decline of its role and importance in relation to the global energy markets and particularly in relation to its traditional markets in Europe.

Despite Russia's vast resources and its history as a significant player in the energy markets, the country has lost much of its clout in comparison to earlier decades. Supplying oil and gas to Europe provided Russia, as well as its predecessor, the Soviet Union, with much-needed cash and political influence during the Cold War. After the Cold War, its export revenue helped sustain newly independent Russia and its fledgling democracy under Boris Yeltsin. In the early years of Vladimir Putin's leadership, Russian oil exports were the primary source of revenue for the state and kept the budget in surplus. Gas exports served to strengthen Moscow's diplomatic and economic ties with key EU member states, including Germany, France, Italy, and the UK. Simultaneously, these exports helped maintain Russia's influence in energy-vulnerable countries across Central and Eastern Europe, as well as in the former Soviet republics.

During the 2000s, until the global financial crisis of 2007–2008, Putin's regime rode the wave of rising oil and natural gas prices and growing global demand for energy resources. Russia was persistently the largest supplier of gas to Europe, while Gazprom and Rosneft acquired European downstream energy assets, grew their influence, and launched new gas pipelines such as Nord Stream and Blue Stream. At the same time, as more countries of the former Soviet bloc joined the EU or NATO, or otherwise shifted away from the Russian sphere of influence—such as the Central and Eastern European states in the 1990s, the Baltic states in the 2000s, and Ukraine, Moldova, Georgia, and others in the 2010s—they forfeited their former privilege of cheaper energy prices. This led to sharp price hikes (especially in gas) and aggravated political tensions. Moreover, Gazprom gained a reputation for wielding significant political leverage and reaping substantial revenues from certain energy-vulnerable European states. The Kremlin's energy diplomacy was increasingly likened to a political tool or even a weapon, leading to growing caution in the EU.

By the mid-2010s, there were increasing signs that the era of Russian gas dominance could be coming to an end in Europe.[4] In the 2010s, during the shale revolution and the so-called "golden age of gas," when the United States emerged as an energy superpower, Gazprom faced considerably less favorable circumstances. In 2014 alone, Gazprom's net profit declined by 86 percent. Moreover, the role of Gazprom in Europe became increasingly constrained owing to evolving global energy markets and EU regulatory efforts. The commercial environment led to increased competition and greater pressure on contract schemes, prices, and margins. Plans to launch exports to China, boost LNG production, and ramp up resource exploration of the Arctic all exemplified Russian efforts to adjust to the new realities. However, Russia's annexation of Crimea and the invasion of the Donbas in 2014, followed by its launch of a full-scale war on Ukraine in 2022, led to widespread sanctions targeting the Russian energy industry.

What is evident by 2024 is that Russia has lost its preeminent position in global energy markets. Gazprom remains a shadow of its former self. In 2023 the former energy giant suffered a record annual net loss of 629 billion rubles ($6.9 billion), compared to a net profit of 1.23 trillion rubles in 2022. The fall is most poignant in Europe, where Russia has taken risky bets by tarnishing its reputation as a reliable energy supplier, even in key markets such as Germany.

The 2022 invasion of Ukraine marked a new era for Putin's regime and led to the emergence of fresh fault lines in the global energy markets. As a result, the European energy policy conversation has shifted from discussing energy security and diversification to broad-scale decoupling from Russia, which is no longer perceived as an acceptable trading partner by many EU members. Instead, Russia is becoming a discounted supplier to non-NATO countries, particularly China and India. While some may argue that Russia is finally reaching the Asian markets and those who have no qualms with their foreign policy, the fact remains that instead of the intended Russian energy policy goal of accessing both European and Asian markets, which might then be played off against each other, Russian oil and gas are now being sold at a discount just to access the remaining available markets in the East.

Loss of Dominance in the European Markets

Russia's loss of its monopoly, then dominance, and subsequently its loss even of market access in many European countries is undoubtedly the largest failure of the Kremlin's energy policy. It marks a departure from policies going back many decades. The Soviet Union had emerged as a key oil and gas supplier to European markets during the Cold War era in 1950s and 1960s.[5] However, in the past decade, Russia's position has consistently deteriorated. Putin's goal from the 2010s on was to secure Europe's largest energy-importing market, Germany, with the Nord Stream 2 natural gas pipeline. However, this plan did not unfold as expected, as discussed in the next section.

The Russian energy strategy adopted in 2015 prioritized "stable relationships with traditional consumers of Russian energy"—in other words, Europe. This priority was driven by concerns about rising competition in the global energy markets as a result of the shale revolution and the emergence of new energy producers. It was also a result of Russia increasingly being perceived as an unreliable energy supplier across its main markets in Europe. Several factors undercut Russia's reputation irrevocably.

From the 1990s, Russia used political pricing and coercion in its gas supply relationship with Central and Eastern European states and the former Soviet republics, especially in markets where Gazprom had a dominant position or a monopoly. The ultimate objective was frequently to shape the foreign policy of the targeted states. Touting the energy-as-a-weapon approach, Russian politicians openly crowed about the importance of Gazprom in Russian foreign policy. Back in 2003, on the occasion of the tenth anniversary of Gazprom's incorporation, Putin had stated that "Gazprom is a powerful political and economic lever of influence over the rest of the world."[6] Moreover, in the same year, a memo written by a team of Russian foreign policy and energy experts pointed out that if "the leaders of this or that country decide to show good will toward the Russian Federation, then the situation with gas deliveries, pricing policy and former debts changes on a far more favorable note to the buyer."[7]

The second damaging factor was Russia's cuts to gas supplies via Ukraine in the winters of 2006 and 2009. The impact on the Ukrainian gas transit system created gas shortages in Europe. In the particularly cold winter of 2008–2009, Gazprom cut supplies to Ukraine, and gas shortages were felt for two weeks in six EU states. As a result, at least ten people in Poland died from exposure to extreme cold and lack of access to gas heating.[8] In response, the EU established a policy and regulatory agenda aimed at reducing the union's reliance on Russian gas, diversifying imports, and enhancing infrastructure for LNG. These events unfolded as the United States was leveraging its shale revolution, rapidly ramping up oil and gas production, and positioning its LNG exports for worldwide markets, including Europe.

At this time, it became increasingly important for the Kremlin to establish direct commercial relationships with key European importers, specifically the largest clients of Gazprom, such as Germany and Turkey. The means to achieve this end involved the planned expansion of the Nord Stream pipeline, the addition of the Nord Stream 2 pipeline, and the eventual completion of the TurkStream gas pipeline to Turkey.

Failure of Nord Stream 2

The primary goal of Nord Stream 2 was to continue exerting Russian energy dominance over the European continent by keeping American LNG out of the continent and keeping German businesses and politicians reliant on Russian gas. The failure to start Nord Stream 2 operations in 2022 could be viewed as a harbinger of the Kremlin's ultimate troubles in the energy markets. In the summer and fall of 2022, in the wake of the February 2022 launch of military operations in Ukraine and rising tensions with Germany and the EU, Russia cut supplies through Nord Stream 1 indefinitely, citing "repair work." The aim was to exert pressure on Germany ahead of the coming winter. It was a tactic that Moscow had used repeatedly over the decades in Eastern Europe, but it would not work this time. By halting gas to its biggest customer, Germany—despite Germany's recent desire to continue purchasing Russian gas—the Kremlin shot itself in the foot.

On September 26, 2022, a series of controversial and unattributed sabotage bombings of Nord Stream 1 and Nord Stream 2 left the pipelines inoperable. With Europe essentially no longer purchasing piped Russian gas, the pipelines became superfluous. In 2023 the only gas Russia was exporting by pipeline to Europe was the 40 million cubic meters per day via the Sudzha station of the Yelets–Kremenchuk–Kryvyi Rih pipeline on the Russia-Ukraine border.[9] This route has remained open in 2024 despite the ongoing war. The European leg of TurkStream likewise continued to supply Hungary and Serbia, Russia's remaining European friends and landlocked countries with few gas alternatives. Europe and the United States continue to enact a host of sanctions against Russia, including plans to completely phase out energy imports from Russia with the rise of alternatives from the global oil and gas markets.

The rise and fall of Nord Stream 1 and 2 reflects in many ways the ebb and tide of the gas relationship between Europe and Russia. As the largest European industrial power, Germany sought to ensure that its gas supplies would not depend on transit through the Ukrainian pipeline system. Designed to get cheap gas directly from Russia, Nord Stream 1 symbolized Germany's period of opportunism under Chancellor Gerhard Schröder, who approved the pipeline before leaving office in 2005. Schröder had developed a close friendship with Putin and, after leaving office, went to work for Russian state-owned companies such as Nord Stream AG, Rosneft, and Gazprom.

When advocating for the Nord Stream 2 addition, Russian interests falsely promoted the idea that Europe's gas needs would continue to rise. Germany's poor execution and planning of its transformational energy policy, dubbed Energiewende (energy transition) and aimed at rapidly eliminating dependence on nuclear power and fossil fuels in the long term, resulted in a short-term energy shortage. Germany's dependence on Russia was the most acute in Europe: not as a percentage of the country's energy mix, as some countries were nearly 100 percent dependent on Russian gas, but because Germany imported by far the largest volume of Russian gas. Germany was Gazprom's long-standing top European customer. Over 90 percent of its gas needs were met by imports, two-thirds of which came from Russia. Thus, as Germany followed plans to close its last nuclear reactors by 2022 and phase out coal by 2038, it faced possible energy shortages and projected power grid blackouts even before the escalation of the war in Ukraine began. Renewables did not close Germany's energy gap, even though the country is a European leader in renewable electricity generation. As a result, despite U.S. sanctions and Russia's annexation of Crimea in 2014, Germany continued with its plans to launch Nord Stream 2 in 2022.

With Russia's 2022 invasion of Ukraine, Chancellor Olaf Scholz had an epiphany regarding the country's energy and foreign policy. Germany postponed the operation of Nord Stream 2 indefinitely. Moreover, Berlin retired its long-held foreign policy doctrine vis-à-vis Russia. During the Cold War, Chancellor Willy Brandt had implemented a policy of Ostpolitik, which entailed improving political relations with Russia through commercial ties, such as the purchase of Russian gas. Germany dashed this doctrine after February 24, 2022. Purchases of Russian "blood oil" or "blood gas" became viewed as a form of financing the Russian war machine by the European public.

Before the start of the war, Germany did not have a single LNG import terminal despite being one of the largest gas importers in Europe. The government immediately launched five floating small-scale LNG import terminals, with three completed by the end of 2022 and two more by the end of 2023. Large-scale, stationary LNG import terminals, on the other hand, take years to develop. Nonetheless, this marked a significant departure in Germany's energy security considerations.

The end of Nord Stream marks a symbolic end to Europe's dependence on Russian gas—a "conscious uncoupling" of sorts, declared Szymon Kardaś of the European Council on Foreign Relations.[10] In 2021, Europe was approximately 45 percent dependent on Russian gas, despite ongoing efforts at diversification. Russia was then the leading supplier of petroleum products and one of the largest crude oil suppliers to the EU. Before the end of 2022, the EU's reliance on Russian gas imports had dwindled from 45 percent to 9 percent, and it fell further in 2023 to 8 percent. EU countries announced they would no longer be purchasing Russian energy. Poland and the Baltic states went from 100 percent dependence ten years ago to not using any Russian gas now. As soon as the beginning of April 2022, Lithuania, followed by Latvia and Estonia, ceased all Russian primary energy imports. This overall trending decline is demonstrated by Estonia's Russian gas imports. In the 2000s, the country was 100 percent dependent on Gazprom for its natural gas imports. By 2020 it was 86 percent dependent, receiving some natural gas via an LNG terminal in Lithuania. Before the war, in 2021, the dependence had fallen to just 11 percent. At the start of 2022, Estonian dependence reached zero. Germany banned Russian oil imports in late 2022, and the EU enacted an embargo on Russian petroleum products in 2023.[11] Having survived the test case winter of 2022–2023 with limited Russian resources, Europe has continued to plan for its winters without the Kremlin's gas and oil.

On the LNG front, Gazprom continuously lost market share to LNG from the United States, Norway, and Qatar. At the same time, it is important to note that Russian LNG exports have increased in Europe since the start of the war as pipeline exports have dwindled. The financial implications of Europe's dependence reduction have been significant. Russia lost the majority of its annual €50–60 billion European gas business. Russia's overall income from energy exports to the EU declined from a monthly €12 billion in 2022 to only €2 billion at the start of 2023.[12]

Russia's loss of its position in the European markets ends the era of Putin's "energy diplomacy." In the past, Putin used energy deals to create personal relationships with leaders such as German chancellor Gerhard Schröder, Hungary's president Viktor Orbán, Turkey's president Recep Tayyip Erdoğan, and Italian prime minister Silvio Berlusconi to create political rapprochements with their respective countries.[13] He successfully employed leading European politicians—Schröder, Austrian foreign minister Karin Kneissl, Italian prime minister Matteo Renzi, Finnish prime minister Esko Aho, and others—in Russian state and private companies after they had departed office. However, those times have irrevocably passed. The extensive EU energy sanctions and ongoing diversification endeavors mark the advent of a new era in which the EU will meet its energy demand from renewable sources and allied countries, leaving Russia no choice but to export its oil and gas to China, India, and other non-NATO countries.

Lagging LNG and Innovation

While Russia has long been a key global supplier of dry natural gas, its LNG industry has significantly lagged despite Putin's promises to the contrary. Nonetheless, despite the war and sanctions, Russia has remained the fourth largest LNG producer in the world and continues to make inroads into the European markets that have largely been closed to Russian piped natural gas.

The Kremlin has stated on numerous occasions that Russia will climb the charts of the world's leading LNG exporters. The Russian 2021 agenda, titled "The Long-term Programme for the Development of Liquefied

Natural Gas Production in the Russian Federation," ambitiously set out to achieve a 20 percent share of the global LNG market by 2035. As of 2021, Australia accounted for a 21 percent share of the global market, Qatar 21 percent, the United States 18 percent, and Russia only 8 percent. In 2021 the Russian government announced its plan to increase LNG exports to 110–190 billion cubic meters (bcm) annually by 2025. In 2021, however, Russia exported only 39.5 bcm of LNG. In 2022 and 2023, Russia's LNG exports rose modestly but remained at about the 45 bcm mark annually. In 2023, about half of these deliveries went to Europe (21.8 bcm) and about half to Asia (20.5 bcm). While for Russia, Europe is still its leading LNG export market, for the EU, only 13 percent of LNG imports (excluding transshipments to non-EU markets) came from Russia in 2023.[14]

The absence of adequate LNG export infrastructure, Western sanctions prohibiting financing and technology transfer, and the scarcity of domestic entities in this sector collectively contribute to Russia's lag in achieving its LNG expansion aspirations. In contrast to other prominent LNG exporters such as Malaysia and Qatar, which initiated their ventures in 1983 and 1997, respectively, Russia inaugurated its first LNG export terminal, the Sakhalin-2 plant, only in 2009.[15] Since then it has played a significant role as a key exporter of LNG to such countries as Japan and South Korea.[16] However, Sakhalin has underscored the difficulties faced in meeting production targets after ExxonMobil and Shell withdrew from the Exxon Neftegas project.

Russia's Yamal LNG terminal, inaugurated in 2017 by Novatek, has been critical in boosting Russia's LNG-exporting capacity and serving the Chinese market.[17] Gazprom's Portovaya and Novatek-Gazprombank's Vysotsk, two small-scale LNG terminals, operate on the Baltic Sea.[18] Arctic LNG 2 became partly operational in 2024 with the help of Chinese technologies after long delays and the postponement of Arctic LNG 1 because of sanctions and the withdrawal of the French multinational company TotalEnergies. Russia has been pushing ahead in the Arctic for strategic rather than solely commercial reasons, and greater shipping via the Northern Sea Route is expected. Russia had plans for two more LNG export terminals, namely the Vladivostok terminal and the Baltic LNG terminal; however, sanctions since Russia's annexation of Crimea and lower global oil prices have resulted in the indefinite postponement of these projects.[19]

The Ministry of Economic Development of the Russian Federation has been revising downward its projection for Russian LNG export volumes, including in 2024 for the 2025–2027 time frame. Current projections and output still do not meet goals set before the launch of the full-scale war. Government deliberations with key Russian energy enterprises such as Gazprom, Novatek, Rosneft, and Rosatom in 2023 underscored the challenges in achieving the objectives outlined in 2021. One of the main reasons is the difficulty in sourcing and producing LNG in the face of sanctions.[20] All existing facilities such as Sakhalin-2 (with the exception of Yamal LNG) were built with the support of Western partners, including APCI, Linde, Shell, and Air Liquide. However, sanctions make such cooperation unlikely in the foreseeable future.

The difficulty of raising capital for new LNG projects, the sanctions following the start of Russia's full-scale war against Ukraine in February 2022, coupled with the shortage of, and lack of access to, technological know-how and advanced equipment, which is predominantly manufactured by Western companies, will prevent the implementation of Putin's LNG ambitions for the foreseeable future. Sanctions have made LNG shipping more difficult, and Russia's LNG export volumes to China and India will not compensate Russia for the sales volumes lost in Europe. Meanwhile, LNG will continue growing in the global gas trade as buyers increasingly prefer it over piped gas. LNG leaders such as Australia, Qatar, and the United States will expand quickly and capture greater market shares because of access to advanced technology and management, leaving Russia further and further behind.

Lagging in Technology and Missing the Shale Revolution

Russia has failed to join the shale revolution and cannot tap into new technologies. A boom in Russian oil or gas production is thus unlikely. Despite Russia having the greatest technically recoverable shale oil resources worldwide and the ninth greatest technically recoverable shale gas resources, Russia has failed to be at the forefront of innovation in the energy markets.[21] It never joined the ranks of countries that have led commercial fracking, such as the United States, Canada, China, and Argentina, since the 2000s. Gazprom has never pursued its shale reserves, stating back in 2013 that at least for the next decade, "its vast conventional reserves are much cheaper to produce."[22] In 2019, Vladimir Putin called shale-derived oil and gas production "barbaric" and reiterated, "In spite of all the economic benefits, we do not need it and we will never do this."[23] Meanwhile, the United States, which has ranked second after Russia for shale oil resources and fourth in the world when it comes to shale gas resources, has embraced fracking and, on the back of its own shale revolution, has emerged as the largest oil and gas producer in the world.

Technological access and progress represent weaknesses for Russia's energy industry. The exit of global oil services firms and other Western oil and gas majors is having a serious impact, especially because a significant portion of Russian equipment was nearing the end of its projected useful life in the 2010s. China has offered some lifelines for the completion of some projects, such as Arctic LNG 2, but does not manufacture some of the equipment Russia needs. For instance, the Rosneft and ExxonMobil joint project in the Kara Sea was suspended after the annexation of Crimea. Meanwhile, Rosneft had to cut production targets in 2022 on Sakhalin Island because of equipment shortages. This technological lag will erode Russia's prospects in the increasingly competitive global markets.

Russian oil and gas extraction has long been inefficient and consequently costly. As a result, American exports have been able to compete in the European markets despite Russian legacy infrastructure and longer shipping distances from North America. For instance, in 2012, Russia produced a ton of oil for 7,500 rubles, whereas by 2022, the cost had risen to 24,600 rubles. Production costs have outpaced inflation as personnel and technology shortages have accumulated, a problem exacerbated by Russia's brain drain and labor shortages consequent on its military operations.

Lost Influence and Isolation in the Global Energy Markets

In the past decade, as energy markets globalized, an unforeseen consequence of Putin's energy policy has been Russia's growing isolation and marginalization rather than integration within the global energy landscape. Numerous factors point toward Russia's waning influence, a situation highlighted by its reduced and sanctioned role in the European and Western energy sectors. Most, if not all, multinational corporations have left or been expelled from Russia's energy industry, rendering Western foreign direct investment in the nation's energy sector unlikely in the foreseeable future. Moreover, the Kremlin's nationalization of assets of foreign companies such as Finland's Fortum and Germany's Unipro serves to dissuade further investment. Within the EU, Russia's strong-arm energy tactics have led to regulatory-driven divestments of Gazprom's assets from the European markets.

The process of Russia's marginalization initially began on a regional scale in the energy markets of the "near abroad" states of the former Soviet Union. The creation of the Eurasian Economic Union failed to grow either in members or in scope, and an energy union with Central Asia and the Caucasus failed to materialize despite the strategic goal formulated back in 2015. In 2022, Russian officials again started pitching a "gas union" to Central Asian states, and with Turkmenistan rebuking Russia in the summer of 2023, a truncated union emerged among Russia, Kazakhstan, and Uzbekistan.

Russia has lost much of its influence in Central Asia and the Caucasus since the 2000s. With Kazakhstan, Uzbekistan, and Turkmenistan reorienting their energy trade away from Russian infrastructure to reach China directly by 2009, the Kremlin has lost a significant amount of its political influence in this region. Russia's declining role in Central Asian energy markets mirrored its loss of the European markets when Putin's regime overplayed its heavy hand and dominant position. In 2006, when Russia purchased Turkmen gas for $60 or $100 per tcm, Gazprom resold that gas via RosUkrEnergo to Ukraine and Europe for at least $250 per tcm.[24] The president of Turkmenistan, Saparmurat Niyazov, had enough and traveled to Beijing to strike a better deal. While Turkmenistan became the most important gas supplier to China, Uzbekistan and Kazakhstan followed suit. At the end of 2009, the first line of the Central Asia–China gas pipeline went into operation. The second line did so in 2010, the third in 2015, and the fourth is uncompleted and seemingly halted.

Moreover, the mysterious explosion on one of the lines of the Central Asia–Center (CAC) gas pipeline between Turkmenistan and Russia on April 9, 2009, was perceived by many in the region to be Russia's doing because it provided Gazprom an excuse to reduce the amount of gas imported from Turkmenistan during a drop in prices following the global financial crisis of 2007–2008.[25] Following Russian-Turkmen disagreements over gas prices and Gazprom's nonpayment for Turkmen gas imports during 2015, Ashgabat ended all gas exports to Russia.[26] By 2016 the Russian–Central Asian gas relationship was largely history. In just a decade after

Niyazov's first visit to Beijing, Central Asia's complete dependence on Russian pipelines and gas markets turned into a heavy dependence on China.

Meanwhile, Azerbaijan began to compete with Russia for the European gas markets. Azerbaijan launched exports to Georgia and Turkey in the mid- to late 2000s. Subsequently the Southern Gas Corridor project from the Caucasus was particularly significant because it brought non-Russian piped gas to Europe through pipelines not owned by Russian companies. The Southern Gas Corridor enabled the diversification of gas imports of southeastern Europe, foremost Greece and Italy, where in 2014, national gas consumption was respectively 63 percent and 37.5 percent dependent on Russian imports.[27] This project was long opposed by the Kremlin, which sought to marginalize it by building the TurkStream pipeline to send Russian gas to southeastern Europe via Turkey. The completion of TurkStream can be counted as one success of Putin in the energy markets, particularly the gas markets. Going forward, Russia will continue to woo Turkey and Azerbaijan, both key states offering a gateway to European energy markets.[28]

Supplier to Asian Markets

The September 2015 unveiling of Russia's energy strategy for the next twenty years marked the pinnacle of Putin's ambition to swiftly secure "access to the Asia-Pacific market." The energy requirements of the developing world were already outpacing those of the developed world, and a significant proportion of this demand emanated from Asia. By 2023, many of the world's top LNG buyers were in Asia—China, Japan, South Korea, India, and Taiwan—in addition to France and Spain.[29]

While Russia aimed to play the European energy markets against the Asian energy markets and allocate its supplies to the highest bidder, the outcome has proved to be quite the opposite. Marginalized in Europe, Russia has emerged as a discounted supplier to India and China. While Russia has augmented its exports to China and India in the aftermath of sanctions, it has struggled to fully replace lost European export volumes in these markets and will never attain a dominant position in them. And though Russia outpaced Saudi Arabia and emerged as the leading crude oil exporter to China in 2023, Russian oil still accounted for less than 19 percent of China's total crude oil imports.

Beijing methodically pursues an energy diversification strategy that seeks to balance its own domestic production of fossil fuels, boosting reliance on renewable sources and diversifying imports. Indeed, China has emerged as a global leader in renewables, particularly in solar, wind, and electric vehicles. When it comes to fossil fuel, China imports supplies from different oil-producing countries, varying between piped gas and LNG, and balances long-term contracts with short-term trades, all from a position of strength. For instance, in 2024, Russia was China's fourth largest gas supplier (piped and LNG), after Australia, Turkmenistan, and Qatar. Russia's exports to Asia will not match the volumes it previously exported to Europe owing to a lack of export infrastructure. Without new pipelines, Russian LNG exports cannot match the volumes delivered to Europe by natural gas pipelines.

Chinese-Russian energy infrastructure has been slow to be implemented. Despite Chinese-Russian efforts at energy cooperation dating back to the 1950s,[30] it wasn't until 2009 that the two countries realized their first project: the East Siberia–Pacific Ocean (ESPO) oil pipeline from Angarsk, Russia, to Daqing, China, which was completed only after China agreed to provide a $25 billion loan to Rosneft and Transneft for its construction. When it comes to natural gas, developments have been similarly slow. Russian and Chinese prime ministers signed off in 1999 on studies for the Altai and the Power of Siberia pipelines. Russia favored the shorter and cheaper Altai pipeline, whereas China preferred the 2,500-mile Power of Siberia pipeline along the eastern route. This latter route, utilizing undeveloped resources in eastern Siberia, had the potential to meet gas demand in China's northeastern industrial region and coastal cities, replace coal, and help reduce severe air pollution. After some delays, the Power of Siberia pipeline launched in 2019 but has reportedly been unprofitable for Russia. Altai has stalled indefinitely. Despite the Kremlin's efforts to revive the Power of Siberia 2 pipeline, no progress was made in 2024. The project would take seven to ten years to build, and there appears to be no serious commitment or interest from China in doing so. Reports suggest that China is requesting gas prices close to Russia's domestic tariffs, making the process unprofitable for Russia.

The market dynamics of the mid-2010s favoring energy buyers over sellers, characterized by low prices and ample supply, followed by subsequent sanctions against Russia after 2022, facilitated China's ability to negotiate with Moscow at rock-bottom prices. China's strategic geographic location, which enables access to both piped gas from Central Asia, Myanmar, and Russia and coastal LNG imports from Qatar, Australia, and potentially Russia and the United States, provides an additional source of leverage.

China's position of strength is further evident in the unfolding Sino-Russian oil relations as evidenced by Moscow's unprecedented willingness to grant Chinese companies equity in oil and gas exploration and production projects in both eastern Russia and third countries, especially in projects operated by the Russian state-owned oil company Rosneft. In 2006, Sinopec and Rosneft established a joint venture, with 49 percent and 51 percent share ownership, respectively, to manage Udmurtneft oil production in Russia's Middle Urals.[31] In 2013, China National Petroleum Corporation (CNPC) and Rosneft agreed to jointly develop oil and gas fields in eastern Siberia, with 49 percent and 51 percent ownership in the project, respectively, and then in 2014, a subsidiary of CNPC gained access to a major oil field in Russia by acquiring a 10 percent stake in the subsidiary ZAO Vankorneft.[32] Chinese involvement in Russian energy projects has been even more crucial after additional sanctions post-2022 when Russia found itself even more isolated.

Meanwhile, India has benefited greatly from Russia's discounted oil exports. It has emerged as the second largest buyer of Russian crude oil after China. In 2023, more than a third of India's oil imports came from Russia; however, these have been discounted from the $60 per barrel price cap imposed by the West by some additional 5–20 percent.

In summary, despite the objectives stated in the *Russian Energy Strategy for the Period up to 2035*, Russia has been unable to replace the European markets with Asian markets, although it has succeeded in tapping the Asian markets. The Asian markets, in particular China and India, have not replaced the European markets either through volumes exported (lack of sufficient infrastructure) or revenues obtained (lower prices). Indeed, the oil markets demonstrate that despite selling a consistent volume of oil, Russia makes far less revenue on each barrel because its oil now trades at discount relative to the global benchmark oil price of Brent crude. Before the war, Russian crude oil traded at a discount of just a few dollars per barrel relative to Brent. In 2023, official price-reporting agency data showed that Russian Urals crude oil traded at a discount of as much as $25–$35 per barrel to Brent.[33] As a sanctioned and isolated country, Russia has become a discounted supplier to meet the supply gaps of China and India.

Repercussions

Over the past few decades, Russia failed to maintain its energy superpower status despite the country's vast resources. In contrast, during this time period, the United States emerged as the largest producer of oil and gas in the world and became a world-leading LNG exporter. Meanwhile, Russia forfeited its special status in Europe as a key oil and gas provider and failed to gain a monopoly or special status in Asia. Excluding Russia's paramilitary group Wagner's takeovers of oil fields in African countries experiencing domestic turmoil, Russia has lost its "energy weapon." Previously, this had been one of Russia's trump cards in Europe.

While Russia has accomplished its "pivot to Asia" and made inroads into supplying the world's rising energy markets in China and India, it has failed to do so on its own terms as originally intended. Facing sanctions and a backlash from Europe and the Western alliance, Moscow can only compete among other suppliers in Asia and often needs to sell its resources at a discount. If Russia had succeeded in having the option to sell to both Europe and Asia, it could have leveraged its position to play off the two markets against each other. However, Russia has lost the European market and is not poised to monopolize the Asian ones. It will continue its "junior partner" status in its relationship with China. However, Russia still retains "energy diplomacy" capabilities, and its oil and gas exports have allowed it to create relationships in Asia and remain relevant in global affairs despite sanctions from the West.

Despite the lucky streak of high energy prices in the 2000s and the early 2010s, Russia failed to leverage two decades of commodity price windfalls to transform its economy. In 2012, oil and gas proceeds accounted for nearly half the country's total budget revenue and over 70 percent of its total export revenue.[34] The situation in 2021, before the further erosive impact of the war, remained essentially unchanged: oil and gas revenues constituted 45 percent of the Russian federal budget.[35] Revenues continued to decline in absolute terms through 2023, but oil and gas tax revenues showed growth in 2024. Nonetheless, this has not been enough, and in May 2024 the Russian Finance Ministry proposed raising income taxes to help cover the costs of the war. However, the oil export revenues continue to finance the Russian war machine. Between February 24, 2022, and June 18, 2024, Russia earned almost €472 billion from oil exports, including crude oil and refined products. Over the same period, EU countries paid around

€107 billion for Russian oil. Russian energy products undoubtedly end up in Western markets despite sanctions—traded in shadow markets, imported and reexported, with their country of origin undisclosed.[36]

Time and global energy market developments have not been on Russia's side. As the world increasingly turns to renewable sources of energy and technological breakthroughs bring new energy suppliers and supplies to markets across the globe, Russia's heyday as an energy supplier with influence is waning. Moreover, the timing of the war and the resulting sanctions have caused Russia to miss the window of relatively high energy prices. The International Energy Agency projects that by 2030 or even earlier, renewables will continue to gain market share even as new oil and gas producers in Africa, Mediterranean, and Latin America enter the markets. The fossil fuel markets will remain buyers' markets with increasing supplies and declining demand.

The Kremlin's mismanagement of the energy sector also led to Russia's failure to develop its economy from that of a raw materials exporter to an economy based on diversified industry, innovation, and higher-value-added production. Nor did Russia utilize its sovereign wealth fund to transform the economy. Trickle-down wealth did not occur beyond the leading cities of Moscow and St. Petersburg and larger cities such as Kazan, Khanty-Mansiysk, and Yakutsk. Standards of living have not improved notably, and the Russian GNP per capita was about $14,000 in 2023, far lower than Portugal's. The window of opportunity to develop the Russian economy on the back of energy exports seems to have closed.

When we consider counterfactuals and what could have been accomplished with Russia's major comparative advantage of having vast resources and an educated labor force, the failures are even more stark. If the state had not come to dominate the Russian energy sector, if profits and progress had led to progress and not corruption, rent-seeking, and coercion through energy deals, the outcome might have been more promising. Private Russian companies might have been able to emerge as global energy leaders, following in the footsteps of Khodorkovsky's Yukos. Collaboration with Western multinational companies could have facilitated development, technology, and managerial best-practice transfers. Russia could have grown more wealthy and developed other sectors of its economy without becoming China's discounted energy supplier.

Instead, Russia is locked into a losing long-term dependence on resource extraction of the classic natural resource curse scenario. On the Norway versus Nigeria scale of successful economic development from the extraction of resources, Russia falls closer to the latter. In addition to paradigm shifts in the global market and competition from new suppliers, the Russian energy sector also faces climate change challenges, the rising demand for renewables, ecological risks from Russia's poorly regulated resource extractions, Western sanctions, and China's slowing economy, which may potentially stunt the growth of its energy demand, all of which may limit any optimism for Russia's energy future.

Domestically, Kremlin authoritarianism and Stalinist-style governance dim prospects for future innovation and the use of advanced technology to address the depletion of Russia's existing oil fields. The incredibly promising but complex development of the Arctic remains elusive. Russia lacks funds to do this anyway. The demographic and brain drain issues, exacerbated by the war in Ukraine, present additional serious limiting factors. The absence of new FDI will limit technological development (see chapter 2).

Nonetheless, for the near term, Russia's energy exports will continue to keep the government afloat and fund the war in Ukraine. The 2024 approved record budget plans for a 30 percent increase in military spending. The energy sector will continue to have to foot most of the bill. Moreover, the Kremlin's control over Russia's energy sector will continue to contribute to Putin's power and ability to remain in office. Yet real questions emerge as to how durable the Russian energy sector is going forward. Thus far the Russian economy has defied expectations largely because of high global energy prices. In the medium term, the economy and the energy sector will carry on, but in the long term, self-cannibalization is becoming increasingly likely.

NOTES

1. Russian Federation, Ministry of Energy (2015).
2. Workman [2024].
3. Data from the U.S. Energy Information Administration (EIA), "Russia," July 28, 2015, and converted by the author from cubic feet to cubic meters using "Natural Gas Volumes Converter."
4. These developments are outlined in Grigas (2017).
5. Ibid., 99–106.
6. Mankoff (2009), 35.
7. Kupchinsky (2009).
8. Grigas (2018).

9. Soldatkin, Astakhova, and Steitz (2023).
10. Kardaś (2023).
11. Ibid.
12. See also Center for Research on Energy and Clean Air (2023).
13. For a discussion, see Grigas (2017).
14. IEA (2022); ExPro Consulting (2024).
15. Tusiani and Shearer (2007), 288; Dargin (2010), 124.
16. Offshore Energy (2015).
17. Griffin (2013); Zvonareva (2015)
18. Novatek is the majority owner-operator of the Vysotsk facility (51 percent), with Gazprombank holding the rest. See LNG Prime (2023b).
19. Gazprom (2013), 4; Gazprom (2015); Zvonareva (2015).
20. Humpert (2024); Rudnik (2023).
21. Data obtained from the EIA (2013, 2015b) and converted by the author from cubic feet to cubic meters using Delek Drilling and Avner Oil, "Natural Gas Volumes Converter" (EIA 2015a).
22. Robertson (2013).
23. Meredith (2019).
24. Russia's 2006 prices paid for Turkmenistan gas from Gould et al. (2008), 11. Gazprom's resale prices from Bahgat (2006), 961.
25. Barkanov (2014), 165–67.
26. Kuvakin (2016); Putz (2015); Reuters (2015).
27. BP (2015), 23, 28.
28. Grigas (2017), 205–34.
29. IEA (2024); LNG Prime (2023a).
30. Paik (2012).
31. Rosneft (2006).
32. Rosneft (2013).
33. U.S. Department of the Treasury (2023).
34. Ladislaw, Leed, and Walton (2014), 5.
35. IEA (2022).
36. Statista (2024).

REFERENCES

Bahgat, Gawdat. 2006. "Europe's Energy Security: Challenges and Opportunities." *International Affairs* 82 (5).

Barkanov, Boris. 2014. "The Geo-Economics of Eurasian Gas: The Evolution of Russia-Turkmen Relations in Natural Gas (1992–2010)." In *Export Pipelines from the CIS Region*, ed. Andreas Heinrich and Heiko Pleines, 165–67. Stuttgart: ibidem.

BP. 2015. "BP Statistical Review of World Energy June 2015."

Center for Research on Energy and Clean Air. 2023. "One Year of Sanctions: Russia's Oil Export Revenues Cut by EUR 34bn." December 5.

Dargin, Justin. 2010. "Qatar's Gas Revolution." *LNG Review, Petroleum Economist*, March.

EIA (U.S. Energy Information Administration). 2015a. "Technically Recoverable Shale Oil and Shale Gas Resources: Russia." U.S. Department of Energy, September.

———. 2015b. "World Shale Resource Assessments." U.S. Department of Energy, September 24.

———. 2013. "Shale Oil and Shale Gas Resources Are Globally Abundant." U.S. Department of Energy, June 10.

ExPro Consulting. 2024. "Russia Continues to Export Most of Its LNG to Europe." ExPro, May 7.

Gazprom. 2015. "Baltic LNG Project to Be Executed in Ust-Luga." Gazprom, January 22.

———. 2013. "Gazprom in Eastern Russia, Entry into Asia-Pacific Markets." Gazprom, June 13.

Gould, Tim, Isabel Murray, Jonathan Sinton, Dagmar Graczyk, Christopher Segar, and Audun Wiig. 2008. "Perspectives on Caspian Oil and Gas Development." Paris: International Energy Agency, 2008.

Griffin, Rosemary. 2013. "JGC Win Tender to Build Russian Yamal LNG Plant." Platts.com, April 1.

Grigas, Agnia. 2018. "Russian Gas and the Case for Sanctions." *American Interest*, September 24.

———. 2017. *The New Geopolitics of Natural Gas*. Cambridge, MA: Harvard University Press.

Humpert, Malte. 2024. "Russia Reduces LNG Forecasts as Western Sanctions Delay Arctic Projects." *High North News*, April 25.

IEA (International Energy Agency). 2024. "Global Gas Security Review 2024: Including the Gas Market Report Q4-2024." Paris: IEA.

———. 2022. "Energy Fact Sheet: Why Does Russian Oil and Gas Matter?" Paris: IEA, March 21.

Kardaś, Szymon. 2023. "Conscious Uncoupling: Europeans' Russian Gas Challenge in 2023." *European Power*. European Council on Foreign Relations, February 13.

Kupchinsky, Roman. 2009. "Russian Energy Strategy: The Domestic Political Factor." Jamestown Foundation, October 8.

Kuvakin, Ilya. 2016. "Gazprom to Suspend Gas Supplies from Turkmenistan." RosBusinessKonsulting, January 4.

Ladislaw, Sarah O., Maren Leed, and Molly A. Walton. 2014. "New Energy, New Geopolitics." Washington, DC: Center for Strategic and International Studies, June.

LNG Prime. 2023a. "Japan Was the World's Largest LNG Importer in 2022, followed by China." January 19.

———. 2023b. "Russia's Novatek Reaches Vysotsk LNG Production Milestone." September 29.

Mankoff, Jeffrey. 2009. *Russian Foreign Policy: The Return of Great Power Politics*. Blue Ridge Summit, PA: Rowman & Littlefield.

Meredith, Sam. 2019. "Russia's Putin Says Shale Oil Technologies Are 'Barbaric.'" CNBC, November 20.

Offshore Energy. 2015. "Sakhalin Energy Hits 1000 LNG Cargoes Milestone." *LNG World News*, August 26.

Paik, Kuen-Wook. 2012. *Sino-Russian Oil and Gas Cooperation: The Reality and Implications*. Oxford Institute for Energy Studies.

Putz, Catherine. 2015. "Russia Takes Turkmenistan to Court Over the Price of Gas." *Diplomat*, July 28.

Reuters. 2015. "Turkmenistan Says Russia's Gazprom Has Not Paid for Any Gas This Year." July 8.

Robertson, Helen. 2013. "Russia Won't Develop Shale Gas for a Decade." *Petroleum Economist*, April 19.

Rosneft. 2013. "Rosneft and CNPC Sign Memorandum to Expand Cooperation in Upstream Projects in East Siberia." Press release, October 18.

———. 2006. "Rosneft and Sinopec to Jointly Control Udmurtneft." RigZone.com, November 17.

Rudnik, Filip. 2023. "Unfulfilled Ambitions: Russia's LNG Sector in the Grip of Sanctions." Centre for Eastern Studies, June 5.

Russian Federation, Ministry of Energy. 2015. "Osnovnie polozheniia proekta Energeticheskoi Strategii Rossii na period do 2035 goda" [Main provisions of the project Energy Strategy of Russia for the period up to 2035]. Moscow.

Soldatkin, Vladimir, Olesya Astakhova, and Christoph Steitz. 2023. "Exclusive: Russia Set to Mothball Damaged Nord Stream Gas Pipelines—Sources." Reuters, March 3.

Statista. 2024. "Volume of Crude Oil Shipments from Russia from January 1, 2022 to January 1 2024, by Declared Destination." Database. June 19.

Tusiani, Michael D., and Gordon Shearer. 2007. *LNG—A Nontechnical Guide*. Tulsa, OK: PennWell Corporation.

U.S. Department of the Treasury. 2023. "The Price Cap on Russian Oil: A Progress Report." Washington, DC, May 18.

Workman, Daniel. [2024]. "Crude Oil Exports by Country." WorldsTop Exports.com.

Zvonareva, Marina. 2015. "Russian LNG: A Five Year Window—and It's Closing." *Natural Gas World*, April 20.

FOUR

Counterpoint

The Rationalization of Russian Agriculture

ALLAN MUSTARD

Russian agriculture has not failed, and will not fail to feed the nation. In contrast to most other sectors of the Russian economy, agriculture and food production have prospered since 1991, and particularly in the last two decades, owing to privatization of production agriculture coupled with government policies and programs of import substitution and food self-sufficiency. A sector noted for its massive grain imports in the 1970s and 1980s was by the mid-2000s a significant wheat exporter and by 2016 had emerged as the world's largest wheat exporter. That said, much of the progress since 1991 has been based on imported technologies, and the international sanctions imposed following the February 2022 invasion of Ukraine threaten to undermine much of what's been achieved.

As a U.S. Department of Agriculture (USDA) field report from Moscow put it in 2018, "Russia has reached self-sufficiency in pork and poultry.... Overall, by 2018, Russia had met or exceeded six of the eight production targets set in its Food Security Doctrine of 2010."

In 2016, Russian agricultural exports exceeded arms exports in value, and in 2020, for the first time in modern history, the value of Russian agricultural and food exports exceeded the value of imports.[1]

Prior to the October Revolution of 1917, Russia was a major grain exporter and competitor of the United States.[2] Collectivization, bad science, and centralized control of production agriculture from the 1930s through 1991 led to generally low productivity that in bad years resulted in famine and, during the Brezhnev era, to massive imports of wheat and corn.[3] How did Russian agriculture rebound after the collapse of communism, and what factors in that rebound pose risks going forward?

Framing the Question

Agricultural economists classically define production as a function of land, labor, capital, and technological progress. Obviously, the land endowment, which includes massive areas of the prime farmland known as "black earth" (chernozem), has not changed significantly, and labor in agriculture has fallen by almost half in the last three decades.[4] The post-1991 uptick in productivity is due to improvements in the way capital is applied to agriculture and in the technologies employed.

From another point of view, agronomists and animal scientists view production as a function of genetics, nutrition, and health. An organism, whether plant or animal, will be more successful and productive if it is blessed with good genes, is fed and watered well, and is protected from diseases and pests. The aforementioned improvements in capital application addressed Soviet-era shortcomings by importing improved livestock and plant genetics and by adopting Western practices in animal and plant nutrition, as well as a focus on animal and plant health.

The Soviet Legacy

We begin by examining what went wrong under the Soviets. During the Soviet period, the leadership of the Communist Party of the Soviet Union (CPSU) and the government it controlled emphasized gross output, to be achieved via mandatory plan targets, but paid relatively little attention to either efficiency or downstream preservation of what was produced. Thus half of all potatoes, a major foodstuff, rotted between the time they were dug and their delivery to market. In years of large grain harvests, up to 20 percent of production rotted owing to lack of proper drying, transportation, and storage capacity. Similarly, production quotas set for agricultural machinery focused on the output of complete units, and not on spare parts. Cannibalization of farm implements for replacement parts was common, leading to overinvestment in the machinery fleet in order to have the minimum needed number of functioning units. In the meantime, chronic underinvestment in storage and processing led to heavy losses of what was produced.[5]

Production agriculture suffered from incompetence in biological research, typified by the charlatan Trofim Lysenko, who for many years headed the Academy of Agricultural Sciences.[6] Lysenko arranged for his predecessor, the eminent biologist Nikolai Vavilov, to be sent to the gulag, where Vavilov was deliberately starved to death in 1943. Likewise, eminent agricultural economists, including Aleksandr Chaianov, the theorist behind agricultural cooperatives that emerged in Germany and the United States during the early 1900s, and Nikolai Kondratev, originator of the Kondratieff wave theory, were shot during the Great Terror of the 1930s. Meanwhile the Bolsheviks' forced collectivization brought about misery and starvation.[7] Access to foreign scientific research was restricted through censorship, inability to travel abroad to scientific conferences, and the risk of imprisonment for corresponding with foreign counterparts. As one Russian scientist ruefully put it to the author, Russian agricultural genetics lags Western genetics by at least a generation, and more likely two.

Following World War II, foreign technology was scarce owing to the lack of foreign exchange. The Soviet ruble was inconvertible, generally placing purchase of imported machinery out of reach.[8] Thus most technologies were either of domestic origin or, in a few cases, imported from Eastern Bloc nations belonging to the Council for Economic Cooperation (Sovet Ekonomicheskoi Vzaimopomoshchi), typically via a clearing account. Tractors seen on collective and state farms ranged from the T-25, a 25hp row-crop tractor produced first in Kharkiv and later in Vladimir, to the massive Kirovets K-700 series, a 300hp, 13.5 metric ton behemoth built at the Kirov Tractor Factory in Leningrad, capable of plowing about three hectares per hour. The real workhorse, however, was the Minsk Tractor Factory's MTZ-80 series, an 80hp general-purpose tractor known today under the Belarus brand, which, owing to its low-price and brand loyalty, remains a mainstay of farm traction across much of the former Soviet Union.⁹

Centralized planning led to gross inefficiencies. The Soviet policy of "proportional development," somewhat akin to but more rigid than the EU's cohesion policy, meant that massive fund flows were devoted to producing meat, milk, fruits, and vegetables in agronomically unsuitable areas. Orders came down from the Kremlin as to when to plant crops based on analysis performed in Moscow but without knowledge of local conditions, and yields often suffered.

By the 1970s the USSR had emerged as the world's largest importer of grain, mainly wheat and corn (wheat for milling into flour and corn for feeding livestock). These imports were a direct consequence of the Communist Party's policy to raise living standards by, in effect, trading export revenues from sales of hydrocarbons and gold for cereals. As a Russian foreign trade official later explained to the author, Soviet communists succeeded in transmuting gold, but in reverse, by converting gold into grain.

Mistargeted incentives under centralized planning, coupled with low compensation for labor, resulted in low labor productivity. In 1989, as Gorbachev was experimenting with agricultural reforms, one of his major agricultural policy advisers told an American audience at Harvard University that a Siberian survey had shown that only 20 percent of agricultural workers were willing to adopt new forms of economic management, 40 percent were vacillating, 20 percent were "categorically opposed" to economic reforms, and 20 percent "don't work now and wouldn't work under any system if they could help it."[10] The policy adviser, Academician Vladimir Tikhonov, noted as well that after seventy years, "the experiment is over and it has turned out a failure."

One result of all this was the rise of private household production, which by the late Soviet period accounted for between a quarter and a half of all food produced in the USSR, mainly high-value products (meat, dairy products, fruits, and vegetables). Despite legal limits on plot size and numbers of livestock one family could own, in 1985, private plots occupying a small fraction of farmland officially produced over 27 percent of meat, 23 percent of milk, 28 percent of eggs, 43 percent of fruits, 29 percent of vegetables, and 60 percent of potatoes.[11] Although government procurement absorbed some of this output, much if not most of it was sold at market prices in so-called collective farm markets, where state-controlled retail prices were not applied. Clearly, the socialist agriculture sector was unable to meet the demand for food.

As post-Soviet Russia entered the new century, this proportion rose, to around half of the food produced nationwide. A study of private plots in Orel oblast showed that in that province, "private plots occupying about 4 percent of all area planted to agricultural crops . . . and having 27% of the bovines, accounted for 45% of all agricultural production, including 91% of potatoes, 80% of vegetables, 79% of fruits and berries, and 48% of milk."[12] Perhaps more to the point, sales of products from these private plots in Orel oblast accounted for 72 percent of family income. By the mid-2000s, the Russian Ministry of Agriculture calculated that nearly half of all food produced came from private plots, and half of that from plots inside city limits.[13]

The Rise of Russian Agriculture

Production agriculture is a form of resource extraction and can to some degree be compared to other extractive industries, such as mining and hydrocarbon extraction. From that point of view, there was no structural reason for Soviet agriculture to have failed. It failed solely owing to the root cause of grossly incompetent, ideological mismanagement of the sector. The sociologist Tatiana Nefedova has attributed the collapse of the livestock sector to the "high cost of production, low quality, unbalanced feed rations, bad breed genetics, and inadequate facilities."[14] Field crop production, particularly grain, continued to suffer from the vagaries of Russia's notoriously risky climatic conditions compounded by withdrawal of much government support. As newly independent Russia moved into the 1990s, it turned to the United States for help, first in the form of Commodity Credit Corporation credit guarantees to buy wheat. Then, in 1993, Russia benefited from the largest U.S. foreign food aid program since the Marshall Plan, worth $800 million.[15] Statistically, output of livestock products bottomed out in 1997, and grain production bottomed out a year later.[16]

Circumstances began to change markedly in the mid-2000s as the Putin government fully turned its back on collectivized and centrally administered agriculture and as Russia began to recover from the 1998 financial crisis. Three major forms of farm organization had by then appeared. In addition to the private plot, called in Russian "personal subsidiary agriculture" (*lichnoe podsobnoe khoziaistvo*, or LPKh), there emerged the smallholder, called in Russian *fermer* (a calque of the English word "farmer"), patterned after the Western ideal of the yeoman farmer, famously lionized by Thomas Jefferson. The third was the corporate farm, typified by the so-called agroholding (*agrokholding*, agricultural holding company), which effectively arose from the rubble of bankrupt collective and state farms.[17]

Land reform was never seriously pursued, despite passage of laws mandating decollectivization of former state and collective farms. Deciding who would get the farmland with good soils, near roads and other infrastructure, versus who would get the swamp, sand hill, or rock pile in the middle of nowhere, was only one of many problems. As a result, the number of "farmers" has remained relatively small. The 2006 agricultural census counted 285,100 out of a rural population of 38.4 million. Smallholder numbers fell to 174,800 by 2016, but total area managed by "farmers" rose from 24.1 million hectares in 2006 to 36.9 million hectares in 2016—almost half again as much land area. In terms of total planted area, in 2016, "farmers" were responsible for a bit more than a quarter, at 27.8 percent.

In the meantime, consolidation was underway among the corporate farms. Though as a rule unable to purchase the land, they negotiated leases with the multitude of owners, the former collective and state farm employees who had received an often undemarcated "land share" (земельный пай, *zemel'nyi pai*) during land reform.[18] In 2023 the one hundred largest of these corporate farms accounted for 40 percent of Russian agricultural production.

As of the 2016 agricultural census, 36,000 corporate farms existed.[19] The hundred largest managed over 100,000 hectares apiece (1 hectare = 2.47 acres); the next two hundred managed over 30,000 hectares each.[20] Between 2006 and 2016, corporate farms' share of area planted fell from just over three quarters to a bit more than two-thirds, from 78.5 percent to 68.9 percent. However, impressively, by 2016, corporate farms dominated poultry (78 percent of production) and pork (81 percent), an improvement from the Soviet and immediate post-Soviet periods.

These large corporate farms are notable for two things: higher education of their managers and a reliance on foreign technologies. The 2016 census showed that 86.9 percent of managers of large corporate farms had a higher education, and in 52.5 percent of cases the education was in agriculture. Another 10.1 percent had a vocational secondary education.

By comparison, only 34 percent of smallholders had a higher education, of whom 15.4 percent were educated in agriculture and 35.4 percent had a vocational secondary education. A quarter of smallholders had earned a secondary school diploma and nothing more. These figures hide, however, an ongoing serious weakness of the corporate subsector. The large agribusinesses often have visionary and well-educated managers at the top, but there is a gap between them and the people who actually do the work. The front-line farm laborers show little loyalty or long-term commitment to the success of the corporate farm.[21]

The labor force's lack of commitment to the success of farms operated by agroholdings had direct ramifications for the adoption of new technologies, which got underway in earnest in the mid-2000s. Crop observation travel during that period revealed that minimum tillage, a foreign approach requiring imported machinery and chemicals, was being adopted. Its broad adoption was confirmed in conversations with dealers of imported implements, such as John Deere, for minimum tillage requires specialized equipment.

Minimum tillage offers multiple advantages once weed pressure is abated. Reduced consumption of motor fuels adds to the bottom line, but minimum tillage also reduces evaporation and thus preserves precious soil moisture. In Russia's semiarid climate, this improves and stabilizes yields, particularly during droughts.[22] Appendix table 4.A1 shows this clearly: grain yields not only stabilized starting in 2001 but began a relatively steady growth thanks to improved moisture retention, fertilization, plant protection, and general agronomic practices.

Table 4.A2 illustrates the impact of yield stabilization through improved agronomic practices. The gross output of cereals rose from a low of 48 million metric tons in 1998, an extraordinarily bad year, to a relatively stable output reliably exceeding 100 million tons since 2014. Remarkably, table 4.A3 shows that this occurred even though Russians took out of grain production roughly one quarter of area planted to grains in 1990. Russian grain producers are harvesting more grain from less area, a clear sign of improved husbandry practices.[23] A major factor in this was the increased application of fertilizer (table 4.A4), up from the low of 15 kilograms per hectare in 1998 to five times as much, 75 kilograms per hectare, in 2021.

Openness to innovation and the adoption of modern practices were major factors in Russia's emergence as the world's largest exporter of wheat (see figure 4.1).

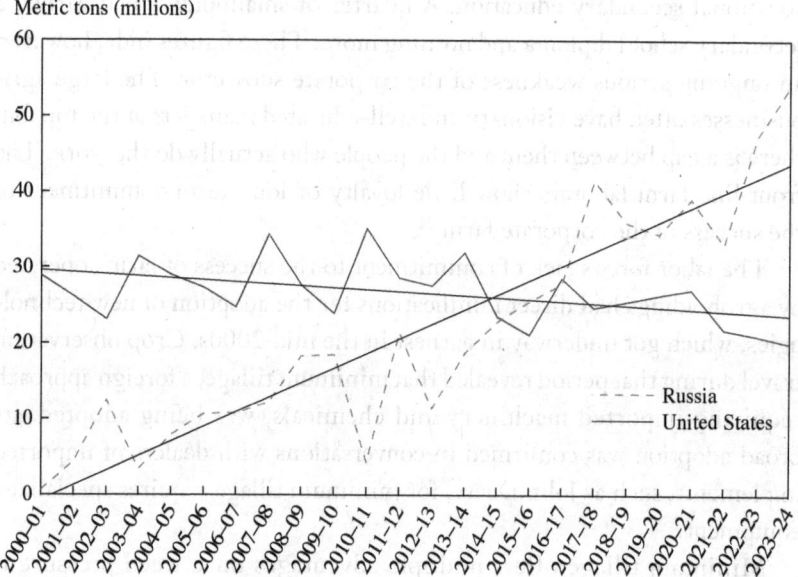

FIGURE 4.1. **Wheat Exports: Russia and the United States, 2000–2001 to 2023–2024, June–May Marketing Years**

Source: U.S. Department of Agriculture, Foreign Agricultural Service (https://apps.fas.usda.gov/psdonline/app/index.html#/app/advQuery).

Genetics is a different story. Although Russian plant breeders had since the nineteenth century developed excellent varieties of wheat, Trofim Lysenko's legacy of incompetence retarded Russian advancement in plant breeding and to this day has blocked the introduction of biotechnology. Russian producers, lacking domestic analogs, quickly shifted to imported hybrid seeds for corn (maize), sugar beets, and sunflower.[24] They also adopted imported agricultural chemicals, particularly herbicides, needed to get weeds under control for the shift to minimum tillage. Now free to plant what they wanted, when they wanted, and to cultivate how they wanted, Russian agricultural producers quickly applied modern inputs.

As one vegetable producer told the author, Russian science had nothing to offer him. He hired foreign consultants when he needed expertise. Russian grain producers the author met refused to buy combines from Rostselmash, preferring Case New Holland and John Deere combines from the United States or Claas from Germany. One of them noted that a single Western combine could do the work of three Russian combines, with a higher mean time between failures—and during the harvest season, downtime due to a mechanical failure is serious.[25] The author also encountered a custom cutter equipped with International Harvester and Deere combines who worked for payment in kind: he accepted 10 percent of whatever his machines harvested for the farmer as his payment. He explained that it was a good deal for the farmer, who would otherwise lose 10 percent of the grain out the back of a Russian combine anyway, so effectively the farmer was getting his grain harvested for free.[26]

The case of livestock production illustrates the impact of improved genetics and nutrition. When the Soviet Union and its administrative controls disappeared, mass culling of livestock followed, with inventories across all categories of farms falling from 57 million bovines (including 20.6 million cows), 38 million swine, and 660 million head of poultry in 1990 to roughly half those levels by 2000 (27.5 million [12.7 million cows], 15.8 million, and 341 million, respectively).[27] Circumstances were initially slow to improve. Nefedova describes the situation in the early 2000s: feed conversion ratios were 1.5 to 2.5 times worse than in developed countries, making it cheaper to import meat than to produce it domestically.[28] Nationally, beef production in 2000 suffered a negative profit—that is, a loss—of 21 percent.[29] In the aggregate, livestock production was unprofitable and was subsidized at the farm level by administrative controls requiring profitable field crop farms also to produce money-losing meat and milk.

Since the collapse of the Soviet Union, bovine numbers, including cow numbers, have continued to decline. Hog and chicken numbers, however, rebounded in the 2000s as imported genetics replaced inferior domestic breeds, entrepreneurial producers saw opportunities to displace imported meat, and modern animal husbandry practices replaced Soviet mismanagement. By 2021, hog numbers had reached 26 million, and poultry inventories totaled 539 million head.[30]

Even more impressive, though, is the output of meat and milk. Total meat production in 1990 was just over ten million metric tons. Following the collapse of animal agriculture in the 1990s, meat production resurged to that level seventeen years later, but did it with less than a third of the number of cattle, only two-thirds the number of swine, and 15 percent fewer chickens (tables 4.A5–4.A8). The livestock had become more productive thanks to imported genetics and better herd and flock management. Between 1990 and 2022, cow numbers imploded from 20.5 million to

7.7 million—a drop of nearly two-thirds—but herd yields nearly doubled over the same period with improvements in genetics, animal nutrition, and herd management, so that milk production stabilized at about 32 million tons per year. Combined with reduced post-harvest losses thanks to ultra-high-temperature technology and modern Tetra Pak packaging, this has given Russians better access to wholesome, drinkable fluid milk than at any point in prior history.[31]

The Russian excuse—"Our livestock are unproductive, but there are a lot of them"—had by circa 2017 finally given way to modern animal husbandry.[32] The livestock sector was by then focused on profitability, and though overall animal inventories were smaller than before, they were more productive. Furthermore, modernization of the downstream chain from farm to consumer meant the Soviet era's massive waste from avoidable losses had finally been curbed. Fixing all that didn't just make sense. It made money.

Demand Conditions

The major external factor influencing Russian crop agriculture was, ironically, the creation of an organization Russia would not join for nearly eighteen years, the World Trade Organization. The WTO came into existence on January 1, 1995, and in preparation for that, the United States and other WTO members-to-be adopted enabling legislation to allow some level of agricultural support that would nonetheless comply with the new trading rules of the WTO's Agreement on Agriculture.

The U.S. approach was embodied in the 1996 "Freedom to Farm" legislation sponsored by then congressman Pat Roberts. It decoupled farm support payments from current production, thereby allowing farmers to produce whatever they wanted without worrying about losing a government check. Many American wheat producers who had been "farming the programs" shifted to more lucrative corn and soybeans, and Russian wheat producers, freed from Soviet Communist meddling, filled that gap. Russia is well suited agroclimatically to produce wheat, and Russian domestic wheat breeders could provide very competitive varieties.

By the mid-1990s the Russian economy had begun to recover, and demand for foodstuffs, particularly animal protein, rebounded. The introduction of U.S.-origin chicken hindquarters, the famous "Bush legs," in

1992 as part of a food aid package resulted in a commercial market for American poultry meat that within a few years was valued at $1.5 billion annually.[33] Over time, Russian poultry producers upped their game by importing improved genetics and adopting better feed compounding, seeing the market opportunity for profits.

As the Russian economy improved, a Russian government policy of "food security" or "food sovereignty" emerged as a major factor. Memories of periodic famines since the 1890s aside, this policy was ostensibly spurred by a desire to ensure Russia would not become dependent on unreliable and potentially hostile foreigners for critical food supplies.[34] However, at least three factors play into this policy. First, in its fear of foreign leverage over food supplies, Russia is in some measure projecting its own willingness to cut off trade as a means of coercing or punishing trading partners, as it has since the mid-2000s with Georgia, Moldova, and Ukraine and more recently with the EU and Kazakhstan. Second, while the role of corruption in these policy decisions has been little explored, it is known that senior Russian government officials' families are heavily involved in agricultural production and food manufacturing, and thus have vested interests in protecting their businesses from competition and maximizing their own revenue streams. Third, Russia's attitude toward food sovereignty is in part shaped by memories of the grain embargo U.S. president Jimmy Carter imposed on the USSR following the Kremlin's 1979 invasion of Afghanistan.[35]

In 2005 the government included agriculture as a national priority project and allocated 30 billion rubles (about $1.1 billion) for expenditure over the period 2006 through 2007. This sum was subsequently increased to 35 billion rubles, and for the period 2007 through 2009 the government authorized 48 billion rubles. The program also authorized protectionist measures in foreign trade to reduce competition with domestic livestock producers, zeroed out import tariffs on machinery for the livestock industry, and expanded low-cost credit facilities for agricultural producers. By 2008 these measures had begun to show results: pork production was up by nearly 20 percent over the 2006 level, and poultry production had grown by over 35 percent. The fact that high officials in the Russian government hold financial interests in Russian agribusiness, coupled with the strategic interest in national food sovereignty for geopolitical reasons, means government support of agriculture and agribusiness has not wavered.

By the mid-2000s, chicken meat, a rare delicacy in Soviet years, had become common, and by the mid-2010s, American chicken was being squeezed out of the Russian market thanks to protectionist veterinary measures taken despite Russia's WTO obligations. The final blow came in August 2014 when, in response to Western sanctions against Russia for its invasion of Ukraine, Russia embargoed food imports from the United States and EU member states.[36] This removed foreign competition and allowed Russian producers of poultry meat and pork to flourish. Growth in the pork and poultry industries led to demand for improved livestock feed, and this resulted in expanded domestic production of corn and soybeans to meet that demand.

Another interesting shift was underway in dairying. In 2005, over half of all livestock products came from private plots, but after that the proportion began to fall. Overall numbers of milk cows dropped, but total output of milk rose—herd yields were rising. One factor was improved genetics; a second factor was improvement in herd management and nutrition, both linked to the emergence of modern, large dairy operations using imported bull semen and frozen embryos as replacements for individually owned cows of legacy Soviet breeds. A third factor was growth in farmgate prices for milk when a new technical regulation defining "dairy products" effectively banned the use of dry milk powder in manufacturing processed dairy products, including reconstituted fluid milk.

By 2018, production agriculture had rebounded sufficiently that the Russian Ministry of Agriculture shifted from an import substitution policy to an export promotion policy.[37] One manifestation of this was a shift in the basic responsibility of Russian agricultural attachés posted abroad from collecting information useful for improving Russian production agriculture, as had been the case since Soviet times, to "expansion of opportunities for exporters in countries with high market potential and representation of interests of the agricultural sector."[38] By this time, Russia had firmly established its position as the world's largest wheat exporter.

Other Externalities

In the post-Soviet period, the near-abolition of centralized control of the agricultural and food economy permitted the rise of entrepreneurship. As one example, even before the collapse of the USSR, a group of entrepreneurs, using the nascent "cooperative" legislation of the time, took over a bankrupt shampoo plant in Alekseevka, a small town in Belgorod oblast, because it had a bottling line that could be converted to packaging sunflower oil. Within fifteen years, the firm they founded, Efko, had become the largest producer of mayonnaise in Russia and was enjoying 50 percent growth year over year. This example illustrates the impact of economic liberalization on the ability of innovators to respond to market signals.

In production agriculture, an unheralded factor was government pressure on processors and merchandisers, as well as investors in other, more lucrative sectors, to adopt dying collective and state farms to keep production going during the "hungry '90s." To buy a grain elevator, for example, you had to take over and manage a bankrupt state farm. To secure access to a seaport, you had to take over a failing collective farm. To take control of a farm's highly profitable sunflower and grain production, you had to agree to maintain money-losing dairying and hog production. These are all specific examples the author encountered. Naturally, such investors had an interest in making their farms at least break even, and maybe even turn a profit, and this aspect of the turnaround was paid for with private funds. It also paved the way for certain favored investors to obtain valuable assets at fire-sale prices.

Initially, such takeovers were done with great reluctance, particularly when the new patrons of husbandry discovered that in addition to managing farms as economic entities they bore responsibility for maintaining roads, telephone service, schools, and myriad other social services and utilities traditionally provided by the collective and state farms rather than by local governments. As time went on, however, and in particular as Russia reintegrated itself with international trade, these new agricultural executives discovered that crop agriculture was quite lucrative and could generate respectable profits in most years, if proper management were applied.

Animal agriculture took more time, in part because it was much less profitable than cropping (in fact, in the aggregate, it was unprofitable in the mid-2000s, and some livestock subsectors remain unprofitable today[39]), and in part because the swine and cattle business cycles are longer than (usually annual) crop cycles, ranging up to twelve years for bovines. However, as noted previously, pork and poultry meat production responded to market demand as well as to rational investment and modernization of management. Poultry production attracted investment in particular because broilers grow to marketable size in less than forty-five days, meaning the return on investment was not only handsome, it was quick, and allowed for rapid expansion. Consumer demand for chicken was all too obvious, given the massive imports of American "Bush legs."

With time, thanks to protection of the domestic market from foreign competition, Russian animal agriculture has even generated some modest exports. The keys were abandonment of Soviet husbandry practices and the adoption of contemporary technologies and genetics from the West.[40]

One should not underestimate the impact of "McDonaldization" (as Russian agricultural experts called it) of consumer behavior in Russia. The introduction of a fast-food and indeed hamburger culture in the 1990s stimulated agriculture in two ways. First, as a result of McDonald's' stringent quality standards, Russian producers of commodities ranging from lettuce and potatoes to beef and chicken under contract to fast-food chains were forced to improve product quality and food safety to Western levels. Second, the younger generation adopted the burger culture, turning away from more traditional Russian cuisine. This boosted demand for quality beef, which, among other things, led the Russian agribusiness company Miratorg to establish the largest proprietary Angus beef herd in the world.[41]

On the negative side, absence of the rule of law, including laws governing such elementary concepts as contract sanctity, retarded integration of the Russian agricultural and food sector both domestically and internationally. Inside Russia, this remains reflected in the widespread vertical integration of enterprises, to a greater degree than is usual in countries with independent judiciaries and a functioning legal system. Simply put, if you cannot rely on contractors, you do it yourself.

In the 2000s, that lack of contract sanctity hurt Russian exporters because of discounts importers applied to contracts for grain deliveries. The Russian penchant for diverting cargoes already under contract because a higher price was offered elsewhere resulted in a roughly $5 per ton penalty compared to goods from competing origins. Russian exporters railed against "ethnic discrimination," but in fact they were being penalized for unreliability.

More broadly, the lack of rule of law engenders distrust. Entrepreneurs distrust government policies and government officials. Business people distrust each other. Labor distrusts management and lacks credible empowerment to negotiate. Nobody trusts capital markets and in particular banks. This distrust hobbles the entire economy, no less in agriculture than elsewhere, with the result that inefficiencies in the form of measures and structures designed to protect oneself are ubiquitous.

The De Facto Food Strategy

Putin has so far had six ministers of agriculture, starting with Aleksei Gordeev, son of Putin's commanding officer at the KGB station in Dresden, whose appointment Putin engineered while he was Boris Yeltsin's prime minister. Gordeev and four of his five successors—Elena Skrynnik, a cardiologist; Nikolai Fedorov, a lawyer; Dmitrii Patrushev, a banker and son of former FSB chairman Nikolai Patrushev; and the current minister, Oksana Lut, a banker sidekick of Dmitrii Patrushev—possessed neither formal education nor significant prior work experience in agriculture or agribusiness prior to joining the ministry.[42] This signifies a sharp departure from the traditionally technocratic approach during Soviet times, when policy was set by the Communist Party apparatus and ministers were drawn from the ranks of technical specialists to implement the party's instructions.[43] Today, agricultural policy is set by Putin's appointees, with strategic guidance from a firm hand in the Kremlin.

The policy directions have been quite clear:

- to limit competition, both domestically and internationally, by promoting champions (particularly those owned at least partially by government officials) and creating obstacles to imports;
- to seek rent through corrupt application of laws and regulations; and
- to promote national self-sufficiency in food, even when economically inefficient, in order to prevent vulnerability to foreign pressure.

To the first policy direction, in discussions with USDA officials in the early 2000s, then minister Gordeev formally asked that the USDA collaborate with his ministry to identify "good companies" in both countries that would receive official support to ensure their success. Then secretary of agriculture Ann Veneman respectfully declined the request, noting that the U.S. government does not pick winners and losers. This attitude of seeking to champion "winners" was in part driven by a desire to squeeze out domestic Russian competitors to enterprises owned or co-owned by Russian officials.

In another case, also in the early 2000s, then chairman of the Federation Council Agrarian and Food Policy Committee, Gennady Gorbunov, patiently and rather naïvely explained to the author that phytosanitary restrictions on imported U.S. rice were imposed purely to protect the interests of Russian rice producers. Similar restrictions on poultry meat imports, beef, and other U.S. commodities, not to mention a ban on products of biotechnology, were not based on sound science but rather on a perceived need to protect domestic producers. Russia also uses geopolitical considerations to promote both its domestic agriculture sector and its geopolitical aspirations. These range from periodic bans on wine from Georgia and Moldova, intended to punish those countries for failing to comply with Russian demands, to the embargo since 2014 on imports of foodstuffs from the EU and United States in response to the sanctions imposed in the wake of Russia's illegal annexation of Crimea.

Regarding the second policy direction, rent-seeking through corruption in agriculture is widespread and well known, if not particularly well documented.[44] On one occasion when the author, then a U.S. diplomat, was awaiting an audience with then minister of agriculture Aleksei Gordeev, the foreign relations official assigned to escort the author commented, "You are very fortunate. You don't have to pay to see the minister." Further inquiry established that the normal fee for a five-minute audience with the minister was $15,000, after which one of the minister's subordinates would negotiate a fee for resolution of the issue at hand—and resolution could cost as much as a million dollars, depending on complexity.

Separately, at a grains conference, during a question-and-answer period an attendee complained that he had been unable to book storage space at the Ministry of Agriculture's proprietary grain elevator in the seaport of Novorossiisk, and asked why not, to the general amusement of the audience. Afterward, an attendee quietly spelled out to the author that elevator space is booked only after payment in advance of a cash bribe of $5 per metric ton of the grain to be stored. In the 1990s the USDA undertook a technical assistance project to establish both an extension system[45] and a market news[46] system in Russia. Minister Gordeev abruptly terminated both projects in 1999 when he learned that extension and market news are cost centers and not revenue generators. To this day, the Russian government offers neither extension nor market news.

The Russian veterinary and phytosanitary service Rosselkhoznadzor is notorious for seeking rent through bribery. Though only rarely are examples of this corruption exposed and prosecuted, it is widespread.[47] In a case personally known to the author, in 2008, a potato producer in Moscow oblast confided that phytosanitary inspectors of Rosselkhoznadzor were known to carry dead nematodes (roundworm pests of crops subject to quarantine) to drop while inspecting farms so that produce from any farm could be quarantined pending "resolution" of the issue. In his case, the potato producer "resolved" the issue for a one-time payment of $11,000.

The author estimated in 2008 that cash income to Ministry of Agriculture officials from bribes and kickbacks amounted to no less than $800 million per year. While a trivial sum compared to corrupt rent-seeking in the oil and gas industry or the defense sector, it nonetheless represents a significant deadweight loss to Russian agriculture, as well as an impediment to economic efficiency—and it likely has only grown since then. Of that sum, well over $300 million came just from sanitary food inspection in Moscow city and Moscow oblast.

These sums are independent of profits generated by agribusinesses owned or co-owned by government officials who, unimpeded by conflict-of-interest laws, promulgate programs and policies that directly benefit their business interests.[48] That these profits far exceed revenue from bribery is without doubt, and that may in fact be a factor in the relative modesty of sums extorted outright. There is simply more money to be made by entering the business and protecting it than by grifting it, as is notoriously the case in the defense industry.[49]

The final policy direction, a goal of national self-sufficiency ("food sovereignty") to thwart external geopolitical pressure, is based mainly on Russia's projection on others of its own propensity to take economic hostages abroad, coupled with memories of past famines and the Carter grain embargo. If there was any shred of doubt about Russia's attitude toward weaponizing food prior to 2022, that doubt was dispelled by Russia's actions to restrict exports of wheat from the Black Sea region after invading Ukraine on February 24 of that year.[50]

Paradoxically, pursuit of this goal has not involved support of science, particularly research, with the possible exception of some successful plant breeding, particularly of wheat. If anything, the Russian Academy of Agricultural Sciences (RAAS), along with its various institutes, has been marginalized as Russian producers and food processors turned to the West for technology and inputs. The ensuing technological lag in Russian agriculture results in greater yield volatility than is found in Canada, which has similar agroclimatic and soil conditions, and an unusually high dependence on imported genetics, both plant and animal.[51]

RAAS is under the authority of the Ministry of Agriculture and has been legendarily behind the times for decades.[52] Russia's most competent agricultural economists do not work at the RAAS's Institute of Agricultural Economics or its Agrarian Institute (the latter founded in 1992 by Aleksandr Nikonov as a liberal counterweight to the hidebound Institute of Agricultural Economics, though unfortunately since degraded) but rather at the Gaidar Institute for Economic Policy, the Russian Presidential Academy of National Economy and Public Administration, and the Higher School of Economics.[53] RAAS, which owns considerable real property in Moscow and environs (laboratories, test plots, experiment stations, and research facilities), has been accused of becoming little more than a real estate agency as its leadership has sought ways to keep the academy financially afloat.

Impact

Russian agriculture contributes between 3 and 4 percent of gross domestic product.[54] On the face of it, that isn't much, but woe betide the government that fails to attend to the economic sector charged with ensuring the populace is fed. Russia has known bread riots. Therein lies concern about the effect of Western sanctions on Russian agriculture.

Since Russia reinvaded Ukraine in February 2022, most Western firms, including providers of machinery, plant and animal genetics, and chemicals, have shuttered their operations in Russia. This withdrawal, coupled with both Western sanctions and an expected reduction in the availability of foreign exchange, will curtail access to inputs on which Russia's production agriculture and food-processing industry have come to depend.

Whether Russian domestic manufacturers can rise to the occasion to create analogs of the same quality is not really in question—they have not in the past, even when resources were thrown at them. In the context of the current brain drain in the wake of the invasion, diversion of resources, including farm labor, to the military establishment, plus isolation from the West and shortages of foreign currency, the notion that Russia will match Western innovation and quality in agricultural productivity, engineering, chemistry, and genetics sounds absurd.[55]

If we assume that Russia's invasion of Ukraine has launched a new cold war that will last as long as the previous Cold War, that is, not merely for decades but for generations, the impact on Russian agriculture will be profound. It will mean that as Western high-technology equipment wears out, as the minimum-tillage seeders and technologically advanced grain combines reach the ends of their service lives, having to replace them with lower-quality domestic machines will reduce both productivity and efficiency. Western hybrid seed will be available only at the sufferance of Western governments. Loss of access to foreign genetics, for both crops and livestock, and to imported agricultural chemicals will certainly hurt as well.

To be sure, Russia will not starve. If in the last three decades Russian politicians-turned-entrepreneurs have learned only one lesson from the USSR's collapse, it is that private agriculture is vastly more productive and efficient than was nationalized socialist agriculture. Barring an improbable renationalization of production agriculture, Russia will continue to produce enough wheat not only to provide bread to its population but likely even an exportable surplus, though over time, yield stability will probably suffer.[56] The same holds true for sunflower and its products, oil and meal. In a pinch, Russians can live off buckwheat, bread, and vegetable oil and revert to producing fruits and vegetables at the dacha, as they have periodically done for centuries.

In that sense, Russian agriculture is not a failure, and will not fail to feed the nation, particularly since it is so heavily protected from foreign competition. It will, however, suffer from being cut off from foreign inputs on which it depends for efficiency and productivity. It will also suffer from endemic corruption that stifles innovation, investment, and entrepreneurship. In the medium to long term, Russian agriculture will stagnate and fall behind Western agriculture, but at least a return to the famines of the 1890s, 1920s, and 1930s is not likely.

Appendix: Agrodata Tables

Table 4.A1. Selected Crop Yields in the Russian Federation, 1990, 2007–2021 (All Categories of Farms; Centners per Hectare of Harvested Area)

	1990	2007	2008	2009	2010	2011	2012
Grains and pulses	19.5	19.8	23.8	22.7	18.3	22.4	18.3
Wheat	21.0	21.0	24.5	23.2	19.1	22.6	17.7
Rye	21.0	19.2	21.1	20.7	11.9	19.5	15.0
Barley	20.5	18.7	24.6	23.1	16.8	22.0	18.2
Oats	14.8	16.3	17.1	17.9	14.4	18.2	14.1
Corn	31.5	29.3	38.6	35.3	30.0	43.4	42.4
Millet	12.3	11.2	13.8	10.0	7.8	13.9	9.9
Buckwheat	7.4	8.4	9.2	9.0	5.9	9.5	7.7
Rice	32.1	45.1	46.0	51.4	52.8	50.9	54.9
Triticale*	...	...	...	27.2	17.6	23.5	20.8
Pulses	15.5	14.1	18.4	16.5	13.9	16.7	12.9
Industrial crops							
Flax (fiber)	3.0	7.2	7.8	8.2	8.2	9.0	9.2
Sugar beet	240	292	362	323	241	392	409
Oilseeds†	12.6	11.0	12.0	11.5	9.9	12.4	11.4
Sunflower	13.7	11.3	12.3	11.5	9.6	12.5	12.2
Soy	11.1	9.2	10.5	11.9	11.8	13.8	12.2
Mustard	8.6	4.3	5.7	4.7	4.8	7.4	5.0
Rapeseed, winter	19.6	15.6	17.6	18.2	19.0	16.9	15.9
Rapeseed, spring	9.4	10.4	10.4	9.3	6.8	10.0	9.0

Source: Rosstat (https://sosstat.gov.ru/storage/mediabank/uroj_.xls).

Notes: One metric centner = 100 kilograms = 0.1 metric tons. *Triticale is a separate line item beginning in 2009. †Until 2011 in raw weight; 2011 and thereafter in processed weight.

2013	2014	2015	2016	2017	2018	2019	2020	2021
22.0	24.1	23.7	26.2	29.2	25.4	26.7	28.6	26.7
22.3	25.0	23.9	26.8	31.2	27.2	27.0	29.8	27.2
18.9	17.7	16.7	20.3	21.7	20.0	17.3	24.4	17.2
19.2	22.7	21.3	22.1	26.2	21.6	24.0	25.3	23.0
16.4	17.1	16.0	17.3	19.6	17.3	18.2	17.7	17.2
50.1	43.6	49.3	55.1	49.0	48.1	57.0	50.8	52.5
11.8	12.3	12.9	15.4	13.4	11.6	12.5	11.0	13.6
9.2	9.3	9.5	10.6	10.2	9.5	10.0	10.9	10.0
49.5	53.6	55.8	53.0	53.1	57.6	57.6	58.3	57.8
24.1	26.4	23.1	27.8	29.1	27.0	26.2	28.1	24.1
12.1	14.6	15.9	17.5	20.1	13.0	16.1	18.1	19.1
8.5	9.0	9.1	9.4	9.2	8.7	8.7	8.6	7.1
442	370	388	470	442	381	480	370	415
13.3	12.4	12.9	13.9	14.1	14.6	16.3	15.2	15.3
14.5	13.1	14.2	15.1	14.5	16.0	18.3	15.9	16.2
12.6	12.3	13.0	14.8	14.1	14.7	15.7	15.9	15.9
4.6	6.0	4.9	5.5	7.2	4.6	5.6	6.1	8.0
16.6	16.8	19.3	18.2	22.7	19.8	22.6	23.0	26.9
9.9	11.2	9.8	10.2	14.5	12.4	13.2	16.3	15.1

Table 4.A2. Gross Production of Selected Crops in the Russian Federation, 1990, 2007–2021 (All Categories of Farms; Thousand Metric Tons)

	1990	2007	2008	2009	2010	2011	2012
Grains and pulses	116676	81478	108188	97024	61007	94247	70941
Wheat	49596	49372	63781	61663	41555	56293	37767
Rye	16431	3909	4504	4333	1635	2971	2133
Barley	27235	15559	23151	17877	8354	16935	13949
Oats	12326	5384	5838	5406	3225	5342	4042
Corn	2451	3795	6672	3953	3068	6937	8187
Millet	1946	417	710	264	133	878	333
Buckwheat	809	1004	924	564	339	800	797
Rice	896	705	738	913	1061	1056	1052
Triticale*	...	...	...	508	258	523	464
Sorghum	62	40	76	13	9	60	45
Pulses	4922	1291	1793	1529	1370	2451	2172
Industrial crops							
Flax seed	48	7	7	9	5	6	7
Flax (fiber)	71	47	52	52	35	43	46
Sugar beet	32327	28832	28984	24863	22241	47609	45031
Oilseeds†	4662	7039	8976	8192	7463	12234	10574
Sunflower	3427	5672	7352	6458	5347	9069	7501
Soy	717	651	747	946	1226	1648	1688
Mustard	192	11	31	24	36	82	38
Rapeseed	258	630	752	667	671	957	945
Rapeseed, winter	105	227	247	308	395	291	157
Rapeseed, spring	153	404	506	359	275	667	789

Source: Rosstat (https://rosstat.gov.ru/storage/mediabank/val_.xls).

Notes: *Triticale is a separate line item beginning in 2009. †Until 2011 in raw weight; 2011 and thereafter in processed weight.

2013	2014	2015	2016	2017	2018	2019	2020	2021
92419	105212	104729	120677	135539	113255	121200	133463	121397
52140	59713	61811	73346	86003	72136	74453	85894	76057
3361	3283	2088	2548	2549	1916	1428	2378	1722
15387	20377	17499	17967	20629	16992	20489	20939	17996
4948	5280	4538	4766	5456	4719	4424	4132	3776
11606	11290	13138	15282	13208	11419	14282	13879	15240
419	493	572	629	316	217	440	396	368
834	662	861	1187	1525	932	786	892	919
935	1049	1110	1081	987	1038	1099	1142	1076
582	654	565	620	501	401	356	310	288
172	219	193	312	104	49	99	53	115
2035	2192	2354	2940	4262	3436	3344	3447	3839
5	6	8	8	8	7	7	8	4
39	37	45	41	39	37	38	39	26
39292	33476	38989	51325	51913	42066	54350	33915	41202
13150	12870	13854	16271	16497	19535	22769	21245	24850
9852	8481	9289	11015	10481	12756	15379	13314	15656
1520	2371	2716	3143	3622	4027	4360	4308	4760
50	93	67	73	98	124	165	103	145
1259	1336	1013	1001	1510	1989	2060	2572	2794
391	452	267	167	339	344	420	693	730
868	884	747	834	1171	1644	1640	1879	2064

Table 4.A3. Area Planted to Selected Crops in the Russian Federation, 1990, 2007–2021 (All Categories of Farms, Thousand Hectares)

	1990	2007	2008	2009	2010	2011
Total planted area	117705	74698	76769	77548	74861	76285
Grain and pulses	63068	44266	46745	47555	43203	43584
of which:						
Wheat	24244	24385	26637	28702	26623	25565
Rye	8008	2103	2166	2147	1762	1551
Barley	13723	9618	9622	9034	7214	7879
Oats	9100	3549	3562	3377	2900	3053
Corn	869	1508	1809	1362	1410	1710
Millet	1936	506	572	521	521	826
Buckwheat	1278	1301	1113	932	1,080	907
Rice	287	162	164	183	203	211
Triticale*	...	...	...	190	165	226
Sorghum	67	41	94	28	20	104
Pulses	3,556	1,094	1006	1,080	1,305	1,552
Industrial crops, total	6,111	8,119	8722	8968	10,909	11848
of which:	418	74	77	69	51	56
Sugar beet	1,460	1,059	818	818	1,159	1291
Oilseeds	4,007	6932	7788	8,027	9,625	10460
of which: Sunflower for seed	2,739	5326	6201	6199	7,159	7621
Soy	675	778	748	877	1,209	1234
Mustard	226	58	59	101	110	134
Rapeseed, winter	57	150	145	178	218	176
Rapeseed, spring (colza)	201	508	535	511	638	718

Source: Rosstat (https://rosstat.gov.ru/storage/mediabank/val_.xls, https://rosstat.gov.ru/storage/mediabank/S_x_2023.rar).

Note: *Triticale is a separate line item beginning in 2009.

2012	2013	2014	2015	2016	2017	2018	2019	2020	2021
75890	77562	77854	78635	79312	80049	79634	79888	79948	80437
44455	45848	46157	46609	47100	47705	46339	46660	47900	47006
24694	25076	25258	26827	27709	27924	27264	28092	29444	28802
1559	1833	1877	1292	1265	1185	980	850	982	1036
8819	9018	9355	8866	8322	8010	8325	8793	8530	8176
3255	3342	3258	3047	2860	2887	2853	2545	2421	2291
2050	2441	2677	2762	2887	3019	2452	2593	2855	2954
474	470	506	595	435	265	260	393	446	295
1270	1096	1008	957	1205	1692	1045	811	873	981
201	190	197	202	208	187	182	194	197	190
233	251	251	251	228	175	154	140	111	125
55	152	176	224	229	141	71	85	81	90
1843	1978	1595	1587	1752	2221	2754	2164	1960	2065
11328	12057	12238	12722	13618	13959	15174	15896	15485	17812
57	55	51	53	49	48	45	50	53	40
1142	903	917	1021	1107	1198	1127	1145	926	1004
10101	11073	11211	11517	12320	12630	13941	14615	14398	16623
6536	7278	6911	7013	7607	7994	8160	8584	8545	9753
1486	1537	2012	2131	2237	2636	2949	3079	2858	3068
118	154	193	192	181	157	334	374	201	213
106	239	276	145	98	154	189	191	307	275
1085	1087	913	876	882	851	1387	1357	1181	1409

Table 4.A4. Mineral Fertilizer Application in the Russian Federation, 1990, 1993–2021

	1990	1993	1994	1995	1996
Mineral fertilizer applied					
Total, million metric tons	9.9	4.3	2.1	1.5	1.5
Kilograms per hectare					
On all planted area	88	46	24	17	17
of which:					
Grain and pulses, excluding corn	81	44	23	16	17
Sugar beet	431	247	150	120	127
Flax	172	86	46	29	27
Sunflower	85	27	9	9	5
Vegetables and curcurbits	163	120	94	79	74
Potatos	265	176	119	113	105
Forage crops	78	37	19	14	13
Fertilized planted area as a percentage of total planted area	66	45	29	25	25
	2007	**2008**	**2009**	**2010**	**2011**
Mineral fertilizer applied					
Total, million metric tons	1.7	1.9	1.9	1.9	2.0
Kilograms per hectare					
On all planted area	32	36	36	38	39
of which:					
Grain and pulses, excluding corn	35	40	40	41	42
Sugar beet	271	274	259	276	268
Flax	44	47	47	50	48
Sunflower	19	22	25	24	23
Vegetables and curcurbits	136	139	144	179	159
Potatoes	242	243	257	263	279
Forage crops	12	13	14	12	15
Fertilized planted area as a percentage of total planted area	39	44	45	42	46

Source: Rosstat (https://rosstat.gov.ru/storage/mediabank/mtb3.xlsx).

Table 4.A5. Production and Trade in Meat, Russian Federation, 1990, 2007–2021 (Thousand Metric Tons)

	1990	2007	2008	2009	2010	2011	2012	2013
Production	10112	5786	6277	6715	7165	7516	8078	8526
Imports	1535	3177	3248	2919	2856	2708	2710	2480
Exports	60	66	90	65	97	76	128	117

Source: Rosstat (https://rosstat.gov.ru/storage/mediabank/Meat.xls).

1997	1998	1999	2000	2001	2002	2003	2004	2005	2006
1.5	1.3	1.1	1.4	1.3	1.5	1.3	1.4	1.4	1.5
18	16	15	19	19	21	21	23	25	27
19	17	16	20	22	25	24	26	29	31
125	112	87	119	139	166	177	223	252	245
32	30	33	73	58	49	49	45	51	38
5	5	5	6	8	12	13	14	15	16
74	88	83	84	82	92	97	115	114	131
126	133	142	155	154	160	186	184	181	213
13	12	12	13	12	11	11	10	9	10
27	**24**	**24**	**27**	**28**	**30**	**29**	**31**	**32**	**34**

2012	2013	2014	2015	2016	2017	2018	2019	2020	2021
1.9	1.8	1.9	2.0	2.3	2.5	2.5	2.7	3.0	3.3
38	38	40	42	49	55	56	61	69	75
40	40	42	45	51	58	60	66	76	83
272	260	255	274	294	300	305	308	316	292
42	38	28	33	42	32	63	60	69	74
26	26	28	25	32	37	34	35	44	48
160	173	172	166	195	198	187	218	260	262
244	268	306	328	326	356	392	405	461	472
14	13	13	14	16	19	20	22	23	24
45	**46**	**47**	**48**	**53**	**58**	**59**	**61**	**67**	**71**

2014	2015	2016	2017	2018	2019	2020	2021
9026	9519	9853.9	10320	10630	10866	11222	11346
1952	1360	1246.4	1085	880	772	648	621
135	143	236.2	307	354	415	609	634

Table 4.A6. Production and Trade in Milk, Russian Federation, 1990, 2007–2021 (Thousand Metric Tons)

	1990	2007	2008	2009	2010	2011	2012	2013
Production	55716	31984	32226	32316	31507	31205	31197	29865
Imports	8043	7134	7315	7005	8159	7955	8525	9455
Exports	335	583	612	520	460	615	645	628

Source: Rosstat (https://rosstat.gov.ru/storage/mediabank/Milk.xls).

Table 4.A7. Herd Yield, Russian Federation, 1990, 2007–2021 (Annual Average of Milk Produced per Cow, Kilograms)

	1990	2007	2008	2009	2010	2011	2012	2013
Herd yield	2731	3501	3595	3737	3776	3851	3898	3893

Source: Rosstat (https://rosstat.gov.ru/storage/mediabank/jiv_prod_643.xls).

Table 4.A8. Livestock Inventory in All Categories of Farms, Russian Federation, 1990, 2007–2021 (in Thousand Head)

	1990	2007	2008	2009	2010	2011	2012
Bovines	57043	21502	20952	20540	19794	19901	19680
Cows	20557	9286	9060	8925	8713	8808	8657
Swine	38314	16371	16217	17288	17251	17263	18785
Sheep and goats	58195	21577	21743	21937	21734	22727	23999
Sheep	55242	19324	19574	19799	19676	20641	21892
Goats	2953	2253	2169	2138	2058	2086	2107
Horses	2618	1307	1325	1330	1284	1288	1287
Poultry	659808	388434	404338	436197	449711	473253	495514
Reindeer	2261	1483	1549	1595	1626	1651	1685
Rabbits	3354	2017	2148	2417	2773	2970	3154
Beehives (thousands)	4503	3072	2946	3012	3019	3221	3255

Source: Rosstat (https://rosstat.gov.ru/storage/mediabank/Jiv1.xls).

Counterpoint

2014	2015	2016	2017	2018	2019	2020	2021
29995	29888	29787	30185	30611	31360	32225	32340
9158	7951	7579	6997	6493	6728	7044	6890
629	606	645	608	576	611	707	806

2014	2015	2016	2017	2018	2019	2020	2021
4021	4134	4218	4368	4492	4642	4839	4988

2013	2014	2015	2016	2017	2018	2019	2020	2021
19273	18920	18621	18346	18294	18151	18126	18027	17650
8431	8263	8115	7966	7951	7942	7964	7898	7784
19010	19452	21406	21925	23076	23727	25163	25850	26193
24131	24445	24606	24717	24389	23129	22618	21660	20959
22053	22353	22443	22662	22347	21136	20655	19785	19148
2078	2093	2163	2054	2042	1993	1963	1875	1811
1266	1249	1241	1216	1239	1283	1311	1303	1299
493945	524252	543914	550169	555827	541447	544691	519779	539097
1746	1652	1764	1788	1839	1780	1734	1650	1570
3211	3516	3750	3626	3745	3562	3588	3445	3430
3312	3446	3425	3317	3182	3094	2983	2890	2790

NOTES

This chapter benefited from comments of Susanne Wengle, David Leishman, Mark Petry, William Liefert, and Fiona Mustard. Any errors or omissions are the responsibility of the author.

1. Federal'nyi tsentr razvitiia eksporta produktsii APK Minsel'khoza Rossii (2021); TASS (2016).
2. Rubinow (1906).
3. Conquest (1986); Morgan (1980); Nikonov (1995).
4. Ayala (2018). Although the land endowment has not changed, after the collapse of the USSR, much marginal land, particularly in non–black earth areas, was abandoned and thus taken out of production. The net result of this was that land that in many cases should never have been cultivated in the first place no longer absorbed resources.
5. Wengle (2022).
6. For a brief overview of Lysenko's impact on Russian biological science, see Sam Kean, "The Soviet Era's Deadliest Scientist Is Regaining Popularity in Russia," *Atlantic*, December 19, 2017. The standard work on Lysenko and Lysenkoism is Zhores Medvedev, *The Rise and Fall of T. D. Lysenko* (New York: Columbia University Press, 1969). For another Russian perspective, see Anton Ivanovich Pervushin, *Okkul'tnye Voiny NKVD i SS* [Occult wars of the NKVD and SS], chapter 2, "Bitvy alkhimikov" [Alchemists' battles], which includes a subchapter on Lysenko titled "Alkhimik Trofim Lysenko" [Alchemist Trofim Lysenko]. Nikonov (1995) mentions Lysenko several times but declines to go into great detail about Lysenko's war against genetics, commenting on page 209, "A description of all the twists and turns of this unreasonable and alien-to-science struggle, which inflicted enormous moral and material damage on our country, costing human lives, is beyond the scope of our work. There is literature about it." Nikonov detested Lysenko so much that, he told the author, he had refused, upon elevation to the presidency of the Academy of Agricultural Sciences, to occupy the office Lysenko used. Lysenko's theories, including "vernalization," that fertilizer is not needed and that genes do not exist, were eventually discredited, but not before inflicting severe damage on the Soviet scientific establishment. A Russian scientist told the author as late as the early 2000s that many Russian biologists continue to dispute the existence of genes, part of the rationale for Russia's rejection of biotechnology in agriculture.
7. The definitive work on this is Conquest (1986).
8. One glaring exception was the importation of Tetra Pak equipment and paper for the production of cartons for fluid milk. Where Tetra Pak was unavailable, milk was sold in plastic bags that were highly inconvenient: once cut open, they threatened to spill the contents whenever handled. Another exception was Pepsi-Cola syrup, for which the USSR paid by granting PepsiCo the license to sell Stolichnaya vodka in the West.

9. *Selkhoztekhnika '78, USSR Exhibits, International Exhibition*. Exhibition catalog in the author's personal collection.

10. *VASKHNIL Academician on Perestroyka*, 89 Istanbul 863, telegram from American Consulate Istanbul to the Department of State, dated February 21, 1989.

11. Finansy i Statistika (1986).

12. Takmakova (2006).

13. In 2006 and 2010, the figure was 48 percent, a high point. Laikam and Petrikov (2020).

14. Nefedova (2003), 130.

15. For an overview of U.S. food assistance to the former USSR, see Jurenas (1993). The author participated in U.S. government missions to Russia in September–October 1991, following the August 19–23 coup attempt, arranged in response to an urgent request from Soviet president Gorbachev that the U.S. Department of Agriculture examine food needs. The missions concluded there was "no threat of famine" but that supplies would be short, and recommended measures be taken to deliver additional U.S.-origin food to Russia and other union republics to alleviate those shortages. During a meeting with the mission, then minister of agriculture Gennady Kulik burst into tears and exclaimed, "My country will starve this winter," reflecting more the mood of the leadership than reality. The mission's summary report is contained in Mustard and Goldthwait (1993).

16. Official Russian statistics on agricultural production may be downloaded in Excel format from https://rosstat.gov.ru/enterprise_economy.

17. Nefedova (2003, chap. 4) describes the emergence of *"fermery"* (small-holding farmers) as an addition to the preexisting private plots and collective or state farms. These last were transformed into the corporate farms or agroholdings. The existence of both private plots and large landed estates predates communism, and in fact dates back at least to the sixteenth century when serfs farmed both their owners' estates and their subsistence plots (Volin 1970, chap. 1). For more on agroholdings, see Uzun et al. (2022).

18. One Russian corporate farmer explained to the author the headache of negotiating annually with a few hundred landlords, each of whom wanted something slightly different. Some wanted only cash. Some wanted payment in kind in addition to cash rent: firewood, mixed feed for livestock, fertilizer, or plowing the private plot in spring. Juggling all these varying demands is a major nuisance.

19. Laikam and Petrikov (2020).

20. *Kommersant'* (2016).

21. The author knows of one corporate farm that instituted Breathalyzer tests of all workers on arrival to and departure from the farm because of the rampant alcoholism, which had destroyed very expensive imported tractors.

22. In agricultural statistics, "yield" denotes quantity produced from a unit of area, such as bushels per acre or metric tons per hectare. It is simply the

arithmetic quotient achieved by dividing production (tons, centners, bales, bushels) by area (acres, hectares).

23. Some of the land taken out of grain production should never have been planted in the first place, such as marginal, fragile, and highly erodible soils. Some of it, however, was shifted to the production of oilseeds as Russian livestock producers learned how to balance rations and to depend less on simply feeding ground grain to livestock. Between 1990 and 2021, area under oilseed crops roughly quadrupled, mostly to meet foreign demand for sunflower oil, but with the happy corollary that this made more sunflower meal available to the livestock industry.

24. Unlike seeds from open pollinated plants, seeds from hybrids cannot simply be saved and planted for the next year's crop. They must be acquired from seed companies. See Texas AgriLife Extension Service, Texas A&M System, *Hybrid Varieties and Saving Seed* (https://aggie-horticulture.tamu.edu/archives/parsons/vegetables/SEED.html).

25. Conversely, the author once visited another farm with nine Don-1500 combines sharing only one engine among them. When the combine with the engine broke down, the engine was transplanted into another, which harvested while the first combine was repaired. If it could not be repaired quickly enough, and if the second combine broke down, the engine would be transplanted to the next in line, and so on. In this way, precious time lost to breakdowns was minimized. The overinvestment in physical capital is obvious.

26. Grain losses from Western combines average about 1.5 percent, with an upper boundary of no more than 4 percent. In the Soviet period, grain combines were often deliberately miscalibrated so that up to 23 percent of grain would be lost out the back. Collective farmers then would turn their private livestock loose on the fields to glean "lost" grain.

27. The terms "bovines" and "cattle" refer to animals of the genus *Bos*, regardless of sex. "Cows" refers to females only, which in the Soviet Union were almost always milked because of the preference for dual-use breeds.

28. The feed conversion ratio is the measure of how much feed you must provide an animal for each unit of meat or milk it produces. In meat production, poultry typically have the best (lowest) ratios, followed by swine, then bovines.

29. Nefedova (2003), 130.

30. One might ask why bovine numbers have continued to fall while hogs and chickens have flourished. First, dual-purpose cattle breeds have given way to more efficient single-purpose breeds, either dairy or beef, and not both. Second, efficient production of beef requires pasturage and outdoor grazing for the first eight to twelve months, followed by six months on concentrates. The alternative technologies are (1) 100 percent grazing (as in Argentina), suitable where pasturage is abundant, or (2) 100 percent confinement and feeding concentrates (as the Soviets did, using nutrient-free straw for roughage

and feeding expensive grain for energy and protein). Ruminants must have roughage or they die. Hogs and poultry don't require roughage and flourish on concentrated feed. Since Russia's land endowment is such that pasturage is scarce, particularly in relatively moderate winter climates (meaning cattle kept outdoors won't freeze to death), and since grain and oilseeds are more valuable products than grass for grazing or haying, the profit motive has focused on grain production followed by poultry and pork produced in confinement (that is, indoors, in barns, out of the cold), plus some dairying. Beef in Russia is now a niche subsector, relatively speaking.

31. In the Soviet period, wholesome, fresh dairy products were virtually unobtainable. Soviet housewives boiled store-bought milk because pasteurization was unreliable and both brucellosis and bovine tuberculosis were epizootic. Much milk spoiled on the shelf because of lack of refrigeration in the distribution system. One legacy of this is the belief among Russian consumers that sterilized long-life UHT milk is superior in quality to pasteurized fluid milk.

32. "Наш скот малопродуктивен, зато его много" [Nash skot maloproduktiven, zato ego mnogo]. Volin put it this way: "The Kremlin made a fetish of large livestock numbers. A great many poorly fed cattle, with low milk and meat yields, were held on farms long after their useful life span and without sufficient regard to feed supply limitations" (1970, 510).

33. See Association for Diplomatic Studies and Training (2021), *Oral History of Ambassador Allan P. Mustard*, for the story of "Bush legs."

34. The 1921 famine in Russia and American efforts to relieve it are described in Patenaude (2002) and Weissman (1974). Conquest (1986) remains the singular authority on the famines of the 1930s.

35. The U.S. grain embargo of the USSR was unsuccessful in punishing the Soviets for invading Afghanistan but succeeded in sowing distrust of the United States as a reliable supplier. See Luttrell (1980).

36. Gataulina et al. (2016).

37. Serova (2020).

38. See the website of the Federal'nyi tsentr razvitiia eksporta produktsii APK Minsel'khoza Rossii (Federal Center for Development of Export of Agroindustrial Complex Products) at https://aemcx.ru/export/attache/.

39. See Rosstat (2023), p. 103, table 6.18: "Rentabel'nost' produktsii, realizovannoyi sel'skokhoziastvennymi organizatsiami" [Profitability of products marketed by agricultural organizations] (https://rosstat.gov.ru/storage/mediabank/Sel_xoz-vo_2023.pdf), which indicates that in 2022, cattle ranching, wool production, and sheep and goat production remained unprofitable, though hog farming enjoyed 12.1 percent profitability.

40. In 2008, a local entrepreneur forced to take over a bankrupt dairy farm asked the author to visit the farm and try to discover why some expensive

imported brood cows were dying. He had imported thirty-three head of Frisian cows from the Netherlands, and four were already dead. During the visit, the author noticed that the animals were locked in stanchions, and had neither feed nor water in front of them (in the West, cows in milk are provided as much as they can eat and drink). The farm manager explained that he did not like these cows because "they eat too much," and so he restricted them to the "scientific norms" of forage and water found in his copy of a 1955 handbook on animal husbandry. The cows were simply starving to death. The author recommended to the entrepreneur that he fire the farm manager and hire someone with more modern outlooks.

41. Levinsky (2019).

42. The outlier under Putin was Aleksandr Tkachev. An engineer by training, Tkachev took advantage of voucher privatization in the early 1990s to take control of the feed mill in Krasnodar krai, at which he was an engineer, and thus entered agribusiness. His family's farming operation today is the fourth largest farm in Russia. See Shagaida and Uzun (2019). Oksana Lut came to the ministry as Patrushev's first deputy and served in that position for six years before being elevated to minister in May 2024, but her background is in banking, not agriculture. *Sel'skaia zhizn'* (2024).

43. See chapter 21 of Volin (1970) for a treatment of relations between the Communist Party and the bureaucracy.

44. Anders Åslund's outstanding treatise on Russian official corruption, *Russia's Crony Capitalism*, does not mention agriculture. Of course, corruption in agriculture is orders of magnitude smaller than in the hydrocarbon or defense industries.

45. Agricultural extension, established in the 1890s in the United States, is the means by which scientific advancement has been delivered to farmers and via a feedback loop farmers' problems have been made known to researchers at state land-grant universities. It is considered one of the cornerstones of American agriculture's success.

46. Market News, run by USDA's Agricultural Marketing Service, provides regular updates on prices and trade volumes for agricultural products to American farmers and agribusiness people.

47. For glowing examples see "Как 'пилят' в Россельхознадзоре во главе с Сергеем Данквертом" [How Rosselkhoznadzor, headed by Sergei Dankvert, "divvies up"], originally published in *Sovershenno sekretno*, September 2011, as well as Синтез и анализ С.А. Данкверта [Synthesis and analysis of S.A. Dankvert], originally published at Б-Ф.Ру, December 24, 2002.

48. A Russian agribusiness man who also served in the Russian parliament informed the author that the only reason he stood for election was to place himself in a position to protect and help his business. He was hardly alone.

49. Officialdom's business interests also protect the agriculture and food sector from renationalization, a fate that has befallen several other sectors of the economy. Then minister Gordeev attempted an abortive renationalization of the grain sector in the mid-2000s but was beaten back, mainly by grain interests, and nobody has tried since.

50. See, for example, Feffer (2022), Schmitt (2022), and *VOA News* (2022).

51. Serova (2020).

52. Nikonov (1995). In the early 2000s, when electronic mail swept Russia, a debate was sparked in the Academy of Agricultural Sciences as to whether email addresses should properly end in a period since in the view of some academy scientists an email address constituted a sentence, and sentences end in a period. The debate raged until senior academicians decreed that indeed email addresses should end in a period. One researcher commented to the author that the debate could have been settled easily by running a simple experiment: send two messages to the same address, one with and one without a period. That this had not occurred to the scientists in the academy, she said, was symptomatic of a much larger malaise.

53. In light of the political crackdown on these institutions since February 2022, their ability to continue high-quality academic research and analysis is in question.

54. In 2019, agriculture accounted for 3.9 trillion nominal rubles out of a GDP estimated at 109.6 trillion nominal rubles for a share of GDP of 3.5 percent. In 2022, the figures were 5.3 trillion nominal rubles and 131.9 trillion rubles, respectively, for a share of GDP of 3.9 percent. Rosstat, *Elektronnye tablitsy* – "*Pokazateli natsional'nykh schetov Rossii v 2014–2021 gg.*" [Electronic tables—"Indicators of national accounts of Russia in 2014–2021"] (https://rosstat.gov.ru/storage/mediabank/naz-chet-tab2014-2021.rar), table 2.4.12: "Schet proizvodstva po otrasliam (detalizirovannaia razrabotka) v 2019 g." [Account of production by sector (detailed workup) in 2019]; Rosstat, *Natsional'nye scheta Rossii v 2015–2022 godakh* [National Accounts of Russia 2015–2022] (https://rosstat.gov.ru/storage/mediabank/Nac-sch_2015-2022.pdf), table 2.4.15: "Schet proizvodstva po otrasliam ekonomiki v 2022 g." [Account of production by sector in 2022], 120–21.

55. Fertilizer availability is not an issue in Russia. Russia is the world's largest exporter by value of nitrogenous fertilizers, and neighboring Belarus is a major exporter of potash.

56. The Russian government's 2024 nationalization of assets of AgroTerra, a Dutch-registered firm operating on 265,000 hectares of farmland, is presumed at this point to be a one-off, singular event rooted in xenophobia and not a bellwether event portending mass nationalization of agricultural land. Vandenboss (2024).

REFERENCES

Association for Diplomatic Studies and Training. 2021. *Oral History of Ambassador Allan P. Mustard.* Foreign Affairs Oral History Project. Arlington, VA: ADST.

Ayala, Deanna. 2018. *Agricultural Economy and Policy Report, GAIN Report RS1819.* July 19.

B-F.Ru. 2022. *Sintez i analiz S.A. Dankverta* [Synthesis and analysis of S. A. Dankvert]. Originally published at Б-Ф.Ру, December 24.

Conquest, Robert. 1986. *The Harvest of Sorrow.* New York: Oxford University Press.

Federal'nyi tsentr razvitiia eksporta produktsii APK Minsel'khoza Rossii. 2021. "Operativnyi obzor eksporta produktsii APK" [Operative overview of export of agroindustrial complex products]. January 17.

Feffer, John. 2022. "The Weaponization of Food." Foreign Policy in Focus, July 27.

Finansy i Statistika. 1986. *Narodnoe khoziaistvo SSSR v 1985 g.* [National economy of the USSR in 1985]. Moscow.

Gataulina, Ekaterina, Renata Ianbykh, Nataliia Shagaida, and Vasilii Uzun. 2016. "Import Substitution in the Conditions of Food Embargo." In *Russian Economy in 2015: Trends and Outlooks.* Moscow: Gaidar Institute for Economic Policy.

Joint Economic Committee. 1993. *The Former Soviet Union in Transition,* vol. 2. Washington, DC: U.S. Government Printing Office.

Jurenas, Remy. 1993. "U.S. Agricultural Exports and Assistance to the Former Soviet Union." In Joint Economic Committee, *The Former Soviet Union in Transition,* vol. 2. Washington, DC: U.S. Government Printing Office.

Kommersant'. 2016. "Agrokholdingi—detishche nashei ekonomiki" [Agroholdings are the brainchild of our economy]. Interview with Dmitry Rylko. October 31.

Laikam, K. E., and A. V. Petrikov, eds. 2020. *Strukturnye izmeneniia v sel'skom khoziaistve Rossii po materialam Vserossiiskikh sel'skokhoziaistvennykh perepisey 2006 i 2016 godov* [Structural changes in Russian agriculture based on materials of the All-Russian agricultural censuses of 2006 and 2016]. Moscow: Vserossiiskii institut agrarnykh problem i informatiki imeni A. A. Nikonova (VIAPI).

Levinsky, Aleksandr. 2019. "Kak 'Miratorg' s pomoshch'iu gosudarstva stal prodovol'stvennym gigantom" [How Miratorg became a food giant with the government's help]. *Forbes Russia,* April 8.

Luttrell, Clifton B. 1980. *The Russian Grain Embargo: Dubious Success.* St. Louis: Federal Reserve Bank of St. Louis.

Morgan, Dan. 1980. *Merchants of Grain.* New York: Penguin Books.

Mustard, Allan, and Christopher E. Goldthwait. 1993. "Food Availability in the Former Soviet Union: A Summary Report of Three Missions Led by the U.S. Department of Agriculture." In Joint Economic Committee, *The Former Soviet Union in Transition*, vol. 2. Washington, DC: U.S. Government Printing Office.

Nefedova, Tatiana. 2003. *Sel'skaia Rossiia na pereput'e* [Rural Russia at a crossroads]. Moscow: Novoe izdatel'stvo.

Nikonov, Aleksandr A. 1995. *Spiral' mnogovekovoi dramy: Agrarnaia nauka i politika Rossii (XVIII–XX vv.)* [Spiral of the centuries-long drama: Agrarian science and policy of Russia (18th–20th centuries)]. Moscow: Encyclopedia of Russian Villages.

PASMI. 2018. "Inspektory-vzyatochniki i rukovoditel' s podozreniem na konflikt" [Inspector-bribetakers and a chief suspected of conflicts of interest]. PASMI.ru, January 19.

Patenaude, Bertrand. 2002. *The Big Show in Bololand*. Stanford, CA: Stanford University Press.

Rosstat. 2023. *Sel'skoe khoziaistvo v Rossii 2023, Statisticheskii sbornik* [Agriculture in Russia 2023, Statistical compendium]. Moscow.

Rubinow, Isaac Max. 1906. *Russia's Wheat Surplus: Conditions under Which It Is Produced*. Washington, DC: U.S. Department of Agriculture, Bureau of Statistics.

Schmitt, Michael N. 2022. "Weaponizing Food." Lieber Institute, United States Military Academy, March 28.

Sel'skaia zhizn'. 2024. "Kandidatury odobreny" [Candidacies approved]. May 16–22.

Serova, Eugenia. 2020. "Challenges for the Development of the Russian Agricultural Sector in the Mid-term." *Russian Journal of Economics* 6 (March 25): 1–5.

Shagaida, Nataliia, and Vasilii Uzun. 2019. "Kak agroholdingi meniaiut sel'skoe khoziaistvo" [How agriholdings are changing agriculture]. *Vedomosti*, January 22.

Sovershenno sekretno. 2011. "Kak 'piliat' v Rossel'khoznadzore vo glave s Sergeem Dankvertom" [How Rosselkhoznadzor, headed by Sergei Dankvert, "divvies up"]. September.

Takmakova, E.V. 2006. "Rol' dokhodov ot vedeniia lichnykh podsobnykh khoziaistv v sovokupnom dokhode sel'skikh zhitelei" [Role of incomes from operating private plots in total income of rural dwellers]. In *Nikonovskie chteniia—2006. Krupnyi i malyi biznes v sel'skom khoziaistve: Tendentsii razvitiia, Problemy, Perspektivy* [Nikonov Lectures—2006. Large and Small Business in Agriculture: Development Trends, Problems, Prospects]. Moscow: VIAPI.

TASS. 2016. "Russian Agricultural Export Outruns Arms Export—Official." August 24.

Uzun, Vasilii, Nataliia Shagaida, Ekaterina Gataulina, and Ekaterina Shishkina. 2022. *Kholdingizatsiia agrobiznesa Rossii* [The holdingization of Russia's agribusiness]. Moscow: Delo.

Vandenboss, Kevin. 2024. "Russia Seizes Over 650,000 Acres of Farmland and Other Assets from Company with Ties to 'Unfriendly' Country." Benzinga, April 10.

VOA News. 2022. "Blinken: Russia 'Weaponizing Food' by Suspending Grain Exports." October 30.

Volin, Lazar. 1970. *A Century of Russian Agriculture: From Alexander II to Khrushchev*. Cambridge, MA: Harvard University Press, 1970.

Weissman, Benjamin M. 1974. *Herbert Hoover and Famine Relief to Soviet Russia: 1921–1923*. Stanford: Hoover Institution Press.

Wengle, Susanne A. 2022. *Black Earth White Bread*. Madison: University of Wisconsin Press.

PART II

Society

FIVE

Who Are We?

Post-Soviet Russia's Identity-Building Failure

MARIA SNEGOVAYA

For a society to survive in changing conditions, without breaking away from its roots and preserving its original identity, it is necessary to understand this very identity and the values on which it is based. The main threat to traditional values and Russian civilizational identity stems not so much from external enemies, but from a lack of understanding by Russian society of itself, from the lack of a unifying worldview and a system of education based on our traditional values.

—Vladimir Aristarkhov[1]

Putin's 2022 decision to launch a war with Ukraine, and Russia's backsliding into authoritarianism and economic regionalism, partially owe to societal failure to create a post-Soviet cohesive identity substantively different from its Soviet predecessor. During the Soviet era, the perception of being a citizen of a feared superpower—one armed with nuclear weapons, exerting control over neighboring countries, and directly competing with the United States—provided ordinary citizens with a sense of unity that compensated for the humiliation and poverty they experienced in their daily lives. During the early post-Soviet period, hampered by the obstinate resilience of Soviet-era elites, beliefs, and institutions, Russia failed to break decisively from its past and forge national and social cohesion around values and ideals other than quasi-Soviet ones. Nation-building efforts reflected this failure as Russia struggled with the challenge of adapting strategies employed by many other post-Soviet states in seeking to erect a state on a titular nationality and in opposition to the Soviet past.

Vladimir Putin understood the void created by the disappearance of the Soviet system and responded by formulating and propagating a resentment-based identity of a humiliated but reborn nation. He borrowed heavily from prior Soviet themes in proclaiming statism, exceptionalism, and great power status for Russia; advancing paramount geopolitical interests; and elevating discourse about the West's existential threat to Russia. This new-old dual identity allowed Russians to reclaim a sense of collective belonging, which provided a psychological shield against harsh realities and helped deflect uncomfortable questions about Russia's past and future. Embracing their great power aspirations, a majority of Russians have supported Putin's "special military operation" in Ukraine.[2] While this perspective is detrimental to Russia's long-term dynamic, the outcome is precisely as intended by Vladimir Putin. In this sense, Russia's identity-building failures are a failure for the society but a success for its leader.

Vladimir Putin's war on Ukraine undid many of Russia's achievements of the past thirty years. Politically, Russia has unambiguously backslid into hard authoritarianism. Institutional checks that had existed since the 1990s have been destroyed.[3] Economically, Western sanctions have acted to detach Russia from the global economy. Internationally, Russia now confronts most of the Western world.

Conventional explanations for Putin launching the Russia-Ukraine War tend to focus on Putin's personality traits, personal biases, predispositions, and worldview, such as his concern with his place in history and his belief that he must "bring together the Russian lands" again.[4] Overly focusing on Putin, however, fails to account for why and how, after a short period of shock and uncertainty, Russian elites and Russian society coalesced, if sometimes reluctantly, around Putin and his war.[5] It is not the first time this has happened. Rather, this phenomenon has occurred after all five wars Putin has initiated during his rule.[6] The failure to address national identity issues and the inability to foster cohesion around values and ideals beyond statism and Russia's great power status led to the acquiescence to war.

Emerging from a communist state and a former empire, both of which were multiethnic rather than nation-state projects, post-Soviet Russia faced acute issues in developing a sense of identity distinct from the Soviet one.[7] During the transition period, Russian elites and society found themselves uncertain about and divided over what Russia was, and where it began and ended. The collapse of the Soviet Union and the economic morass that immediately followed provoked cynicism about what basic parameters of community and values should shape the future Russian state. The urge to develop a modernized state and economy conflicted with the desire to indulge post-Soviet nostalgia. An alternative strategy used by many other post-Soviet states—that of a nationalizing state built in opposition to the Soviet past—did not work for Russia. As a result, Russia failed to develop a distinct alternative identity to its Soviet one.

To say that Russians after the fall of the Soviet Union had no sense of identity, however, would be wrong. Rather, a number of factors contributed to the formation of a resentment-based identity that focused on lost empire and the humiliation that followed. This identity drew extensively on aspects of Russia's Soviet-era identity and provided fertile ground for Vladimir Putin to till as he sought to boost popular support for his leadership. Putin offered Russians a new vision in which both *ressentiment* and affirmative elements reinforced each other. Featuring a combination of restoration and nostalgic anticipation, his vision suggested that Russia's future would look more like its past, with the country restoring its international standing, pride, and respect from others.[8] This vision has also provided justification for the wars Putin has launched as a means of regaining Russia's great power status.

"What a Great Country We Lost!"

Understanding how crucial Soviet collective identification was to its citizens helps shed light on the traumatic effect that its disappearance had on Russian society. Soviet rulers might have failed on many accounts, but there was one area where they succeeded: in instilling in their citizens a distinct sense of identity. Soviet citizens shared ideas and beliefs about themselves as a collective body. These ideas and beliefs, often internalized to the extent of being taken for granted, helped shape their perceptions of themselves and the world around them.[9] One such idea, promulgated from above and rooted in a historical worldview that dated back to the Soviet Empire, was a sense of Soviet exceptionalism. The Soviet Union actively propagated the notion of its distinctive status as a mighty superpower, a huge country with nuclear weapons that "everyone in the world used to fear and respect" and that had only one competitor, the United States.[10]

In the Soviet context, the perceived individual dependence on (and chronic dissatisfaction with) the authorities often paradoxically transformed into a form of approval of the social order. This experience is not unique to Russia. Comparative studies show that people who are most disadvantaged by an existing social order are more inclined to make excuses for it[11] to compensate themselves psychologically.[12] Similarly, in Russia, as Lev Gudkov discusses, a sense of belonging to an exceptional "great power" compensated Soviet "little men" for their daily humiliation, chronic poverty, lack of rights and agency, and dependence on despotic authority.[13] Unable to change the existing social reality, people had no choice but to accept it psychologically by making excuses for an autocratic, repressive Soviet state. Soviet propaganda helped people find those justifications: it portrayed a strong repressive state as indispensable to preserve the Soviet Union's might and defend its interests on the international scene.[14]

To Russians, who formed the ethnic core of the system "largely viewed as Russian communism,"[15] their leading position within the Soviet Union served as an additional compensatory mechanism. Soviet propaganda characterized ethnic Russians as "the elder brother" in the Soviet "family of nations," placing them above other ethnic groups and societies in the system.[16] This sense of superiority provided an extra source of collective pride and self-respect in a context where other sources of self-esteem, such as republic-level structures separate from federal structures, as had been granted to other Soviet republics, were lacking. While in theory, Russians were meant to assume the role of a tolerant elder sibling to other Soviet citizens, in reality, significant divisions and power imbalances existed between the ethnically Russian center and the non-Russian periphery. Deliberate discrimination was widespread, and this left a lasting imperialist mark.[17] Post-Soviet Russia embraced this legacy by adopting a patronizing role toward the non-Russian post-Soviet space. As Jade McGlynn points out, this attitude is not primarily based on ethnicity but rather constitutes "social racism, the imperial elitism towards a lesser culture."[18] This perspective is reflected in the term "near abroad," which implies that neighboring countries are not as "foreign" as others and therefore are subject to different rules or treatment by Russia—in essence, forming a Russian sphere of influence.[19]

The Soviet Union's collapse, its defeat in the Cold War, and the loss of its superpower status led to the sudden and traumatic disappearance of many important constructions that had occupied a central place in the Soviet collective identity.[20] As an adviser to Yeltsin said, "When totalitarianism was being destroyed, the idea of ideology was being destroyed, too. . . . But our Kremlin polls show that people miss this."[21] In the early years of post-Soviet Russia, nothing filled the void left by a disappearing state identity. In a 2004 poll conducted by the Russian Academy of Sciences, less than one-third of respondents self-identified with Russia (while another third of respondents continued to occasionally associate themselves with the then nonexistent Soviet community). Self-identification with Russia was more widespread among big city residents, but even among this group, more than 40 percent did not consider themselves as citizens of their own country.[22]

After the dissolution of the Soviet Union, the Russian Federation lost much of its influence on the international stage and even had to accept aid from its archrival, the United States.[23] The majority of Russian respondents (72–74 percent) at that time recognized their country's loss of its great power status,[24] which caused something akin to a withdrawal syndrome, a deep frustration often expressed in a popular saying repeated like a mantra: "What a great country we lost!" ("Какую страну потеряли!").[25] One of the earliest signs of this deeply held sense of resentment, anger, and revanchism in Russian society was the electoral victory of Vladimir Zhirinovsky's imperialist and xenophobic Liberal Democratic Party (LDPR). In the 1993 Duma elections, the LDPR garnered 22.9 percent of the vote, more than any other party (next was the liberal party Russia's Choice, with 15.5 percent, and the Communist Party, with 12.4 percent). Among his many controversial demands, Zhirinovsky called for Russia to restore its great power status by extending its reach to the shores of the Indian Ocean and the Mediterranean.[26] Against the backdrop of the 1998 financial crisis, which further deepened existing grievances, the post-Soviet nostalgia peaked.[27] Even ten years after the Soviet Union's dissolution, as many as 73 percent of Russian respondents still expressed regret over its collapse.

Table 5.1. Russians' Views on Russia's Great Power Status, 1992–2017 (Percent)

	1992	1999	2008	2016	2017
Russia should maintain its great power status	72	78	86	76	82
Russia should not pretend to a great power status	14	9	6	17	13
Don't know	13	13	8	7	5

Source: Data from Levada Center. Survey respondents' answer to the question, "Which of the two opinions would you agree with more?"

Among younger generations, those who were twenty-seven to twenty-eight years old or older at the time of the Soviet Union's collapse, 70 percent continued to lament a decade later that during Soviet times, they had felt a sense of belonging to a large community (only 10–15 percent said they did not experience that feeling). Over half of respondents in the twenty-five- to thirty-five-year-old age cohort (who were age twenty-two or younger at the time of the USSR's collapse) voiced the same emotion.[28]

Even as they lamented the decline of Russia's international standing after the Soviet Union's collapse, many Russians clung to a persistent belief in their country's exceptionalism. For example, in 1994, among a total of three thousand respondents surveyed by the state-owned Russian Public Opinion Research Center, VTsIOM, 40 percent emphasized Russia's uniqueness (32 percent thought that Russia was developing along its own special path and could not be compared with other countries, while 8 percent thought that "Russia has always been among the first and will not give up this role").[29] In a 2001 VTsIOM survey, 71 percent of Russians believed that Russia belonged to the "Eurasian" or "Orthodox civilization" and the Western path of development was unfit for it (with only 13 percent of participants considering Russia "part of Western civilization").[30] The independent pollster Levada Center's long-term data confirm this trend (see tables 5.1 and 5.2). In other words, the belief in Russia as a special, and great, power and in Russia's exceptionalism long preceded Putin's rise.[31]

The difficulties experienced in the transition from a Soviet republic to a nation-state, the void resulting from the disappearance of the Soviet identity, and a perceived decline in the nation's status in the context of a persistent belief in their country's exceptionalism all contributed to a heightened perception of injustice. This, in turn, resulted in widespread resentment akin to a national trauma. In *Russian Talk: Culture and Conversation during*

Table 5.2. Russians' Views on Russia's Exceptionalism, 1992–2017 (Percent)

	1992	1999	2016	2017
Russians are a great people of particular significance in the world's history	13	57	57	64
Russians are a people like any other	80	36	34	32
Don't know	7	7	9	4

Source: Data from Levada Center. Survey respondents' answer to the question, "Which of these two opinions would you agree with more?"

Perestroika, Nancy Ries shows how everyday conversations, which frequently wove narratives about the poverty, hardship, and social decay that Russians had to endure during the perestroika period, served to fabricate a common worldview casting Russian society at the time as an inescapable realm of absurdity and suffering.[32] This sense of perceived humiliation was therefore internal, not imposed on Russia from the outside.[33]

Psychological studies have established that injustice perceived by members of a social group often creates negative emotions.[34] This is hardly unique to Russia. For example, a similar status-resentment dynamic is linked to the emergence of a populist phenomenon. Studies have shown that a dominant group often develops a sense of resentment bound up with issues of entitlement when it perceives loss of social dominance.[35] While not being unique to Russia, however, this accumulated resentment is more dangerous in the case of a country with a large military and nuclear arsenal. Indeed, while the injustice or threat to a group's position may be imagined, the ramifications that follow are often real. Perceived injustices to their collective status often provide groups with the moral ground to take restitutive actions to achieve redemption. In simpler terms, "It is when a dominant group positions itself as a potential or actual victim that the most toxic consequences follow."[36]

Searching for a New Identity

Lack of Alternatives

For Russians, the lack of an alternative, non-Soviet self-identification aggravated the status-resentment dynamic. In contrast, some other former socialist republics did much better. In the Baltic states, for example, a sense of common history and values predated their incorporation into the Soviet Union.[37] Politicians in those societies could rebuild their own nations in opposition to the Soviet Union, which was viewed as a threatening "other" that had imposed communism on them through occupation. In such contexts, the anti-Soviet liberation movements adopted distinct national overtones, and non-Soviet national identities formed with relative ease. In Russia, however, the Soviet system was a homegrown phenomenon that emerged after the Bolshevik Revolution. The intertwining of Russian and Soviet identities made it difficult for Russians to sort out who they were in distinction to their Soviet past, which made the construction of a positive collective self-image more problematic.[38] While other countries could redefine themselves by externalizing communism, Russia struggled with the challenge of "othering itself," as Gulnaz Sharafutdinova has it.[39] Attempts to radically reassess the Soviet past during the troubled transition in the 1990s were too painful (and politically costly) for Russia's insecure national self-esteem, a reality reflected in Yeltsin's team's identity-building failures.[40] As the historian Geoffrey Hosking explains, "With the end of the Soviet Union, Russia had gained its freedom but lost its birthright. As a political entity, Russia came into being as a negative: 'not-the-USSR.' So there was no symbolic moment when Russia broke with the Soviet past and created its own institutions."[41]

Several factors contributed to the lasting imprint of the Soviet identity on the new Russia. First, more than seventy years of communism had left few people who could recall a non-Soviet Russia at the time of the USSR's dissolution. In many Eastern European countries, by contrast, the communist period lasted only thirty to forty years.[42] Second, many Soviet institutions continued in post-Soviet Russia in different forms. The reproduction of Soviet culture and symbols, the reproduction of elements of the Soviet educational system, and the inertia of Soviet mass attitudes and opinions continued to influence new generations. Most ideological movements in new Russia were oriented to the past in some fashion, be they post-Soviet populism, left-wing movements passionate about egalitarian justice, or nationalist and focused on Russia's past greatness.[43]

These factors complicated Russia's search for a viable alternative identity. Boris Yeltsin's administration struggled to find ideological foundations for the new post-Soviet Russian state. Many liberals in Yeltsin's government believed that ideology building pertained strictly to the totalitarian past and had no place in a newly democratized Russia.[44] Early on, however, some Yeltsin-aligned liberals, such as Yegor Gaidar and Galina Starovoitova, did attempt to develop a vision for Russia's Europeanness and civic society.[45] Yet this vision turned out to be too divisive. Decidedly pro-Western liberal groups made up less than 7–8 percent of the population.[46] With condemnation of Soviet history being unappealing for large swaths of the society, Yeltsin was left with trying to popularize the idea of national reconciliation in the post-transition period. Rather than intensifying efforts to formulate a more distinct vision of a civic European Russia, Yeltsin opted for the politically less contentious approach of depoliticizing national history. As the historian Kathleen Smith writes, "In effect, he endorsed forgiving with a dose of forgetting."[47] This stance prevented Yeltsin's team from taking steps to evict Lenin's body from the mausoleum: public opinion polls indicated a split over whether to bury Lenin, and the issue repeatedly incited protests. Yeltsin's own imperfect record and the absence of prerevolutionary exemplars of democratic virtue further complicated matters. His invocation of imperial symbols, such as the use of czarist sites, emblems, and traditions, made many democrats uncomfortable.[48] Last, the objective of building a civic Russian identity came into conflict with the simultaneous effort to protect the ethnic constituency of Russian speakers in the post-Soviet region, a lasting imperial legacy borne by the post-Soviet Russian state.[49] The confusion that characterized Russia's nation-building effort at the time was best illustrated by *Rossiiskaia gazeta*'s desperate offer in 1996 to pay an equivalent of $2,000 to any caller who could come up with a "unifying national idea."[50] This contest produced no winners.

Elite Continuity

For these various reasons, the Russian anticommunist movement also found it difficult to present the Soviet legacy as something external and hostile to Russia and to frame anti-incumbent, anticommunist conflicts in ways that resonated with broader society.[51] This impasse contributed to the overall weakness of the anti-Soviet movement in Russia, the electoral defeat of liberals, and the eventual domination of old elites in Russian power structures. Independent opposition groups achieved only isolated victories, mostly in big cities: opposition politicians were unable to fully capture a single regional legislature. Moscow and St. Petersburg, for example, were surrounded by predominantly rural regions that remained in the hands of local political elites composed of Communist Party and state officials who had previously held power. In other parts of Russia, regional leaders also mostly came from the ranks of the old apparatchiks.[52]

In the inaugural, relatively free parliamentary elections of the 1990 Supreme Soviet, Russia's Communist Party candidates secured the highest share (86 percent) of votes in comparison to the rest of Eastern Europe, second only to Belarus.[53] Almost all executive, representative, regional, economic, and military structures in Russia remained in the hands of those who had run them during the late Soviet period.[54]

Former Soviet leadership elements, including the security services, gradually reasserted their dominance in Russia and further complicated the formation of an anti-Soviet identity.[55] Socialized in Soviet nomenklatura and resentful of the weakening of their social standing in post-Soviet Russia, these groups "were inevitably filled with old-style ideas and attitudes, nostalgic for Russia's superpower or imperial status," writes Andrei Kozyrev.[56] Most lacked an alternative vision of Russia's future and merely regurgitated old Soviet themes, slightly repackaged. As observed by Deputy Prime Minister Sergei Shakhrai, "Many of them have shed their communist apparel but have not, on that account, become different people."[57] The accepted ways of thinking and acting, past patterns of culture and behavior, and the desire to retain a relatively secure and privileged mode of life continued. As the historian Mikhail Suslov points out, for the vast majority of Russia's political establishment, the Soviet past was an important identity-defining anchor as in their view, "it reflected the peak of the development of Russian civilization."[58] These groups sought to restore traditional forms of statehood. After an initial period of disarray, by the mid-1990s, Communist and nationalist opposition reconsolidated and gained strength in Yeltsin's government. As liberals' influence weakened, the nation-building emphasis began to revert toward selective adoption of elements of the Soviet legacy, avoiding critical reassessment of it and adopting more imperial reconceptualizations of the new Russian state as a homeland for Russians and Russian speakers across the former USSR territory.[59] These trends accelerated under Vladimir Putin, who himself was once a member of the Soviet elite and a KGB officer.[60]

Putin's Response

The Identity of Resentment

In a society marked by collective narcissism and resentment over its diminished status, influential leaders play a pivotal role in skillfully constructing and disseminating narratives among dominant groups who perceive themselves as victims.⁶¹ Such leaders give voice to existing grievances and also offer solutions as to how to address these problems. In Russia's case, Vladimir Putin was just such a leader. As Sharafutdinova elucidates, "The top-down leadership and bottom-up collective identity-driven processes coalesced to produce a newly revanchist Russia."⁶² Putin's propagandist frames worked by reinforcing existing societal emotions and prejudices.⁶³

Putin recognized the void left by the disappearance of Soviet collective identity. He successfully identified narratives and emotions that resonated with Russian society and articulated preexisting and long-entrenched configurations of mass beliefs.⁶⁴ Putin constructed and propagated its substitute: an identity of a humiliated but "reborn" Russia. To cultivate that resentment, it is necessary to highlight a period of national humiliation. In this context, the significance of the "dashing 1990s" became crucial. According to that narrative, Russia was perceived to have suffered defeat and humiliation owing to a combination of domestic traitors (including the last Soviet leader, Mikhail Gorbachev; Yeltsin and his administration; and corrupt businessmen and politicians) and foreign enemies (such as the United States and the broader West, which were seen as capitalizing on a weakened Russia).⁶⁵ Putin bore down on this point to underscore Russia's humiliation.

Putin presents his administration's restitutive actions to achieve Russia's long-awaited redemption by promoting so-called patriotism.⁶⁶ The language used to construct this restored identity reflects its revanchist orientation: "*re*viving" Russia, which is "*getting up* off its knees" and ready to "*re*play" certain episodes of its past greatness, and so on. Appealing to Russia's alleged, mythologized past, this identity borrows heavily from Soviet themes while offering a new vision encompassing both resentment-based and affirmative elements that serve to reinforce each other. This vision is not fully backward-looking; it has a futuristic element in that it holds that Russia's future will look more like its past, with the country reclaiming its international posture, restoring pride, and recapturing all the great things it had lost.⁶⁷ The gradual restoration of many Soviet myths and ideas under Putin's rule reflected its backward orientation.⁶⁸ In that respect, Putin's most memorable line was describing the collapse of the USSR as "the greatest catastrophe of the twentieth century."⁶⁹ In Russia, gradual re-Sovietization followed. Soviet symbols, including the state coat of arms and the national anthem, were selectively adopted. Stalin-era repressions were either reinterpreted as a necessary evil or forgotten entirely in newly adopted history books. Additionally, monuments to Stalin were re-erected in Russian cities.⁷⁰

The main themes of Putin's propaganda echoed central pillars of the Soviet collective identity: statism, Russia's exceptionalism and great power status, the decisive importance of its geopolitical interests, a sense of entitlement over neighboring countries, antiliberalism, and the existential foreign threat posed to Russia and its people by the West.[71] A key pillar of this identity is statism, a worship of a strong, stable state that unites and protects Russians.[72] The idea of Russia's exceptionalism is premised on the assumption that to secure its stable development and international might, Russia needs to preserve and protect its existential, cultural, and ideological distinctness from the influence of others.[73] This theme found receptive ground in Russian society: multiple polls conducted in the mid- to late 2000s showed that Russians consistently prioritized the promotion of "traditional" and "historically Russian" ideas and values over "liberal" or "socialist" alternatives. For example, in a January 2009 VTsIOM poll, most respondents (31 percent) selected "Russian values, sovereignty and independence, reinforcing a strong state, and protecting the interests of Russians" as their preferred "ideological and political trend" for the country. In another poll, such concepts as "patriotism" and "*derzhavnost'*" (statism) were supported by 34 percent of respondents, while "communist" and "socialist ideals" were selected by 25 percent and "capitalist" by only 5 percent.[74]

Unlike other countries, such as the Baltic states, which successfully redefined themselves in opposition to the Soviet other, in Russia, much as in the Soviet Union, the West was assigned that role. Western values, including liberalism, diversity, and tolerance, came to be portrayed as decidedly "non-Russian."[75] Societal resentment over "defeat" in the Cold War and perceived humiliation by the West throughout the 1990s provided state propaganda a wide range of themes to draw on to develop this narrative. The claim of the West's existential threat to Russia reinforced this tendency toward othering. This narrative conveys that Russia is so exceptional and unique that Europe, the United States, and NATO desperately and persistently attempt to encroach on its countless treasures, be they its vast territory, natural resources, unique culture, or spirituality. The Kremlin employed this argument to decrease the appeal of Western-style democracy, consolidate society around the authoritarian state, and silence dissent.

The Kremlin's vision of a resurgent Russia, however, is derived from a deep-seated inferiority complex.[76] Various polls suggest that Russian collective identity correlates with such negative attributes as fear, hatred, and derision on the part of the West.[77] Stronger identification with Russia among respondents is associated with higher levels of collective narcissism (an unrealistic belief in a group's greatness contingent on external validation) but also with a collective resentment (a perception that Russians are miserable and maltreated). In extreme cases, believing that "we are very good but no one loves us" among Russians leads to a higher war approval and even support for the use of nuclear weapons. For example, a 2024 study by Gulevich, Osin, and Chernov demonstrated that sociopsychological variables in Russia reflecting group identification and attitudes, such as secure national identification, national narcissism, system justification, and perceived international threat, all positively correlated with support for a military operation in Ukraine, mobilization, and even violence against civilians.[78]

The Role of War

This brings us to the role of war in the Putinist propaganda-constructed national identity. The mythology around war is highly important for the Putin regime. This is another element of the lasting Soviet legacy. During the Brezhnev era, the state deflected attention from the regime's increasingly visible inability to fulfill the promised communist society by leaning hard on a war narrative of society's enormous sacrifice and victory during the Great Patriotic War, as World War II came to be known in Soviet history books. The Great Patriotic War thus served to legitimize the Soviet system.[79] In post-Soviet Russia, divided and confused about its past, the remaining national consensus and source of pride centered on the victory perceived as the most important event of the twentieth century (by 77 percent of respondents in 1989 and 73 percent in 1994) and united all Russians, irrespective of political and ideological cleavages.[80] Since the early days of post-Soviet Russia, this belief compensated for the country's economic failures and loss of great power status as more than 80 percent of Russians consistently identified the victory in the Great Patriotic War as a key source of national pride.[81] Even before Putin came to power, Victory Day remained the second or third most popular holiday in Russia, after the New Year's celebration.[82]

Because most Russians agreed on its symbolic significance, Putin early on used the war myth to unify a fragmented Russian society. Putin versatilely incorporated various cultural frames, ranging from "heroic sacrifice," "national glory," "defense of freedom," and "salvation of civilization" to "mass suffering," "unrecoverable losses," and "national victimhood."[83] Two days after his inauguration as president in May 2000, Putin began his congratulatory speech on Victory Day with "Brothers and sisters," in reference to the opening words of Stalin's radio address to the Soviet people following the Nazi invasion of the Soviet Union.

The importance of the victory in the Great Patriotic War metamorphosed beyond a simple symbolic significance when the somewhat critical attitude toward the Soviet past adopted during the 1990s was increasingly replaced by its selective appropriation. The Great Patriotic War became the linchpin of a new concept of Russian history that conflated the idea of the great state (statism) with the heroism of the Russian people who achieved their triumphant victory, allegedly liberated half of Europe, and made the USSR a superpower. In the 2000s, this triumphalist narrative became the main pillar of the propaganda-constructed post-Soviet Russian identity. The commemoration of Russia's World War II victory gradually turned into a pompous celebration of state grandeur with quasi-religious overtones.[84] Victory Day celebrations, which became increasingly lavish, eventually equaled New Year celebrations in importance.[85] No other event in Russia's history approaches the depiction of victory in terms of its salience for Putin's state rhetoric. Olga Malinova in *War and Memory in Russia, Ukraine and Belarus* estimates that speeches on various war anniversaries and memorial dates made up over 30 percent of all commemorative addresses by Presidents Putin and Medvedev between 2000 and 2014.[86] Throughout Putin's presidencies, the victory myth has remained the top reason for pride in Russia, as named by respondents in polls, as the importance of other factors declined.[87] The backward orientation of this identity-building effort resonates in the Immortal Regiment parades, started in 2012, in which people across Russia march bearing portraits of their deceased relatives who fought in World War II.

The Kremlin used the wartime memory to unite the Russian society against a perceived enemy and boost Putin's support, but also as a geopolitical tool and a source of inspiration for Russia's great power ambitions.[88] This propagandist plot revolved around Russia's moral superiority, demonstrated historically by its victory over fascism, and today by its readiness to struggle against a revisionist vision of World War II and the new Western order.[89] State propaganda also reinterpreted the war narrative to criticize "hegemonic" Western policies and to emphasize Russia's historical struggle against the predatory West, symbolized by Nazi Germany's attack on Russia (the Western allies' contribution to the Soviet Union's victory was conveniently omitted). This trend accelerated in the post-2014 period, after Putin launched his first war against Ukraine.

State propaganda also presented the wars Putin launched through the same lenses of Russia's exceptionalism, its historic struggle against the predatory West (Russia's latest war in Ukraine is no exception), and its postimperial claims on spheres of influence. The perception of external threat led to societal consolidation, which helped create a sense of the "collective us"[90] and boosted a sense of unity among Russians. According to polls, each of the wars launched by Putin has led to a temporary spike in his popularity (above his average approval levels)[91] and an increase in patriotism and pride in Russia, as well as greater overall optimism about the country's direction (despite the associated economic cost of war that the population had to bear). Russia's 2022 invasion of Ukraine proved no exception.[92]

How Russia's annexation of Crimea affected mass opinion best illustrates this trend. State propaganda amplified anti-Western sentiment and led to a dramatic increase in pride and a sense of belonging to Russia. In October 2014, a peak of 86 percent of poll respondents reported being proud of Russia (as opposed to 48 percent in 2006), and 64 percent agreed that "Russia is better than most other countries." Between 70 percent and 80 percent considered themselves patriots. While in 2011, opinions were about equally divided (47:47 percent) as to whether Russia had regained its status as a great power, after the Crimea annexation, 63–68 percent of Russians described their country as "great" once again.[93] These data demonstratively reflect a national consolidation that emerged in which Russians experienced a sense of mutual connection and a feeling of belonging to a national community.[94]

This propaganda-injected sense of collective unity with one's own country is emotive and addictive. Russian identity has been constructed so that individuals derive their sense of worth from the feeling of belonging to a large and strong state, that is, "their country." It is very telling that at the height of the post-Crimea annexation euphoria, respondents' self-respect spiked from 27 percent in July 2012 to 45 percent in August 2014.[95] In mass culture, there is a clear connection between individual identity, statism, patriotism, and support for war. A striking example of this occurred after the 2022 invasion of Ukraine. The pop-rock song "Я русский" (Ia russkii, I am [ethnically] Russian), performed by singer Yaroslav Yuryevich Dronov (better known by his stage name, Shaman), has effectively become Russia's new anthem. It resonates in every Russian school; it is listened to, taught, loudly sung, and was even played during Vladimir Putin's 2023 presidential New Year's address to the nation. The song's refrain repeats, "I am Russian, and I persevere to the end!"[96]

What Is Next?

The analysis presented in this chapter does not inspire optimism. Over the past thirty years, there has been a persistent failure to decisively break with the Soviet legacy. Additionally, there is an unwillingness to address challenging questions related both to the Soviet past and to Russia's future. Disagreements persist regarding what truly defines Russianness. Compounding the problem, Kremlin propaganda narratives have reinforced existing societal emotions and prejudices, creating a significant obstacle to fully disentangling from the Soviet past.

Putin has constructed and propagated a very different type of identity: one based on the feeling of resentment prevalent in Russia after the dissolution of the Soviet Union. This is the identity of a humiliated but reborn nation, a meme that borrows heavily from well-worn Soviet themes. This new-old identity presumably allows Russians to regain a sense of collective belonging while offering a comfortable psychological shield against reality. The psychological embrace of an imperialistic past, one that readily supported military actions across Russia's deemed sphere of interests and "rightful parts" of its former empire, tragically culminated in the 2022 war in Ukraine.

As long as an insecure Russian identity persists, the Kremlin will endeavor to create pseudo-realities to match a mythologized past. For Russian society to recognize the realities of the present, its vision of the past must change.[97] The collective self-perception that emerged and became entrenched in Russia during Vladimir Putin's reign does not allow much space for alternative nation building by forging national and social cohesion around liberal democratic values and ideals. A nonimperial concept of Russian statehood is yet to be created. This is particularly true after the 2022 invasion of Ukraine: the regime actively suppressed the promotion of narratives that challenge its reading of Russian identity, particularly ones that offer more liberal alternatives.[98] Since the start of the war, many individuals who might have supported such narratives have left Russia.[99]

The Kremlin's ideology derives its strength from the state's bygone glory and cannot provide alternative sources of authority or different perspectives on a desirable future for the country.[100] This pushes the country into a vicious circle of resentment-driven conflicts. Until Russian society can escape this paradigm, any attempt at consolidating democracy in Russia is unlikely to succeed.

NOTES

1. Aristarkhov (2021). Vladimir Aristarkhov is a Kremlin-linked personage responsible for the formulation of the new Russian ideology.

2. Polls run by a variety of methods and companies reveal a consistent support for war at the level of about 60–70 percent. See, for example, Levada Center (2023, 2024), Russian Field (2024), and Chronicles' survey results at https://www.chronicles.report/dynamics. Moreover, multiple studies run over the last two and half years in Russia did not reveal consistent evidence of either significant change in response rates (that is, the number of respondents willing to talk to pollsters), an increase in the share of respondents who answered "don't know" (that is, persons who may be unwilling to answer sensitive questions), or evidence of preference falsification (see, for example, Rosenfeld 2023; Volkov and Kolesnikov 2023; Zvonovsky and Khodykin 2024). Moreover, the dynamics of many social ratings in Russia follow the patterns revealed during Putin's previous wars, and no additional evidence (either from polling data or from antiwar protests inside or outside Russia) has emerged suggesting that the polling numbers are radically distorting reality. This suggests that the polling data are broadly indicative of the situation on the ground. See Rosenfeld (2023), 38–48; Volkov and Kolesnikov (2023); and Zvonovsky and Khodykin (2024).

3. Kolesnikov (2022).

4. Frye (2022); Gessen (2012); Hill and Gaddy (2015); McFaul (2020); Myers (2015); Ostrovsky (2015); Taylor (2018).

5. Rustamova (2022); Snegovaya (2022).

6. These wars initiated by Putin are the 1999 Second Chechen War, the 2008 Russo-Georgian War, the 2014 war with Ukraine, the 2015 intervention in Syria's war, and the 2022 full-scale war with Ukraine.

7. Kolstø and Blakkisrud (2016).

8. Snegovaya, Kimmage, and McGlynn (2023).

9. Sharafutdinova (2020).

10. Gudkov (2015b).

11. Henry and Saul (2006); Jost (2019).

12. Sengupta et al. (2017); Vargas-Salfate (2017).

13. Gudkov (2015b), 38.
14. Gudkov (2015a).
15. Beissinger (2009), 342.
16. Mirsky (1997).
17. "Elder brother" and leading nation in a "family of nations": Koplatadze (2019).
18. McGlynn (2023), 175.
19. Kubicek (1999), 556.
20. Gudkov (2015), 37.
21. Quoted in Smith (2002), 159.
22. Tikhonova (2008), 118, 122.
23. Laine (2021), 16.
24. Gudkov (2015a), 202.
25. Eggert (2015).
26. Zhirinovsky (1997).
27. Levada Center (2018).
28. Tikhonova (2008), 103–36, 117–18.
29. Dubin (2010), 2.
30. The data are from Dunlop (2010), 91.
31. Levada Center (2017), 33.
32. Ries (1997).
33. Pomerantsev (2022).
34. Gudkov (2015b); Malinova (2014); Sengupta, Osborne, and Sibley (2015); Sharafutdinova (2020).
35. Van Zomeren, Postmes, and Spears (2008), 504.
36. Reicher and Ulusahin (2020), 277.
37. Darden and Grzymala-Busse (2006); Way (2005).
38. During Soviet times, the absence of the republic-level structures in the RSFSR, which were granted to the other Soviet republics, further obstructed the development of a strong Russian national identity. Malinova (2017), 43.
39. Sharafutdinova (2022).
40. Malinova (2017), 46.
41. Hosking (2006), 388.
42. Pop-Eleches and Tucker (2020).
43. Gudkov (2015a), 194.
44. Smith (2002).
45. Shevel (2011).
46. Zhilyaeva (2023). This number is consistently reproduced across multiple polls. For example, in 2023, the independent media broadcasting from outside Russia had a combined audience of 7 percent of Russians (https://spektr.co/glukhaya-oborona-levada-spektr/).
47. Smith (2002), 172.

48. Smith (2002), 169, 171–72.
49. Shevel (2011).
50. Remnik (2022).
51. Way (2005).
52. Snegovaya (2023b), 110.
53. In the 1990 Supreme Soviet elections in Ukraine, Communist Party candidates received a total of 74 percent; in Moldova, they received a total of only 44 percent, while in Belarus, they received 88 percent. Interestingly, Belarus had experienced similar challenges moving away from the Soviet identity. See, for example, Shraibman (2018): "The House That Lukashenko Built: The Foundation, Evolution, and Future of the Belarusian Regime."
54. Snegovaya (2023b), 109–10.
55. Libman and Obydenkova (2021).
56. Kozyrev (2019), 150.
57. Shakhrai quoted in Tucker (2019), 10.
58. See Orlov (2023).
59. Malinova (2017); Pain (2009); Snegovaya and Lanoszka (2022).
60. In May 1990, shortly after Anatoly Sobchak was elected chairman of the Leningrad City Council of People's Deputies, Putin became his adviser, and subsequently chairman of the Committee for External Relations of the Leningrad City Hall and head of the Mayor's Office Commission on Operational Issues.
61. Reicher and Ulusahin (2020), 280.
62. Sharafutdinova (2020), 18.
63. McGlynn (2023), 206; Shirikov (2022).
64. Shirikov (2022).
65. Garner (2023).
66. Snegovaya (2016).
67. Snegovaya, Kimmage, and McGlynn (2023).
68. Snegovaya (2023b).
69. *NBC News* (2005).
70. Snegovaya (2018).
71. Gudkov (2015b); Sharafutdinova (2020), 27.
72. Snegovaya, Kimmage, and McGlynn (2023). According to William Pomeranz (2016), the state historically occupies such a prominent place "largely because it remains the only institution that has traditionally held the country—and empire—together."
73. Chebankova (2016).
74. Popov (2009).
75. Gudkov (2021), 34.
76. Gudkov (2015a, 2015b); Levinson (2023).
77. Gudkov (2015a), 201.
78. Gulevich, Osin, and Chernov (2024).

79. Snegovaya (2020).
80. Gudkov (1997).
81. Ibid.
82. In the 1990s and in the early 2000s.
83. Malinova (2017), 43–70.
84. Gudkov (2015a); Snegovaya (2018).
85. TASS (2018).
86. Malinova (2017), 43–70.
87. Levada Center (2020).
88. Malinova (2017), 45.
89. Laruelle (2021, 161).
90. Gudkov (2015a, 2015b).
91. Radio Svoboda (2022).
92. Maksimova (2022).
93. Gudkov (2015a), 176–77.
94. Ibid., 164.
95. Gudkov (2015b), 39.
96. Caprio (2023).
97. McGlynn (2023), 206.
98. Snegovaya and McGlynn (2024).
99. Snegovaya (2023a).
100. Kolesnikov (2015).

REFERENCES

Aristarkhov, Vladimir. 2021. "Kharakteristika ugroz natsional'noi bezopasnosti Rossii v normativnykh aktakh po gosudarstvennoi kul'turnoi politiki" [Characteristics of threats to Russia's national security in regulations on state cultural policy]. *Redakstsionnaia kollegiia*, 5–6.

Beissinger, Mark R. 2009. "Nationalism and the Collapse of Soviet Communism." *Contemporary European History* 18 (3).

Caprio, Stefano. 2023. "Singing Russia's Identity." AsiaNews.it, April 22.

Chebankova, Elena. 2016. "Contemporary Russian Conservatism." *Post-Soviet Affairs* 32 (1): 28–54.

Darden, Keith, and Anna Grzymala-Busse. 2006. "The Great Divide: Literacy, Nationalism, and the Communist Collapse." *World Politics* 59 (1): 83–115.

Dubin, Boris. 2010. "'Osobii put'' i sotsial'nii poriadok v sovremennoi Rossii" [A "special path" and social order in modern Russia]. *Vestnik obshchestvennogo mneniia. Dannye. Analiz. Diskussii* 1 (103).

Dunlop, John B. 2010. "Alexander Dugin's 'Neo-Eurasian' Textbook and Dmitri Trenin's Controversial Response." *Forum of Contemporary Eastern European History and Culture* (Russian edition) 1:79–113.

Eggert, Konstantin. 2015. "Rossiiane eshche otseniat Den' Rossii" [Russians will still appreciate Russia Day]. *Deutsche Welle*, June 12.

Frye, Timothy. 2022. *Weak Strongman: The Limits of Power in Putin's Russia*. Princeton, NJ: Princeton University Press.

Garner, Ian. 2023. *Z Generation: Into the Heart of Russia's Fascist Youth*. London: Hurst & Co.

Gessen, Masha. 2012. *The Man without a Face: The Unlikely Rise of Vladimir Putin*. New York: Riverhead Books.

Gudkov, Lev. 2021. "Kak my dumaem: Stat'ia L'va Gudkova i obsuzhdenie" [How we think: Article by Lev Gudkov and discussion]. Levada Center. February 5.

———. 2015a. "Ressentimentnii natsionalizm" [Resentment nationalism]. *Politicheskaia kontseptologiia: Zhurnal metadistsiplinarnykh issledovanii* 4:102–87.

———. 2015b. "Russian Public Opinion in the Aftermath of the Ukraine Crisis." *Russian Politics & Law* 53(4) (2015).

———. 1997. "Pobeda v voine: K sotsiologii odnogo natsional'nogo simvola" [Victory in the war: Toward the sociology of one national symbol]. *Monitoring obshchestvennogo mneniia: Ekonomicheskie i sotsial'nye peremeny* 5:12–19.

Gulevich, O., E. Osin, and D. Chernov. 2024. "Dark Triad and the Attitude toward Military Violence against Civilians: The Role of Moral Disengagement." *European Journal of Social Psychology*, March.

Henry, P. J., and Andrea L. Saul. 2006. "The Development of System Justification in the Developing World." *Social Justice Research* 19:365–78.

Hill, Fiona, and Clifford G. Gaddy. 2015. *Mr. Putin: Operative in the Kremlin*. Washington, DC: Brookings Institution Press.

Hosking, Geoffrey. 2006. *Rulers and Victims: The Russians in the Soviet Union*. Cambridge, MA: Harvard University Press.

Jost, John T. 2019. "A Quarter Century of System Justification Theory: Questions, Answers, Criticisms, and Societal Applications." *British Journal of Social Psychology* 58 (2): 263–314.

Kolesnikov, Andrei. 2022. *Putin's War Has Moved Russia from Authoritarianism to Hybrid Totalitarianism*. Washington, DC: Carnegie Endowment for International Peace.

———. 2015. *Russian Ideology after Crimea*, vol. 22. Washington, DC: Carnegie Endowment for International Peace.

Kolstø, Pål, and Helge Blakkisrud, eds. 2016. *The New Russian Nationalism: Imperialism, Ethnicity and Authoritarianism 2000–2015*. Edinburgh: Edinburgh University Press, 2016.

Koplatadze, Tamar. 2019. "Theorizing Russian Postcolonial Studies." *Postcolonial Studies* 22 (4).

Kozyrev, Andrei. 2109. *The Firebird: The Elusive Fate of Russian Democracy*. University of Pittsburgh Press.

Kubicek, Paul. 1999. "Russian Foreign Policy and the West." *Political Science Quarterly* 114 (4).

Laine, Veera. 2021. "Nationalism as an Argument in Contemporary Russia: Four Perspectives on Language in Action." *Commentationes Scientiarum Socialium*, no. 16.

Laruelle, Marlène. 2021. *Is Russia Fascist? Unraveling Propaganda East and West*. Ithaca, NY: Cornell University Press.

Levada Center 2024. "Konflikt s Ukrainoi: Otsenki kontsa 2023 – nachala 2024 goda" [Conflict with Ukraine: Assessments from the end of 2023–beginning of 2024]. Press release, February 6.

———. 2023. "Konflikt s Ukrainoi: Otsenki oktiabria 2023 goda" [Conflict with Ukraine: The October 2023 assessments]. Press release, October 31.

———. 2020. "Gordost' i identichnost'" [Pride and identity]. Monitoring obshchestvennogo mneniia. Press release, October 19.

———. 2018. "Nostal'giia po SSSR" [Nostalgia for the USSR]. Monitoring obshchestvennogo mneniia. Press release, December 19.

———. 2017. "Obshchestvennoe mnenie—2017" [Public opinion—2017]. Monitoring obshchestvennogo mneniia. Press release.

Levinson, Aleksei. 2023. "'Nevelikost' zhizni dolzhna byt' kompensirovana velichiem derzhavi': Zachem vlasti tsenzura" [The smallness of life must be compensated for by the greatness of the power: Why the authorities need censorship]. *Forbes Russia*, February 28.

Libman, Alexander, and Anastassia V. Obydenkova. 2021. *Historical Legacies of Communism: Modern Politics, Society, and Economic Development*. Cambridge: Cambridge University Press.

Maksimova, Kseniia. 2022. "RAN: Opros vyiavil paradoksal'nyi i rost optimizma rossiian po povodu budushchego strany [RAN: The survey revealed a paradoxical increase in Russians' optimism about the country's future]. Gazeta.ru, December 22.

Malinova, Olga. 2017. "Political Uses of the Great Patriotic War in Post-Soviet Russia from Yeltsin to Putin." In *War and Memory in Russia, Ukraine and Belarus*, ed. Julie Fedor, Markku Kangaspuro, Jussi Lassila, and Tatiana Zhurzhenko, 43–70. New York: Palgrave Macmillan.

———. 2014. "Obsession with Status and Ressentiment: Historical Backgrounds of the Russian Discursive Identity Construction." *Communist and Post-Communist Studies* 47 (3/4): 291–303.

McFaul, Michael. 2020. "Putin, Putinism, and the Domestic Determinants of Russian Foreign Policy." *International Security* 45 (2): 95–139.

McGlynn, Jade. 2023. "Russia's War: Unravelling the Kremlin's narrative." National Digital Repository Center on Defence Studies, General Sir John Kotelewala Defence University, Dehiwala-Mount Lavinia, Sri Lanka.

Mirsky, Georgiy. 1997. *On Ruins of Empire: Ethnicity and Nationalism in the Former Soviet Union*. Westport, CT: Greenwood.
Myers, Steven Lee. 2015. *The New Tsar: The Rise and Reign of Vladimir Putin*. New York: Penguin Random House.
NBC News. 2005. "Putin: Soviet Collapse a 'Genuine Tragedy.'" April 25.
Orlov, A. 2023. "Interv'iu s istorikom Mikhailom Suslovym: Kreml' khochet, chtoby putinizm stal universal'noi ideologii" [Interview with the historian Mikhail Suslov: The Kremlin wants Putinism to become the universal ideology]. *Novaia gazeta*, June 22.
Ostrovsky, Arkady. 2015. *The Invention of Russia: The Rise of Putin and the Age of Fake News*. New York: Penguin Books.
Pain, Emil'. 2009. "Russia between Empire and Nation." *Russian Politics & Law* 47 (2): 60–86.
Pomerantsev, Peter. 2022. "Ukraine Is the Next Act in Putin's Empire of Humiliation." *New York Times*, July 26.
Pomeranz, William. 2016. "How 'The State' Survived the Collapse of the Soviet Union." *Kennan Cable*, September.
Pop-Eleches, Grigore, and Joshua A. Tucker. 2020. "Communist Legacies and Left-Authoritarianism." *Comparative Political Studies* 53 (12): 1861–89.
Popov, N. 2009. "Poiski natsional'noi idei Rossii prodolzhaiutsia" [The search for the national idea of Russia continues]. Russkie.org, November 27.
Radio Svoboda. 2022. "'Reiting Putina vsegda ros vo vremia voyny': Sotsiolog Lev Gudkov o nastroeniiakh rossiian" ["Putin's rating always increased in wartime": Sociologist Lev Gudkov on the mood of Russians]. March 1.
Reicher, Stephen, and Yasemin Ulusahin. 2020. "Resentment and Redemption: On the Mobilization of Dominant Group Victimhood." In *The Social Psychology of Collective Victimhood*, 277. Oxford: Oxford University Press.
Remnik, David. 2022. "What Is Putin Thinking?" *New Yorker*, March 27.
Ries, Nancy. 1997. *Russian Talk: Culture and Conversation during Perestroika*. Ithaca, NY: Cornell University Press.
Rosenfeld, Bryn. 2023. "Survey Research in Russia: In the Shadow of War." *Post-Soviet Affairs* 39 (no. 1–2): 38–48.
Russian Field. 2024. "'Spetsial'naia voyennaia operatsiia' v Ukraine: Otnoshenie rossiian. 5 volna (23 maia – 2 iunia 2024)" ["Special military operation" in Ukraine: The attitude of Russians. Wave 5 (May 23–June 2, 2024)].
Rustamova, Farida. 2022. "'Now We're Going to F*ck Them All': What's Happening in Russia's Elites after a Month of War." Substack, March 31.
Sengupta, Nikhil K., Lara M. Greaves, Danny Osborne, and Chris G. Sibley. 2017. "The Sigh of the Oppressed: The Palliative Effects of Ideology Are Stronger for People Living in Highly Unequal Neighbourhoods." *British Journal of Social Psychology* 56 (3): 437–54.

Sengupta, Nikhil K., Danny Osborne, and Chris G. Sibley. 2015. "The Status-Legitimacy Hypothesis Revisited: Ethnic-Group Differences in General and Dimension-Specific Legitimacy." *British Journal of Social Psychology* 54 (2): 324–40.

Sharafutdinova, Gulnaz. 2022. "Is Politics Always the Same? Response to Comments on *The Red Mirror: Putin's Leadership and Russia's Insecure Identity.*" *Nationalities Papers* 50 (3).

———. 2020. *The Red Mirror: Putin's Leadership and Russia's Insecure Identity.* Oxford: Oxford University Press.

Shevel, Oxana. 2011. "Russian Nation-Building from Yel'tsin to Medvedev: Ethnic, Civic or Purposefully Ambiguous?" *Europe-Asia Studies* 63 (2): 179–202.

Shirikov, Anton. 2022. "How Propaganda Works: Political Biases and News Credibility in Autocracies." PhD diss., University of Wisconsin.

Shraibman, Artyom. 2018. "The House That Lukashenko Built: The Foundation, Evolution, and Future of the Belarusian Regime." Washington, DC: Carnegie Endowment for International Peace.

Smith, Kathleen E. 2002. *Mythmaking in the New Russia: Politics and Memory in the Yeltsin Era.* Ithaca, NY: Cornell University Press.

Snegovaya, Maria. 2024. "Russian Identity and War Support." PONARS Eurasia Policy Memo no. 901. PONARS, June 14.

———. 2023a. "Russian Emigration." In Andrea Kendall-Taylor, Richard Connolly, Siemon Wezeman, et al., *Identifying Russian Vulnerabilities and How to Leverage Them.* Washington, DC: Center for a New American Security, December.

———. 2023b. "Why Russia's Democracy Never Began." *Journal of Democracy* 34 (3): 105–18.

———. 2022. "Why Russians Support Putin's War against Ukrainians." *National Interest*, March 14, 2022.

———. 2020. "A Backward Looking Nation." Washington, DC: Center for European Policy Analysis, May 11.

———. 2018. "Reviving the Propaganda State: How the Kremlin Hijacked History to Survive." Washington, DC: Center for European Policy Analysis.

———. 2016. "Slepye piatna liubvi k rodine" [Blind spots of love for the motherland]. *Vedomosti*, July 11.

Snegovaya, Maria, and Jade McGlynn, 2024. "Dissecting Putin's Regime Ideology." *Post-Soviet Affairs*, 1–22.

Snegovaya, Maria, Michael Kimmage, and Jade McGlynn. 2023. "The Ideology of Putinism: Is It Sustainable?" Washington, DC: Center for Strategic and International Studies.

Snegovaya, Maria, and Alexander Lanoszka. 2022. "Fighting Yesterday's War: Elite Continuity and Revanchism." SSRN 4304528.

TASS. 2018. "Rossiiane nazvali svoi liubimye prazdniki" [Russians named their favorite holidays]. October 31.

Taylor, Brian D. 2018. *The Code of Putinism*. Oxford: Oxford University Press.

Tikhonova, N. E. 2008. Nasledie imperii v obshchestvennom soznanii rossiian" [The legacy of empire in the public consciousness of Russians]. In *Nasledie imperii i budushchee Rossii* [The legacy of empires and Russia's future], 103–36. Moscow.

Tucker, Robert C. 2019. "Post-Soviet Leadership and Change." In *Patterns in Post-Soviet Leadership*, ed. Timothy J. Colton and Robert C. Tucker, 5–28. New York: Routledge.

van Zomeren, Martijn, Tom Postmes, and Russell Spears. 2008. "Toward an Integrative Social Identity Model of Collective Action: A Quantitative Research Synthesis of Three Socio-psychological Perspectives." *Psychological Bulletin* 134 (4): 504.

Vargas-Salfate, Salvador. 2017. "The Palliative Function of Hostile Sexism among High and Low-Status Chilean Students." *Frontiers in Psychology* 8:1733.

Volkov, Denis, and Andrei Kolesnikov. 2023. "Dom na bolote: Kak rossiiskoe obshchestvo spriatalos' ot ukrainskogo konflikta" [House on a swamp: How Russian society hid from the Ukrainian conflict]. Carnegie Endowment for International Peace, November 22.

Way, Lucan A. 2005. "Authoritarian State Building and the Sources of Regime Competitiveness in the Fourth Wave: The Cases of Belarus, Moldova, Russia, and Ukraine." *World Politics* 57 (2): 231–61.

Zhiliaeva, Yana. 2023. "Aleksey Levinson: 'Nevelikost' zhizni dolzhna byt' kompensirovana velichiem derzhavy': Zachem vlasti tsenzura" [Aleksei Levinson. "The smallness of life must be compensated for by the greatness of the power": Why do the authorities need censorship?]. *Forbes Russia*, February 24.

Zhirinovsky, V. V. 1997. *Poslednii brosok na iug* [The last push to the south]. Moskva.

Zvonovsky, Vladimir, and Aleksandr Khodykin. 2024. "Rossiiskoe obshchestvennoe mnenie v usloviiakh voennogo konflikta, 2022 – 2023" [Russian public opinion in conditions of military conflict, 2022–2023]. Chişinău: Historical Expertise.

SIX

Protests in Civil Society in Russia

ALFRED B. EVANS JR.

Some of the largest protests in Russia since the beginning of this century took place during the winter of 2011–2012, provoked by the perception of fraud in the elections to the Duma in November 2011.[1] The largest crowds of demonstrators gathered in Moscow, although there were also vigorous protests in other cities in Russia at the same time. Reliable sources indicate that as many as 100,000 discontented citizens took part in each of the largest rallies in the capital in December 2011 and February 2012. Commenters have devoted a great deal of attention to those protests. However, very few have attempted to provide an overview of trends in change in the movements that have carried out protests in Russia in more recent years. This chapter tries to convey a general sense of those trends and to suggest how they reflect the underlying tension between Putin's regime and the Russian people.

Trends in Change

The largest demonstrations in the winter of 2011–2012 reflected change in the growth in the relative importance of protest activity in the largest cities in Russia, especially in Moscow. After the breakup of the Soviet Union, protests arose at various locations in Russia, but by the latter part of the decade of 2000–2010, there was an increase in the percentage of protests that took place in Moscow and St. Petersburg.[2] Graeme Robertson has reported that, while "protests in that country were once largely confined to Russia's vast provinces," by 2011 the capital had "become the dominant location for protests to be organized."[3] The largest and most important protests were those in Moscow in the winter of 2011–2012, though there were demonstrations for the same cause in many other cities on the same dates.[4] As a result of a second trend leading up to 2011–2012, those demonstrations also reflected a change in the types of demands made by most protesters. Most protests in the 1990s had focused on specific, concrete goals, usually of an economic character and often in the form of a demand for the payment of wages or the delivery of benefits.[5] In contrast, the large protest rallies of 2011 and 2012 demanded clean and fair elections. The slogans of those protests were framed in terms of abstract principles of justice and democracy. But they did not lead to any substantial progress toward the realization of those principles. Instead, they were followed by increased repression of dissent. A third feature of the large-scale protests of 2011 and 2012 was that their participants consisted primarily of people who lived in Moscow or St. Petersburg and had a high level of education.[6] Some commenters have referred to the section of society to which those protesters belonged as the "creative class."

It is striking that in more recent years, each of the trends that reached their climax in 2012 has been reversed, partially or almost completely. In the first place, there has been a tendency toward the decentralization of protest activity in Russia.[7] It is no longer the case that Moscow is the main center of protests. A precedent for interregional protests had been created by the widespread eruption of anger against the reform of social benefits (the antimonetization movement) in 2005.[8] More recently, protest movements that have mobilized participants in many regions have included the movement since 2017 against a new tax on long-haul truckers and the one in 2018 opposing proposed changes in eligibility for pensions.[9] Since 2018, vigorous movements have produced public actions in Ekaterinburg,

Arkhangelsk, Ingushetia, Khabarovsk, Bashkortostan, and other locations, and some of those movements have been successful in winning concessions from the authorities. Vehement protests against overloaded landfills have erupted in such towns as Volokolamsk in Moscow oblast, and in towns in other regions.[10] The movements against landfills in those locations created linkages for mutual communication.[11] In addition, those movements provided encouragement and advice to a movement that opposed the storage of a huge amount of waste from Moscow at the remote site of Shies in Arkhangelsk region.[12] In turn, the activists at Shies were in contact with the leaders of a movement in Bashkortostan that strived to protect a mountain named Kushtau ("Twin Mountain" in Bashkir) from mining that would have destroyed it.[13] Of course, some movements still stage protests in Moscow and St. Petersburg; for instance, a large number of people have been moved to action by critics of the program of resettlement of residents in apartments in Moscow,[14] and thousands have resisted encroachments on green spaces in that city and St. Petersburg. But those cities do not dominate the landscape of protest in Russia as they did in 2011 and 2012, and sometimes movements of discontent transmit influence from the periphery to the capital instead of the reverse direction.[15]

A second trend that has been evident since the protests of 2011 and 2012 has been a change in the types of demands presented by most movements that generate protests. Clearly, the momentum of movements calling for fundamental changes in Russia's political regime has decreased greatly since its peak in the winter of 2011–2012.[16] At times, thousands of people have shown up for opposition protests, such as those that took place after the assassination of Boris Nemtsov in 2015, the disqualification of many candidates in the elections for Moscow's Duma in 2019, and the poisoning and arrest of Alexei Navalny in 2021. Yet participation in such demonstrations has had an increasingly higher cost as Russia's political leadership has increased its repression of the political opposition. In 2020, Anton Barbashin and Olga Irisova wrote, "Politically motivated protests in the past decade have consistently brought additional repression and innovations in limiting freedom of speech and assembly by the state."[17] That tendency was intensified to a high degree after Russia's invasion of Ukraine in February 2022. As a result, the potential for movements that might engage in open political protests has been virtually eliminated.

Today, most protests do not explicitly call for the realization of democratic principles and the protection of human rights. Instead, most protesters voice their indignation over disruptions to people's everyday lives and call for remedies in the form of concrete, specific, and limited changes. A few years ago, this author argued that "most of the groups engaging in protests have focused on issues that are relevant to the everyday lives of most people and usually are grounded in the self-interest of average citizens."[18] Samuel Greene and Graeme Robertson emphasize that "the greater part of protests are connected with much more localized dissatisfaction, both physical and material, and therefore their ideational basis has a much less abstract character."[19] Lisa McIntosh Sundstrom, Laura A. Henry, and Valerie Sperling agree that "in the current environment, citizens are most likely to support and participate in public mobilization efforts when they concern everyday social problems: concrete, material, local concerns that affect them directly."[20] András Tóth-Czifra observes that protesters who address such issues typically complain that injustices have been perpetrated by local officials, and ask higher authorities to intervene to correct the problem.[21] As this author has said, "Typically, such protests over specific issues do not openly challenge the legitimacy of the national political regime but appeal to the authorities at the highest level to intervene to solve problems."[22]

During the last few years, the protests in Ekaterinburg, at Shies, and at Kushtau mountain did win satisfaction for the essence of their demands,[23] with intervention by Vladimir Putin, the president of Russia, ultimately proving decisive in overcoming resistance to the protesters' wishes. Of course, we should realize that even if a group of discontented citizens concentrates its demands on a narrow, specific problem, it will not always achieve success.[24] But even though a movement's dramatic victory may be unusual, such a triumph of ordinary people is remembered by those in other movements and serves as a model for them. The protests at Volokolamsk and other sites encouraged the people who took up the cause of Shies, and the success of the movement focused on Shies later inspired the defenders of Kushtau. Though anyone who resorts to protest to try to gain any change in Russia faces formidable obstacles, the trend since 2012 has been toward greater importance for movements that aim to counter specific actions by agents of the state that create problems affecting people in their daily lives.[25] And some protesters have succeeded in putting particular issues on the government's agenda for policymaking when no formal institutions offered opportunities for them to be heard.[26]

It is likely that there has also been a third trend in protests in Russia since 2012. Researchers have shown that in 2011 and 2012, most of the people who took part in the large protests against fraud in elections were drawn from the middle class, and the majority of those participants were residents of the largest cities and had high levels of education. As Denis Volkov has put it, "They were atypical of Russians in general, and even of Moscow residents."[27] They were much more likely than other Russians to rely on the internet as a key source of information, and much less likely to receive news from television. Their political attitudes also differed from the attitudes of the majority of Russians. While 89 percent of the protesters supported the slogan "Not one vote for Vladimir Putin!," only 24 percent of Russians agreed. After the protests of the winter of 2011 and 2012, Volkov charged that the "active minority" that was represented in those demonstrations had been "sadly inactive when it comes to bridging the gap between itself and the passive majority."[28]

Since 2012, the opponents of Putin's regime, most prominently Alexei Navalny, have attracted thousands of participants in protests. Those protesters are distinguished from the majority of their fellow Russians most clearly by their political attitudes. Navalny's supporters have "an unequivocally negative attitude towards Russia's political regime"[29] and have lost all faith in the Russian state's potential to represent them, so they continue to demand fundamental political change and do not hope to improve the state's handling of concrete issues. Volkov estimates that the citizens who are "the most politicized part of society, who have a critical attitude toward the state," are about 10 percent of the population of Russia.[30] Part of Putin's strategy in countering political opposition since the protests in 2012 has been to stigmatize his most vocal critics as a minority who serve the interests of foreign powers and reject the values of the patriotic majority in Russia.[31] The degree of success of the media controlled by the state in conveying that perception is suggested by the fact that in a survey conducted by the Levada Center in Russia in January 2021, only 19 percent expressed a favorable view of Alexei Navalny.[32] Nevertheless, the thousands of Russians who attended Navalny's funeral in Moscow on March 1, 2024, dramatically underscored his huge appeal to a segment of society.

As the number of those taking part in protests calling for regime change has gradually dwindled, however, there are signs that support for protests focused on problems at a practical level comes from wider circles in Russian society and is not confined to the creative classes in the largest cities. As Laura Henry has pointed out, "Those engaged in everyday activism may represent a broader swath of social groups in terms of level of education, profession, age, and political orientation than participants in opposition rallies."[33] The participants in such grassroots protests are found in large cities, small towns, and rural areas and in various regions of Russia. And although the results of research on the social composition of the movements that produce such protests have not yet appeared, it seems very likely that support for protests focused on problems at a practical level comes from a variety of sectors of Russian society.

That conclusion is implied by the issues that have sparked many movements that have carried out protests. The people who have felt the impact of a new tax on long-haul truckers are most likely small business owners and highly skilled manual workers. Most of the residents of Moscow who are affected directly by the city's program of resettlement live in small apartments, including the very compact *khrushchevki*, which are the main property that most of them own, so they probably represent a cross section of people with middle and lower incomes. When poisonous fumes penetrate the air of a small city, people with different levels of education and different occupations are affected painfully. When the cost of heating homes rises sharply in Bashkortostan, the people with lower incomes will feel the greatest stress, and some of them will complain.[34] The broader social base for the expression of discontent by groups of Russians is particularly significant since many of those groups are also part of Putin's base; these groups include residents of smaller cities and rural areas, people with lower levels of education and income, and older Russians. Putin has enjoyed some success in branding the protesters of the creative class as hostile to the values of the silent majority and servants of sinister Western powers, but such accusations could not be convincingly applied to those who are protesting at Volokolamsk, Shies, and Kushtau. Movements that engage in protests against problems that affect people's daily lives can draw support from various groups belonging to the majority in Russian society.

Interpretation: Different Opportunity Structures

The opportunity structure for protests that demand change in the political regime in Russia is different from that for protests that call for solutions to specific problems, and that difference has become greater in recent years.[35] Since the protests against election fraud in 2011 and 2012, the state has steadily increased the harshness of suppression of protests by the political opposition, raising the costs for those who take part in such demonstrations.[36] Through such repression, as Tomila Lankina and Katerina Tertytchnaya observe, the Russian government has sent the message that "as long as ordinary Russians shy away from joining political protest, they should be less concerned about coercive sanctions."[37] But overtly repressive measures have been only one part of the regime's strategy to create a more hostile environment for movements that attempt to challenge its legitimacy. The Putin leadership has also carried out a campaign to achieve the ideological isolation of the type of opponents who led the protests of 2011 and 2012 by portraying them as disdainful of the majority of Russians and lacking in loyalty to their nation. Opinion surveys indicate that its campaign has had some success. In addition, the leadership has refused to make concessions that would satisfy the demands of the political opposition. A major problem for activists who try to recruit Russians to participate in protests that would continue the legacy of the winter of 2011–2012 is that such protests have failed to produce tangible, positive results.

On the other hand, the opportunity structure for specifically targeted protests in Russia is significantly different, and though it is not completely favorable, it is not as inhospitable. The suppression of protests that seek solutions to specific problems is usually not as severe as it is for antiregime political protests. Lankina and Tertytchnaya have found that the government of Russia is more likely to use violence against citizens who take part in openly "political" protests. In contrast, they report that the government is more tolerant of protests focused on social, economic, or "civic" issues, including environmental problems.[38] Ellie Martus comments that antiwaste protests "were for the most part depoliticized and not linked to broader criticisms of the regime," and "as a result, they were more tolerated than other large-scale protests in Russia in recent years have been."[39] Tomila Lankina, Kohei Watanabe, and Yulia Netesova have found that state-controlled media in Russia frame large-scale antiregime protests with an emphasis on disorder but provide more favorable coverage of some other protests, allowing recognition of the problems that such demonstrations identify.[40] The media's treatment of different types of protests signals the regime's attitude toward them, which suggests that national leaders are less disturbed by movements that do not pose more serious challenges. Perhaps the more astute social activists may get the message from such coverage. That should not lead us to assume that the activists in protests driven by specific issues never encounter any resistance. The people who have led such protests are often harassed in various ways, even if some of their demands have been satisfied. But usually the majority of those who take part in a protest seeking a solution to a specific problem are not going to be beaten or arrested. The decision by local officials and business executives in Bashkortostan to use violence openly against the protesters at the foot of Kushtau in August 2020 seems to have been seen by the top leaders of Russia as unwise and embarrassing.[41]

The opportunity structure for movements that give rise to protests in Russia is influenced not only by the strategy of the state but also by changes in technology and society.[42] One development that apparently has contributed to the proliferation of organized groups of protesters is the growth of the technology and tactics of communication within each group and among such groups. Sundstrom, Henry, and Sperling point out that "recent environmental campaigns to preserve green space or protest landfills have been coordinated primarily on-line, through social media."[43] And as we have seen, citizens who protested about pollution caused by landfills near their towns contacted activists in northern Russia who opposed the plan to store trash at Shies. Also, Geir Flikke has revealed that some of the activists who were focused on Shies "launched an interactive map, where the VKontakte sites of all related actions were available,"[44] facilitating communication among interested citizens in different parts of the regions that would be directly affected and also making it feasible to attract the attention of potential supporters living in other regions of Russia. In turn, social media helped to create links between the activists who were concerned about Shies with those in Bashkortostan who sought to counter the threat to Kushtau.[45] Of course, agents of the state tried to disrupt communications through social media among groups of environmental activists at every step, but the more technologically adept participants among the environmentalists were able to work around most of the obstacles they encountered.[46] Use of the internet by the leaders of a movement of protesters in Russia for communication and coordination can be traced at least as far back as 2005,[47] but access to the internet in Russia has increased greatly since then, and some members of social movements have developed much more expertise in using online media. In the words of Perrine Poupin, "every new struggle was able to draw on the knowledge of previous groups,"[48] so that guidance about strategy has been accumulating. Poupin also remarks that "social networking platforms have been an important support for this dynamic." Dedicated activists have used social media to build numerous communities of protesters and create links among those communities. That is one way in which the opportunity structure for protests has been reshaped.

The three trends in protests in recent years traced in this chapter were displayed in a movement that reached a peak in the winter of 2021–2022, when it had a dramatic impact on the national government's decision-making.[49] A problem that led to an attempt to change policy was the slow growth in the number of Russians who had been vaccinated against COVID-19. By October 2021, only 36 percent of the people in Russia had been fully vaccinated against the virus.[50] On November 12, 2021, the draft of a law that was introduced in the Duma would have required proof of vaccination to enter public places such as restaurants, bars, stores, theaters, and stadiums. Another piece of proposed legislation would have mandated proof of vaccination to gain access to intercity transportation on trains and planes. Before that time, the responsibility for dealing with the COVID-19 pandemic had been left primarily with the regional authorities. There already had been some signs of resistance to vaccination mandates, but the draft legislation provoked a widespread expression of anger toward the proposed restrictions. Vladimir Putin distanced himself from the proposals, and the bills requiring proof of vaccination were subsequently withdrawn by the Duma.[51] The government had backed down in the face of protests from the grass roots.

The trend toward greater decentralization of movements engaging in protests was exemplified to a high degree by the actions of Russians who opposed vaccination mandates. The first eruption of discontent with such measures (which the regional government had imposed) occurred in Kazan, the capital of Tatarstan, where there was an organized boycott of public transportation and a group helping people without the required QR codes was formed. After that, protests against QR codes and mandatory vaccination were seen in at least sixty different cities in Russia.[52] The number of people who took part in each in-person demonstration was usually small, but there were many of those protests. The opponents of vaccination mandates seemed to place their main emphasis on videos (*videoroliki*) that were sent through social media and often were addressed to President Putin and other officials in the national government.[53] Hundreds of such videos arrived, and they came from many different locations in Russia. The similarity among those videos suggested a great deal of horizontal communication, since there was no indication that a single center had coordinated protests in widely separated cities. And the pattern in which protests may originate in many different locations in Russia rather than spreading from the capital to the provinces was quite evident in the activities of those who opposed vaccination mandates.

A second trend that has been noted is for more protests to concentrate on issues that touch on experiences in people's everyday lives. In the perception of many Russians, regulations that made proof of vaccination necessary for engaging in activities that were a familiar part of daily life were extremely offensive. Polls showed that the percentage of Russians who were opposed in principle to vaccination against the coronavirus was lower than the percentage saying that it was wrong for the state to make vaccination mandatory.[54] The QR codes that would have been required for access to restaurants, stores, trains, or airplanes were seen by many citizens as symbols of unacceptable interference in their familiar activities. According to Aleksandr Konfisakhor, many Russians saw the imposition of QR codes as "crossing personal boundaries" and moving into "an intimate zone."[55] The movement against mandatory vaccination channeled resentment that was provoked by an issue that was closely related to everyday life.

A third trend, highlighted earlier in this chapter, was for participants in many protests targeting specific policies to come from wider circles in society compared with participants in demonstrations by the political opposition. That trend was also evident in the movement opposing vaccination mandates. Clearly, people who voiced indignation against the restrictions symbolized by QR codes lived in a wide variety of geographic locations in Russia, with a majority not residing in the largest cities. This contrasted with the demographics of those who participated in the large demonstrations in the winter of 2011–2012. Also, it is important to note that the movement of opposition to vaccination mandates drew support from Russians with a variety of political orientations. As one observer put it, "The refusal to accept QR codes was a position on which the most varied political forces could be united."[56] It even appears that those who felt irritated by vaccination requirements included Russians who were part of the base that is loyal to Putin's regime.[57] A number of commenters have reported that conservative, nationalistic groups that support Putin enthusiastically have played a prominent role in the campaign against QR codes.[58] According to Meduza, much of the support for that campaign can be traced to "conservative Orthodox groups and other organizations that promote so-called traditional values."[59] But some sources have also said that even citizens who previously were apolitical were motivated to protest against compulsory vaccination and required QR codes.[60] The main point that should be emphasized about the anti-QR codes campaign is that a movement that engages in protests against a policy of the Russian state may draw support from citizens in different parts of society and with widely varying political views, not just from the members of society who support protests by opponents of the regime.

Conclusion

The opportunity structure for protests that demand change in the political regime in Russia is different from the opportunity structure for protests that call for solutions to specific problems, and that difference has become greater in recent years. Since the protests against election fraud in 2011–2012, the state has consistently increased the harshness of suppression of protests by the political opposition, raising the costs for those who take part in such demonstrations.[61] That tendency has intensified even further since the full-scale invasion of Ukraine. Now, any criticism of Russia's actions in Ukraine may bring harsh punishment.[62] In the first few weeks after February 24, 2022, at least 498 protests were held in 154 cities in Russia, and approximately 15,000 protesters were detained.[63] As Katerina Tertytchnaya observes, "The authorities' response to anti-war protests was more violent than their response to previous waves of protest in Russia's post-Soviet history."[64] Open political protests in Russia have become almost impossible, except for the actions of brave individuals who know that they will be sent to prison.[65] Before the invasion of Ukraine, Putin's regime had spent years increasing restrictions on the organizational structures that were capable of coordinating large-scale political protests, culminating in the systematic destruction of Alexei Navalny's Anti-Corruption Foundation in 2021.[66]

While open political dissent has become very rare, quiet resistance is represented by activism in networks that help many Russians avoid conscription into the military or assist them in leaving the country.[67] Even voluntary activity assisting refugees from Ukraine who have come to Russia may be a form of "an anti-war civic initiative that, while humanitarian in nature, has a strong political sentiment," implying rejection of the war.[68] Some of those who have opposed the invasion of Ukraine have left Russia since February 2022.⁶⁹ For some, emigrating might have been intended as a form of protest. Their departure has decreased the base of support for the political opposition inside Russia and increased the number of potential anti-Putin protesters in exile. It is too soon to assess the impact of those changes on protests taking place in Russia.

Another development reflecting the impact of the war in Ukraine is the Put' Domoi (The Way Home) movement, which first became visible in November 2023. Some wives and other relatives of men who had been drafted into the Russian army in the fall of 2022 in a "partial mobilization" began to appear, wearing white scarves, to lay flowers at the Tomb of the Unknown Soldier in Moscow and other memorials and monuments around Russia. Those women asked that their men be sent home.⁷⁰ Apparently that movement was uncoordinated and became known largely through a Telegram channel.⁷¹ The state was cautious in dealing with the movement, as the police usually refrained from arresting women who took part in such actions, though reporters who covered such actions were often arrested.⁷² The state did not immediately bring criminal charges against them, in contrast to its treatment of those who protested openly against the war. The state's discomfort with the movement was signaled on May 31, 2024, when it classified Put' Domoi as a "foreign agent."⁷³ The number of women who joined in such demonstrations had increased rapidly, and some men took part with them. It was reported that the women who participated in the movement initially had various political orientations, and many of them were supporters of Putin.⁷⁴ One source characterized them as the "flesh and blood of Putin's electorate."⁷⁵ Within a short time, however, some of those in the Put' Domoi movement became more explicitly political, as some women in it began to criticize Putin and some encouraged others to vote against him.⁷⁶ One of them explained that it had become impossible to stay outside politics, since "with the beginning of the war, politics came to us in our home."⁷⁷ She added a plea for recognition of "the right to return to a normal, peaceful life." One commenter argued that the strategy of the Put' Domoi movement resembled that of the movement against mandatory vaccination, which had been quite successful.⁷⁸ We might point out, however, that the movement opposing vaccination mandates and QR codes felt free to be bolder and more demanding, and that the movement demanding the return of soldiers who were drafted in the fall of 2022 has not extracted a concession from the state that would satisfy its demand.⁷⁹ Apparently, some of those who oppose Russia's war in Ukraine or sympathize with the wives of men who had been drafted in 2002 found a way to signal their wishes by joining with the hundreds of thousands of citizens who stood in line to give their signatures in support of Boris Nadezhdin, an antiwar candidate for president.[80] (It should be noted, however, that Nadezhdin's application for candidacy was disqualified, so his name did not appear on the ballot.)

Despite the change in the political atmosphere in Russia since February 2022, protests against local problems have continued. As Katerina Tertytchnaya said in early 2023, "Russians continued to take to the streets to advance local, environmental, and other socio-economic demands."[81] Leyla Latypova reports that "permitted rallies tend to focus strictly on local politics or social and environmental issues, like urban planning decisions, new landfill sites or working conditions," and adds that "as long as there is no criticism of Russia's invasion of Ukraine or the Kremlin, activists have said, police are likely to leave demonstrators alone."[82] Should we conclude that the Putin regime has a successful approach for dealing with movements that seek improvements in specific conditions without explicitly challenging the nature of that regime? The picture may not look good from the point of view of lower levels in the state. Local and regional officials must find it difficult to deal with protests by such movements. Those officials face contradictory imperatives. They are expected to implement the policies that have been chosen by superior leaders and disregard demands for different policy choices. Yet they also should avoid provoking the open expression of discontent among the local population, which may flare up because of the implementation of unpopular policies. The effects of those contradictory imperatives are evident in some of the examples mentioned in this chapter. At Volokolamsk, Shies, and Kushtau, regional leaders were committed to one course of action, which presumably fit with the wishes of the central leaders. But protests changed the calculations of the highest national leaders, making it necessary for the regional leaders to reverse course.[83]

Since the beginning of the large-scale war in Ukraine, Putin's regime has placed a high priority on the preservation of stability in Russian society and has devoted "huge" economic resources to ensuring tranquility among the public.[84] Apparently those efforts have succeeded, at least so far, in reassuring most Russians that the conditions that directly affect their daily lives will not change noticeably. Volkov observes that "the feeling of socio-economic stability, together with the ability to maintain a more or less familiar way of life, has so far allowed the majority of Russians to cope with anxieties."[85] The need for domestic stability might explain why some protests over local issues are not crushed if the authorities do not expect that they will take on a broader political character.[86] But if deteriorating economic conditions and ill-advised actions by local leaders should provoke more widespread expressions of discontent at the grassroots level, local leaders would face the question of whether to engage in harsh repression of a wide range of protests supported by average citizens.[87] Such a reckless choice by local leaders might disturb the stability in society that is important to the national regime. It would increase the risk that the movements focusing on issues pertaining to daily life could become more challenging. Volkov suggests that if the authorities become less successful in maintaining socioeconomic stability, "the hitherto unfocused worry and anxiety, characteristic under the surface for many Russians, may crystallize and find an outlet at a moment that is most unsuitable for the regime."[88]

The opportunity structure for protests focused on local problems is not as hopeless as that for protests by the political opposition in Russia. But that does not mean that the state usually solves the problems that trouble protesting citizens. The regional and local officials who are responsible for dealing with protests are accountable to the highest leaders, not to local citizens. Whether the governor of a region stays in office depends on Vladimir Putin, not on the will of voters in that region. As a result, as Nikolai Petrov has observed, "the state machine has the goal, not of resolving the problems of citizens, but of defending the state from citizens."[89] Power has been centralized even more and representative institutions have become even more ineffective as warfare has become the main preoccupation of the political regime. The absence of institutional mechanisms that people at the grassroots level might use to put pressure on leaders is felt not only when protests occur but also when there is no adequate solution to the demands of the protesters.

The typical lack of response by the authorities to protests by groups in the majority of the population shows that the state is indifferent to their needs. The authorities cannot credibly fit the issues raised by those protests into the framework of a global struggle between Russia and the West. The Putin regime's view of its relationship with Russian society has been implied by that regime's actions during two especially challenging periods. At the height of the COVID-19 pandemic, the leadership hastily backed off in the face of a widespread and vehement reaction against vaccination mandates. Second, as losses of life by Russian soldiers in the war in Ukraine took a rising toll, and after the mobilization of reservists alarmed many Russian citizens, the leaders refrained from calling for another mobilization and found other ways of replenishing the ranks of their soldiers. The actions (or lack of actions) of the nation's leaders in those two situations seemed to show that they viewed support for their regime among most people in Russian society as tentative and conditional.

Russia's political leadership knows how it wants to deal with protests from the political opposition, and it has been effective in silencing most of those protests. But the regime is not sure how it should react to protests by groups formed by a broader representation of the population, especially groups that constitute the base of its support, so it is inconsistent and often ineffective in responding to those protests. The Russian state now considers waging war to be of overriding importance, but most Russians do not feel that way. Although polls in Russia find that most Russians will say they support the war effort in Ukraine, some commentators have pointed out that the dominant attitude of most Russians toward the war is one of indifference.[90] For the greatest part, Russians try to shut themselves off from news about the war and hope it does not touch their everyday lives.[91] That disparity between the viewpoint of the political leadership and the viewpoint of the majority of Russians has created a tension between society and state. That tension underscores the state's failure to address numerous demands from society, which could potentially lead to widespread discontent—a prospect Russia's leaders undoubtedly fear.

NOTES

1. Evans (2019), 95.

2. Dmitriev (2015), 225, 229; Lankina (2015), 26, 34; Robertson (2013), 12, 18.

3. Robertson (2013), 12.

4. Robertson in "Protesting Putinism" says of the election protests of 2011–2012, "There were protests in the regions and St. Petersburg, but by far the largest and most significant protests were in the capital" (2013, 19). Mikhail Dmitriev in "Lost in Translation" reports that on the date of the first major protests against election fraud, December 10, 2011, the number of those taking part in the protest in Bolotnaya Square in Moscow was estimated to have been one-third of all the participants in protests in forty-two cities in Russia (2015, 228).

5. Robertson (2013), 12.

6. Volkov (2012), 57.

7. Dmitriev (2015), 229; Tóth-Czifra (2021a), 1.

8. Ananyeva (2021), 221; Wengle and Rasell (2008), 740. Robertson in "Protesting Putinism" characterizes those protests as "a key turning point" (2013, 22). Gabowitsch in *Protest in Putin's Russia* remarks that those protests "left traces in Russia's protest culture" (2017, 129). It is likely that hundreds of thousands of Russians participated in those protests.

9. Ananyeva (2021), 221.

10. Martus (2020), 2–3; Weir (2018).

11. Geir Flikke in "Dysfunctional Orders: Russia's Rubbish Protests and Putin's Limited Access Order" reports that there was "migration of eco-activists from Kuchino to other dumping sites" (2021, 476), and András Tóth-Czifra in "Russia's (Canceled) Ecological Referenda" says that antilandfill movements from various regions "coalesced" (2021b, 1).

12. Flikke writes that activists at Shies "employed a broad repertoire of action derived from the Volokolamsk events" (2021, 478).

13. Evans (2021); Tóth-Czifra (2020), 5; Tóth-Czifra (2021b), 3.

14. That project is officially billed as a program of "renovation" of housing; its opponents call it a program of "demolition" (*snos*) of housing.

15. Recently, activists who have voiced their opposition to some construction projects in Moscow that are planned by the company Tashir have made a film titled *Moskovskii Kushtau* (Moscow's Kushtau). See Suslova (2020). Also, in December 2020, a representative of an "initiative group" that strives to defend the Troitskii Forest in Moscow from proposed road construction said, "There are successful examples of the defense of natural territories, for example, Shies or the Shikhans." Ol'ga Slastunina, quoted in Dar'ia Alifanova (2020).

16. The decline of enthusiasm for protests of that type had already begun by the end of the summer of 2012. As Gabowitsch has written, "Over the summer, what euphoria had been left gave way to a sense of disillusionment and routine" (2017, 9). A major reason for that disillusionment surely was the lack of substantial accomplishments from the protests in favor of fair elections. Similarly, subsequent protests by the political opposition have produced almost no substantive changes.

17. Barbashin and Irisova (2020), 117.

18. Evans (2019), 95.

19. Greene and Robertson (2016), 11. See also Semenov (2022).

20. Sundstrom, Henry, and Sperling (2022), 1378.

21. Tóth-Czifra (2020), 3. See also Evans (2019), 95. Scholars who study collective actions in China refer to protests of that type as "rightful resistance." O'Brien and Li (2006), 2–3.

22. Evans (2019), 95. See also Henry (2022), 145.

23. Barbashin and Irisova (2020), 117; Evans (2021); Henry (2022).

24. Scholars who study protests in Russia emphasize that the authorities are inconsistent in responding to the demands of groups that protest about specific problems. Greene (2014), 160; Evans and Plantan (2023), 127.

25. A law that discourages nongovernmental organizations from getting financial support from abroad may also have influenced the choice of issues on which a movement focuses. Elizabeth Plantan in "A Tale of Two Laws: Managing Foreign Agents and Overseas NGOs in Russia and China" suggests that the "foreign agents" law in Russia "could incentivize domestic Russian organizations to pay more attention to simpler, local issues that directly affect the population, rather than going after international grants that tend to finance abstract or broader-reaching campaigns" (2020, 175).

26. See, for example, Martus (2020), 4, and Tóth-Czifra (2021b), 4.

27. Volkov (2012), 57. See also Evans (2019), 96.

28. Volkov (2012), 60.

29. Erpyleva and Zhuravlev (2021), 4. See also Zhuravlev, Alexandrova, and Lupenko (2020), 9.

30. Meduza (2022).

31. Evans (2109), 97–98.

32. Semenov and Dollbaum (2021).

33. Henry (2020). See also Evans (2019), 102, and Henry (2022), 149.

34. For more on heating costs in Bashkortostan, see Saifranova (2021).

35. Tilly and Tarrow in *Contentious Politics* offer this definition: "*Political opportunity structure* refers to features of regimes and institutions (e.g., splits in the ruling class) that facilitate or inhibit a political actor's collective action and changes in those features" (2007, 49).

36. Evans and Plantan (2023), 122, 127.

37. Lankina and Tertytchnaya (2019), 30.

38. Ibid., 21, 29.

39. Martus (2020), 3.

40. Lankina, Watanabe, and Netesova (2020), 157.

41. Gorbacheva (2020); Mel'nikova (2020); Rakhmatullin (2020).

42. This chapter does not attempt to discuss all the changes in society in recent years that may have had an impact on social movements in Russia.

43. Sundstrom, Henry, and Sperling (2022), 1385.

44. Flikke (2021), 478.

45. Evans (2021), 19–20; Tóth-Czifra (2021b), 3.

46. Poupin (2021), 8–10. Of course, we may expect that the Russian state will make more efforts to obstruct online communication among movements that organize protests.

47. Greene (2014), 174. Communication through social media and websites also played a crucial role in recruiting participants in the protests in the winter of 2011–2012.

48. Poupin (2021). Also, activists found it necessary to rely more on social media "because of the increase in state repression of political and civic activism during the Putin era." Sundstrom, Henry, and Sperling (2022), 1383.

49. Evans (2022).

50. Roshchina, Roshchin, and Rozhkova (2022), 5739.

51. Pertsev (2021a, 2021b, 2021c).

52. Evans (2022).

53. Korbat (2021); Rusova (2021); Solodovnikov (2021). Also, many online appeals were addressed to officials at the local and regional levels.

54. In December 2021, the Levada Center reported that 36 percent of Russians said they were not ready to be vaccinated; 56 percent opposed general, required vaccination; 76 percent opposed the introduction of electronic passes for the use of public transportation; and 67 percent opposed using QR codes to determine admission to restaurants, museums, stores, and large gatherings.

55. Konfisakhor quoted in Griaznevich and Vorob'eva (2022).

56. Danilovich (2021).

57. Griaznevich and Vorob'eva (2022).

58. Danilovich (2021); Garmonenko (2021); Kurkin (2021); Lobanova (2021); Rusova (2021); Solodovnikov (2021).

59. Hart (2021). We should note that extreme right-wing groups in the West also have opposed anti-COVID-19 measures: Rusova (2021). It is likely that instruments of Putin's regime have given assistance to anti-vaccination campaigns in the West. For more than ten years, the government of Russia has placed a high priority on developing connections with right-wing movements and parties in Europe and North America.

60. Lobanova (2021).

61. Evans and Plantan (2023), 116, 119, 122.

62. Margarita Zaslavskaia (2021) has commented: "Recently with the background of a sharply increased level of state repression, the price of protest has greatly grown."

63. De Vogel (2023).

64. Tertytchnaya (2023).

65. In the assessment of Vladimir Gel'man (2023), "We do not see any kinds of serious mass demonstrations (*vystupleniia*) against that which is taking place in the country."

66. De Vogel (2023); Gel'man (2023); Vladimir Gel'man, interviewed in Liutova (2022).

67. Evgenia Olimpieva, Irina Olimpieva, and Masha Golenko in "Russia's Antiwar Movement Goes Far beyond Street Protests" characterize such activity as "acts of *stealth resistance*" and "an alternative to street protests" (Olympieva et al., 2022).

68. Meyer-Olimpieva (2023). See also Ekaterina Moroko (2023), which makes it clear that some Russians who take part in such efforts do not see their work as antiwar activity.

69. At least several hundred thousand and perhaps as many as one million Russians have left their country since February 2022. Ebel and Ilyushina (2023). It has been reported that those who have emigrated recently have had a variety of reasons for leaving.

70. *Moscow Times* (2024a); Petrov (2023). Some of the women had previously sent appeals to high-ranking officials and had sought permission to hold protests (with denial of approval for demonstrations in almost all cases).

71. Kuznetsov (2023); *Moscow Times* (2024a).

72. Knight (2024); Stanovaya (2024).

73. *Moscow Times* (2024b).

74. *Moscow Times* (2024a).

75. Petrov (2023).

76. *Kholod* (2024); Petrov (2023).

77. *Kholod* (2024).

78. Kuznetsov (2023).

79. However, we might note that the state has found ways to avoid another partial mobilization, which may partly reflect the influence of that movement. Such information would not satisfy the wives and mothers of men who were mobilized in September 2022.

80. Knight (2024); Kuznetsova (2024); *Novaia gazeta Evropa* (2024).

81. Tertytchnaya (2023). See also Semenov (2022).

82. Latypova (2023).

83. Those contradictory pressures may also be reflected in the record of inconsistency in the state's responses to the demands of protesters, as mentioned earlier.

84. Volkov (2023). Michael Kimmage and Maria Lipman in "Wartime Putinism" point out that "the government has been spending money lavishly on pensioners, poorer Russians, and those connected to the war effort" (2023).

85. Volkov (2023).

86. Guzel Yusupova, quoted in Latypova (2023).

87. In "Why Is There No Antiwar Mobilization?," Andrei Semenov (2022) says about policy-focused protests: "If and when such initiatives gather momentum due to the deepening economic crisis and bad governance, they will be harder to control with the means developed to constrain civic protests."

88. Volkov (2023).

89. Nikolai Petrov, interviewed by Liubov Borisenko and Sof'iia Kanevskaia (2024).

90. Gozman (2024); Inozemtsev (2024).

91. Pertsev (2024).

REFERENCES

Alifanova, Dar'ia. 2020. "V Novoi Moskve mogut unichtozhit' desiatki gektarov Troitskogo lesa" [In New Moscow dozens of hectares of the Troitsky Forest may be destroyed]. *Moskovskaia gazeta*, December 24.

Ananyeva, Ekaterina. 2021. "The Kremlin Learns to Strike Back: Assessing Reactions to Protests in Russia." *Russian Politics* 6 (2).

Barbashin, Anton, and Olga Irisova. 2020. "Protesting in Russia in the 2010s: Rising Risks, Rising Costs." *SAIS Review of International Affairs* 40 (2): 111–19.

Borisenko, Liubov', and Sof'iia Kanevskaia. 2024. "Chinovniki pytaiutsia sozdat' khoroshee vpechatlenie u Putina, a ne u grazhdan" [Officials are trying to make a good impression on Putin, and not on citizens]. *Novaia gazeta Evropa*, April 11.

Danilovich, Mikhail. 2021. "Po-nashemu obiazatel'no budet" [It will definitely be our way]. Holod Media, November 25.

de Vogel, Sasha. 2023. "A Promise Unfulfilled: Scholar Sasha de Vogel Explains Why Russia Lacks Massive Antiwar Protests." Meduza, February 13.

Dmitriev, Michael. 2015. "Lost in Transition? The Geography of Protests and Attitude Change in Russia." *Europe-Asia Studies* 67 (2).

Ebel, Francis, and Mary Ilyushina. 2023. "Russians Abandon Wartime Russia in Historic Exodus." *Washington Post*, February 13.

Erpyleva, Svetlana, and Oleg Zhuravlev. 2021. "What's New about Russia's New Protests?" OpenDemocracy.net, June 3.

Evans, Alfred B. Jr. 2022. "The Movement against Vaccination Mandates as a Reflection of Trends in Protests in Russia." Paper presented at the National Convention of the Association for Slavic, East European, and Eurasian Studies, November.

———. 2021. "The Struggle for Kushtau: The Movement to Protect a Mountain in Russia." Paper presented at the Annual Meeting of the Western Political Science Association, April.

———. 2019. "Civil Society and Protest." In *Putin's Russia: Past Imperfect, Future Uncertain*, ed. Stephen K. Wegren. Lanham, MD: Rowman and Littlefield.

Evans, Alfred B. Jr., and Elizabeth Plantan. 2023. "Civil Society and Social Movements." In *Putin's Russia: Past Imperfect, Future Uncertain*, 8th ed., ed. Darrell Slider, 111–38. Lanham, MD: Rowman and Littlefield.

Flikke, Geir. 2021. "Dysfunctional Orders: Russia's Rubbish Protests and Putin's Limited Access Order." *Post-Soviet Affairs* 37 (5): 470–88.

Gabowitsch, Mischa. 2017. *Protest in Putin's Russia*. Cambridge, UK: Polity Press.

Garmonenko, Daria. 2021. "Kreml' pytaetsia depolitizirovat' QR-kody" [The Kremlin is trying to depoliticize QR codes]. *Nezavisimaia gazeta*, November 16.

Gel'man, Vladimir. 2023. "Kak voina izmenila putinskii rezhim?" [How has the war changed Putin's regime?]. *Meduza*, January 8.

Gorbacheva, Karina. 2020. "Vstali goroi za bashkirskii Shies: Kak spasaiut Kushtau" [Standing up for Bashkir's Shies: How to save Kushtau]. *Real'noe vremia*, August 12.

Gozman, Leonid. 2024. "Polovina Velikoi Otechestvennoi" [Half of the Great Patriotic]. *Novaia gazeta Evropa*, February 24.

Griaznevich, Vladimir, and Iuliia Vorob'eva. 2022. "Kak Brestskaia krepost': Chto skazal QR-protesty o rossiiskom obshchestve?" [Like the Brest Fortress: What did the QR protests say about Russian society?]. St. Petersburg: RBK, January 27.

Greene, Samuel A. 2014. *Moscow in Movement: Power and Opposition in Putin's Russia*. Stanford, CA: Stanford University Press.

Greene, Samuel, and Graeme Robertson. 2016. "Sposobnost' k protestu sokhraniaetsia" [Capacity for protests remains]. *Kontrapunkt* 3 (April).

Hart, Eilish. 2021. "'This Only Takes 20 Minutes!'" *Meduza*, November 18.

Henry, Laura A. 2022. "People Power in Putin's Russia: Social versus Political Protests." In *The Power of Populism and People: Resistance and Protest in the Modern World*, ed. Nathan Stoltzfus and Christopher Osmar, 137–61. London: Bloomsbury Academic.

———. 2020. "The Politics of Waste in Russia: Everyday Environmentalism and Shifting State-Society Relations." Paper presented at the Annual Meeting of the Association for Slavic, East European, and Eurasian Studies, November.

Inozemtsev, Vladislav. 2024. "Zhdet li Rossiiu novaia mobilizatsiia?" [Is Russia awaiting another mobilization?]. *Riddle*, April 11.

Kholod. 2024. "Zheny mobilizovannykh vpervye vystupili protiv Putina" [Wives were the first to mobilize for protest against Putin]. March 15.

Kimmage, Michael, and Maria Lipman. 2023. "Wartime Putinism." *Foreign Affairs*, January 13.

Knight, Amy. 2024. "A Movement Builds against Putin's War in Ukraine." *Washington Post*, February 6.

Korbat, Irina. 2021. "Protesty antivakserov dobavliaiut massovost' za schet chuzhogo mitinga" [Antivaccine protest increased in size because of an unrelated meeting]. Fontanka.ru, November 16.

Kurkin, Boris. 2021. "Prokremlevskie politologii zhdut, chto antivaksery nachnut massovye protest" [Pro-Kremlin politologists are waiting for antivacciners to begin a mass protest]. *Moskovskaia gazeta*, July 19.

Kuznetsov, Pavel. 2023. "Est' vse zhe chuvstvo iumora u nashevo prezidenta!" [Our president still has a sense of humor!]. *Novaia gazeta Evropa*, December 1.

Kuznetsova, Alisa. 2024. "Liudi khotiat, chtoby zakonchilas' voina" [People want the war to end]. *Vazhnye istorii*, January 26.

Lankina, Tomila. 2015. "The Dynamics of Regional and National Contentious Politics in Russia." *Problems of Post-Communism* 62 (1).

Lankina, Tomila, and Katerina Tertytchnaya. 2019. "Protest in Electoral Autocracies: A New Dataset." *Post-Soviet Affairs* 36 (1).

Lankina, Tomila, Kohei Watanabe, and Yulia Netesova. 2020. "How Russian Media Control, Manipulate, and Leverage Public Discontent: Framing Protest in Autocracies." In *Citizens and the State in Authoritarian Regimes*, ed. Karrie J. Koesel, Valerie J. Bunce, and Jessica Chen Weiss. Oxford: Oxford University Press.

Latypova, Leyla. 2023. "Russia's Local Activists Find Room for Protest—Just Don't Mention the War." *Moscow Times*, April 19.

Levada Center. 2021. "Koronavirus, vaktsinatsiia, QR-kody" [Coronavirus, vaccinations, QR codes]. Press release, December 7.

Liutova, Margarita. 2022. "Pochemu rossiiane tak pokorno otpravliaiutsia na front? I mogut li regiony nachat' protestovat' vsled za Dagestanom?" [Why are Russians so resigned to being sent to the front? And could regions begin to protest like Dagestan?]. Meduza, September 26.

Lobanova, Aleksandra. 2021. "Politologii sprognozirovali izmenenie protestnoi aktivnosti v sluchae priniatiia zakona o QR-kodakh" [Politologists predict a change in protest activity if the law on QR codes is adopted]. *Moskovskaia gazeta*, November 17.

Martus, Ellie. 2020. "Municipal Solid Waste Management in Russia: Protest, Policy, and Politics." *Russian Analytical Digest* 261 (December 23): 2–3.

Meduza. 2022. "Pochemu rossiiane ravnodushny k proiskhodiashchim segodnia repressiam?" [Why are Russians indifferent to the repression taking place today?]. October 30.

Mel'nikova, Anastasia. 2020. "Vladimir Vladimirovich ne liubit, kogda mestnye problemy masshtabiruiutsia na federal'nyi uroven'" [Vladimir Vladimirovich does not like it when local problems become large scale at the federal level]. Znak.com, September 8.

Meyer-Olimpieva, Irina. 2023. "Helping Ukrainian Refugees as an Alternative to Street Protest." *Russian Analytical Digest* 291 (January).

Moroko, Ekaterina. 2023. "From Russia with Peace." *Riddle*, April 22.

Moscow Times. 2024a. "White Scarves and Flowers: Wives and Mothers of Mobilized Soldiers Take Resentment to the Kremlin." January 17.

———. 2024b. "Russia Labels Wives of Mobilized Soldiers Group 'Foreign Agent.'" June 1.

Novaia gazeta Evropa. 2024. "Bol'shaia malenkaia voina" [A big little war]. February 3.

O'Brien, Kevin J., and Lianjiang Li. 2006. *Rightful Resistance in Rural China*. Cambridge: Cambridge University Press.

Olimpieva, Evgenia, Irina Olimpieva, and Masha Golenko. 2022. "Russia's Antiwar Movement Goes Far beyond Street Protests." *The Monkey Cage, Washington Post*, October 18.

Pertsev, Andrey. 2024. "Poslanie ot lobbistov" [A message from lobbyists]. *Riddle*, March 1.

———. 2021a. "QR Codes? Not Worth It. A Draft Bill on Introducing Vaccine Proof on Public Transport Was Removed from the Russian State Duma's Agenda. Here's Why." Meduza, December 14.

———. 2021b. "Kak vyiasnila 'Meduza,' zakon o QR-kodakh otlozhili iz-za konflikta mezhdu 'sanitarami' i 'ekonomistami,' v pravitel'stve RF" [Meduza ascertained that the law on QR codes was put aside due to conflict between "sanitaries" and "economists" in the Russian government]. Meduza, November 23.

———. 2021c. "Kak vyiasnila 'Meduza,' Kreml' sobiraetsia perezapustit' kampaniiu massovoi vaksinatsii" [Meduza learned that the Kremlin is preparing to restart a massive vaccination campaign]. Meduza, November 16.

Petrov, Nikolai. 2023. "Mobilized Soldiers' Wives against Putin." *Russia.Post*, December 1.

Plantan, Elizabeth. 2020. "A Tale of Two Laws: Managing Foreign Agents and Overseas NGOs in Russia and China." In *Citizens and the State in Authoritarian Regimes*, ed. Karrie J. Koesel, Valerie J. Bunce, and Jessica Chen Weiss. Oxford: Oxford University Press.

Poupin, Perrine. 2021. "Social Media and State Repression: The Case of VKontakte and the Anti-Garbage Protest in Shies, in Far Northern Russia." *First Monday* 26, no. 5 (May 3).

Rakhmatullin, Timur. 2020. "Top-100 elit Bashkirii: 'Svoi liudi' Khabirova, faktor Kushtau i ukrepivshiesia siloviki" [The 100 top Bashkir elite: "Our people" Kahbirova, the Kushtau factor and strengthening siloviki]. *Real'noe vremia*, September 15.

Robertson, Graeme. 2013. "Protesting Putinism: The Election Protests of 2011–2012 in Broader Perspective." *Problems of Post-Communism* 60 (2): 11–23.

Roshchina, Yana, Sergey Roshchin, and Ksenia Rozhkova. 2022. "Determinants of COVID-19 Vaccine Hesitancy and Resistance in Russia." *Vaccine* 40, no. 39 (September 16).

Rusova, Sof'ia. 2021. "Molitvy potiv QR-kody i protesty protiv politiki gosudarstva" [Prayers against QR codes and protests against government policy]. Activatica, November 16.

Saifranova, Elina. 2021. "V Ufe obshchestvennoe dvizhenie 'Stop BashRTS' prizyvaiut ne platit' za otoplenie sleduiushchie 3 mesiatsa" [In Ufa the social movement "Stop BashRTS" is calling for not paying for heat for the next 3 months]. Mkset.ru, October 18.

Semenov, Andrei. 2022. "Why Is There No Antiwar Mobilization in Russia?" *Russia.Post*, September 6.

Semenov, Andrei, and Jan Matti Dollbaum. 2021. "Tsifrovoe soprotivlenie" [Digital resistance]. *Riddle*, June 2.

Solodovnikov, Vladimir. 2021. "Novye protest protiv QR-kodov idut po vsei Rossii" [New protests against QR codes are taking place all across Russia]. FederalCity.ru, November 15.

Stanovaya, Tatiana. 2024. "As Election Looms, Putin Is in a Wartime Trap of His Own Making." Washington, DC: Carnegie Endowment for International Peace, January 15.

Sundstrom, Lisa McIntosh, Laura A. Henry, and Valerie Sperling. 2022. "The Evolution of Civic Activism in Contemporary Russia." *East European Politics and Societies* 36 (4): 1377–99.

Suslova, Lora. 2020. "'Moskovskii Kushtau': Pochemu moskvichi protestuiut protiv stroek 'Tashira'?" ["Moscow's Kushtau": Why are Muscovites protesting against building "Tashira"?]. MBKh Media, October 6.

Tertytchnaya, Katerina. 2023. "Russian Protests Following the Invasion of Ukraine." PONARS Eurasia Policy Memo no. 841. PONARS, April 17.

Tilly, Charles, and Sidney Tarrow. 2007. *Contentious Politics*. New York: Oxford University Press.

Tóth-Czifra, András. 2021a. "What Pro-Navalny Protests Tell Us about Russian Regions." Institute of Modern Russia, March 3.

———. 2021b. "Russia's (Canceled) Ecological Referenda" [in Russian]. *Riddle*, October 25.

———. 2020. "How Russia's Environmental Issues Increase Risks for the Kremlin." Institute of Modern Russia, December 2.

Volkov, Denis. 2023. "Ne vidno kontsa: Pochemu rossiiane ne zhdut skorogo zaversheniia konflikta na Ukraine" [No end in sight: Why Russians do not expect an end to the Ukraine conflict soon]. Forbes.ru, June 4.

———. 2012. "Putinism under Siege: The Protesters and the Public." *Journal of Democracy* 23 (3).

Weir, Fred. 2018. "Russian Consumerism May Be Poisoning This Town. But Nascent Civil Society Is Pushing Back." *Christian Science Monitor*, April 12.

Wengle, Susanne, and Michael Rasell. 2008. "The Monetization of L'goty: Changing Patterns of Welfare Politics and Provision in Russia." *Europe-Asia Studies* 60 (5).

Zaslavskaia, Margarita. 2021. "Pochemu rossiiane ravnodushny" [Why Russians are indifferent]. Meduza, October 30.

Zhuravlev, Oleg, Violetta Alexandrova, and Darya Lupenko. 2020. "In Russia's New Protest Cycle, a Demand for a Democratic State Emerges." OpenDemocracy.net, August 3.

SEVEN

Russian Human Capital
Decline or Demise?

HARLEY D. BALZER

Vladimir Putin insists that Russia's version of "reform and openness" under Gorbachev and Yeltsin ravaged Russia's population, lost control of the borders, and nearly destroyed Soviet achievements in education, science, and technology. In Putin's narrative, his regime successfully restored Russia's great power status while simultaneously addressing Russia's human capital and knowledge economy challenges.

Substantial evidence demonstrates the reality is quite different. Even after the failed coup in August 1991, Gorbachev was not able to separate himself from the Communist Party. The Yeltsin presidency was a period characterized by economic stringency and new possibilities. After Putin became president in 2000, rising oil prices and important reforms created the potential to address demographic decline, curb anti-immigrant hysteria, improve health care and education, and use Yeltsin's opening to international cooperation to build on what remained of the Soviet legacy in science and technology. Over a quarter century, Putin's policies have failed in each of these crucial realms.

Unlike some economic and trade issues where Putin blames hostile powers or global trends, the failures described here are overwhelmingly of his own making. Even in demography, where Russia resembles Europe in birth rates, Russia remains an outlier on many indicators. The rapid declines in science and technology are unprecedented for a country with high income and high levels of educational attainment that is not suffering a major natural disaster or military defeat.

Rather than investing the windfall from rising hydrocarbon prices in human capital to make Russia's natural resources the drivers of technology development in a diversified economy, Putin chose policies that have squandered opportunities.[1] His real but limited market reform era ended in 2003. By 2019, many of his hydrocarbon-fueled positive achievements from the early 2000s had been reversed. Following a decade of conflict that became full-scale war in Ukraine, negative trends in social policy have accelerated.[2] Putin has mortgaged Russia's future in an attempt to redefine authoritarianism as "sovereign democracy," upend global systems, and restore Russia as a great power.

The bills are coming due. Even if Putin achieves some of his goals in Ukraine, Russia and Russians will pay a long-term price. After years of war and more than a decade of sanctions, a large swath of the commentariat continues to focus on Russia's "resilience." Putin's regime has found creative ways to work around many of Russia's problems. Far less attention has been devoted to the long-term costs of these policies. The sanctions and Russia's response are like termites: the serious damage is not fully visible until it is too late.

The human capital failures begin with demography and health. The Russian population could be half its current size by 2100, and that smaller number will likely be more vulnerable. The second section describes Russia's declining educational system, increasingly disrupted by the Ukraine war. The third section recounts how the uneven, costly, yet genuine Soviet science and technology achievements have been seriously degraded. The conclusion focuses on the long-term implications of Putin's choices. They presage a diminished Russia.

Russia's government has not failed at everything, and Putin boasts of successes on his own terms. Yet Putin's positive results are based on short-term solutions to long-term problems. The most consequential failures begin with the declining number and physical condition of Russia's population.

For decades to come the population will be smaller, the dependency ratio will be higher, and the number of invalids will be greater. Ethnic Russians and Russian Orthodox believers are likely to constitute a smaller proportion of the population.

Demographics and Health

Russia's population has been declining since 1992 owing to low birth rates, high adult mortality, and emigration. Immigration offset much of the decline into the early 2000s. Russia's invasion of Ukraine and wartime policies since 2022 have reduced voluntary immigration into Russia while prompting a new exodus of Russians who refuse to serve in the war or reject Putin's increasingly repressive policies. The regime has sought to compensate by distributing Russian passports to people living in occupied Ukrainian territories, offering pardons to prisoners willing to serve as soldiers, conscripting migrant workers to fight in Ukraine, and raising salaries for foreign mercenaries. These are not long-term solutions.

Demographic policy during Putin's presidency has been marked by four important inflection points. In 2006 Putin issued a decree mandating a demography program to 2025 that was implemented along with his first four national projects.[3] The second important shift came in 2014 with the annexation of Crimea, adding people living in the occupied territory but narrowing the already limited number of countries supplying labor to Russia. The third and most serious shock was the February 2022 full-scale invasion of Ukraine, turning an exploitative relationship with immigrants into a massive, state-supported criminal enterprise.

The fourth inflection point came with the formation of a new government in mid-2024. Putin's reelection to a fifth term was accompanied by a shift from ad hoc wartime measures to a longer-term approach that began to acknowledge Russia's new political and demographic realities. Analysts at some government think tanks have focused on the need for a more comprehensive demographic policy and a more balanced screening system to attract desperately needed labor while excluding potential criminals. Yet, as in many countries, immigration is a fraught political issue. In August 2024 Putin signed new laws making it easier to deport unwanted migrants.[4] Competing interests in Russia's legislative and administrative systems continue to struggle with these issues.

FIGURE 7.1. UN Russian Population Projection, 2023

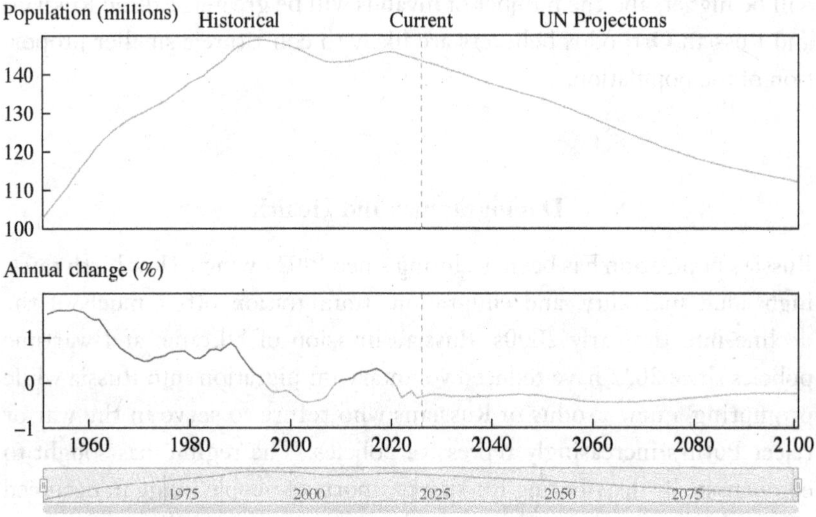

Source: Macrotrends.net (https://www.macrotrends.net/countries/RUS/russia/population), based on United Nations data.

Declining Numbers

Russia's population peaked in 1992–1993 and is not likely to recover to that level in this century. Declining numbers and aging will prevail for at least the next two decades, and likely far longer (figure 7.1).[5] Neither natural increase nor exogenous factors appear capable of substantially altering the equation.

Natural population size is determined by natality and life expectancy. Russia's low birth rate is not unusual among European countries, nor is the population decline. However, Russia is an outlier among high-income countries (a status it was accorded in 2024) in the death rate among working-age adults and the net loss of highly skilled personnel to emigration. The war inevitably increases adult mortality. Policies since 2014 have exacerbated the serious qualitative and increasingly quantitative immigration-emigration imbalances.

Russia will need between 390,000 and 1.1 million immigrants *per year* to prevent irreversible demographic decline, according to experts at Russia's Higher School of Economics Institute of Demography. United Nations scenarios project Russia's population in 2100 to be between 74 million and 112 million, compared with the current 146 million.[6]

Natural decline in the size of Russia's population began after 1993 and accelerated for a decade (table 7.A1). The number of women of childbearing age peaked in 2012–2014, depending on which statistics one believes. The total fertility rate (TFR, number of births per woman) improved from 1.3–1.5 to nearly 1.8 in the decade after 2006 but peaked in 2015 and has declined since. Population replacement generally requires a TFR of 2.1; growth requires more. Russia's persistently high rate of adult mortality means that a TFR of 2.2 to 2.4 could be needed for full replacement.[7]

Despite higher fertility rates, birth rates have been nearly level since 2013 owing to a smaller number of women in the childbearing-age cohort. Low birth rates in the 1990s, the extreme effects of the COVID-19 epidemic in Russia, more than a decade of declining living standards since 2013, and Putin's war will have negative repercussions for decades.[8]

Russia's population declined every year between 1994 and 2008 (see table 7.A1). In the early 2000s the Russian government discussed population policy options, debating among policies to increase immigration, improve life expectancy, or raising the birth rate. As in many countries, immigration was deemed to be too fraught politically. Extending life expectancy is slow, challenging, and costly, requiring major investments in social policy and health care. Increasing the birth rate appeared to be the most promising and politically acceptable choice.[9]

Putin cited demography as a crucial problem after he was appointed prime minister in 1999. In his first address to the Federal Assembly of the Russian Federation as president in July 2000, Putin stated that "the demographic situation is one of the most alarming that the country faces."[10] Apparently, other concerns became more alarming.[11] It was not until 2006 that the government finally addressed the problem. In his annual address to the legislature in May of that year, President Putin cited population decline as "the most acute problem" facing Russia.[12] The government responded with a "demography program" for 2007–2025. The major component was maternity capital, mandating payments to mothers for birth of a second and subsequent children. Other elements included a special allowance for unemployed women, help for those with no insurance, compensation if children enrolled in preschool programs, and, beginning in 2011, new regional programs offering land and other incentives to large families.[13]

A review of the program's first decade by scholars at the Russian Presidential Academy of the National Economy and Public Administration (RANEPA) assessed achievements and shortcomings. The Russian population increased slightly (less than 0.10 percent) in 2010 and 2011. Population growth reached 0.30 percent in 2016, but then slowed, turning negative again in 2019. This reflected reaction to changes raising the pension age immediately after the 2018 presidential election, deteriorating economic conditions, and the impact of COVID-19 beginning in 2020.[14]

The Russian data are confusing in part because a smaller number of women in the childbearing cohort meant more births per woman would not necessarily result in significant population growth unless women gave birth to more than two children. The maternity capital program did stimulate more women to have a second or third child, but the number was not large enough to offset the smaller cohort of women.

The monetary incentives encouraged births in families with low incomes. (Johnson provides details on the program and its expansion over time in chapter 9.) In the best year, the increase was 0.30 percent. Women in rural areas and towns with relatively small populations responded to the financial incentives. In more populous urban centers, home to 76 percent of Russia's population, the cost of living and housing prices meant the payments were insufficient to influence birth rates in most families. The maternity capital program had no significant impact in Moscow, St. Petersburg, and other large cities.

Except for some private clinics, Russia's health care system fails to provide a level of care that encourages multiple births. Many young women are discouraged from having a second child after their initial experience giving birth in Russian hospitals. A study in St. Petersburg concluded: "If increasing the birthrate is to be the main way to mitigate Russia's daunting demographic situation, prospective mothers' emotional and psychological needs must be taken into account. Without serious attention to improving the care provided during pregnancy and childbirth, no financial incentives will induce educated and empowered women to have a second child, much less to become 'hero-mothers.'"[15]

A (temporary) increase in the number of women in the prime childbearing age cohort (eighteen to thirty-five years) likely was more important than the maternity capital program in raising birth rates (table 7.A2). Russia's TFR peaked just below 1.8 in 2015 and has declined since, despite the maternity capital program continuing and the benefits being extended to include first and all subsequent children.[16] The ruble amounts have been increased, but wartime inflation may limit the incentives.

In a detailed account of these government policies, the RANEPA authors note that in practically every realm, the measures were far from constituting a coherent program.[17] While the pro-natal emphasis was politically acceptable, the specific measures were far from adequate. France and Sweden managed to increase birth rates with packages of programs that included parental leave, pre- and postnatal care, free or affordable childcare, housing, guaranteed return to employment, and other incentives.[18] Financial incentives alone cannot overcome the reluctance of many Russian women to raise large families.[19]

Nicholas Eberstadt questions the impact of the pro-natal policies, noting that the birth rate began to decline after 2014 while the policies remained in place.[20] The RANEPA authors concur that the impact of maternity capital declined beginning in 2015, suggesting that higher incomes and improved social stability had played an important role in decisions to have children.[21] Yet they also note that the share of women having a second child rose from 31 percent to 37 percent, and the proportion having a third child increased from 11 percent to 20 percent.[22] Data on the age of women having more than one child support the argument that the policy achieved some modest results. Policies adopted in 2024 mandating that women should have three or more children to provide soldiers in wartime while also encouraging women to join the labor force and assume combat roles are clearly contradictory.[23]

Sustaining a TFR of 1.8 is not sufficient for population replacement. It would result in a decline of about 25 percent in the size of each subsequent generation.[24] Yet the national project "Demography" approved in 2024 set targets of 1.6 for 2030 and 1.8 for 2035.[25] This means the new goal is to regain the level of 2015 within two decades.

Some societies, such as Japan, have managed to cope reasonably well with a declining population,[26] but Russia's economy and military continue to depend on inputs of capital and personnel. Automation and robotics remain significant challenges.

Russia's low birth rates in the 1990s produced long-term consequences. The smaller cohort of women aged eighteen to thirty-five years in the 2020s means that even without the Ukraine war, deaths would exceed births at least into the early 2030s. COVID-19 and the war have extended this time frame. The current number of children under age five is the smallest age cohort below the age of sixty-five for males and seventy-five for females in Russia's 2023 population pyramid, a significant change from a decade earlier (figures 7.2 and 7.3).

In the period 2003–2016, Russia's draft-age male population declined by half.[27] Putin's war in Ukraine has accentuated competition among education, military needs, and labor force demands. This has led to widespread

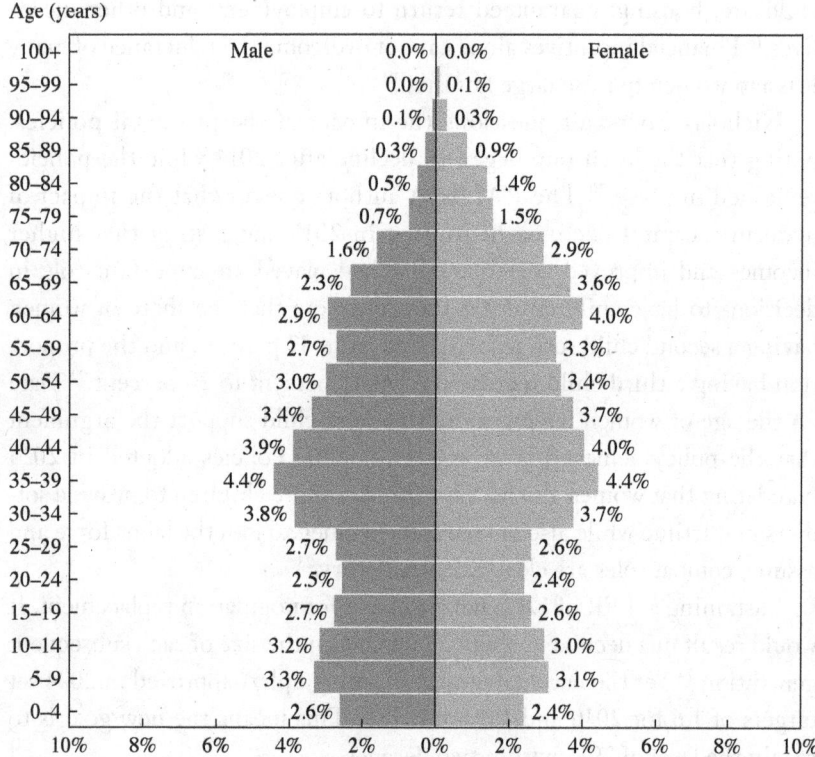

FIGURE 7.2. Russian Population Pyramid, 2023
(Population = 144,444,358)

Source: PopulationPeriod.net (https://www.populationpyramid.net/russian-federation/2023/).

abuses, including mobilizing older men and fathers with large families.[28] Many Russians responded by leaving the country. While no one has precise data, estimates are that somewhere between 300,000 and 700,000 draft-age men left Russia between February 24, 2022, and the end of that year. This estimate does not include male children whose families relocated. Many assessments put the number at well over one million.[29]

Regardless of official pronouncements, indicators show the war lowering birth rates. In the summer of 2022, sales of at-home abortion products increased 50–60 percent. The government has responded with policies to limit birth control.[30] Elizaveta L'vova at the Samara office of SCORA IFMSA noted the threat of new laws, an unstable economy, and the continuing military conflict as factors in women preferring to make their own choices.[31] Yet the government persists in encouraging women to marry earlier and have

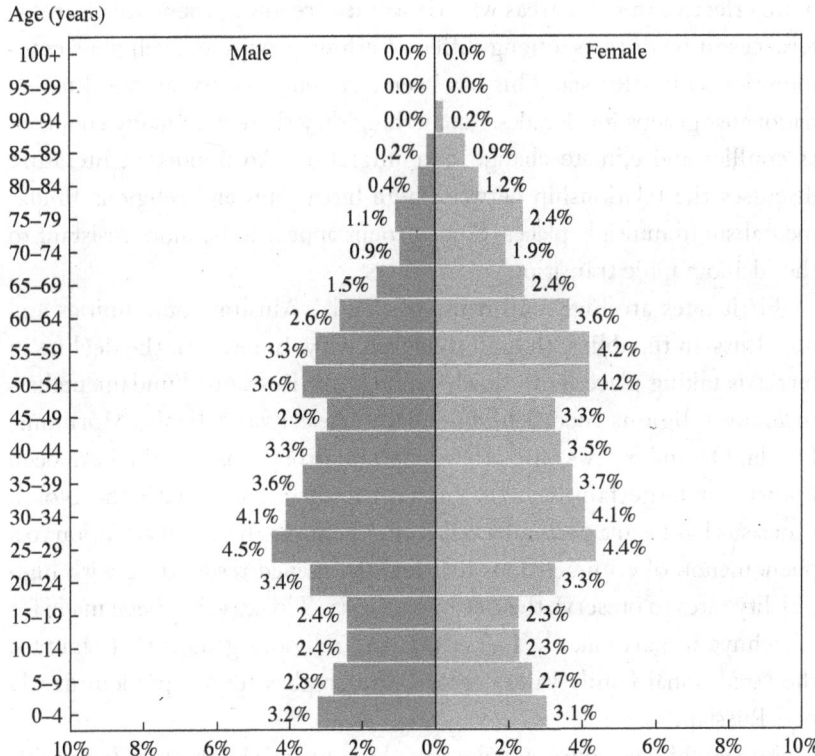

FIGURE 7.3. Russian Population Pyramid, 2013 (Population = 144,664,836)

Source: PopulationPyramid.net (https://www.populationpyramid.net/russian-federation/2013/).

children at a younger age. The new norm for families should be at least three children. Legislation now designates information encouraging children to limit family size as "extremism," punishable by long prison terms.[32]

Abortions have declined in recent years, but this does not mean women are responding to calls for them to produce more potential soldiers. Rather, more women are opting for sterilization, auguring longer-term population decline.[33]

A majority of Russian physicians, 59 percent, oppose efforts by the Ministry of Health and Duma legislation to limit sales of medications to terminate pregnancy. They fear it will result in more back-alley abortions and encourage medical tourism. Fewer than 20 percent of doctors support the new laws, despite ministry claims they are designed to protect women's health.[34]

Russian demographic policy is complicated by significant regional and ethnic differences. In addition to the maternity capital program being far more effective in rural areas where incomes are lower, there are clear differences in birth rates among different ethnic groups and religious communities within Russia. This has been a serious concern among Russian nationalist groups for decades,[35] something they share with many countries as conflict and climate change spur migration. An important literature discusses the relationship between high birth rates and religious fundamentalism in multiple places. Some groups appear to be more resistant to the "demographic transition" than others.

Birth rates are higher in many of Russia's Muslim communities and non-Russian republics, though the levels vary. In general, the decline in births is taking place more slowly among non-Russians. Fundamentalists in many religions record higher birth rates: Evangelicals, Mormons, Hindu, Orthodox Jews, and others. Certain groups historically have been known for large families. In Russia, the differential with the North Caucasus has been a particular concern.[36] Some analysts call attention to a phenomenon of ethnic groups that feel threatened responding with high fertility rates to preserve their ethnic identity. This case has been made for Chechnya in particular.[37] The ethnic and religious groups that embrace the "traditional family values" that Putin emphasizes are predominantly non-Russian.

Russian official sources stress that the country's birth rates do not differ significantly from those of many other countries that were once Soviet Union republics or from rates in most EU and OECD nations. This is correct. In addition to low birth rates, Russia's intractable demographic problems reflect a level of adult mortality unprecedented in a country with high levels of educational attainment and incomes. Russia continues to be an outlier in emigration by highly skilled individuals. While Russian birth rates may be comparable to those of many developed nations, adult mortality, particularly among the working-age population, is at the level of the third or fourth world.[38] The RANEPA authors stated that "the limited potential for increasing births" means Russia must improve life expectancy and increase immigration.[39] Putin's wartime policies are undermining all of the possible solutions. Battlefield losses and stressed families do not promote longevity. Forcing migrant workers to join the war in Ukraine discourages immigration.

Life Expectancy

Despite generating serious criticism for focusing on technology rather than outcomes, Russia's "health care" program combined with economic stabilization during Putin's first two presidential terms generated improvements (short-lived) in life expectancy.[40] After declining each year from the Soviet-era peak of 69.13 years in 1988, Russian life expectancy turned positive in 2004 (table 7.A3). Increases of about four to six months were seen each year from 2005 to 2015. Gains continued at a slower rate after 2017. The adult mortality differential with OECD countries was reduced by about half.[41] Official Russian statistics continued to report improved life expectancy despite COVID-19 and the war (see table 7.A3 and figure 7.3). These data are questionable given that official statistics likely omit a large share of the war casualties. In mid-2024 both the U.S. Department of Defense and Ukrainian sources claimed Russian casualties had reached half a million, including 200,000 deaths.[42]

Life expectancy for Russians peaked in 2019, the year before COVID-19.[43] Official data report slight increases in 2020–2022 (see table 7.A3). Yet COVID-19 hit Russia harder than most countries in 2020 and 2021. Russian sources reported 1.3 million excess deaths in these two years, but the government attributed just 300,000 of these deaths to COVID-19.[44] This was precisely when Putin chose to attack Ukraine. Putin may have calculated that worsening economic and demographic data, along with sanctions' impact on technology, meant that Russia would not be in as strong a position any time in the next two decades. This is one of several plausible explanations.

Russia's older population in general is better educated and healthier than previous generations, suggesting increased life expectancy if normal conditions return.[45] Yet the modest projected life expectancy increase of 0.19 percent per year to 2100, reaching close to ninety years, appears implausible. The war is killing and maiming an enormous number of Russia's young and middle-aged men, while hundreds of thousands have left the country since 2022. This exodus and the war casualties will produce a growing dependency ratio (ratio of dependents—people younger than fifteen, disabled, or older than sixty-four—to the working-age population) in the coming years. Like the losses in World War II, the reduced birth rate will echo for several generations. Putin's failures include reversing modest improvements achieved in his first decades in power.

While Russia achieved genuine improvements between 2005 and 2019, increasing life expectancy by eight years overall and ten years for males, concurrent improvements in these indicators in OECD nations mean Russia's gap remains significant. More alarming, Russian life expectancy declined again after 2019 owing to COVID-19.[46] Russia continues to have elevated rates of HIV and tuberculosis infections, yet the overwhelming causes of adult deaths before the war were cardiovascular disease and injuries/poisoning.[47] The war is not encouraging healthy lifestyles. Alcohol consumption has increased.[48]

Another persistent Russian failure, not unique to Putin but increasingly costly, is inadequate attention to the disabled and handicapped population. A country facing serious demographic decline cannot afford to neglect drawing on all potential contributors to the labor force. Beginning with Stalin's program to disappear the disabled from Russian cities after World War II, the USSR and, subsequently, the Russian Federation consistently failed to draw on this significant share of its human capital. For several years in the 1990s, Russian media focused on providing services for people with special needs. However, this responsibility has fallen primarily on civil society efforts, as discussed by Johnson (see chapter 9). In spring 2024 media reported efforts to employ invalids and people with disabilities to compensate for labor shortages, but also noted serious limitations.[49]

A regime that favors silver bullets in the guise of national programs and hero projects rather than complicated, multifaceted solutions is not likely to change character during a war.[50]

While government economic and social policies play an important role in the incentive structure for having children, individual decisions about family and lifestyle determine the results. Life expectancy is similar in being a product of individual lifestyle decisions. The realm where government policy has the most significant impact is the immigration-emigration equation. Conflict and climate change, increasingly in combination, are driving growing numbers of people to risk their lives in search of safer places to live, creating growing concern about migrants in many countries. Far from taking advantage of the growing migration surge, Russia's wartime policies represent a failure of stunning magnitude.

Exogenous Factors: Immigration-Emigration and Brain Drain-Brain Circulation

Despite Russians being ambivalent about welcoming immigrants, even before the Ukraine war most independent analysts viewed immigration as the only path to replacement level for Russia's population.[51] Yet Russia rarely is the preferred destination for people with high human capital. Attracting compatriots or immigrants is challenging when Russians are leaving in large numbers to escape the war and the government is forcibly conscripting foreign workers to avoid mobilizing Russians.

IMMIGRATION AND EMIGRATION. Writing in 2018, RANEPA analysts saw no alternative to migration. Yet the share of labor migrants in total personnel employed was just 6 percent, and there was no visible means of increasing the proportion. Even before the Crimean annexation, workers from Moldova and Ukraine preferred the EU, citing "increasing Russian economic backwardness compared with developed countries."[52] Sanctions and Russia's economic difficulties after 2014 further curtailed immigration. In 2018, 95–96 percent of labor migrants came from CIS countries. Russia had been recruiting 150,000–170,000 workers each year from China, North Korea, and Vietnam, but ruble devaluation has made this less feasible.[53]

Since the attack on Ukraine, few individuals from Belarus, Azerbaijan, Kazakhstan, or Georgia have sought Russian passports. The already small numbers in the first quarter of 2023 compared with 2022 declined further. Applications from Ukraine, including the Russian-occupied areas, were down 60 percent. The vacuum was filled only partially by Tajiks, Kyrgyz, and Uzbeks. Tajiks constituted 42 percent of Russia's new citizens in the first half of 2023, compared with 23 percent in 2022 and 12.5 percent in 2021. Total in-migration in the first quarter of 2023 was 106,320, compared with 141,663 a year earlier. Of these, 97 percent were from former USSR republics.[54] Increasing pressure on Central Asians to fight in Ukraine caused a marked decline in the numbers willing to work in Russia. By the end of 2023, Tajiks constituted half of the new migrants to Russia.[55]

No agency tracks total emigration from Russia. The Ministry of Internal Affairs records only individuals who have applied for citizenship elsewhere. In 2022 this number was 50,000. Using data from countries reporting Russian arrivals, Re-Russia.net put the number exiting at between 820,000 and 920,000.[56] The FSB tracks border crossings, which may or may not represent emigration.

Sources reporting data from receiving countries often omit some of the regions where Russians now live. Israel reports growing numbers, as do countries in Latin America.[57] The threat of being mobilized for military service in Ukraine is a major reason foreign workers now avoid Russia. Accounts in Russian media and blogs describe attempts to pressure labor migrants into enlisting or joining paramilitary groups fighting in Ukraine. In late 2022, advertising appeared in Moscow public transit in Uzbek language to recruit fighters. This created tensions, and most were removed.[58]

In the summer of 2023, Communist Party deputy Mikhail Matveev introduced Duma legislation to revoke citizenship for migrants who refuse military service. While some experts say new laws are unnecessary, reports indicate that pressure on migrants is a visible political trend. In many cities, large groups of migrant workers have been rounded up and forced to register for military service.[59]

Despite the significance of remittances that workers send home, most Central Asian regimes now seek to limit recruitment of their citizens for the war in Ukraine by either side. Even before Russia invaded Ukraine, Kazakhstan imposed a three-year (suspended) sentence on a citizen for providing noncombat help to Russian fighters in eastern Ukraine. The Civic Assistance Committee, a group designated as a foreign agent in Russia, tracks data on migrants. It reported a major shift away from encouraging work in Russia by Central Asian and other CIS governments in the first quarter of 2023.[60]

Kazakhstan in 2023 issued warnings about its citizens participating in the war and investigated ten individuals suspected of fighting in Ukraine. Kazakh prosecutors sought to ban goods featuring the Russian "V" and "Z" war symbols. The Kyrgyz Republic sentenced one citizen to ten years' imprisonment for serving as a mercenary. The Kazakh, Kyrgyz, and Uzbek governments all have issued warnings that engaging in combat in Ukraine would be viewed as mercenary activity, a criminal offense making participants ineligible for dual citizenship. The implication of the new policies is that citizens of these nations who fight in Ukraine could lose their citizenship rights in their native countries or encounter difficulties if they returned home.[61]

At the June 2024 St. Petersburg Economic Forum, Investigative Committee head Alexander Bastrykin requested amendments to the law on citizenship, adding language to facilitate depriving "new Russians" of citizenship for planning, attempting, or committing any serious crime. The Investigative Committee also insists that all migrants register for the draft at the same time they receive their Russian passports.

The Duma responded in the summer of 2024, adopting new rules and restrictions for migrants that likely will further discourage all but the most desperate. In addition to making it easier to deport illegal migrants and those who violate Russian laws, a more comprehensive identification and registration system is being instituted. It includes obligatory biometrics, fingerprinting, and genomic registration, along with digital registration of each individual's workplace and residence.[62]

Bastrykin did not mention ongoing programs to hire mercenaries from Central Asia and elsewhere. British intelligence reported that in the summer of 2023, Russian online advertising in Armenia and Kazakhstan offered a one-time payment of $5,140 and monthly salaries of nearly $2,000. Recruiters in Kazakhstan's northern Qostanai region, home to a large Russian population, were particularly active. In Uzbekistan recruiters offered a fast path to citizenship and salaries of more than $4,000. At the same time, Uzbek construction workers recruited to rebuild Mariupol in Ukraine have had their passports seized and have been forced to join the Russian forces in combat.[63]

Predatory practices have extended beyond Russia's usual sources of migrant workers. Individuals from Nepal, India, and other countries have been recruited to work in factories or as guards at various venues in Russia. After they arrive, their passports are confiscated, and they are sent to fight in Ukraine. Punishment squads are deployed to prevent soldiers from retreating. These devious tactics differ from the treatment of Cuban and African mercenaries, who are attracted by the money.[64]

An invaluable, stunning, and alarming description of life in the Russian military system during the war by Sarah Topol appeared in the *New York Times Magazine* in September 2024. Topol's account illustrates why Russia's war in Ukraine relies so heavily on impressment, fraudulent labor recruitment, and mercenaries to limit dependence on mobilizing more Russians to fight.[65]

In a late July 2024 interview, Bastrykin cited the story of a Moscow oblast entrepreneur who built a hotel to provide decent housing for foreign workers. The new living quarters attracted not only foreigners but also Russians from neighboring regions. Rather than viewing this as evidence that employers need to provide better conditions for all their workers, Bastrykin cited it as proof that enough labor was available without foreigners. He proposed imposing a tax on businesses using foreign labor, along with requiring employers to pay for transportation, housing, and an escrow account in case it became necessary to deport labor migrants.[66]

The Federal Agency for Ethnic Affairs has developed a special "adaptation course" for migrants. It includes a seventy-minute lecture explaining "all they need to know" about Russia's laws on migration and labor. The content covers guidance regarding behavior in Russia and in particular regions. Migrants are warned not to whistle at women and not to comment in their own language about people they pass on the street. Sacrificing animals in public is not permitted. The course includes a history component emphasizing the amount of money the USSR spent to develop its Central Asian republics.[67]

The Duma in late July 2024 passed legislation proposed by a group composed of members of all parties to tighten laws on migration. The new rules make it much simpler to expel migrants. A second law grants police full authority to deport foreign citizens and individuals without Russian citizenship and creates a register of these individuals. Police will have the authority to deport offenders within forty-eight hours unless a court intervenes.[68]

Foreign nationals placed on the expulsion register will be prohibited from changing their place of residence in Russia without authorization from the Ministry of Internal Affairs; traveling outside their place of residence; driving vehicles or obtaining a driver's license; acquiring or disposing of immovable property, vehicles, and self-propelled machines, or registering such property with state authorities; marriage; and opening bank accounts, transferring money, or disposing of funds in their accounts.[69]

Political scientist Mikhail Vinogradov notes that Russia's attractiveness for migrants had decreased even without these new policies, owing to economic conditions and the risk of being sent to the special military operation. Difficulties crossing the border, and the possibility of being deprived of Russian citizenship even if someone is naturalized are further disincentives. Vinogradov concludes that the new provisions assume all migrants are guilty rather than providing incentives for the honest ones to work in Russia.[70]

Concerned that even these measures might not be sufficient, the Duma proposed creating a new Commission on Migration Policy[71] Without major shifts in treatment of non-Russian migrants, the only exogenous source of population growth would be returning Russian compatriots. This is not sufficient to meet Russia's needs.

BRAIN DRAIN AND BRAIN CIRCULATION. Highly skilled individuals have left Russia in repeated waves of emigration over the past half century. An even larger number have abandoned careers in education and science for more highly paid employment in Russia, often in the informal sector. Some find tutoring a more profitable activity than teaching.[72]

While Central Asians increasingly are wary of going to Russia, wartime mobilization resulted in Russians flocking to Central Asia and other former Soviet republics by the tens of thousands. Kazakhstan, the Kyrgyz Republic, Georgia, and Armenia initially did little to restrict large numbers of Russians from crossing borders to escape military service. The influx of relatively wealthy Russian refugees has stimulated economic growth along with serious social problems. These economies benefit from Russian spending, but scarce housing has become more expensive, along with growing inflation in other sectors.[73]

Not all the Russian arrivals have managed to find long-term employment, and some have returned home.[74] Openness following the demise of the USSR resulted in many Russian professionals becoming full participants in international epistemic communities. This created tensions with those whose skills were suited to the Soviet system and resisted change.[75] As post-Soviet openness increasingly gave way to restoring control, exit became more attractive to many. Some high-level officials and talented specialists now regret not leaving when they might have had the opportunity.[76]

A Boston Consulting Group survey in 2018 reported that more than half of Russia's highly educated specialists expressed a desire to work abroad. This was true for half of Russian scientists, 54 percent of top managers, 54 percent of IT specialists, 49 percent of engineers, and 46 percent of medical personnel. Among potential émigrés, 65 percent were individuals with "digital talent."[77] This was confirmed by reports of a significant exodus of IT personnel after February 24, 2022.[78] When the Duma introduced legislation to increase taxes on IT workers living outside Russia, the minister of digitization objected, stating that Russian firms would have difficulty replacing these workers.[79]

While Russian policies increasingly deter immigration, the country continues to lose talented people in astonishing numbers. The damage to Russia's future stems not just from the sheer number of people who have departed but from their high human capital. Those leaving are scientists, engineers, and creative individuals with higher education and good prospects for employment elsewhere.[80] Many were reasonably well-off and have managed to move some of their wealth abroad. One result is that Russia's tax base will shrink. The government's response is to raise taxes.

Emigration from Russia increased after Putin's return to the presidency in 2012, which was followed by punitive measures against the protestors during the 2011–2012 election cycle. Emigration continued to increase in the wake of the Crimean annexation. The February 2022 invasion of Ukraine stimulated a far larger wave of Russian emigration, initially to former Soviet republics or satellites that still are open to Russians. While no one has precise data, estimates are that more than one million people left Russia in 2022.[81] Some families anticipated the war. Their bags were packed to leave the day of the invasion.[82] Traffic jams at border crossings to Georgia, Kazakhstan, and elsewhere were reported in Russian media. The price of airline tickets out of Russia skyrocketed.

The "near abroad" increasingly is a way station en route to the diminishing list of countries that continue to welcome Russians. Russians who can afford relocating to the UAE, China, Thailand, Serbia, and other countries are managing to settle there, though far from all have been able to find long-term employment. Argentina, a popular destination for Nazis after World War II, has become another popular destination, especially for pregnant women.[83]

Many of those leaving are draft-age males or families with male children. Putin's saying "good riddance" to supporters of democracy (except for those murdered or imprisoned) resulted in the regime not preventing departures, even by persons in some key professions or subject to conscription.

Military mobilization paid little attention to where people worked. In some instances, key employees, including educators and skilled workers or managers, were sent to fight in Ukraine. The combination of emigration and combat casualties is reducing the already limited share of Russia's population in the eighteen- to forty-year-old age cohort, further undermining prospects for increasing the birth rate in the coming decades.

Developing countries lose a significant share of STEM (science, technology, engineering, and math) personnel seeking higher pay and creative opportunities elsewhere. Russia is unique among nations with high levels of education in the one-sided character of its emigration-immigration equation. Russia's brain drain is only minimally ameliorated by brain gain or brain circulation.[84] Russia continues to experience a net loss of human capital.

By 2024, economic difficulties and less welcoming environments were inducing some compatriots to return home. However, glaring examples of mistreatment make many wary. A woman with dual Russian and American citizenship who visited family in Russia was arrested and sentenced to twelve years' incarceration for having made a $51 donation to a charity aiding Ukrainians.[85] New rules include a requirement that returning compatriots speak Russian. Fear of being conscripted or being accused of disloyalty is reducing the attractiveness of returning.

In sum, Putin's war will reduce birth rates for several generations, significantly increase mortality, shrink the able-bodied population, deter immigration to Russia, and increase emigration by young males and skilled professionals. The slight improvements in life expectancy, birth rates, and health stalled after 2015 and now are being reversed by the war and regime policies. Despite indexing social benefits, inflation in many sectors, particularly food costs, has put pressure on a majority of consumers. Social stress has escalated. While women are choosing to avoid pregnancy, the shortage of males of marriageable age is growing as a result of war-induced deaths, injuries, and emigration. Life expectancy and labor market participation for those injured physically or psychologically will be a persistent concern.

Fewer, but Not Better: Health and Health Care

Russia's smaller population has experienced a decade of declining nutrition, physical conditions, health, and education. War exacerbates each of these challenges. Beginning in 2014, declining real incomes and Russia's countersanctions against European food producers resulted in many items being more expensive and lower in quality.[86] Many Russians are eating a less healthy diet. Wages have been rising owing to unprecedented labor shortages, but these wage increases combined with global food supply problems cause inflation. Russia's government and Russian employers must constantly play catch-up. The share of food in wholesale trade turnover rose from 76 percent in 2018 to 82 percent in 2022. The war has amplified problems of higher prices and lower quality.[87]

Health care for Russia's increasingly fragile and ageing population is less available, more expensive, and less capable of meeting people's needs. Sanctions, both Western and Russian, have limited the availability of some medicines. Russia's pharmaceutical industry cannot fill the gaps. Russia depends on imports for many medicines, and more than half of the drugs sold in Russia before 2022 were based on foreign intellectual property.[88] In Saratov, the NGO providing insulin to diabetics was declared a "foreign agent" because it was receiving support from several international drug firms.[89] This illustrates another of Putin's serious failures: suppressing civic activity that improves the economy, saves lives, and helps achieve government goals. (Evans addresses these issues in chapter 6.)

Much of the funding allocated for the national project "Health Care" went to purchase advanced medical equipment, frequently at graft-inflated prices. Some perpetrators of such scams were eventually convicted and sent to prison. According to Reuters, two Putin cronies similarly involved suffered no penalties.[90] Some analysts credit the national project "Health Care" with Russia's modest GNP growth since 2009.[91]

Despite public health being one of the four initial priority national projects (along with education, housing, and agriculture), most doctors' salaries are comparable to those of workers in the retail or food service sectors. This means "healthcare providers are still paid in ways that encourage them to waste money and disregard health outcomes."[92]

Costly equipment has not improved overall health. The "healthy lifestyle" program is credited with some reduction in cardiovascular disease, a major cause of early death in Russia. Yet Russia continues to struggle with a host of illnesses that are not prevalent in other high-income nations. HIV/AIDS remains a major threat. Russian medical authorities retained a number of Soviet norms rejecting international best practices. HIV continues to be viewed as a criminal problem rather than a medical issue. Foreign-supported NGOs providing needle exchanges and substitution therapy were increasingly harassed and then labeled foreign agents. In the decade 2007–2017, AIDS grew from the twenty-third most common cause of death in Russia to number ten. This was not the result of lower numbers for other diseases.[93]

TB infection rates remain high, and the Soviet practice of institutionalizing patients rather than providing drug treatment persists. *This is yet another way government policies contribute to growing labor shortages.* Russia is one of four countries where multidrug-resistant (MDR) and extensively drug-resistant (XDR) TB variants are widespread and increasing. In 2016, one quarter of TB cases were MDR. The trajectory is for one-third of cases to be MDR and another 10 percent XDR by 2040. TB patients increasingly have coinfection with HIV or hepatitis C.[94] The drug-resistant strains of TB are particularly prevalent in prisons, where inmates often fail to take their full course of medication. This aspect of the health situation was apparently not considered when Yevgeny Prigozhin began promising pardons for convicts willing to fight in Ukraine.

Health targets established for 2019–2024 were immediately threatened by COVID-19 and Russia's economic downturn in 2020. An analysis by Russian scholars published a year after Russia invaded Ukraine concurs. While Russia has made some efforts to replicate European models relying on primary care physicians rather than hospital treatment, this effort remains problematic. Primary care is the weakest element of Russian medicine, resulting in extensive reliance on prolonged hospital and clinic stays. Increased funding and improved medical education, accompanied by structural changes in government administration of health care, are key to reducing costly reliance on inpatient care.[95]

COVID-19 revealed in stark ways the accumulating financial, structural, and ethical problems in Russia's health care system. Despite the resources devoted to the national project "Health Care" since 2007, Russia remained short of medical personnel, lacked modern equipment, and spent far less on health per capita or as a share of GDP than EU or OECD nations. Even before COVID-19, Russia lagged in mortality, life expectancy, and rates of illness. Russia's system was totally unprepared for the pandemic. Yet despite the lack of preparation, the share of GNP devoted to health care *declined* from 7.1 percent in 2020 to 6.3 percent in 2021.[96]

Financial and structural problems intensified as weak vaccines were rushed to market. Being first came at a cost in efficacy. The more effective MRNA vaccines developed in Europe and the United States were denigrated by Russian official media, resulting in many Russians refusing all vaccines. The pandemic created new opportunities for corrupt activity.[97] Russia in 2020 suffered the highest excess mortality rate per million population of any developed nation.[98]

As the war strains Russia's government budget, health programs are increasingly threatened. Russian leaders boast of an economic revival as the economy shifts to support the war. A more sober analysis would focus on the distortions resulting from excessive defense spending and growing reliance on imports that are driving Russian products from the market. A government decree in June 2021 established a pilot program for 2021–2022 to increase salaries for medical personnel in just seven regions.[99] The federal budget for 2024 includes a 70 percent increase for defense.

While Russia's food supply has not been threatened (as noted in chapter 4), a number of Russian specialists have cited the declining quality and higher cost of many important food products. Russian sources report that western sanctions had less impact on Russian consumers than Putin's countersanctions due to increasing concentration of both production and food distribution in a small number of large conglomerates.[100]

Poor health and diet, plus the need for many students to work while enrolled in education programs, have accentuated negative trends in the quality of education. In education, science, and technology, Putin's war in Ukraine is adding to the damage to Russia's' knowledge economy.

Education

A shrinking population creates challenges for schooling at all levels. Declining numbers often result in amalgamating and closing institutions, making education less accessible, especially in rural areas. Costs per student increase, while financial support declines.[101] Differences between families and regions have become far more pronounced. Military veterans and their families increasingly are being privileged in access to higher education, upward social mobility, and government positions. Prior to the Ukraine war, Russia's elite preferred foreign or private educational and medical services. As a result, demand for these public goods has remained relatively weak among important constituencies in Russia.[102] Putin's war created problems for wealthy Russians whose spouses and children were living abroad. Their return to Russia has increased demand for private services, putting additional strains on provision of public goods.

Preschool, elementary, and secondary education have become unfunded mandates for financially strapped local governments. Training for skilled workers and technicians remains problematic. The higher education system has zig-zagged in numbers of institutions and enrollments while struggling to maintain quality. The share of Russia's population enrolled in higher education peaked in 2010–2011 and likely will decline for the foreseeable future (table 7.A4). The network of higher education institutions expanded rapidly during the years of economic stringency in the 1990s. However, the number of institutions peaked along with enrollments in 2010–2011 and has declined since (tables 7.A5 and 7.A6).

Preschool access has been a consistent problem for all but affluent or well-connected Russians. Elementary and secondary education varies widely in quality. Experiments with diverse curricula after 1991 have been replaced with standardized content emphasizing patriotic themes and military preparedness.[103] With education abroad options limited, Russia's remaining private schools increasingly compete with state institutions. Private institutions face growing scrutiny.[104] The Political Science Faculty at the European University at St. Petersburg was the only Russian political science department in Russia to have been ranked in the top one hundred in Europe. In July 2024 the university rector closed it.[105]

As in the Soviet era, Russia lacks adequate training for skilled workers and technicians. Soviet professional-technical schools (PTUs) were consistently the least prestigious level in the "worker's paradise." Students who studied in specialized secondary education institutions to become technicians frequently took advantage of provisions allowing them subsequently to enroll in engineering institutes without taking entrance exams.[106] The "flight from production," described by Kendall Bailes for the Stalin era, continued into the twenty-first century.[107] Technicians' training remains a weak link, though it has received increased attention in the early 2020s.[108] Beyond competing for qualified students, education for workers and technicians continues to be short of resources and personnel. Factories facing labor shortages because of the war are more likely to put students and apprentices to work than to focus on their education. Several Russian colleagues of the author have shared concerns about forcing fourteen-year-olds to choose their future careers.[109]

Faced with widespread shortages of skilled workers and mid-level technical personnel, Russia is encouraging students to choose vocational education while struggling to improve its quality. This remains challenging. New programs and a significantly larger budget announced in 2024 fail to address the most serious challenges.

The number of universities and other institutions of higher education (*vysshee uchebnoe zavedenie*, or VUZy) peaked in 2010–2011 and has declined precipitously since. About one-half of the institutions were closed or amalgamated during a "cleansing" in 2014–2018. Russia's Deputy Minister of Education Sergei Kravtsov announced that the "peak" of the process had been reached in 2018.[110] The number of institutions did increase over the next three years but has declined again during the war (see table 7.A6).

By 2020 the number of higher education openings matched the total number of secondary education graduates. If all graduates chose higher education, vocational schools, civilian employers, and the military would have no new personnel. A majority of Russia's private higher education institutions have been closed since 2010 (see table 7.A6). While state

VUZy were closed or amalgamated less frequently, a growing number of Russian regions have no universities.[111]

Despite retaining some strength in math and physics, Russian education fails in preparing students for a twenty-first-century economy. Lifelong learning is a slogan rather than a widespread practice. By 2016 the qualitative decline was severe enough that some experts considered it irreversible.[112] Politicization was increasingly intrusive before the Ukraine war.[113] Since February 24, 2022, controls on personnel and content have become stifling. Every student is now a potential Pavlik Morozov.[114] Accounts of young students who raise questions about the war being separated from their parents and the parents punished have proliferated.

In the same manner that Russian economic data emphasize inputs rather than outputs, education data focus on attainment (number of students completing programs) rather than quality. Yet even on this indicator, the proportion of Russians with higher education has declined since 2010, reflecting the smaller number of young people (see table 7.A4 and figures 7.1 and 7.2).

The Soviet system emphasized memorization rather than critical thinking. Efforts to alter teaching styles initiated during perestroika and widespread in the 1990s have been replaced by educators once again avoiding attempts to address difficult questions. War has made this mandatory, with increasingly strict enforcement of required curricula.

Russia briefly became a global leader in higher education attainment in 2010, but the quality of that education suffers from limited resources. Russia allocates far less of its consolidated (federal and local) budget to education than other nations with comparable enrollment rates, spending just 3.5 percent of its GNP compared to an average of 5.2 percent. Russia lags significantly in contributions from the private sector, which amount to just 0.8 percent of GNP, a figure below that of all OECD member nations in 2021.[115] Russia spends 1.7 times less per student in higher education and two times less in general education than OECD member countries. In a 2018 study, experts calculated that Russia needed to invest an additional 1–1.5 percent of its GNP to begin to be globally competitive.[116]

Higher education has experienced an exceptionally chaotic policy environment. Massive expansion in the 1990s was followed by significant contraction beginning in 2010–2011 (see table 7.A5). The curriculum at all levels passed through a century's worth of changes in just three decades. After 1991, reformers sought to jettison Soviet educational approaches, but had to wait nearly a decade for new textbooks. As proponents of internationalizing the curriculum gained influence, Russia attempted to adopt the Bologna system.[117] This level of internationalization was never fully embraced, with many institutions operating hybrid systems offering multiple degree options. The struggles between legacy Soviet and other approaches have now been resolved in favor of the former, with near total rejection of foreign models.[118]

The declining number of applicants to higher education has forced institutions to admit students with lower scores on the country's Unified State Exam (*Edinyi Gosudarstvennyi Ekzamen*). The scores on this entrance exam determine not only who is admitted but how much funding the government provides for their education.[119] One indication of declining quality and turning inward is that Russian institutions have been vanishing from international rankings. After major international ranking systems dropped "reputation" as an indicator, Russian universities scored less well.[120] Despite programs to place five Russian universities in the global top one hundred, success was elusive.[121] Putin's advocacy of "sovereign education" no longer requires international linkages beyond a limited number of partners who share authoritarian concerns about critical thinking.

Prior to the war, Russian authorities continued to focus on prestige more than performance. As Russian universities disappeared from international rankings, officials responded by gaming the QS World University Rankings.[122] New "sovereign" Russian ranking systems include the number of students and graduates along with vaguely defined institutional "social contributions."[123] In 2023, Moscow State University returned to the top one hundred in Times Higher Education (THE) World University Rankings, but descriptions of all Russian universities disappeared from THE's website.[124] In 2024, no Russian university was included in some top two hundred lists.

Despite a number of programs designed to foster research at VUZy, including some jointly funded by U.S. philanthropic foundations and the Russian government, Russia's higher education system has not become a sustainable contributor to R&D.[125] Leading math and physics programs continue to produce some talented graduates with the skills needed for IT, but many graduates aspire to work abroad. Policies mandating use of Russian processors and software at leading engineering institutions illustrate the continued impact of sanctions in this priority sector. Legislation now requires that Russia's top engineering schools use Russian hardware, operating systems, and programs, but the requisite domestic equipment and software are not yet ready. Deadlines for "sovereign technology" in IT have been repeatedly postponed.[126]

The COVID-19 pandemic exacted a toll at all levels of education in many countries. Online instruction reduced attendance. Students with computers and good internet connections could cope if they wished. Many who could not easily join virtual class meetings became bored or used it as an excuse to skip lessons. In the United States, media covered the stories of parents who drove their children to locations where they could find an open network. The challenges in Russia were far greater.

Some 70 percent of Russian university faculty dislike virtual education and believe it undermines quality.[127] The educational system had not recovered from the COVID-19 pandemic before Russia invaded Ukraine. The combination of low salaries, inadequate pensions, and emigration by younger scholars makes Russian university departments and research organizations increasingly resemble retirement communities. The average age of VUZ faculty and academy researchers remained around sixty or above for many years. Young people avoid working in higher education, while older personnel cannot afford to stop working, though wartime conditions are offering them new options. If in the 1990s, talented mid-career scientific personnel with international connections left Russia, now it is promising younger scholars who seek opportunities abroad.[128]

Wartime labor shortages are altering many Russians' professional orientation. Beginning with perestroika and continuing in the 1990s, the private sector offered more remunerative if less secure opportunities than state employment. Putin's policies shifted priority back to the state sector. The Ukraine war is disrupting labor markets in sometimes astonishing ways. Wages in most state occupations are fixed. In the private sector, severe labor shortages have created bidding wars for workers that confound previous expectations. In Moscow and St. Petersburg in 2024 food delivery personnel could earn 100,000–200,000 rubles per month, far more than physicians. Teachers and professors are switching to higher-paying jobs in services, retail, and other non-white-collar professions.

No discussion of Russian education can be complete without attention to pervasive ethical problems. Russia is hardly alone in this respect, but Russia's rot begins at the top, making it exceptionally difficult to cure. While posted in Dresden, Vladimir Putin acquired his stereo equipment from the terrorist Red Brigades.[129] His candidate of science dissertation was written by the rector of the Mining Institute (now St. Petersburg Mining University) and includes eighteen and one-half pages of material plagiarized from an American economics textbook.[130] Putin is hardly alone in this behavior. About one-third of Russian Duma deputies have academic credentials produced for a fee. Disrespect for academic integrity begins early. Teachers in Russian schools often leave the classroom during exams, creating an opportunity for students to access various varieties of cheat sheets (*shpargalki*).[131]

Some scholars describe a massively corrupted Russian academic system, where everything from school admissions at all levels (beginning with preschool) to passing grades and advanced degrees now have fixed market prices.[132] This literature has been summarized by Dmitrii Trubnikov and Ekaterina Trubnikova, Higher School of Economics (HSE) scholars now living outside Russia.[133] While their description of Russia's predatory state fostering predatory universities may exaggerate the extent to which the entire system and all of its participants have succumbed to temptations, this detailed account of the "predatory ecosystem" for admissions, diplomas, publications, and university rankings illustrates serious challenges to academic integrity in Russia and beyond. As in the high-pressure Chinese academic environment, the extreme pressure to publish encourages plagiarism, dubious lists of multiple authors, and other abuses.

Shortly before the February 2022 start of the full-scale war in Ukraine, Finnish scholar Sirke Mäkinen published a comprehensive analysis of the struggles over internationalizing Russia's education and R&D systems, identifying proponents of neoliberal, state control, and status-focused models. Mäkinen concluded that Russian educators retained a desire to deepen international integration *provided it could be done more on Russia's terms*.[134] Putin has chosen to do everything on Russia's terms. The Ukraine war has dramatically altered the discourse on education. Internationalization now must be based on a "sovereign internet" and use "sovereign technology," while collaborative projects are limited to authoritarian partners. As noted in the discussion of science below, even these efforts entail serious dangers. Among the nations still willing to work with Russia, few are major global science and technology innovators.

The war with Ukraine has produced a reversion to many of the practices that contributed to Gorbachev's decision to restructure the Soviet system. Changes are being introduced at all levels of education. Despite overall themes of sovereignty, nationalism, and adaptation to the needs of the war, competing institutional and ideological interests are generating confusion and contradictions.

In preschool, kindergarten, and elementary schools, the major change is a focus on patriotic themes and early familiarity with weapons. Preschoolers are being introduced to assault rifles. Kindergarten classes include military drills. At all levels, the mandatory curriculum now is based on state standards, ostensibly to facilitate students transferring to other schools if needed. The emphasis on ease of transfers may be an excuse for limiting diversity but could also reflect the need to move Russian students away from regions bordering Ukraine that are under attack.

Older students are called on to engage in activities that were familiar in the USSR. "Labor education" requires cleaning the school grounds, sometimes including washing the floors. The *"subotniki"* requiring "voluntary" Saturday work have been revived. Previously, parents could refuse permission for their children being required to do janitorial work at their schools. Now the task is mandatory. The "basics and security of Russia" requirement includes learning emergency medical care as well as personal health and fitness. History courses must use a new textbook emphasizing Russia's point of view and presenting the official version of what Putin insists on calling a "special military operation." Soviet literature is again part of the curriculum.[135]

In the summer of 2023, President Putin approved a pilot project for six universities to adopt a new program with four to six years of "basic higher education." Graduates could seek employment or continue in a "specialist" program of one to three years (depending on the specialty) to earn a master's degree or could choose *"ordinatura,"* a program of individual study to become a specialist. The advanced academic option will remain graduate study (*aspirantura*), with various sources suggesting this could be one to three years or as much as five years, again depending on the discipline. While the pilot project is slated to run until 2026, some accounts suggest it could become the norm more quickly.

Creating a new ministry responsible for elementary and secondary education, the Ministry of Enlightenment (a name harking back to nineteenth-century appellations), and separating it from the Ministry of Science and Higher Education has resulted in contradictory proposals. The new government formed after Putin's reelection in 2024 appears to have recognized this problem, moving secondary technical education back to the Ministry of Science and Higher Education.

Yet many proposed policy changes fail to address Russia's most serious needs. How the new, often longer education programs will fare in a system facing high demand for soldiers to fight in Ukraine, an overheated labor market, and the continuing exodus of men to avoid military service has not been addressed. One increasingly popular solution is to have more students work while studying. About half the students in Soviet Union and Russian Federation higher education institutions were enrolled part-time in evening and correspondence (*zaochno*) programs. Concerns about the quality of these programs persist.

Putin has increasingly demanded changes in higher education admissions to privilege veterans of the special military operation and their families. Like Stalin with the early five-year plans, he appears to be endeavoring to create a new elite based on loyalty rather than competence or willingness to think independently about solving problems.

The constantly disrupted education system will have difficulty producing the personnel needed to compete in an expanding global science and technology community. Russia is increasingly the junior partner in collaboration with China.[136]

Science and Technology

Sputnik established an enduring myth of Soviet capacity in education, science, and technology.[137] Yet after Gagarin became the first person in space, the Russian program lagged behind the U.S. effort in most areas. The International Space Station was an exception, as was atomic energy. The USSR did well in basic research in traditional strengths, particularly math and physics, and was competitive in atomic weaponry and some military technology. Life sciences, medicine, interdisciplinary research, and social science were weaker. Translating research achievements into commercial technology has been a persistent challenge.[138]

Most Soviet R&D was carried out at the Russian Academy of Sciences and in a large network of industrial research institutes within various ministries. In the 1990s, as many of these institutions deteriorated, a number of programs supported developing research capacity at universities. The Academy and many university faculty resisted these efforts. The Academy sought to protect its privileged role. VUZ faculty carried heavy teaching loads, many had little experience conducting research, and funding was limited. Higher education continues to receive targeted research funding, but this has not been reflected in sustainable improved outputs.[139] Many VUZ faculty continue to regard research as a burden.[140] This has fostered an epidemic of articles with multiple authors, ghostwritten papers, and for-fee publications. The Academy and other research institutions continue to lose personnel and status.

Bad management, institutional decay, and corruption have undermined much of what remained of Soviet science. Many of the leading researchers who left in the 1990s thought their departure might be temporary. In the first decade of the 2000s, some returned to Russia or divided their time between Russia and their new positions abroad. Enthusiasm generated by election protests in 2011–2012 caused some to consider resuming work in Russia. A program of generous "megagrants" encouraged dozens to repatriate, but conditions were far from favorable.[141] Putin's return to the presidency in 2012 and subsequent crackdown on political opposition deflated hopes for change.[142] Compatriots living abroad are divided in their allegiances, with some continuing to support Putin despite the war. But, as noted above, only a limited number have returned to Russia. Wartime policies and new requirements do more to discourage than encourage repatriation.

Neither Russians abroad nor new partner countries (China, Iran, North Korea) are providing the assistance sorely needed to improve science and technology. Russia has achieved some improvements in weaponry, primarily by modifying old equipment, and electronic and cyber capabilities continue to be adequate. But genuine innovation remains a challenge. It requires melding basic research with technological development. Success remains elusive. The Putin regime continues the Soviet approach, emphasizing quantitative inputs rather the quality of outputs.

The Soviet system conferred high prestige for scientific and technical achievements and, after Stalin died, allowed a certain amount of leeway for its scientists, a practice sometimes mistaken for genuine autonomy. The Soviet-era Academy elected its president and new members, managing on occasion to limit political interference. In 1970 the Academy rejected the government's attempt to organize the election of Sergei Trapeznikov, the Central Committee official responsible for science, as a member.[143] Despite pressure from the authorities, the Academy never deprived Andrei Sakharov of membership.

Since 1992 the Academy has suffered diminished funding and status and increasingly has lost important administrative battles. As with other somewhat independent institutions, Putin has used KGB-style "salami tactics" to curtail its role. After the Academy's research institutes were shifted to the Ministry of Education and Science in 2013, the Academy was assigned a new role providing expert opinions regarding research funding.[144] Academy researchers have persisted in using their Academy titles, which still confer some prestige. In 2023, Putin broke with a long-standing policy by imposing his preferred candidate as Academy president.[145]

The cumulative impact of Putin-era changes has left many Academy institutes increasingly less able to support cutting-edge research. Low salaries compel Academy researchers to increase their income by teaching or tutoring. In place of budget funding, they now must seek grants to cover research expenses. Foreign funding has become scarce and risky, even when the sources are "friendly" countries like China and Iran, leaving limited state funds as the only option. Starting before the war, state funding was increasingly directed to applied research; now the military-industrial complex is the overwhelming funding priority.

One encouraging development in post-Soviet education and research was institutions establishing endowments to provide funding independent of government budgets. New private VUZy required this for long-term sustainability; state institutions increasingly sought discretionary funds. The fate of these endowments is now in question. As the government increasingly develops new policies to fund Putin's war, any pot of money becomes a target.

The most impressive private Russian effort supporting scientific research was the Dynasty Foundation, established in 2002 by scientist-turned-telecom mogul Dmitry Zimin. He placed the endowment funds in foreign banks to protect them from Russian inflation and currency value fluctuations. This caused the Dynasty Foundation to be declared a foreign agent in 2015. Zimin and his son Boris continued their philanthropic efforts outside Russia. Despite touting public-private partnerships, Putin's regime has failed to accept compromises that could make this a significant contributor to R&D. Rejecting private efforts to augment Russia's education and R&D capacity, like the closure of foreign-supported medical programs, underlines the Putin regime's failure to utilize available resources to achieve its purported goals.

Since 2000, Russian researchers have increased their total number of scientific publications but publish fewer articles in top international journals. Russian publications are cited less frequently than work by Western and Chinese colleagues. In 2023, only five Russians ranked among Clarivate's list of the 6,849 most highly cited scientists in the world.[146]

Russia's share of global publications and citations continues to decline.[147] In March 2022 the minister of science and higher education announced that publications in journals listed on Web of Science and Scopus would no longer be prioritized in evaluating Russian scholars' scientific work.[148] Russian scientific journals rank about even with Brazil's for citations and the h-index measure of citations and impact factor. Russia's rank for citations per paper demonstrates a shocking contrast with other countries producing large numbers of research papers.

Russia ranks low in international coauthorship and collaborative projects, although highly cited scientific papers involving Russian authors tend to be the product of collaborative work.[149] In 2021 the United States and Germany were Russia's major partners, accounting for 20 percent of the country's collaborative research projects. By 2024 this figure had been cut nearly in half. Cooperation with most European countries has declined. Collaboration with Chinese colleagues, touted as the new direction for Russian international collaboration, grew from 7.1 percent in 2021 to 7.7 percent in 2022, but declined slightly to 7.4 percent in 2023. Collaborations with colleagues in India have not changed. Overall, Russian scientists are increasingly isolated from most leading research centers.[150] As noted below, Russian punitive action against scientists who have worked with colleagues in what are deemed friendly countries has made collaborative work increasingly risky.

World Intellectual Property Organization (WIPO) data show Russia performing far less efficiently than China in terms of the returns it derives from its investments in R&D for innovation (table 7.A7). This continues a long history of Russian industry lacking the investment capital and infrastructure for producing domestic inventions.[151]

As at educational institutions, the war in Ukraine is generating a plethora of damaging denunciations against specialists. Accusations of treason have been leveled against researchers for collaborating with colleagues abroad, including some against scientists communicating with Iranian and Chinese colleagues. Scientific institutions in Novosibirsk's Akademgorodok, once a thriving bastion of creative activity, have been particularly hard-hit.

In the summer of 2022, two Novosibirsk physicists were arrested. In July, Dmitry Kolker died following his arrest for treason. He was in poor health, battling advanced pancreatic cancer. Kolker died two days after being taken from his apartment and transported to Moscow's Lefortovo prison. His son Maxim believes he was detained because of a lecture he delivered in China in 2018. The case is now closed. The family has demanded investigations into the prosecutor and the judge who authorized his arrest. Colleagues question why a man his age (fifty-four) with a serious illness was dragged to Moscow instead of simply being put under house arrest.[152] In July 2022 Anatoly Maslov, in his mid-seventies, was arrested and charged with treason. He survived two years in custody, despite suffering a heart attack. In May, 2024 the St. Petersburg Appeals Court confirmed a fourteen-year sentence for the seventy-eight-year old physicist.[153]

Sixteen more scientific workers at the Siberian branch of the Academy were arrested in the spring of 2023.[154] The roundup included three scientists who worked on Putin's hyperweapons. They, too, are suspected of treason for sharing information with Chinese colleagues.[155]

Reminiscent of the Stalin era, personal grudges, quotas for prosecutors, or simple bad luck may result in people being imprisoned. One notable difference is that during World War II, the Stalin regime established special prisons where talented scientists and engineers worked on projects to aid the Soviet war effort.[156] A significant breakthrough could earn freedom. Stalin understood that their talent was important. Putin's victims languish or disappear. That the list of victims includes specialists who have worked on some of Putin's most highly publicized priority projects remains a conundrum. In place of R&D achievements, Putin's pardons go to convicted criminals who agree to join the war in Ukraine.

Despite purporting to value education, science, and technology and choosing to acquire an advanced academic credential, Putin's approach to the knowledge economy has been as contradictory as his overall economic policies. Enriching himself and his cronies has been a significant component of priority projects.[157] Funds allocated for education and R&D frequently are purloined or used inefficiently. Incentives are far from adequate.[158]

Putin's value system is perhaps his greatest failure. Boris Yeltsin summarized the problem nicely when he dismissed three close associates, saying, "They took too much and gave too little." Russia is hardly the only country where politicians seek to enrich themselves. Putin has established a system based on extensive predation, and his example has been followed by cronies, their families, and countless government officials.[159]

Funding for science in 2023 was at the level of 2020, representing a reduction of about one-third in real terms.[160] Loss of expertise, technical capacity, and access to essential inputs at Russia's industrial research establishments has received far less attention. Mastering increasingly complex serial production of advanced technology requires long-term collaboration with market leaders. Merely stealing intellectual property is insufficient for producing sophisticated equipment. Know-how is difficult to acquire, and capacity may be lost with stunning rapidity.

Technological Retrogression

A weak capacity for technological innovation has been a persistent feature in imperial Russia, the Soviet Union, and the post-1991 Russian Federation. Exceptions, significant but limited, resulted from creative individuals and/or priority projects in privileged, primarily defense-related sectors.[161] The Soviet Union exported a large amount of basic equipment while importing an increasing volume of more expensive advanced technology.[162]

When the Soviet Union dissolved, crucial technology chains were disrupted. The Soviet regime linked USSR republics and "fraternal" communist nations in Eastern Europe through industrial production dependencies. Personal computer production assigned specific components to each Comecon (Council for Mutual Economic Assistance) country. Pharmaceuticals were primarily from Romania. Within the USSR, engines for helicopters and airplanes were produced at Motor Sich in Ukraine,[163] while Sumgaitmash in Azerbaijan supplied oil and gas well Christmas tree heads.[164] The events of 1989 and 1991 dissolved many of these networks, requiring Russia to rely on imports for key technologies.

Beginning with perestroika after 1985, economic stringency as a result of low oil prices and insider privatization undermined Russia's R&D sector. Gorbachev's efforts to improve science and technology, including providing higher salaries and additional funding, resulted in many new "temporary collectives" that used state resources for their private enterprises.[165] Through the economically troubled 1990s, capacity to manufacture a growing range of critical equipment declined. *Yet it did not disappear.* Russia's legislature, elected in 1990 and dominated by Soviet-era managers and factions opposed to market reforms, refused to permit shuttering factories or making workers redundant. Regional governors enforced these policies to avoid social unrest.

Russia's economic recovery after the 1998 crisis could have provided an opportunity to revive at least some of what remained. This was not deemed a priority.[166]

Reforms in 2000–2003 put Russia's macroeconomic policy and at least part of its legal code on a solid footing, providing favorable conditions for development (see chapter 1). Positive changes were curtailed beginning in 2003, when the Kremlin acted against the Yukos Oil Company and initiated policies of renationalization, renewing emphasis on the state's role in Russia's economy.[167]

The most compelling example of Putin's failure is the energy industry, the sector that he repeatedly touted as key to Russia's development in the twenty-first century. If there is any sector of the economy that a Russian leader bent on territorial aggrandizement should have prioritized for wise policy choices, it is hydrocarbons. As described in chapter 3, Putin did not succeed in making hydrocarbons the basis for a vibrant Russian economy. Russia now faces more serious and growing constraints.

Gazprom, the gigantic majority-state-owned gas enterprise, suffered from malfeasance and policies focused on geopolitics that at times curtailed revenue. Sanctions have revealed the costs of mismanagement. Gazprom reported a loss of about $7 billion in 2023. The coal industry fared even worse in 2024, projecting a deficit of 450 billion rubles, equal to its total profits in 2020 and 2021.[168] Chinese demand for Russian coal has declined significantly.

A disheartening example of the possibilities had Putin created a different environment is the saga of the Rybinsk aircraft engine plant.[169] Renamed UEC Saturn, under the leadership of economist Yuri Lastochkin the enterprise established a partnership with the French firm Snecma. The company developed the capacity to produce engines meeting world standards. UEC Saturn won the tender to build engines for the Sukhoi Superjet 100, Russia's alternative to Canada's Bombardier and Brazil's Embraer regional jets.

In 2007–2008, as UEC Saturn was achieving success, Rostec CEO and long-time Putin crony Sergei Chemezov determined it should become a jewel in his mushrooming Rosoboroneksport/Rostec agglomeration. Lastochkin resisted the takeover. Eventually Putin visited Rybinsk, making it clear that this was an offer Lastochkin could not refuse. Lastochkin attempted to remain with UEC Saturn but found that functioning effectively in the new environment was impossible. After resigning, he ran successfully for mayor of Rybinsk, but his term in office was short. He was incarcerated for corruption, a fate he shared with numerous others who opposed Putin's decisions.[170]

The UEC Saturn case suggests that, given Russia's improving finances, some of the country's surviving technology enterprises could have played a role in reindustrialization. Reporting by the courageous Russian investigative journalists who recounted the case implies that other viable technology firms were stifled through absorption into the massive, crony-controlled holding companies that dominate Russia's defense industry.

Large firms were not the only victims of empire building by Putin associates. Viktor Cherkesov befriended Putin at St. Petersburg University, joined the KGB, and moved to Moscow with Putin. He was disappointed when Putin chose Nikolai Patrushev to head the FSB, consigning Cherkesov to the Federal Drug Control Service. In 2006 Cherkesov sought to raise the service's profile by establishing a monopoly in Russia's chemical and pharmaceutical industries. This was achieved by reclassifying many of the chemicals used in these industries as narcotics. The change led to the destruction of many small and medium-size enterprises (SMEs) as private entrepreneurs were arrested for using substances that were now classified as illegal.[171]

Russia's industrial decline accelerated during Putin's initial years as president, despite the concurrent oil-based economic windfall. Putin's government by 2003 reached a decision similar to the choice made by Leonid Brezhnev: as global oil and gas prices soared, Soviet investment policy prioritized hydrocarbon exports while importing advanced technology.[172] In an article published in 1999, Putin proposed relying on this strategy as the key to rebuilding Russia's entire economy.[173] He has reiterated this policy several times, despite his faith in the military-industrial sector as the source for Russian high technology not being vindicated.

Dependence on imports increased significantly while rising oil prices fueled Russia's economic recovery.[174] Choosing to sell commodities and buy foreign technology resulted in entire industrial sectors becoming reliant on imported equipment, components, and intermediate goods. Putin's virtual economy focused on resource rents without serious attention to moving up the technology ladder.[175] The competitiveness of Russian industry declined fourfold between 1998 and 2015, as use of the most advanced technologies diminished.[176] Putin spoke repeatedly about the need to reduce dependence on technology imports. Yet despite trillions of rubles invested in import substitution after 2013, dependence on imports increased. *The sector most dependent on imports is the oil and gas industry.*[177] In the four years prior to Putin's full-scale attack on Ukraine in 2022, surveys of Russian businesses showed Russia continuing to lose the domestic capacity to manufacture equipment, produce components, and provide needed materials (see table 7.A9).

The list of components and machinery that Russian enterprises *prefer* to import is even more extensive. Despite more than a decade of import substitution efforts, Russian dependence on imports in crucial high-technology sectors has remained overwhelming. Russian state media have repeatedly claimed that 70 percent or more of the technology in many sectors is produced in Russia. Russian business associations report that the 70 percent figure has not changed much over the past two decades.[178] Yet there are situations where having even 99 percent of the required components is not sufficient. In 2022, 15 percent of Russian companies reported they could not acquire necessary machinery from Russian manufacturers or "friendly" countries.[179]

The "for want of a nail" problem remains acute in guidance systems, high-altitude electronics, and other sophisticated systems. Technologies as basic as engine transmissions and reliable tires have proved problematic. In wartime, Russian industry acquires much of the technology it needs through gray markets and "parallel imports."

While Russia may legitimately claim important advances in several fields of natural science, beyond nuclear reactors, Kalashnikov rifles, and Soyuz rockets, it is increasingly challenging to identify technologies where Soviet achievements have been preserved, much less surpassed. When Russian designers manage a breakthrough, serial production often presents overwhelming challenges. Vladimir Putin has repeatedly boasted of developing superweapons that are not matched by anything that exists elsewhere. The best explanation for Russia being alone in developing these hyperweapons is that they are largely hype.[180]

Russian industry continues to produce and export inexpensive basic machinery. Advanced technology is imported, along with components and intermediate goods (table 7.A8). Multiple Russian accounts describe a process of technology regression as the country loses the personnel and equipment necessary to replicate foreign machinery, much less generate innovation.[181]

After Prime Minister Dmitry Medvedev replaced Putin as president in 2008, Russia contracted with the Massachusetts Institute of Technology to create a "Russian Silicon Valley" at Skolkovo, just outside Moscow. The Russian government invested significant resources to build the new facility, including a golf course. Returns have been modest at best. The project failed to attract the anticipated private capital. Despite a requirement that private firms contribute at least half the funding for projects, government support ultimately averaged close to 95 percent.[182] When Putin returned to the presidency in 2012, two new priority projects competed with Skolkovo. One is a new R&D corridor in southwest Moscow involving Putin's younger daughter and her thesis adviser, Moscow State University rector Viktor Sadovnichii. The second project, also involving Putin's daughter, is a military R&D campus located at Anapa on the Black Sea coast. Funding for these competing projects consumes resources needed by existing facilities.[183]

While Putin's return reinforced official emphasis on developing domestic technology, the new programs called for less reliance on foreign help. A decree in late 2013, presaging Crimean annexation, called for import substitution, requiring Russia's defense industry to use domestic components when available.[184] Like many of Putin's edicts, his decrees mandating domestic technology development have generated limited accomplishments.[185]

Russian reliance on imported components and machinery increases directly with the sophistication of the technology involved. This means high costs and high vulnerability to sanctions. Putin cronies have benefited from taking over subsidized enterprises in sectors receiving generous state funding. Poor management, loss of skilled personnel, and corruption have limited their capacity to deliver.[186] Stealing from the state dwarfs the Soviet ethos of stealing for the state.[187] Cutthroat competition exists in acquiring assets, but competition is limited in production, where enormous holding companies monopolize key sectors.[188]

Russian analysts reported that between 2006 and 2013, Russian dependence on imported technology grew rapidly.[189]

- Overall the share of imported inputs for production increased from 8.5 percent to 14.7 percent.
- The share of imported components for communications equipment rose from 7 percent to 22.3 percent.
- The share of imported components for machine building increased from 14.4 percent to 36.5 percent.

- The share of imported electronics for missiles and rockets amounted to 65–79 percent.

Western sanctions in 2014 stimulated Russia to make major investments in import substitution. Despite plentiful funding, some successes, and massive propaganda, the import substitution efforts have failed to reduce Russian dependence on advanced technology imports. After Russia annexed Crimea, studies by independent Russian analysts evaluated Russia's dependence on imported technology and the potential for producing comparable equipment domestically. These projections should have been a warning.[190]

Specialists estimated that import substitution could make it possible for Russia to produce close to 90 percent of required textile machinery but just 20 percent of necessary chemicals, 22 percent of transportation vehicles and equipment, and 34 percent of electrical and optical components. Russian domestic production accounted for 85 percent of cement mixers and 69 percent of off-road vehicles, but a mere 6.5 percent of numerically controlled metal cutting machines and just 1 percent of laser and ultrasound cutters deployed in industrial production.[191]

These analysts gauged the situation remarkably well. Reports by Russian scholars and business organizations at the end of 2022 confirmed the lack of success in developing advanced technology. Despite more than 3 trillion rubles allocated to over 1,500 projects after 2015, in many branches of industry dependence on imports remained at 90 percent or more.[192] Data from 2023 illustrate growing dependence in crucial sectors (table 7.A9).

Russia's civilian enterprises lack the financial resources, components, intermediate goods, and skilled personnel to develop and manufacture a growing variety of high-tech products. Russian defense industry enterprises, despite receiving an influx of new funding, resisted import substitution directly and in a host of less visible ways. Managers and technical staff colluded with government officials to "prove" there were no Russian analogs to the imports.[193] Faced with a choice between failing to meet deadlines to use Russian technology or failing to produce required products, managers calculated that it was safer to rely on imports. They chose correctly. Every deadline set by Putin's government for achieving domestic production of specific products has been extended.[194]

Russian managers' preference for imports is understandable. In addition to reliability, imports solved a host of difficulties. Foreign firms offer extended payment terms at low interest rates. Russia's Finance Ministry requires that equipment be delivered in the budget year it is purchased, but few Russian manufacturers maintain significant stocks of expensive equipment. Lack of inventory means delivery delays are common. Foreign suppliers not only offered credit and on-time delivery (when not stopped by Russian customs officials demanding bribes), but many provided installation and servicing. Some Russian sources hint at kickbacks—Russian purchasing agents benefited from the contracts beyond simply delivering the product. Everyday business in Russia routinely involves side payments for many ordinary transactions, and unsurprisingly, priority projects have higher and often much higher costs.[195]

Despite the sanctions imposed on Russia owing to the war in Ukraine, many businesses continue to insist that they must rely on parallel imports because Russian substitutes are less reliable.

Western sanctions against Russia have been dismissed by many commenters as ineffective. Yet sanctions have delayed or derailed Putin's highest-priority projects. In March 2018, Putin presented an election campaign video featuring six new hyperweapons that would put Russia's military capacity beyond anything the rest of the world could match. Six years later, only one of the six new weapons, the Kinzhal missile, has been produced in any quantity. It has been deployed in Ukraine, with no significant strategic impact. The other five weapons are not ready for deployment. On Victory Day in both 2023 and 2024, the Yars and Iskander missiles, revised versions of Soviet-era weapons, were displayed and touted for their effectiveness in Ukraine. None of the new weapons was displayed.[196]

At about the same time Putin publicized his ostensibly game-changing missiles, Russian industrial policy shifted from the failing import substitution effort to "leasing" and "localization."[197] Neither has generated the hoped-for impact. The leasing model is highly institutionalized in the oil and gas industries. Global services firms provide equipment and maintenance for many companies. Their departure from Russia as a result of sanctions after February 24, 2022, has had a growing impact.

Leasing is widespread in global aviation. After February 24, 2022, the Russian government refused to return hundreds of aircraft leased from foreign companies. This at best represents a short-term solution. Landing these aircraft in countries honoring sanctions risks their confiscation. These illegally seized aircraft will not be serviced by the manufacturers or leasing companies. Replacement parts are available primarily via informal channels or the cannibalization of other aircraft. Third countries that provide these parts to Russia risk secondary sanctions. The situation generates informal supply chains with varying reliability.[198]

As in Soviet times, a growing share of equipment becomes unusable as spare parts are diverted to maintain other aircraft. China is of some help, but most Chinese aircraft have a significant share of imported components.[199] Safety has become an increasingly dire issue in sectors including aviation, rail transport, and trucking. Shifting exports to the Far East has put a serious strain on shipping capacity and road maintenance. Similar problems have appeared in agricultural machinery and other sectors. Russian forces looted food and equipment from territory they occupied in Ukraine in 2022. Subsequently they worked with criminal organizations to steal farm equipment in England and Ireland.[200]

Russian enterprises increasingly have relied on leasing and localizing to circumvent sanctions. Once foreign factories began production in Russia, Russian companies sought to have them "localized" as legal Russian entities.[201] Foreign firms were slow to understand that their Russian "branches" could become competitors. Data on production at these enterprises since February 2022 are scarce. Reports of the extent of parallel imports and sanctions evasion suggest these "Russian" factories are producing some goods, but not fully replacing previous imports.[202] Foreign companies have increasingly found ways to block at least some parallel imports.[203]

Localization was defined with minimal rigor. The preferred model is having a foreign firm build a factory and begin production in Russia, then turn the facility over to Russian control. Ironically, this is precisely what Russian entrepreneurs accused the Chinese of demanding in the early 2000s as a way to acquire proprietary technology. Localization relied on European countries, particularly Italy, Germany, Sweden, and Switzerland, to build the factories Russia needed. The Ukraine war has curtailed these opportunities. Even Switzerland has imposed technology sanctions.

Neither leasing nor localization reduced Russian dependence on imports. In preparing for the 2022 attack on Ukraine and inevitable additional sanctions, attention again focused on import substitution, but Russia now has a far more limited choice of partners. Russian efforts to circumvent sanctions increasingly depend on countries seeking profits rather than partnerships. A Bank of Finland report in late 2023 provided data on the inflated prices Chinese companies demand for equipment sold to Russia.[204] It remains unclear what prices or other rewards the North Koreans have exacted for the arms they provided to Russia.

While some recent studies cite examples of growing Russian capacity in developing technology, in almost every case the developments fail to demonstrate an ability to compete in crucial high-technology sectors. Data provided by Russian manufacturers and government sources is contradicted by surveys of Russian businesses and reports by Russian business associations.

Putin has claimed that Russia is finding new partners. As in the case of new customers for Russian hydrocarbons, these countries are not meeting all of Russia's needs, and some, particularly Turkey and China, have become serious competitors in Russia's domestic markets.

China Disappoints

Before 2022, Russians involved in technology businesses cited substantial benefits derived from cooperation with European firms compared with minimal returns from Chinese collaboration.[205] Sanctions have curtailed, though not entirely eliminated, cooperation with Russian businesses' preferred partners.

While much is made of the close relationship between Putin and Xi Jinping, China has persistently failed to fulfill Russian hopes for significant investment. China's investments in Pakistan dwarf its investments in Russia.[206] Equally important, China lacks the capacity to supply many of the crucial advanced technologies that Russia needs. Transmissions for missile chassis, electronic components hardened against high-altitude radiation, and the most advanced chips are not made in China.

China's impressive success in consumer technologies, from solar panels to EVs, is not evidence of high-technology development. Only one percent of China's high-technology exports come from state-owned enterprises.[207] While this may be changing, the private and foreign-invested enterprises producing advanced technology in China are subject to secondary sanctions if their products are sent to Russia. The same is true for Chinese financial institutions underwriting trade. New sanctions introduced in late 2023 and early 2024 have disrupted the payment systems crucial to conducting Sino-Russian trade.[208] From December 31, 2022 to December 31, 2024, the ruble depreciated against the Chinese renminbi by nearly 30 percent.

Climbing the technology ladder generally requires capacity in basic research. This has not been a Chinese strength. Yet few Chinese now go to Russia to study science, suggesting they have concluded the Soviet reputation for excellence in fundamental research is now history.[209] China is an increasingly important science and technology partner for Russia, but Russia plays a minor role in Chinese scientific collaboration.[210] Russia's Academy of Sciences provided an assessment of the leading nations in technology sectors as of 2017. America dominates, Russia ranked in the top five only in military/security technology, and China was not a leader in high technology.[211] These assumptions continue to influence Russian expert opinion despite evidence that China is developing increasing capacity in some high-tech sectors.

Despite repeated claims in Russian and Western media, there is limited evidence that China is helping Russia evade sanctions beyond what is legal. China is not a signatory to the sanctions regime. Increasing use of secondary sanctions has limited the willingness of major banks and corporations to aid Russia directly. In many cases, less reliable firms have filled the gaps, sometimes providing inferior or defective products. China has been buying Russian hydrocarbons at a discount while selling Russians vehicles, mobile phones, electronics, and other products at prices that are inflated yet often undercut Russian competitors. Technology imports from China are accelerating Russia's deindustrialization.

Some Chinese companies have developed ways to circumvent the sanctions, but this does not guarantee a stable supply chain.[212]

Sanctions' Impact

Russia's leaders have belittled the impact of sanctions while simultaneously blaming sanctions for Russia's economic difficulties. The contradiction inherent in this rhetoric has not received enough attention. Some Western sources report, and sometimes seem to take delight in describing, the extent to which Russia has managed to evade restrictions. The situation requires a broader context. At least five questions should be part of the discussion:

- Would so many accounts of sanctions evasion be appearing if Russia's own import substitution efforts were even moderately effective?
- Will Russian industry and other sectors remain equally reliant on imports or become even more dependent after the war ends?
- Does the size of Russia's domestic market make it impossible for Russian companies to achieve economies of scale that would allow them to compete with imports?

- To what extent have Chinese and other foreign producers garnered enough market share and brand loyalty to be positioned to dominate Russian markets in the future? Some European and other foreign businesses have increased their efforts to sell goods to Russia via third countries as a way to secure their own place in the postwar Russian market, creating additional challenges for Russian companies.
- What impact will the declining ruble exchange rate have on Russia's capacity to continue paying for crucial technology imports in the future?

Parallel imports and illicit transactions demonstrate Russian capacity to obtain some, and sometimes much, of what they need. Yet informal channels have serious limitations. Parallel imports from third countries are not covered by manufacturers' warranties, which are valid only in the country that initially imported the product. Defects or repairs in Russia are not covered. Replacing worn or damaged parts can be challenging. Russian government agencies review the technical documentation that must accompany imports. The requirements are particularly stringent in the defense industry, but parallel imports often lack the required documentation. At best, side payments solve the problem, but the risks are significant. Delivery delays were frequent even before the war.[213]

Illicit supply routes generally are more expensive. Russians boast that they can buy washing machines, laptop computers, or vehicles from China and remove the chips to use elsewhere. These solutions inflate prices while failing to guarantee reliability. When the volume of chips from China more than doubled after February 24, 2022, the proportion of defective chips increased from 10 percent to 40 percent. Sanctions caused many regular suppliers to cease exports to Russia, while the alternative sources proved less reliable.[214]

Smuggling requires obtaining product, moving it using covert methods, and bribing customs officials. There are no assurances that crucial items will be available when, where, and in the quantity needed. Espionage and the black market are not reliable alternative supply chains. Sanctions violations have resulted in fines and prison terms. For complex technology, the efficacy of stealing information without personnel who know how to use it remains limited.

Russia has assembled a "ghost fleet" of tankers to transport the hydrocarbon cargoes that are no longer insured by major international firms. Russia's ships manage some successful deliveries. Whether this represents a long-term solution remains an open question. No amount of shipping can replace the volume of gas exports Russia sent to Europe via the now unusable Nord Stream pipelines. Maintenance, reliability, cost, and the threat of detection will continue to present challenges. So will safety. The ghost ships derive their name from shutting off systems broadcasting their location. Higher prices could support Russia's efforts, but oil prices are always volatile. Tightening sanctions is persistently under discussion.[215]

Most European countries have adjusted reasonably well to life without Russian oil and gas. New suppliers have been identified, while growth in renewables has accelerated. China is now Russia's most important hydrocarbon customer, but China is also a leading global producer of solar and wind equipment, EVs, and other green technologies. In 2024 a Chinese firm launched the world's first battery-powered container ship.[216] If the International Energy Agency is correct in projecting a surplus of oil and gas in global markets by the late 2020s, China's need for Russian hydrocarbons could be far less. China has reduced its purchases of Russian coal.

If Russia failed to build domestic capacity in technology industries when commodity prices were high and OECD nations were willing to help, the situation is not likely to improve under wartime conditions and sanctions. Most Russian manufacturing is not globally competitive, enabling Chinese, Iranian, Turkish, and other foreign firms to gain market share in Russia. Chinese firms have increasingly opened their own stores to sell their merchandise in Russia.[217]

Countersanctions imposed by Russia in response to Western policy have had a greater negative impact on the Russian population than on "enemy" economies.[218] U.S. officials focused sanctions on key individuals and industrial sectors in ways designed to be cumulative. Russian media, the blogosphere, and reports from the business community bemoan a significant and growing impact from the sanctions. Partial solutions and informalization will impair Russia's capacity to restore "normal" economic activity in the future.

Putin's government continues to view the defense industry as *the* source of innovation but also has adopted policies to stimulate greater R&D collaboration between the prioritized defense industry and private companies.

One effort involves encouraging SMEs to work with state conglomerates. This is challenging, requiring integration of significantly different business cultures and structures while coping with issues Russian SMEs face, including rising prices, shrinking markets, labor shortages, difficulties accessing components, and demands from government agencies with differing vested interests.[219]

Foreign investment in Russian technology enterprises was limited even before 2014. Fisher provides detailed data on declining FDI in chapter 2. Sanctions have increasingly constrained investors and sellers. Putin's solution has been for state enterprises to develop dual-use technology, relieving pressure on the government budget by mandating that 50 percent of defense enterprise production consist of products for the civilian market. This approach resembles the Soviet "defense conversion" program developed in the 1980s. It faces similar challenges as the war necessitates increased defense production.[220]

The demographic constraints discussed above are causing serious difficulties in Russia's wartime military enterprises. Media accounts report that at some factories operating three shifts for round-the-clock arms production, workers are averaging far more than forty hours per week. At some plants, the average workweek is sixty to seventy hours, indicating that workers work one and one-half shifts. Instead of overtime pay, they are required to make "voluntary" contributions to the "special military operation."[221]

In the USSR, military enterprises performed somewhat better than the civilian sector not only by being a separate entity receiving more generous funding, with some situated in closed "monotowns," but also by appropriating the best-quality production from the civilian sector. As technology has become more complicated, this is less effective. No Russian enterprise produces significant volumes of advanced processors or chips.[222]

Technology Trauma

Beyond the energy sector, Russian weaknesses are particularly pronounced in IT, electronics, machine tools, and other sectors requiring sophisticated technology.[223]

As Russian troops moved to the Ukrainian border in 2021, the Russian government sought to reduce if not eliminate dependence on foreign chips and software, including operating systems. Leading engineering schools were instructed to use Russian hardware and software, which meant that all of the equipment and programs would need to be produced in Russia.[224]

The plan was for Russia's Baikal and El'brus processors to be fabricated by TSMC, and for Russian engineers to develop the required software. Sanctions rendered the TSMC option impossible. Russian companies have repeatedly insisted that they need more time to develop the software. Far from delivering in 2022, the time frames have slipped to 2025–2027. Many Russian IT personnel have expressed concerns about the demands, recognizing that rejecting foreign systems would cut them off from participating in global technology development. The technical challenges of creating new operating systems and security programs compatible with both existing and new software have proved particularly daunting.[225]

As the situation in IT indicates, electronic components remain a serious problem. Open-source information about satellites and guidance systems is limited, requiring caution in making assessments. Published accounts indicate weaknesses in electronics have been a significant impediment to developing key systems.

One serious casualty has been satellite production for GLONASS, Russia's satellite positioning/navigation system. The initial GLONASS system used low-altitude satellites. Replacing them with high-altitude satellites would expand the area each could cover, halving the number needed. The cost savings and reduced need for imported electronic components would be significant. But high-altitude systems require radiation-hardened integrated circuits (RHICs).[226] In 2018 both Russia and China obtained RHICs from a Texas businessman who was subsequently incarcerated for violating sanctions.[227] On another occasion, a Chinese firm sold the Russians supposedly hardened components that quickly failed.[228] The latest proposal is a new partnership of GLONASS with Gazprom Space Systems to build a new low-orbit GPS system. The initial stage will be seventy-eight low-orbit satellites, with plans for three hundred low-orbit satellites by the end of 2027. Covering the entire planet would require a larger number of higher-altitude satellites and cost 150 billion rubles, a price that is currently prohibitive.[229]

Fraud

Russian media have increasingly reported malfeasance in import substitution efforts. Abuse has been particularly prevalent in the defense sector, given the volume of funding available.[230]

One well-publicized case was particularly embarrassing for Vladimir Putin. During a televised visit to a defense plant in Kazan, Putin was shown a machine tool purchased from another Russian enterprise, hailed as successful import substitution. Knowledgeable viewers quickly identified the equipment as Italian machinery purchased by a Russian company in Moscow oblast, repainted, and sold in Kazan for more than double the original price.[231]

The Kazan case was hardly an outlier.[232] Inept and predatory business practices were described in the design, delays, and quite limited production of Armata tanks[233] and mobile missile chassis. The latter involved both failure to acquire the technology from Belarus and Russia's own problems.[234] Putin's 2018 media performance demonstrating threatening new hyperweapons aroused concerns that have not been justified. Most of the new, supposedly unique weapons systems do not yet exist, are still being tested, or have been produced in small numbers.[235]

The Sarmat hypersonic missile, Putin's "unstoppable" weapon, illustrates both venality and import dependence. Initially announced in 2015 as a replacement for the Soviet-era R-36 (named SS-18 "Satan" by NATO), Sarmat development was delayed when sanctions prevented the purchase of crucial American chips.[236] A flight test finally was scheduled in 2019, more than a year after Putin showcased Sarmat. Three billion rubles were allocated for a test launch. One-third of the funds disappeared within twenty-four hours via a labyrinth of opaque electronic transfers.[237] A successful flight test finally was conducted in April 2022, and Russian media announced that "serial production" had begun at the end of that year.

However, a second test in 2023 failed. It is not clear whether this was due to problems with electronics or to other difficulties. Russian defense industry standards require far more successful flight tests before approving a new missile for deployment. Full evaluation usually requires a year *after* at least six successful flight tests. Yet Russian media continued to report that serial production was underway. Initial plans for serial production of the Sarmat projected six to seven missiles per year through 2027.[238] Subsequent flight tests failed, including one in September 2024 that damaged the test launch facility. Since the Voevoda (the heavy missile Sarmat is supposed to replace) has not flown for a decade, Russia's heavy-missile program is in an uncertain status.[239]

In sum, Russia's technology capacity has been seriously degraded by Putin's policies, leaving the country highly vulnerable to sanctions. While Putin insists that sanctions are making Russia stronger, evidence from the technology sector demonstrates acute failure. Putin clearly acknowledged this at the St. Petersburg International Economic Forum in June 2023. He suggested that Russia should adopt supply-side economics in hydrocarbon production, focusing on creating demand inside Russia. A long article in *Ekspert* reporting on Putin's speech made a similar argument.[240]

Conclusion

Putin has failed to foster a sustainable increase in the Russian population's size, health, life expectancy, educational quality, or economic and environmental security. Despite spending trillions of rubles on import substitution and technology development, he has failed to create a Russian military capable of achieving the promised "short, victorious" conquest of a country with one-third the population and one-eighth the GDP of Russia. Putin's record in fostering the human capital and knowledge economy crucial to guaranteeing Russia's future as a major power is an unmitigated disaster. Regardless of how the war in Ukraine ends, the accumulated challenges will persist for decades, as Russia faces an expanded NATO alliance while relying on partners whose relationships are transactional rather than genuinely collaborative.

Before February 24, 2022, Russia was experiencing a demographic decline accelerated by the world's worst per capita COVID-19 mortality rate. Russia now hemorrhages talented human capital with scant potential for replacement. The education and health care systems were underfunded and deteriorating before the war. Mobilization has created massive disruptions in all Russian institutions. Russian science, in decline for decades, now is severed from interaction with most of the world's leading research centers. The hydrocarbon industries that fuel Russia's economy face increasingly serious challenges as equipment ages and replacement is difficult. Even before the war, Russia's technology capacity increasingly evoked the 1950s rather than the twenty-first century.[241] The Novosibirsk scholars who reported this would not have been surprised by Russia now relying on tanks manufactured more than half a century ago.

If neither the quantity nor the quality of human capital will bolster Russia's economy in the next two decades, the remaining hope is greater productivity derived from technology. Could there be some breakthrough or technological revolution that might change the trajectory? While surprises should not be ruled out, the history of technology includes few examples of any research group moving significantly beyond the existing knowledge frontier. This explains the many instances of disputed simultaneous discoveries.[242]

The danger that continuing reliance on imports will further undermine Russia's domestic industrial potential does not appear to be a serious concern for President Putin. Chinese firms are gaining market share in key sectors. Former CIA director William Burns was correct in suggesting that Russia's future is likely to be as a resource colony for China.[243] Yet China may need fewer of those resources in the future. Putin until recently ignored China's emergence as a major producer of renewable energy technologies. As urban development and climate change reduce arable farmland, China's greatest need will be more land for agriculture. Chinese museums feature maps showing the territory seized by Russia in the seventeenth, eighteenth, and nineteenth centuries.[244] Putin's good friend Xi Jinping insists Chinese maps include the Chinese names of former Chinese territory, along with the new (perhaps temporary?) Russian appellations.

Agriculture is driving one of the few sources of new migrants to Russia as Chinese are again arriving in the Far East in significant numbers. This time they are attracted not by trade or higher pay but rather by opportunities in agriculture. As Russians leave eastern regions in search of better lives or to become cannon fodder in Ukraine, Chinese are acquiring land through Russian front men and are farming soybeans and other crops needed to feed China.[245] The post-1991 pattern of local residents protesting the Chinese incursions while local officials and Moscow elites reap economic benefits has reappeared.

On the eve of the Ukraine war, Russian analysts reported that Russia's economy had lost 0.5 percent of GNP because of the declining quality of human capital. This included "worsening health, education and declining levels of professional skills."[246] Disruptions from the "special military operation" have amplified these problems. As mobilization removes men from the labor force and drives a massive exodus, specialists and skilled workers are increasingly scarce. The Putin regime's policies are curtailing the availability of foreign labor. Wages have soared to levels that may be unsustainable when the war ends.

In the first year of the war, the sectors facing the greatest labor shortages were construction and agriculture, which rely heavily on migrant labor. By mid-2023, the defense industry faced a shortage of 50,000 specialists. In

May 2023, Ekaterina Ponomareva, personnel director at Finbridge Financial Services, stated, "Today, when many of the factors favorable for economic growth are exhausted, human capital is our most valuable economic resource."[247] Another Russian analysis in mid-2023 foresees bleak prospects for Russia's "most valuable economic resource":

> We can state with a high degree of confidence that the stock of human capital in Russia has already been reduced due to departure of qualified personnel. The education and health care systems face new constraints that will hinder further accumulation of human capital. The prospects for a return to previous incentives and possibilities remain dim.[248]

The unevenness of Russia's economic growth described by Sergei Guriev in chapter 1 has been magnified by wartime policies. Growth *doubled* in the years 1999–2008. For the period 2009–2021, *total* growth was only 15 percent.[249]

In July 2024 Sergei Kirienko, first deputy chief of staff in the presidential administration, stated publicly what a growing number of Russia watchers have been saying. The Ukraine war is doing more than the conflicts in Afghanistan, Chechnya, Georgia, and Syria to alter Russian society.[250] The soldiers who survive their extended terms fighting in Ukraine are returning with serious emotional and psychological damage. The criminals who return were hardly model citizens, and many are reverting to their pre-incarceration behavior. Some are forming new criminal organizations. Many of the mercenaries who have been promised citizenship if they get out of Ukraine alive are not ethnic Russians. If they are permitted to enjoy the promised citizenship they are likely to have larger families, making Russia less Slavic and less Russian Orthodox.

Improvements in Russian economic performance require major investments in education, health, programs to enhance skills for those already in the labor force, and the R&D infrastructure essential for developing key technologies. These long-term needs compete with funding the current war and social programs. In an increasingly challenging budget environment, it will be impossible to satisfy all claimants. Thus far, choices continue to favor Putin's cronies. At some point, Russians may finally demand an accounting for these failures.

Table 7.A1. Russia Historical Population Data, 1985–2024

Year	Population	Population growth rate (%)
2024	143,957,079	−0.34
2023	144,444,359	−0.19
2022	144,713,314	−0.27
2021	145,102,755	−0.35
2020	145,617,329	−0.09
2019	145,472,286	0.06
2018	145,652,293	0.14
2017	145,452,536	0.24
2016	145,109,157	0.30
2015	144,668,389	0.27
2014	144,285,070	0.23
2013	143.956,866	0.23
2012	143,629,362	0.18
2011	143,364.543	0.09
2010	143,242,599	0.06
2009	143,163,643	0.05
2008	143,086,549	−0.02
2007	143,117,693	−0.15
2006	143,338,669	−0.32
2005	143,800,049	−0.38
2004	144,353,636	−0.41
2003	144,946,723	−0.44
2002	145,590,136	−0.44
2001	146,235,530	−0.41
2000	146,844,839	−0.33
1999	147,336,388	−0.23
1998	147,672,728	−0.18
1997	147,939,972	−0.20
1996	148,233,411	−0.22
1995	148,557,451	−0.18
1994	148,829,113	−0.05
1993	148,897,270	0.12
1992	148,725,601	0.18
1991	148,455,402	0.30
1990	148,005,704	0.45
1989	147,341,508	0.60
1988	146,464,378	0.79
1987	145,312,019	0.88
1986	144,046,482	0.80
1985	142,896,392	0.71

Source: Macrotrends.net (macrotrends.net/countries/RUS/russia/population). Used by permission of Macrotrends. Data for 2024 are as of August 2024.

Table 7.A2. Russian Birth Rates and Total Fertility Rates

Year	Birth rate	Change (%)	Rosstat TFR	Change (%)	Reliable TFR
2023	11.329	−2.48	1.825	0.05	1.45
2022	11.617	−2.42	1.824	0.05	1.50
2021	11.905	−2.37	1.823	0.05	1.50
2020	12.194	0	1.823	0.05	1.50
2019	12.194	−4.51	1.822	0.05	1.50
2018	12.770	−0.33	1.821	1.39	1.60
2017	12.812	−0.33	1.796	1.35	1.60
2016	12.854	−0.33	1.772	1.43	
2015	12.897	−0.32	1.747	1.39	
2014	12.939	−0.32	1.723	1.47	
2013	12.981	2.46	1.723	1.47	
2012	12.669	2.52	1.650	3.06	
2011	12.357	2.60	1.601	3.09	
2010	12.044	2.66	1.553	3.26	
2009	11.732	2.37	1.504	3.30	
2008	11.420	2.90	1.456	2.25	
2007	11.098	2.99	1.424	2.23	
2006	10.776	3.07	1.393	2.35	
2005	10.455	3.18	1.361	2.33	
2004	10.133	3.20	1.330	2.47	
2003	9.811	1.87	1.298	0.78	
2002	9.631	1.90	1.288	0.78	
2001	9.451	1.93	1.278	0.87	
2000	9.272	1.98	1.267	0.80	
1999	9.092	2.02	1.257	0.80	
1998	8.912	−4.17	1.247	−4.59	
1997	9.300	−4.00	1.307	−4.32	
1996	9.688	−2.85	1.366	−4.21	
1995	10.076	−3.71	1.426	−3.97	
1994	10.426	−3.58	1.485	−3.88	
1993	10.852	−8.94	1.545	−6.93	
1992	11.917	−8.20	1.660	−6.48	
1991	12.982	−7.59	1.775	−6.13	

Source: Compiled by the author using UN data, usually based on official Rosstat reporting. The "Reliable TFR" data for years after 2015 are from the World Bank (https://data.worldbank.org/indicator/SP.DYN.TFRT.IN?locations=RU). Russia's new, five-pronged National Demography Project aims for a TFR of 1.6 by 2030 and 1.8 by 2035.

Notes: Table shows percent change year over year. The birth rate shows total births each year per 1,000 population. The percent change is year over year. The total fertility rate (TFR) represents births per woman each year. The rate considered necessary to maintain population size (replacement) is 2.1. The Russian SSR reached that level in 1987 and 1988.

For the years after 2016 (shaded area), TFR data represent UN estimates, with no attempt to adjust for the effects of COVID-19.

Table 7.A3. Russian Life Expectancy at Birth

Year	Value	Year	Value
1988	69.13	2004	65.39
1989	68.62	2005	65.83
1990	68.11	2006	66.26
1991	67.60	2007	66.70
1992	67.09	2008	67.14
1993	66.58	2009	67.77
1994	66.40	2010	68.39
1995	66.23	2011	69.02
1996	66.05	2012	69.64
1997	65.88	2013	70.27
1998	65.70	2014	70.67
1999	65.55	2015	71.08
2000	65.40	2016	71.48
2001	65.25	2017	71.89
2002	65.10	2018	72.29
2003	*64.95 (Low point)*	2019	72.43
		2020	72.57
		2021	72.70
		2022	72.84
		2023	72.98
		2030	*73.97 (Projected)*
		2050	*77.02*
		2099	*83.62*

Source: Compiled by the author with data from https://www.macrotrends.net/countries/RUS/russia/life-expectancy and using UN World Population Prospects. Data from Macrotrends, used by permission.

Note: The break between years 2003 and 2004 indicates a shift from a decline to an increase in life expectancy. The data for 2022 and 2023 are what Russia reported. Their accuracy is not confirmed. The projections beyond 2023 do not take into account combat deaths or injuries. Russian demographer Rakshev estimates that official Russian data omit about 40 percent of the war casualties (personal communications with colleagues).

Table 7.A4. Number of Students in Higher Education per 10,000 Population

Decadal, 1950–51 to 2010–11		Annual, 2011–12 to 2023–24	
1950–51	77	2011–12	454
1960–61	124	2012–13	424
1970–71	204	2013–14	393
1980–81	219	2014–15	356
1990–91	190	2015–16	325
2000–01	324	2016–17	300
2010–11	493	2017–18	289
		2018–19	284
		2019–20	277
		2020–21	277
		2021–22	278
		2022–23	282
		2023–24	

Source: *Rossiiskii statisticheskii ezhegodnik*, an open-source statistical handbook, various years.

Table 7.A5. Number of Higher Education Institutions in Russia

Year	Total (N)	State (%)	Students (%)	Private (N)
1970–71	457			
1980–81	494			
1985–86	502			
1990–91	514			
1991–92	519			
1992–93	535			
1993–94	626	548 (88)		78
1994–95	710	553 (78)	96	157
1995–96	762	569 (75)	95	193
1996–97	817	573 (70)	94	244
1997–98	880	578 (66)		302
1998–99	914	580 (64)		334
1999–00	939	590 (63)		349
2001–02	965	607 (63)	90	358
2003–04	1044	652 (63)		392
2005–06	1068	655 (61)	85	413
2007–08	1108	658 (59)		450
2009–10	1114	662 (59)		452
2010–11	1115	653 (59)	83	462
2011–12	1080	634 (59)	84	446
2012–13	1046	609 (58)	85	437
2013–14	969	578 (59)	84	391
2014–15	950	548 (58)	85	402
Start of massive contraction				
2015–16	896	530 (59)	88	366
2016–17	818			
2017–18	766			
2018–19	741			
2019–20	724		99	229
2020–21	710	497 (70)	99	213

Source: Data from *Rossiiskii statisticheskii ezhegodnik*, an open-source statistical handbook, various years.

Note: The number of institutions does not include branches. Discrepancies in the data in tables 7.A5 and 7.A6 are because the Rosstat data are based on the beginning of the school year, while other sources use data from January 1. There are also differences in which institutions are included. Some small online institutions are listed at postupi.online but not in the official Rosstat publications. Data were not available for some years in the early 2000s.

Table 7.A6. Reduction in the Number of Higher Education Institutions, 2014–2024

Type of institution	January 2014	January 2018
State	567	484
State branches (*filialyi*)	908	428
Nonstate (private)	371	178
Nonstate branches	422	81
Total	2,268	1,171

Source: Makeeva (2018).

Note: For the years 2018–2021, data on total number of institutions are as follows: 2018: 998; 2019: 1,057; 2020: 1,080; 2021: 1,096 (Source: Ditkovskiy et al., *Science and Technology Indicators in the Russian Federation*, 2023). Data for 2024 are from Postupi.online (2024: "Куда поступать: Число вузов: актуальная цифра в 2024") and are as follows: 1,056 total, of which 853 were state and 203 were private.

Table 7.A7. WIPO Global Innovation Rankings, Russia and China, 2016 and 2021

	2016		2021	
Efficiency	China	Russia	China	Russia
Input subindex	29	44	25	43
Output subindex	15	47	7	52
Efficiency ratio rank	7	69	—	—

Source: Data from WIPO (https://www.wipo.int/en/web/global-innovation-index).

Note: The WIPO index annually provides data ranking each country on a number of indicators, including efficiency. The efficiency rankings include subindexes for inputs and outputs, as well as an overall ranking of efficiency based on calculations of outputs relative to inputs. What is notable here is that China is one of the few countries that receive significantly higher ranking for outputs compared to inputs. Russia consistently ranks lower in outputs compared to inputs, and the differential has increased over time. Russia moved up from forty-fourth in inputs to forty-third, but dropped from forty-seventh place to fifty-second in outputs.

WIPO did not provide the efficiency ratio rankings for 2021, as indicated by dashes. Data for the war years are not reliable.

Table 7.A8. Russia Trade Data, 2021 (Percent of Exports and Imports)

Product	Exports (%)	Imports (%)
Food products and agricultural raw materials	7.3	11.7
Mineral products	56.4	1.9
Chemical products, rubber	7.7	18.5
Wood and pulp-paper products	3.4	1.4
Textiles, textile products, and footwear	0.4	6.4
Metals, precious stones, and products made with them	16.8	7.4
Machinery, equipment, and vehicles	6.5	48.6
Other goods	1.5	4.1

Source: *Torgovlia v Rossii* (2023): 151 Russia/NIS Statistical Publications. EastView.

Note: For a more detailed breakdown of specific products, see WorldsTopExports.com.

Table 7.A9. Increase in Russian Import Dependence: A Comparison of 2018 and 2022

Type of import	2018 (%)	2022 (%)
Machinery and equipment		
Using imports, Russian analogs available	37	30
Using imports, no Russian analogs	8	**39**
Details, components, assemblies		
Using imports, Russian analogs available	41	27
Using imports, no Russian analogs	9	**34**
Raw materials, materials		
Using imports, Russian analogs available	43	20
Using imports, no Russian analogs	19	**31**

Source: Simachev et al. (2023), 17.

Note: Bold indicates an increasing independence on imports in this sector.

NOTES

Multiple iterations of the material in this chapter have been improved by generous advice from many colleagues, including Marjorie Mandelstam Balzer, Chris Bort, Jonathan Coopersmith, Paul Goble, Thane Gustafson, Robert Otto, Valerie Sperling, and two reviewers for Brookings Institution Press.

1. Wright and Celusta (2002) present a strong case for the natural resource sector as the initial driver of technology development. Putin's policies closely resemble the wasteful policies described in Ascher (1999).

2. Balzer (2017), 113–61.

3. Putin began to talk about the serious need to address Russia's demographic challenges while serving as prime minister, but it took six years to take action. *Rossiiskaia gazeta* (2007). The 2007 demography program was overseen by the same agency monitoring national projects. It became a national project in 2018, with an expanded portfolio (https://национальныепроекты.рф/projects/demografiya/).

4. Radio Free Europe / Radio Liberty (2024); Kremlin.ru (2024).

5. This section draws on three excellent studies: Khasanova et al. (2019), Twigg (2021), and Eberstadt (2022).

6. Gorbacheva and Skorobogatyi (2024).

7. Nicholas Eberstadt, personal communication.

8. Comparing the UN data on Russian birth rates and fertility rates illustrates the issue. The UN data show an increase in the fertility rate *every year* from 1998 to 2022. The data on *birth rates* show increases each year from 1998 to 2013, but then an annual decline in births each year from 2014 to 2023 (see table 7.A2).

9. Balzer (2003a).

10. Putin (2000).

11. For example, in August 2000 the nuclear-powered *Kursk* submarine sank as the result of an explosion onboard, killing all hands.

12. Putin (2006).

13. Khasanova et al. (2019), 6–8.

14. Ibid.

15. Temkina and Zdravomyslova (2008). For recent confirmation of the persistent problem, see Yusopova (2024).

16. Khasanova et al. (2019), 8–12.

17. Ibid.

18. The initial Russian program centered on payments to women for having children. The money could be used for education, housing, or retirement funds. In early 2023, Prime Minister Mishustin announced that the program would provide a subsidy for all needy families. Government.ru (2023).

19. Markov and Alekseeva (2019).

20. Eberstadt (2022), 9.

21. Khasanova et al. (2019), 8.
22. Ibid., 12.
23. Kurmanaev and Bodyagina (2024).
24. Eberstadt (2022), 12.
25. Intellinews.com (2024).
26. Eberstadt (2022), 4.
27. Twigg (2021), 100.
28. Abuses have been covered extensively in Russian media and more than a dozen shocking examples have been confirmed in personal communications.
29. Aminov et al. (2022).
30. Kostarnova (2023), 5.
31. L'vova cited in Kostarnova and Rakitina (2023a), 5.
32. Averbakh (2024). Deputy Chair of the Duma Irina Iarovaia is a strong supporter. Her name is associated with the legislation adopted in 2016 requiring telecommunications companies to retain information about phone calls, messages, and other communications for at least six months and granting the security services access to this information. It has been used to indict people for "extremism" and has been deployed against a number of religious groups. If the legislation is adopted, anyone suggesting girls should not have large families could be accused of extremism.
33. Kostarnova (2024).
34. Kostarnova and Rakitina (2023b), 5.
35. Balzer (2003a).
36. Ibid.
37. Iliyasov (2024).
38. Eberstadt (2022), 14–21.
39. Khasanova et al. (2019), 25–36.
40. Avdeeva (2022); Khasanova et al. (2019), 8.
41. Eberstadt (2022), 21.
42. A retired U.S. Army colonel has been working with the Ukrainian military since the war began. In daily reports he states that in Russia's summer 2024 offensive, Russian casualties averaged about one thousand per day.
43. Eberstadt (2022), 16.
44. Ibid., 7.
45. Twigg (2021), 106.
46. Eberstadt (2022), 16.
47. Ibid., 19.
48. Sukhankin (2024).
49. Kucherenko (2024).
50. On the role of "hero projects" in Soviet and post-Soviet policy, see Josephson (2024).
51. Khasanova et al. (2019), 47–49.

52. Ibid., 50.
53. Ibid., 50.
54. Shcherbakova (2024).
55. Ibid.
56. Re: Russia (2023).
57. Ibid.
58. Bisenov (2023).
59. Latypova (2023); Baranovskaya (2023).
60. Gabdullina (2023).
61. Gabdullina (2024), 3.
62. Ibid.
63. Zoria (2023), 4; Leiba and Veretennikova (2023).
64. Sharma and Gettleman (2023); *Moscow Times* (2024).
65. Topol (2024).
66. Kozlova (2024).
67. Gabdullina and Chernykh (2024), 5.
68. Belousov (2024).
69. Chupik (2024); Tiazhlov (2024), 1.
70. Gabdullina (2024), 3.
71. Veretennikova (2024).
72. Solov'eva (2022); Herbst and Erofeev (2019).
73. Aminov et al. (2022).
74. *Bloomberg News* (2024); Balzer (2024), 13.
75. Balzer (2020), 130–31.
76. Personal communications shared with the author.
77. Solov'eva (2022).
78. Aminov et al. (2022).
79. Ibid.
80. Snegovaya (2023).
81. Personal communications with Russians who left the country. The desire to leave the country remains significant. Uzhvak (2023).
82. Personal communications.
83. Frydlewsky and Forero (2023).
84. Balzer (2020), 141. Brain gain refers to immigration into the country by highly qualified specialists. Brain circulation refers to specialists who work in more than one country, moving back and forth for fixed periods.
85. Kirby and Drenon (2024).
86. Volchkova and Kuznetsova (2019).
87. Along with the rising share of food products in total wholesale trade, in late August 2023 consumers had shifted to purchasing smaller or larger packages of food products in an effort to avoid waste or stretch food budgets. See Rakitina (2023), 7.

88. Twigg (2021), 117.
89. Mukhina (2019).
90. Grey, Bush, and Anin (2014).
91. Komrakov (2023).
92. Twigg (2021), 115.
93. Ibid., 111.
94. Ibid., 111. Most of the MDR and XDR infections originate in prisons. Deploying convicts as soldiers in Ukraine could alter this equation. Mobilized convicts who survive their military service and return to Russia could spread these dangerous variants.
95. Shishkin et al. (2022); Schetnaia palata (2023).
96. Klepach and Luk'ianenko (2023).
97. One horror story involves Epi-Vax, a vaccine developed at the Vector Lab in Novosibirsk, infamous for Soviet bioweapons research. Created with the support of (and investment from) a high official in the Ministry of Health, Epi-Vax was touted as the "elite" vaccine. It took more than two years for Russian officials to finally admit it was useless (personal communications). Another stunning revelation is a reference to the need to restore ambulance service. Klepach and Luk'ianenko (2023), 87.
98. Ibid., 82. The number in Russia was 2,323 per million. Italy counted 1,618; the United States 1,481; Germany 473.
99. Ibid., 84.
100. Balzer (2021a), 74.
101. Reddaway (1946), 189–92.
102. Balzer (2003b). A recent issue of *Europe-Asia Studies* (75, no. 2, 2023) is devoted to social policy.
103. A new history was produced rapidly to present the Kremlin's view of the war in Ukraine. It has received scathing reviews. Kovalov (2023); Poliak (2023).
104. Personal communications. See also Marokhovskaya and Dolinina (2022).
105. Dergacheva (2024). For a valuable listing of the ongoing attacks on Russian academic institutions, see "Khroniki presledovaniia uchenykh" (Chronicles of the persecution of scholars) at https://www.t-invariant.org/category/timeline/. The author served on the International Advisory Committee for the department for several years and was a member of the European University Board of Trustees for more than a decade. He received an honorary doctor of sciences degree from the university.
106. Balzer (1990), 289–305.
107. Bailes (1978).
108. Roshchin (2023). For coverage of the critical content, see Astapenkova (2023).
109. Author's personal email communications with former Russian professors.

110. Makeeva (2018).
111. Liubimov, Lysiuk, and Gvozdeva (2018).
112. Akindinova, Kuz'minov, and Iasin (2016), 29.
113. Balzer (2020), 142.
114. Pavel (Pavlik) Morozov became a Soviet hero for turning in his father for corrupt behavior. After his father was executed, Pavel was killed by his family, and they were also executed. Pavel's heroism became a major Stalinist propaganda effort that included songs, stories, and even a full-length opera. Research during perestroika and after 1991 has convincingly shown that most of the account was fiction.
115. OECD (2021).
116. Higher School of Economics (2018), 18.
117. The Soviet system of higher education admitted students for a five-year program after eleven years of general education. The most common advanced degree was the candidate of science, usually based on three years of research to produce a dissertation. The highest degree, a doctor of science, resembled the French or German thesis, usually written by a senior scholar. The Bologna program BA, MA, and PhD made it easier for Russian students and academics to integrate into the U.S. and European systems. But it encountered fierce resistance from many older academics and from employers. The result was a plethora of programs, with some institutions seeking to offer "all of the above," both the Russian candidate of science and the new MA. Since 2014, and especially since February 2022, the system is increasingly reverting to the Soviet model. "Sovereign" science is discussed below.
118. Balzer (2020), 156. The author was told this in no uncertain terms by Russia's minister of education and science in mid-2015.
119. The Soviet Union's constitution mandated free higher education to those who achieved top scores on entrance exams. The Russian constitution mandates that the state provide free higher education to a fixed proportion of high school graduates. Most institutions after 1991 began to charge tuition for applicants who did not qualify for state support. The massive repressed demand for higher education from the Soviet era resulted in many students finding ways to cover the costs. By 2010, about two-thirds of students in higher education paid tuition. As the number of high school graduates declined, government "budget" students fill most openings, limiting the tuition revenue.
120. Balzer (2020), 133–34; Higher School of Economics (2018), 63.
121. Dezhina and Efimova (2022).
122. Quacquarelli Symonds (QS) is an international ranking system established in 2004. Initially in partnership with the Times Higher Education (THE) system, in 2009 QS went its own way. Where THE and others have dropped subjective indicators such as "reputation" from their rankings, QS continues to include reputation for 30 percent of an institution's score.

Russian universities have sought to game the QS ranking system. In the 2024 QS rankings, Moscow State University is number 87. No Russian institution is in the top one hundred in the other major ranking systems. QS includes five Russian institutions in the 300s and five more in the 400s (https://www.topuniversities.com/university-rankings/world-university-rankings/2024). In its 2023 list, THE has no Russian institutions in the top one hundred. Moscow State ranks 163. One institution is in the 201–250 rank, one in 301–350, and two more in 401–500 (https://www.timeshighereducation.com/world-university-rankings/2023/world-ranking#!/length/25/locations/RUS/sort_by/rank/sort_order/asc/cols/stats).

123. Gaming the system sometimes succeeds. Targeted efforts enabled Russia to move up in the World Bank "Doing Business" rankings while doing little to improve the domestic business climate. Aleksashenko (2018), 289–90.

124. See the website at https://www.timeshighereducation.com/world-university-rankings/2023/world-ranking.

125. Trofimova (2021).

126. Semchenkov (2018).

127. Sobolevskaia (2022); Semchenkov (2018).

128. At universities the author worked with in Russia, senior faculty with apartments, dachas, children, and sometimes grandchildren still living in Russia are reluctant to move. Junior faculty perceive limited possibilities in Russia and have emigrated in large numbers. Families with male children at or near conscription age have left in droves.

129. Dawisha (2015). The Red Brigades became the Baader-Meinhof Gang.

130. Danchenko and Gaddy (2006). The author was the first speaker at this event. Owing to technical problems, the Brookings website staff had to reconstruct the page. In the process they mixed up the date, removed some of the content, and changed the names of some participants.

131. Personal communications with Russian students. Websites offer detailed how-to instructions.

132. Personal communication with a colleague who taught in southern Russia. See also Popravko and Rykun (2002).

133. Trubnikov and Trubnikova (2024).

134. Mäkinen (2021). In a more recent article, Mäkinen has acknowledged the difficulties in scholarly collaboration with colleagues in China and Russia. He reaches the conclusion many of us have come to: Continue communication with colleagues we have known for many years but avoid research collaboration in the current environment (2024, 51–65).

135. Gerasimova (2023a, 2023b).

136. Johnson, Adams, Grant, and Murphy (2022); Balzer and Askonas (2016).

137. Siddiqi (2010); Gerovitch (2011).

138. Graham (2013).

139. Izotova (2020), 15–17.

140. This issue came up repeatedly during the author's visits to dozens of Russian VUZy between 1991 and 2019. The data showing that VUZ faculty regarded research as a burden are from Sobolevskaia (2022) and Semchenkov (2018).

141. The author was invited to work with one of these projects and was in a position to observe the administrative pressures and stringent financial controls involved.

142. The author attended several meetings in Russia that were organized to encourage émigré scientists to engage in more collaborative work and perhaps agree to work at least part-time in Russia. Interest in doing this declined after 2012, was seriously curtailed in 2014, and now has almost vanished.

143. Stanovaya (2013).

144. Ibid.

145. Berg (2017).

146. See the Clarivate web page "Highly Cited Researchers 2023" (https://clarivate.com/highly-cited-researchers/).

147. Scimago Journal and Country Rank (https://www.scimagojr.com/countryrank.php). The annual Scimago Journal and Country Rankings list countries by the number of documents published, citations per document, and the Hirsch index (h-index) score. The h-index is calculated based on the total number of publications in recognized journals and the number of citations per publication. Many small countries with a small number of publications have high rankings for citations of their limited number of publications. The material referenced shows the changes in Russia's rankings for publications, citations, and impact factor since Putin became president in 2000. The slight improvement in the number of publications during Putin's first decade was followed by more significant gains from 2010 to 2021. These gains have been undermined by the Ukraine war.

Russia's position in rankings of number of documents contrasts sharply with its scores for citations per document and the h-index impact factor. Russia consistently underperforms compared with other nations ranked in the top dozen for number of publications. For comparison, in 2020, before the full-scale war, the United States ranked sixty-ninth in number of citations per document, China ranked seventieth, and Ukraine ranked 220th.

148. Wetsman (2022).

149. Mokhnacheva and Tsvetkova (2019).

150. Jack (2024).

151. Graham (2013).

152. Voronov (2022).

153. Meduza (2024); Mediazona (2024).

154. Vedneeva (2023).

155. *Moscow Times* (2023). My reading of the case is that they engaged in normal scientific communication with Chinese colleagues at a time when Russian scholars in all fields were being encouraged to "learn Chinese."

156. Siddiqi (2015). Alexander Solzhenitsyn described the sharashka in his novel *The First Circle*, published in 1968.

157. Aleksashenko (2018); Åslund (2019); Balzer (2019).

158. Polovinkin (2023).

159. Among the most blatant examples was diverting the entire $1 billion designated for renovating the St. Petersburg port to construction of his palace on the Black Sea. See Belton (2020), 319.

160. *Novye izvestiia* (2023).

161. Graham (2013); Siddiqi (2010).

162. Berry and Cooper (1977); Luke (1985).

163. Hurska (2019).

164. Thane Gustafson, personal communication.

165. Jones and Moskoff (1991), 46–48. Balzer (1989), 174–79.

166. Balzer (2020), 157.

167. Balzer (2005).

168. Milov (2024), 5; Zainullin and Skorlygina (2024), 1.

169. Aleksashenko (2018), 226–32.

170. A massive cadre of FSB and Ministry of Justice investigators arrived in Rybinsk and "unearthed" evidence of serious financial malfeasance. Lastochkin was sentenced to 8½ years in 2015. Il'iushenkova (2015).

171. Pomerantsev (2014), 79–100.

172. Gustafson (1989).

173. Balzer (2006), 54.

174. Shirov, Iantovskii, and Potapenko (2015).

175. Gaddy and Ickes (2002).

176. Zhironkin, Gasanov, and Kolotov (2018), 141; Mekhanik (2014).

177. Melnikov (2014); Shirov, Iantovskii, and Potapenko (2015).

178. RSPP (2024).

179. Simachev et al. (2023), 18.

180. Latynina (2022).

181. For the Soviet technology balance, see Amann, Cooper, and Davies (1977). For the Putin era, see Shirov, Iantovskii, and Potapenko (2015). Fisher provides patent data in chapter 2.

182. Personal communications with Skolkovo staff.

183. See the Wikipedia page for Katerina Tikhonova at https://en.wikipedia.org/wiki/Katerina Tikhonova. Several of the Russian sources I accessed earlier are no longer available.

184. Putin and his staff almost certainly assumed that the sanctions imposed following Sergei Magnitsky's death in prison would be augmented if Russia seized Ukrainian territory.

185. Kazaev (2023).

186. Balzer (2020), 141–45; Falichev (2021). Wartime difficulties may finally be requiring some limits, but serious problems remain. Dixon (2024).

187. Berliner (1957)

188. Balzer (2019); Galeotti (2021).

189. Shirov, Iantovskii, and Potapenko (2015).

190. Ibid. These data are available in Balzer (2020), 197–98.

191. Ibid.

192. The Higher School of Economics held a "master class" presenting data from a report by the Russian Union of Industrialists and Entrepreneurs. See HSE.ru (2022). The document was removed from the HSE and sponsors' websites.

193. Personal communications.

194. The requirement that engineering schools and enterprises producing products for the government use Russian operating systems and software provides a striking example.

195. Personal communications; Krylova (2018).

196. Van Brugen (2023); Army Recognition (2024).

197. Shagina (2020).

198. Some Western media sources claim Russia now has few problems. Russian media citing Russian entrepreneurs and survey data continue to report serious problems in key sectors.

199. Balzer (2021b), 11.

200. Fylyppov and Lister (2022); Riegel (2023); Tingle (2023).

201. Shagina (2020).

202. Trifonova (2023).

203. Kornev and Litvinenko (2024), 7.

204. Simola (2023), 10–13.

205. Yakunin and Vilisov (2020), 251.

206. Balzer (2020), 13. The situation has not improved during the war. Despite Xi Jinping continuing to make friendly statements and China abstaining on UN resolutions critical of Russia, Chinese leaders continue to eschew direct financial support. Alienating Europe would deprive Chinese businesses of important customers at a time of economic difficulty.

207. Kennedy (2022); Xiang (2021).

208. Prokopenko (2024).

209. Balzer (2020), 173.

210. Data from https://www.natureindex.com/country-outputs/China.

211. Doklad RAN (2021), 35.
212. Rappeport (2024), B5.
213. Kornev and Litvinenko (2024); Trifonova, (2023).
214. Kornev (2022a), (2022b), 7; Shen (2022).
215. A report in the summer of 2024 suggested that the Biden administration was holding back on enhancing the ghost ship sanctions to avoid an increase in gas prices before the November 2024 elections. Tankersley and Rappeport (2024).
216. Chik (2024).
217. Balzer (2020), 9; Edovina (2024); Johnson (2024).
218. Piper (2014); Kara-Murza (2018).
219. See Golts's chapter 12. Duel' and Sugarova (2023).
220. Gorbachev's team failed to study the literature on defense conversion. In the United States, the average successful project lost money for three years and managed to break even for another seven years before beginning to report profits. Far from reducing pressure on the budget, conversion requires significant initial investments with little prospect of short-term success. Balzer (1989), 199–203.
221. Leiba (2023); *Verstka* (2023); TagilCity.ru. (2022).
222. Stepanova (2021).
223. On electronics, see Tuchkov (2020a). On machine tools, see Simonova (2021). On 5G, see Tishina and Zhabin (2023). On IT, see the next paragraph.
224. Korolev (2021).
225. Korolev (2024); Intellinews.com (2024).
226. InsideGNSS (2020).
227. Langford (2018).
228. InsideGNSS (2020).
229. Ustinova (2024), 8. The two partners have not yet agreed regarding funding.
230. Kul'manov (2022); Beliakova and Perlo-Freeman (2018).
231. Terent'ev (2020), 8.
232. Terent'ev (2020) provides many other examples.
233. Privalov (2020).
234. Tuchkov (2020b).
235. Kaushal (2021).
236. Republic.ru (2023); Starchak (2023).
237. Tuchkov (2020c).
238. TASS (2023); Uvarchev (2023).
239. Kaushal (2024); Starchak (2024).
240. Ogorodnikov (2023).
241. Zhironkin, Gasanov, and Kolotov (2018).
242. Kroeber (1923), 342–43.
243. Burns (2023).
244. Balzer (2021b), 7–8.

245. Nakazawa (2024).
246. Komrakov (2023).
247. Ibid.
248. Avdeeva (2023).
249. Ibid.
250. Goble (2024).

REFERENCES

Some Russian sources were accessed using the EastView Database. These references provide full publication information and identify EastView as the source.

Akindinova, N., Ia. Kuz'minov, and E. Iasin. 2016. "Ekonomika Rossii: Pered dolgim perekhodom" [The Russian economy: Before the long transition]. *Voprosy ekonomiki* 6:5–35.

Aleksashenko, Sergey. 2018. *Putin's Counterrevolution*. Washington, DC: Brookings Institution Press.

Amann, Ronald, Julian Cooper, and R. W. Davies, eds. 1977. *The Technological Level of Soviet Industry*. New Haven, CT: Yale University Press.

Aminov, Khalil, Aleksandra Mertsalova, Georgii Dvali, Arshaluis Mgdesian, and Aleksandr Konstantinov. 2022. "Na kogo rabotaet trudovoi front: Kuda resotsirovalis rossiiskie spetsialisty i ikh dengi" [For whom does the labor front work: Where Russian specialists and their money relocated]. *Kommersant'*, no. 244 (December 30).

Army Recognition. 2024. "Analysis: Armored and Combat Vehicles Showcased at Russia's Victory Day Military Parade 2024." ArmyRecognition.com, April 29.

Ascher, William. 1999. *Why Governments Waste Natural Resources: Policy Failures in Developing Countries*. Baltimore: Johns Hopkins University Press.

Åslund, Anders. 2019. *Russia's Crony Capitalism: The Path from Market Economy to Kleptocracy*. New Haven, CT: Yale University Press.

Astapenkova, Tamara. 2023. "Sistema SPO prakticheski prekratila podgotovku kvalifitsirovannykh rabochikh – sleduet iz doklada NIU VShE" [The system of secondary professional education has practically ceased to prepare qualified workers, according to a report by the Higher School of Economics]. *Uchitel'skaia gazeta*, April 12.

Avdeeva, D. A. 2023. "Vklad chelovecheskogo kapitala v rost ekonomiki – issledovat' slozhno, no mozhno" [Researching the contribution of human capital to economic growth—complicated but possible]. Moscow Higher School of Economics, March 27.

———. 2022. "Pokazateli chelovecheskogo kapitala v issledovaniiakh ekonomicheskovo rosta: Obzor" [Human capital indicators in economic growth studies: An overview]. *HSE Economic Journal* 26 (2).

Averbakh, Zhenia. 2024. "V Rossii gotoviatsia zapretit' 'ideologiiu chaildfri'. Zakonproekt uzhe v razrabotke" [Russia prepares to prohibit "the ideology of child-free": The law is already being drafted]. Fontanka.ru, June 27.

Bailes, Kendall. 1978. *Technology and Society under Lenin and Stalin*. Princeton, NJ: Princeton University Press.

Balzer, Harley. 2024. "A Russia without Russians: Russia's Disastrous Demographics." Washington, DC: Atlantic Council, August.

———. 2021a. "Sanctions Are Undermining Putin's Economy." *Baltic Rim Economies* 4 (October): 74.

———. 2021b. "Axis of Collusion: The Fragile Putin-Xi Partnership." Washington, DC: Atlantic Council, December 21.

———. 2020. "Can Russia Catch Up/Keep Up? Russian Science and Education in Putin's Fourth Term." In *Putin's Russia: Economy, Defence and Foreign Policy*, ed. Steven Rosefielde, 127–97. Singapore: World Scientific.

———. 2019. "Are the Siloviki More Corrupt Than Other Russian Elites?" Paper presented at ASEEES Annual Meeting, San Francisco, November.

———. 2017. "Russia's Knowledge Economy Decline: Views from Inside." In *Russia in Decline*, ed. S. Enders Wimbush and Elizabeth M. Portale, 113–61. Washington, DC: Jamestown Foundation.

———. 2006. "Vladimir Putin's Academic Writings and Russian Natural Resource Policy." *Problems of Post-Communism* 53 (1): 48–54.

———. 2005. "The Putin Thesis and Russian Energy Policy." *Post-Soviet Affairs* 21 (3): 210–25.

———. 2003a. "Demography and Democracy in Russia: Human Capital Challenges to Democratic Consolidation." *Demokratizatsiya* 11 (1): 95–109.

———. 2003b. "Routinization of the New Russians?" *Russian Review* 62 (1): 11–36.

———. 1990. "Secondary Technical Education in Russia/USSR: The Muddled Middle Level." In *Education and Economic Development Since the Industrial Revolution*, ed. Gabriel Tortella, 289–305. Valencia: Generalitat Valenciana.

———. 1989. *Soviet Science on the Edge of Reform*. Boulder, CO: Westview Press.

Balzer, Harley, and Jon Askonas. 2016. "The Triple Helix after Communism: Russia and China Compared." *Triple Helix* 3 (1).

Baranovskaya, Marina. 2023. "How Russia Drafts Migrants to Fight in Ukraine." *Deutsche Welle*, September 12.

Beliakova, Polina, and Sam Perlo-Freeman. 2018. "Corruption in the Russian Defense Sector." World Peace Foundation at the Fletcher School of Diplomacy, Tufts University, Medford, MA, May 11.

Belousov, Evgenii. 2024. "Gosduma odobrila uzhestochenie migratsionnogo zakonodatel'stva" [The state Duma approved harsher migration laws]. *Kommersant'*, July 23.

Belton, Catherine. 2020. *Putin's People: How the KGB Took Back Russia and Then Took On the West*. New York: Farrar, Straus and Giroux.

Berg, Evgenii. 2017. "Vybran novyi president RAN. Samoe vazhnoe kandidatov vperevye utverzhdano pravitel'stvo, no blizkii k Koval'chukam pretendent vse ravno proigral" [A new president of the Academy of Sciences was elected. Most important, the candidates were approved by the government, but the candidate close to Kovalchuk still lost]. Meduza, September 26.

Berliner, Joseph. 1957. *Factory and Manager in the USSR*. Cambridge, MA: Harvard University Press.

Berry, M. J., and J. M. Cooper. 1977. "Machine Tools." In *The Technological Level of Soviet Industry*, ed. Ronald Amann, Julian Cooper, and R. W. Davies, 121–98. New Haven, CT: Yale University Press.

Bisenov, Naubet. 2023. "Russia, Central Asia Locked in Tug of War over Ukraine Recruiting." Asia.Nikkei.com, August 29.

Bloomberg News. 2024. "Russians Who Fled Abroad Return in Boost for Putin's War." Bloomberg.com, May 2.

Burns, William. 2023. "A World Transformed and the Role of Intelligence." 59th Ditchley Annual Lecture, Oxfordshire, July 1.

Chik, Holly. 2024. "World's Largest Electric Container Ship Starts Service between China's Major Coastal Cities." *South China Morning Post*, April 29.

Chupik, Valentina. 2024. "How Russia Plans to Make Life Hell for Migrants." *Moscow Times*, June 27.

Danchenko, Igor, and Clifford Gaddy. 2006. "The Mystery of Vladimir Putin's Dissertation." Washington, DC: Brookings Institution.

Dawisha, Karen. 2015. *Putin's Kleptocracy: Who Owns Russia?* New York: Simon and Schuster.

Dergacheva, Daria. 2024. "One of the Last Liberal Universities in Russia Shuts Down Its Political Science Department." GlobalVoices.org, July 9.

Dezhina, I. G., and G. Z. Efimova. 2022. "Riski Proekta 5-100: Otsenki nauchno-pedagogicheskikh rabotnikov razlichnyhh pokolenii" [Risks of 5-100 project: Evaluations of academic staff from different generations]. *Vysshee obrazovanie v Rossii* 31 (3): 28–39.

Ditkovskiy, K., et al. 2023. *Science and Technology Indicators in the Russian Federation, 2023: Data Book*. Moscow: National Research University, Higher School of Economics, February.

Dixon, Robyn. 2024. "In Putin's Wartime Russia, Military Corruption Is Suddenly Taboo." *Washington Post*, June 10.

Doklad RAN. 2021. "O realizatsii gosudarstvennoi nauchno-tekhnicheskoi politiki v Rossiiskoi Federatsii utverzhden resheniem obshchevo sobraniia RAN 20–21 aprelia 2021" [Report of the Russian Academy of Sciences 'On realization of the state scientific technical policy for the Russian Federation,' approved by the general meeting of the academy, April 20–21, 2021].

Duel', Aleksei, and Elina Sugarova. 2023. "Rabotat nekomu. Ombudsmen Titov rasskazal o problemakh biznesa v RF" [No workers. Ombudsman Titov described the problems for Russian business]. AIF.ru, September 3.

Eberstadt, Nicholas. 2022. "Russian Power in Decline: A Demographic and Human Resource Perspective." AEI Foreign and Defense Policy Working Paper Series, August 24.

Edovina, Tat'iana. 2024. "Oborot s vostokom: Rost torgovli Kitaia s Rossei ne compensiroval emu poter' na global'nom rynke" [Turnover with the East: Growth in China's trade with Russia did not compensate for losses on global markets]. *Kommersant'*, January 15.

Falichev, Oleg. 2021. "Nadezhnyi zaslon na puti korruptsii" [A reliable barrier to corruption]. *Voenno-promyshlennyi kur'er* 7, March 2. (The journal, which frequently published sharp criticism of problems, ceased publication after February 24, 2022. The material is archived on the site vpk.name.)

Frydlewsky, Silvina, and Juan Forero. 2023. "Russian Women Flock to Argentina to Give Birth." *Wall Street Journal*, February 26.

Fylyppov, Olexsander, and Tim Lister. 2022. "Russians Plunder $5M Farm Vehicles from Ukraine—to Find They've Been Remotely Disabled." CNN, May 1.

Gabdullina, Emiliia. 2024. "Po mestu genomnoi registratsii: SKR prizval Gosdumu uzhestohit' migratsionnoe zakonodatel'stvo" [The place for genomic registration: The Russian Federation Investigative Committee called for the State Duma to toughen migration laws]. *Kommersant'*, no. 128 (July 19): 3.

———. 2023. "Ukraintsev i belorusov importozamestili tadzhikistantsami: Eksperty fiksiruiut izmeneniia interesa k rossiiskomu grazhdanstvu" [Tajiks import substituted for Ukrainians and Belarussians: Experts identify the changes of interest in Russian citizenship]. *Kommersant'*, no. 138 (July 31): 4.

Gabdullina, Emiliia, and Aleksandr Chernykh. 2024. "Ne svistet', ne tsykat', baranov ne rezat: B izuchil materialy novogo adaptatsionnogo kursa dlia migrantov" [No whistling, no shouting, no slaughtering sheep: B studied the materials for the new course on adaptation for migrants]. *Kommersant'*, no. 123P (July 15): 5.

Gaddy, Clifford, and Barry W. Ickes. 2002. *Russia's Virtual Economy*. Washington, DC: Brookings Institution Press.

Galeotti, Mark. 2021. "The Silovik-Industrial Complex: Russia's National Guard as Coercive, Political Economic and Cultural Force." *Demokratizatsiya: The Journal of Post-Soviet Democratization* 29 (1): 3–30.

Gerasimova, Elena. 2023a. "Zolotoi standart obrazovaniia pridet v shkoly s sentiabria" [The gold standard of education will come to schools in September]. *Nezavisimaia gazeta Evropa*, May 7. EastView.

———. 2023b. "Srednee obrazovanie prodolzhaiut perestraivat'" [Perestroika of secondary education continues]. *Nezavisimaia gazeta* 132 (June 29): 8. EastView.

Gerovitch, Slava. 2011. "'Why Are We Telling Lies?' The Creation of Soviet Space History Myths." *Russian Review* 70 (3): 460–84.

Goble, Paul. 2024. "Russian Army Degrading in Ukraine, Threatening Moscow Both There and at Home." *Eurasia Daily Monitor* 20 (July 29).

Gorbacheva, Elena, and Petr Skorobogatyi. 2024. "Nuzhny li migranty rossiiskomu 'oliv'e'" [Does Russian olive oil [salad dressing—eds.] need migrants?]. *Monokl'*, no. 15 (April 8).

Government.ru. 2023. "Meeting with Deputy Prime Ministers on Current Issues." February 6.

Graham, Loren. 2013. *Lonely Ideas: Can Russia Compete?* Cambridge, MA: MIT Press.

Grey, Stephen, Jason Bush, and Roman Anin. 2014. "Special Report: Billion-Dollar Medical Project Helped Fund 'Putin's Palace.'" Reuters, May 21.

Gustafson, Thane. 1989. *Crisis amid Plenty: The Politics of Soviet Energy under Brezhnev and Gorbachev*. Princeton, NJ: Princeton University Press.

Herbst, John E., and Sergei Erofeev. 2019. "The Putin Exodus: The New Russian Brain Drain." Atlantic Council, February.

Higher School of Economics. 2018. *Dvenadtsat' reshenii dlia novogo obrazovaniia: Doklad Tesntra Strategicheskikh razrabotok i Vysshei Shkoly Ekonomiki*. Moscow.

HSE.ru. 2022. "O master-klasse Vdovina Igoria Aleksandrovicha." November 22.

Hurska, Alla. 2019. "The Motor Sich Factory and Its Covert Ties to Russia." *Eurasia Daily Monitor* 16, no. 128 (September 19).

Il'iushenkova, Natal'ia. 2015. "Iurii Lastochkin golodovka, shizo i noveishie rakety" [Iurii Lastochkin: Hunger strike, isolation ward and the latest missiles]. *Rybinskaia pravda*, June 6.

Iliyasov, Marat. 2024. "Chechen Demographic Growth as an Indicator of Unresolved Conflict." Presentation at George Washington University, Washington, DC, March 5.

InsideGNSS. 2020. "Third GLONASS-K—The First in Six Years—to Launch in October." September 8.

Intellinews.com. 2024. "Demographics and Equality Main National Goals in Putin's latest May Decrees." May 13.

Izotova, G. S. 2020. "Rezul'taty ekspertno-analiticheskogo meropriiatiia 'Opredelenie osnovnykh prichin, sderzhivaiushchih nauchnoe razvitie v Rossiiskoi Federatsii: Otsenka nauchnoi infrastruktury, dostatochnost' moitvatsionnykyh mer, obespechenie privlekatel'nosti raboty vedushchikh uchenykh'" [Results of the expert-analytical analysis "Determining the basic reasons holding back scientific development in the Russian Federation: Evaluation of the scientific infrastructure, adequacy of means of motivating and attracting leading scientists to work"]. Moscow: Schetnaia palata (Accounting Chamber).

Jack, Patrick. 2024. "Russian Research 'Increasingly Isolated' amid Ukraine War." TimesHigherEducation.com, July 31.

Johnson, Jo, Jonathan Adams, Jonathan Grant, and Daniel Murphy. 2022. "Stumbling Bear, Soaring Dragon: Russia, China and the Geopolitics of Global Science." London: Kings Policy Institute; Cambridge, MA: Harvard Kennedy School, July.

Johnson, Keith. 2024. "The Very Real Limits of the Russia-China 'No Limits' Partnership." *Foreign Policy*, April 30.

Jones, Anthony, and William Moskoff. 1991. *Ko-ops: The Rebirth of Entrepreneurship in the Soviet Union*. Bloomington: Indiana University Press.

Josephson, Paul. 2024. *Hero Projects: The Russian Empire and Big Technology from Lenin to Putin*. Oxford: Oxford University Press.

Kara-Murza, Vladimir. 2018. "Russia Sanctions the West—Hurting Its Own Citizens." *Washington Post*, April 25.

Kaushal, Sidharth. 2024. "Russia's Sarmat Test Failure: Implications for the Strategic Balance." RUSI.org, October 22.

———. 2021. "Putting the Russian Hypersonic Threat in Perspective." RUSI.org, September 28.

Kazaev, Timur. 2023. "Pochemu 'maiskie ukazy' Vladimira Putina tak i ne byli ispolneny" [Why were Vladimir Putin's "May decrees" not implemented]. *Verstka*, no. 22 (June 12).

Kennedy, Scott. 2022. "Data Dive: The Private Sector Drives Growth in China's High-Tech Exports." CSIS.org, April 28.

Khasanova, R. R., T. M. Maleva, N. V. Mkrtchian, and Iu. F. Florinskaia. 2019. *Proaktivnaia demograficheskaia politika: 10 let sputstia* [Proactive demography policy: 10 years later]. Moscow: Izdatel'skii dom DELO.

Kirby, Paul, and Brandon Drenon. 2024. "US-Russian Woman Jailed for 12 years for $51 Charity Gift." BBC, August 15.

Klepach, Andrei, and Raisa Luk'ianenko. 2023. "Rossiiskoe zdravokhranenie: Makroekonomicheskie parametry i strukturnye problemy" [Russian health care: Macroeconomic parameters and structural problems]. *Problemy prognozirovaniia* 2:76–77. EastView.

Komrakov, Anatolii. 2023. "Snizhenie kachestva rabochei sily tormozit razvitie: Vklad chelovecheskogo kapitala v VVP strany stal otritsatel'nym" [Declining quality of the labor force is holding back development: Human capital's contribution to GNP has become negative]. *Nezavisimaia gazeta*, May 29.

Kornev, Timofei. 2022a. "V Rossii rastet populiarnost' braka: Proizvoditelei elektroniki poluchaiut vse bol'she negodnykh komponentov" [The popularity of defects grows in Russia: Electronics producers are receiving far more worthless components]. *Kommersant'*, no. 192P (October 17): 7.

———. 2022b. "'Nedostatok parallel'nogo importa v tom, chto on ochen' nestabilen': Anton Gus'kov, predstavitel' RATEK" ["The shortcoming with parallel imports is that they are highly unstable": Anton Gus'kov, representative of the Association of Trade Companies and Manufacturers of Household Electrical and Computer Equipment]. *Kommersant'*, no. 214 (November 18): 10.

Kornev, Timofei, and Iurii Litvinenko. 2024. "I chainik ne proskochit: Inostrannye postavshchiki nachali blokirovat' parallel'nyi import v RF" [Even the tea kettle will not slip though: Foreign suppliers have begun blocking parallel imports to Russia]. *Kommersant'*, no. 45 (March 15): 7.

Korolev, Nikita. 2024. "'Vse kogda-to chego-to nachinali rasti': Prezident 'Elementa' Il'ia Ivantsov o mechtakh realiakh rossiiskoi mikroelektroniki" ["Everything began growing from something": Ilya Ivantsov, president of Element, on the dreams and realities of Russian microelectronics]. *Kommersant'*, no. 49 (March 21): 10.

———. 2021. "Protsessory zachisliat na biuzhet: Pravitel'stvo khochet peresadit' studentov za 'Baikaly' i 'El'brusy'" [Processors to be on the budget: The government wants to shift students to Baikal and Elbrus]. *Kommersant'*, no. 226P (December 13): 9.

Korolev, Nikita, and Iurii Litvinenko. 2022. "Subsidii kommutiruiutsia: Vlasti khotiat profinansirovat' zapasy zarubezhnykh elektronnikh komponentov" [Subsidies switched: The powers that be want to finance reserves of foreign electronic components]. *Kommersant'*, no. 204 (November 2): 9.

Kostarnova, Natal'ia. 2024. "Vo vse bolee steril'noi obstanovke: Rosstat otmechaet rost chisla meditsinskikh sterilizatsii na fone snizheniia chisla abortov"[An increasingly sterile condition: Rosstat cites an increased number of medical sterilizations accompanying the decline in abortions]. *Kommersant'*, no. 4 (January 12): 4.

———. 2023. "Preparat zakryt na uchet: Minzdrav izdal prikaz o kontrole za sredstvami dlia medikamentnogo aborta" [The medicine is closed for registration: The Ministry of Health issued a decree to control means of medical abortion]. *Kommersant'*, no. 185 (October 5): 5.

Kostarnova, Natal'ia, and Ekaterina Rakitina. 2023a. "Eshche ne narozhali: V 2022 godu v poltora raza vyros spros na preparaty dlia pereryvaniia bremennosti" [Still not having children: Demand for abortion medications increased 1.5 times in 2022]. *Kommersant'*, no. 139 (August 2): 5.

———. 2023b. "Mediki otsenili mery stimulirovaniia rozhdaemosti: Vrachi ne podderezhivaiout zapret svobodnoi prodazhi preparatov dlia pereryvaniia bremennosti" [Medics assessed measures to stimulate the birth rate: Doctors do not support banning the open sale of abortion drugs]. *Kommersant'*, no. 147P (August 14): 5.

Kovalov, Alexey. 2023. "New Russian Schoolbooks Preach Hatred of Ukraine and the West." *Foreign Policy*, September 3.

Kozlova, Natal'ia. 2024. "Bastrykin: V usloviakh provedeniia SVO obshchestvo osobenno ostro reagiruet na korruptsiiu chinovikov" [Bastrykin: In conditions of the special military operation, society pays particular attention to corrupt officials]. *Rossiiskaia gazeta* 163 (July 24).

Kroeber, Alfred. 1923. *Anthropology: Culture Patterns and Processes*. Cambridge, MA: Harvard University Press.

Krylova, Yulia. 2018. *Corruption and the Russian Economy: How Administrative Corruption Undermines Entrepreneurship and Economic Opportunities*. London: Routledge.

Kucherenko, Dar'ia. 2024. "Kak izmenilsia rynok truda na fone voiny" [How the labor market has changed due to the war]. Verstka Media, April 12.

Kul'manov, Aleks. 2022. "Razval dostigaet epichekikh razmerov, kogda treshchat poslednie skrepy" [The collapse reaches epic proportions, when the last braces crack]. Kasparov.ru, November 1.

Kurmanaev, Anatoly, and Ekaterina Bodyagina. 2024. "Family Values or Fighting Valor? Russia Grapples with Women's Wartime Role." *New York Times*, May 4.

Langford, Cameron. 2018. "Tech Smuggler to Russia & China Gets 46 Months." CourtHouseNews.com, January 25.

Latynina, Iuliia. 2022. "Arkhangel 'Satana'" [Archangel "Satan"]. *Novaia gazeta*, July 16.

Latypova, Leyla. 2023. "Russia Pressures Migrant Workers with Raids, Military Summons." *Moscow Times*, September 7.

Leiba, Gregorii. 2023. "Putin: Defitsit kadrov v OPK meshaet vypolniat' gosoboronzakaz" [Putin: Personnel deficit in the defense industrial complex hinders fulfilling the state military order]. *Kommersant'*, March 14.

Leiba, Grigorii, and Kseniia Veretennikova. 2023. "Uklonisty s inostrannym aktsentom: 'Novykh rossiian' predlagaiut lishat' grazhdanstva za neispolnenie voinskogo dolga" [Draft dodgers with a foreign accent: Proposal to deprive 'New Russians' of citizenship if they fail to perform military service]. *Kommersant'*, no. 158 (August 28): 3.

Liubimov, I. L., M. V. Lysiuk, and M. A. Gvozdeva. 2018. "Atlas ekonomicheskoi slozhnosti rossiiskikh regionov" [Atlas of economic complexity of Russian regions]. *Voprosy ekonomiki* 6: 71–91.

Luke, Timothy W. 1985. "Technology and Soviet Foreign Trade: On the Political Economy of an Underdeveloped Superpower." *International Studies Quarterly* 29 (3): 327–53.

Makeeva, Anna. 2018. "Polovina VUZov Rossii ne sdali zachet" [Half of the higher education institutions in Russia did not pass the exam]. *Kommersant'*, March 27, 13.

Mäkinen, Sirke. 2024. "Akademisk frihet og sikkerhet i fare? Finlands forskningssamarbeid med autoritære stater." *Internasjonal Politikk* 82 (1): 51–65.

———. 2021. "Global University Rankings and Russia's Quest for National Sovereignty." *Comparative Education* 57 (3): 417–34.

Markov, Sergei, and Anastasiia Alekseeva. 2019. "Materinskii kapital: Sushchnost', mekhanizm, problemy i perspektivy razvitiia" [Maternity capital: The nature, mechanism, problems and prospects of development]. *Voprosy studencheskoi nauki* 8:77–87.

Marokhovskaya, Alesya, and Irina Dolinina. 2022. "Before, It Never Occurred to Anyone to Consider Education as a Threat to Security." IStories, April 8.

Mediazona. 2024. "Apellatsionnyi sud utverdil 14-letnii srok 78-letnemu novosibirskomu uchenomu Anatoliiu Maslovu po delu o gosizmene" [The appeals court affirmed the 14-year sentence for 78-year-old scientist Anatoly Maslov for state treason]. September 9.

Meduza. 2024. "Novosibirskogo uchenogo Anatoliia Maslova prigovorili k 14 godam kolonii po delu o gosizmene" [Novosibirsk scientist Anatoly Maslov sentenced to 14 years for treason]. May 21.

Mekhanik, Aleksandr. 2014. "Bez svoikh cheviakov ne oboidemsia" [We can't do it without our own worms]. *Expert* 37 (Sept. 8): 32–37. EastView.

Melnikov, Aleksandr. 2014. "Chto esli Zapad prekratit postavki tekhniki dlia neftedobychi v Rossii?" [What if the West stops supplying technology for oil extraction in Russia?]. Kapital-rus.ru, July 23.

Milov, Vladimir. 2024. "Oil, Gas and War: The Effect of Sanctions on the Russian Energy Industry." Atlantic Council Eurasia Center, May.

Mokhnacheva, Iu. V., and V. A. Tsvetkova. 2019. "Russia in the Global Array of Scientific Publications." *Herald of the Russian Academy of Sciences* 89 (4): 370–78.

Moscow Times. 2024. "Indian Men 'Tricked' into Fighting in Ukraine Appeal for Help." March 6.

———. 2023. "Razrabotchikov giperzvukovykh raket Putina arestovali za gosizmenu" [The developers of Putin's hypersonic rocket were arrested for treason]. May, 173.

Mukhina, Anna. 2019. "'This Isn't a Panic—It's a Catastrophe' as Saratov Region Runs Out of Insulin, 'Meduza' Discovers Medicine Shortages All Over Russia." Meduza, June 5.

Nakazawa, Katsuji. 2024. "Analysis: Xi-Putin Honeymoon at Risk as Chinese Flood into Russia." *Nikkei Asia*, March 21.

Novye izvestiia. 2023. "Dmitrii Peskov rasskazal, kak ne vernut'sia v srednie veka v oblasti nauki" [Dmitry Peskov described how to avoid returning to the Middle Ages in science]. March 14.

OECD. 2021. "Education at a Glance 2021." Paris: OECD Publishing.

Ogorodnikov, Evgenii. 2023. "Smotrite: Eto zakat Rossiiskogo neftegaza" [Look: This is the sunset of Russian oil and gas]. *Ekspert*, no. 26, June 25.

Piper, Elizabeth. 2014. "Crunch Time: As Sanctions Bite, Putin Ally Gets into Apples." Reuters, December 28.

Poliak, Rimma. 2023. "Edinyi uchebnik istorii ot Medinskogo: Uchit' po nemu—eto presuplenie protiv sevodniashnykh shkol'nikov: Kak propaganda pobedila obrazovanie" [Medinsky unified history textbook is a crime against today's students: How propaganda defeated education]. *Respublik*, August 11.

Polovinkin, Valerii. 2023. "Pochemu rossiiskaia nauka po mnogim pokazateliam po-prezhnemu nedostatochno effektivna: Fundamental'naia, poiskovaia i prikladnaia" [Why is Russian science by many indicators still insufficiently effective: Fundamental, exploratory and applied]. *Nezavisimaia gazeta*, August 2.

Pomerantsev, Peter. 2014. *Nothing Is True and Everything Is Possible: The Surreal Heart of the New Russia*. New York: PublicAffairs.

Popravko, N. V., and A. Iu. Rykun, 2002. *Stanovlenie i razvitie rynka dopolnitelnykh obrazovatelnykh uslug na territorii Tomskogo regiona: Analiz povedeniia potrebitelei*. [Creation and development of the market for supplementary educational services in the Tomsk region: Analysis of consumer behavior]. Tomsk: Izdatel'stvo Tomskogo universiteta.

Postupi online. 2024. "Kuda postupat': Chislo vyzov: Aktual'naia tsifra v 2024" [Where to enroll: Number of VUZy: Actual figures for 2024].

Privalov, Aleksandr. 2020. "O glavnykh avtobronetankovykh sobytiiakh i novinkakh MVTF 'Armiia 2020'" [On the main armored vehicle events and what is new at the International Armored Vehicles Exhibition "Army 2020"]. GruzovikPress.ru, October.

Prokopenko, Alexandra. 2024. "What Are the Limits to Russia's 'Yuanization'?" *Carnegie Politika*, May 27.

Putin, Vladimir. 2006. "Annual Address to the Federal Assembly." May 10. http://en.kremlin.ru/events/president/transcripts/23577.

———. 2000. "Annual Address to the Federal Assembly of the Russian Federation." July 8. http://en.kremlin.ru/events/president/transcripts/21480.

Radio Free Europe / Radio Liberty. 2024. "New Russian Laws Will Dramatically Restrict Migrants' Rights, Activist Says." RFERL.org, July 25.

Rakitina, Ekaterina. 2023. "Potrebiteli pereshli k krainim meram: Rossiiane stali pokupat' libo ochen' malo, libo slishkom mnogo" [Consumers have switched to extreme measures: Russians are buying either very little or a lot]. *Kommersant'*, no. 159 (August 30): 7.

Rappeport, Alan. 2024. "U.S. Imposes Sanctions on Chinese Companies for Aiding Russia's War Effort." *New York Times*, May 1, B5.

Re: Russia. 2023. "Escape from War: New Data Puts the Number of Russians Who Have Left at More Than 800,000 People." Re-Russia.net, July 28.

Reddaway, W. B. 1946. *The Economics of a Declining Population*, 2nd ed. London: George Allen & Unwin.

Republic.ru. 2023. "Moia zhizn' s 'Sarmatom': Pochemu raketa strashna tol'ko v propagandistskikh SMI. Byvshii sotrudnik 'Roskosmosa'–o kremlevskom 'chudo-oruzhii'" [My life with "Sarmat": Why the rocket is frightening only in media propaganda. A former Roskosmos staffer on the Kremlin's "miracle weapon"]. Republic.ru, October 3.

Riegel, Ralph. 2023. "Gangs Targeting Valuable Farm Equipment to Sell on the Russian Black Market." *Independent* (Ireland), June 18.

Roshchin, S. Iu., ed. 2023. "Vypuskniki srednego professional'nogo obrazovaniia na rossiiskom rynke truda" [Graduates of secondary professional education on the Russian labor market]. Moscow: Higher School of Economics.

Rossiiskaia gazeta. 2007. "Pravitel'stvo odobrilo demograficheskuiu programmu i obvinilo chinovnikov v nerestoropnosti" [The government approved the demography program and accused officials of sluggishness]. May 24.

RSPP. 2024. "Kliuchevye napravleniia politiki v oblasti obespecheniia tekhnologicheskogo suvereniteta, importozameshcheniia i eksporta: Vzgliad biznesa" [Key directions of policy in supporting technological sovereignty, import substitution and exports: The view from business]. Russian Union of Entrepreneurs and Industrialists.

Schetnaia palata [Accounting Chamber]. 2023. "Galina Izotova: Trebuetsia sovershenstvovat' gospolitiku v sfere zdravookhraneniia" [Galina Izotova: It is necessary to update state policy in the sphere of health care]. Press release, July 18.

Semchenkov, Iuri. 2018. "Vuzy vs nauka. Chto meshaet prepodavateliam zanimat'sia issledovaniiamim" [VUZy vs. science: What prevents teachers from doing research]. *Argumenty i Fakty*, November 14.

Shagina, Maria. 2020. "Drifting East: Russia's Import Substitution and Its Pivot to Asia." CEES Working Paper no. 3 (April).

Sharma, Bhadra, and Jeffrey Gettleman. 2023. "A Small Country Far from Ukraine Is Sending Hundreds to War, on Both Sides." *New York Times*, October 20, 1.

Shcherbakova, E. M. 2024. "Migratsiia v Rossii, predvaritelnye itogi 2023 goda" [Migration to Russia, preliminary results 2023]. *Demoskop Weekly*, no. 1025–1026 (March 26–April 10), 8.

Shen, Xinmei. 2022. "Defect Rate of Chinese Chips Shipped to Russia Surged to 40 Percent after Western Sanctions, Local Newspaper Says." *South China Morning Post*, October 20.

Shirov, A. A., A. A. Iantovskii, and V. V. Potapenko. 2015. "Otsenka potentsial'nogo vliianiia sanktsii na ekonomicheskoe razvitie Rossii i EC" [Evaluation of the potential impact of sanctions on the economic development of Russia and the EU]. *Problemy prognozirovaniia* 4: 3–16.

Shishkin, Sergey, et al. 2022. "Structural Changes in the Russian Health Care System: Do They Match European Trends?" *Health Economics Review* 12 (29).

Siddiqi, Asif. 2015. "Scientists and Specialists in the Gulag: Life and Death in Stalin's Sharashka." *Kritika* 16 (3): 557–88.

———. 2010. *The Red Rockets' Glare: Spaceflight and the Soviet Imagination, 1857–1957*. Cambridge: Cambridge University Press.

Simachev, Iu. V., et al. 2023. "Rossiiskie promyshlennie kompanii v usloviakh 'vtoroi volny' sankstionnykh ogranichenii: Strategii reagirovaniia" [Russian industrial firms in conditions of the "second wave" of sanctions: Adjustment strategies]. *Voprosy ekonomiki* 12 (December): 5–30.

Simola, Heli. 2023. "Latest Developments in Russian Imports of Sanctioned Technology Products." Bank of Finland BOFIT Policy Brief no. 15. Helsinki.

Simonova, Kristina. 2021. "Stankostroitel'nye zavody Rossii: Vozrozhdenie otrasli" [Russia's machine-building plants: Resurrection of the sector]. Vestsnab24.ru, April 2. (Accessed May 9, 2021. Site no longer operating.)

Snegovaya, Maria. 2023. "Russian Emigration." In Andrea Kendall-Taylor et al., *Identifying Russian Vulnerabilities and How to Leverage Them*, 41–44. Washington, DC: CNAS, December.

Sobolevskaia, O. V. 2022. "Publikatsionnaia passivnost': Pochemu prepodavateliam vuzov slozhno mnogo zanimat'sia issledovaniiami" [Publication passivity: Why is it difficult for VUZ teachers to conduct much research]. HSE.ru, February 15.

Solov'eva, Ol'ga. 2022. "Emigratsiiu uchenykh pritormozila pandemiia: Spetsialistov v Rossii sposobny uderzhat' tol'ko oboronnaia i atomnaia promyshlennost'" [The pandemic slowed emigration of scientists: Russian specialists are able to support only the defense and atomic power industries]. *Nezavisimaia gazeta*, January 26.

Stanovaya, Tatiana. 2013. "Reform of the Russian Academy of Sciences: Checkmate in Two Moves." Institute of Modern Russia, July 15.

Starchak, Maksim. 2024. "Rossiia teper na dolgoe vremia okazhetsia bez tekhnicheski gotovoi tiazheloi rakety" [Now Russia will be without technologically ready heavy rockets for a long time]. Meduza, September 25.

Starchak, Maxim. 2023. "Russia's Sarmat Missile Saga Reflects an Industry in Crisis." *Carnegie Politika*, October 18.

Stepanova, Iuliia. 2021. "V gossektore skvozit elektronika: Rossiiskie protsessory rvutsia v novye proekty" [Electronics seen through the state sector: Russian processors are eager for new projects]. *Kommersant'*, no. 201 (March 11): 2.

Sukhankin, Sergey. 2024. "Russia Faces Spike in Crime and Alcoholism as War Nears Two-Year Mark." *Eurasia Daily Monitor* (Jamestown) 21 (January 29): 13.

TagilCity.ru. 2022. "Direktor UVZ v Tagile nachal aktsiiu po sboru pozhertvovanii na SVO iz zarplaty zavodchan" [The director of Uralvagonzavod in Tagil began an action to collect contributions for the special military operation from the salaries of factory personnel]. TagilCity.ru, December 6.

Tankersley, Jim, and Alan Rappeport. 2024. "New Plan to Target Russia's Oil Revenue Brings Debate in White House." *New York Times*, July 7.

TASS. 2023. "First Sarmat ICBMs Regiment to Go on Combat Duty in December 2023—Source." November 19, 2023.

Temkina, Anna, and Elena Zdravomyslova. 2008. "Patients in Contemporary Russian Reproductive Health Care Institutions." *Demokratizatsiya* 16 (4): 277–93.

Terent'ev, Denis. 2020. "Skrobnyi mulisz proizvodstva: Proizvodstvo Stankov v Rossii sokratil'os v 20 raz po sravneniu s sovetskimi vremenami'" [Sad mock production: Production of machine tools decreased by 20 times compared to the Soviet era]. *Argumenty nedeli*, no. 42 (736), October 28–November 5.

Tiazhlov, Ivan. 2024. "'My real'no ne znaem, kto k nam edet': Pervyi zamestitel' ministra vnutrennikh del Aleksandr Gorovoi o sviazannykh s migratsei riskakh" ["We really do not know who comes to us": First Deputy Minister of the Interior Aleksander Gorovoi on the risks related to migration]. *Kommersant'*, no. 171 (September 19): 1.

Tingle, Rory. 2023. "Ukraine War Sparks Rural Crime Wave in UK: Machinery Thefts Soar by 300% as Criminal Gangs Trade Farm Equipment with Russia on the Black Market after Moscow Was Hit by Import Sanctions." *Daily Mail*, June 8.

Tishina, Iuliia and Aleksei Zhabin. 2023. "Pravitel'stvo vyshlo na sviaz' s budushchim: Strategicheskimi zadachai otrasli do 2035 goda stali oborona i bezopasnost'" [Government is connected with the future: Strategic sectors to 2035 are defense and security]. *Kommersant'*, no. 226 (Dec. 5): 7.

Topol, Sarah A. 2024. "The Deserter." *New York Times Magazine*, September 22, 22–61.

Trifonova, Polina. 2023. "Faktory vstali na tsepochki: Otras' ishchet novye resheniia v parallel'nom importe" [Factories have taken to the chains: Industry is looking for new solutions in parallel imports]. *Kommersant'*, no. 32 (February 2): 8.

Trofimova, I. N. 2021. "Rossiiskaia obrazatoval'naia politika i konflikty interesov v sfere innovatsii'" [Russian education policy and conflicts of interest in the sphere of innovation]. *Polis. Politicheskie issledovaniia* 5:25–38.

Trubnikov, Dmitrii, and Ekaterina Trubnikova. 2024. "From Bogus Journals to Predatory Universities: The Evolution of the Russian Academic Sphere within the Predatory Settings of the State." *Minerva*, 62:49–68.

Tuchkov, Vladimir. 2020a. "Bombu pod otechestvennuiu elektroniku podlozhili polveka nazad" [The bomb under fatherland electronics was placed there half a century ago]. *Voenno-promyshlennii kuri'er*, March 24.

Tuchkov, Vladimir. 2020b. "'Yars' s belorusskim aktsentom: RVSN Rossii nakhodiatsia v zavisimosti ot tiagachei Lukashenko. Svoiu promyshlennost' v RF slomali" ["Yars" with a Belorusian accent: The Russian Strategic Rocket Forces are dependent on Lukashenka for haulers. Our own industry in the Russian Federation is broken]. *Voenno-promyshlennii kuri'er*, August 4.

Tuchkov, Vladimir. 2020c. "Doletit li 'Sarmat' do postanovki na dezhurstvo" [Will "Sarmat" make it to active duty]. VPK-news, September 1.

Twigg, Judyth. 2021. "Russian Health and Demographic Trends and Prospects." In *Putin's Russia: Economy, Defence and Foreign Policy*, ed. Steven Rosefielde, 95–126. Singapore: World Scientific.

Ustinova, Anna. 2024. "Glonnass i 'Gazprom kosmicheskie sistemy' zaimutsia nizkoorbital'nymi sputnikami" [GLONASS and Gazprom Space Systems will develop low-orbit satellites]. *Vedomosti*, no. 192 (October 11): 8. EastView.

Uvarchev, Leonid. 2023. "Komanduiushchii RVSN: Sozdanie novogo shakhtnogo kompleksa 'Sarmat' pochti zaversheno" [Command of Strategic Rocket Forces: New silos for the Sarmat are almost complete]. *Kommersant'*, December 16.

Uzhvak, Polina. 2023. "Administratsiia prezidenta i ministerstva zakazali opros studentov ob otnoshenii k voine i Putinu. My poluchili pervye rezultaty. Bolee treti oproshennykh khoteli by uekhat' iz strany, a kazhdyi chyetvertyi priznalsia, chto samoe podkhodiashchee slovo dlia situatsii v Rossii—'krizis'" [The presidential administration and ministry ordered a survey of students about their view of the war and Putin. We received the first results. More than one-third wanted to leave the country, and one in four say that the most appropriate description of the situation in Russia is—"crisis"]. IStories.news, May 18.

van Brugen, Isabel. 2023. "Russia Had Just One Tank at Its Victory Day Parade." *Newsweek*, May 9.

Vedneeva, Nataliia. 2023. "V Sibirskom otdelenii RAN silovki podvergli presledovaniiam 16 chelovek" [The siloviki opened prosecution of 16 people at the Siberian Branch of the Russian Academy of Sciences]. *Moskovskii komsomolets*, May 16.

Veretennikova, Kseniia. 2024. "V Dume poiavitsia komissiia po voprosam migratsionnoi politiki" [The Duma will have a commission on migration policy]. *Kommersant'*, no. 130 (July 24): 3.

Verstka. 2023. "'Eshche i zastavliaiut v samodeiatel'nosti uchastvovat': Sotrudniki rossiiskogo VPK rasskazali 'Verstke' o problemakh svoei raboti i o tom, chto meshaet narashchivat' proisvodstve oruzhiia" ["And they also make you do amateur shows": Staff in Russia's defense industry told *Verstka* about problems in their work and what hinders expanding weapons production]. May 4.

Volochkova, N. A., and P. O. Kuznetsova. 2019. "Skol'ko stoiat kontrasanktsii: Analiz blagosostoianiia" [How much do countersanctions cost: A welfare analysis]. *Zhurnal NEA* 43 (3): 173–83.

Voronov, Konstantin. 2022. "Mera presecheniia okazalas' smertel'noi: Uchenyi umer cherez dva dnia posle aresta po delu o gosizmene" [A preventive measure turned out fatal: A scientist died two days after being arrested for treason]. *Kommersant'*, no. 117P (July 7): 4.

Wetsman, Nicole. 2022. "Russian Government Bars Its Scientists from International Conferences: Scientific Schools Will Also De-emphasize Publication in International Databases." TheVerge.com, March 21.

Wright, Gavin, and Jesse Czelusta. 2002. "Exorcizing the Resource Curse: Minerals as a Knowledge Industry, Past and Present." Stanford University Faculty Workshop.

Xiang, Nina. 2021. *US-China Tech War: What Chinese Tech History Reveals about Future Tech Rivalry*. Independent.

Yakunin, Vladimir, and Maxim Vilisov. 2020. "Belt vs. Road: Eurasian Dilemma for Infrastructure Development." In *The "Roads" and "Belts" of Eurasia*, ed. Alexander Lukin, 237–59. Singapore: Palgrave Macmillan.

Yusupova, Olga. 2024. "Learning, Performance, Fatigue and Regret: Tales of Motherhood on Russian Social Media in the 2010s–2020s." *Europe-Asia Studies* 76 (2): 247–64.

Zainullin, Evgenii, and Natal'ia Skorlygina, 2024. "Skvoz' tuman uglictyi put' blestit: Vlasti ishchut dlia otrasli puti vykhoda iz budushchego krizisa" [The coal road shines through the fog: The authorities seek a way for the sector to avoid a future crisis]. *Kommersant'*, no. 67 (April 16): 1.

Zhironkin, S. A., M. A. Gasanov, and K. A. Kolotov. 2018. "Vozmozhno li v Rossii neoindustrial'noe impotozameshchenie?" [Is neo-industrial import substitution possible in Russia?]. *EKO* 5:139–57.

Zoria, Yuri. 2023. "British Intel: Russia Recruits Foreign Nationals against Ukraine, Offering Payments, Fast-Track Citizenship." Euromaidan Press, September 3.

EIGHT

Ethnic Diversity

GUZEL YUSUPOVA

The Russian Federation came into existence as a multinational federation celebrating diversity in various forms. However, under Vladimir Putin's leadership, ethnically diverse Russia has gradually transformed into a nationalizing, assimilationist state constructed around an ideology that emphasizes the culture of the dominant ethnic group. Rather than building on the rich experience and advantages of the Soviet nationalities policy and the federalization trends of the 1990s, Putin's approach to diversity management has increasingly led Russia toward homogenization, the highlighting of its core ethnicity, and the creation of institutional incentives for xenophobia and racism. This outcome stems from Putin's perception of diversity not as a value but as a threat.

This chapter examines issues of diversity and inequality in the Russian Federation during Putin's tenure. The first section outlines the main trends in ethnic and migration politics and provides a brief overview of the policies and discourses that define authoritarian diversity management. It describes how the Putin regime dismantled federative relations to transform a once viable multiculturalism into a culturally unified nation. The next section explores the impact of Russia's war against Ukraine and related decolonization discourses on Russia's internal diversity issues. The final section focuses on the treatment of immigrant minorities and racial issues within the country.

Overall, the changes resulting from Putin's policies have created ethnic hierarchies that may become more pronounced, potentially leading to ethnic cleavages and instability. This ethnic hierarchization may in turn lead to greater dissatisfaction with the regime among the broader citizenry and potentially serve as a precondition for regime change.

Managing Ethnic Diversity in Russia

The vast territory known as the Russian Federation has been a culturally diverse space for centuries. Russia's extensive and complex history has played a significant role in shaping its distinct framework of ethnic relations. While most of the population identifies as ethnically Russian, the 2021 population census indicates that there are more than 190 ethnic groups, both indigenous and immigrant, that together constitute about 20 percent of the population. To this day, the Russian constitution recognizes the "multiethnic people" (*mnogonatsional'nyi narod*) as the custodian of national sovereignty, acknowledging the population's diversity.[1] However, recent constitutional amendments have effectively established a symbolic ethnic hierarchy by designating ethnic Russians as the "state-forming nation," thereby subordinating other ethnic groups. Official mass media, legislation, and speeches by political elites and state officials frequently depict Russia's cultural diversity as a distinctive national trait to be cherished. Concurrently, however, the state implements assimilationist policies on the ground.[2] This countermovement complicates diversity management in Russia. The failure of diversity management under Putin's regime, which does not value cultural diversity but instead has restricted it, has contributed to regional wars and instability.

Political discourses that support authoritarian politics frequently portray diversity as a threat to the state's integrity, using it as a means to justify police state control. There are three major pro-Kremlin media narratives related to managing diversity that underwrite assimilationist politics and state control. The first concerns titular indigenous groups within ethnic republics that could call for separation, which in turn could lead to the disintegration of the Russian state, as happened in the 1990s. The second pro-Kremlin media discourse addresses incoming migrants from Central Asian countries and the South Caucasus, who are depicted as endangering social safety because of purported involvement in drug trafficking or the transmission of diseases. The third narrative concerns demographic growth trends in the traditionally Muslim regions of the Russian Federation. This growth is seen as potentially leading to the Islamization of Russia, possibly even fostering Islamic religious extremism, and posing a risk to the country's core identity. These media themes shape the directions of diversity management policies.

Social scientists typically commence an overview of race and ethnicity in Russia by reviewing Soviet nationalities politics and its impact on contemporary ethnic relations. Only recently has more distant history come into consideration. It is still barely acknowledged that colonial relations had been established not just between the metropole and its territorially defined provinces but also with the racially defined, diverse groups of people who populated this vast space.[3] This history still shapes the present. Russia's attempts to legitimize its war in Ukraine by referring to Russians and Ukrainians as one nation and "brothers" offer the best example. The war also instigated the decolonial narrative explaining the failure of diversity management in Russia: representatives of ethnic minorities recognized the overlap between poverty and ethnicity, which became especially visible when the war started as participation in the "special military operation" offered the promise of a somewhat better financial livelihood. Unemployment and poverty could explain the war's higher death toll for some ethnic groups, but not others.[4] Yet very little research has addressed this overlap in depth, its reasons and consequences, and the actual significance of ethnic factors in comparison to territorial and other elements in accounting for the various inequalities associated with diversity.

The imperial legacy in Russia's contemporary ethnic landscape is prominent and also affects knowledge production about diversity, particularly as the majority of academic perspectives originate in Moscow because of greater funding available for research. The result is often a lack of data and pauce research on certain issues. Nonetheless, there exist superficial measures for the Kremlin to showcase equality and diversity. For instance, the central government often co-opts provincial political elites and includes some ethnic minority representatives in important state decisions or in leadership roles. Examples include Elvira Nabiullina, a Tatar who heads the

Russian Central Bank, and Sergei Shoigu, a half-Tuvan who most recently served as the minister of defense and was appointed secretary of Russia's National Security Council in May 2024. These appointments are used to highlight diversity and inclusion, despite the lack of substantial measures to genuinely promote these values at all levels.

At the same time, the Soviet legacy still has a positive impact on the negotiation of ethnic relations. Before the Russian invasion of Ukraine, Russia was a magnet for immigration from states of the former Soviet Union. Some ethnic republics still possess some traits of quasi-states (such as their own constitutions and official languages). Legislation provides protection, including exemption from mandatory military conscription, for representatives of disappearing ethnic groups. However, field reports indicate concerns persist about the effective enforcement of such legislation.[5]

In light of such legislative protections and at least the appearance of diversity and inclusion efforts (however de minimis), why argue that diversity management in Russia has failed? Diversity management is successful when effective policies for the integration of immigrants bear results, when the principle of federalism to suit diversity provides some form of equality in social conditions and political perspectives for representatives of various groups, and when political and symbolic representation of the diverse groups constituting a multinational state is based on equal terms. Is this the case for Putin's Russia?

Failed Federation

The Russian Federation was built on the legacy of the nationalities policies of the Soviet Union, which distinguished people by race and assigned ethnicity to territories. In other words, ethnicity was institutionalized in various official forms and daily practices.[6] These routines were largely replicated in the Russian Federation. For example, up until 1997, Russian passports still specified an individual's ethnicity. Accordingly, the Russian Federation could claim its multinational people were protected under its sovereign power and could tout diversity as an important feature of the new country. Initially the ethnic regions and later the nonethnic provinces of the Russian Federation acquired significant political, fiscal, and other autonomy from the federal center. However, as Konstantin Zamyatin argues, ethnic federalism pursued a limited accommodationist strategy that targeted only territorially concentrated groups.⁷ The policy toward indigenous small-numbered peoples combined accommodationist and integrationist elements by providing very limited territorial autonomies within broader regions—for example, indigenous peoples such as Evenks in autonomous territories within the Sakha Republic and Buryatia. Moreover, nonterritorial national-cultural autonomies intended to integrate territorially dispersed groups. To the extent the latter remained ineffective, a federal laissez-faire policy amounted to a de facto assimilationist approach toward the smaller groups. Nevertheless, the institutional design of an asymmetric ethnic federation, in which some groups or territories enjoyed more autonomy from the federal center than others, was crucial in balancing presidential power in Russia in the 1990s. Regional leaders, especially the leaders of ethnic republics, were able to limit the consolidation of power into one hand. Ideological association of the right to self-determination with democracy in the 1990s legitimized regional elites and empowered them to promote real federalism in Russia and to counterbalance presidential power.

Vladimir Putin came to power, built his power vertical, and eliminated the federative institutional design of Russia. He centralized legislative, judicial, fiscal, and executive powers in Moscow and instituted mechanisms that subordinated the regional heads under this central authority, without encountering much resistance from them. Additionally, Putin's power vertical cut horizontal ties among regional elites. This proscribed and limited any possibility of aligning behind common goals. As Marjorie Mandelstam Balzer shows, even cultural and civilizational bonds among citizens of the culturally similar ethnic republics have been alternately ignored or considered threatening by various levels of government.⁸

Gulnaz Sharafutdinova explains this quick submission of powerful regional elites to Putin's centralization policies by both structural determinants and legitimizing ideas.⁹ The latter are especially important and are still used to expound Putin's almost unlimited presidential power and the importance of security services in sustaining the Russian state. In the early years of his presidency, in dealing with Chechen terrorist attacks and challenges to Russia's integrity, Putin used the discourse on the need to protect the state's security (and therefore the need for public surveillance) to defend his steps to centralize the government and to consolidate power in his own hands. Similarly, Putin capitalized on the 1998 financial crisis, the renewal of the war in Chechnya in 1999, and a wave of terrorist bombings in Moscow and in several other cities in Russia the same year to shift public focus away from the values of democratic development. The Russian populace perceived these principles as having led to unsatisfactory economic outcomes, unmet welfare infrastructure needs, and an increased sense of insecurity (discussed in chapter 5). Instead, Putin proffered the value of a needed strong hand to ensure social security and reestablish the country's integrity.[10] As Konstantin Zamyatin has noted, "Regional separatism was among the threats that Putin envisaged when justifying his move towards recentralization and undermining of the autonomy of regions."[11] Other threats were seen in pan-Turkic, pan-Mongolic, pan-Circassian, and pan-Finno-Ugric movements, which were especially popular in the early 2000s but were later labeled as extremist by the Kremlin.[12]

However, as with most of Putin's policies, the centralization of power did not happen immediately but was implemented gradually over the course of more than a decade. Putin first created seven federal districts in May 2000 to coordinate federal agencies in the regions. A "plenipotentiary representative" of the president would monitor these agencies. Putin next instituted a legal campaign to bring regional constitutions in line with federal legislation and to subordinate them to the federal constitution. In this process, appointees, rather than elected officials, would populate the Federation Council (in many cases, nontitular Moscow-based representatives were appointed instead of local ones), significantly reducing its role as a channel of ethnic political representation.[13] In 2004 tax reform was introduced, centralizing financial resources. That same year Putin made the decision to abolish gubernatorial elections, which he justified in the aftermath of the Beslan tragedy. Subsequently, new legislation was enacted in 2005 that granted the president the right to dismiss regional governors. Last, certain ethnic territories traditionally regarded as ethnically labeled regions were merged with nonethnically labeled regions. Gulnaz Sharafutdinova argues that Putin's institutional, legal, fiscal, and other reforms of Russia's federal system were widely interpreted as countering the *disintegrative* tendencies of the Yeltsin period. She explains that the power vertical that subordinated Russia's governors was conceived as a mechanism for *strengthening the Russian state*.[14] This has dramatically affected the country's diversity management over the past thirty years and has resulted in building a de facto culturally homogeneous nation-state instead of a multinational federation.

In 2017, measures of assimilation in the name of power centralization were implemented through a language reform. This reform changed the requirement to learn the official languages of the titular groups in national republics from mandatory to voluntary, potentially leading to their eventual disappearance. Crucially, social mobility was restricted to Russian language proficiency, especially via access to higher education, which was almost absent in indigenous languages.[15] This was followed by a prohibition against using the title "president" for the heads of regions in 2021. Although these recent measures instigated popular protests in ethnic republics, the regional elites did little to nothing to counter the new policies. Preemptive actions of the security services made social resistance almost invisible to the national public (see chapter 6).[16] Taken together, the aforementioned steps transformed the Russian Federation into a unitary state with only one de facto autonomous region, Chechnya. Thus, while some regions enjoyed special financial relations with the federal center in exchange for silence regarding greater political autonomy, other regions, such as the Sakha Republic or Bashkortostan, experienced financial losses due to this centralization of power.[17] The ideological basis for legitimizing assimilationist policies has remained the same throughout Putin's reign: the federal system of center-region relations and great regional autonomies make Russia weak in the face of terrorism and separatism, and this inevitably will lead to regional wars and instability. Ironically, these very steps *have* led to war and instability. Overall, the ideological legitimization of Putin's centralization of power and its limitation of political representation for nondominant ethnic groups have precariously compromised diversity management and the role of ethnicity and race in Russian society.

Failed Multiculturalism

Some scholars argue that the Soviet nationalities policy favored indigenous groups, whereas some say the Soviet Union was a prison for nations. The Soviet Union sometimes featured contradictory policies: the waves of *korenizatsiia* (indigenization) followed by waves of Russification.[18] More important, greater appreciation of diversity in the USSR also correlated with the periods of more liberal policies in other domains. The same logic applies to diversity management in the Russian Federation. I argue that the more authoritarian Putin's regime has become, the more assimilationist policies it has imposed on indigenous groups. Moreover, some scholars contend that Russian ethnonationalist movements grew precisely because of the rise of minority ethnic nationalisms in the ethnic regions of

Russia in the 1990s and early 2000s. As a consequence, the proliferation of Russian nationalist organizations has contributed to the promotion of assimilationist politics.[19]

The Russian Federation today lacks legislation dealing systematically with the problems of ethnic minority groups other than indigenous peoples (*korennye narody*).[20] However, legislation on cultural and language rights of titular indigenous groups in ethnic republics has been reconsidered throughout Putin's presidency. Konstantin Zamyatin provides the most systematic account of three stages of diversity management in Russia up until the 2010s.[21] He argues that the defederalization of Russia and the centralization of power were accompanied by nation building and de-ethnicization politics, which sought the removal of ethnicity from the political domain and its restriction to a cultural sphere.[22] He describes how the promotion of the Russian nation without the necessary civic foundation has happened in Russia's legal domain with consequences in both political discourse and everyday life.

The first official document that introduced the term "Russian nation" building was the *Concept of the State Nationalities Educational Policy*, which emerged as part of the education reform. This document intended to "consolidate the multinational people of the Russian Federation into a single Russian political nation."[23] The official introduction of the term in this document is emblematic because education had to become the principal tool of identity building directed at the homogenization of citizenry. The education reform significantly curtailed the possibility of regional authorities promoting regional identities and languages. Although different policy patterns were applied to different regions and groups, the supply of public services in non-Russian languages in education was cut everywhere.[24]

The first decade of Vladimir Putin's presidency was characterized by the exclusion of ethnicity from the public sphere and elimination of the discussion of local cultures in educational curricula. At the same time, the symbolic link between ethnicity and territories persisted in ethnic regions. The principal ambiguity underlying debates concerning Russia's nation building arises from confusion over two dichotomies embedded in formulating the country's identity. The first dichotomy is between the conceptualization of Russia as a classic nation-state with a core ethnic identity or as a multinational state without a dominant culture. This debate is not about civic versus ethnic understandings of nationhood or exclusive or inclusive citizenship (immigrants are not taken into account in the debate) but rather whether the country is defined by a single ethnic group or by many different ethnic groups. The second dichotomy involves whether Russia, a federative state on paper, should remain an ethnofederation in practice or not. Those living in ethnic republics are still more likely to experience the presence of federal symbolism and to be aware of ethnic hierarchies, on both the regional and national level, than those living in nonethnic regions.

These two ways of describing what the "Russian nation" means are usually ordered hierarchically, in the sense that both opponents and proponents of contemporary nation-building policies base their argumentation on prioritizing one or the other dichotomy and their choice within this dichotomy. Can Tatars force ethnic Russians to learn the Tatar language in Tatarstan? The answer may be no because Russia is a classic nation-state based on the culture and values of the core Russian ethnicity. Or the answer may be yes because Russia is an ethnofederation in which ethnic republics have rights allowing them to confer identity elements on their residents. It is a classic chicken-or-egg dilemma, even though both sides discuss two closely related questions that differ in their essence.

From 2012 onward, nation building in Russia became increasingly oriented toward privileging the core ethnic group—ethnic Russians (see chapter 5).[25] As part of his strategy of power legitimization, Putin has increasingly highlighted the importance of Russian culture and language by appealing to patriotism imbued with ethnocultural content. The populations in nonethnic regions and Russians in ethnic regions perceive this policy as commonsensical and typical of a nation-state. Meanwhile, the adult citizens in ethnic regions have experienced a gradual transformation from being titular minorities (or majorities within their territories), with privileged rights within their territories, to experiencing a step-by-step abolition of these rights without clear top-down articulation of these policies. This has occurred for the most part without public debate.[26] The author's research shows that in recent years, ethnicity in Russia has been politicized from both sides. The dominant Russian ethnicity is being highlighted from the top down,[27] in legislation, symbolic politics, and in nation-building policies in general, while ethnic minorities are creating their ethnic symbolism from the bottom up.[28] Ethnic minority identification becomes a highly valued social resource to showcase some sort of opposition to an authoritarian regime as well as an additional value in neoliberal settings for cultural entrepreneurs. Ethnic minorities in Russia develop new, and adjust old, practices of ethnic reproduction in the context of a plexus of nationalizing authoritarianism, incipient market economy, and globalization.[29] As Marjorie Mandelstam Balzer notes in her piece for Russia.Post, indigenous people in ethnic republics also have resentment around ecological issues, in addition to language and land rights, thus making the current system fragile, although these resentments are repressed and invisible on the surface.[30] Furthermore, ecological concerns have led to the increasing importance of ethnic identification for representatives of indigenous groups.[31]

The contemporary everyday life of Russia's indigenous groups consists of various ethnically labeled activities in the social sphere, on the internet, and within the local economy. Ethnic minority culture today extends beyond the portrayal of folk dancing in traditional costumes, as often depicted on Russian television. Instead, it encompasses practical, everyday, locally rooted customs and practices initially introduced by ethnic entrepreneurs and later adopted by ordinary people. The revitalization of minority languages, the incorporation of ethnic symbolism into fashion, and the proliferation of small enterprises targeting ethnically oriented customers and tourists may reach a tipping point when ethnicity becomes an essential source for self-identification.[32] These mundane practices and ethnicity commodification gradually politicize ethnicity in the ethnic regions. The disproportionately high (relative to the Russian general population) death toll of men from ethnic regions at the beginning of the war in Ukraine exacerbates this trend of politicizing ethnicity.[33] Moreover, the importance of preserving ethnic culture is tied to globalization and glocalization trends, the role of local politics, and growing internal tourism, which often promotes ethnic tourism or pays tribute to local culture and specific local heritage.

Russia's Wars and Decolonization

Russia's war in Ukraine has prompted academic and public discussions about the enduring imperial nature of the Russian state. On the one hand, decolonization is promoted by the Kremlin as justification for the war, meaning Russia wants to decolonize a world that has been colonized by the West, specifically the United States. On the other hand, Kremlin propaganda portrays decolonizing initiatives as extremist, alleging that they seek to cause disintegration of the Russian Federation by dividing it into smaller pieces. According to Russian propaganda, activists engaged in decolonizing work conceal their true intentions behind slogans advocating greater autonomy for ethnically labeled territories.

At the same time, the decolonization of the Russian Federation has emerged as a significant political prospect for the country's future. Although various interpretations exist regarding how this decolonization might unfold, whether through the refederalization of Russia into a new union or its dissolution into several independent states, the significance of ethnicity and recognition of cultural diversity lie at the heart of these discussions. Moreover, the war in Ukraine has surfaced such issues as the unequal allocation of the war's burden based on ethnic background and the role of ethnic divisions in Russia's future social and political order as the most pressing issues related to the war's impact on Russian society.[34] Ethnic minority diaspora members living abroad organize media campaigns to raise awareness of racism and ethnicity-based inequality in Russia. They call for reconsideration of historical memories, recognition of the colonial past, and an acknowledgment of the violent conquest of their native territories. Altogether, these developments reinterpret historical memories of Russia's distant past and the history of its territorial expansion, as well as periods of ethnic oppression during the Soviet period. Ethnic minority activists claim that ethnic inequalities persisting today have deep roots in history. They challenge how historical heritage is presented and highlight the "inconvenient" memories that are kept silent. Indeed, Russian history textbooks and national art predominantly portray Russia's history of colonization as inclusive and peaceful. In other words, the colonial nature of Russian territorial expansion was never acknowledged.[35]

Until recently, the challenges of accommodating cultural diversity were seldom a focal point in public discourse inside Russia.[36] Instead, the idea of the friendship of peoples, predominant in the USSR, persists in official narratives about diversity in contemporary Russia and nurtures nostalgia for the days of the now lost USSR.[37] Thus the war in Ukraine (over a "brotherhood of peoples") has instigated a reevaluation of diversity issues in Russia and recognition of the values of diversity and equality among the political opposition, both abroad and inside Russia. While the grievances related to multilayered inequalities based on minority origin are more than relevant, they also have some distinctive, emotional foundations. In the absence of any available means to influence Putin and the Kremlin, critically minded people in Russia, along with those who have recently emigrated, direct their emotions toward ethnic others with whom they can actually engage and may actually influence (for better or for worse). For ethnic activists, these may be representatives of the liberal intelligentsia, who often fail to recognize ethnic issues as important ones, and vice versa. The March 22, 2024, terrorist attack on Crocus City Hall in Moscow is the best illustration of how this works. Incited by ominous propaganda narratives, people readily channeled their anger toward labor immigrants from Central Asia, a vulnerable group they could immediately seek to punish, instead of questioning and demanding accountability from the security services that failed to prevent the terrorist attack and protect innocent lives.

Failed Friendship of People

Russian diversity, however, is not limited to indigenous peoples but is also constituted in part by the large number of immigrants, mostly coming from the less economically developed former republics of the Soviet Union. Until recently, Ukraine, Moldova, and the Central Asian and South Caucasian states were the main countries of origin for labor immigrants to Russia. Chinese immigration is also growing gradually but inconsistently. Vladimir Malakhov argues that immigration from the post-Soviet "near abroad" to Russia actually started circa 1970.[38] Jeff Sahadeo's book, *Voices from the Soviet Edge: Southern Migrants in Leningrad and Moscow*, supports this thesis with stories that shape this complicated nature of migration into narratives of racial discrimination and ethnic hierarchies.[39] While in the 1990s, the vast majority of immigrants were ethnic Russians who had fled former union republics because of various nationalizing policies that negatively affected them in the newly independent states, immigration under Putin was distinguished by large and predominantly male labor migration from former Soviet Union countries because of structural dependence on and economic disparity with Russia. However, from the very beginning, immigration policies under Putin were characterized by restrictions placed on immigration. An example of this is Russia's naturalization policy, implemented in 2002, which has made acquiring Russian citizenship more complex.[40] Moreover, research by Marthe Myhre shows that the State Program for Voluntary Resettlement of Compatriots prioritized compatriots of Slavic origin over others.[41] That might either reveal racist attitudes in the individual practices of state officials or perhaps indicate a well-thought-out strategy. Research by Sergei Abashin confirms that the proportion of immigrants from Central Asian countries has been declining since 2012. He explains as follows:

> First, in 2013–15 new changes in laws that restricted migration were enforced, including norms on foreign citizen residency in Russia for 90 instead of 180 days without special documents extending this period, on prohibited entry (in effect for three to five years) for those who have violated administrative rules several times, and on restricting work in certain spheres of the economy. We can include expanding police practice of expelling and deporting foreign citizens for these and other violations of migrational legislation. Starting in 2013, prohibitions on entry and numbers of those expelled or deported began to rise sharply; in all, 1.6 million foreign citizens received a prohibition on entry in 2013–15, of whom 340,000 were expelled or deported. No publicly available figure reveals what proportion of this number consists of citizens from Central Asian countries but judging from mass information media and individual statements by officials, they predominate. . . . The second significant factor is the economic crisis in Russia, which began in 2014 and led to a reduction in jobs, and, most important, to a nearly twofold decline in the ruble relative to the dollar, the principal currency for migrant transfers. . . . The decline in migrants' incomes because of the crisis was accompanied by an increase in the cost of legalizing residency and obtaining employment in Russia.[42]

Why can the limits on migration from Central Asia be an intended unofficial policy? Based on demographic and immigration statistics, Marlène Laruelle observes that Russia is becoming increasingly a Muslim country since birth rates are high in traditionally Muslim regions of Russia and some of the sending countries are traditionally Muslim.[43] Currently about 25 million people of Muslim background are living in Russia, or 18 percent of the population. While the majority are not fervent believers, and only a minority practice Islam routinely, this significant portion of the population is steadily growing in numbers. Moscow already has the largest Muslim community in Europe. According to Laruelle, by approximately 2050, Muslims will represent between one-third (the most conservative estimate) and one-half (the most generous estimate) of the Russian citizenry (for more on demography, see chapter 7). While the official discourse regarding Muslims is Islamophilic, this creates a challenge to Putin's nation-building strategy, which prioritizes ethnic Russians and bases authoritarian politics on the conservative values of Orthodox Christianity. From the bottom up, ethnic violence against people with Muslim backgrounds accounts for a considerable portion of all ethnic violence data collected by the Moscow-based SOVA Center, and increases every year.[44] This trend is not unique, however, since Islamophobia is widespread across the globe on various levels. Other religious groups also suffer from prejudice and are even considered to pose threats by the Kremlin. For example, cross-international Buddhist ties have become stronger and more threatening to the Kremlin, as have Finno-Ugric Christian non-Orthodox groups, the Mari "pagan-Christian" religious revitalization, and many other nondominant religious groups.[45]

Racial Issues

The large numbers of visible minorities, whether indigenous or of immigrant origin, make racial issues particular important in daily life and in the public sphere. However, there are few scholarly studies of contemporary racism in Russia. The few accounts that exist highlight the importance of the legacy of the Soviet nationalities policy, which has affected the current understanding of race in Russia.[46] They also study the postcolonial nature of the Russian state, which contributes to the flourishing of racism.[47] Sahadeo notes, for example, that official publications designed for broader consumption show residents of multiethnic Moscow and St. Petersburg as uniquely white and Slavic.[48] Most scholars who address race, citizenship, and nationhood in Russia highlight that the differences in the attitudes of the local citizens from those of former compatriots from the post-Soviet space are hierarchical and depend on many factors, such as Slavic or non-Slavic origin, religion, and region. Labor migrants coming from the former republics of the Soviet Union *and* indigenous minorities in Russia negotiate their racial differences vis-à-vis the "whiteness" of ethnic Russians that itself is still in the process of construction, depending on constantly evolving economic and political contexts. However, the concept of race was almost absent from both public and academic debates until recently.[49]

This racialized hierarchy stems from the idea of ethnic Russians as the elder brother in the friendship of people declared in the Soviet Union, but also exceeds it.[50] As Peter Rutland has noted, casual racism is fairly widespread in post-Soviet Russia,[51] with polls showing the strongest hostility toward Roma, Chechens, and other peoples of the Caucasus.[52] Large numbers of labor migrants from Central Asia and the Caucasus have been increasingly treated as a racialized other.[53] This group of humanity numbers 10 to 15 million people (7–10 percent of Russia's population) and represents the second largest absolute number of immigrants in the world after immigration to the United States.[54] The Black Lives Matter (BLM) movement and the protests after the killing of George Floyd in the United States have sparked debates over racial issues across the globe and in Russia. While reaction to the BLM movement in Russia had a strong impact on political debates among Russian intellectuals, they were hesitant to open Pandora's box and discuss racism in Russia itself. As Peter Rutland argues, for pro-Kremlin figures,

> It was quite easy to incorporate BLM into their narrative, using it to criticize structural racism in America while at the same time echoing racist attitudes. For the reasons outlined above, this was much more challenging for Russian liberals. In recent decades, liberalism in the West has evolved to become a more open and contested discourse, very different from the monolithic grand liberal narrative of the Cold War. Russian liberals remain somewhat trapped in binary categories (the corrupt elite versus their righteous critics) and feel uncomfortable with the self-criticism of contemporary liberalism.[55]

Nikolay Zakharov rightly argues that it is important to pay attention not just to forms of racial difference but also to the ways the racialized subjects negotiate them: "Since the migrant is an agent, she may develop strategies for the de-racialization or negotiation of her perceived racial belonging, and these strategies may vary depending on the dominant ideology, the economic situation, and other factors. . . . Racialization can support an unequal distribution of resources, but it also leads to the formulation of counter-ideologies by racialized minorities."[56]

Popular celebrities and a bottom-up reaction brought domestic racial issues into the public agenda. For example, pop singer Manizha Sangin represented Russia in the international Eurovision song contest in 2021 with a song questioning the racialized understanding of Russian nationhood. The ban of comedian Idrak Mirzalizade for a supposedly insulting joke[57] that depicted situations that contribute to prejudices about non-Russians living among Russians has sparked another wave of debate over racism in Russia.[58] Another example is Russia's largest advertising website, Avito, which has banned ads with potentially racial connotations. Decolonial narratives voiced by various groups within and without Russia after February 24, 2022, have linked racism with colonialism and acknowledged the consequences of the broader social inequalities that racism causes. This encouraged greater debates on racial issues and other bottom-up developments.

Conclusion

Ethnic diversity in Russia has been managed under Putin's rule in a way that diminishes its significance and value. Instead of celebrating the polyethnic nature of common nationhood, state policies and their implementation resulted in cultural homogenization and an understanding of national belonging not in a civic but rather in a primordial sense. This conception of nationhood facilitates the emergence of ethnic hierarchies and will inevitably lead to ethnic cleavages and instability. Failing to build on the rich experience and advantages of the Soviet nationalities policy's legacy and the federalization trends that flourished in the 1990s, Putin's diversity management has increasingly led Russia to homogenize, to highlight its core ethnicity, and to create institutional incentives for xenophobia and racism. The idea of greater cultural rights for ethnic minorities is associated with the potential disintegration of the country and legitimizes the police state and power vertical that Putin has built. Instead of treating diversity as a useful resource in a globalized world, he diminishes it further in the name of stability. Ironically, the rejection of diversity as a value and the normalization of homogeneity have instead led to legitimization of the Russo-Ukrainian war and consequent social instability.

Despite its increasing isolation and repressive environment, however, Russia is still a part of a global world and participates in the overall trend toward glocalization of minority cultures.[59] Therefore, issues of diversity and equality, including ethnic and racial diversity and political representation of various minority groups, are expected to become increasingly prominent, particularly at the grassroots level, despite and sometimes because of repressions. This trend is already unfolding inside Russia but remains occluded to outsiders because of self-censorship in an increasingly repressive environment in the country.[60] The Russian Federation, however, is not the USSR in any sense, a fact especially noticeable in the differences in the institutionalization of ethnicity and the relative proportions of the dominant and nondominant groups. Therefore, it is unrealistic to expect a collapse akin to that of the USSR. Instead, growing ethnic, religious, and racial issues will likely become one of many factors contributing to dissatisfaction with the regime among the broader citizenry, which is a necessary condition for regime change but not for the breakup of the country.

NOTES

I wish to thank Marjorie Mandelstam Balzer, Harley Balzer, and Steven Fisher for their thoughtful comments on this chapter.

Although the knowledge production about ethnic diversity in the Russian Federation is dominated by Moscow and St. Petersburg perspectives, this chapter references several studies done by colleagues of minority origin who grew up in and were educated in ethnic republics of Russia.

1. *Constitution of the Russian Federation*, accepted December 12, 1993. Official text. Moscow: Omega-L, 2021.
2. Malakhov and Osipov (2023).
3. Etkind (2011); Tolz (2001).
4. Lenton (2022).
5. Walker (2024).
6. Brubaker (1996).
7. Zamyatin (2014).
8. Balzer (2021).
9. Sharafutdinova (2013).
10. Sharafutdinova (2020).
11. Zamyatin (2016), 34.
12. Shtepa (2021).
13. Ross and Turovsky (2013), 64–67, 71–73.
14. Sharafutdinova (2013).
15. Prina (2016); Suleymanova (2018a); G. Yusupova (2021, 2023).
16. G. Yusupova (2021).
17. Gontmakher (2021).

18. For example, Gorenburg (2006); Martin (2001).
19. Kolstø (2016); Pain (2013).
20. Bowring (2013).
21. Zamyatin (2016).
22. Codagnone and Filippov (2000), 282; Prina (2016); Zamyatin (2016).
23. Ministry of Education Order, August 3, 2006 (https://elementy.ru/library9/pr201.htm).
24. Zamyatin (2016), 37.
25. Kolst (2016).
26. Zamyatin (2016).
27. *Kommersant'* (2018).
28. Yusupova (2018).
29. Ibid.
30. Balzer (2023).
31. Balzer (2020a, 2020b).
32. Balzer (2021); Suleymanova (2018b); Yusopova (2018).
33. Mediazona (2022).
34. Bessudnov (2023).
35. Tolz (2001).
36. Pain and Fediunin (2020).
37. Sullivan (2022).
38. Malakhov (2007).
39. Sahadeo (2019).
40. *Federal Law on Citizenship of the Russian Federation* (http://www.rg.ru/2002/06/05/zakon-gragdan.html).
41. Myhre (2017).
42. Abashin (2019), 158.
43. Laruelle (2016).
44. SOVA Center (n.d.).
45. Balzer (2011).
46. For example, Malakhov (2007); Shnirel'man (2011, 2022); Zakharov (2015).
47. Abashin (2015); Sahadeo (2019). Kishlak is a general term for a Central Asian village.—eds.
48. Sahadeo (2019).
49. M. Yusupova (2021).
50. Yusupova (2024).
51. Rutland (2022).
52. Alexseev and Hale (2016).
53. Roman (2002); Sahadeo (2019).
54. Rutland (2022).
55. Rutland (2020).

56. Zakharov (2015), 157.
57. Meduza (2021).
58. Yusupova (2024).
59. Amin (2019).
60. Balzer (2023); G. Yusupova (2021).

REFERENCES

Abashin, Sergey. 2019. "Returning Home and Circular Mobility: How Crises Change the Anthropological View of Migration." *Anthropology & Archeology of Eurasia* 58 (3): 155–68.

———. 2015. *Sovetskii kishlak: Mezhdu kolonializmom i modernizatsiei* [Soviet Kishlak: Between colonialism and modernization]. Moscow: Novoe literaturnoe obozrenie.

Alexseev, Michael, and Henry Hale. 2016. "Rallying 'Round the Leader More Than the Flag: Changes in Russian Nationalist Public Opinion." In *The New Russian Nationalism*, ed. Pål Kolstø and Helge Blakkisrud. Edinburgh: Edinburgh University Press.

Amin, Sarah. 2019. "Cultural Socialization and Ethnic Consciousness." In *The Palgrave Handbook of Ethnicity*. Singapore: Palgrave Macmillan.

Balzer, Marjorie Mandelstam. 2023. "Polarization in Siberia: Thwarted Indigeneity and Sovereignty." Russia.Post, March 4.

———. 2021. *Galvanizing Nostalgia? Indigeneity and Sovereignty in Siberia*. Ithaca, NY: Cornell University Press.

———. 2020a. "Editor's Introduction: Arctic Issues and Identities." Special issue, *Anthropology & Archeology of Eurasia* 58 (4): 205–14.

———. 2020b. "Introduction: Ecology Lessons: Community Solidarity, Indigenous Knowledge, Civic Society in Crisis." Special issue, *Anthropology & Archeology of Eurasia* 59 (3–4): 167–76.

———. 2011. "Religious Communities and Rights in the Russian Federation." In *Religion and the Global Politics of Human Rights*, ed. Thomas Banchoff and Robert Wuthnow. Oxford: Oxford University Press.

Bessudnov, Alexey. 2023. "Ethnic and Regional Inequalities in Russian Military Fatalities in Ukraine: Preliminary Findings from Crowdsourced Data." *Demographic Research* 48 (31): 883–98.

Bowring, Bill. 2013. *Law, Rights and Ideology in Russia*. London: Routledge.

Brubaker, Rogers. 1996. *Nationalism Reframed: Nationhood and the National Question in the New Europe*. Cambridge: Cambridge University Press.

Codagnone, Cristiano, and Vassily Filippov. 2000. "Equity, Exit and National Identity in a Multinational Federation: The 'Multicultural Constitutional Patriotism' Project in Russia." *Journal of Ethnic and Migration Studies* 26 (2): 263–88.

Etkind, Alexander. 2011. *Internal Colonization: Russia's Imperial Experience.* Cambridge: Polity Press.

Gontmakher, Evgeny. 2021. "Russia's Uneven Economic Development." Liechtenstein: Global Intelligence Services, September 16.

Gorenburg, Dmitry. 2006. "Soviet Nationalities Policy and Assimilation." In *Rebounding Identities: The Politics of Identity in Russia and Ukraine*, ed. Dominique Arel and Blair A. Ruble, 273–303. Baltimore: Johns Hopkins University Press.

Kolstø, Pål. 2016. "The Ethnification of Russian Nationalism." In *The New Russian Nationalism: Imperialism, Ethnicity and Authoritarianism*, ed. Pål Kolstø and Helge Blakkisrud, 18–45. Edinburgh: Edinburgh University Press.

Kommersant'. 2018. "Russkomu narodu nashli mesto v rossiiskom" [The Russian people found a place among (nonethnic—ed.) Russians]. October 24.

Laruelle, Marlène. 2016. "Russia in Decline: How Islam Will Change Russia." Jamestown Center, September.

Lenton, Adam C. 2022. "Who Is Dying for the 'Russian World'?" *Riddle*, April 26.

Malakhov, Vladimir. 2007. "Ponaekhali tut: Ocherki o natsionalizme, rasizme i kulturnom pliuralizme" [Came here. Essays about nationalism, racism, and cultural pluralism]. Moscow: Novoe literaturnoe obozrenie.

Malakhov, Vladimir, and Alexander Osipov. 2023 "Managing Ethnic Diversity in Post-Soviet Context: The Cases of Russia, Ukraine, and Kazakhstan." *Problems of Post-Communism*, August 28.

Martin, Terry Dean. 2001. *The Affirmative Action Empire: Nations and Nationalism in the Soviet Union, 1923–1939.* Ithaca, NY: Cornell University Press.

Mediazona. 2022. "Kto gibnet na voine s Ukrainoi: Issledovanie Mediazoni" [Who is dying in the war with Ukraine: Mediazona investigation]. April 25.

Meduza. 2021. "'Undesirable' Comedy Stand-up Comedian Idrak Mirzalizade Made an 'Insulting' Joke. Now He's Banned from Russia for Life." August 30.

Myhre, Marthe Handå. 2017. "The State Program for Voluntary Resettlement of Compatriots: Ideals of Citizenship, Membership, and Statehood in the Russian Federation." *Russian Review* 76 (4): 690–712.

Pain, Emil. 2013. "The Ethno-political Pendulum: The Dynamics of Relationship between Ethnic Minorities and Majorities in Post-Soviet Russia." In *Managing Ethnic Diversity in Russia*, ed. Oleh Protsyk and Benedikt Harzl, 153–72. Abingdon: Routledge.

Pain, Emil, and Sergey Fediunin. 2020. "Intercultural Policies and Practices: Perspectives for Implementation in Russia" [in Russian]. *Polis. Political Studies* 1:114–34.

Prina, Federica. 2016. *National Minorities in Putin's Russia: Diversity and Assimilation.* New York: Routledge.

Roman, Meredith. 2002. "Making Caucasians Black: Moscow Since the Fall of Communism and the Racialization of Non-Russians." *Journal of Communist Studies and Transition Politics* 18 (2): 1–27.

Ross, Cameron, and Rostislav Turovsky. 2013. "The Representation of Political and Economic Elites in the Russian Federation Council." *Demokratizatsiya* 21 (1): 59.

Rutland, Peter. 2022. "Racism and Nationalism." *Nationalities Papers* 50 (4).

———. 2020. "Do Black Lives Matter in Russia?" *PONARS Eurasia*, July 13.

Sahadeo, Jeff. 2019. *Voices from the Soviet Edge: Southern Migrants in Leningrad and Moscow*. Ithaca, NY: Cornell University Press.

Sharafutdinova, Gulnaz. 2013. "Gestalt Switch in Russian Federalism: The Decline in Regional Power under Putin." *Comparative Politics* 45 (3): 357–76.

———. 2020. *The Red Mirror: Putin's Leadership and Russia's Insecure Identity*. Oxford University Press.

Shnirel'man, Viktor. 2022. *Sovremennyi rasizm: Ideologiia i praktika. Sbornik statei* [Contemporary racism: Ideology and practice. Collected essays]. Dashkov i Ko.

———. 2011. *"Porog tolerantnosti": Ideologiia i praktika novogo rasizma* [The tolerance threshold: Ideology and practice of the new racism]. Moscow: Novoe literaturnoe obozrenie.

Shtepa, Vadim. 2021. "Kremlin's Geopolitical Fears Divide Finno-Ugric Peoples." *Eurasia Daily Monitor* (Jamestown Foundation) 18 (100), June 23.

SOVA Center. n.d. "Baza dannykh: Akty vandalizma" [Database: Acts of vandalism]. http://www.sova-center.ru/database/vandalism/ (last viewed September 4, 2023).

Suleymanova, Dilyara. 2018a. "Between Regionalisation and Centralisation: The Implications of Russian Education Reforms for Schooling in Tatarstan." *Europe-Asia Studies* 70 (1): 53–74.

———. 2018b. "Creative Cultural Production and Ethnocultural Revitalization among Minority Groups in Russia." *Cultural Studies* 32 (5): 825–51.

Sullivan, Charles J. 2022. *Motherland: Soviet Nostalgia in the Russian Federation*, 22–39. Singapore: Palgrave Macmillan.

Tolz, Vera. 2001. *Russia: Inventing the Nation*. New York: Oxford University Press.

Walker, Tommy. 2024. "Myanmar's Youth Leaders Fear Conscription Law." Voice of America, March 2.

Yusupova, Guzel. 2024. "The Digital Contestation of Racialized Nationhood in Russia: Manizha's Eurovision Performance." *Communist and Post-Communist Studies* 57 (2): 135–55.

———. 2023. "The Promotion of Minority Languages in Russia's Ethnic Republics: Social Media and Grassroots Activities." In *Varieties of Russian Activism: State-Society Contestation in Everyday Life*, ed. Jeremy Morris, Andrei Semenov, and Regina Smyth. Bloomington: Indiana University Press.

———. 2021. "How Does the Politics of Fear in Russia Work? The Case of Social Mobilisation in Support of Minority Languages." *Europe-Asia Studies* 74 (4): 620–41.

———. 2018. "Cultural Nationalism and Everyday Resistance in an Illiberal Nationalising State: Ethnic Minority Nationalism." *Nations and Nationalism* 24 (3): 624–47.

Yusupova, Marina. 2021. "The Invisibility of Race in Sociological Research on Contemporary Russia: A Decolonial Intervention." *Slavic Review* 80 (2): 224–33.

Zakharov, Nikolay. 2015. *Race and Racism in Russia.* London: Palgrave Macmillan.

Zamyatin, Konstantin. 2016. "Russian Political Regime Change and Strategies of Diversity Management: From a Multinational Federation Towards a Nation-State." *Journal on Ethnopolitics and Minority Issues in Europe* 15 (1): 19–49.

———. 2014. *An Official Status for Minority Languages? A Study of State Languages in Russia's Finno-Ugric Republics.* Helsinki: Finno-Ugrian Society.

NINE

How Putin's Sexism and LGBTQ-Phobia Endanger Russia's and the World's Future

JANET ELISE JOHNSON

Putin's regime has failed women in Russia. When Putin came to power, the situation was already beginning to look worse than under Soviet rule, with the promises of emancipation, especially the broad-based social policies supporting mothering, having been undermined by the weakened state and economy. By 2024, women's rights had been decimated, with Russia rejecting all sorts of international norms of gender justice, including rights to live free from domestic and sexual violence, rights around sexuality or mothering for those who are queer, and rights to organize as women, especially as feminists or lesbians. These reversals were compounded by increased racism directed toward women who were not ethnically Russian (or who were married to men who were not) and by warlordism for women in Chechnya (and eastern Ukraine). Starting in 2006, when Putin announced the maternity capital program to incentivize women to have more children, and again more markedly in the 2010s, Putin fostered a complicated but significant alliance with the Russian

Orthodox Church leadership and ultraconservative forces, both of which reject international norms of gender justice. Despite the claims to protect women and families, this alliance did not lead the Putin regime to address the underlying structural problems facing women, such as in the economy, health care, or social services.

Putin's Russia has also failed gay and transgender men. While male homosexuality was decriminalized in 1993 and limited opportunities for gender-affirming care and legal gender recognition had been created, Putin's Russia has enacted no laws banning discrimination, and no institutions have been set up to protect LGBTQ rights. Instead, with nudging from its new ideological allies, Putin's Russia started targeting LGBTQ people explicitly in 2013 with its vaguely worded ban on "propaganda" among minors of "nontraditional sexual relations," the so-called gay propaganda law. Recently, this law was expanded, a new law eliminating gender recognition was passed, and the "international LGBT movement"—which does not exist as a singular entity—has been labeled an extremist organization.

To substantiate these arguments and to assess Putin's Russia on its own merits, this chapter examines gender- and sexuality-related policy changes since 2000. Formal policy changes, such as legislation, bureaucratic procedural changes, or executive orders, are easier to see, but to the extent possible, I include informal policy shifts as these also indicate the regime's approach. I also understand that policies in hybrid or authoritarian regimes—in which there is rule by law, not rule of law—are not to be taken at face value. Instead, new policies are often worded in expansive or vague ways to allow arbitrary enforcement so that citizens self-censor their behavior or to signal to regime supporters that they have more leeway to threaten or harm people.

Theorists argue that gender and sexuality are analytically distinct, though often intersecting, identities and structures constructed by rules—norms and conventions that shape people's lived experiences in their human bodies. Gender refers to the status of and relations between women and men, affecting and shaping the experiences also of transgender and gender-nonconforming people. Sexuality refers to rules and norms that almost always privilege heterosexuality over other sexualities. However, because of the Soviet legacy of conflating transgender issues with sexuality, along with the human rights coalition that has been created around LGBTQ politics, this chapter includes transgender issues in the LGBTQ category.[1] In other words, when I write about gender equality and women's rights below, I am mostly considering issues of cisgender and heterosexual women's status, while lesbian and trans women are more explicitly included in the discussion of LGBTQ rights.

The common wisdom is that Putin's Russia has been backtracking on matters related to gender and sexuality since 2006, with an outright conservative turn by 2012, followed by an ultraconservative shift in the year leading up to the 2022 full-scale invasion of Ukraine. This chapter supports this description of the overall trend but also acknowledges Putin's ambivalence toward the conservatives' traditionalist agenda, which resulted in some minor policy reforms regarding women's rights even recently. However, most other postcommunist and many "traditionalist" authoritarian regimes have done more to promote women. On LGBTQ issues, the chapter acknowledges that the Putin regime mostly ignored them until 2013.

Many observers connect these shifts over time to Russia's demographic crisis, but this crisis has been ongoing since at least the 1990s, and there is little evidence that policies such as Russia's have an impact on the birth rate. Instead, Putin's changing takes on gender and sexuality are tactical, reflecting the mixed signaling Putin uses to keep elites and the population in line behind his rule.[2] They indicate a regime more focused on maintaining power than on any ideological or policy commitment.

In the following sections, I discuss women's rights and then LGBTQ rights. For both, I put forth models for assessing Putin's Russia, review whether Putin has supported these models, discuss the various types of policy issues, and then examine policy changes since 2000. I then briefly examine Russia's approaches to gender and sexuality in comparison with other postcommunist and authoritarian regimes. I consider what these findings mean for the lived experiences of (cis-hetero) women, gay men, lesbians, and trans and nonbinary people, as well as the stability of the Russian regime.

This analysis provides the basis for the claim that Putin's Russia has failed most of its people and that this failure endangers Russia's and the world's future. In Russia, its approach to gender and sexuality, tactical and self-serving as it is, has not just affected women and LGBTQ people, it has also fostered an informality of politics and the fossilization of a personalist regime. Those politics, in turn, have contributed to Russia's waging of war in Syria, Georgia, and Ukraine, where there is increasing evidence of the use of sexual and gender-based violence by Russia's military or Russia-backed armed forces. The consequences of these wars are devastating for these societies, including for women and LGBTQ people there, but also for those in Russia as a result of the mix of militarism, sexism, and LGBTQ-phobia the regime has embraced to justify its wars to its population. Even without waging war, in its attempt to destabilize democracies and strengthen its role in the world, Putin's Russia has been undermining gender and LGBTQ justice globally through its support of illiberal populist leaders in their "antigender" efforts.[3]

Women's Rights

To create a framework to assess Putin's Russia's impact on women's rights, I discuss three models related to gender equality, the Soviet (and early post-Soviet) legacy, and the various categories of gender-related policy. Feminist political scientists define gender-related policies as "measures through which governments can accelerate progress toward" the ideal of gender equality, a situation in which "all women and men have similar opportunities to participate in politics, the economy, and society; their roles are equally valued; neither suffers from gender-based disadvantage; and both are considered free and autonomous beings with dignity and rights."[4] I then use this framework to assess gender-related policy changes since 2000.

Three Models to Assess Putin's Russia on Gender

The first model is based on international women's rights and requires not just supporting women along essentialist lines but questioning gendered norms. This is not just a Western feminist assessment but something that Putin has periodically embraced, as can be discerned from studying Putin's annual public speeches.[5] In his first two terms as president, he sometimes said things that can been seen as promoting gender justice (such as decrying the lack of women in government positions or women being the only ones to take care of children), or at least not being gendered in expected ways (through the use of such elocutions as bringing up "people in the military" instead of "men in the military" or talking about parents, not just mothers).

The second model is based on Soviet approaches to women's emancipation, which understood women as the primary caretakers of children, but also as workers. This model relies on a stereotypical understanding of gender and calls for public policies or special "privileges" to balance these competing demands. Some on the left find this Soviet/stereotypical model more progressive in practice than liberal feminist approaches because issues of class are directly addressed.[6] Until the summer of 2021, the study of Putin's speeches found, this was the position he most often championed.

However, in the buildup to the full-scale invasion of Ukraine, Putin's formal rhetoric on women became more regressive. It shifted from merely advocating for "traditional families" to adopting an antigender and ultra-conservative stance, actively attacking feminist ideas.[7] At the October 2021 gathering at Valdai, he expressed "amazement at the processes underway in the [Western] countries . . . [such as] the demand to give up the traditional notions of mother, father, family and even gender," deeming efforts to support children's flexibility in embracing gender roles as "truly monstrous" and "verg[ing] on [being] a crime against humanity."[8] At the December 23, 2021, annual big press conference in Moscow, he declared that he would "uphold the traditional approach that a woman is a woman, a man is a man, a mother is a mother, and a father is a father."[9] These pronouncements exemplify the third, regressive model.

Soviet and Early Post-Soviet Legacies with Respect to Different Types of Gender-Related Policy

Establishing a framework for analysis of Putin's Russia also requires being clear about what came before. Putin came to power in Russia on the vestiges of the Soviet model of woman's emancipation. There has been much debate about whether women were better off during or after Communist Party rule, with important complexity gained when the lenses of ethnicity, race, and colonialism are included.[10] The 1990s then brought colossal economic devastation but also new rights for women. Here I consider these legacies and experiences, noting that they vary among seven categories of gender-related policy.

The first category comprises all types of violence against women, including domestic violence between current and former partners or other family members, rape and other forms of sexualized violence or harassment, stalking in person or online in pursuit of a romantic or sexual relationship, female genital mutilation (FGM), and the intentional killing of women related to their being women (femicide). I include forced dress codes, such as compelling women to wear or not wear hijab or niqabs, but there is no clear international norm: some European feminists see only compelling women to wear hijab as violent, and some Islamic feminists would not include the compulsion to wear hijab as a violation of gender justice.

Though the Soviet Union was the first country to address workplace sexual harassment in law in the 1920s, Soviet authorities did little—and Russian authorities in the 1990s did less—to hold men accountable for inflicting violence on women (other than when the public order was also disturbed).[11] The Soviet Union also held violent unveiling campaigns in the Caucasus and Central Asia.

Before Putin, because of the Soviet legacy, Russia was relatively progressive on the next four sets of gender-related policy issues with regards to cis-hetero women. In the second category of gender-related policies are family laws regarding inheritance, guardianship, marital property, right to work, marital names, divorce, custody, and adultery law. The current Family Law was codified in 1995, before Putin, affirming these rights but leaving women with many more financial and care responsibilities for children in the case of divorce. In the third category of policies are those related to women's workplace equality, with many Bolshevik-initiated policies encouraging women to work and requiring equal pay for equal work, but also prohibitions on when women could work or in what professions—ostensibly to protect them—and, after communism, increased gender gaps in wages. The fourth category includes policies related to reproductive justice, including the right to contraception (but also abortion rights for most feminists in Central and Eastern Europe) and maternity care, and the freedom from being compelled to have children. The Soviet Union was the first modern country to legalize abortion, in 1920 (though it recriminalized abortion between 1933 and 1955), and it was widely used by women as contraception. For the overwhelming majority of women who chose to or were compelled to become mothers, there was universal, state-funded care from preconception to postpartum. The fifth category comprises policies that support women who are mothers, especially those without financial resources, such as paid family leave, subsidized child care, and child allowances from the state. Feminists debate the opportunity costs for women's careers of long maternity leave and payments for women to stay home to care for children instead of funding daycare and preschool but tend to support the addition of paternity and family leave for men to help shift the caregiving balance. The Soviet system included paid maternity leave and publicly funded daycare and kindergartens, in addition to full-day schooling. Medical and social services were underfunded during the Soviet period, and funding was significantly reduced in real terms during the economic collapse of the 1990s.

In the sixth category of gender-related policies are those concerning women's rights to participate in the political process, including the right to vote, to serve in elected office, and to organize collectively, with most countries around the world now having implemented some type of gender quota to fast-track women into politics. The Soviet system had an informal quota for women in rubber-stamp legislatures, but these opportunities became meaningful only in the 1990s. In the seventh category are the commitments to the principle of equality, the banning of discrimination, and the establishment and maintenance of institutions responsible for addressing gender equality. Before Putin, there was a foundation of formal commitments to the principle of equality of the sexes, including in the 1993 constitution and all major legal codes.[12] There were also several institutions related to the status of women, such as the Duma Committee on the Family, Women and Youth, but only one committed to gender equality, the Commission for the Advancement of Women's Status, established under the Government of the Russian Federation in 1996.[13]

In sum, by 2000, most women in Russia had many civil, political, and economic rights, but not the right to live free from bodily harm, and the practice of these rights was severely limited by the lack of state capacity and commitment.

Women's Rights Policy Changes in Putin's Russia

Table 9.1 summarizes Russia's gender-related policy changes since 2000, categorizing them both by type of policy and according to the three assessment models. The first column includes the reforms assessed to be progressive in terms of international norms of gender justice and the last column lists reforms that are regressive by that standard but that traditionalist or antigender ultraconservatives are likely to extol as being "pro-family." In the middle column are policy reforms that reflect the Soviet approach to women's emancipation, which Putin embraced through much of his tenure. These policies can be seen from various angles as either beneficial for or detrimental to women.

ASSESSMENT BASED ON INTERNATIONAL WOMEN'S RIGHTS NORMS. Several patterns are evident in this analysis from the perspective of international feminist norms. First is the trend that, in general, the situation gets worse for women over time, with more progressive and meaningful policies in the early part of Putin's rule and more regressive policies later. This trend reflects the common wisdom among gender scholars that Putin has increasingly failed women. However, this is not the whole story as some tiny progressive policy changes were made in the past decade, including in 2022—2024.

Table 9.1. Women's Rights Policy Changes by Issue and Assessment Model, 2000–2024

Policy issues	Progressive reforms according to international norms	Soviet-like reforms with mixed assessments	Regressive policy changes according to international norms
All types of violence against women	Criminalization of trafficking in persons (2003)[14] Establishment of public women's crisis centers for violence in the family (mid-2000s) Criminalization of battery between close persons (2016)[17] Clarification of the badly written partial decriminalization of battery to apply only to the first instance (2022)[20]	None	Ceding authority to regions of Chechnya, Dagestan, and Ingushetia on issues such as FGM, honor killings, domestic violence, dress codes, and kidnapping by men or authorities (after 2007)[15] Refusal to sign the Council of Europe's Istanbul Convention on violence against women (2011)[16] Partial decriminalization of domestic violence (2017), which signaled tolerance, including of femicide;[18] only 3% of the recommended shelter spaces existed by 2021[19]
Family law	None	None	Ceding authority to Chechnya, Dagestan, and Ingushetia regarding custody, divorce, polygamy, and child marriage (after 2007)[21]
Women's workplace equality	Ban on sex-specific and physical appearance–based job advertisements (2013) Shortened list of professions banned for women (2019)	None	None
Reproductive justice	Introduction of "childbirth vouchers" program allowing women a choice of obstetrician and facility and small incentives to register early in a pregnancy (2006)[22]	None	Creation of the annual Day of Family, Love and Fidelity on top of an Orthodox holiday to support "traditional values" (2008) and fines for "propaganda against childbearing" (2024)

	Fathers allowed to attend births in public clinics if there is no other birthing parent in the room (2011)[24] Two popular emergency contraception drugs made available over-the-counter (2024)	Ban on advertising about abortion in public places where children might be (2009)[23] Abortion on socioeconomic grounds limited to the first 12 weeks of gestation and a required waiting period introduced (2011) Procedural changes to require counseling to dissuade women from having abortions (2020–)[25] Drugs used for medical abortions recategorized as controlled substances, pressures on private clinics to cease providing abortion, and unnecessary tests required (2023–2024)
Paid family leave and subsidized childcare	Maternity leave procedural reform that made it easier for women to be compensated if fired while pregnant (2011)[26] Stipulation that all children from 2 months to 8 years of age are guaranteed access to a public daycare/preschool (2012), though notable gaps in practice for children 18–36 months (most women take 18 months of partially funded childcare leave)[28]	Introduction of maternity capital program ($7,000–$11,000) for second and subsequent children (2006) and amendments extending program to the first child (2020)[27] Monthly child benefits for young children in low-income families introduced (2006) and then expanded from 18 months to age 3 (2017), to age 7 (2020), and to age 17 (2022) Resurrection of the Soviet Mother Heroine rank for raising 10 kids (2022)

(continued)

Table 9.1. *(continued)*

Policy issues	Progressive reforms according to international norms	Soviet-like reforms with mixed assessments	Regressive policy changes according to international norms
Right to participate in political processes	Obligation to create equal opportunities for women's representation (2001)[29]	An increase in women in politics from 2000, with a significant jump (especially in the appointed upper house) after 2012 as the regime consolidated as authoritarian[30]	Pressure against foreign donors and increased regulation of women's and feminist NGOs while supporting pro-regime conservative groups (2006) Increasing repression of feminist groups and activists, marked by Pussy Riot arrests, using a variety of laws, such as foreign agents law (2012), "insulting believers' religious feelings" law (2013), and "undesirable organizations" law (2015)
Principle of gender equality or banning of discrimination or institutions responsible for addressing gender equality	A fine introduced (but rarely used) for discrimination based on sex (and race, ethnicity, language, origin, etc.) (2011)[31] National Action Strategy plans periodically adopted, including in 2022, stating a commitment to "ensure the principle of equal rights and freedoms for men and women and create equal opportunities for their implementation"[33]	None	Disbanding of Commission for the Advancement of Women's Status (2004)[32] Increasing alliance with ultraconservative Russian Orthodox Church leadership, philosophers, politicians, oligarchs, and paramilitary groups (2009–)[34] Withdrawal from the Council of Europe, depriving women of a variety of gender equality mechanisms (2022)

Second, there is important variation by policy issue. Most positively, working women, especially working mothers, received some new support throughout the period. There were also attempts to improve maternity care, which gave women a bit more choice, but the system remained paternalistic, and some neoliberal reforms undermined care in rural regions.[35] More mixed was the significant increase in women in politics starting in the 2010s as a result of Kremlin input, though this was not done to promote women's rights but to increase regime support.[36] When women in the media brought credible claims of sexual harassment against Duma deputy Leonid Slutsky in 2018, several women deputies supported him. The committee appointed to investigate exonerated him, highlighting the constraints faced by women in public life.

Most troubling were the partial decriminalization of battery, which signaled lack of concern for domestic violence, and the repression of women's and feminist activists, which made feminist activism incredibly difficult if not impossible by 2024. Despite this pressure, feminists were increasingly active in the 2010s through 2022, not just online with grassroots feminist schools and social media campaigns but also through what appears to be the largest feminist protest in a century, the 2019 demonstration in support of the Khachaturyan sisters, who killed their father after years of abuse and police apathy. After the full-scale invasion of Ukraine, women's groups, including the Feminist Anti-War Resistance and the Put' Domoi group of wives and mothers of mobilized soldiers, have been the most active presence in resisting the war, but the visible members of the former live in exile, and by June 2024, both groups had been branded "foreign agents."

Third, certain categories of women fared much worse than others. Women in the North Caucasus faced extreme forms of gendered violence and patriarchal family law as the Kremlin ceded authority over those issues to Chechen president Ramzan Kadyrov, a warlord embraced by Putin. There appear to be no gender-related policies that addressed the concerns of other ethnic minorities or the millions of immigrants from Central Asia. (Lesbian and transwomen are discussed below.)

Not covered in the table are gender equality policymaking failures. Not only was the only high-level gender equality–promoting institution disbanded in 2004, but efforts to pass meaningful gender equality legislation, On State Guarantees of Equal Rights, Freedoms and Equal Opportunities for Men and Women in the Russian Federation, were stymied in 2003 and then proponents faced intense backlash in 2012–2013, with opponents arguing the legislation threatened "traditional values."[37] Similarly, there have been many attempts to pass comprehensive reform addressing domestic violence, most notably in 2013 and 2019, that were blocked and then pilloried by antigender ultraconservatives. Unsurprisingly, Russia is certainly not a feminist regime.

ASSESSMENT BASED ON SOVIET/STEREOTYPICAL NORMS. From the perspective of Soviet/stereotypical norms, 2006 marked a success, a shift back to paternalistic approaches toward women but ones that supported mothers with an assumption that they would be working. Many feminist Russianists have been critical of Putin's signature gender-related policy, the maternity (family) capital, for its application only to mothers with more than one child and for signaling that women should mother many children. Yet the funds were intentionally allocated to mothers, and, much like the Soviet approaches, the policy offers financial support for those having children, which has proven helpful for some mothers in the poorer, rural regions (see chapter 7).[38] The increase in women in politics in the 2010s is also a success from this perspective. Women gained more appearance of representation, bringing more equality to men, who constitute the overwhelming majority in politics.

Seen through this lens, where Putin fails most women is in the inability to address the deeper structural problems in the social and health services and society, which sets Russia far apart from the achievements of social democracies. The maternity capital policy is superficial, not structural, and it has been used by only half of those eligible because it is difficult or impractical to use.[39] Instead of a cash payment, it is given as a certificate for use in buying or renovating housing, to pay for a child's education or assistance if disabled, or for a mother's pension, but these benefits are receivable only once the child reaches the age of three. Most poor families have more immediate needs, such as food and clothing, that are not covered under the policy. The policy also fell prey to the informal systems that undermine most formal governance in Russia. Networks of bureaucrats, realtors, and financial entities for illegally cashing out these certificates emerged almost immediately; in other cases, fake births were registered to secure certificates.

In addition, while socialist approaches demand treating all women equally, Putin's Russia has failed women in the North Caucasus by abdicating its authority. Similarly, Putin's claim to care about women and their children is undermined by the officially organized and ordered kidnapping of children from their parents in Ukraine into Russia.[40]

LGBTQ Rights

On LGBTQ issues, this analysis is much simpler. There is only one progressive model, international LGBTQ human rights norms, which I use below. Putin never publicly embraced these norms, but he also did not say much against them until 2012 when he started aligning with ultraconservatives.[41] In the last few years, he has been proclaiming the dangers of gay pride marches and gender fluidity as "perversions that lead to degradation and extinction."[42]

In contrast to the Soviet promises of women's emancipation, Putin had virtually no positive Soviet legacy to draw on regarding sexuality. Though the Bolsheviks had decriminalized male homosexuality in 1922, this relaxation of repression was short-lived; within a decade Stalin had reversed course, and male homosexuality remained criminalized until after the Soviet collapse.[43] Tens of thousands of gay men were convicted and sent to labor camps, where many faced sexual violence. Thousands of lesbians were institutionalized as mentally ill, and all LGBTQ people were surveilled by their families, schools, and workplaces. The Soviet legacy was more progressive for trans people, with some quietly allowed surgery and legal gender recognition, and the Soviet Ministry of Health developed a formal policy in 1991.[44]

As with gender, there are several types of LGBTQ-related policies with which to assess Putin's impact, and there was some progress on LGBTQ issues in the 1990s. The first is all types of violence against LGBTQ people related to their sexuality or non-conventional gender, often understood as hate crimes and including murder. While international pressures led to decriminalization of male homosexuality in 1993, the reform of the criminal code, while trying to broaden notions of sexual assault from heterosexual rape, also created troubling crimes, such as "forced lesbianism." Although Russia developed a legal framework regarding hate crimes, courts systemically refused to recognize anti-LGBTQ violence as such.[45]

In the second category are family laws, such as legalization of same-sex unions or marriages and facilitation of coparenting by same-sex partners, and laws allowing sex changes on legal documents. In the 1990s, as was only beginning to happen globally, no laws facilitated legal partnerships, and neither the Soviet nor the Russian state recognized lesbians', gay men's, or trans people's rights to have a family. In 1997, another law was passed regarding changing one's gender on formal documents, but the required form was not created, leading to legal gender recognition on an ad hoc basis.

Third are workplace equality, such as laws requiring equal treatment regardless of LGBTQ status, and no such protections were passed in the 1990s. Fourth are medical and reproductive rights, such as gender-affirming care and access to assisted reproductive technologies for everyone regardless of marital or LGBTQ status. In 1999, the Ministry of Health no longer categorized homosexuality as mental illness and formalized rules for (limited) gender-affirming care.[46] Fifth are LGBTQ people's rights to participate in the political process, including the right to vote, to serve in elected office, and to organize collectively. This perhaps was the area of greatest improvement in the 1990s, as advocacy and support groups began to emerge.

Sixth are the commitments to the principle of equality, the banning of discrimination in general, and the creation of institutions responsible for addressing LGBTQ equality. In the 1990s, no policies were passed banning discrimination against LGBTQ individuals, and no significant state-based institutions charged with fostering LGBTQ rights were created.

Table 9.2 outlines Russia's LGBTQ-related policy changes since Putin came to power. The pattern is straightforward on gay rights: there were no positive reforms, only regressive policies. Most far-reaching was the ban on "propaganda about nontraditional sexual relationships," which is often called the "gay propaganda" law but has been applied to all LGBTQ identities.[47] While there had been attempts to criminalize homosexuality again in the early 2000s, they did not pass, but this ban, which claims to prevent harm to children, does not address any real question of harm. Instead, it was a signal that LGBTQ people were threats to Russian society, and it authorized backtracking on all sorts of rights that LGBTQ citizens should theoretically have on the basis of their citizenship. The ban was expanded in several ways starting in 2022, leading to a new wave of repression of LGBTQ entities and venues such as gay bars and drag shows, restrictions on social media, and the emigration of LGBTQ people.

More complicated were trans rights. In 2022, one expert claimed that "Russia has a surprisingly developed system of medical care for trans people. . . . The procedure of LGR [legal gender recognition] is among

Table 9.2. LGBTQ Rights Policy Changes by Issue and Assessment, 2000–2024

Policy issues	Progressive changes relative to international norms	Regressive changes relative to international norms
All types of violence against LGBTQ people	None	"Gay propaganda" ban (2013) and its extension (2022), which authorized court cases against gay people and hate crimes, including murder[49] Gay purges in Chechnya in which hundreds of gay and bisexual men were imprisoned and tortured by law enforcement; lesbian and bisexual women were targeted with violence by family members, and some LGBTQ persons were kidnapped back "home" (2017, 2019–)[50] Government tolerance for parents paying thugs to kidnap LGBTQ children for conversion therapy (2023–)[51]
Family law and laws allowing document changes[52]	Form adopted to standardize legal gender recognition, creating more opportunities for trans people (2017)[53]	Ban on adoption of Russian children by nationals of countries with legal same-sex marriage (2013) or gender transitions (2024) Constitutional amendment limiting marriage to between a man and a woman (2020)
LGBTQ workplace equality	None	"Gay propaganda" ban authorizing unequal treatment at work
Medical and reproductive rights	None	"Gay propaganda" ban making "public lesbian parenting" impossible and trans parenting increasingly difficult[54] Law banning surgery and hormone treatment for transgender people (2023)

(continued)

Table 9.2. *(continued)*

Policy issues	Progressive changes relative to international norms	Regressive changes relative to international norms
Right to participate in political processes	None	Pressure applied to foreign donors and increased regulation of LGBTQ NGOs while supporting pro-regime conservative groups (2006)
		Increasing repression of LGBTQ groups and activists using a variety of laws such as foreign agents law (2012), "gay propaganda" law (2013), and "undesirable organizations" law (2015), with all major LGBTQ organizations listed as foreign agents by the end of 2021
		Declaration by Supreme Court that the "international LGBT movement" should be listed as extremists (2023), and it was (2024)[55]
Principle of LGBTQ equality or banning of discrimination or institutions responsible for addressing LGBTQ equality	None	Increasing alliance with ultraconservative Russian Orthodox Church leadership, philosophers, politicians, oligarchs, and paramilitary groups (2009–)[56]

the easiest and quickest in the world and requires no medical interventions."[48] These de facto trans rights resulted from the Soviet legacy of medicalization of gender variance and loopholes in regulation that allowed hormones to be acquired without a prescription. This situation formally ended in 2023 when the State Duma passed a law banning both medical assistance in gender transition and legal gender recognition.

By 2024, all LGBTQ rights had been eliminated across Russia, with impunity granted to individuals and groups to harass and harm LGBTQ people, most horrifically in Chechnya. In addition to the decade-long arguments about LGBTQ rights being only Western values that Russia must resist, anti-gender forces added claims that allowing gender transitions was creating opportunities for men to evade being drafted to fight in Ukraine.

Comparisons with Other Postcommunist and Traditionalist Authoritarian Regimes

The Putin regime's policy changes regarding gender appear much worse when placed in a comparative context. While Russia has not passed any gender equality law, Ukraine passed one in 2005, Kazakhstan in 2009, and Georgia in 2010, along with two of the three Baltic countries. While Russia has passed no comprehensive legislation on domestic violence, virtually all other postcommunist countries have. While Russia has had no women presidents or prime ministers, such women firsts have become relatively commonplace in the region, not just in Central and Eastern Europe (Serbia, Romania, Poland, Croatia, Slovenia, Kosovo, Latvia, Lithuania, Estonia, and Finland) but also in non-Baltic states of the former Soviet Union (Georgia, Ukraine, Moldova, and Kyrgyzstan).

Given the variation in postcommunist regime types, a more realistic comparison is with other authoritarian regimes, but even those outshine Russia on women's rights. In the twenty-first century, "dictatorships are actively enacting women's rights legislation at rates that surpass democracies."[57] Saudi Arabia, for example, having prohibited women from voting or running for its Consultative Assembly, changed course in the 2010s, and in 2023, women made up nearly one-fifth of its members, matching the average for the Middle East and North Africa, which has tripled since 2000.[58] In the Maghreb, comprehensive constitutional and legislative reforms have created more equitable family laws, new laws against violence against women, and new protections of reproductive rights.[59] Other authoritarian regimes, such as those in Laos, Ethiopia, Malaysia, and Uganda, have adopted legal reforms or set up entities supposedly to represent women or to make policy decisions that promote gender equality.[60] Of course, these regimes are likely undertaking these reforms to burnish their reputations and distract from "persistent authoritarian practices,"[61] but the comparison clarifies changing international norms even for traditionalist authoritarian regimes.

In contrast, Russia has not enacted major reforms aimed at addressing gender inequality. One could argue that women in Russia entered the twenty-first century with many more rights than women in Arab autocracies, suggesting such reforms were less necessary. However, Russia is now doing badly in terms of the proportion of women in politics despite having been a forerunner during the Soviet period. As of May 2023, Russia was ranked 139 out of a total 185 countries for the proportion of women in the lower (or single) house parliament. If only authoritarian regimes were included, Russia was thirty-ninth, behind the United Arab Emirates, Uganda, Iraq, Egypt, Saudi Arabia, and Turkey, including countries with similar communist legacies (Belarus, Uzbekistan, Kazakhstan, Azerbaijan, Turkmenistan, and China).[62]

On LGBTQ issues, Russia looks less regressive in comparison to these regimes. Unlike on women's rights, there is no pattern of authoritarian regimes enacting progressive reforms on LGBTQ issues. In 2023, Uganda, for example, added the death penalty to possible punishments for homosexuality, and also introduced the possibility of twenty years' imprisonment for "promoting" homosexuality. Most other Communist Party–led regimes decriminalized homosexuality after Stalin's death—many became more progressive than their Western counterparts at the time—but homosexuality was still seen as pathological, and all these regimes have been slow to progress since 1989. Still, it's worth noting that, as of August 2023, Slovenia and Estonia have legalized same-sex marriages, and many other postcommunist countries in Central Europe recognize civil unions, while Russia has been pushing the gay propaganda ban in the South Caucasus and Central Asia.

Implications of Russia's Two Decades of Policy Changes on Gender and Sexuality

From the perspective of feminist and queer political science, governments succeed when they create public policy that helps solve collective problems for all categories of people—in this case, those disempowered as a result of gender and sexuality—and create sustainable institutions and practices likely to solve those problems in the future. For those working within intergovernmental organizations or transnational social movements, this is often understood as protecting human rights. States are seen as more responsible for their own citizens and residents than for those outside the state, but at the very least, success means not creating problems for others, and perhaps sometimes helping people in other countries through humanitarian assistance, human rights advocacy, and diplomacy. Of course, these are ideals that few, if any, states meet, so failure is more than just not meeting these ideals but doing so in a marked way. Failure is not meeting the standards set in state rhetoric or in comparison to other similarly situated states or doing worse over time. Worse than failure is perpetrating or sanctioning mass violence or deprivation based on people's gender or sexuality inside or outside the country.

So what does this evidence of Russia's policymaking since 2000 suggest about Putin's success or failure in addressing the problems faced by those disempowered by gender and sexuality? While there were a few promising policies for heterosexual women outside the North Caucasus—and more if your perspective is Old Left—Russia's two-decade pattern suggests no commitment to gender justice. Steeped in Soviet approaches, Putin was open to more progressive policies in the early 2000s when Russia was still trying to cast itself within global norms. After the economy faltered during the 2007–2008 global financial crisis and the glow of Russia's 2014 annexation of Crimea faded, the regime's policies became more traditionalist on women's rights, and more homophobic. In the lead-up to and during the full-scale invasion of Ukraine when more support was needed, Russia adopted some ultraconservative policies, and all along condoned ultraconservative justifications for state violence against women and gay men in parts of the North Caucasus. However, Putin doesn't seem to be committed to any of these approaches to gender, even the more traditionalist approach he has taken recently. His personal life is anything but traditional: Putin has been divorced since 2014 and has had extramarital relationships and children, it seems, during and after his marriage.[63] Given the Soviet legacy, Putin may be more LGBTQ-phobic than sexist, but gender and LGBTQ politics are mostly being used for tactical reasons, not ideological commitments, to maintain his power.

This argument about the tactical use of gender and sexuality echoes arguments by other scholars about the Kremlin's image-making around Putin. With staged photos of his "manly" hobbies and images of his naked chest, Putin has been cast as the hypermasculine erotic superleader in order to justify his power and Russia's authoritarianism.[64] A "cult of personality" has been constructed, creating "complete fusion between the man and the state."[65] In these ways, gender and sexuality have been part and parcel of the creation of a personalist autocracy with weak institutions and little promise of long-term stability in light of Putin's age.

While this chapter focuses on the policies related to those in Russia, it would be irresponsible to ignore the impact abroad. With the conservative turn in the 2010s, gender and sexuality also became a tool in Russia's foreign policy.[66] In terms of so-called soft power, hundreds of millions of dollars' worth of rubles were spent on anti-gender campaigns as part of efforts to destabilize democratic politics in other countries and to justify its warmongering and war-waging, with much of the money coming from Konstantin Malofeyev (a warlord who pioneered mercenary Russian forces in eastern Ukraine).[67] In 2015 the Kremlin established a government-organized nongovernmental organization (GONGO), the Eurasian Women's Forum, to advance its increasingly traditionalist version of gender equality globally, with meetings that included right-wing European women politicians while simultaneously calling for women to fight against Nazism.[68] These efforts have had a concrete and devastating impact as they became part of the justification for the war against Ukraine. Not just in the former Soviet bloc or Europe, the Kremlin disinformation campaign helped get Donald Trump elected in the United States, playing on sexist tropes and fears of his women opponents. Trump's 2016 election laid the groundwork for the biggest rollback in decades of women's rights in the overturning of *Roe v. Wade* and what the Human Rights Campaign calls a national state of emergency for LGBTQ Americans.[69]

I would also argue that sexism (and LGBTQ phobia) is a part of Russia's hard power foreign policy. There is some evidence of the tolerance of sexual violence in Russia's 2008 war against Georgia.[70] Such violence appears to be more systematic in Ukraine, with the use of sexual violence by Kremlin-sponsored groups in rebel-controlled areas of Ukraine from 2014, the seeming impunity with which Russia's soldiers raped and sexually tortured women in 2022, and the imposition of sexualized violence as a means of control within detention centers.[71] Without addressing issues of gender and LGBTQ justice within Russia, Russia gave its military, Wagner mercenaries, Chechen Kadyrovites, and Kremlin-backed leaders impunity to use sexual and LGBTQ-phobic violence. Contrary to Putin's claim to care about Russian women, these consequences have been disastrous for Russian-speaking women in Ukraine.

This evidence shows that Putin's Russia has failed women (including lesbians), gay men, and transgender people, who collectively constitute more than half of Russia's population. In most places in Russia, the state has done practically nothing to protect their rights or solve their real problems, but instead has sometimes sanctioned violence by citizens (with the "gay propaganda" law or the partial decriminalization of domestic violence) and sometimes committed violence (with its unlawful imprisonment of feminist and LGBTQ activists). The policies have gotten worse over time, in contrast to authoritarian regimes globally, which are at least paying lip service to gender equality.

Putin's Russia has not even met Putin's own standards that he established in formal rhetoric in the 2000s. For those in the North Caucasus, it is far worse, with more state-perpetrated or more widespread state-sanctioned violence targeting these populations. For those in Syria and Ukraine, where Russia has targeted civilian infrastructure if not civilians themselves, it is too soon to know the extent of gendered and sexualized violence, but it looks like war crimes.

This chapter has not addressed the concerns of Russia's cisgender, heterosexual men, yet it is easy to see failures for this population, too, with millions fleeing Russia to avoid being sent to kill or used as cannon fodder in Russia's unjustified war in Ukraine (especially ethnic minority and Central Asian men). When people say they admire Putin for his strongman rule of Russia for more than two decades, they are ignoring his impact on the lives of most Russians, let alone those outside Russia.

NOTES

For comments on drafts of this chapter, the author thanks Alexandra Novitskaya, Valerie Sperling, Valeria Umanets, Steven Fisher, Harley Balzer, and George Andreopoulos, as well as the participants on the conference panel "Women and Power/Politics in Soviet and Post-Soviet Russia" at the 2023 ASEEES convention and the Spring 2024 CUNY Human Rights Workshop.

1. On the Soviet legacy of conflating these various terms and issues, see Novitskaya et al. (2024).
2. Johnson et al. (2021).
3. Datta (2021).
4. Htun and Weldon (2018).
5. Johnson et al. (2021).
6. Ghodsee (2018).
7. Novitskaya et al. (2024).
8. "Vladimir Putin Meets with Members of the Valdai Discussion Club. Transcript of the Plenary Session of the 18th Annual Meeting," Valdai Club, October 22, 2021, cited in Novitskaya et al. (2024).

9. Kremlin, "Vladimir Putin's Annual News Conference," December 23, 2021, cited in Novitskaya et al. (2024).
10. Johnson, Fabian, and Lazda (2022).
11. Johnson (2009)
12. Hoare and Muravyeva (2019).
13. Hoare and Muravyeva (2019), 24.
14. Johnson (2009).
15. See the website for Stichting Justice Initiative at https://srji.org/en/; see also OC Media (2020).
16. Muravyeva (2022).
17. Johnson (2023).
18. Johnson (2023).
19. WAVE (2021).
20. Ibid.
21. Lokshina (2017, 2021).
22. Temkina, Novkunskaya, and Litvina (2023).
23. Chandler (2013), 125.
24. Ibid.
25. Luxmoore (2021).
26. Johnson (2016).
27. Roberts (2020).
28. Bodrova and Yudina (2018).
29. Hoare and Muravyeva (2019), 23.
30. Johnson (2016).
31. Hoare and Muravyeva (2019), 23.
32. Hoare and Muravyeva (2019), 24.
33. Russian Federation (2022).
34. Novitskaya et al. (2024).
35. Temkina, Novkunskaya, and Litvina (2023), 3, 51.
36. Johnson (2016).
37. Hoare and Muravyeva (2019), 23.
38. The policy is now officially the "maternity (family) capital" and can be given to men in families with male-headed households.
39. Roberts (2023).
40. Ryzhkova and Gamalova (2023).
41. Novitskaya et al. (2024).
42. Kremlin, "Signing of Treaties on Accession of Donetsk and Lugansk People's Republics and Zaporozhye and Kherson Regions to Russia," September 30, 2022, cited in Novitskaya et al. (2024).
43. Novitskaya et al. (2024).
44. Kirey-Sitnikova (2022).
45. Kondakov (2022).

46. Kirey-Sitnikova (2022), 58.
47. Kondakov and Novitskaya (2022).
48. Kirey-Sitnikova (2022), 68.
49. Ibid.
50. Lokshina and Knight (2021).
51. Dixon (2023); Queer Women of the North Caucasus (2018).
52. Note a possible regressive policy banning legal gender changes, passed on the first reading on June 14, 2023, and reported by Meduza (2023).
53. Kirey-Sitnikova (2022), 5.
54. Zhabenko (2019).
55. Reuters (2024).
56. Novitskaya et al. (2024).
57. Donno, Fox, and Kaasik (2022).
58. Inter-Parliamentary Union (2023).
59. Tripp (2019).
60. Donno, Fox, and Kaasik (2022).
61. Bjarnegård, Håkansson, and Zetterberg (2022).
62. Inter-Parliamentary Union (2023).
63. Kovalenko and Rothrock (2023).
64. Riabov and Riabova (2014); Sperling (2014); Wood (2016).
65. Gaufman (2023, 37).
66. Gaufman (2023).
67. Datta (2021).
68. Gradskova (2023).
69. See the web page of the Human Rights Campaign titled "Anti-LGBTQ+ Laws? Know before You Go," at https://www.hrc.org/campaigns/national-state-of-emergency-for-lgbtq-americans.
70. Human Rights House Foundation (2010).
71. Gall and Boushnak (2023).

REFERENCES

Bjarnegård, Elin, Sandra Håkansson, and Pär Zetterberg. 2022. "Gender and Violence against Political Candidates: Lessons from Sri Lanka." *Politics & Gender* 18 (1).

Bodrova, Elena, and Elena Yudina. 2018. "Early Childhood Education in the Russian Federation." In *Handbook of International Perspectives on Early Childhood Education*, ed. Jaipaul L. Roopnarine, James E. Johnson, Suzanne Flannery Quinn, and Michael M. Patte, 56–69. Abingdon: Routledge.

Chandler, Andrea. 2013. *Democracy, Gender and Social Policy in Russia: A Wayward Society*. Houndsmills: Palgrave Macmillan.

Datta, Neil. 2021. *Tip of the Iceberg: Religious Extremist Funders against Human Rights for Sexuality and Reproductive Health in Europe 2009–2018*. Brussels: European Parliamentary Forum for Sexual & Reproductive Rights, June 15.

Dixon, Robyn. 2023. "In Russia, Parents Are Having Gay Children Abducted to Be 'Cured.'" *Washington Post*, December 22.

Donno, Daniela, Sara Fox, and Joshua Kaasik. 2022. "International Incentives for Women's Rights in Dictatorships." *Comparative Political Studies* 55 (3): 454.

Gall, Carlotta, with photographs by Laura Boushnak. 2023. "'Fear Still Remains': Ukraine Finds Sexual Crimes Where Russian Troops Ruled." *New York Times*, January 5.

Gaufman, Elizaveta. 2023. *Everyday Foreign Policy: Performing and Consuming the Russian Nation after Crimea*. Manchester: Manchester University Press.

Ghodsee, Kristen R. 2018. *Why Women Have Better Sex under Socialism: And Other Arguments for Economic Independence*. New York: Random House.

Gradskova, Yulia. 2023. "From Defending Women's Rights in the 'Whole World' to Silence about Russia's Predatory War? The (Geo)politics of the Eurasian Women's Forums in the Context of 'Traditional Values.'" In *Post-Soviet Women: New Challenges and Ways to Empowerment*, ed. Ann-Mari Sätre, Yulia Gradskova, and Vladislava Vladimirova, 29–49. Cham, CH: Palgrave Macmillan.

Hoare, Joanna, and Marianna Muravyeva. 2019. *Achieving Balanced Participation of Women and Men in Political and Public Decision Making in the Russian Federation*. Strasbourg: Council of Europe, October.

Htun, Mala, and S. Laurel Weldon. 2018. *The Logics of Gender Justice: State Action on Women's Rights around the World*. Cambridge: Cambridge University Press.

Human Rights House Foundation. 2010. "Victim of Sexual Abuse during the August War in Georgia Appeals to the ECHR." March 9.

Inter-Parliamentary Union. 2023. "Monthly Ranking of Women in National Parliaments" (database) as of May 1, 2023. https://data.ipu.org/women-ranking?month=5&year=2023 (accessed June 15, 2023).

Johnson, Janet Elise. 2023. "Authoritarian Gender Equality Policy Making: The Politics of Domestic Violence in Russia." *Politics & Gender* 19 (4): 1035–60.

———. 2016. "Fast-Tracked or Boxed In? Informal Politics, Gender, and Women's Representation in Putin's Russia." *Perspectives on Politics* 14 (3): 643–59.

———. 2009. *Gender Violence in Russia: The Politics of Feminist Intervention*. Bloomington: Indiana University Press.

Johnson, Janet Elise, Katalin Fabian, and Mara Lazda. 2022. "The Gendered Ambiguity of the Postcommunist Transitions." *Russian Review* 81 (2): 344–53.

Johnson, Janet Elise, Alexandra Novitskaya, Valerie Sperling, and Lisa McIntosh Sundstrom. 2021. "Mixed Signals: What Putin Says about Gender Equality." *Post-Soviet Affairs* 37 (6): 507–25.

Kirey-Sitnikova, Yana. 2022. "Access to Trans Healthcare in Russia." In *Trans Health: Global Perspectives on Care for Trans Communities*, ed. M. N. Appenroth and Castro Varela. Bielefeld: transcript Verlag.

Kondakov, Alexander Sasha. 2022. *Violent Affections: Queer Sexuality, Techniques of Power, and Law in Russia*. UCL Press.

Kondakov, Alexander, and Alexandra Novitskaya. 2022. "The Politics of Gender and Sexuality." In *Russian Politics Today: Stability and Fragility*, ed. Susanne A. Wengle. Cambridge: Cambridge University Press.

Kovalenko, Ania, and Kevin Rothrock. 2023. "Putin's Private Life and Off-the-Books Family." Meduza, June 9.

Lokshina, Tanya. 2021. "European Court Rules to Reunite Chechen Woman with Her Children." Human Rights Watch, November 25.

———. 2017. "In Chechnya, a Ruthless Strongman Orders Family Reunification." Human Rights Watch, September 6.

Lokshina, Tanya, and Kyle Knight. 2021. "No End to Chechnya's Violent Anti-Gay Campaign." Human Rights Watch, August 31.

Luxmoore, Matthew. 2021 "Russia Announces Plan to Halve Abortion Rates to Spur Population Growth." Radio Free Europe / Radio Liberty, September 22.

Meduza. 2023. "State Duma Approves First Reading of Bill Banning Legal Gender Changes." June 14.

Muravyeva, Marianna. 2022. "Russia and the Istanbul Convention: Domestic Violence Legislation and Cultural Sovereignty." *Osteuropa-Recht* 68 (1): 147–64.

Novitskaya, Alexandra, Valerie Sperling, Lisa McIntosh Sundstrom, and Janet Elise Johnson. 2024. "Unpacking 'Traditional Values' in Russia's Conservative Turn: Gender, Sexuality and the Soviet Legacy." *Europe Asia Studies* 76 (2): 173–97.

OC Media. 2020. "Chechen Women Scolded and Forced to Remove Niqabs on State TV." December 2.

Queer Women of the North Caucasus. 2018. *Violence against Lesbian, Bisexual and Transgender Women in the North Caucasus Region of the Russian Federation*. Moscow: Heinrich Böll.

Reuters. 2024. "Russia Adds 'LGBT Movement' to List of Extremist and Terrorist Organisations." March 22.

Riabov, Oleg, and Tatiana Riabova. 2014. "The Remasculinization of Russia? Gender, Nationalism, and the Legitimation of Power under Vladimir Putin." *Problems of Post-Communism* 61 (2): 23–35.

Roberts, James McMeehan. 2023. "Obnalichivanie (Russia)." Global Informality Project.

———. 2020. "Putin's Pursuit of the Baby Boom—The Next Chapter." UCL SSEES Post-Soviet Brief.

Russian Federation. 2022. "Natsional'naia Strategiia deystvii v interesakh zhenshchin na 2023–2030 gody" [National Strategy of Action for Women 2023–2030]. Moscow. http://static.government.ru/media/files/ilHtVCkhskBAE9DAflD3Akpd787xAOc4.pdf (accessed June 11, 2024).

Ryzhkova, Anna, and Regina Gamalova. 2023. "'Just Call Me Masha': The International Criminal Court Issued Warrants for the Arrest of Putin and One of His Appointees, Maria Lvova-Belova. She's Clearly No Ordinary Mom of 22." *Meduza*, March 18.

Sperling, Valerie. 2014. *Sex, Politics, and Putin: Political Legitimacy in Russia*. Oxford: Oxford University Press.

Temkina, Anna, Anastasia Novkunskaya, and Daria Litvina. 2023. *Pregnancy and Birth in Russia: The Struggle for "Good Care,"* chap. 3. New York: Routledge.

Tripp, Aili Mari. 2019. *Seeking Legitimacy: Why Arab Autocracies Adopt Women's Rights*. Cambridge: Cambridge University Press.

WAVE (Women Against Violence Europe). 2021. *WAVE Country Report 2021: Women's Specialist Support Services in Europe and the Impact of COVID-19 on Their Provision*, 151. Vienna, December.

Wood, Elizabeth A. 2016. "Hypermasculinity as a Scenario of Power: Vladimir Putin's Iconic Rule, 1999–2008." *International Feminist Journal of Politics* 18 (3): 329–50.

Zhabenko, Alisa. 2019. "Russian Lesbian Mothers: Between 'Traditional Values' and Human Rights." *Journal of Lesbian Studies* 23 (3): 321–35.

PART III

Governance and Security

TEN

The Siloviki

BRIAN D. TAYLOR

Vladimir Lenin, on the eve of the October 1917 revolution that brought the world's first "socialist" government to power, declared, "A standing army and police are the chief instruments of state power."[1] The next Vladimir to rule Russia, Vladimir Putin, also relies heavily on state coercive organizations to control the Russian state and pursue his policies. In Russia these coercive organs—military, security, and law enforcement structures—are known as the power ministries. The power ministries and their personnel—known in Russian as *siloviki*, from the Russian word for power—are among the big winners of Putin's rule. He has granted them considerable power and showered them with money. The siloviki were supposed to help Putin rebuild the Russian state, restore and maintain order, and make Russia a "respected great power."

This chapter evaluates the role of the siloviki in the Putin era. The task is complicated by the fact that, although frequently treated as a coherent collective, in reality, the siloviki encompass multiple people and organizations with often disparate objectives. Conflict is at least as common in intrasiloviki relations as cooperation. Still, the siloviki label exists for a reason, and there are some general features of the siloviki we can point to. In general, the siloviki have been on board with Putin's stated objectives of strengthening the state, establishing internal political control, and standing up to the West and expanding Russia's global influence. They have backed the Russian war against Ukraine. At the organizational level, each of the power ministries has fought for more power and resources for itself. At the individual level, regardless of whatever other ideas they might hold, siloviki have sought to increase their power and wealth.

The siloviki certainly have had some notable successes, from both the individual and the collective perspective. Many of the most powerful people in Russia have siloviki backgrounds. Some of them have acquired stupendous wealth. More generally, many siloviki may believe they have helped Putin build a strong state, restore order, and elevate Russia's status as a great power. Security and law enforcement organs have suppressed opponents of Putin's authoritarian and corrupt regime, thus helping Putin maintain power. Putin's anti-Western, assertive foreign policy also has considerable siloviki support.

Though the siloviki may claim successes, these alleged achievements have actually contributed to a larger story of failure. Russia, with its corrupt and inefficient state apparatus, cannot be considered truly "strong." By most measures of good governance and state quality, Russia is misruled. At the grassroots level, disorder prevails, and state accountability is absent. Siloviki input and activity have adversely affected Russian economic performance and contributed to Russia's strategic failure in Ukraine. Putin's imperialist war stands as the most tragic consequence of over two decades of his rule and that of his siloviki associates. These so-called successes ultimately exacted a heavy toll on both Russia and its people, as well as on Ukraine and its citizens.

This chapter begins with an overview of the literature on the Russian siloviki—who they are, what they think, and how we should conceptualize their role in Russian politics. The second section examines the results of giving so much political power to the siloviki. I argue that most of the purported achievements of Putin came not because of but despite the role of the siloviki in the regime. The third section considers the argument that the biggest problem of the siloviki is that they are thieves who built a kleptocratic regime. The fourth section argues that the siloviki are motivated not just by money but also by a geopolitical agenda to restore what they consider Russia's rightful global status. The fifth section looks at the siloviki's role in Putin's disastrous decision to invade Ukraine in February 2022, and the threat to Putin and the siloviki posed by the Prigozhin mutiny of June 2023.

The Siloviki: A Primer and a Review

Vladimir Putin decided as a teenager to pursue a career in the Soviet KGB (the Committee on State Security), and when he finished university, the KGB did indeed come calling. He served about sixteen years, up until the collapse of the Soviet Union in 1991, and left with the rank of lieutenant-colonel. When President Boris Yeltsin chose Putin as his successor in late 1999, he said that Russian society was demanding a leader who was both "democratic" and "new thinking" but also a "firm military man."[2]

Indeed, Yeltsin had started the trend toward appointing more siloviki to important positions in his second term as president—for example, his last three prime ministers all had power ministry connections. This trend accelerated when Putin became president in 2000. Russian sociologist Ol'ga Kryshtanovskaya's pathbreaking article on "Putin's militocracy"— her term for a siloviki-dominated regime—was published in Russian in 2002 and in English in 2003. She documented the spread of siloviki to positions throughout the Russian state, including in the government, the parliament, and as regional governors. During his more than two decades as Russia's ruler, Putin has continued to rely heavily on siloviki. Public opinion polls consistently show that Russians think that Putin represents the interests of the siloviki more than any other group—more than big business, more than state officials and bureaucrats, more than the middle class, and certainly more than "simple people."[3]

Who exactly are the siloviki? The word, as noted, comes from the Russian word for "power" or "force." The origin of the word comes from the term "force structures" (*silovye struktury*)—the state's military, security, and law enforcement bodies. Siloviki, then, are those who work or worked for one of the force structures, or "power ministries." Sometimes the term is used to refer to the power ministries themselves, as opposed to the individuals with that background. Some of the key power ministries include the Ministry of Defense, the Federal Security Service (FSB, the main domestic successor agency to the Soviet KGB), the Foreign Intelligence

Service (SVR), the Federal Guards Service (FSO, responsible for leadership security), the National Guard (Rosgvardiya), the Ministry of Emergency Situations (MChS), and the Ministry of Internal Affairs (MVD, responsible for the police). The Procuracy and the Investigative Committee, two important law enforcement agencies, also are often considered force structures.

To take some specific examples, someone like Yevgeny Prigozhin, the deceased head of the quasi-private military company the Wagner Group, who led a mutiny against the Russian military leadership in 2023, would not be considered a silovik. He spent his twenties in prison and his thirties selling hot dogs and used cars before moving into the restaurant business. Although he was eventually put in charge of the Wagner Group, he never worked in or for one of Russia's state military or security bodies. In contrast, his informal boss, Putin, who was recruited into and trained in the KGB, and his nemesis, Chief of the General Staff Valery Gerasimov, a professional military man, would both count as siloviki. Prigozhin's other nemesis, Sergei Shoigu, then minister of defense and now secretary of the Security Council, is an interesting case. He was a civil engineer with Communist Party connections and not a professional officer, yet he should still be considered part of the siloviki because he headed two power ministries, the MChS and the Ministry of Defense, and was given the rank of general when he headed the MChS.

Putin has been remarkably loyal to the leaders of the power ministries (table 10.1). Since he was first inaugurated as president in May 2000, there has been very little turnover at the top of these agencies (Dmitry Medvedev served as president from 2008 to 2012, but even then, Putin, who was prime minister at the time, played the key role in siloviki appointments and in controlling the siloviki in general). In contrast to the longevity of power ministry heads under Putin, when Boris Yeltsin was president (1992–1999), most of these positions saw considerable turnover. For example, Yeltsin appointed nine different Security Council secretaries, four different defense ministers, seven different FSB heads, and four different MVD ministers—all in only eight years as ruler compared to Putin's twenty-four.[4] Putin is loyal to his siloviki, even when they underperform, and they in turn have been loyal to him.

At the beginning of his fifth term as president in May 2024, Putin mostly left the top siloviki officials in place. He did replace Minister of Defense Shoigu and Security Council secretary Nikolai Patrushev. Shoigu had served almost a dozen years as minister of defense, and Patrushev had

Table 10.1. Power Ministry Leaders under Putin

Agency	Tenure of current leader (as of June 2024)	No. of agency heads under Putin (since May 2000)*
Security Council	1 month	6
Federal Security Service (FSB)	16 years, 1 month	2
Foreign Intelligence Service (SVR)	7 years, 8 months	3
Federal Guards Service (FSO)	8 years, 1 month	2
Ministry of Defense	1 month	5
Ministry of Internal Affairs (MVD)	12 years, 1 month	4
Ministry of Emergency Situations (MChS)	2 years, 1 month	5
Rosgvardiya	8 years, 2 months	1 (agency created 2016)
General Procuracy	4 years, 6 months	3
Investigative Committee	13 years, 6 months†	1 (made an independent agency in 2011)

Notes: *The president of Russia is the head of the Security Council. For this table I count secretaries of the Security Council. †The current head of the Investigative Committee has been in that position since June 2007, but formally it was previously part of the General Procuracy.

served sixteen years as secretary of the Security Council. Putin maintained his loyalty to both men by appointing Shoigu secretary of the Security Council and naming Patrushev an aide and leaving him as a permanent member of the Security Council.

In *State Building in Putin's Russia*, I proposed that there are three different ways to think about the siloviki and the role they play in Russian politics. I called these three approaches the cohort, corporate, and clan approaches. The cohort approach treats everyone with a siloviki background as part of a large collective group, often assumed to have similar values or interests; this is the method Kryshtanovskaya used in her research on the "militocracy." The corporate or organizational approach focuses on the different power ministries and services, and thus compares the way the values or interests of the military, for example, might differ from those of the secret police (FSB) or regular police (MVD). Finally, the clan approach starts from the premise that the real action in Russian politics involves battles between different informal elite groupings, often referred to as clans, for power and resources. Under Putin, observers have frequently referred to a siloviki clan or group in high politics, usually seeing this group as battling with more "liberal" groupings of civilian economists or lawyers. In reality, there are multiple siloviki clans that compete for influence.[5]

Consistent with Kryshtanovskaya's conception of the Russian regime as a militocracy, many observers have pointed to the dominance of the siloviki as central to understanding Putinism. As early as 2003, *New York Times* columnist William Safire stated, "Russia today is ruled by Vladimir Putin's *siloviki*, former KGB men and military officers who have the nation by the throat." Not only do siloviki dominate the important Security Council, a key interagency advisory body that brings together most of Russia's top officials, but they also played a central role in implementing key Putin goals, such as reducing the influence of the so-called oligarchs, weakening regional governors, and controlling civil society.[6]

The militocracy argument is both numerical and ideological. The assertion is twofold: first, that the number of siloviki in top positions in politics and the economy has increased notably under Putin, and second, that they have a distinct mindset that has led Russia in a particular direction. Two aspects of this mindset have drawn particular attention. First, in terms of domestic politics, siloviki are believed to prioritize control and order and a strong state. Consequently, other values, such as freedom, pluralism, and democracy, are seen as less important. They are also overwhelmingly male (no woman has ever led one of the power ministries), and Putinism as a political style and mentality is marked by hypermasculinity and macho displays (see chapter 9). Second, siloviki are more inclined to believe Russia is a unique civilization that is threatened from the outside, especially by the West. They see Russia as a besieged fortress. As Putin once memorably put it, "We want to survive and to fight . . . or we want our skin to hang on a wall. That is the choice we face."[7]

Other scholars have criticized both aspects of the militocracy argument, the numerical and the ideological. David Rivera and Sharon Werning Rivera showed in a series of articles that some of the claims about the dominance of siloviki in state positions were misleading, overstating the number of siloviki across top levels of government. The ideological argument has been challenged by scholars such as Bettina Renz, who argues that a siloviki professional background does not necessarily lead to more authoritarian political views and that it is a mistake to treat them as a coherent grouping.[8]

These criticisms have some merit. The number of siloviki in the Russian political and economic elite has been exaggerated by many scholars and analysts, and it is obviously true that not everyone with the same professional background shares the same political views. At the same time, the evidence is convincing that the number of siloviki in top political and economic positions increased under Putin (especially those who had prior connections to Putin from his time in the KGB or in the St. Petersburg mayor's office), that the most important siloviki tend to have authoritarian and hawkish views, and that in general, siloviki elites tend to hold those views more than civilian elites. For example, Putin not only appointed siloviki associates to the top position in various power ministries, which perhaps was not surprising, he also put them in such positions as head of Russia's largest oil company, Rosneft; head of the state pipeline monopoly, Transneft; head of the state arms conglomerate, Rostec; and head of Russia's largest employer, Russian Railways. Daniel Treisman coined the term *silovarch*—a portmanteau of siloviki and oligarch—to refer to these siloviki taking control of large businesses.[9] During his third term as president (2012–2018), Putin began to advance the careers of his former bodyguards, moving no fewer than six of them into important political positions at the regional and national level.[10]

In terms of the mentality of the siloviki, there is evidence both from social science surveys and from close analysis of the statements of leading siloviki elites that their views tend to be more hawkish and authoritarian than those of other officials. Data from the Survey of Russian Elites show that siloviki are "significantly less sympathetic towards liberal democratic values.... A distinct *siloviki* mindset in the realm of domestic politics persists."[11] A detailed analysis of the political views of two of Putin's closest siloviki allies, Nikolai Patrushev and SVR head Sergei Naryshkin, also identifies a distinct worldview that sees Russia as an "anti-Western power that is a 'besieged fortress.'"[12]

The examples of Patrushev and Naryshkin bring us to a final important point about the siloviki. The category of siloviki links together a large group of people with some important commonalities—military ranks, uniforms, access to weapons—but also some important differences. Historically in Russia, there have been key differences, sometimes quite bitter, between the military and the secret services, and between the regular police and the secret police. A young Vladimir Putin took great offense when someone suggested that he was headed toward a career in the police, retorting, "I won't be a cop!"[13] Instead, Putin wanted to be in the secret services, the KGB. Secret police personnel are collectively known as

"Chekists," after the name for a KGB predecessor organization, the Cheka, created under Lenin. Arguably, to understand Putinism, one should look not at the siloviki in general but at the Chekists in particular. Patrushev, Naryshkin, the head of the FSB, Aleksandr Bortnikov, and the head of Rosgvardiya, Viktor Zolotov, to name just four important examples, are not just siloviki but Chekists. Putin, too, is a proud Chekist. If the siloviki writ large are among the big winners under Putinism, then the Chekists are the crème de la crème.

The Siloviki in Charge

What do the siloviki and the Chekists do with all the power they have been granted by Putin? The official version, of course, is that they have restored order and stability, made Russia more prosperous, and "raised Russia from its knees" in the international arena. Putin and his siloviki colleagues may view themselves as successful in achieving these three goals. Consistent with the overall theme of this book, I contend that Putin and the siloviki have failed at these goals and have set Russia back.

First, let's look at the central claim of Putin and his defenders that he restored order and has rebuilt the Russian state. There were notable achievements in some areas. For example, tax collection is much more efficient than before, and the homicide rate has dropped considerably since spiking after the Soviet collapse, although there are real questions about both the reliability of the data and whether changes in policing and law enforcement had anything to do with the decline. It also is true that the Russian state under Putin has been able to effectively repress threats to Putin's continued rule, although the Wagner mutiny revealed a stark vulnerability to challenges from within the system. Putin and the siloviki have built a police state fully capable of arresting protestors and shutting down opponents, whether in politics, the media, or civil society.[14]

Putin's Russia, though, is not a well-ordered police state but a disordered one. A variety of international assessments of state performance, such as rankings of the quality of governance, institutional effectiveness, the level of corruption, or the state's ability to deliver socially desirable outcomes to citizens such as well-being and opportunity, demonstrate that Russia seriously underperforms what might be expected from its level of income.

Detailed case studies show that, although there might be pockets of competence here and there, in general, the Russian state governs poorly. A wide variety of scholars, using different methods, have come to similar conclusions about bad governance in Russia. Long-time Russia watchers Fiona Hill and Clifford Gaddy conclude in a major biography that Putin "has not built a truly strong state.... People with personal connections to Mr. Putin and his inner circle, and others who have been given positions of power in the system or in the state apparatus, often do not use their positions in the service of the state or society."[15]

The siloviki played an important role in building this disordered police state. Kryshtanovskaya described the way in which the siloviki mentality affected their approach to governing: "What is 'disorder' in the eyes of a man in uniform? It's the absence of control. If there is not control, there is the possibility of independent influence. And siloviki perceive the presence of alternative centers of power in the country as a threat to the country's integrity."[16] The prioritization of hierarchy and order led to a form of state building that vested power in the executive branch and eliminated forms of accountability that are important for good governance. Without real opposition political parties, a vibrant free press, strong civil society organizations, and an independent judiciary, an unconstrained executive often works for its own benefit rather than the citizens'.

We see a similar picture with the economy (see chapter 1). Russia experienced significant economic growth during Putin's first two terms. Since that time, however, growth has slowed down considerably: since 2008, average annual growth is less than 1 percent per year. This is well below average global growth rates. Putin's political system makes it hard to increase investment, productivity, and innovation. The economy is thus highly dependent on resource exports and their prices.

The state interferes in the economy in harmful ways, and much of this has to do with the siloviki. State law enforcement agencies routinely shake down both average citizens and businesses. They participate in corporate "raiding," using their investigative power to participate on one side of a business dispute—for a cut of the profits, of course. In 2015, Putin stated that in 2014, investigators had opened nearly 200,000 cases related to business crimes, but only 15 percent of these cases had received any kind of verdict. At the same time, fully 83 percent of these entrepreneurs lost some or all of their business. As Putin put it, "They were squeezed, robbed, and let go."[17]

Of course, Putin himself created the political and legal conditions that make such behavior possible. For example, Putin's 2003 decision to imprison Russia's richest man, Mikhail Khodorkovsky, and basically transfer the assets of his private oil company, Yukos, to the state oil conglomerate, Rosneft, was taken as a signal by law enforcement to target business. It was the FSB, after all, that arrested Khodorkovsky, the Procuracy that led the criminal case against him, and Putin's silovik ally Igor Sechin who controlled Rosneft and benefited from the takeover. Even worse, the prosecutor-general of Russia at the time, Vladimir Ustinov, was a close associate of Sechin, the architect and beneficiary of the Yukos case; Ustinov's son was married to Sechin's daughter. After the Yukos affair, Russian academic researchers documented a 50–70 percent increase in economic crime cases. Putin continues to call for an end to law enforcement harassment of private business, as he has done throughout his rule, but such harassment is a feature and not a bug of the political and legal order he and the siloviki have built.[18]

If we place the Russian case in a broader comparative context, it is not surprising that a personalist autocracy with a large component of security personnel in top positions would be badly governed. Personalist autocracies and military strongmen regimes have generally performed poorly in such matters as economic growth, political stability, and domestic repression. They also are more internationally belligerent than other regimes.[19]

Finally, Russians and some external observers give credit to Putin for rebuilding Russia's global power and status. Elements of the siloviki, such as the military and intelligence services, are also central to this story. We return to this issue in our discussion of the Russia-Ukraine War and argue that Putin's global security policy also has been a failure.

Police and Thieves

One of the most common frames for thinking about Putin's Russia is as a "militocracy" or a "neo-KGB state." A second common approach to the study of Putinism is found in the literature on kleptocracy. Kleptocracy means the rule of thieves. Corruption is a global problem and was a particular problem in many postcommunist countries. Venelin Ganev has explained the weakness of many postcommunist states as a consequence of an "elite predatory project" of "extraction from the state." The Russian Federation has had high levels of corruption since it became the successor state to the USSR on December 26, 1991, and has made little headway in combating it. Putin consistently receives low marks from the Russian public regarding fighting corruption.[20]

That Putin receives low marks for fighting corruption is not surprising. There is no evidence that he has any interest in fighting corruption, rhetoric notwithstanding—particularly among his cronies. Indeed, Putin's ability to control what Clifford Gaddy and Barry Ickes call the "rent management system" helps buttress Putin's power. Monitoring illicit cash flows also gives Putin a way to keep state officials in line because they know that they can be dismissed or imprisoned for stepping out of line or challenging the system.[21]

The kleptocracy literature goes beyond these observations and asserts that the primary function of the system is to enrich Putin and his close associates. On the analytical and journalistic side, the notion that Putinism is primarily kleptocratic is the central argument of two prominent books on the era: Karen Dawisha's *Putin's Kleptocracy* and Catherine Belton's *Putin's People*.[22] On the activist side, this was the fundamental message of Alexei Navalny and his team at the Anti-Corruption Foundation. Their work resulted in the Russian government designating the foundation as both a "foreign agent" and an "extremist organization," and ultimately cost Navalny his life.

Belton's work, more than any other book in English, pulls all of the corrupt threads together. Much of the evidence is convincing. Putin and his cronies have stolen a lot, a fact well documented by Belton and a large number of Russian activists and journalists. But the book has larger ambitions, advancing an argument about how, as the subtitle has it, "the KGB took back Russia and then took on the West." This larger argument is problematic for the simple reason that the KGB has not existed for more than thirty years. It was broken into separate parts with separate missions. Obviously, many people who previously served in the KGB continued to work for the Russian state, from Putin on down, but after 1991 there was no KGB directing their activities or implementing plans.

This notion of an enduring, unified, and all-powerful KGB network ignores all the research that shows that Chekists frequently fight among themselves, that the remnants of the KGB—currently the FSB, the SVR, and the FSO—have different missions, different personnel, and different priorities, and that even the core successor agency, the FSB, is also riven by factional infighting.[23] As one anonymous FSB officer told Russian investigative journalist Sergei Kanev, "At the Lubyanka [FSB headquarters] there is a constant battle between influential clans and the friends of Putin standing behind them. . . . The second floor fights with the third, the fourth with the first, and the fifth with all of them simultaneously. Each clan tries to place its people in the key posts."[24]

Finally, and most important, there is a deeper tension between arguments claiming simultaneously that Russia is a kleptocracy and that former KGB networks have a coherent plan to take on the West. A lot of corrupt Russian money is in fact squirreled away in Western banks and Western property. Leaving all of one's money in Russia is risky, subject to possible appropriation by a greedy state and a fickle ruler. In contrast, there are many brokers in the West—bankers, lawyers, accountants, property managers—happy to profit from helping Russians secure potentially ill-gotten gains abroad. Once secured, these assets are somewhat protected by the property rights regimes and legal systems of the capitalist and democratic West.

If the primary goal is to steal, then, decent relations with the West would seem to be essential. Yet Putin has pursued a series of increasingly aggressive policies that have led to massive sanctions against Russian state entities, Russian business interests, and Russian individuals. Many of his closest associates are now locked out of keeping their assets in the West or traveling to those countries. This has been true since the annexation of Crimea in 2014. For example, one of Putin's closest associates, the billionaire gas trader Gennady Timchenko, complained in August 2014 that U.S. sanctions meant that he could not vacation in southern France with his family and that he was cut off from them, including his favorite dog.[25] Russia's rich and well-connected frequently sent their kids to foreign schools and universities and their families for medical care in Western hospitals and clinics, in addition to locating their financial and physical assets in the West. This easy access to the West for Russia's wealthy depended on maintaining at least a minimally functional relationship with Western governments. Such a relationship was seriously undermined by the 2022 full-scale invasion of Ukraine. That said, it is also worth noting that the children of some of the most prominent Chekists and siloviki—including the children of Patrushev, Bortnikov, Naryshkin, and Shoigu—have received lucrative positions inside Russia, often working in state-connected banking or energy companies.[26]

There is, then, a fundamental incompatibility between turning Russia into a kleptocracy and pursuing a confrontational and aggressive foreign policy that challenges core Western interests and principles. Thieves would typically prefer to hide from or ingratiate themselves with those who handle their money rather than yell loudly at and punch in the face those who hold their assets. Putin and Russia's Chekist elites like money, but they have bigger plans beyond theft.

A Mafia or a Junta?

Throughout the Putin era, there has been a submerged battle between different siloviki clans, and among Chekists in particular, over the tension between thieving and ruling a great power. In 2007, one of Putin's former KGB allies from Leningrad, Viktor Cherkesov, published an article titled "Warriors Should Not Be Traders."[27] Cherkesov claimed that the involvement of security and law enforcement agencies in various economic schemes to enrich themselves was undermining their ability to protect Russian sovereignty and security. The Russian political scientist Kirill Rogov noticed a similar dynamic in 2015, when two other top Putin allies and Chekists—then Security Council secretary Nikolai Patrushev and former Security Council secretary and minister of defense Sergei Ivanov—spoke out on Russia's future direction in light of the annexation of Crimea in 2014 and worsening relations with the West. Rogov summarized the gist of their message in the following way: "We are not a mafia, we are a junta. A mafia is about money and dealing, and we care about ideology, we are a junta, we care about geopolitics and we will speak through geopolitics."[28]

Patrushev, one of Putin's closest allies, has long claimed that Chekists are motivated by a higher calling. He said in 2000, "Our best colleagues, the honor and pride of the FSB, don't do their work for the money. They all look different, but there is one very special characteristic that unites all these people, and it is a very important quality. It is their sense of service. They are, if you like, our new nobility."[29]

At the same time, Navalny's team showed in 2014 that Patrushev's wife owned a mansion outside Moscow worth far more than their combined salaries could ever afford.[30] Despite Patrushev's claim that this "new nobility" of Chekists does not care about money, many Chekists, including Putin himself, seem to enjoy money quite a bit. There is abundant evidence that Putin has personally enriched himself and his friends and family considerably. But this does not mean that Putin, Patrushev, and other siloviki do not have a self-image based on noble service to the state. One can imagine that they think they deserve to live at least as well as wealthy oligarchs, given their self-perception as saviors of the Russian state.

The answer to the question "Are the siloviki elite a mafia focused on money or a junta concerned with geopolitics?" is "Why not both?" The siloviki from top to bottom are riddled with corruption. As Peter Reddaway has observed, "Law-enforcement officers [fight] each other like criminal gangs."[31] Many of them are more likely to engage in corruption than fight it. But it is also true that the siloviki are much more inclined to think that Russia should partner with China, and much less inclined to think that they should partner with the West, compared to civilian elites. The siloviki think Russia is a besieged fortress, while also wanting their own personal fortresses to be elegant and well furnished.[32]

One of the common tropes in analyzing Putinism is to contrast an alleged tug-of-war between hard-liners and soft-liners, statists and marketeers, or siloviki and so-called *civiliki* (civilian officials). In many ways, the tug of war is real: clear policy differences on important political and economic issues do exist. Yet in a larger sense the imagery is misleading. It implies that Putin is somehow in the middle of these two camps, sometimes tacking one way, sometimes tacking the other. The image of Putin is one in which he has a siloviki devil (Patrushev or Sechin, say) on one shoulder whispering in his ear and a liberal angel (such as former finance minister Alexei Kudrin or current Central Bank of Russia head Elvira Nabiullina) on the other shoulder whispering in his other ear. But this would be a misleading image. Putin is generally with the siloviki devils. The liberals had one key job, to uphold Russia's economic sovereignty by pursuing conservative fiscal policies that would allow Russia to pay down its external debt quickly in the 2000s and never become dependent on Western financial assistance after that. The liberals did their job well, but they have had little influence on the overall political course of Putin's Russia.

This view of Putin as at a midway point between hard-liners and soft-liners also is based on the notion that Patrushev is much more hawkish than Putin. But the evidence for this idea is weak. Putin stated in 2000, before he was elected to his first term, that Patrushev was one of his most trusted comrades.[33] He put Patrushev in charge of the FSB for his first two terms and then placed him in charge of the Security Council for sixteen years. It is not so much that Patrushev has a big influence on Putin as that Putin and Patrushev share a similar worldview. As Russian political analyst

Andrei Kolesnikov put it in 2022, Patrushev "is the one allowed to explain and clarify Putin's thoughts."[34] They agree on Russia's mission in the world, and on the threat to Russia's position and purpose from the West. They are both Chekist hawks. Putinism has strong elements of kleptocracy, but what really matters to Putin and his siloviki is their goal of "making Russia great again."

Fight Test: Putin's Disastrous War

Russia invaded Ukraine in February 2014, a nation with which it had multiple agreements recognizing Ukraine's sovereignty and territorial integrity. Russia first annexed Crimea with military force, and then sponsored and controlled a so-called "separatist war" in southeastern Ukraine, the Donbas. Putin had long believed that Russia must maintain political control over Ukraine and prevent its economic and political integration with the West. Putin's 2014 actions actually made Ukraine's break with Russia much more likely because annexing Crimea removed the most pro-Russian voters from the Ukrainian electorate and alienated the rest of the Ukrainian electorate from Russia. After eight years of military and political pressure failed to bring Ukraine back under Moscow's control, Putin opted for a full-scale invasion of all of Ukraine in February 2022.

Putin bears ultimate responsibility for the Ukraine war (see also chapters 12 and 13). Also culpable are the siloviki, who went along with the war and Putin's overall foreign policy and provided poor analytical and operational support for his endeavors. The decision to annex Crimea in 2014 was made with a very small group of siloviki insiders—reportedly Minister of Defense Shoigu, Security Council Secretary Patrushev, FSB head Bortnikov, and long-time Putin ally from the KGB, Sergei Ivanov. Allegedly Shoigu, Chief of the General Staff Gerasimov, and the SVR opposed the annexation of Crimea but were overruled by Putin.[35] Others were shut out. The Ministry of Finance, for example, was not consulted about the potential economic costs of the move.[36]

Similarly, it seems the decision to launch a full-scale invasion in February 2022 was also a closely held decision confined to a small group of siloviki. In particular, the department of the FSB responsible for Ukraine played an important role in shaping Putin's confidence that Ukraine would quickly fall. The FSB had been placing agents inside Ukraine and bribing officials for years. The security service believed it had a government-in-waiting ready to take power and that Ukrainians would not resist; even though its own polling generally suggested otherwise, it apparently cherry-picked the most favorable results. A combination of a failure to understand Ukrainian national identity, contempt for the Ukrainian state, wishful thinking, and strong incentives to align its analysis with Putin's preconceived ideas meant that the FSB failed in its job to provide accurate intelligence and analysis to the president.[37] One Western intelligence official told the *Financial Times*, "The FSB had built a whole system of telling the boss what he wanted to hear. There were huge budgets given out and corruption at every level. You tell the right story up top and you skim off a bit for yourself."[38]

On the eve of the February 2022 invasion, the evidence suggests that even some of the siloviki and Chekists were unsure of Putin's plan. For example, Naryshkin of the SVR got dressed down on national television for suggesting to Putin that Russia continue negotiations.[39] Reports differ on whether Patrushev, a perceived hawk known to peddle conspiracy theories about how the United States wants to break Russia apart, supported or opposed the invasion. Allegedly such top officials as the foreign minister, Putin's spokesman, his chief of staff, and the Kremlin's main domestic policy official were in the dark.[40] Foreign Minister Sergei Lavrov reportedly told one oligarch the day of the invasion that Putin "has three advisors. Ivan the Terrible. Peter the Great. And Catherine the Great."[41]

More generally, the 2022 full-scale invasion of Ukraine was the culmination of a decades-long process in which a group of siloviki and Chekist hawks, most importantly Putin himself, had built a foreign policy around a sense of Russia's alleged humiliation after the Soviet collapse and the need to reclaim its role as one of the world's great powers and reassert its control over its neighbors. Russia under Putin has been in a state of semiwar with the West for a long time. In 2004, Putin accused the United States of making common cause with Chechen terrorists to dismember Russia. In 2007 he went to the Munich Security Conference and delivered a blistering attack on U.S. global predominance, and in 2008 he created two Russian protectorates from legally Georgian territory after a short war with that country. After the 2014 annexation of Crimea, Russian methods became more aggressive. Russian intelligence services intervened in the 2016 U.S. presidential election on the side of Donald Trump by hacking and strategically leaking emails from Hillary Clinton's campaign, and in 2018, two assassins were sent to kill a former double agent in Great Britain with an illegal nerve agent. Typically, in both cases their tradecraft was so sloppy that Russia's involvement was easily detected.[42]

The problems with Russia's intelligence services that helped pave the way to the 2022 full-scale invasion were also of long standing. Specialists such as Mark Galeotti have covered in detail the infighting, recklessness, corruption, obsequiousness in the face of presidential pressure, and poor analytical coordination that marked the work of the special services. Galeotti in 2016 summarized the situation this way:

> Putin has the intelligence and security community he wanted: a powerful, feral, multi-headed, and obedient hydra. But it is Putin himself, and his dreams of Russia as a renewed great power, that is the real victim of this aggressive and badly managed beast. The agencies reinforce his assumptions and play to his fantasies rather than informing and challenging his worldview, as good intelligence services should.[43]

Corruption and recklessness took a nearly fatal form for the regime in the June 23–24, 2023, mutiny of Yevgeny Prigozhin. His Wagner Group, a quasi-private military company closely connected to the Russian state, rebelled against the Russian military. Wagner forces seized control of the Southern Military District's headquarters in Rostov-on-Don and advanced largely unimpeded toward Moscow. During the drive to Moscow, Wagner forces shot down multiple Russian military aircraft, killing more than a dozen people. Eventually the Wagner insurgents turned around when they were little more than one hundred miles from Moscow, having struck a deal to end the rebellion. Two months later, on August 23, Prigozhin and two of Wagner's most important personnel (along with seven other people) were killed when Prigozhin's private plane fell out of the sky while en route from Moscow to Saint Petersburg. The most likely explanation for Prigozhin's death is that Russian president Vladimir Putin considered Prigozhin's treachery in launching a mutiny in the middle of a war an unforgivable act, and took his revenge when the time was right.

The June 2023 Wagner mutiny was the closest Russia had come to an armed struggle for power near the capital since the early 1990s. One of the most striking features of this bizarre episode was the inactivity of Russia's security and military structures during the mutiny. Nothing was heard from the minister of defense, the chief of the General Staff, the secretary of the Security Council, the director of the Federal Security Service, the minister of internal affairs, and the director of the Rosgvardiya until after the mutiny was over.[44] One European security official, commenting on the Russian government's inept response to the mutiny, said, "There was paralysis on all levels. . . . There was absolute dismay and confusion."[45] The agreement to end the mutiny averted a potential military confrontation on the outskirts of Moscow.

For over two decades, Vladimir Putin and his siloviki supporters have boasted that he restored stability to Russia after a period of disorder following the collapse of the Soviet Union. In 2007, Putin named "strengthening the state" as one of his primary achievements.[46] Putin, said one ally in 2020, was a "guarantee of stability, both internally and externally."[47] Yet in June 2023, the Russian state seemed paralyzed, and the security and military forces looked hapless and helpless in the face of an uprising by a quasi-mercenary army led by Prigozhin, a former restaurateur and caterer who was known as "Putin's chef" (Prigozhin said the nickname "Putin's butcher" would have been more fitting).[48] One Kremlin insider told a journalist that the security forces had "slept through" the danger Prigozhin presented to the Russian state, but Western intelligence sources later claimed that Putin had apparently been warned about a possible rebellion in advance, but took no action. The absence of clear orders from the top led many military and security officials at various levels to take a wait-and-see approach during the mutiny.[49]

Putin was the most oblivious to the potential threat posed by Prigozhin. For months, Prigozhin had verbally attacked Minister of Defense Shoigu and Chief of the General Staff Gerasimov in increasingly vituperative fashion, all while Putin turned a blind eye. Yet the power ministries also were culpable. These agencies, which ruthlessly crack down on peaceful expressions of discontent with Putin and the war in Ukraine, proved completely unprepared for an armed challenge to state power from one of Putin's trusted cronies. As former CIA director William Burns said, "What we saw was Russian security services, the Russian military, Russian decision-makers adrift, or they appeared to be adrift, for those 36 hours. The question was, 'Does the emperor have no clothes?' Or at least, 'Why is it taking so long for him to get dressed?'"[50]

As in other spheres, loyalty was rewarded more than competence, although treason has always been rewarded with death. The war in Ukraine is another Putin failure. Regardless of when and how the war ends, the 2022 invasion has cost Russia a massive amount of blood and treasure while guaranteeing a Ukrainian society intensely hostile to Russia for generations to come. This is a failure not only objectively but in Putin's own terms—the desire to bring Ukraine under Russian control and show that Russians and Ukrainians are "one people."

Conclusion

Boris Yeltsin said he viewed Putin as his successor because he wanted someone who was a "firm military man" while also being "democratic" and "new thinking." However, Putin's regime of siloviki strongmen has been defined by autocracy and old thinking. They built an ineffective and corrupt state that failed to provide sustainable economic growth and a better life for Russian citizens. Their vain quest to rebuild the empire and take on the West has brought death to hundreds of thousands and hardship to millions and set Russia back in almost every imaginable respect—economically, demographically, politically, and globally. "The myth of autocratic competence," in the words of Kathryn Stoner, a myth that helped buoy Putin during his first decade in power as the Russian economy grew quickly, has been badly damaged by more than a decade of economic stagnation and a disastrous war.[51] State repression, led by the siloviki, has always been an important part of Putinism, but the scale and intensity of the repression have grown even as performance legitimacy has faded.

Perhaps Putin and his Chekist cronies do not care—they are rich and have immense power—although the evidence suggests Putin is obsessed with his place in history. The Prigozhin mutiny, however, showed that even the force structures that are supposed to be the bedrock of Putin's rule might prove to be unreliable and indifferent when the regime's fate is on the line. The rank and file in such force structures as the police service and the armed forces probably do not see themselves as either a powerful political constituency within the regime or a big winner from Putin's reign; though they are paid well enough, they are certainly not treated like the "new nobility" of the security services. One highly placed military intelligence officer told a journalist after the mutiny that many in the military and elsewhere in the state "are tired of this war and want it to stop, one can feel the discontent." It is hard to know how widespread these feelings are, but if nothing else, the Prigozhin mutiny showed how quickly Putin could lose control and everything could fall apart. That may yet prove to be a lesson for others.[52]

Putin has been very loyal to his siloviki associates. There appear to be no consequences for failure if you are loyal to the boss. Whether the boss will face consequences for his failures, potentially even from the siloviki themselves, remains to be seen.

NOTES

I would like to thank Harley Balzer, Fabian Burkhardt, Peter Clement, Renée de Nevers, Alfred Evans, Steven Fisher, Janet Elise Johnson, Robert Otto, David Rivera, Maria Snegovaya, and the external reviewers for very helpful comments on earlier drafts of this chapter.

1. Lenin (1968), 268.
2. Putin (2000), 24–25, 38; Yeltsin (2000), 254.
3. Kryshtanovskaia (2002); Kryshtanovskaya and White (2003); Levada Center (2023).
4. The figures for the FSB include its predecessor organizations, the Ministry of Security and the Federal Counter-Intelligence Service.
5. Galeotti (2016); Meakins (2018); Reddaway (2018); Taylor (2011).
6. William Safire quoted in Rivera and Rivera (2018): "The Militarization of the Russian Elite under Putin: What We Know, What We Think We Know (but Don't), and What We Need to Know." This article provides an excellent overview of the academic literature on the siloviki.
7. "We want to survive and to fight": Putin (2014). Some accounts of the siloviki worldview include Kryshtanovskaya and White (2005), Rivera and Rivera (2019), Soldatov and Rochlitz (2018), 95–97, and Taylor (2011), 61–64.
8. Renz (2006); Rivera and Rivera (2014, 2018).
9. Taylor (2018); Treisman (2007).
10. RTVI (2022).
11. Rivera and Rivera (2019); Rivera, Rivera, and Nemeth (2022). The data set for the Survey of Russian Elites is available at https://www.icpsr.umich.edu/web/ICPSR/studies/3724.
12. Kragh and Umland (2023), 4.
13. Putin (2000), 25.
14. Taylor (2011), 91–102; Lysova (2020).
15. Hill and Gaddy (2013), 268. The literature on this point is massive. Some examples include Gel'man (2022, 2017); Melville (2023); Taylor (2011); Taylor (2018), 131–65; Treisman (2018); and Wilson (2023), 63–74.
16. Ol'ga Kryshtanovskaia interviewed in Khamraev (2007).
17. Putin (2015).

18. Tompson (2005); Fortescue (2006); Volkov, Paneiakh and Titaev (2010); Volkov (2013); Putin (2019).
19. Geddes, Frantz, and Wright (2014); Kendall-Taylor, Frantz, and Wright (2017); Frye (2022), 37–49.
20. *Economist* (2007); Ganev (2005); Gudkov (2021).
21. Gaddy and Ickes (2015), 35–56.
22. Dawisha (2015); Belton (2020).
23. Meakins (2018); Reddaway (2018).
24. Kanev (2018).
25. Vandenko (2014).
26. Legucka and Bieliszczuk (2019).
27. Cherkesov (2007).
28. Rogoff quoted in Davydov (2015).
29. Patrushev quoted in Soldatov and Borogan (2010), 5.
30. Navalny (2014).
31. Reddaway (2018), 107.
32. Rivera et al. (2020), 19–21.
33. Putin (2000), 181.
34. Belton (2022).
35. See Aleksei Zuyev's film *Krym: Put' na rodinu*, first posted on the state-owned Russian-language YouTube channel Rossiya-24 on March 15, 2015; Zygar' (2015), 336; Gershkovich et al. (2022); Taratuta and Tovkaylo (2015). It is not clear how much top officials such as then prime minister Dmitry Medvedev or Foreign Minister Sergei Lavrov knew about the planned Crimean annexation in advance.
36. Taratuta and Tovkaylo (2015).
37. Anin (2022); Dylan, Gioe, and Grossfeld (2023); Gershkovich et al. (2022); Miller and Belton (2022); Saito and Tsvetkova (2022); Seddon, Miller, and Schwartz (2023).
38. Seddon, Miller, and Schwartz (2023).
39. Kremlin.ru (2022).
40. Gershkovich et al. (2022); Seddon, Miller, and Schwartz (2023).
41. Sergei Lavrov quoted in Seddon, Miller, and Schwartz (2023).
42. See, for example, Taylor (2018), 14–18, 30–34, 166–94.
43. Galeotti (2016), 15.
44. On the behavior of the siloviki during the mutiny, see, for example, Belton, Harris, and Miller (2023), Soldatov and Borogan (2023), and *Insider* (2023).
45. Quoted in Belton, Harris, and Miller (2023).
46. Putin (2007).
47. Balmforth (2020); Federal Duma (2020).
48. Faulconbridge (2023).

49. Belton, Harris, and Miller (2023); Pertsev (2023).
50. Myre (2023).
51. Stoner (2023).
52. "*Vse uvideli, kak Putin oslab. . . .*"

REFERENCES

Anin, Roman. 2022. "Kak Putin prinial resheniie o voine" [How Putin made the decision to go to war]. *Vazhnye istorii*, May 16.

Balmforth, Tom. 2020. "First Woman in Space Brought Down to Earth by Anger over Bid to Prolong Putin Rule." Reuters, March 13.

Belton, Catherine. 2022. "The Man Who Has Putin's Ear—and May Want His Job." *Washington Post*, July 13.

———. 2020. *Putin's People: How The KGB Took Back Russia and Then Took On the West*. New York: Farrar, Straus and Giroux.

Belton, Catherine, Shane Harris, and Greg Miller. 2023. "Putin Appeared Paralyzed and Unable to Act in First Hours of Rebellion." *Washington Post*, July 25.

Cherkesov, Viktor. 2007. "Nel'zia dopustit', chtoby voiny prevratilis' v torgovtsev" [Warriors should not be traders]. *Kommersant'*, October 9.

Davydov, Ivan. 2015. "My ne banda, my—khunta" [We are not a gang, we are a junta]. *New Times*, June 30.

Dawisha, Karen. 2015. *Putin's Kleptocracy: Who Owns Russia?* New York: Simon and Schuster.

Dylan, Huw, David V. Gioe, and Elena Grossfeld. 2023. "The Autocrat's Intelligence Paradox: Vladimir Putin's (Mis)management of Russian Strategic Assessment in the Ukraine War." *British Journal of Politics and International Relations* 25 (3): 385–404.

Economist. 2007. "The Making of the Neo-KGB State." August 23.

Faulconbridge, Guy. 2023. "Mercenary Prigozhin Warns Russia Could Face Revolution Unless Elite Gets Serious about War." Reuters, May 24.

Federal Duma. 2020. "Valentina Tereshkova predlozhila rassmotret' vopros o snyatii ogranichenii po chislu prezidentskikh srokov" [Valentina Tereskova proposed considering the removal of limits on the number of presidential terms]. Duma.gov.ru, March 10.

Fortescue, Stephen. 2006. *Russia's Oil Barons and Metal Magnates: Oligarchs and the State in Transition*. New York: Palgrave Macmillan.

Frye, Timothy. 2022. *Weak Strongman: The Limits of Power in Putin's Russia*. Princeton, NJ: Princeton University Press.

Gaddy, Clifford G., and Barry Ickes. 2015. "Putin's Rent Management System and the Future of Addiction in Russia." In *The Challenges for Russia's Politicized Economic System*, ed. Susanne Oxenstierna. New York: Routledge.

Galeotti, Mark. 2016. *Putin's Hydra: Inside Russia's Intelligence Services*. European Council on Foreign Relations.

Ganev, Venelin I. 2005. "Post-communism as an Episode of State Building: A Reversed Tillyan Perspective." *Communist and Post-Communist Studies* 38 (4): 425–45.

Geddes, Barbara, Erica Frantz, and Joseph G. Wright. 2014. "Military Rule." *Annual Review of Political Science* 17:147–62.

Gel'man, Vladimir. 2022. *The Politics of Bad Governance in Contemporary Russia*. Ann Arbor: University of Michigan Press.

Gel'man, Vladimir, ed. 2017. *Authoritarian Modernization in Russia: Ideas, Institutions, and Policies*. London: Routledge.

Gershkovich, Evan, et al. 2022. "Putin, Isolated and Distrustful, Leans on Handful of Hard-Line Advisers." *Wall Street Journal*, December 23.

Gill, Graeme, ed. 2023. *Routledge Handbook of Russian Politics and Society*, 2nd ed. London: Routledge.

Gudkov, Lev. 2021. "Balans dostizhenii i neudach Putina" [Balance sheet of Putin's successes and failures]. Levada Center, April 8.

Hill, Fiona, and Clifford G. Gaddy. 2013. *Mr. Putin: Operative in the Kremlin*. Washington, DC: Brookings Institution Press.

Insider. 2023. "'Vse uvideli, kak Putin oslab, tak chto stoit zhdat' vtoroga akta'" [Everyone saw how Putin was weakened, so we should expect a second act]. July 20.

Kanev, Sergei. 2018. "Poslednii spetsnazovets Sechina" [Sechin's last spetsnaz]. *TSURrealizm* (blog), Media.com, May 14.

Kendall-Taylor, Andrea, Erica Frantz, and Joseph Wright. 2017. "The Global Rise of Personalized Politics: It's Not Just Dictators Anymore." *Washington Quarterly* 40:7–19.

Khamraev, Viktor. 2007. "'Polozhenie chekistov segodnia fantastitecheski ustoichivo'" [The Chekists' position today is fantastically stable]. Interview with Ol'ga Kryshtanovskaia. *Kommersant'-Vlast'*, March 19.

Kragh, Martin, and Andreas Umland. 2023. "Putinism beyond Putin: The Political Ideas of Nikolai Patrushev and Sergei Naryshkin in 2006–20." *Post-Soviet Affairs* 39 (5): 366–89.

Kremlin.ru. 2022. "Zasedanie Soveta Bezopasnosti" [Security Council meeting]. February 21.

Kryshtanovskaia, Ol'ga. 2002. "Rezhim Putina: Liberal'naia militoktratiia?" [The Putin regime: Liberal militocracy?]. *Pro et Contra* 7 (4): 158–80.

Kryshtanovskaya, Ol'ga, and Stephen White. 2005. "Inside the Putin Court: A Research Note." *Europe-Asia Studies* 57 (7): 1065–75.

———. 2003. "Putin's Militocracy." *Post-Soviet Affairs* 19 (4): 289–306.

Legucka, Agnieszka, and Bartosz Bieliszczuk. 2019. *Kremlin Kids: The Second Generation of the Russian Elite*. Warsaw: Polish Institute of International Affairs, November.

Lenin, V. I. 1968. "The State and Revolution." In *Lenin: Selected Works*. Moscow: Progress Publishers.

Levada Center. 2023. "Otnoshenie k Vladimiru Putinu" [Attitude toward Vladimir Putin]. July 7.

Lysova, Alexandra. 2020. "Challenges to the Veracity and the International Comparability of Russian Homicide Statistics." *European Journal of Criminology* 17 (4): 399–419.

Meakins, Joss I. 2018. "Squabbling Siloviki: Factionalism within Russia's Security Services." *International Journal of Intelligence and Counter Intelligence* 31 (2): 235–70.

Melville, Andrei. 2023. "State Capacity and Russia." In *Routledge Handbook of Russian Politics and Society*, 2nd ed., ed. Graeme Gill. London: Routledge.

Miller, Greg, and Catherine Belton. 2022. "Russia's Spies Misread Ukraine and Misled Kremlin as War Loomed." *Washington Post*, August 19.

Myre, Greg. 2023. "CIA Chief: The Uprising in Russia Shows 'Signs of Weakness' in Putin's Rule." NPR, July 21.

Navalny, Aleksei. 2014. "Dniu bor'by s korruptsiei posviashchaetsia. Zhena sekretaria i ee dom za milliard" [Anti-Corruption Day is dedicated to the Secretary's wife and her billion-ruble house]. Navalny.com, December 9.

Pertsev, Andrey. 2023. "Eshche rannim utrom 24 iiunia Kreml', sudia po vsemu, pytalsia dogovorit'sia s Prigozhinym. Iz etogo nichego ne vyshlo" [The Kremlin, it seems, even during the early morning of June 24 tried to agree with Prigozhin. Nothing came of it]. Meduza, June 24.

Putin, Vladimir. 2019. "Poslanie Prezidenta Federal'nomu Sobraniiu" [Presidential Address to the Federal Assembly]. Kremlin.ru, February 20.

———. 2015. "Poslanie Prezidenta Federal'nomu Sobraniiu" [Presidential Address to the Federal Assembly]. Kremlin.ru, December 3.

———. 2014. Bol'shaia press-konferentsiia Vladimira Putina" [Vladimir Putin's annual press conference]. Kremlin.ru, December 18.

———. 2007. "Interv'iu zhurnalistam pechatnykh sredstv massovoi informatsii iz stran—chlenov 'Gruppy vos'mi'" [Interview with print journalists from G-8 countries]. Kremlin.ru, June 4.

———. 2000. *Ot pervovo litsa: Razgovori s Vladimirom Putinym* [First person: Conversations with Vladimir Putin]. Russia: Vagrius, 2000.

Reddaway, Peter. 2018. *Russia's Domestic Security Wars: Putin's Use of Divide and Rule against His Hardline Allies*. London: Palgrave MacMillan.

Renz, Bettina. 2006. "Putin's Militocracy? An Alternative Interpretation of Siloviki in Contemporary Russian Politics." *Europe-Asia Studies* 58 (6): 903–24.

Rivera, David, and Sharon Werning Rivera. 2019. "Are Siloviki Still Undemocratic? Elite Support for Political Pluralism during Putin's Third Presidential Term." *Russian Politics* 4 (4): 499–519.

———. 2018. "The Militarization of the Russian Elite under Putin: What We Know, What We Think We Know (but Don't), and What We Need to Know." *Problems of Post-Communism* 65 (4): 221–32.

———. 2014. "Is Russia a Militocracy? Conceptual Issues and Extant Findings Regarding Elite Militarization." *Post-Soviet Affairs* 30 (1): 27–50.

Rivera, Sharon Werning, David Rivera, and Alexander Nemeth. 2022. "Elite Support for Political Pluralism in 2020: Comparing Civilians and Siloviki in the Survey of Russian Elites." Paper presented at the Annual Convention of the Association for Slavic, East European, and Eurasian Studies, November 30.

Rivera, Sharon Werning, et al. 2020. *Survey of Russian Elites 2020: New Perspectives on Foreign and Domestic Policy*. Hamilton College, July 28.

RTVI. 2022. "Iz ad"iutantov v ministry. Kem stanovilis' ofitseri FSO pri prezidente Putine" [From adjutants to ministers. What FSO officers became under President Putin]. May 26.

Saito, Mari, and Maria Tsvetkova. 2022. "How Russia Spread a Secret Web of Agents across Ukraine." Reuters, July 28.

Seddon, Max, Christopher Miller, and Felicia Schwartz. 2023. "How Putin Blundered into Ukraine—Then Doubled Down." *Financial Times*, February 22.

Soldatov, Andrei, and Irina Borogan. 2023. "Putin's Real Security Crisis." *Foreign Affairs*, July 6.

———. 2010. *The New Nobility: The Restoration of Russia's Security State and the Enduring Legacy of the KGB*. New York: PublicAffairs.

Soldatov, Andrei, and Michael Rochlitz. 2018. "The Siloviki in Russian Politics." In *The New Autocracy: Information, Politics, and Policy in Putin's Russia*, ed. Daniel Treisman. Washington, DC: Brookings Institution Press.

Stoner, Kathryn. 2023. "The Putin Myth." *Journal of Democracy* 34 (2): 5–18.

Taratuta, Yuliya, and Maksim Tovkaylo. 2015. "Minfin ne sprashivali, vo skol'ko oboidetsia reshenie po Krymu" [The Finance Ministry was not asked how much the Crimea decision would cost]. *Forbes Woman*, March 5.

Taylor, Brian D. 2018. *The Code of Putinism*. Oxford: Oxford University Press.

———. 2011. *State Building in Putin's Russia: Policing and Coercion after Communism*. Cambridge: Cambridge University Press.

Tompson, William. 2005. "Putting Yukos in Perspective." *Post-Soviet Affairs* 21 (2): 159–81.

Treisman, Daniel, ed. 2018. *The New Autocracy: Information, Politics, and Policy in Putin's Russia*. Washington, DC: Brookings Institution Press.

Treisman, Daniel. 2007. "Putin's Silovarchs." *Orbis* 51 (1): 141–53.

Vandenko, Andrei. 2014. "Gennadii Timchenko: Za vse v zhizni nado platit'" [Gennadiy Timchenko: Everything in life has a price]. TASS, August 3.

Volkov, V. V., E. L. Paneiakh, and K. D. Titaev. 2010. *Proizvol'naia aktivnost' pravookhranitel'nykh organov v sfere bor'by s ekonomicheskoi prestupnost'iu:*

Analiz statistiki [Arbitrary activity of law enforcement agencies in combating economic crime: A statistical analysis]. IPP EUSPB.

Volkov, Vadim. 2013. "Delo Naval'nogo: Predelyi proizvola razdvigaiutsia" [The Navalny case: Pushing the limits of arbitrary despotism]. *Slon*, April 27.

Wilson, Kenneth. 2023. "Vladimir Putin: Great Leader or Ordinary Authoritarian?" In *Routledge Handbook of Russian Politics and Society*, 2nd ed., ed. Graeme Gill. London: Routledge.

Yeltsin, Boris. 2000. *Prezidentskii marafon: Razmyshleniia, vospominaniia, vpetchatleniia* [Presidential marathon: Reflections, memories, impressions]. Moscow: AST.

Zygar', Mikhail. 2015. *Vsia kremlevskaia rat': Kratkaia istoriia sovremennoi Rossii* [All the Kremlin's men: A short history of contemporary Russia]. Moscow: Intellektual'naia literatura.

ELEVEN

"Dictatorship of Law" or Just Dictatorship?

IVAN PAVLOV

The Putin era began with high hopes for legal reform. Shortly after taking office, President Vladimir Putin promised a "dictatorship of law." In 2001, Russia adopted a new Code of Criminal Procedure that incorporated many aspects of a Western adversarial system, including trial by jury in certain cases and the exclusion of statements given by suspects in the absence of counsel. Reforms that made the commercial courts more transparent and reliable were also introduced. However, throughout the Putin era, another tendency has been present—revision of the law in order to allow it to be used to suppress political dissent in the name of protecting "national security." Over time, this tendency has become stronger, especially after the protests of 2011, the annexation of Crimea in 2014, and in the lead-up to, and aftermath of, the invasion of Ukraine in February 2022. As a result, the key legal reforms or, more aptly, counterreforms of the Putin era have created a situation in which, as in the Soviet era, the government can use the law arbitrarily and indiscriminately to punish political dissent. The regime has thus failed to deliver a "dictatorship of law," delivering instead only a dictatorship.

This chapter traces some of the key milestones in the evolution of the manipulation of national security for purposes of legal counterreform during the Putin era. Throughout, the same pattern is evident: introduction into the law of broad and vaguely worded provisions that give maximum discretion to enforcement authorities and application of these norms to suppress political dissent rather than to protect national security.

The Law on Extremism: 114-FZ (July 2002)

At the same time that the Putin administration was supporting a new liberal Code of Criminal Procedure in the early 2000s, fear of the populace and the desire to use the law to suppress dissent was already evident. One of the first steps in this direction was the adoption, in July 2002, of Federal Law 114-FZ, entitled "On Counteracting Extremist Activity."[1] The law defines "extremist activity" broadly to include, among other things, acts aimed at "the subversion of the security of the Russian Federation" and "the making of mass disturbances, ruffian-like acts, and acts of vandalism for the reasons of ideological, political, racial, national or religious hatred or hostility toward any social group," thus permitting it to be used for political purposes.[2] With such a broad and vague definition, the law gave the government the power to label almost any protest movement as "extremist."

At the same time, two new and overlapping articles were added to the Criminal Code—Article 282.1, entitled "Organization of an extremist organization," and Article 282.2, "Organization of the activity of an extremist organization." These two articles collectively criminalize almost any activity related to an "extremist" organization, including, among other things, creation, organization, participation, or recruitment, and carry a penalty of up to twelve years' incarceration, depending on the circumstances. As a result, the government now had new and powerful tools to use the criminal justice system to suppress dissent.

Over time, the law on extremism has been expanded and applied more aggressively. As Aleksandr Verkhovsky, the director of the SOVA Center, said in 2021, since passage in 2002, "the law has changed, there've been lots of amendments and it's become significantly much harsher."[3] According to statistics from the Supreme Court of the Russian Federation, in 2012 there was only one conviction under Article 282.1, in 2013 there were four, and in

2014 there were four. However, in 2019 there were fourteen, in 2020 there were nine, and in 2021 there were twenty-one. Similarly, in 2012, there were thirty-seven convictions under Article 282.2, in 2013 there were thirty-eight, and in 2014 there were thirty-six. By contrast, in 2019, there were fifty-eight convictions, in 2020 there were seventy-one, and in 2021, 125. The war has also seen a sharp increase in the use of this statute, with 212 and 265 convictions in 2022 and 2023, respectively.[4]

Over time, the law has also been applied more clearly for political purposes. For example, in 2021, after the arrest of Alexei Navalny, his Anti-Corruption Foundation (known in Russian by its initials, FBK) was designated an extremist organization, which led to the subsequent criminal prosecution of many of its members, including Navalny. Navalny's organization was engaged in classic political activity, including participation in electoral campaigns and organization of peaceful political protests. However, the authorities clearly viewed him as a political threat and used criminal prosecution to force his supporters to cease their activities in Russia. The FBK was the most influential and well-known opposition organization, and when the authorities did not see strong civil society resistance to the closure of the FBK, they began to purge the remaining independent political structures and media organizations (discussed more below).

Internal Enemies: The "Foreign Agents" Law, 121-FZ (July 2012)

In July 2012, against the backdrop of the Bolotnaya protests and shortly after resuming the presidency, President Putin signed 121-FZ, which allows the government to designate organizations that receive foreign funding and that engage in "political activity" as "foreign agents."[5] The law does not require that the foreign funding come from a government source. In contrast to the U.S. Foreign Agents Registration Act (FARA), it does not require that the political activity be undertaken at the direction of, or in the interests of, the foreign funder. It thus turns any recipient of funding, even funding that is provided with no conditions and "no strings attached," into an "agent." Political activity is defined in the law as activity designed to influence government policy or to influence popular opinion about government policy. Designated foreign agents are required to, among other things: (1) produce quarterly financial reports about their activities, file semiannual documents describing their activities and the composition of their management bodies, and submit to an annual state audit, (2) obtain prior authorization before participating in any political activity, and (3) label all materials distributed in the media, including on the internet, as having been produced by foreign agents. Failure to fulfill these obligations can be criminally prosecuted under Article 19.34 of the Code of Administrative Violations, which carries a penalty of up to five years' incarceration, and administratively under Article 330.1 of the Criminal Code, both of which were introduced simultaneously with the Foreign Agents law.

Starting in 2014 and coinciding with the beginning of the war in eastern Ukraine, the legislation on foreign agents gradually became more repressive. Originally, only registered NGOs could be designated foreign agents. However, in 2017, after the United States required Russia Today to register under the U.S. FARA, the Duma adopted legislation creating the category of "Foreign Media Agents," and in 2019 the law was further amended to allow individuals, in addition to organizations, to be designated foreign agents. As the legislation has expanded, so has the number of foreign agents. For example, in 2013, just one organization was included in the register of foreign agents. In 2014, twenty-nine more were added. In December 2022 the various registers of foreign agents were combined into one. By the end of 2023, according to the official Ministry of Justice of the Russian Federation list, 742 individuals and/or organizations had been declared foreign agents, with 108 more added in the first eight months of 2024 (figure 11.1).[6]

Data from the official registry show the dramatic increase in registrations over time and especially in connection with the war in Ukraine.[7]

Over time, the law has also been used more to silence independent media. In 2021, many major independent media organizations were added to the register of foreign agents, including Meduza, Mediazona, TV Rain, *The Insider, Important Stories*, and others. In the same year, journalists from the BBC, Mediazona, and Radio Freedom, activists from Pussy Riot, lawyers from Team 29, and various environmental and LGBTQ+ activists were designated foreign agents, and many fled Russia as a result. Many important civil society organizations and human rights organizations, including OVD-Info, Zone of Law, Doctors' Alliance, the election observer organization Golos, and a number of LGBTQ+ organizations, have also been designated foreign agents. As of August 30, 2024, according to the Ministry of Justice, 850 individuals and organizations were registered as foreign agents.[8]

In July 2022 the law was further amended when the Duma adopted a set of amendments titled "On Control over Activities of Entities/Persons

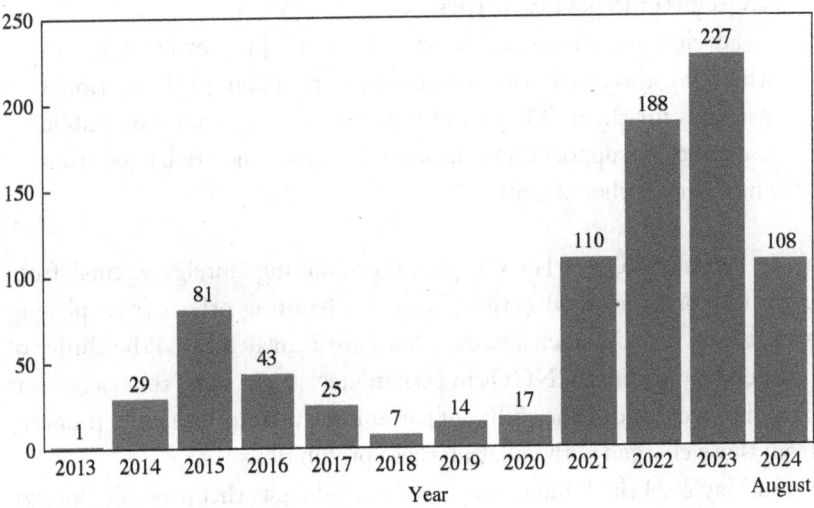

FIGURE 11.1. Number of Individuals and Organizations Declared to Be Foreign Agents in Russia, 2013–August 2024

Source: Official Registry of Foreign Agents, Ministry of Justice, Russian Federation (https://minjust.gov.ru/ru/activity/directions/998/).

under Foreign Influence."[9] As Human Rights Watch reports, the July 2022 law replaces the various categories of foreign agents

> with a consolidated, simplified, but endlessly broad definition to cover any person—Russian, foreign or stateless; any legal entity, domestic or international; or any group without official registration, if they are considered to have received foreign support and/or are considered to be "under foreign influence" and engaged in activities that Russian authorities would deem to be "political." It also covers anyone who gathers information about Russia's military activities or military capabilities, or creates or publicly disseminates information or funds such activities.[10]

Designation as a foreign agent has especially serious consequences for individuals. As Human Rights Watch explains, the July 2022 law excludes "foreign agents" from key aspects of public life and bans them from

> joining the civil service, participating in electoral commissions, acting in an advisory or expert capacity in official or public environmental

impact assessments, in independent anti-corruption expertise of draft laws and by-laws, or electoral campaigns or even donating to such campaigns or to political parties.

Foreign agents are also banned from teaching or engaging in other education activities for minors or producing informational materials for them. They cannot participate in organizing public assemblies or support them through donations and are barred from a number of other activities.[11]

In February 2024, a law was passed prohibiting "foreign agents" from earning money from advertising and also banning others from placing advertisements with such agents. This significantly limited the ability of independent media and NGOs to earn money. At the same time, a law was passed that expanded the ability of law enforcement to confiscate property from those charged with violating these prohibitions.[12]

In May 2024 the Duma also passed amendments that prohibit "foreign agents" from participating in elections. Now individuals listed in the registry of foreign agents cannot be a candidate at any level, from local to federal. This directly contradicts the Russian constitution and is a clear example of abuse of the concept of "foreign agent" to exclude opposition politicians from participating in the political life of the country.[13]

Treason, Espionage, and State Secrets: 190-FZ (November 2012)

As challenges to the regime mounted, the regime gave itself more legal tools to repress dissent. On November 12, 2012, in the wake of large-scale protests over the rigged Duma elections of 2011 and Putin's return to the presidency in May 2012, the Duma adopted Federal Law No. 190-FZ, which made it significantly easier to criminally prosecute political dissent. Federal Law No. 190-FZ contained four main amendments to the Criminal Code, discussed in turn below.

Treason—Article 275 of the Criminal Code

Prior to the passage of 190-FZ, treason was defined under Article 275 of the Criminal Code as "disclosure of a state secret or the rendering of other assistance to a foreign government, foreign organization, or their representatives in the conduct of hostile actions causing damage to the external security of the Russian Federation." However, with the passage of 190-FZ, "assistance to international organizations and their representatives" was also included in the definition of treason. This amendment radically altered the Russian legal definition of treason, which, consistent with international norms and practice, had always focused on cooperation with foreign governments and intelligence services. With the addition of "international organizations and their representatives," anyone who worked with anyone connected with any international organization could be prosecuted for treason, provided that the other elements of the statute were satisfied.

At the same time, the element of "damage to the external security of the Russian Federation" was replaced by the element of "damage to the security of the Russian Federation," thus allowing the government to define any perceived threat to its security as treason. As human rights activist Lev Ponomarev explained on the law's passage, "The term 'security' in contrast to the term 'external security' which was used in the previous version of the statute, can mean anything—commercial security, internal security, legal security, etc. and the revised statute can be used to prosecute any interaction between political opponents of the regime and foreigners, including presentations on human rights at international conferences."[14]

Unfortunately, Ponomarev's words proved prophetic as the law has consistently been abused to silence dissent. In April 2023, political opposition leader Vladimir Kara-Murza was sentenced to twenty-five years on various charges, including treason, based on a speech he gave in Arizona to the Phoenix Committee on Foreign Relations in which he denounced the "kleptocracy and thievery" of the Putin regime.[15] In September 2022, journalist Ivan Safronov was sentenced to twenty-two years, one of the longest sentences ever imposed under the treason statute, for allegedly (1) disclosing state secrets about Russian arms sales to a Czech journalist and (2) sharing information about Russia's operations in Syria with a political scientist from Germany. Safronov was prosecuted for treason even though he did not have access to state secrets and even though all the information he used for his articles was publicly available. Given its legal infirmity, Safronov's case was clearly designed to intimidate independent Russian media.

In July 2022, new amendments were adopted qualifying switching to the side of the enemy as treason. This statute has been used to prosecute citizens attempting to leave the country. For instance, twenty-one-year-old Saveliy Frolov was detained at the Russian-Georgian border and charged with "treason" when the FSB searched his backpack and found subscriptions to some Ukrainian media channels and camouflage pants.[16]

On April 18, 2023, Federal Law No. 157-FZ introduced more substantive changes. For example, Article 275 of the Russian Criminal Code was amended to provide life imprisonment for "high treason," which is not even clearly defined.[17]

Cooperation on a Confidential Basis with Foreigners in Activities against the Security of the Russian Federation—Article 275.1 of the Criminal Code

On July 14, 2022, under a new package of amendments to the Criminal Code that purportedly "simplified" the law on treason, Article 275.1 was adopted. Article 275.1 introduced a potential punishment of up to eight years' imprisonment for "confidential cooperation with a foreign government, international or foreign organization in order to assist them in activities knowingly directed against the security of the Russian Federation." Again, given the vague definition of "cooperation," it can be used to intimidate, restrict engagement by, and criminally prosecute individuals who communicate with international bodies, including the United Nations.[18]

It could also be interpreted as applying to the preparation of reports for international organizations or the dissemination of information that, in the opinion of Russian law enforcement, could undermine Russian national security. According to official data, in 2023, three people were convicted under this article, with one being sentenced to compulsory measures for those with mental health issues.[19]

Espionage—Article 276 of the Criminal Code

Federal Law No. 190-FZ also made significant changes to Article 276 of the Criminal Code, which criminalizes espionage. Previously, a prosecution for espionage required proof of direct work for a foreign intelligence service. However, as a result of the amendments, espionage was defined also as work "in the interests of" a foreign intelligence service, a definition that allows for prosecution based on acts that may have the incidental effect of benefiting a foreign intelligence service, even if the subject did not know that he was working with a foreign intelligence service or intend to directly benefit a foreign intelligence service. As with Article 275, the element of damage to "external security" was replaced by the element of damage to "security" generally.

One example of how the revised version of Article 276 has been used is the case of Karina Tsurkan. Tsurkan, a Moldovan citizen, worked for the Russian state-owned energy company InterRAO and allegedly shared classified information with a business contact who allegedly had ties to the Moldovan intelligence services.[20] According to the Memorial Human Rights Defense Center, the charging documents failed to specify how Tsurkan obtained access to state secrets, how she passed the secret information to Moldovan intelligence, or what, if anything, she received as compensation from Moldova.[21] In fact, the charges were so vague that Tsurkan stated in a media interview, "I'd comment on the charges, if I understood them."[22] Nevertheless, in 2020 Tsurkan was convicted of espionage and sentenced to fifteen years' incarceration.

In 2023, nine people were convicted of espionage under Article 276, surpassing the previous record of four in 2018.[23]

Disclosure and Receipt of State Secrets—Articles 283/283.1 of the Criminal Code

Federal Law No. 190-FZ also made important changes to Articles 283 and 283.1 of the Criminal Code that criminalize, respectively, the disclosure and receipt of state secrets. Prior to 190-FZ, only those who had official access to state secrets through their work or official government positions were considered holders of state secrets, and only they could be prosecuted for disclosure of state secrets. However, 190-FZ expanded the list to include those who have access to state secrets by virtue of academic work or "other situations covered by the legislation of the Russian Federation," even if they have not been officially informed that they have authorized access to state secrets.

Moreover, it is hard to know whether one has access to state secrets because the law that defines what constitutes a state secret, aptly named "On State Secrets," lacks a clear definition and lists only general categories of information. For example, the definition of "state secrets" includes, among other things, information about (1) the Russian military and its capabilities and plans, (2) the Russian economy and Russian science and technology, (3) Russian foreign policy, including any information "about Russian foreign policy and foreign economic policy, the premature disclosure of which could undermine national security," and (4) information about intelligence gathering and counterintelligence activities.[24]

As a result, a person can easily be prosecuted for receiving and/or disclosing state secrets without proof of knowledge or intent. The cases of Anton Kolomytsyn and Viktor Ryzhanov are illustrative. Kolomytsyn, a historian, was prosecuted for buying a 1970s era Soviet military topographical map, which the FSB considered a "state secret," even though similar maps can easily be found in libraries (including the U.S. Library of Congress), stores, and on the internet. Viktor Ryzhanov, a resident of Bryansk oblast, which is located on the border with Ukraine, was friends with a border guard, with whom he had previously served in the army. In several discussions, Ryzhanov's friend discussed whether he would be going on patrol that day. Unbeknownst to Ryzhanov and his friend, information about border patrols is considered a state secret. Ryzhanov's friend was prosecuted under Article 283 for disclosure of state secrets and sentenced to 1.5 years' probation. Ryzahnov was prosecuted under Article 283.1 for illegal receipt of state secrets and sentenced to three years and three months. At the time, I was serving as Ryzhanov's lawyer. I explained the legal conundrum this way: "In order to know what is a state secret and what is not a state secret, you would have to be familiar with all the secret instructions and orders that regulate access and only those who have authorized special access to state secrets can do so. Ryzhanov never had such access."[25]

According to human rights organization Department One, although the articles on treason and espionage were first amended in 2012, because of the prolonged investigation period for such cases, the increase in corresponding convictions and sentences became noticeable only in 2014. The 2014 increase in treason and espionage prosecution was also related to the annexation of Crimea and Russia's invasion of eastern Ukraine. The Department One report also points out that since then, the article on treason has increasingly been used against elderly scientists as this is the easiest way for the FSB to present "success." For example, the physicist Alexei Vorobyov, who was represented by Department One, was sentenced to twenty years in prison for treason because of "Chinese dust" allegedly found on the memory card of his smartphone. However, as noted above, the most striking example of a political case masquerading as a legitimate treason prosecution is that of journalist Ivan Safronov, who did not have any access to state secrets and published only publicly available data. Safronov was prosecuted simply because he was dealing with a touchy subject, namely, military investigations, including those in Ukraine, for the daily publication *Kommersant'*. In September 2022, Ivan Safronov was sentenced to the maximum allowable term of twenty-two years in prison.

Recent statistics show that the number of cases of high treason is growing in all regions, but the greatest increase is recorded in the occupied territories of Ukraine, in particular in Crimea and Sevastopol, and in

Moscow, as well as in the Kaliningrad, Belgorod, Rostov, Samara, and Sverdlovsk regions. In 2023, seventy individuals were convicted under Article 283 for disclosing state secrets, surpassing the previous record of sixty-six convictions in 2022. Similarly, fifteen and sixteen individuals were convicted under Article 283.1 in years 2022 and 2023, respectively.[26]

External Enemies: The Law on "Undesirable Organizations": 129-FZ (May 2015)

On May 23, 2015, President Putin, partly in response to the Crimea sanctions, signed 129-FZ, also known as the law on "undesirable organizations." This law prohibits the existence of foreign organizations that, in the opinion of the prosecutor general, threaten the "constitutional structure, defense capability and security of the state." Designations of organizations as "undesirable" are made by the prosecutor general with the consent of the Ministry of Foreign Affairs, with no requirement of judicial approval. Participation in an "undesirable" organization is punishable under Article 20.33 of the Code of Administrative Offenses by a fine of up to 15,000 rubles, and under Article 284.1 of the Criminal Code, which provides for up to four years' incarceration.

Although the government announced that the undesirable organizations law would be used against commercial organizations, from the very beginning it was used primarily against foreign NGOs advocating for democratic reform. For example, in 2015, the Washington, D.C.–based U.S. Russia Foundation and the National Endowment for Democracy, the latter of which is partly funded by the U.S. Congress, and two organizations founded by George Soros, the Open Society Foundation and Open Society Institute (both of which the Russian government accused of being the "puppet masters" of color revolutions), were designated "undesirable." In subsequent years the list expanded to include many European NGOs, including some financed by the EU.

On February 17, 2017, the Duma passed amendments prohibiting undesirable organizations from creating Russian legal entities, and on October 26, 2017, the Duma passed additional restrictions that gave the prosecutor general's office the authority to block, without judicial authorization, the internet sites of undesirable organizations. At the same time, the state media monitoring agency, Roskomnadzor, forbade the mass media to publish materials of undesirable organizations and threatened to block any sites that even linked to them.

In 2021, Article 284.1 of the Criminal Code, which criminalizes participation in foreign undesirable organizations, was amended to increase the penalties and to make it easier to bring charges by expanding the scope of liability. Shortly thereafter, on May 27, 2021, during the preparation of the amendments, Andrei Pivovarov, the director of Mikhail Khodorkovsky's organization Open Russia, announced that Open Russia, which had not been declared undesirable, would be closing.[27] Four days later, Pivovarov, who had declared his candidacy in the September 2021 Duma elections, was arrested as he was preparing to leave Russia on vacation.[28] He was charged with cooperating with an undesirable organization under the expanded version of Article 284.1 even though Open Russia had never been declared an undesirable organization.[29] In July 2022, he was sentenced to four years' incarceration and an eight-year ban on involvement in social-political activity.

In August 2021, several other Khodorkovsky-linked organizations, including Pravozaschita Otkrytki, MBK Media, and Open Media, were also closed. Other organizations, including Project (in Russian, Proekt), which conducts investigations into corruption, and Team 29 (in Russian, Komanda 29), which is representing Alexei Navalny's Anti-Corruption Foundation in a case brought against it for "extremism," were also designated "undesirable."

By the end of 2022, seventy-two organizations had been designated undesirable. The statistics have nearly doubled since then, with an additional fifty-eight undesirable designations in 2023 and sixty in 2024 as of August 30, 2024.[30] These include:

- Greenpeace International
- Transparency International
- Woodrow Wilson International Center for Scholars
- Central and East European Law Initiative (CEELI)
- Bellingcat
- Heinrich Böll Foundation
- Bard College
- Jamestown Foundation
- Atlantic Council
- German Marshall Fund

In 2021, one of the authors of the "undesirables" law, Alexander Tarnavsky, was asked by the independent media outlet Meduza whether he was happy with how the law was being implemented. He answered:

> Absolutely not. Initially, the law was designed to address commercial conflicts, which exist in all countries. But as it turned out, the law was not applied to economic or commercial organizations, but only to the NGO sector. When we were drafting the law, we were very happy that the main government agency responsible for designating organizations as undesirable was the Ministry of Foreign Affairs (MFA). But it turned out that there is no difference between the FSB and the MFA.[31]

Taken together, the "foreign agent" and "undesirable organizations" laws allow the FSB to ban anybody who expresses disagreement with official government policy and to deprive potential antiwar movements of structure, organization, and leadership.

"Special Operations" and Presidential Decree Number No. 273 (May 2015)

On May 28, 2015, President Putin signed Decree No. 273, which further revised the law on state secrets.[32] Among other things, Decree No. 273 classified as state secrets information about military losses "in peacetime and during the conduct of special military operations."[33] By virtue of Decree No. 273, the term "special operation" became enshrined in the law, though without a clear definition, which meant that information about military casualties ceased to be accessible to civil society and journalists. As a result, the government can declare any military action a "special operation," and any journalistic or academic research about the "operation" can result in criminal prosecution, regardless of the fact that, for the reasons discussed above, those researching or writing about it have no way of knowing what exactly is legally considered a state secret. As also discussed above, collecting and/or disseminating such information can be prosecuted under Articles 283 and 283.1 of the Criminal Code. Theoretically, even the parents of soldiers who have died can be criminally prosecuted for organizing a public funeral. In fact, the only safe form of reporting on military operations is the simple retransmission of official statements from the Ministry of Defense. Considered in light of the wars in the Donbas and Syria (both recently underway at the time that Decree No. 273 was adopted), the goal was obvious: to prevent the dissemination of any objective information about military conflicts that could undermine the official version. As discussed in more detail below, the Russian government has used this tool aggressively with respect to the war in Ukraine.

The FSB and the Internet (2014–2019)

In 2014, after the beginning of the conflict in Ukraine, a number of laws were adopted that expanded the access of the intelligence services to personal data and established their control over the internet. In 2014, Prime Minister Dmitry Medvedev signed a resolution that required social networks and other internet platforms to install equipment and software that would allow the FSB to automatically receive information about users' activity, and also required the FSB to designate a specific squad that would be responsible for cooperation with each site.[34] In 2016 the Duma adopted the so-called "Yarovaya Law," which, among other things, required operators to collect and maintain recordings of conversations and correspondence, and required operators that used encryption to provide "encryption keys" to the intelligence services.[35] As a result, the FSB obtained unlimited access to the personal data and correspondence of Russian citizens. Finally, in 2019, the Duma passed a series of laws, collectively known as the Sovereign Internet Law, that further expanded the powers of the FSB over the internet. The law(s) had three main aspects:

- The compulsory installation of technical equipment for counteracting threats;
- Centralized management of telecommunication networks in case of a threat and a control mechanism for connection lines crossing the border of Russia; and
- Implementation of a Russian national Domain Name System (DNS).[36]

As one commenter wrote, "Officially, the amendments aim to protect the internet within Russia from external threats. In fact, they provide the crucial legal framework for creating a centralized management system of the internet by the state authority—theoretically enabling the isolation of Russia's network from the global internet."[37]

The FSB aggressively used its new powers. For example, in 2017 the FSB demanded decryption codes from the messenger service Telegram. After Telegram refused to provide them, the site was blocked in April 2018 (though it was unblocked in 2020 with no explanation). In 2019, against the backdrop of wide-scale protests in Moscow over the rigging of the Moscow City Duma elections, the FSB demanded that Yandex and ten other Russian sites, including Avito, Habrahabr, and Rutube, provide de-encryption keys.[38] The letters sent to the companies informed them that they were required to provide the FSB with "round the clock remote access to the organization's information system" and to "ensure, in the shortest possible time, technical capacity to provide the Center [i.e., the FSB] with information necessary for decoding electronic communications of users of their internet services."[39] According to publicly available information, Yandex and other companies reached an agreement with the FSB on implementation of the Yarovaya Law, but the exact details of what they agreed to are not publicly available.

FSB "Professional Secrets": 279-FZ (2020), and Military "Work Secrets": 172-FZ (2021)

On July 21, 2020, the Duma passed Federal Law No. 279-FZ, which, among other things, prohibits current and former FSB employees from disclosing "professional secrets." The concept of professional secrets had never existed previously in Russian law and its definition in 279-FZ is extremely vague: "information that does not include information that constitutes a state secret or the secrecy of which is otherwise protected by the law, the disclosure of which could create a threat to the security of the FSB and/or harm the reputation of the FSB."[40]

Although ostensibly directed at current and former FSB employees, the real purpose of the law is clear: to allow the FSB to conceal information from the public. Duma deputy Dmitry Vyatkin acknowledged as much when he explained that although disclosure of state secrets is already a crime, certain sensitive information the disclosure of which could harm the interests of the FSB is not always covered by the law on state secrets and is not always clearly identified as "secret."[41] In other words, according to Vyatkin, the FSB needed a law that would allow it to hide information that would otherwise be available to the public. Mikhail Fedotov, the former chairman of the Presidential Council for Civil Society and Human Rights, explained that the law, in addition to being vague, contradicts other laws. For example, he pointed out that the Supreme Court has held that information about violations of the law cannot be withheld from the public. But, under the professional secrets law, the FSB could prohibit the disclosure of information about crimes if such disclosure could harm the reputation of the FSB, and such disclosure could even result in criminal prosecution.[42]

In another indication of a potential military action, in June 2021 the Duma passed 172-FZ, an amendment to the law "On Defense" that introduced the concept of "work secrets" in the defense sector.[43] Federal Law No. 172-FZ defines "work secrets" in the area of defense as information that does not constitute a state secret but that is not "generally accessible" and authorizes all defense-related agencies (including the Ministry of Defense, the FSB, the SVR, the Federal Protection Service, the Military Procuracy, and military investigative agencies) to determine exactly what information constitutes a defense "work secret." In November 2021 the Ministry of Defense published its list of "work secrets," which contained 689 categories of information that, collectively, include almost all defense-related information that is not already classified as a "state secret." For example, the list includes "information about international cooperation in the area of collective security," "materials about the investigation of the deaths of military personnel," "information about the number of those called for military service, their point of departure and arrival," "financing of expenditures in the defense sector," "information about military procurement," and many others.

The legislative history of the law also makes clear that it is intended to give these agencies the authority to issue "prior restraints" with respect to the publication of any information related to the military. Violations of the law on work secrets are punishable as administrative offenses under the Code of Administrative Violations; civilians are subject to fines and military personnel are subject to disciplinary punishment.

As a result of the passage of 279-FZ and 172-FZ, by January 2022 (one month before the invasion of Ukraine) the categories of information that were prohibited to be disclosed had expanded substantially to include information about military operations, including information about mobilization, troop movements, and casualties, as well as information about corruption in state procurement and financial violations.

Expansion of MVD Powers: 424-FZ (December 2021)

In December 2021, two and a half months before the Russian invasion of Ukraine, the Duma passed another law, 424-FZ, which amended the basic law "On the Police" and significantly expanded the powers of the Ministry of Internal Affairs (MVD).[44] Specifically, 424-FZ empowered MVD officers to:

- dismantle and search automobiles at their discretion, including for the purposes of ensuring public security during mass protests;
- cordon off residences and other buildings with only executive branch (rather than judicial) authorization and conduct physical searches of people in the cordoned-off area (previously this had been allowed only to prevent physical harm or threats to life);
- not identify themselves in interactions with citizens by name or rank in case of a threat to the life or security of an MVD officer or if necessary to prevent the commission of a crime or administrative violation; and
- forcibly enter a residence to arrest someone who likely committed a crime based only on a single uncorroborated witness statement (previously this had been possible only if it was established that someone who had officially been designated a suspect was in the residence).

Thus 424-FZ essentially gives the police martial law–like powers to suppress protests and interfere in the private lives of citizens, with no judicial oversight.

Law on "Discrediting" the Armed Forces (March 2022/March 2023)

On March 4, 2022, in what became known as the "fake news" law, the Duma adopted amendments to the Criminal Code penalizing the dissemination of false information about the Russian Armed Forces and also for public calls for sanctions against Russia.[45] Three weeks later, on March 22, 2022, the Duma adopted amendments expanding the scope of the law and establishing criminal and administrative liability for disseminating false information about the work of any Russian government agencies overseas.[46] The law was further amended in March 2023 to prohibit discrediting of voluntary formations, organizations, and individuals who are assisting the Russian Armed Forces (such as the Wagner Group).[47]

As a result, Article 207.3 of the Criminal Code now criminalizes the "public dissemination . . . of knowingly false information about the armed forces of the Russian Federation, the activities of state organs of the Russian Federation outside the territory of Russia and voluntary formations, organizations or individuals providing assistance to the Russian armed forces." Penalties range up to fifteen years' incarceration and fines of up to 5 million rubles. In 2022 and 2023 respectively there were fourteen and fifty-nine convictions under this article.[48] (Statistics for 2024 were unavailable at the time the book went to press.)

Article 207.3 has been used aggressively to silence political opposition. As noted above, opposition leader Vladimir Kara-Murza was sentenced in April 2023 to a total of twenty-five years on three separate counts for discrediting the armed forces. In December 2022, opposition politician Ilya Yashin was convicted under Article 207.3 based on a YouTube stream that he posted about Russian war crimes in Ukraine and was sentenced to eight and one-half years in prison. On August 1, 2024, Russia released Vladimir Kara-Murza and Ilya Yashin, among others, in a prisoner exchange with the West.

The Kara-Murza and Yashin cases are only the tip of the iceberg. According to information compiled by OVD-Info, 164 people are currently being investigated or prosecuted for violations of Article 207.3, while there are 6,839 administrative cases open under the equivalent provision of the Code of Administrative Violations.[49] According to a Supreme Court report, in 2022, courts ordered citizens to pay fines for discrediting the military 4,439 times.[50] In comparison, in 2023, under Article 20.3.3 there were 2,361 administrative charges, with 2,353 fines imposed.[51] Many of these cases appear to have had little to do with actually protecting the Russian military. For example, in March 2023, Alexei Moskalyov was sentenced to two years in prison for discrediting the Russian military based on a series of social media posts criticizing the war in Ukraine and after his thirteen-year-old daughter drew an antiwar picture at her school.[52] Olga Lakhman, a teacher, was fined 30,000 rubles for printing a Wikipedia article about Russia's invasion of Ukraine, and Anastasia Chernysheva, a baker, was fined 35,000 rubles for baking a cake with antiwar slogans.[53]

Conclusion

A modern legal system should be focused, in the commercial realm, on ensuring fair and impartial adjudication of disputes, and, in the area of criminal justice, on balancing the need to protect society from crime while simultaneously protecting the rights of those accused of crimes. A healthy legal system appropriately directed toward these goals is a fundamental pillar of a vibrant economy and civil society. While the Putin regime made some steps toward progressive legal reform, especially in the commercial courts, ultimately politics triumphed and the goal of building a dynamic economy and polity was supplanted by the more primitive goals of preventing dissent and simply maintaining power. This shift in priorities is reflected in the judicial system, where, over time, reform devolved into simply providing the government with more tools of repression. A legal system focused on protecting state power begets corruption as it prevents investigation into misconduct. Corruption, in turn, stifles economic development and begets more repressive laws. In this sense, legal reform under Putin has been a failure.

If history is any guide, we may yet see Stalinist-style show trials in which the defendants confess to participation in fantastic plots organized by foreign intelligence services to overthrow the regime. Such show trials have been, and can once again be, used by the Kremlin to foster an atmosphere of paranoia about internal enemies in order to make the populace more deferential to the government.

NOTES

The author would like to thank Tom Firestone of Squire Patton Boggs for his contributions to this chapter. The chapter is based in part on data compiled by the human rights organization Department One.

    1. Federal Law of the Russian Federation, "On Counteracting Extremist Activity," 114-FZ, as of 25 July 2002 (see the complete report of the European Commission for Democracy Through Law, 5 March 2012, at https://www.venice.coe.int/webforms/documents/default.aspx?pdffile=CDL(2012)024-e).

2. The complete text of Law 114-FZ can be found on the official website of the Ministry for Digital Development, Communications and Mass Media of the Russian Federation (in Russian) (digital.gov/ru/ru/documents/3075).

3. Eckel (2021).

4. Statistics of the Supreme Court of the Russian Federation for the year 2022 (https://stat.xn----7sbqk8achja.xn--p1ai/stats/ug/t/14/s/17); statistics of the Supreme Court of the Russian Federation for the year 2023 (https://stat.xn----7sbqk8achja.xn--p1ai/stats/ug/t/14/s/17).

5. The complete text of Federal Law No. 121-FZ, "On Amendments to Legislative Acts of the Russian Federation Regarding the Regulation of the Activities of Nonprofit Organizations Performing the Functions of a Foreign Agent," dated 20 July 2017, can be found on the Official Internet Portal of Legal Information of the Russian Government (in Russian) (http://pravo.gov.ru/).

6. The Foreign Agents Registry can be found on the official website of the Ministry of Justice of the Russian Federation (in Russian) (https://minjust.gov.ru/ru/activity/directions/998/) (requires VPN).

7. Ibid.

8. Ibid.

9. The complete text of Federal Law No. 255-FZ, "On Control over Activities of Entities/Persons under Foreign Influence," dated 8 July 2022, can be found on the Official Internet Portal of Legal Information of the Russian Government (in Russian) (http://publication.pravo.gov.ru/document/view/0001202207140018) (requires VPN).

10. Human Rights Watch (2022).

11. Ibid.

12. Mass Media Defense Center (2024).

13. State Duma (2024).

14. Vinokurova (2012).

15. Associated Press (2023).

16. OVD-Info (2023b).

17. Kropman (2023).

18. BBC News Russia (2022).

19. Statistics of the Supreme Court of the Russian Federation for the year 2023.

20. Her citizenship is relevant because, in contrast to the treason statute, the espionage statute applies only to non-Russian citizens. On the case, see *Deutsche Welle* (2020).

21. Memorial Human Rights Defense Center (2020).

22. Meduza (2018).

23. Statistics of the Supreme Court of the Russian Federation for the year 2023.

24. The complete text of the Law of the Russian Federation No. 5485-1, dated 21 July 1993 (as amended on 4 August 2023), "On State Secrets" (as amended and supplemented on 1 February 2024), can be found on the Consultant Plus website (in Russian) (https://www.consultant.ru/document/cons_doc_LAW_2481/b6a297f676cd64a5eea867c45fb375fcb1dee3a5/).

25. Zarembo (2017).

26. Statistics of the Supreme Court of the Russian Federation for the year 2023.

27. Meduza (2021b).

28. *Current Time* (2021).

29. Amnesty International (2022).

30. The list of foreign and international nongovernmental organizations whose activities are recognized as undesirable on the territory of the Russian Federation can be found on the official website of the Ministry of Justice of the Russian Federation (in Russian) (https://archive.ph/2023.04.17-175048/ https:/minjust.gov.ru/ru/documents/7756/).

31. Meduza (2021a).

32. The complete text of Decree No. 273 of the President of the Russian Federation as of 28 May 2015, "On Amendments to the List of Information Classified as State Secrets, Approved by Decree of the President of the Russian Federation on 30 November 1995 No. 1203," can be found on the Official Internet Portal of Legal Information of the Russian Government (in Russian) (http://publication.pravo.gov.ru/Document/View/0001201505280001?index=1).

33. Ibid.

34. The complete text of the Resolution of the Government of the Russian Federation as of 31 July 2014 No. 473, "On Approval of the Rules for Interaction Between Organizers of Information Dissemination in the Information and Telecommunications Network 'Internet' with Authorized Government Agencies Carrying Out Operational and Search Activities or Ensuring the Security of the Russian Federation" (with Amendments and Additions), can be found on the Information and Legal Provisions Portal Garant (in Russian) (https://base.garant.ru/70709018/#:~:text=%D0%B8%D1%8E%D0%BB%D1%8F%202014%20%D0%B3.-,N%20743).

35. Complete texts of the Federal Law as of 6 July 2016 No. 374-FZ, "On Amendments to the Federal Law 'On Counteracting Terrorism' and Certain Legislative Acts of the Russian Federation in Terms of Establishing Additional Measures to Counteract Terrorism and Ensure Public Safety," and Federal Law as of 06 July 2016 No. 375-FZ, "On Amendments to the Criminal Code of the Russian Federation and the Criminal Procedure Code of the Russian Federation in Terms of Establishing Additional Measures to Counter Terrorism and Ensure Public Safety," can be found on the Official Internet Portal of Legal Information of the Russian Government (in Russian)

(http://publication.pravo.gov.ru/Document/View/0001201607070016; http://publication.pravo.gov.ru/Document/View/0001201607070042).

36. See the Russian Wikipedia article, "Russian Sovereign Internet Law."
37. Epifanova (2020).
38. Meduza (2020).
39. Idel.Real (2019).
40. The complete text of the Federal Law as of 31 July 2020 No. 279-FZ, "On Amendments to Article 7 of the Federal Law 'On the Federal Security Service,'" can be found on the Official Internet Portal of Legal Information of the Russian Government (in Russian) (http://publication.pravo.gov.ru/Document/View/0001202007310049).
41. RBC (2020).
42. Ibid.
43. The complete text of the Federal Law as of 31 May 1996 No. 61-FZ (as amended on 25 December 2023), "On Defense," is available on the Consultant Plus website (in Russian) (https://www.consultant.ru/document/cons_doc_LAW_10591/407560ca13761004ca7027afca04f5053a28528a/).
44. The complete text of the Federal Law "On Amendments to the Federal Law 'On Police,'" dated 21 December 2021, No. 424-FZ (latest revision), is available in on the Consultant Plus website (in Russian) (https://www.consultant.ru/document/cons_doc_LAW_404061/).
45. State Duma (2022a).
46. State Duma (2022b).
47. Archived bill No. 253972-8, "On Amendments to Articles 13.15 and 20.3-3 of the Code of the Russian Federation on Administrative Offenses (in Terms of Establishing Administrative Liability for Disseminating Information in the Media Containing Instructions for the Illegal Manufacture of Ammunition for Firearms, and Clarifying Liability for Discrediting Volunteer Formations)," can be found on the Legislative Activity Support System website (in Russian) (https://sozd.duma.gov.ru/bill/253972-8) (requires VPN).
48. Article 207.3 of the Criminal Code of the Russian Federation with Comments, "Public Dissemination of Knowingly False Information about the Use of the Armed Forces of the Russian Federation, the Exercise of Powers by State Bodies of the Russian Federation, the Provision of Volunteer Formations," can be found on the Article-by-Article Comments to the Criminal Code of the Russian Federation Portal (in Russian) (https://ukodeksrf.ru/ch-2/rzd-9/gl-24/st-207-3-uk-rf).
49. Ibid.
50. OVD-Info (2023a).
51. Statistics of the Supreme Court of the Russian Federation for the year 2023.
52. Litvinova (2023).
53. OVD-Info (2023a).

REFERENCES

Amnesty International. 2022. "Russian Federation: Activist Sentenced to Four Years in Prison: Andrei Pivovarov." July 29.

Associated Press. 2023. "Top Kremlin Critic Convicted of Treason, Gets 25 Years." April 18.

BBC News Russia. 2022. "The State Duma Decides to Supplement the Criminal Code in Case of Military Actions" [in Russian]. May 25.

Current Time. 2021. "Andrey Pivovarov Registered as Candidate for State Duma Elections" [in Russian]. August 5.

Deutsche Welle. 2020. "Russia Jails Ex-Energy Executive for Spying." December 29.

Eckel, Mike. 2021. "'Extremism' as a Blunt Tool: Behind the Russian Law Being Used to Shut Navalny Up." Radio Free Europe, April 29.

Epifanova, Alena. 2020. "Deciphering Russia's 'Sovereign Internet Law.'" German Council on Foreign Relations, January.

Human Rights Watch. 2022. "Russia: New Restrictions for 'Foreign Agents.'" December 1.

Idel.Real. 2019. "RBK: FSB Demands Encryption Keys for User Correspondence from Yandex" [in Russian]. June 4.

Kropman, Vitaly. 2023. "The State Duma of the Russian Federation Adopts a Law on Life Sentence for Treason" [in Russian]. *Deutsche Welle Russia*, April 18.

Litvinova, Dasha. 2023. "Russia Convicts Father of Teen Who Drew Antiwar Picture." *AP News*, March 28.

Mass Media Defense Center. 2024. "Advertising Ban for Foreign Agents: Explanations Made by Lawyers." February 28.

Meduza. 2021a. "It Doesn't Work Properly, It Is Wrong: How the Co-Author of the Law on 'Undesirable Organizations' Assesses It Today" [in Russian]. March 16.

———. 2021b. "Open Russia Announces Shutdown Due to Pressure on Activists." May 27.

———. 2020. "FSB Demanded Keys to Decrypt Correspondence from Avito, Rutube, Habr and a Dozen Other Websites. This Happened at the Height of Moscow Protests" [in Russian]. February 11.

———. 2018. "I'd comment on the charges, if I understood them." August 13.

Memorial Human Rights Defense Center. 2020. "Karina Tsurkan, a Former Senior Manager at Inter RAO, Is a Political Prisoner." October 15.

OVD-Info. 2023a. "Wartime Repressions Report. May 2023." May 24.

———. 2023b. "Resident of the Moscow Region Sentenced to 6 Years of Strict Regime in the Case of Preparation for Treason" [in Russian]. October 25.

RBC. 2020. "Why the Law on Professional Secrecy of the FSB? Will Journalists Be Able to Write about the Special Service?" [in Russian]. July 21.

State Duma. 2024. "The President Signs a Bill into a Law Prohibiting Participation of Foreign Agents in Elections" [in Russian]. Official website of the State Duma of the Russian Federation, May 15 (http://duma.gov.ru/news/59314/).

———. 2022a. "Liability Introduced for Disseminating 'Fakes' about the Actions of the Russian Armed Forces" [in Russian]. Official website of the State Duma of the Russian Federation, March 4. (http://duma.gov.ru/news/59314/).

———. 2022b. "Amendments Adopted to Liability for 'Fakes' about Actions of Russian Government Agencies Abroad" [in Russian]. Official website of the State Duma of the Russian Federation, March 22 (http://duma.gov.ru/news/53773/).

Vinokurova, Ekaterina. 2012. "The Point Action Law" [in Russian]. Gazeta.ru, October 23.

Zarembo, Igor. 2017. "The Supreme Court Lightens a Sentence of a Man Convicted of Obtaining State Secret" [in Russian]. Russian Agency for Legal and Court Information, December 20.

TWELVE

Russia's Military Failures in Ukraine
Causes and Consequences

ALEKSANDR GOLTS

The hostilities in Ukraine that Russia began on February 24, 2022, resulted in significant military defeats for Moscow during 2022 and Russia's inability to achieve strategic goals in 2023 and 2024. Two decades of uncompleted military reforms thwarted by the inherent contradictions of Vladimir Putin's militarist state are to blame. The weakness of the Russian armed forces, now glaringly revealed, has pushed the Kremlin to abandon the modernization of Russia's army and return to the concept of mass mobilization. This will fail in the long term because of Russia's worsening demographic and economic situation, and any drastic attempt at military rebuilding can only result in chaos.

The war is still ongoing, and its outcome is unknown, but it is already clear that none of the likely options for ending hostilities will achieve the war goals originally proclaimed by the Kremlin. The notorious "denazification" and "demilitarization" declared by Putin as the goals of the operation masked ultimatums for Kyiv to abandon its intention to integrate into the Euro-Atlantic community and ensure its sovereignty through defense preparations. Moscow was seeking regime change. But Kyiv showed high-level resilience, won a series of significant victories in 2022, and demonstrated the ability to withstand the superior forces of Russia in 2023 and 2024. NATO countries are supplying (though with delays, caused by internal political struggles in the United States and some European countries) Ukraine with state-of-the-art intelligence, massive amounts of weapons, and training for its servicemen.[1] Contrary to the Kremlin's goals, Ukraine has become much more integrated into NATO's military structure than it was before Russia's aggression, which aimed to prevent just such integration. Finland and Sweden have joined NATO. Although it cannot be ruled out that Russia will be able to maintain control over the territories it currently occupies, ending the conflict on Russia's terms is highly unlikely.

A Military (Mis)adventure

In military planning, Putin's "special military operation" was a classic example of a military (mis)adventure. The Russian armed forces, whose official authorized strength was 1.2 million servicemen (estimates of the actual number vary from 750,000–800,000[2] to 900,000[3]), were able to create a grouping of only 200,000 troops.[4] This grouping from the beginning was incapable of taking over a large European country of approximately 600,000 square kilometers and a population of over 42 million that was unwilling to accede to the Kremlin's demands. In a strange way, Russia intended to defeat the Ukrainian army not by concentrating its forces but rather by dispersing them. Russia attacked the territory of Ukraine from four directions, which determined the failure of its offensive plans.[5] Russian air and missile strikes, moreover, failed to defeat the Ukrainians. Most likely the Russian forces did not possess the required quantity of high-precision strike weapons and guidance systems to demoralize Ukraine to the same extent as the initial days and weeks of American operations in Afghanistan and Iraq had. The pre-invasion reports by Russia's Defense Ministry that the military had increased by "thirty times" the number of cruise missiles during the years under Sergei Shoigu's leadership were a bluff or showed the very low base of missile supplies before the war started.[6] In any case, the quantity of cruise missiles, as well as of other ammunition, was insufficient to meet the operational objectives. Nor did the Russian military have a decisive superiority in personnel numbers.[7]

Russia's expectation of a quick victory was based not on military analysis but on false intelligence reports that Ukrainians would joyfully welcome the "liberation." It is no coincidence that in his televised address after the start of the invasion, Vladimir Putin directly appealed to Ukrainian generals to take power away from the "drug-addicted Nazi regime."[8] Those who planned the operation were clearly assuming that in the first hours the Russian armed forces would destroy Ukraine's organized centralized defense and the Ukrainian leadership would flee. This error alone can explain the aborted landing of several Russian brigades in the suburbs of Kyiv. These forces had no chance of capturing a city of two million inhabitants. Significantly, the hope for a disorganized, weak resistance could explain the advance of Russian army columns without proper reconnaissance and air defense. As a result, numerous Ukrainian artillery ambushes and air strikes decimated Russian formations. The fact that the first echelon of the advancing troops included Rosgvardiya (riot-control law enforcement agency) columns, which had no heavy weapons, showed the obvious unpreparedness for a serious fight against an enemy. The purpose of those columns was to control the already occupied territories, not to capture them militarily.

The obvious adventurism of military planning turned into inevitable defeats in 2022. Russian troops unsuccessfully tried to overrun Kyiv, Kharkiv, and Chernihiv but got bogged down on the approaches to these important centers. As a result, the Kremlin had to withdraw its troops from Kyiv, Kharkiv, Chernihiv, and Sumy, declaring it "an act of goodwill."

The siege and subsequent capture of Mariupol resulted in its complete destruction. However, there was no significant advance of Russian troops. The Russian army lacked necessary reserves to maintain the offensive to capture the entire Donetsk oblast.

In autumn 2022, Ukrainian armed forces took the initiative. Kyiv succeeded in mass mobilization and achieved, if not superiority, then at least relative equality with Russia in the number of troops engaged in combat operations. Faced with an obvious shortage of manpower, the Kremlin had to take extreme measures. A "partial" mobilization was announced in September 2022. According to official statements, about 300,000 reservists were called up. The Wagner private military company created large military formations with 50,000 hardened criminals released from prisons.[9]

At the same time, the Ukrainian army began to receive large quantities of long-range artillery systems, targeting and fire-control systems, and unmanned aerial vehicles from Western countries. These weapons systems used Western countries' satellite reconnaissance data, enabling the Ukrainian side to significantly disrupt the logistical support of the Russian troops. Ukraine took advantage of the Russian command's inability to effectively cover the 1,600-kilometer-long combat front and launched a successful offensive in the direction of Kharkiv, as a result of which Russian troops, threatened by encirclement, retreated into the former Luhansk oblast. Ukraine then launched an offensive in Kherson oblast that forced the withdrawal of Russian formations to the left bank of the Dnipro river. Unable to prevail, Moscow announced a partial mobilization, and by calling up (according official reports) about 300,000 reservists, Moscow managed to stabilize the situation.

Following the defeats of 2022, Russia switched to strategic defense—the type of warfare for which the Soviet army was organized since the time of the Cold War. During the winter of 2023, Russia created a line of defensive fortifications to protect its foothold in the captured territories. Russia began launching powerful missile strikes against Ukraine's infrastructure, primarily its energy system. By attempting to deprive Ukrainians of heat and light, Russia mistakenly hoped that the Ukrainian population would lose its will to resist. The main hostilities concentrated in the town of Bakhmut in Donetsk oblast, which had no significant strategic importance. The forces of the Wagner private military company, which had been besieging Bakhmut since early March 2023, eventually succeeded in capturing the city in late May, though at a huge cost in terms of casualties. During this time, Western countries continued large-scale arms deliveries to Ukraine that, in addition to long-range artillery systems, included a substantial number of tanks and armed vehicles.

The Ukrainian counteroffensive began in June 2023. It did not achieve its intended goals. These objectives included severing supply routes from Russia to the occupying forces and liberating a substantial portion of the occupied territories. Although Ukrainian troops managed to penetrate the Russian defenses, they ultimately failed to break through, and lost their strategic initiative. Disappointment in the Ukrainian army led to delays in the West's delivery of further military assistance.

The military initiative passed to Russia. Taking advantage of Ukraine's lack of troops and ammunition, Russia launched an offensive and captured

Avdiivka, a Ukrainian fortified settlement near Donetsk. The front line will now most likely be stabilized indefinitely and the fighting become positional. Hostilities took on the character of a war of attrition. Former Ukrainian commander in chief Valery Zaluzhny named the situation the "stalemate" in his interview with the *Economist* in November 2023.[10] It is possible that Zaluzhny's assessment of the situation was one of the main reasons why he was dismissed by President Zelensky on February 8, 2024.

The war of attrition now begun could clearly have significant consequences for the course of Russia's war against Ukraine. It appears that neither side possesses significant strategic reserves that would enable a swift victory. Consequently, it is increasingly evident that each side will be doomed to a protracted war of attrition. Russia will experience the greatest challenges in terms of replenishing its weaponry and military equipment, while Ukraine will see its human resources stretched.

The Russia-Ukraine War bears little resemblance to the "war of the future," as some experts have described it. In fact, the fighting looks more like the battles of the industrial rather than the digital era. The achievements of the revolution in military affairs—the ability to control the battlefield comprehensively, the use of high-precision weapons, and the use of drones—do not play a decisive role on the battlefield in this war. Both sides possess such weapons in approximately equal quantities. A situation of relative equality of combat capabilities and resources is characteristic of the strategic deadlocks of World War I and, in part, the Korean War, rather than the American swift defeat of the Iraqi army. Most warfare utilizes weapons systems—tanks, multiple rocket launchers, artillery, aircraft—that are advanced versions of those used in the wars of the middle of the last century. If so, this leads to the conclusion that quantity is no less important in this war, and perhaps even more important than quality. It is not a coincidence that both the Ukrainian and the Russian commands began to attach such importance to the issue of mobilization.

Russia possesses the largest nuclear arsenal in the world, and Putin constantly hints at the possibility of using nuclear weapons if Ukraine or the West crosses certain "red lines." Yet the West has been relatively successful in countering the Kremlin's nuclear blackmail. On October 7, 2022, U.S. president Joe Biden said, "For the first time since the Cuban Missile Crisis, we have a direct threat of the use [of a] nuclear weapon, if in fact things continue down the path they've been going."[11] Shortly before Biden's statement, however, U.S. national security adviser Jake Sullivan said that despite Moscow's nuclear hints, the United States had seen no signs that Russia was immediately preparing to use a nuclear weapon. A month later, a White House official said that Central Intelligence Agency director William Burns had warned Sergei Naryshkin, head of Russia's SVR foreign intelligence service, about the consequences of any use of nuclear weapons: "He is conveying a message on the consequences of the use of nuclear weapons by Russia, and the risks of escalation to strategic stability."[12] However, at the same time, the West restricted Ukraine in the use of advanced weapons, and as of today, still puts restrictions on their use on internationally recognized Russian territory.[13]

Unfinished Reforms

If we approach Russia's war on Ukraine by the standards of the last century, Russia should have won: its population is at least four times larger than Ukraine's and the Russian defense industry is many times larger as well. This theoretically should provide a huge superiority in manpower and firepower.

Despite its advantages, however, the Russian army failed to secure any victories that could lead to a swift peace settlement on Russian terms. The clear failures of the Russian army during the military operation came as a surprise to most experts, who had long preferred to believe the bravura reports of the Russian Defense Ministry about the constantly growing power of the Russian armed forces and their large stocks of the latest military equipment. These reports probably impressed Vladimir Putin as well.

Russia's strategic defeats in Ukraine are grounded in the way the Russian army developed after the collapse of the Soviet Union. In 1991 the newly independent Russian Federation received most of the Soviet armed forces (about 2.8 million servicemen), which in terms of structure and organization were a mass mobilization army. The country's defense relied on the ability to mobilize millions of reservists on the eve of war, in the so-called "threatened period." The peacetime Soviet army was a school of military training for these reservists. Military formations consisted of enlisted men, with almost no professional NCOs. The degree of personnel manning, not the level of combat training of the troops, determined the degree of combat readiness of these formations. No strategic operation could be launched without first "mobilizing": conscripting reservists, manning incomplete formations with conscripts, and distributing and readying weapons and equipment from their storage bases. Such an army could be effective only if the entire economy of the country worked for it, with the entire male population immediately available as a "mobilization resource." Such a system could function only in a totalitarian state.

Russia developed a market economy after the fall of the Soviet Union, though a very specific one, that declared, but only selectively enforced, basic rights and freedoms and the rule of law. A capitalist market economy, however, immediately challenged the basic principles by which the Russian army was maintained, and a structural crisis resulted. First and foremost, this concerned the manning of the armed forces. Although universal compulsory service was formally in effect in Russia, young men of conscription age saw military service not without reason as a form of legalized slavery and tried to avoid it by all available means. The Ministry of Defense could not fill the required positions of conscripts as new recruits often fell short of meeting the minimum intellectual, physical, and moral standards. Morals in the Russian army differed little from those in prison. The leadership of the armed forces basically showed itself incapable of fighting the so-called *dedovshchina*, the system of humiliation and abuse of first-year conscripts by second-year soldiers. (Hazing, or barracks violence, in its Russian variant, was not a breach of discipline but a system for maintaining discipline in the most barbarous and savage way, by using physical violence.) Fleeing unbearable conditions, soldiers deserted military units in platoon and company numbers, which, unsurprisingly, created a crime epidemic.

Two wars in Chechnya demonstrated the monstrously low combat effectiveness of the Russian armed forces. Vladimir Putin recognized this: "In order to effectively repel the terrorists, we needed to put together a group of at least 65,000 men, but the combat ready units in the entire army came to only 55,000 men, and they were scattered throughout the entire country. Our armed forces came to a total of 1,400,000 men but there were not enough men to fight. This is how kids who had never seen combat before were sent in to fight. I will never forget this."[14] The privatized Russian industry could not, if called upon, begin mass production of weaponry to equip an army of millions. The so-called mobilization preparation of industry in the 1990s became extortion. Military officials demanded bribes for releasing enterprises from fulfilling state defense orders.

Vladimir Putin watched with obvious irritation as his annual mandatory military budget increases, averaging around 20 percent since 2000, did not lead to any positive changes in the army. Only after the war with Georgia in 2008 did the Russian military-political leadership realize that despite the continuous increase in funding since the beginning of Putin's presidency, the armed forces remained ineffective, and that if the Georgians had been just a little stronger, Russia's incursion might have ended in defeat.

Anatoly Serdyukov, appointed minister of defense in 2007, quickly understood the essence of the problem and began a radical military reform. Serdyukov decisively rejected the concept of a mass mobilization army, which Russia had adhered to for the previous 150 years. He and Chief of the General Staff of the Armed Forces of Russia Nikolai Makarov sought to create a different kind of army: a compact, mobile army, with fully manned units and formations. Taking into account Russia's challenging demographics, this could only be achieved by drastically reducing the number of armed forces units and manning them mostly on a contract (volunteer) basis. Serdyukov succeeded in sharply reducing the total number of units and formations and managed to fully staff the remaining ones. His successor, Sergei Shoigu, later began the gradual "contractization," or conversion to volunteer enrollment in the armed forces. At the beginning of 2020, the number of contract servicemen amounted to 405,000, and significantly exceeded the number of conscripts for the first time.[15] At that point, compulsory service in the armed forces could be canceled without any harm to the national security.

As a result of Serdyukov's reforms, the Kremlin had at its disposal several dozen fully staffed brigades, which made it possible to execute combat orders within hours of their receipt. Putin, who had long suffered from the humiliation caused by his inability to use military force, immediately used these formations to further his geopolitical goals. Victory time for Putin began in February 2014, when some "polite green men" blockaded the local parliament building in Crimea, cut off all transportation communications linking the peninsula to Ukraine, and surrounded Ukrainian troop locations. A year later, Putin acknowledged the participation of Russian troops in the "return" of Crimea.[16] By then, observers had noted significant changes in the Russian army since the war with Georgia in 2008.

Well-equipped and disciplined Russian army units conducted a carefully prepared operation in Crimea. The impressive sudden deployment of Russian troops to Ukraine's Donbas region followed at the end of February 2014. In 1999, it took the Russian General Staff more than two weeks to form and send two battalions of paratroopers to Dagestan, where Chechen fighters had advanced. In contrast, fifteen years later, Russia deployed over 40,000 troops to the Ukrainian border within just a day and a half. In September 2015 the Kremlin announced its intention to launch an armed fight against global terrorism in Syria. Russian aircraft and air defense systems spectacularly appeared and helped Bashar al-Assad's battered army launch a counteroffensive and lay siege to Syria's second most important city, Aleppo. Moscow forced Washington to negotiate on coordination in Syria. The revived Russian army became the most important effective instrument of foreign policy, as well as a significant aid in domestic policy by dramatically increasing support for the president. However, these military successes, stemming from the Serdyukov reform, led Putin and his military experts to overestimate the effectiveness and combat capabilities of Russia's armed forces.

Serdyukov succeeded only partially. He could not reform the armed forces' command-and-control system. In Russia, the military and political leadership of the country remain unseparated. The Russian Armed Forces have still not seen a clear division of functions between the Defense Ministry and the General Staff. The chain of command is extremely confusing. The Main Combat Training Directorate of the armed forces, for example, is part of the Defense Ministry, while the Main Organization and Mobilization Directorate is part of the General Staff. The current system of "special military operation" command resembles a strange improvisation. At first, a unified command did not exist. The commands of each of the four military districts individually exercised leadership and led their own formations. The air force and navy were subordinate to their own superiors. For this reason, it was apparently necessary to create a hitherto unknown body—"the joint staff of military branches involved in special military operation," whose existence only became known from the news reports on Putin's visit to it.[17] The very existence of the joint staff indicates that the idea of a "joint operation," where the command system is constituted and navy and aviation combat units are included, has never been implemented. Instead, the units and formations of the various branches of the armed forces retain their own systems of command, support, supply, and communications. Thus the headquarters "coordinated" the use of formations of different branches of the armed forces, as well as the orders coming from different commands. Naturally, such coordination takes time, and the degree of confusion increases.

In its attempt to achieve success in combat operations, the Kremlin abandoned in 2022–2023 its state monopoly on violence and allowed the existence of parallel military structures not directly subordinated to its command. Private military companies (the largest of which was the Wagner Group) have played a significant role in the combat operations in Ukraine. Though they depend heavily on the military for equipment, logistics, and the ammunition of the regular army, these organizations are not part of the structure of the armed forces and do not report to the Russian military command. Private military company Wagner has never had a formal relation to the Russian army; it "is a private army that has operated, operates and will operate around the world," declared the late Yevgeny Prigozhin, the owner of Wagner.[18] During the storming of Bakhmut, Prigozhin had outrageously demanded that Minister of Defense Shoigu and Chief of the General Staff Gerasimov provide ammunition and, if they did not, threatened to withdraw his own troops from battle positions. Prigozhin, who held no military rank or official position, claimed that high-ranking Russian generals, both retired and active duty, were under his operational command. According to him, Sergei Surovikin, previously commander of Army Group "South" of the Russian Armed Forces, was responsible for supplying Wagner with ammunition. Colonel General Mikhail Mizintsev, dismissed from his post of deputy defense minister in late April 2023, became Prigozhin's deputy a week later.

Trying to regain control over the command system, Shoigu issued an order according to which all "volunteer" formations must sign a contract with the Ministry of Defense. According to Deputy Defense Minister Pankov, the order intended to give "the necessary legal status to volunteer formations, create unified approaches to the organization of comprehensive support and fulfilment of their tasks."[19] Prigozhin immediately rejected the possibility of signing such a contract, noting that Wagner did not obey the Ministry of Defense.[20] In the end, Prigozhin unleashed a direct military mutiny. Several thousand Wagner fighters marched on Moscow, and the Kremlin did not have enough troops to stop them with military force. Putin was forced to negotiate with the organizers of the rebellion. Prigozhin and his commanders did not suffer any legal punishment despite Wagner units having shot down several Russian helicopters and a plane, killing at least thirteen Russian military personnel.[21] When the mutiny ended, Putin even met with its organizers and offered them to continue their service. When, under pressure from Prigozhin, who participated in this meeting, they refused, again no legal punishment followed.

Prigozhin and Wagner military commander Dmitry Utkin (along with eight others) were killed in an aircraft crash two months later in what many considered a direct punishment from Putin. The Ministry of Defense then managed to somehow include different "volunteer" units in its command structures. Wagner is now under the umbrella of the Russian military intelligence (GRU) service.[22] Nevertheless, Prigozhin's mutiny opened a real Pandora's box. Going forward, in a situation of serious crisis, any military commander under whose command there are several thousand armed fighters will know that that commander can use military force not only by order, but also in his own interests.

On March 23, 2024, the Criminal Code of the Russian Federation was amended, outlining a procedure whereby those suspected or accused of petty and minor crimes can be freed from potential prison sentences if they are called up for military service through mobilization or in wartime, or if they sign a contract with the Ministry of Defense.[23] In addition, the exemption is supposed to be extended to those who have been convicted and are already serving time. Convicted criminals who decide to fight in Ukraine are to have their sentences changed to a suspended sentence.

One of the main reasons for Russia's military failures is the desire to preserve its archaic military culture at all costs. Particularly noteworthy in this respect is the requirement to carry out fully and unconditionally any order of a senior commander. General Zaluzhny, then commander in chief of the Ukrainian army, accurately described this situation when he characterized his then opponent, Sergei Surovikin, thus: "The Soviet Army welcomed and enforced one concept: the commander. But being a commander and being a leader is not the same. With all due respect to Mr. Surovikin, if you look at him, he is an ordinary Petrovite commander from Peter the Great's time, shall we say, a Derzhimorda [a brutal martinet in Gogol's *The Government Inspector*]. You look at him and understand that either you complete the task or you're f---ed."[24]

Battlefield situations in modern warfare change so rapidly that scrupulous adherence to orders inevitably leads to defeat. The requirement to follow orders deprives Russian officers of initiative, personal responsibility, and the ability to make independent decisions. It is self-reliance in solving combat tasks, however, that is the key to success in network-centric warfare. This concept recognizes that achievements in the revolution in military affairs—such as the ability to conduct satellite reconnaissance and communications and the use of drones—require each participant in combat operations to receive timely, comprehensive information and make decisions based on it. The Russian Ministry of Defense has tried for many years to create a modern combat management system, with no success. This failure is logical. The concept of network-centric warfare is fundamentally incompatible with Russia's archaic military culture, which, centered on a mass mobilization army, requires and prioritizes numerical superiority over the enemy.

The officer corps owns its military culture and cannot quickly change it. Serdyukov faltered when he tried to initiate changes in military education. He and his subordinates decided to convert all military higher educational institutions—in 2008, there were sixty-eight of them—into ten educational and research centers corresponding to the branches of the armed forces. Serdyukov planned to concentrate leading researchers in relevant fields of military science there and to provide opportunity for cadets and officers to become familiar with the most modern methods of warfare. They decided to abandon the academies of the branches of the armed forces and to reduce training at the Military Academy of the General Staff of the Armed Forces of the Russian Federation to a few months. The reformers proceeded from the assumption that a graduate, having received a basic military education, would later acquire new knowledge without having to leave his place of service for an extended period. In order to obtain a new position and rank, an officer would have to take short courses to master new knowledge and skills in a particular field. Seniority alone would no longer be sufficient.

Serdyukov wanted to radically overhaul the core professional military education curriculum to incorporate broader civilian disciplines. Drawing on insights from foreign experience that the skills to use even sophisticated military equipment—ships, planes, rockets—can be acquired in specialized training centers, he intended to reduce the emphasis on acquiring specific military skills. The program was to include the humanities, especially the study of foreign languages, with the aim of enhancing commanders' capacity for continuous learning and a deeper understanding of the world.

Putin fired Serdyukov in November 2012 and replaced him with a former minister of emergency situations and loyal ally, Sergei Shoigu. Shoigu reversed Serdyukov's reforms. Meeting the demands of the generals, the Defense Ministry decided to preserve twenty-six military academies and nine of their branches. The military educational institutions, which during the time of Serdyukov were under the control of the Department of Education of the Defense Ministry, were returned to the general commands of the armed forces branches. In pursuing their narrow departmental objectives, these commands began to demand that the military universities equip cadets not with fundamental knowledge but with more "practical skills." Unsurprisingly, the first of these skills was unconditional obedience.

Serdyukov's reduction of the number of military units between 2009 and 2012 had created an oversupply of lieutenants, who were injudiciously assigned to sergeant positions. Under Shoigu, however, the creation of more and more skeleton units led to a shortage of officers, and an accelerated "reproduction" of officers began. The term of service of officers was extended by five years. In 2012, military universities admitted only 8,000 people, but in 2023 they accepted 15,000.[25] Starting in 2019, the duration of basic education was shortened by one year, for a new total of four years. The planned expansion of the armed forces, along with the associated mobilization requirements, further amplified the demand for junior officers, but this expansion came at the expense of quality.

It is no accident that the government rejected military education reform. Let us imagine that educated, independent, self-confident, and self-righteous people join the army. It is unlikely that they would be satisfied with the current system, under which an officer must execute any, even criminal, order, or otherwise face court-martial (it is possible to appeal, but only after the order is executed). Officers with a modern education, therefore, would be problematic for the present authorities. A cardinal reduction in the effectiveness of the armed forces resulted.

Corruption, which has plagued the Russian army since its creation over three hundred years ago, has also significantly contributed to Russia's military failures. The war in Ukraine revealed the extent to which the Russian Armed Forces lack vital matériel reserves, which, obviously, were either stolen or not manufactured in the first place. The guise of secrecy prohibited any form of public oversight, and the number of crimes in the sphere of state defense orders in recent years has exceeded all imaginable limits.[26]

Return to Mass Mobilization Concept

Serdyukov's reforms envisioned the creation of effective armed forces with a clear purpose: to win a short-term local conflict. The rejection of the concept of mass mobilization was also a rejection of the idea of winning a large-scale war without resorting to nuclear weapons. However, Russia's actions in Ukraine led to a direct military confrontation with the West.

As a result, the army received tasks it could not fulfill. Such a war requires far more troops, weapons, and military equipment than Russia has at its disposal. After Russia captured Crimea and began the proxy war in the Donbas, a new cold war started. Russia began to confront the whole of NATO, and this required the creation of new divisions. In 2016, Shoigu announced the creation of eight armies, which would include more than twenty-five divisions (combined arms, aviation, air defense, and surface ships) and fifteen brigades.[27] In the succeeding years, Shoigu regularly announced the creation of more and more divisions and regiments.[28]

Before 2022, the number of troops did not increase significantly. However, the number of units increased permanently after 2014, which meant that all established "armies," "divisions," and "brigades" were only skeleton units. Ministry of Defense official reports may have counted the number of units two or three times by establishing an army headquarters, and then subordinating to it two or three skeleton divisions. In fact, these skeleton divisions might consist of only one or two brigades.

During a Ministry of Defense board meeting held at the end of December 2022, Shoigu announced plans for an unprecedented buildup of the armed forces, insisting on the need to increase the size of the armed forces to 1.5 million soldiers.[29]

Shoigu intended to form three new motorized rifle divisions and two airborne assault divisions and an army corps, and to convert seven motorized rifle brigades and five marine brigades into divisions. For each of the nine combined-arms armies and one tank army, Shoigu wanted to create a mixed aviation division and another army aviation brigade numbering eighty to one hundred attack helicopters. In addition, Shoigu planned to form eight bomber aviation regiments, one fighter aviation regiment, and six army aviation brigades, as well as an artillery division and a "high-powered" artillery brigade in each of the military districts.

It was clear that without drastically changing the laws and lengthening the term of draft service, it would be impossible to increase the size of the armed forces. The necessary amendments to the laws were adopted in the first half of 2023. First, in April, laws were passed that eliminated the need for military registration and enlistment offices to deliver draft notices in person and obtain the conscript's signature. Now the notice is considered served once it is sent to the conscript's personal account on the public services portal, Gosuslugi.

From that moment until he shows up at the enlistment office, the conscript has his rights seriously restricted: he is forbidden to leave the country, conduct real estate transactions, register a car, or obtain a driver's license. The fines for violating the rules of military registration have been increased manyfold. In addition, huge fines of half a million rubles are to be paid by employers who do not ensure that their employees turn up when conscripted. In July 2023, another law was enacted extending the reserve service duration by five years. Now, privates and sergeants are in the first-category reserve (that is, they are the first to be mobilized) up to the age of forty years, and junior officers up to the age of fifty years.[30] Last, lawmakers expanded the draft age for conscription, maintaining the lower limit at eighteen years old and raising the upper limit to thirty."[31]

The only logical conclusion is that the Defense Ministry intends to draw its replenishment from a "mobilization resource," and make mobilization permanent. The chair of the Duma Defense Committee, General Andrey Kartapolov, told the truth about the Kremlin's intentions: "This law was written for a big war, for a general mobilization. It already smacks of such a big war."[32] According to Rosstat, as of January 1, 2022, there were 7.2 million men between seventeen and twenty-nine years of age in Russia. They will account for most of those whom Shoigu expected to draft into the armed forces. Assurances from the Russian authorities that conscripted soldiers would not fight in Ukraine are hardly worth taking seriously. Indeed, on the same day, the Duma adopted a law "permitting" conscripted soldiers to sign a contract with the Ministry of Defense (which would make them "professionals" and lift the prohibition on them fighting) as soon as a month after the start of service. The Russian military long ago learned how to force conscripts to sign these contracts, through psychological pressure and sometimes physical violence. In theory, another approximately 18 million men between thirty and forty-four years of age can be mobilized.[33] At the same time, fewer than two million of the 7.2 million in the first group have been drafted and have at least some kind of military training.[34] Thus a return to the model of a mass mobilization army would require the armed forces to replenish themselves with conscripts who have no military training at all. Moreover, most of the formations will be incomplete.

Volunteer Mobilization

In 2023, a significant shift occurred in Russia's military buildup strategy. Although the Kremlin had returned to the mass mobilization concept that had dominated Russian military planning for 150 years, this mobilization took place on a "voluntary basis." This marked a true revolution in Soviet military culture. The Kremlin returned to the practice of the czarist government in World War I, paying the families of mobilized reservists monthly sums comparable to the earnings of the men sent to the front line.[35] Soldiers began to be paid monthly salaries of at least 210,000 rubles (€2,200),[36] significantly more than the average salary of civilians. The Kremlin also pays about 12.5 million rubles (€124,000) for each soldier killed—more than the average Russian male will earn in a lifetime.[37] For this reason, public pressure on the authorities looks unlikely. Zaluzhny has honestly admitted that Kyiv misjudged the sociopolitical situation in Russia: "That was my mistake. Russia has lost at least 150,000 dead. In any other country, such casualties would have stopped the war."[38] In fact, huge Russian losses have turned out to be entirely acceptable to the Kremlin, as well as to the wider Russian society. As a result of its mobilization efforts, the Kremlin has managed to concentrate 700,000 troops on the battlefield, which is about half the official strength of the Russian armed forces.[39]

Tanks from Soviet Depots

The transition to a mass mobilization army will inevitably require fundamental changes in the organization of industry and property rights, and such a pivot will change the internal structure of the Russian state. The current level of military production is inconsistent with plans to increase the size of the armed forces. Russian industry is clearly unable to provide equipment and armaments to more than two dozen new divisions. For example, eight hundred helicopters are needed to supply the envisioned army aviation brigades, but only four hundred are available. Russia produces no more than one hundred per year.[40]

Thanks to the Soviet concept of defensive warfare using conventional weapons, the Kremlin has managed to equip its troops with weapons despite heavy losses, and continues to do so successfully. Soviet-era leaders were well aware that Western military equipment was far more advanced than Soviet equipment. They also took into account the fact that the productivity of the NATO countries' military industries was significantly higher. Their answer was to produce and stockpile the maximum amount of equipment and armaments in peacetime in case of war. The Soviet armed forces were equipped with 63,900 tanks, 66,880 artillery pieces and mortars,

76,520 infantry fighting vehicles (IFVs) and armored personnel carriers (APCs), 12,200 combat aircraft and helicopters, and 435 warships.[41] The Soviet Union had as many tanks, APCs, and IFVs as all the other countries in the world combined and three times more than the United States. Stockpiles of armaments created decades ago have not yet been exhausted. Since the production of new weapons is a labor-intensive and costly process, Russian troops are given hastily repaired tanks and guns produced forty to fifty years ago to replace those destroyed in combat operations in Ukraine. As of the beginning of 2023, more than 5,000 tanks, 4,000 IFVs, 6,000 APCs, and 11,000 artillery pieces were still in storage.[42] If, according to British military intelligence, during two years of war the Russian army lost 2,600 tanks and 4,900 other armored vehicles (and, owing to the defensive nature of the fighting in 2023, lost 40 percent less than in 2022),[43] it can safely be assumed that the stored weapons will be sufficient for at least another two to three years of fighting.

Industry must be organized in a certain way to provide a mass mobilization army with huge quantities of weapons and military equipment. Soviet industry, based on a planned economy and autarky, was an ideal example of such production organization. The USSR did not feature separate civilian and military industry sectors. Final assembly plants belonged to the official defense industry, but civilian factories manufactured the vast majority of components for military production. The quality and price of civilian goods naturally reflected a production system under the administration of the State Planning Committee (Gosplan), which allocated funds and artificially set all prices: for raw materials, for the component base, and for various components, thus ensuring the necessary "profitability." In the 1990s, most Soviet industry died, with only a small part converted to other production. The current owners of private enterprises do not need a Defense order at all, and an attempt to fulfill it would inevitably make their main products more expensive and less competitive. It is no coincidence that before the Ukraine war, there were government proposals to obligate private producers to manufacture military products, which they tried to avoid. In the spring of 2022, the Duma passed a law according to which the owners "regardless of the organizational-legal form and form of ownership do not have the right to refuse to sign contracts and fulfill government contracts. In addition, the government may, at its will, increase or decrease the quantity of goods, the amount of work or services within the framework of the State Defense Order, upon presentation by the security agencies."[44] These are only the first steps in the structural militarization of the country's economy. An attempt to quickly transfer industrial production to military production under the pressure of Western sanctions, however, is likely only to significantly exacerbate the economic crisis.

Not surprisingly, government officials from the economic sector are skeptical of the very idea of mobilizing the economy. Then first deputy prime minister Andrey Belousov admitted in December 2022: "I think there is no point in creating a mobilization economy right now; we simply cannot do it. . . . A mobilization economy is part of a mobilization society," he explained, adding that it is "always a militarized story, a rejection of personal interests over state interests, a rigid prevalence of state [interests]."[45] In other words, a high-ranking official, far from being a liberal, quite rationally believes that Russian society, having embraced the fruits of the market economy, is not yet ready to abandon them. Belousov was appointed minister of defense on May 12, 2024. Putin stressed that the main task of the new minister was "to incorporate the economy of our defense and security sector, and the Defense Ministry as its core element, into the national economy."[46] In other words, the task was to militarize the country's economy, the need for which Belousov earlier denied.

Furthermore, the Ministry of Defense would need to restore a Soviet-type mobilization infrastructure and reestablish a network of dozens of military schools (that were closed between 2008 and 2012) to provide for mass training of reserve officers in universities and institutes. Rebuilding this infrastructure might take years if not decades to accomplish.

The Militarist State

The relatively successful military reforms carried out between 2008 and 2012 by Serdyukov in the absence of general democratic reforms (which guarantee the rule of law, the changeability of power, and free elections, as well as the provision of citizens with basic political rights and freedoms, such as freedom of speech, assembly, political activity, etc.) inevitably led to Russia becoming a militarist state, just as happened with Prussia in the early nineteenth century.[47] For the last fifteen years, political scientists have refused to consider the regime established in Russia as totalitarian (see Maria Snegovaya's discussion of hard authoritarianism in chapter 5), pointing out that it has no obvious ideology. I suggest that this ideology is militarism. It is a system of beliefs regarding the state's structure, its institutions, and the political and spiritual aspects of society. In this system, military methods of governance, military views, and military values take precedence over all else. In the militarist state, the most important political decisions are based on military calculations rather than on a comprehensive analysis from the point of view of state interests; and military approaches dominate peoples' attitude to certain problems. At the same time, military relations and military values deeply penetrate all spheres of society.[48] Anthony Giddens defines militarism as the tendency of the elites in some societies to seek military solutions to political conflicts and a corresponding tendency of the lower social strata to accept such solutions.[49]

Paradoxically, having made the military the foundation of the state, militarists will make disastrous mistakes in the very area of military planning, as Russia's invasion of Ukraine shows. Arthur Vagts, author of *A History of Militarism: Civilian and Military*, points out the fundamental difference between militarism and the drive to strengthen defense capabilities to prepare the army for possible war, which is natural for any country: "The military way is marked by a primary concentration of men and materials on winning specific objectives of power with the utmost efficiency. . . . Militarism, on the other hand, presents a vast array of customs, interests, prestige, actions, and thought associated with armies and wars, and yet transcending true military purposes."[50]

Vagts identifies the most dangerous source of militarism: "Civilian militarism might be defined as the unquestioning embrace of military values, ethos, principles, attitudes; as ranking military institutions and considerations above all others in the state; as finding the heroic predominantly in military service and action, including war—to the preparation of which the nation's main interests and resources must be dedicated. . . . With the soldier militarist, the civilian militarist shares the contempt for civilian politics, parliamentarianism, parties, the hatred of civilian supremacy, of trade, of labor, of diplomacy."[51] Vladimir Putin embodies those characteristics of a civilian militarist. His militarism has developed quite naturally from Russian traditions. For three centuries, Russia has known practically no other way to concentrate state resources than through military mobilization. The Russian state has been interested in man primarily as a soldier, and secondarily as a source of funds to maintain the army. The peculiarities of this national military culture, which thoroughly penetrated society, most likely explain the dual attitude of the Russian people toward the army.

On the one hand, no one challenges the right of the state to conscript people into the army and to dispose of their lives without bearing serious responsibility for their deaths. Russian military leaders consider this acceptance to be a natural characteristic of the Russian people. On the other hand, society does not condemn those who evade military service by any means.

After the collapse of the USSR, it seemed to many researchers that as a result of objective processes of the country's development, the "old militarism," based on conscription—the ability to use a constantly renewable human mass of recruits—was dead. The concept of a mass mobilization army cannot be implemented in principle: Russia's current demographics cannot provide the necessary mass of soldiers, and Russian industry would have to return to the model of a planned economy to begin the mass production of weapons sufficient to equip a multimillion-strong army. It seemed that with more changes in military leadership, generations poisoned by militarist propaganda would pass away, and this historical atavism would disappear. But militarism was revived, and that happened, sadly enough, as a result of a "progressive" military reform. This "new" militarism undoubtedly concentrates the most conservative trends and is in fact the main obstacle to Russia's modernization.

Putin began to create his notorious vertical of power from his first days in the Kremlin. He envisioned the best system of governing Russia as a strict hierarchy, similar to the army hierarchy. At the top of this pyramid was the president, aka the commander in chief, while below, level by level, were executive and loyal (or frightened) officials capable of conveying the will of the supreme leader to every corner of the vast country. As a result of this system, power in Russia once again follows the military-feudal principle. In the eyes of the Kremlin leadership, this power is monolithic in nature, its division (sharing or delegation) is seen as heresy, and the principle of undivided authority also applies to the political system of the state.

By removing all checks and balances, thus concentrating enormous power, and by arrogating all decisions of any significance to himself, the leader becomes a hostage to the information he receives. Consequently he becomes hostage to his own underlings and confidants, who fear the consequences of delivering bad news the leader wishes not to hear. Putin decided to conduct a "special military operation" in Ukraine under the influence of distorted information that was manipulated to suit his preconceived ideas. The FSB's forecast of the Ukrainian population's reaction to the invasion had nothing to do with reality. Likewise, the bravura reports of the heads of the Ministry of Defense about the high degree of combat readiness of the armed forces were myths.

Conclusion

Russia's failed war in Ukraine was the natural, and indeed the only possible, development of the domestic and foreign policy of the militarist state created by Vladimir Putin. In full accordance with the typical scheme of development of such a state, Russia's armed forces were assigned tasks they cannot fulfill. The demands of Russian militarism contradict the need to reform the archaic nature of the Russian armed forces. The Kremlin now seeks a way out by completely abandoning the modernization of the armed forces and returning to the concept of mass mobilization. This cannot work, however, owing to Russia's worsening demographic and economic situation. An attempt at a drastic upturn in military buildup would inevitably cause chaos.

Russia's inability to win its war in Ukraine will sooner or later turn into a crisis. Vladimir Putin will have to face an unruly mass of armed men from among the mobilized and freed criminals, among other existential threats.

NOTES

1. Masters and Merrow (2024). According to then U.S. secretary of defense Lloyd Austin, by the end of May 2023, the West had provided $65 billion in military assistance to Ukraine, which exceeds the Russian military budget. Austin (2023).

2. Luzin (2023).

3. International Institute for Strategic Studies (2022). *The Military Balance 2022*, 193.

4. Wilkie (2022).

5. In modern military history there are examples of victories achieved when the attacking side had significantly fewer forces than the defending one. An example is the American intervention in Iraq in 2003, when a 100,000-strong American contingent defeated Saddam Hussein's 400,000-strong army. However, the U.S. military had a qualitative technological advantage over the Iraqi forces. The American absolute knowledge of the battlefield, complete air superiority, and ability to react instantaneously to any change in the combat situation had a powerful psychological effect on the enemy. The Russian Armed Forces do not have the overwhelming technological superiority over the Ukrainian army that the U.S. forces had in Iraq.

6. TASS (2020).

7. *New York Times* (2022).

8. Kremlin (2022a).

9. "Rodinu lyubliu, Putina slushaius', Shojgu na mylo, voevat' budem dal'she" [I love my Motherland, I listen to Putin, I give Shoigu soap, we will continue to fight]: words of Evgeny Prigozhin on May 24, 2023, one month before he launched a rebellion against Russian military leadership, in an interview with Konstantin Dolgov that was published by Meduza on May 24. See Meduza (2023).

10. *Economist* (2023).

11. Reynolds (2022).

12. Faulconbridge and Pamuk (2022).

13. Kluth (2023).

14. Putin (2006).

15. Mislivskaia (2020).

16. Sheval'e (2015).

17. Kremlin (2022b).

18. *Kommersant'* (2023).

19. TASS (2023).

20. Prigozhin's Press Service (2023).

21. See the Russian Wikipedia entry for Miatezh ChVK "Vagner" (Wagner PMC Mutiny) at Мятеж ЧВК «Вагнер» — Википедия (wikipedia.org) (last accessed July 21, 2024).

22. Inwood and Tacchi (2024).

23. Konsul'tant Plius (2024).

24. *Economist* (2022).

25. The 2012 figure of 8,000 is from Gavrilov (2012). The 2023 figure of 15,000 is from *RIA Novosti* (2023).

26. TASS (2021).

27. Poroskov (2016).

28. RBK (2022a).

29. RBK (2022b).

30. RBK (2023a).

31. RBK (2023b).

32. General Andrey Kartapolov quoted in Fontank (2023).

33. Rosstat (2022).

34. Data for 2021 from https://rosstat.gov.ru/storage/mediabank/Ejegodnik_2023.pdf.

35. Pushkareva and Shcherbinin (2005).

36. Petrov (2023).

37. Erlikh (2023).

38. *Economist* (2023).

39. President of Russia, "Встреча с участниками программы 'Время героев.'" http://www.kremlin.ru/events/president/news/74292.

40. Nikol'skii (2022).
41. Zolotarev, Saksonov, and Tiushkevich (2002), 414.
42. International Institute for Military Studies (2023). *The Military Balance 2023*, 185.
43. UK Ministry of Defence (2024).
44. Interfax (2022).
45. TASS (2022).
46. Kremlin (2024).
47. In 1807–1813, "liberals in uniform" undertook a famous military reform in Prussia. They were the first who established a conscription system and general staff as permanent military institutions. They believed that military modernization would go along with constitutional reform, which would make Prussia similar to Great Britain. Yet, other than military reforms, all other reforms failed, resulting in a profoundly authoritarian Prussian state and an almost perfect military machine that blindly followed the orders of the kaiser and, a century later, the führer.
48. Danopoulos and Watson (1996), 143.
49. See Giddens (1985), 80. Although Giddens rightly points to the impact of militarism on social and economic processes, he is, in my view, not very convincing when he argues that militarism is not a consequence but one of the causes of industrial capitalism.
50. Vagts (1959), 13–15.
51. Ibid., 453.

REFERENCES

Austin, Lloyd J. III. 2023. "Opening Remarks by Secretary of Defense Lloyd J. Austin III at the 12th Ukraine Defense Contact Group (As Delivered)." Speech, U.S. Department of Defense, Washington, D.C., May 25.

Danopoulos, Constantine P., and Cynthia A. Watson. 1996. *The Political Role of the Military: An International Handbook*. Westport, CT: Greenwood Press.

Economist. 2023. "Ukraine's Commander-in-Chief on the Breakthrough He Needs to Beat Russia." November 1.

———. 2022. "An Interview with General Valery Zaluzhny, Head of Ukraine's Armed Forces." December 3.

Erlikh, Mariia. 2023. "Gonki na grobovykh" [Coffin racing]. *Novaia gazeta*, August 3.

Faulconbridge, Guy, and Humeyra Pamuk. 2022. "CIA Boss Talks Nuclear Weapons and Prisoners with Putin's spy Chief." Reuters, November 15.

Fontanka. 2023. "'Bol'shoi voinoi uzhe popakhivaet': Kartapolov ob'iasnil tsel' popravok v zakon o voinskoi sluzhbe" ["It already smells like a big war": Kartapolov explained the purpose of the amendments to the law on military service]. Fontanka.ru, July 25.

Gavrilov, Yurii. 2012. "V 2012 godu v voennie vuzy primut vosem' tysiach abiturientov" [In 2012, eight thousand applicants will be admitted to military universities]. *Rossiiskaia gazeta*, June 19. https://rg.ru/2012/06/19/vuzy-site.html?ysclid=lclsw2y3t7959341419.

Giddens, Anthony. 1985. *The Nation-State and Violence. Volume Two of a Contemporary Critique of Historical Materialism*. Cambridge: Polity Press.

Interfax. 2022. "Putin podpisal zakon o spetsmerakh v ekonomike pri silovykh operatsiiakh za rubezhom" [Putin signed a law on special measures in the economy during military operations abroad]. July 14.

International Institute for Strategic Studies. 2023. *The Military Balance 2023*. London: Taylor and Francis.

———. 2022. *The Military Balance 2022*. London: Taylor and Francis.

Inwood, Joe, and Jake Tacchi. 2024. "Wagner in Africa: How the Russian Mercenary Group Has Rebranded." BBC, February 20.

Kluth, Andreas. 2023. "Thanks for the Tanks, but Send the Abrams and Leopard Too." Bloomberg, January 7.

Kommersant'. 2023. "Prigozhin otritsaet sviaz' ChVK 'Vagner' s rossiiskoi armii" [Prigozhin denies the connection between the Wagner PMC and the Russian army]. February 18.

Konsul'tant Plius. 2024. "Podpisan zakon ob osvobozhdenii ot ugolovnoi otvetstvennosti v sviazi s prizivom na voennuiu sluzhbu po mobilizatsii ili v voennoe vremia libo zakliucheniem kontrakta o prokhozhdenii voennoi sluzhby" [A law has been signed on exemption from criminal liability in connection with conscription for military service on mobilization or in wartime, or the conclusion of a contract for military service]. March 23.

Kremlin. 2024. "Meeting with Military District Commanders" [in Russian]. Press release. Moscow, May 15.

———. 2022a. "Soveshchanie s postoiannimi chlenami Soveta Bezopasnosti" [Meeting with the permanent members of the Security Council]. Press release. Kremlin.ru, February 25.

———. 2022b. "Poseshchenie ob'edinionnogo shtaba rodov voisk, zadeistvovan-nykh v SVO" [Visit to the joint headquarters of the branches of the armed forces involved in the SVO]. Press release. Kremlin.ru, December 17.

Luzin, Pavel. 2023. "The Russian Army in 2023." *Riddle*, January 18.

Masters, Jonathan, and Will Merrow. 2024. "How Much U.S. Aid Is Going to Ukraine?" Council on Foreign Relations, May 9.

Meduza. 2023. Evgeny Prigozhin, interview by Konstantin Dolgov, May 24.

Mislivskaia, Galina. 2020. "Shoigu: Chislo kontraktnikov previsilo 400 tysiach chelovek" [Shoigu: The number of contract soldiers exceeded 400,000 people]. *Rossiiskaia gazeta*, March 25.

New York Times. 2022. "Russia-Ukraine Tensions: Citing U.S. Intelligence, Biden Says Putin Has Decided to Invade Ukraine." April 13.

Nikol'skii, Aleksei. 2022. "Minoborony ob"iavilo ob uvelichenii chislennosti armii do 1,5 mln chelovek" [The Ministry of Defense announced an increase in the size of the army to 1.5 million people]. *Vedomosti*, December 22.

Petrov, Ivan. 2023. "Minimal'nii oklad boitsa SVO vyros do 210 tysiach rublei" [The minimum salary of an air defense soldier increased to 210,000 rubles]. *Rossiiskaia gazeta*, October 23.

Poroskov, Nikolai. 2016. "Nekolokol'nye interesy Rossii" [Nonparochial interests of Russia]. *Nezavisimoe voennoe obozrenie*, February 19.

Prigozhin's Press Service. 2023. "Press-sluzhba Prigozhina #1788: Publikuem zapros ot redaktsii proekta 'Strazhi Rodiny' i otvet." Telegram, June 11.

Pushkareva, Nataliia, and Petr Shcherbinin. 2005. Organizatsiia prizreniia semei nizhnikh chinov v gody pervoi mirovoi voini" [Organization of charity for families of lower ranks during World War I]. *Zhurnal issledovanii sotsial'noi politiki* 3 (2): 147–62.

Putin, Vladimir. 2006. "Poslanie Federal'nomu Sobraniiu Rossiiskoi Federatsii" [Address to the Federal Assembly of the Russian Federation]. Transcript. Kremlin.ru, May 10.

RBK [RosBizn'esKonsulting]. 2023a. "Putin povysil predel'nie sroki prebyvaniia v zapase na piat' let" [Putin raised the maximum period for remaining in the reserves by five years]. July 24.

———. 2023b. "Sovfed prinial zakon o prizive na srochnuiu sluzhbu s 18 do 30 let" [The Federation Council adopted a law on conscription for military service from 18 to 30 years old]. July 28.

———. 2022a. "Shoigu zaiavil o sozdanii novoi divizii na iuge Rossii" [Shoigu announced the creation of a new division in southern Russia]. *RIA Novosti*, May 20.

———. 2022b. "Zasedanie kollegii Ministerstva oboron" [Meeting of the board of the Ministry of Defense]. Kremlin.ru, December 21.

Reynolds, Nick. 2022. "Fact Check: Is Putin First 'Direct' Nuke Threat since Cuban Missile Crisis?" *Newsweek*, October 7.

RIA Novosti. 2023. "Shoigu rasskazal o priemnoi kampanii v voennie vuzy" [Shoigu spoke about the admission campaign to military universities]. July 31.

Rosstat. 2022. "Chislennost' naseleniia Rossiiskoi Federatsii po polu i vozrastu na 1 ianvar'ia 2022 goda" [Population of the Russian Federation by sex and age as of January 1, 2022]. Database. https://rosstat.gov.ru/storage/mediabank/Bul_chislen_nasel-pv_01-01-2022.pdf.

Sheval'e, Ekaterina. 2015. "O chom rasskazal Putin v interv'iu dlia fil'ma Krym: Put' na Rodinu?" [What did Putin say in an interview for the film *Crimea: The Way to the Motherland*?]. *Argumenty i fakty*, March 16.

TASS. 2023. "Dobrovol'cheskie otriady, ikh pravovoi status, kontrakty s MO RF" [Volunteer units, their legal status, contracts with the RF Ministry of Defense]. June 10.

———. 2022. "Belousov: RF ne nuzhna mobilizatsionnaia ekonomika, tak kak u nee est' neobkhodimye rezervy" [Belousov: The Russian Federation does not need a mobilization economy since it has the necessary reserves]. December 27.

———. 2021. "Rosfinmonitoring vyiavil v sfere gosoboronzakaza prestupleniia na 9 mlrd rublei" [Rosfinmonitoring revealed crimes worth 9 billion rubles in the sphere of state defense procurement]. February 19.

———. 2020. "Shoigu: Chislo vysokotochnykh krylatykh raket v voiskakh za vosem' let vyroslo v 30 raz" [Shoigu: The number of high-precision cruise missiles in the army has increased 30 times in eight years]. February 11.

UK Ministry of Defence. 2024. "Latest Defence Intelligence update on the situation in Ukraine." Twitter post, January 29. https://x.com/DefenceHQ/status/1751898118436655191.

Vagts, Alfred. 1959. *A History of Militarism: Civilian and Military*. New York: Meridian Books.

Wilkie, Christina. 2022. "Nearly All of Russia's Initial Invasion Forces Now in Ukraine, Pentagon Says." CNBC, March 7.

Zolotarev, V. A., O. V. Saksonov, and S. A Tiushkevich. 2002. *Voennaia istoriia Rossii* [Military history of Russia]. Russia: Kuchkovo Pole M. Zhukovskii.

FURTHER READING

Arbatov, Alexei. 1998. "Military Reform in Russia: Dilemmas, Obstacles and Prospects." *International Security* 22 (4).

Blank, Stephen F. 2002. "The Great Exception: Russian Civil-Military Relations." *World Affairs* 165:91–105.

Craig, Gordon A. 1955. *The Politics of the Prussian Army 1640–1945*. Oxford: Clarendon Press of Oxford University Press.

Dalsjö, Robert, Michael Jonsson, and Johan Norberg. 2022. "A Brutal Examination: Russian Military Capability in Light of the Ukraine War." *Survival* 64 (3): 7–28.

Dolman, Everett Carl. 2005. *The Warrior State: How Military Organization Structures Politics*. Gordonsville, VA: Palgrave Macmillan.

Farrell, Theo, and Terry Terriff, eds. 2002. *The Sources of Military Change: Culture, Politics, Technology*. Boulder, CO: Lynne Rienner.

Forster, Anthony, Timothy Edmunds, and Andrew Cottey, eds. 2003. *The Challenge of Military Reform in Postcommunist Europe: Building Professional Armed Forces*. Gordonsville, VA: Palgrave Macmillan.

Geyer, Dietrich. 1987. *Russian Imperialism: The Interaction of Domestic and Foreign Policy, 1860–1914*. New Haven, CT: Yale University Press.

Holden, Gerard. 1991. *Soviet Military Reform: Conventional Disarmament and the Crisis of Militarised Socialism*. London: Pluto Press.

Levinson, Aleksei, and Stepan Goncharov. 2015. "Voina vmesto budushchego: Reshenie dlia anomicheskogo soznaniia" [War instead of the future: A solution for anomic consciousness]. *Vestnik obshchestvnnogo mneniia* 3–4 (121): 45–66.

McDermott, Roger N. 2011. *The Reform of Russia's Conventional Armed Forces: Problems, Challenges and Policy Implications*. Washington, DC: Jamestown Foundation.

McDermott, Roger N., Bertil Nygren, and Carolina Vendil Pallin, eds. 2012. *The Russian Armed Forces in Transition: Economic, Geopolitical and Institutional Uncertainties*. London: Routledge.

Menning, Bruce. 2000. *Bayonets before Bullets: The Imperial Russian Army, 1861–1914*. Bloomington: Indiana University Press.

Moran, John P. 2002. *From Garrison State to Nation State: The Russian Military and Political Power under Gorbachev and Yeltsin*. Westport, CT: Praeger.

Odom, William E. 2000. *The Collapse of the Soviet Military*. New Haven, CT: Yale University Press.

Serra, Narcís. 2010. *The Military Transition: Democratic Reform of the Armed Forces*. Cambridge: Cambridge University Press.

Shanahan, William Oswald. 1945. *Prussian Military Reforms 1786–1813*. Columbia University Press.

Szayna, Thomas S., and F. Stephen Larrabee. 1995. *East European Military Reform after the Cold War: Implications for the United States*. Santa Monica, CA: Rand Corporation.

Taylor, Brian D. 2003. *Politics and the Russian Army: Civil-Military Relations, 1689–2000*. Cambridge: Cambridge University Press.

Zabrodskyi, Mykhaylo, Jack Watling, Oleksandr V. Danylyuk, and Nick Reynolds. 2022. "Preliminary Lessons in Conventional Warfighting from Russia's Invasion of Ukraine: February–July 2022." Royal United Services Institute for Defence and Security Studies, November 30.

THIRTEEN

How Putin Turned Foreign Policy Success into Strategic Defeat

PETER CLEMENT

This chapter provides a chronological overview of key events that influenced the evolution of Putin's foreign policy thinking from 2000 to 2024, with an eye to these two guiding questions:

- Were there clear turning points in the hardening of Putin's thinking about policy toward the United States and the West more broadly?
- Why did Putin eschew twenty-one years of relatively successful foreign policy pragmatism from 2000 to 2021 in favor of the biggest land invasion in Europe since World War II? Specifically, what factors figured into Putin's fateful decision to reinvade Ukraine?

Putin's fateful move into Ukraine exacerbated long-term vulnerabilities that call into question Putin's foreign policy record. The chapter's conclusion, "Assessing Success or Failure: Whose Yardstick?," examines Putin's foreign policy record through a different lens, one in which foreign policy is a critical element of Putin's broader plan for building a Russia that mirrors his view of Russia's history, culture, and values.

A Little-Known New President Arrives

Boris Yeltsin's announcement of Vladimir Putin as prime minister in August 1999, along with noting that Putin was his choice to succeed him, caught most observers by surprise. Little was known about the forty-six-year-old former KGB officer who only twelve months earlier had emerged from obscurity when he was named director of the Federal Security Service (FSB). And little was known about Putin's foreign policy views. Did his KGB/FSB work predispose him to hard-line views of the United States and the West? And if so, did his five years as a senior official working under the reform-minded mayor of St. Petersburg, Anatoly Sobchak, leaven his thinking?

Some early clues to Putin's views on international issues could be gleaned from his manifesto, "Russia at the Turn of the Millennium" (in Russian, "Россия на рубеже тысячелетий"), published in Russian newspapers on December 30, 1999, and a book that followed shortly thereafter designed to introduce Putin to the world (and the Russian people) titled *First Person: An Astonishingly Frank Self-Portrait by Russia's President Vladimir Putin*.

Putin's five-thousand-word millennium manifesto offered a candid and sobering assessment of Russia's significant economic and social challenges, noting that Russia needed fifteen years of substantial economic growth to achieve the level of Portugal or Spain and that Russia's GDP was a tenth that of the United States and a fifth of China's. His manifesto barely mentioned foreign policy, with one notable exception: that Russia must *"integrate the Russian economy into world economic structures* . . . to incorporate Russia into the international system of regulating foreign economic operation, *above all the WTO"* (emphasis in original text).[1] This emphasis on the economic component of foreign policy was reiterated in a section titled "Belief in the Greatness of Russia": "In the present world the might of a country as a great power is manifested more in its ability to be the leader in creating and using advanced technologies, ensuring a high level of people's well-being, reliably protecting its security and upholding its national interests in the international arena, than in its military strength."[2] Oddly, there was no mention of the war in Chechnya, though Putin's surprise New Year's Eve trip to that war zone clearly signaled Chechnya was a top domestic priority.

The series of interviews in *First Person* were conducted before the March 2000 presidential election, but, public posturing aside, the book provides some important insights into Putin's thoughts about international issues. For example, when asked whether "we will again have to search for Russia's special path," Putin replied, "We don't have to search for anything. It's already been found. It's the path of democratic development. Of course, Russia is a very diverse country, but we are part of Western European culture. *No matter where our people live, in the Far East or the south, we are Europeans*" (emphasis added).[3] Putin discussed his experience as a KGB officer in Dresden, where he witnessed angry crowds as the East German regime was collapsing, and his view that the Soviets had retreated from Eastern Europe too hastily.

Closer to home, Putin compared the situation in the North Caucasus to the collapse of the Soviet Union. Defending his tough military response to the extremists in the North Caucasus, Putin said their activities would lead to a "second Yugoslavia on the entire territory of the Russian Federation—the Yugoslavization of Russia."[4] He then batted away questions about international peacekeepers or Organization for Security and Cooperation in Europe (OSCE) observers by citing parallels with Kosovo—implying that NATO's initial stabilization mission ultimately resulted in Kosovo's secession from Serbia. While open to consideration of Russia joining NATO, it would have to be a different NATO, not the one that went into Kosovo in violation of UN decisions.

One American diplomat who interacted with Putin in the 1990s during his tenure in the St. Petersburg mayor's office summed up Putin's worldview then: Russia needed to regain its status as a superpower, and the "near abroad constituted Russia's sphere of influence—and . . . those countries should not be reabsorbed by Russia, but they were bound to Russia by tradition and it is natural they should act in concert with Russia." Interestingly, the diplomat assessed that Putin was not a gambler in the classic sense, much less a reckless one, since gambling involves the risk of losing—and Putin did not like taking such risks.[5]

Putin's First Years as President: Into the Maelstrom

Consistent with his stated millennial address goals of "integrating Russia into the world economy and gaining WTO membership," Putin visited key Western capitals in 2000: London (April), Rome (June), Madrid (June),

Berlin (June), Tokyo (September), New York City (September), Paris (November), and Ottawa (December). In contrast, Putin's other trips to Beijing and Pyongyang (July), New Delhi (October), and Havana (December) were more attuned to the multipolar world view espoused by former Russian foreign minister Yevgeny Primakov. Geopolitics aside, if Russia were to be seen as a major power, Putin recognized he would need to quickly introduce himself to key global counterparts. He traveled to twenty-four different capitals between May and December 2000.[6]

Putin's early focus was on priority domestic issues: managing the war in Chechnya, strengthening his political power, and carrying out economic reform. He quickly put Russia's oligarchs on notice that the rules had changed: to keep their grip on their wealth, they would have to stay out of politics.[7] Meanwhile, the media gradually came under state control, a process initially sparked by negative coverage of Putin's belated response to the August 2000 *Kursk* submarine disaster and accelerated by critical media accounts of the government's response to domestic terrorist events, including the Chechen hostage-taking of Dubrovka Theater attendees in Moscow in October 2002 and the Beslan school hostage crisis in September 2004. Over four hundred died in these events.

Early Grievances: The Chechen Thread

The early August 1999 Chechen separatist incursion into Dagestan, two days before Putin was named prime minister, revived the unresolved question of Chechnya's status. Those behind the incursion—including a radical Islamist from Saudi Arabia—called for uniting Chechnya and Dagestan into an Islamic emirate. During an August 12 meeting with President Clinton at the Asia-Pacific Economic Cooperation summit in New Zealand, Putin grimaced at the suggestion of placing international monitors in Chechnya. He countered by stressing that the events in Dagestan were an invasion of Russia not just by Chechens but also by the forces of international Islamic terrorists. Putin later told the U.S. ambassador to Russia, James Collins, that Osama bin Laden had been to Chechnya several times and was providing funds to the Chechen separatists. A senior Clinton adviser viewed the reference to Osama bin Laden as calculated to enlist U.S. sympathy, given al-Qaeda's August 1998 attacks on two U.S. embassies in East Africa.[8]

In the wake of four still controversial apartment building bombings in Buynaksk, Moscow, and Volgodonsk in August and September, Putin escalated the military campaign against the Chechen separatists, including carpet bombing, artillery attacks, and later missile strikes on Grozny.[9] The ensuing destruction and civilian deaths elicited a barrage of criticism from U.S., German, and French leaders. In a November meeting in Oslo, Clinton urged Putin to combine his military strategy with a political track. Putin stressed that Moscow was dealing with "Muslim extremists" but noted Russia "will try to find someone to have a dialogue with." Later, in response to Secretary of State Madeleine Albright's suggestion of finding a third party as an intermediary, Putin asked, "How can I negotiate with terrorists?"[10]

Putin's first meeting with the new U.S. president, George Bush, on June 16, 2001, in Slovenia generated mutual hopes for improving the bilateral U.S.-Russia relationship. Bush famously stated that he "was able to get a sense of Putin's soul," while Putin said the two leaders were starting with "a clean sheet of paper" and had forged a "very high level of trust." Bush even mentioned the possibility of a deal on missile defense.[11]

Shortly after al-Qaeda struck New York City's World Trade Center on September 11, 2001, Putin was one of the first foreign leaders to call the White House to express his condolences and offer support. Washington soon asked the Kremlin to endorse the deployment of U.S. military forces in Central Asia. Putin faced strong resistance from his own military and security advisers; indeed, just three days later, Defense Minister Sergei Ivanov had told TV reporters that he saw "absolutely no basis for even hypothetical suppositions about the possibility of NATO military operations on the territory of Central Asian nations."[12] On September 22, Putin informed Bush that Moscow would support the United States "in the war on terror."[13] Less noted at the time was an important caveat in Putin's televised announcement of that decision, namely, that the "depth and character" of that support would "depend on the level of *mutual understanding in the fight against international terrorism*" (emphasis added).[14] That phrase conveyed Putin's view, albeit implicitly, that his support was quite transactional—that he expected unquestioning support for his own response to terrorism in Russia.

The apogee of this growing friendship was the November 2001 first Bush-Putin summit in Washington, D.C., and the follow-on trip to Bush's ranch in Crawford, Texas. Some observers noted the chemistry between the two leaders, calling them "soul-mates"—even though Bush informed Putin the United States would withdraw from the Anti-Ballistic Missile (ABM)

Treaty. Still, both did agree on new cuts to strategic nuclear arsenals, reducing them to between 1,700 and 2,200 warheads; the formal Strategic Offensive Reductions Treaty (SORT) was signed during Bush's May 2002 trip to Moscow. Russia's role in a proposed NATO-Russia Council (NRC) sparked some discussion after Bush signed the SORT accord in Moscow, but both sides recognized Moscow would not really be satisfied until it had a truly equal voice in NATO decisions.[15]

Putin made little of the U.S. withdrawal from the ABM Treaty in February 2002, publicly acknowledging the United States had a legal right to do so. But his subdued anger over that decision frequently surfaced over the years, both publicly and in private exchanges with U.S. interlocutors.

The March 2003 U.S. invasion of Iraq highlighted other areas of conflicting interests. Moscow felt stung that Washington had ignored Russian—and some European countries'—counsel and offers to mediate. As important, perhaps, was the near-term loss of a key Middle East state with which Russia had long-standing economic and political equities.

Meanwhile, Chechnya remained a stubborn burr that deepened Putin's suspicions about the degree of the U.S. commitment to supporting Putin in dealing with Russia's terrorist threat. The breaking point was the Beslan hostage-taking incident in September 2004, when Chechen separatists took hostage North Ossetian schoolchildren, demanding an end to the war, Russian recognition of Chechen independence, and Putin's resignation. The three-day siege ended with the deaths of 333 people, including 186 children.[16]

Faced with domestic and international criticism of the harsh government tactics that ended the Beslan hostage tragedy, Putin met with angry parents and acknowledged that there was "no excuse for officials' improper fulfillment of their duties." While not naming the United States explicitly, Putin went on to assert that "some would like to tear from us a 'juicy piece of pie.' Others help them. They help, reasoning that Russia still remains one of the world's major nuclear powers, and as such still represents a threat to them. And so they reason that this threat should be removed. Terrorism, of course, is just an instrument to achieve these aims."[17]

In a four-hour meeting with Western foreign policy experts days later, Putin angrily lashed out at the United States for urging negotiations with the Chechens, which he likened to asking the United States to talk to Osama bin Laden. Putin also noted that each time Russia complained to the Bush administration about meetings held between U.S. officials and

Chechen separatist representatives, the U.S. response had been "We'll get back to you" or "We reserve the right to talk with anyone we want." (Some U.S. officials had in fact talked with Chechen representatives, including the separatist regime's putative foreign minister, Ilyas Akhmadov, in October 2000 in New York and again in March 2001; he was later granted U.S. asylum in 2004.)[18]

Multiple senior Bush administration officials believed the Beslan attack marked a turning point, with one saying, "We never got back on track after Beslan, and . . . Putin concluded that U.S. counterterrorism policy was just a smokescreen to cover U.S. geopolitical advances in Eurasia."[19]

In short, Putin believed his politically difficult decision to support the United States after 9/11 warranted commensurate, unqualified U.S. reciprocity for his war on terrorism in Russia. This explains his mounting anger over earlier U.S. criticism of his ruthless tactics in dealing with the terrorist methods employed by Chechen separatists and their al-Qaeda-linked allies, such as the controversial apartment bombings in August–September 1999 or the hostage-taking of hundreds of theatergoers at Moscow's Dubrovka Theater in October 2002.

Apart from the Beslan school hostage crisis, two other major developments in 2004 significantly contributed to Putin's hardening view of the United States and the West: NATO enlargement and Ukraine's Orange Revolution.

NATO Enlargement

In February 2004, seven new members entered NATO, including the Baltic states—the first former Soviet republics to be admitted. At an April ceremony in Brussels, Foreign Minister Sergei Lavrov called NATO's expansion a mistake, stating, "The presence of American soldiers on our border has created a kind of paranoia in Russia." Days later in Berlin, Putin grudgingly offered a subdued response, warning that "Russia would closely monitor the deployment of NATO forces and build our defense and security policy correspondingly."[20]

Ukraine's Orange Revolution

The events of November–December 2004 represented an especially bitter personal setback for Putin. He had directly injected himself into a contentious Ukrainian presidential election whose initial result sparked massive protests in the streets of Kyiv. Putin had publicly endorsed Viktor

Yanukovych and made trips to Kyiv just before the first two rounds of voting. Domestic and international election observers declared that the second-round run-off vote—won by Yanukovych—was marred by massive fraud and thus invalid. The ensuing protest, dubbed the Orange Revolution, led to a new second run-off vote in December, won by the West-leaning Viktor Yushchenko.

Smarting from these setbacks, Putin took steps to preempt or forestall similar events, particularly on the question of NATO enlargement. In October 2006, for example, he warned U.S. secretary of state Condoleezza Rice about NATO-aspirant Georgia: "Saakashvili is nothing more than a puppet of the U.S.—you need to pull back the strings before it is too late. . . . If Georgia causes bloodshed in Ossetia, I will have no alternative but to recognize South Ossetia and Abkhazia, and responding with force. . . . I want you to understand, if Saakashvili starts something, we will finish it."[21]

The NATO Question and the War in Georgia

Russia's improving economic and fiscal picture contributed to Putin's more assertive posture, as it allowed for a needed rebuilding of Russia's military, evidenced by a steady growth in defense spending. Unlike Gorbachev and Yeltsin before him, Putin benefited from higher global oil prices—energy export revenues accounted for some 40–45 percent of state revenue, according to the International Energy Agency.

Putin's strident remarks to Western security officials at the February 10, 2007, Munich Security Conference marked one of the first public manifestations of this growing assertiveness. He bemoaned a unipolar world that witnessed the "almost uncontrolled use of hyper-force—military force . . . where no one feels safe," and named the United States as the "one state, and, of course, first and foremost" that "has overstepped its national borders in every way." Putin characterized the OSCE as a "vulgar instrument" to promote other states' interests, and informed the audience that Russia was developing "asymmetric capabilities" to counter U.S. anti-missile systems. On NATO enlargement, he predictably asked, "Against whom is this expansion intended?"[22]

One year later, this NATO question came into sharper focus as Georgia and Ukraine—with U.S. backing—were pushing hard for Membership Action Plan (MAP) status. At the fateful April 2–4, 2008, Bucharest NATO summit, NATO members reached an unsatisfying compromise: Ukraine and Georgia would not be granted MAP status, but members agreed to state that "Ukraine and Georgia *will* become members of NATO" (emphasis added). In his public remarks at the summit, Putin conveyed a measured response:

> But I want that all of us, when deciding such issues, realize that we have there our interests as well. Well, seventeen million Russians currently live in Ukraine. Who may state that we do not have any interests there? South, the South of Ukraine, completely, there are only Russians. The Crimea was merely received by Ukraine with the decision of the KPSS Political Bureau. There were not even any state procedures on transferring this territory. We have been calm and responsible about these problems. We are not trying to provoke anything, we have been acting very carefully, but we ask our partners to act reasonably as well.[23]

However, in a subsequent closed-door session, Putin angrily vented, "Ukraine is not even a country. . . . If Ukraine joins NATO, it will do so without Crimea and the eastern regions. It will simply fall apart." Those comments were leaked and appeared in both Russian and Ukrainian media days later.[24]

Barely four months after the Bucharest summit, Putin flexed his military muscle in Georgia in the wake of Saakashvili's aggressive moves against South Ossetia separatists. In the wake of fighting between Tbilisi and South Ossetia separatists, Russian forces responded, disproportionately, by marching to the outskirts of Tbilisi. They ultimately withdrew, but the invasion represented a physical manifestation of Putin's red line: Georgia cannot enter NATO. To underscore that point, Moscow recognized South Ossetia and Abkhazia as independent states, further complicating NATO consideration of Georgia for membership.

Despite the continued clash of views on NATO expansion and Moscow's temporary invasion of Georgia, the arrival of two new faces in U.S.-Russian relations began a brief hiatus from these growing tensions. Dmitry Medvedev won the March 2008 Russian presidential election and announced Putin would be his prime minister. While most observers believed Putin was essentially primus inter pares, the younger and technologically savvy Medvedev offered some hope for improved relations.

On the U.S. side, President Barack Obama was inaugurated in January 2009, looking to navigate the U.S. through the 2007–2008 global financial crisis and the U.S. wars in Iraq and Afghanistan.

The Reset: A Brief Respite

Medvedev and Obama initiated the "reset" in March 2009, which produced a wide variety of positive gains: expanding the Northern Distribution Network (NDN) allowing U.S. forces to transit to Afghanistan, signing the New START Treaty, and cooperating to impose new UN sanctions on Iran for nuclear proliferation violations.[25] NATO expansion tensions temporarily subsided. At the Lisbon NATO summit on November 19–20, 2010, President Medvedev openly praised the fact that "we have traveled down a long path from illusions and mistrust to the development of a strategic partnership" and that "the period of a cooling of relations and the cold period of claims has ended."[26]

Medvedev's bonhomie in Lisbon likely reflected the fact that Viktor Yanukovych had won Ukraine's January 2010 presidential election and fulfilled his campaign promise to eschew NATO aspirations and improve relations with Russia. In June the Ukrainian Rada passed a law barring membership in any military bloc, while not ruling out "cooperation" with NATO. Earlier, in April, Yanukovych had extended Russia's lease to the naval base in Sevastopol, Crimea, home of the Black Sea Fleet, through 2042; this move technically was not needed, as the original lease did not expire until 2017. In return, Russia reduced natural gas prices. Prime Minster Putin called the deal a "breakthrough in bilateral relations," stressing that "the main thing here is not the money, not gas and not even the fleet" but "relations between the two peoples, relations of trust towards each other, the realization of common interests and historic purposes, a feeling of fellowship." Yanukovych's predecessor, Viktor Yushchenko, publicly had stated he wanted the Black Sea Fleet gone from Sevastopol as it undermined Ukraine's sovereignty. In short, Yanukovych's election augured a degree of stability for at least the duration of his five-year term.

The issue of EU membership, however, was not addressed in the new law eschewing military blocs. Indeed, when the law on military blocs was passed, Ukrainian prime minister Mykola Azarov highlighted that EU membership remained a priority.[27]

A Key Turning Point: The Arab Spring and the Contested 2011 Duma Election

The U.S.-Russia reset was soon severely tested, if not entirely undone, in 2011 because of two major issues: the Arab Spring uprisings and the domestic protests in Russia following the September announcement that the Medvedev-Putin tandem would again do a "job swap."

Arab Spring

As the Arab Spring pulsed into Libya, strongman Muammar Gaddafi threatened to destroy Benghazi, home to many of his opponents. On March 17, 2011, the United Nations Security Council (UNSC) voted to create a no-fly zone over Libya and take "all necessary measures" to protect the city. Apparently swayed by Western entreaties, including from U.S. vice president Joe Biden, Medvedev directed the Russian ambassador to the UN to abstain from voting—which enabled a subsequent NATO-led intervention and, ultimately, Gaddafi's demise.[28] Despite Prime Minister Putin's repeated claim that foreign policy was not in his purview, he publicly condemned the intervention, calling it a "medieval crusade in which somebody calls upon somebody to go to a certain place and liberate it." Medvedev publicly retorted, saying references to a clash of civilizations or "crusades" was inadmissible and that he had fully intended to support the UNSC resolution.[29] In 2014, Putin told an interviewer, "You know, it's not correct that it [the reset] has ended now over Crimea. I think it ended even earlier, right after the events in Libya."[30]

Most observers agree the Putin-Medvedev public clash about the Libya UNSC vote sealed Medvedev's fate on his already limited chance to run for reelection. Arguably, the last straw for Putin was Medvedev's comment about Ukraine at a press conference in May 2011: "I am absolutely not worried about Ukraine's European integration. After all, this is a sovereign country, and it is up to you to choose where to integrate."[31]

In late September, Medvedev and Putin revealed they would again swap positions—and Medvedev explicitly acknowledged that "an agreement over what to do in the future was reached between us several years ago."[32] Though not a surprise to many Russians, the announcement dashed the hopes of those Russians hoping for a different future. Their disappointment became palpable when tens of thousands demonstrated in Moscow after domestic and international observers declared the parliamentary elections on December 4 were tainted by ballot stuffing and fraud on behalf of Putin's party, United Russia.[33]

The large, multiweek protests represented the very scenario Putin feared most: a threat to his power from the street. An Arab Spring zeitgeist seemed quite evident, as some protest banners declared "This is our Tahrir Square." Apart from protesters, who Putin felt were not appreciative of all he had done for them, Putin also fingered an external culprit: the United States, specifically U.S. nongovernmental organizations (NGOs) and U.S. secretary of state Hillary Clinton. He angrily reacted to Clinton's comment that the Russian people "deserve to have their voices heard and their votes counted, and that means they deserve fair, free transparent elections and leaders who are accountable to them." Putin asserted that Clinton "had set the tone for some actors in our country and gave them a signal . . . they heard the signal and with the support of the U.S. State Department began active work."[34] Putin later declared that Russia needed to safeguard itself from "interference in our internal affairs," and soon new draconian laws and regulations were passed constraining crowd sizes and effectively minimizing the prospect of any new public protests.[35]

The extent of Putin's wrath toward Clinton would become clear in the 2016 U.S. presidential election. Interestingly, as early as 2013, a key tool in Russia's interference in that election was created, the internet trolls and actors housed in the St. Petersburg–based Internet Research Agency.[36]

Despite these serious bilateral tensions and continuing differences about dealing with the Arab Spring uprisings in Libya and later Syria, progress in select areas of mutual interest was still possible. In 2012, for example, Russia completed the final steps for formal entry into the WTO; Putin and Obama met on the margins of the June 2012 Los Cabos, Mexico, G20 summit, where Putin acknowledged U.S. help in its accession to the WTO.[37] The two sides also reached a deal in 2013 to remove chemical weapons from Syria, Russia continued to support access to the NDN, Russia-U.S. International Space Station launches from Baikonur continued, and talks on Iran's nuclear programs grew more serious (later culminating in the 2015 Joint Comprehensive Plan of Action to contain Iran's nuclear program).

Ukraine's Maidan

These positive gains aside, the issue of Ukraine's geopolitical orientation was still festering. Shortly after the April 2010 lease deal on Sevastopol was signed, Yanukovych tried to fend off domestic critics by providing assurances that he still sought EU integration and that "in the triangle of EU-Russia-U.S., Ukraine will find its place and national interest."[38]

Ultimately, this geopolitical tug-of-war between the EU and Russia ignited the Maidan Revolution of Dignity of November 2013–February 2014 that culminated in Putin's annexation of Crimea and intervention in eastern Ukraine. Faced with prolonged Russian pressure to enter Putin's Eurasian Economic Union (EEU) and unhappy over EU terms for Association member status, Yanukovych abruptly suspended Ukraine's negotiations with the EU on November 21, triggering large protests on Kyiv's Maidan Square.[39] In mid-December, Yanukovych went to the Kremlin, where he and Putin announced that Moscow was extending $15 billion in loans and natural gas discounts to help Kyiv address its financial crisis. Putin, moreover, said the question of EEU membership was not discussed.[40] Nonetheless, protests and mounting violence led to Yanukovych's flight from Kyiv on February 22, 2014. Putin declared the new interim leadership was illegal, put into power by "nationalists, neo-Nazis, Russophobes and anti-Semites." Within days, Russian forces began taking control of Crimea, and assisted pro-Russian fighters in the later self-declared Luhansk and Donetsk "People's Republics" (LPR and DPR, respectively).

In his long March 18, 2014, address to the nation, Putin announced the formal incorporation of Crimea into the Russian Federation.[41] While touting a popular referendum (managed by Russia) as the legal basis for this annexation, Putin also cited the need to protect ethnic Russians in Crimea and in eastern Ukraine, and the need to ensure the security of the Black Sea naval base in Sevastopol. Unstated was the utility of LPR and DPR, as they further complicated a territorial dispute that precluded Ukraine from consideration for NATO membership. In contrast to his later July 12, 2021, treatise, "On the Historical Unity of Russians and Ukrainians," Putin did *not* say at that time that Ukraine did not exist; on the contrary, he assured Ukrainians that he harbored no ambitions beyond Crimea: "Do not believe those who want you to fear Russia, shouting that other regions will follow Crimea. We do not want to divide Ukraine; we do not need that."[42] At the same time, he did not acknowledge Russia's direct role in setting up the LPR and DPR, saying merely that ethnic Russians there only sought to protect their identity and local autonomy within Ukraine.

Turning to China and the Global South: Putin against the West and with the Rest

Putin's quick realization of the strategic impact of Western sanctions wrought by the Crimea annexation led him to Beijing in early May.[43] His two-day talks with Chinese president Xi Jinping in Shanghai yielded several major energy agreements, notably a thirty-year, $400 billion natural gas export deal; the trip signaled the beginning of a strategic pivot of Russia's energy market toward China—and later India.[44] While needing to mitigate the potential loss of most of the European energy market, Moscow was not blind to the downside risks of tethering too closely to China. In preparing to pivot even closer to China, the Kremlin conducted an internal policy review to assess three perceived risk areas: the Chinese presence inside Russia's Far East (not really a problem), the sale of advanced military technologies to China (better to make money now before China produces its own), and the potential growth of Chinese influence in Central Asia (lay down markers about observing Russian economic interests and role as security guarantor).[45]

With Western sanctions seemingly manageable, Putin faced another big decision: in the summer of 2015, Syrian president Bashar al-Assad requested Russian and Iranian military assistance to rescue his besieged regime, now in its fourth year of civil war. Russian air and naval power, complemented by Iranian and Hezbollah foot soldiers, saved the Assad regime. By 2017, Russia's compensation included a forty-nine-year lease to the Tartus naval facility and the right to operate the Hmeimin Air Base. Differences among Turkey, the United States, and other NATO members about which Syrian opposition groups to support probably made Putin's decision easier, as did Assad's definition of enemy combatants: all regime opponents were "terrorists." This low-risk gambit yielded other important benefits for Putin: it stabilized Moscow's key Middle East client, ensured Moscow a seat at any peace talks about Syria, and, over time, provided Russian generals, aviators, and naval officers with battlefield experience and a testing ground for their new weapons systems. Nine years later, however, this seemingly low-risk, high-gain intervention in Syria fell prey to the ever-changing kaleidoscope of Middle East conflicts as the Assad regime was toppled in December 2024 by Islamist opposition fighters, who swept through Aleppo, Homs, and Damascus in less than two weeks.

Less dramatic, perhaps, but critical to Russia's oil and gas export revenues was another Middle East success: the breakthrough in Russian-Saudi relations, which led to a Russian seat at the OPEC+ table.[46] In short, during the two years after the intervention in Ukraine and the Crimea annexation, Putin had bolstered his defenses against new Western economic pressures. After the February 2022 second invasion, Putin expanded the rationale for the invasion, elaborating on earlier themes of war with the West and Western civilization. This war increasingly is portrayed as involving the entire world. The global south, especially the BRICS countries, thus became a major audience to cultivate, largely to promote alternative financial and trade mechanisms to counter and reduce the influence of such U.S.- and EU-dominated entities as the IMF, the World Bank, and the SWIFT system for interbank transactions; these were key issues raised in late October 2024 at the Putin-hosted BRICS summit in Kazan, Russia.

New Opportunities and Unfinished Business: Putin's March to Ukraine

This section briefly reviews the period since the annexation of Crimea to address the bigger question about Putin's ambitions in Ukraine: What factors may have led Putin to begin seriously considering a much bigger move to acquire parts or the entirety of Ukraine?[47] Putin hardly kept secret his view that Ukraine wasn't really a country. In April 2008, Putin rhetorically asked Bush after the Bucharest NATO summit, "What is Ukraine? Ukraine isn't even a country. Part of it lies in eastern Europe, and the other, more significant part was given by us as a gift."[48] This outburst was later leaked to the Russian and Ukrainian media to rebut any idea that Moscow had accepted the Bucharest statement.[49] Believing such things, of course, is not the same as acting on them.

Many Russia watchers effectively argue that a key factor underlying Putin's concerns about functioning democracies on Russia's borders is their potentially destabilizing impact on his authoritarian regime, whereby Russian citizens might be led to question why their leaders couldn't match the political and economic gains of their neighbors.[50]

Beyond the broad threat posed by a future healthy Ukrainian democracy, several other specific factors since 2016 likely figured in Putin's shifting calculations about Ukraine: growing Russian security concerns about NATO and Ukraine, the failure of the Minsk Process to yield decisive Russian political influence inside Ukraine, a perceived window of opportunity to advance broader geostrategic goals against the West, and a desire to secure his place in Russian history.[51]

Concerns about NATO

In his statements of February 21 and 24, 2022, to justify Russia's renewed invasion of Ukraine, Putin asserted he had information that Ukraine's accession to NATO had already been decided and that deployment of NATO facilities was "only a matter of time."[52] Of course, it was Putin's 2014 invasion that fostered Ukraine's growing ties to NATO, including training in military doctrine and tactics, command structures, and annual defense exercises.[53]

Failed Influence-Building Campaigns inside Ukraine

According to an April 2023 article based on multiple well-placed Ukrainian and Russian sources, Volodymyr Zelensky's surprising landslide victory over Petro Poroshenko in April 2019 sparked some optimism in Ukraine that a breakthrough in the stalled Minsk Process might be within reach. Candidate Zelensky had talked of coming to an agreement with Putin to pursue peace in Ukraine and was probably viewed in Moscow as unprepared to deal with the wily Putin. Such optimism dissipated at the Zelensky-Putin December 2019 talks in Paris, hosted by Emmanuel Macron and Angela Merkel. Zelensky yielded little on key aspects of the Minsk Accord and even tried to alter text to make the special status of the Donbas temporary, not permanent.[54] The final straw for Putin was the Ukrainian government's crackdown on the pro-Russian oligarch and Rada member Viktor Medvedchuk and three strongly pro-Russian television stations, which essentially deprived the Kremlin of key soft power tools in eastern Ukraine.[55]

Window of Opportunity

Apart from Russia's security angst about NATO enlargement, Putin likely assessed that geopolitical circumstances had opened a once-in-a-lifetime window of opportunity to decisively break the seven-year stalemate in eastern Ukraine and maybe even push NATO to a breaking point: (1) the United States was increasingly politically polarized throughout the Trump presidency, Trump publicly questioned NATO's raison d'être, and the

American public was largely indifferent to Ukraine and wary of new foreign wars after the messy U.S. departure from Afghanistan; (2) Europe was trying to navigate a very complicated divorce, Brexit; (3) German chancellor Angela Merkel, a tough interlocutor since the Crimea annexation, was leaving office; (4) the world was still preoccupied with the COVID-19 pandemic; and (5) Europe, especially Germany, was still heavily dependent on Russian oil and gas.

Legacy

Putin has a fixation on Russian history. He is determined to secure his legacy as the great leader who restored core Slavic territories to Russia along with its rightful place as a global power.

Putin's 2014 invasion of Ukraine and annexation of Crimea likely were also part of a grander design, the first step toward incorporating much of Ukraine back into "Mother Russia." Just months after the annexation of Crimea, Putin made public references to "Novorossiya"—the territory north of the Black Sea that was annexed by Catherine the Great in the eighteenth century—which, he noted, included Kharkiv, Kherson, Luhansk, Donetsk, Mykolayiv, and Odesa, areas that he described as "not part of Ukraine." At that time, however, a large-scale invasion of Ukraine was out of the question; by Putin's own account, Moscow had had to act quickly after the February 2014 fall of Viktor Yanukovych, the pro-Russia Ukrainian president, just to secure Crimea.

Moreover, events elsewhere likely redirected Putin's focus away from Ukraine—for example, Syrian president Bashar al-Assad's request to rescue his tottering regime in the summer of 2015. Of greater consequence was the outcome of the 2016 U.S. presidential election. Moscow was surprised, like most observers, by Donald Trump's win, despite its major efforts to influence the U.S. vote against Hillary Clinton, including through information operations, the use of false personas on U.S. social media, and leaking hacked U.S. personal information, among other nefarious activities.[56]

William Burns, a former American ambassador to Russia and then director of the CIA, has described Putin as the "apostle of payback." He had not forgotten about Hillary Clinton's perceived interference in the 2011 Duma elections. Though Putin publicly has denied Russian interference in the 2016 U.S. election, the highly unusual public celebrations of Trump's victory suggested Putin was savoring a vengeful payback. Burns had noted in a June 2007 cable that Putin explicitly threatened a response if the United States interfered in Russia's elections.[57] Putin didn't want "outside interference" that might undo his mastery of a system of "managed democracy" to ensure electoral victories.[58]

Putin likely concluded the Trump presidency presented potentially big new opportunities, ones not to be jeopardized by new moves on Ukraine. Along with exploiting the growing political polarization in the United States, he could play to Trump's skepticism of NATO and distrust of the U.S. intelligence community and possibly even reach a deal on Ukraine that was favorable to Russia. Even months before Trump was elected, backchannel talks and emails between a former senior Trump campaign official, Paul Manafort, and Konstantin Kilimnik, a former Manafort employee the FBI said had ties to Russian intelligence, discussed a possible deal on Ukraine. In a December email, for example, Kilimnik told Manafort that a "very minor 'wink' (or slight push) from DT"—an apparent reference to president-elect Trump—could "start the process" and that "DT could have peace in Ukraine, basically within a few months after inauguration."[59]

In Europe, Putin considered Europe's institutional foundation was severely stressed on several fronts, and saw major possibilities: Britain's protracted economic divorce (Brexit) from the continent suggested a weakening EU; Arab Spring refugees had sparked anti-immigrant sentiment and strengthened populist parties, reinforcing leaders like Hungary's Viktor Orbán, whose views on social values and national identity aligned nicely with Putin's; and Trump's questioning of NATO's raison d'être appeared to raise existential doubts within NATO. Moreover, Putin may have assumed a modest but manageable German reaction to a new move in Ukraine, given Germany's major investment in the Nord Stream 2 pipeline and its long-standing business ties with Russia—former German chancellor Gerhard Schröder was on the board of Rosneft, Russia's oil giant, and had ties to Gazprom as well.

This confluence of promising developments likely contributed to Putin's growing sense of confidence, clearly in evidence during a remarkable March 2018 state of the nation address to a large Moscow audience in the Manezh exhibition hall. Putin devoted nearly half of his two-hour speech to Russia's security, boastfully unveiling several new strategic nuclear weapons systems, among them a hypersonic glide vehicle with a nuclear payload, a nuclear-powered cruise missile of global range, and a nuclear-powered underwater drone. Accompanied by videos of these weapons' capabilities, including a simulated flight over Florida, Putin thundered, "No one listened to us then, so listen to us now." That remark generated a standing ovation and stormy prolonged applause. Putin asserted that the need for these new weapons arose from the United States' withdrawal from the ABM Treaty in June 2002 and that these new weapons promised to ensure Russia could evade America's missile defense systems.[60]

Other factors played an important role in Putin's decision to act on his "unfinished business" with Ukraine: his strict self-isolation following the onset of the coronavirus pandemic in early 2020 and faulty intelligence reporting about Ukraine.

Impact of Coronavirus Isolation

The Russian journalist Mikhail Zygar, citing multiple well-connected insiders, described an isolated Putin whose belief in "domination over Ukraine" was reinforced by the extremely limited access to his normal interlocutors. One exception was an old friend and longtime adviser from St. Petersburg, Yuri Kovalchuk; the two were reportedly "inseparable" since the summer of 2020 and shared conservative views on Russia's "greatness" and orthodox Christianity.[61]

French president Emmanuel Macron, who met with Putin in 2019 and again two weeks before the February 24, 2022, invasion of Ukraine, offered his aides an insight into the impact of this isolation by comparing two meetings he had had with Putin: in 2019, Putin seemed less tough and less focused on history, whereas in 2022, Putin delivered a five-hour diatribe characterized by "historical revisionism" and grievance over the West's "broken commitments."[62]

Faulty Intelligence

Important information about Russia's intelligence gathering inside Ukraine has surfaced since the invasion, mostly from FSB polling data and the subsequent analysis provided to Western analysts and media by Ukraine. Overall, these materials suggest the FSB misread the implications of the polling data. Key examples: January 2022 data showed that 48 percent of respondents said they would defend Ukraine in the event of an invasion, consistent with an early February poll in which 40 percent said they would not serve in the military or resist an invader. Apart from the fact that such data suggest a high level of resistance to an invading force, the data also showed that those who said they would not defend were disproportionately concentrated in Ukraine's South and East—home to many ethnic Russians.

The February poll also offered contradictory insights about support for Zelensky: while 67 percent of respondents said they distrusted the presidency, large numbers said they would still vote for Zelensky.[63]

Such complicated poll data likely contributed to the FSB thinking that a lightning strike on Kyiv would topple the government and create a political vacuum that could be filled by FSB assets.[64] One wonders if anyone considered the local resistance to the 2014 efforts of the Moscow-backed Ukrainian separatists in Donetsk and Luhansk, regions with a high percentage of ethnic Russians. How much of the FSB data or other intelligence and analysis was seen by Putin is uncertain, though his own intelligence background makes it likely he would ask for such reports. Another key question here is just how such reporting was presented. If Zygar's many sources are accurate, few people dared to offer Putin different or contrarian views. In any event, the politically prudent Putin shrewdly portrayed that decision as a collective one. The highly unusual February 21 televised meeting of Russia's Security Council allowed each member to voice their concurrence with the proposal to recognize the independence of the Donetsk and Luhansk "republics." And, in his February 24 statement explaining the immediate cause for Russia's "special military operation," Putin said Moscow was responding to calls for assistance from those new states.[65]

The precise moment when Putin gave his military the "prepare for an invasion" order remains a mystery, but military exercises along the Ukrainian border throughout 2021 make early 2022 a distinct possibility. Those activities did lay the military groundwork to make an invasion a viable option. Moscow's planned military exercises provided both a pretext for the activity and cover for a significant buildup of Russian forces from an estimated 87,000 in February 2021 to some 150,000–190,000 on the eve of the February 2022 invasion.[66] Some 30,000 of that number were in place following an unscheduled military exercise with Belarus in mid-February, putting those troops on Ukraine's northern border and in a direct line to Kyiv.

A good case could be made that such military activity was classic compellence theory in practice: the physical display of military preparation as part of a negotiating strategy to achieve one's goals without the actual use of force, particularly since Moscow presented the United States with a specific set of demands in mid-December 2021 to resolve the crisis.[67] They included the removal of NATO infrastructure from the East European states admitted to NATO since 1997, no deployment of offensive weapons in states bordering Russia (not just NATO states), and NATO forswearing, in writing, any expansion to Ukraine or other states of the former USSR.[68] These demands would essentially rewind the clock to the world of 1997, before any post-Cold War NATO enlargement. While arguably a maximalist opening position negotiating tactic, most observers saw these demands as designed to be rejected and a move to put the onus on the United States and NATO for failure to negotiate. This view was largely confirmed when Foreign Minister Sergei Lavrov later stated that these maximalist terms were not negotiable—a convincing signal the decision to invade had been made.

Putin provided another clear signal on November 18, 2021, in comments to the Russian Foreign Ministry Collegium: "Our concerns and warnings regarding NATO's eastward expansion have been totally ignored." He further complained about the West's "superficial approach to our warnings about redlines."[69]

Putin's startling July 12, 2021, treatise, "On the Historical Unity of Russians and Ukrainians," when combined with the military buildup throughout 2021, makes a case for Putin having made the invasion decision before July, if not earlier. In his review of over one thousand years of Russian history, Putin stated that historically, "Russians and Ukrainians were one people—a single whole"; that Ukraine had never existed as a state; and that Ukraine's current government was under "direct external control," as demonstrated by the presence of "foreign advisers" and the "deployment of NATO infrastructure" on Ukrainian territory.

Putin's references to Russian history were nothing new, but for the leader of a major nuclear power to state so baldly that a neighbor didn't really exist and was actually part of that leader's territorial domain represented a clear marker that military action was in the works.

Putin, Russian History, and Solzhenitsyn

Putin's July 2021 treatise was only the latest manifestation of Putin's obsession with Russian history.[70] He has publicly cited conservative Russian thinkers, such as Ivan Ilyin, who wrote of Russia's unique history, identity, and mission. During Putin's tenure, moreover, a veritable statuary of famous Russian leaders appeared across Russia. Most politically relevant to the Ukraine issue were three statues erected since the 2014 annexation of Crimea: those of Vladimir I, Ivan III, and the Soviet-era dissident and literary giant Aleksandr Solzhenitsyn.

- In 2016, Putin unveiled a massive sixty-foot statue of Prince Vladimir I (an early ruler of Kyivan Rus' from 980 to 1015) outside the Kremlin grounds. This was a pointed barb directed toward Ukraine, since Russia and Ukraine both claim Vladimir as a founding figure.
- The statue of Ivan III (1462–1505) unveiled in Russia's Kostroma region in 2017 was the first one devoted to "Ivan the Great," dubbed by Russian historians "the gatherer of the Russian lands." Ivan ended the Mongols' nearly 250-year rule, and his defeat of other competing principalities—including parts of modern Ukraine—made Moscow the center of a growing Russian state.
- Most curious, however, was Putin's personal unveiling of Solzhenitsyn's statue in Moscow in December 2018. Putin evinced a strong personal interest in Solzhenitsyn just months into his presidency, visiting him in September 2000 and again in June 2007 to award him the Russian Federation National Award, the country's highest civilian honor. Putin also attended Solzhenitsyn's funeral in August 2008, renamed a Moscow street after him, and in 2010 made Solzhenitsyn's *Gulag Archipelago* required high school reading. Solzhenitsyn's criticism of Western materialism, moral corrosion, and spiritual emptiness, conveyed in his 1978 Harvard University commencement address, undoubtedly attracted Putin, who often asserts Russia's traditional values as morally superior to those of the West.

Putin's clear affinity with Solzhenitsyn likely stems from Solzhenitsyn's 1990 book, *Rebuilding Russia*, in which he argued that the Russian Empire and its Soviet successor had lost their Russianness by incorporating many disparate ethnicities. To rebuild a strong Russia, Solzhenitsyn said, Russia needed to integrate its Slavic core, and he explicitly defined this as Russia, Belarus, Ukraine's Novorossiya region, and the northern and northeastern parts of Kazakhstan.[71] Acknowledging the intertwined demography of Ukraine, Solzhenitsyn wrote, "If the Ukrainian people should *genuinely wish* to separate, no one would dare to restrain them by force. But the area is very heterogeneous indeed, and only the *local* population can determine the fate of a particular locality" (emphasis in original).[72] In a 1994 interview, Solzhenitsyn supported a "separate" Ukraine: "If you want to be separate, by all means, go ahead, please. But within the borders of the true Ukraine. The historical Ukraine, the place where Ukrainians really live."[73]

Putin's 2014 annexation of Crimea initially suggested a more modest vision than Solzhenitsyn's. As noted earlier, Putin assured Ukrainians he had no other territorial designs beyond Crimea.

Putin's Foreign Policy Record to 2021

A 2021 assessment of Putin's foreign policy record since he became president in 2000 might have accorded him fairly good grades. Overall, he had advanced Russian security interests in key areas abroad that strengthened Moscow's global geopolitical position.

Putin had forcefully kept NATO and the EU from expanding further into the former Soviet space through military interventions in Georgia (2008) and Ukraine (2014) and had created territorial disputes that precluded them from immediate consideration for NATO membership; he had annexed Crimea and thus ensured (barring a future return of Crimea to Ukraine) permanent access to the Russian Navy's Black Sea home base in Sevastopol; and he had rebuilt Russia's strategic nuclear arsenal to credibly preserve the reality of mutually assured destruction.

Putin also restored Russia's role as a major international actor. In the Middle East, military intervention helped rescue Moscow's key regional client, Syria, garnering in the process naval and air bases and a guaranteed seat at the table in any international settlement of the Syrian war. Putin's courtship of Saudi Arabia yielded a seat at the OPEC+ table. And Moscow's diplomatic lines to all of the region's key players involved in conflicts and factional disputes led many Western experts to depict Moscow as the region's new power broker.

Putin's deepening relationship with China, meanwhile, helped Moscow redirect its critical energy exports away from Europe, where it had lost its markets, mitigate the impact of post-Crimea Western sanctions, and give some credence to Putin's view of a multipolar world that would reduce American influence around the globe.

Moreover, Putin had been a prudent and successful risk-taker in three foreign interventions that advanced Russian foreign policy interests: in Georgia (2008) and Crimea (2014), Russian forces had overpowered an undermatched and surprised adversary. In Syria (2015), Russia had provided matériel and air and naval power while Iran and Hezbollah had provided the manpower to ensure Assad's survival, thus solidifying Russia's main Middle East client. In short, all three cases were relatively low-risk, high-gain challenges (opportunities) with little chance of mass Russian casualties.

In Africa, Russian private military organizations had helped Russia shore up or expand its influence, notably in Sudan, Libya, Mali, and the Central African Republic; in May 2024, private military companies also supplanted a U.S. force in Niger. Russia continued other influence-building activities elsewhere in the world through arms and nuclear energy reactor sales, both of which provide offshore training and access to Russian technicians and intelligence officers.

However, Putin's gains before the 2022 invasion—most significantly the annexation of Crimea and intervention in eastern Ukraine—were not without major negative consequences. On the security side, Putin's 2014 invasion sparked Ukraine's greatly expanded relationship with NATO. The resulting NATO training and exercises, as well as military assistance from NATO member states, helped better prepare the Ukrainian military for the current conflict. On the economic side, Western sanctions hurt Russia's economic growth. Experts differ on just how much sanctions, as opposed to other factors, affected Russia's economy, but a good case has been made that economic growth averaged 0.3 percent between 2014 and 2021, in contrast to global growth of 2.3 percent. Western sanctions also led some wealthy Russian businessmen to move their assets—and sometimes their families—out of Russia.[74]

On balance, then, prior to the 2022 full-scale invasion of Ukraine, Putin could have been accorded generally good marks for strengthening Russia's overall geopolitical position. Other factors, some of his own doing, others serendipitous, assisted. Major increases in world oil prices from 2000 through 2008 provided much of the financial wherewithal to rebound from the tumultuous 1990s. That, plus the fiscal responsibility exercised by Russia's Ministry of Finance and Central Bank, enabled Moscow by 2006 to pay off all Soviet-era foreign debt and in 2008 to set up Russia's National Wealth Fund. The 2007–2008 global financial crisis, however, hit Russia hard, with major inflation increases, diminished energy export revenue, and a 20 percent drop in foreign currency reserves.[75] The rainy day Reserve Fund and the National Welfare Fund did provide some assistance to help cushion the blow for Russian households. But, as noted by Sergei Guriev in chapter 1, it reinforced Putin's view that the state should be the main driver of the economy.[76] Since the 2014 annexation of Crimea, the Central Bank of Russia had again built up its foreign reserves, which had nearly doubled by 2022; combined with gold holdings, this amounted to approximately $630 billion.

Ironically, Russia's seemingly large financial reserves and Putin's poor understanding of the state of his military forces may well have solidified in Putin an unwarranted sense of strength that contributed directly to a belief that he could successfully invade Ukraine and weather a new round of Western sanctions.

It seems Putin was unaware that almost half of Russia's currency reserves resided in Western financial institutions and didn't comprehend the potentially crippling impact of a much broader sanctions regime. That may explain his "very matter of fact" response to CIA director Burns's warning in early November 2021. In Moscow, Burns told Putin that the United States knew what Putin was up to, that he shouldn't invade, and that if he did, he would pay a huge price.[77] Burns also delivered a letter from President Biden, reaffirming the consequences of an invasion. [78]

Putin's braggadocious display of Russia's new strategic nuclear weapons in March 2018 in hindsight may have revealed a significant blind spot. Irrespective of the actual capabilities offered by the new strategic nuclear weapons systems, they were not relevant to an extended ground war. As noted by Aleksandr Golts in chapter 12, the Ministry of Defense's touted military reforms refashioned Moscow's traditional mass land army into a smaller one designed for short-term local conflict. While such forces worked easily in the takeover of Crimea in 2014, they were a woefully wrong fit for a prolonged conventional war with Ukraine in 2022. It is possible this factor didn't figure in Putin's thinking or in that of Russian military planners. If things had gone as planned—if the Zelensky regime had fallen within days or weeks, as Putin assumed it would—the mismatch between Russian and Ukrainian military forces might have ensured a quick Russian victory. Because Putin assumed this invasion would end quickly with Zelensky's ouster, he likely viewed this move as akin to his "low-risk, high-gain" interventions in Georgia, Crimea, and Syria. Hence it is more accurate to describe his invasion decision as a disastrous miscalculation, not a high-risk gamble.

Putin's Foreign Policy Record since 2022: Strategic Failure

Putin's invasion of Ukraine has resulted in at least four major changes that negatively affect Russian national security and, more broadly, Russia's future. The strategic implications of these changes have largely negated Putin's pre-2022 foreign policy gains and will be difficult if not impossible to reverse.

NATO EXPANSION WITH FINLAND AND SWEDEN. Putin's war of choice has added over eight hundred miles to the NATO-Russia border (Finland) and breathed new life into an organization whose mission was being questioned by some in the West. The great irony, of course, is that halting NATO enlargement was one of Putin's stated reasons for invading Ukraine.

DEMOGRAPHIC AND HUMAN CAPITAL DECLINE. The large exodus of young Russians to evade conscription (and of other Russians critical of or threatened by the Putin regime) is estimated at somewhere between 400,000 and 1,000,000 according to various sources. This loss will magnify Russia's long-standing demographic crisis, one that Putin has regularly highlighted, as Russia's population remains below its 1991 level of 148 million. The loss of a tech-savvy young generation cohort (through the exodus as well as through losses on the battlefield) will also diminish Russia's competitiveness in the global digital world, where innovation and new technologies determine the winners.

INCREASED DEPENDENCE ON CHINA. Russia is unquestionably the junior partner, if not a supplicant, in this "no limits" relationship with a rising China, a country with which it shares a 2,600-mile border. As of 2022, there were some 7.9 million Russians living in Russia's Far East Federal District, while the neighboring Chinese provinces numbered some 57 million.[79] As the primary importer of Russian energy and key ally of Russia on the UNSC and in the increasingly tense relationship with the United States, China has gained a strong upper hand. Russia's dependence on China and India for energy sales in particular is unlikely to diminish anytime soon. Russia also is accessing banned imports, notably microchips, through firms based in China and elsewhere, although this trade will not resolve Russia's import substitution woes.[80] Putin's high-profile visits to Beijing months after annexing Crimea in 2014, and again in October 2023 and

May 2024—after invading Ukraine again in 2022—underscore Putin's dependence on China.

UKRAINE IS LOST. Irrespective of the outcome of the war, Ukrainians will forever remember Putin as a ruthless leader whose war of choice rained death and destruction on Ukraine. Putin has firmly solidified Ukrainians' sense of a distinct national identity, one fully separated from Russia. To the extent that postwar Ukraine seeks to protect itself via pursuit of NATO membership and/or a massive military buildup, Putin has transformed Ukraine from an opportunity to a national security concern, and now to a national security threat.

Ironically, Putin's projected February 2022 quick victory in Ukraine morphed into a prolonged bloody war that has left Moscow overextended, as Moscow's war burden left it unable to again salvage its key Middle East client, Assad's Syria. Neither could Assad be rescued again by Russia's collaborators in Syria, Iran and Hezbollah, who were now struggling to deal with a more assertive Israel on their home turf. Absent these critical lifelines, Syrian forces literally evaporated when surprised by the lightning offensive of Islamist fighters in late 2024. Russia was complicit in Assad's downfall as it failed to pressure him onto a political off-ramp that might have ended the thirteen-year civil war; instead, Assad and Putin discovered that calling all your opponents "terrorists" and pursuing a policy of "bomb, bomb, and bomb again"—one that even employed chemical weapons—is not a strategy for victory. In a fitting coda to Putin's 2015 intervention in Syria, Assad now resides in Moscow, while the future of Russia's key geostrategic assets—its naval and air facilities in Tartus and Hmeimim—remains uncertain. In sum, what began as a foreign policy success for Putin in Syria has now shifted to a glaring failure, marking a significant reversal on his geopolitical ledger.

The war in Ukraine revealed Russia's unpreparedness for a prolonged ground war, leading Moscow to expand ties not only with China but with Iran and North Korea, which have provided missiles, drones, and even ammunition. Moreover, Putin visited Pyongyang in June 2024—his first trip there in twenty-four years—to sign a mutual defense accord; this paved the way for the surprise dispatch of some 10,000 North Korean troops in late October, primarily to assist in Moscow's campaign to recover its Kursk region.

Domestically, the war in Ukraine also posed some political problems for Putin, notably the late June 2023 mutiny of Yevgeny Prigozhin's Wagner

Group. Putin's initial response to the mutiny and his seeming compromise with Prigozhin raised questions about Putin's decision-making and judgment.[81] It was Putin, after all, who had enabled the very public and nasty feud between Prigozhin and Minister of Defense Shoigu and Chief of the General Staff Gerasimov. Moreover, Prigozhin directly challenged Putin's rationale for the invasion, asserting that corrupt officials seeking Ukraine's resources and generals seeking additional stars were behind the invasion, not an imminent NATO threat and neo-Nazi leaders in Kyiv being manipulated by the United States.

Within two months, however, Putin had firmly reinforced his political position. Dozens of suspected senior-level sympathizers within the Russian military were arrested, as well as the hard-line, pro-war blogger Igor Girkin, a former Russian army veteran prominent in the 2014 invasion of Ukraine. An arguably more powerful message was the August 23 plane crash that killed Prigozhin and several other Wagner leaders. Putin's critics believe he had a hand in that event.[82]

Since his March 2024 reelection as president, Putin has made additional moves signaling his unhappiness with the Ministry of Defense. After he replaced Defense Minister Shoigu with a top bean-counting economic adviser, Andrey Belousov, in April 2024, a slow-rolling purge swept up five deputy defense ministers on corruption charges—ironically, the very corruption that Prigozhin had vocalized had come back to haunt the Defense Ministry.

Since the onset of the war, Putin has placed Russia on a wartime footing, ostensibly to better prosecute his proxy war against NATO to ensure Russia's "survival" but also as a precautionary measure to protect his power and regime cronies.[83] Similarly, Putin shrewdly had the February 21, 2022, meeting of his Security Council televised, thus depicting the invasion of Ukraine as a collective decision.

Putin has taken other steps to reinforce his power. How else to explain Putin's draconian muzzling of Russian society—his near total control of the media, outlawing of the word "war" (which must be referred to as a "special military operation"), and the reported arrests of some 20,000 people for their opposition to the war? Sadly, the onset of related denunciations and snitching on such war critics is reminiscent of the deeds of the Stalin-era youngster Pavlik Morozov, who turned in his father for anti-Soviet comments.[84]

Assessing Success or Failure: Whose Yardstick?

Assessing Putin's foreign policy record is a tricky business. As a Western Russia watcher, my assessment, that the negative strategic consequences of Putin's second invasion of Ukraine negate twenty-one years of a generally successful foreign policy, is just that: an outsider's analysis. Moreover, a compartmented approach to measure "success" in foreign policy is, by definition, narrow and violates a cardinal rule of diplomatic historians: don't put foreign policy and domestic policy or politics in separate bins, as they often are intertwined. In that context, Putin likely sees his foreign policy as a success, admittedly a costly one, but one critical to a much broader goal. While his fateful move into Ukraine was part of an ambitious "gather the Russian lands" foreign policy project, it also is a piece of his bigger mission: to build a Russian state and society in line with Putin's view of Russia's history, its culture, and its traditional values. That vision has long been evident in Putin's annual addresses, interviews, and in state documents, but the 2022 invasion has significantly accelerated its implementation.[85]

Ironically, Russia's failure to quickly decapitate the Zelensky government arguably has advanced this broader Putin vision. Initial Russian military setbacks sparked an immediate crackdown on any criticism of the war and a massive campaign to infuse in—more accurately, perhaps, to impose on—Russian citizens an intense sense of patriotism and national purpose. Putin has employed near total control of media and the Russian education system to promote a wartime narrative in which Russia is besieged by a NATO-backed Nazi regime in Ukraine and by a U.S.-led Western liberal order that threatens Russia's societal and religious norms and its territorial integrity. In sum, Putin has used the war to militarize an already strong police state, moving it ever closer to a Stalin-era totalitarian system characterized by the atomization of society. The startling reach and magnitude of this system were formalized in Putin's November 9, 2022, executive order, "Fundamentals of State Policy to Preserve and Strengthen Traditional Russian Spiritual and Moral Values."[86]

Putin's fixation on Russia's history attests to a fierce desire to secure a legacy, to be remembered as a modern-day gatherer of the Russian lands who protected Russia from an encroaching NATO. The fixation on history and historical grievances was highlighted in his maximalist demands of December 2021, an unmistakable effort to turn back the clock to the world of 1997, a world without NATO enlargement. Similarly, current Russian efforts to cultivate clients in Africa with arms and security training and to enlist the global south in Russia's anti-U.S., anti-West campaign reflect this attempt to rewind the clock and recreate the world of Putin's KGB days. This was a time when the United States had recognized the USSR as its nuclear power equal and when KGB comrades believed "the world was going their way" in the "Third World."[87] Another variation on this "back to the future" theme is seen in Putin's expanded ties not only with China but also with North Korea, Iran, and even Hamas—the so-called "axis of chaos"—as a means to expand the Russia-Ukraine "battlefield" and divert U.S. and NATO attention away from Ukraine and toward other potential threats and conflict areas.

Putin's March 2024 reelection as president and the subsequent shuffling of his national security team attest to the unabated strength of his political power, putting to rest any doubts that may have arisen following the June 2023 Prigozhin mutiny. During his remaining tenure, Putin, like Stalin, will be heralded in the controlled media and in children's history books as one of Russia's greatest leaders, someone who fended off NATO and a Western-led campaign to dismember Russia and destroy Russia's unique national identity.

The November 2024 election of Donald Trump, who vowed to end the Ukraine war in a day, understandably sparked widespread talk of a ceasefire or negotiated settlement in 2025. It is far too soon to speculate on an end to the war, given the wide range of variables here. That said, Putin does appear to hold a strong negotiating hand—and he has repeatedly stated he will settle for nothing less than the territory he has already annexed, though not fully controlled, in eastern Ukraine. Indeed, politically, Putin must show such tangible gains, given the enormous costs Russians have endured as a result of Putin's war of choice: some 700,000 casualties, a defense budget that now consumes an estimated 33 percent of the budget, and the imposition of totalitarian-type control of citizens' talk about the war or perceived political activism. Moreover, Russian officials stress the need for resolution of other security concerns, presumably the ones raised in late 2021 about Ukraine's status and the need for a new European security architecture.

In the short term, then, Putin could well emerge with a "victory" and his great leader image could remain intact for years, possibly a decade or two. However, whatever successor regime emerges, whether it is one that maintains Putin's narrative of reality or one that undertakes some form of de-Putinization, will face the harsh realities bequeathed by Putin's war on Ukraine: a revitalized NATO that includes more of Russia's neighbors, an exacerbated demographic decline and distorted economy, and an unhealthy dependency on China. In sum, then, the longer-term consequences of Putin's war with Ukraine and the West will more likely render Putin's "victory" a strategic failure—one that will severely tarnish his legacy.

NOTES

I thank Stephen Sestanovich, Kimberly Marten, Brian McCauley, and Greg Whisler for their thoughtful comments on an early draft of this chapter.

1. Putin (1999).
2. Ibid., 6.
3. Putin (2000), 169.
4. Ibid., 139–41.
5. Goodman (2022), 1–3.
6. *Wikipedia*, "List of International Presidential Trips Made by Vladimir Putin" (https://en.wikipedia.org/wiki/List_of_international_presidential_trips_made_by_Vladimir_Putin), last accessed June 26, 2023.
7. For accounts of this key meeting, see Zygar (2016), 48–50, and Baker and Glasser (2005), 86–87.
8. "Memorandum of Conversation—Prime Minister Vladimir Putin of Russia" (Clinton Digital Library, 1999), presidentiallibraries.us, 7–8. See also Talbott (2002), 359–60.
9. The apartment bombings remain the subject of great controversy. There were four apartment building bombings—the first in Buynaksk, Dagestan, two in Moscow, and one in Volgodonsk (600 miles southeast of Moscow). A fifth bombing may have been attempted in Ryazan. Two men carrying sacks into an apartment building in Moscow were detected by residents. A local expert said they contained the explosive hexogen; FSB director Patrushev later said the sacks contained sugar and that this was an FSB antiterrorism training exercise. This incident has sparked serious questions of possible FSB involvement in the other bombings. The limited—and sometimes contradictory—factual data on the bombings and the government's failure to launch a thorough investigation have given rise to numerous conflicting theories about possible culprits and motives behind the bombings. A former student of mine, Christina Harward, described the historiography on this topic as "a conspiracy theorists' paradise." Many experts assess there was government culpability in the bombings; see Knight (2012), which provides an excellent review of John Dunlop's book, *The Moscow Bombings of September*

1999: Examination of Russian Terrorist Attacks at the Onset of Vladimir Putin's Rule. Robert Bruce Ware argues that Dagestani extremists were responsible for the four bombings in "Revisiting Russia's Apartment Block Blasts" (2005, 599–606). Robert Otto (2023) recently put forth another intriguing hypothesis involving Boris Berezovsky and MVD actors. One fact is clear: Putin's tough military response to the bombings propelled him from being a little-known government official to a competitive candidate for the presidency.

10. "Memorandum of Conversation—Prime Minister Vladimir Putin of Russia" (Clinton Digital Library, 1999), presidentiallibraries.us, 7.

11. Baker and Glasser (2005), 128–29.

12. Ibid., 129–30.

13. Ibid., 132. See pages 129–34 for a detailed chronology of events surrounding Putin's decision, based on interviews with U.S. and Russian advisers or participants.

14. Putin (2001).

15. Short (2022), 378–79.

16. See *BBC News* (2005).

17. Putin (2004).

18. Dougherty (2004). Despite initial differences within the U.S. government, Akhmadov eventually gained political asylum in August 2004. For an assessment of Russian assertions of U.S. financial and other support to the Chechen separatists, see "Claim (in 2004, 2015 and 2017): The U.S. Government Supported Chechen Separatism" (Russia Matters, 2024).

19. Ignatius (2023).

20. Myers (2004).

21. Burns (2019), 201–02.

22. For the full text of Putin's February 10, 2007, Munich address, see Kremlin (2007).

23. UNIAN (2008).

24. Zygar (2016), 153–54; Yasmann (2008).

25. White House (2010).

26. Medved quoted in Borisov (2010).

27. *BBC News* (2010).

28. Stent (2014), 248–49.

29. Anishchuk (2011).

30. *Moscow Times* (2014).

31. Myers (2015), 385. See also *Kyiv Post* (2011).

32. Medvedev's statement and Putin's subsequent revelation at the United Russia Party Congress can be found in the transcripts of the congress (Kremlin 2011) and in Medvedev (2011). See also Myers, who in *The New Tsar* astutely notes this swap was actually a *"rokirovka,"* a chess move called castling, in which the rook and king swap places to better protect the king (2015, 391).

33. Barry (2011).
34. Herszenhorn and Barry (2011). See also Crowley and Ioffe (2016).
35. Human Rights Watch (2013).
36. Krever and Chernova (2023).
37. The range of issues discussed is covered in the White House archives. See White House (2012).
38. *Deutsche Welle* (2010).
39. Piper (2013).
40. Herszenhorn and Kramer (2013).
41. Putin (2014).
42. Putin (2021).
43. Thanks to Angela Stent for her superb examination of Putin's foreign policy, region by region, in *Putin's World: Against the West and with the Rest* (2019).
44. Perlez (2014).
45. Gabuev (2018).
46. Reed (2016).
47. Thanks to Eugene Rumer and Andrew Weiss for the perfect phrase "unfinished business" in Ukraine. See Rumer and Weiss (2021).
48. Zygar (2016), 153–54; Short (2022), 785.
49. Short (2022), 785.
50. See, for example, Person and McFaul (2022), 18–27.
51. Clement (2022).
52. Putin (2022a).
53. Michaels (2022).
54. Zhegulev (2023).
55. Ibid., 20.
56. ODNI (2017).
57. Burns (2019), 286.
58. Ibid., 228–29.
59. U.S. Department of Justice (2019), 2:143.
60. For the full text of Putin's March 1, 2018, address, see Putin (2018).
61. Zygar (2022).
62. Rose (2022).
63. Miller and Belton (2022); Reynolds and Watling (2022).
64. Miller and Belton (2022).
65. Putin (2022b).
66. Jones (2022).
67. On compellence theory, see Biddle (2020) and Betts and Biddle (2016)
68. The full text of Russia's draft treaty proposal, *Treaty between the United States of America and the Russian Federation on Security Guarantees*, is available at https://mid.ru/ru/foreign_policy/rso/nato/1790818/.

69. For Putin's comments at the November 18, 2021, meeting of the Foreign Ministry board, see Kremlin (2021).

70. For a fine summary of Putin's obsession with Russian history, see Hill and Stent (2022).

71. Solzhenitsyn (1991), 7–9. I want to thank two Columbia University students, Ilona Rand Dotson and Lola Seibert, for their insights, research, and rich discussions related to my longtime interest in Putin's relationship with Solzhenitsyn and possible links between Putin's July 12, 2021, treatise, "On the Historical Unity of Russians and Ukrainians," and Solzhenitsyn's 1991 book, *Rebuilding Russia*.

72. Solzhenitsyn (1991), 18.

73. Remnick (1994).

74. Åslund and Snegovaya (2021).

75. Desai (2010).

76. Seager (2006).

77. Harris et al. (2022).

78. Ibid.

79. Population statistics on Russia and China from Statista (2023).

80. Bush (2023).

81. Observers wondered why Putin seemed to be relatively lenient in dealing with Prigozhin, though most believed some vengeful payback was inevitable. Putin probably chose to be patient so as to avoid any disruption of Prigozhin's various activities, activities that generate important benefits for Putin and Moscow's foreign policy: the Wagner Group's military activities in Syria and multiple African states, gaining access to new revenue streams from those states' natural resources, or, in the past, the utility of the Wagner Group as a "nongovernmental actor," as this professed private entity helped build Russian influence abroad. Prigozhin's Internet Research Agency also plays an important role in Russian information operations and disinformation activities abroad, notably in Russia's interference in the 2016 U.S. presidential election.

82. Grove (2023); Roth (2023); Troianovski and Hopkins (2023).

83. For a fuller appreciation of how Putin utilizes his national security establishment to strengthen his hold on power and how those organs will play a key role in any Putin succession, see Sestanovich (2020).

84. Dixon (2023).

85. For two excellent early 2022 assessments of Putin's personality and broader foreign policy goals, see Roger Cohen's "The Making of Vladimir Putin: Tracing Putin's Slide from Statesman to Tyrant" (2022) and Angela Stent's "The Putin Doctrine: A Move on Ukraine Has Always Been Part of the Plan" (2022).

86. Government of Russia, Ministry of Foreign Affairs (2022).

87. Andrew and Mitrokhin (2006).

REFERENCES

Andrew, Christopher and Vasilii Mitrokhin. 2006. *The World was Going Our Way: The KGB and the Battle for the Third World*. New York: Basic Books.

Anishchuk, Alexei. 2011. "Russia's Medvedev Raps Putin's Libya Crusade." Reuters, March 21.

Åslund, Anders, and Maria Snegovaya. 2021. "The Impact of Western Sanctions on Russia and How They Can Be Made Even More Effective." Atlantic Council Report, May 3.

Baker, Peter, and Susan Glasser. 2005. *Kremlin Rising: Vladimir Putin's Russia and the End of Revolution*. New York: Scribner.

Barry, Ellen. 2011. "Rally Defying Putin's Party Draws Tens of Thousands." *New York Times*, December 10.

BBC News. 2010. "Ukraine's Parliament Votes to Abandon NATO Ambitions." June 3.

———. 2005. "Putin Meets Angry Beslan Mothers." September 2.

Betts, Richard K., and Stephen Biddle. 2016. "Deterrence in Foreign Policy." Council on Foreign Relations, YouTube channel, November 16.

Biddle, Tami Davis. 2020. "Coercion Theory: A Basic Introduction for Practitioners." *Texas National Security Review* 3 (2), February 20.

Borisov, Sergey. 2010. "Medvedev Is 'More Optimistic' about Russia-NATO Relations after Summit." *RT*, November 20.

Burns, William. 2019. *The Back Channel: A Memoir of America Diplomacy and the Case for Its Renewal*. New York: Random House.

Bush, Daniel. 2023. "Russian Military Uses China in Sourcing Banned Tech from 59 US Firms." *Newsweek*, June 21.

Clement, Peter. 2022. "Putin's Risk Spiral: The Logic of Escalation in an Unraveling War." *Foreign Affairs Online*, October 26.

Cohen, Roger. 2022. "The Making of Vladimir Putin: Tracing Putin's Slide from Statesman to Tyrant." *New York Times*, March 26.

Crowley, Michael, and Julia Ioffe. 2016. "Why Putin Hates Hillary." *Politico*, July 25.

Desai, Padma. 2010. "Russia's Financial Crisis: Economic Setbacks and Policy Responses." *Journal of International Affairs* 63 (2, Spring/Summer): 141–51.

Deutsche Welle. 2010. "Eastern Rapprochement." April 22.

Dixon, Robyn. 2023. "Russians Snitch on Russians Who Oppose War with Soviet-Style Denunciations." *Washington Post*, May 19.

Dougherty, Jill. 2004. "Putin Blasts U.S. on Terror Stance." *CNN International*, September 7.

Gabuev, Alexander. 2018. "Why Russia and China Are Strengthening Ties: Is the U.S. Driving Them Closer?" *Foreign Affairs*, September.

Goodman, Andrew. 2022. "Putin the Planner." *Texas National Security Review*, April.

Government of Russia, Ministry of Foreign Affairs. 2022. "On approving the Fundamentals of State Policy to Preserve and Strengthen Traditional Russian Spiritual and Moral Values" [in Russian]. Press release, November 9.

Grove, Thomas. 2023. "Russia Detained Several Senior Military Officers in Wake of Wagner Mutiny." *Wall Street Journal*, July 13.

Harris, Shane, Karen DeYoung, Isabelle Khurshudyan, Ashley Parker, and Liz Sly. 2022. "Road to War: U.S. Struggled to Convince Allies, and Zelensky, of Risk of Invasion." *Washington Post*, August 16.

Herszenhorn, David M., and Ellen Barry. 2011. "Putin Contends Clinton Incited Unrest over Vote." *New York Times*, December 8.

Herszenhorn, David M., and David E. Kramer. 2013. "Russia Offers Cash Infusion for Ukraine." *New York Times*, December 17.

Hill, Fiona, and Angela Stent. 2022. "The World Putin Wants: How Distortions about the Past Feed Delusion about the Future." *Foreign Affairs*, September–October.

Human Rights Watch. 2013. "Laws of Attrition: Crackdown of Russia's Civil Society after Putin's Return to the Presidency." April 24.

Ignatius, David. 2023. "When Putin Turned from the West." *Washington Post*, March 9.

Jones, Seth. 2022. "Russia's Ill-Fated Invasion of Ukraine: Lessons in Modern Warfare." Center for International and Strategic Studies Briefs, June 1.

Knight, Amy. 2012. "Finally, We Know about the Moscow Bombings." *New York Review of Books*, November 22.

Kremlin. 2021. "Expanded Meeting of the Foreign Ministry Board" [in Russian]. Kremlin.ru, November 18.

———. 2011. "United Russia Party Congress" [in Russian]. Transcript. Kremlin.ru, September 24.

———. 2007. "Speech [by Putin] and the Following Discussion at the Munich Conference on Security Policy" [in Russian]. Transcript. Kremlin.ru, February 10.

Krever, Mike, and Anna Chernova. 2023. "Wagner Chief Admits to Founding Russian Troll Farm Sanctioned for Meddling in U.S. Elections." CNN, February 14.

Kyiv Post. 2011. "Medvedev Not Worried by Ukraine's Possible European Integration." May 18.

Medvedev, Dmitry. 2011. "Comments to United Russia Party Congress." Kremlin.ru, September 24.

Michaels, Daniel. 2022. "The Secret of Ukraine's Military Success: Years of NATO Training." *Wall Street Journal*, April 13.

Miller, Greg, and Catherine Belton. 2022. "Russia's Spies Misread Ukraine and Misled Kremlin." *Washington Post*, August 19.

Moscow Times. 2014. "'Reset' with U.S. Ended with Libya, Not Crimea, Putin Says." April 17.

Myers, Steven Lee. 2015. *The New Tsar: The Rise and Reign of Vladimir Putin.* New York: Knopf.

———. 2004. "As NATO Finally Arrives on Its Border, Russia Gambles." *New York Times*, April 3.

ODNI (Office of the Director of National Intelligence). 2017. U.S. Intelligence Community Assessment, "Assessing Russian Activities and Intentions in Recent U.S. Elections." January 6, 2–3. ICA_2017_01.pdf (dni.gov).

Otto, Robert. 2023. "The 1999 Moscow Bombings Reconsidered." *Russian Politics 8* (appeared online in August 2023).

Perlez, Jane. 2014. "China and Russia Reach 30-Year Gas Deal." *New York Times*, May 21.

Person, Robert, and Michael McFaul. 2022. "What Putin Fears." *Journal of Democracy* 33 (2): 18–27.

Piper, Elizabeth. 2013. "Special Report: Why Ukraine Spurned the EU and Embraced Russia." Reuters, December 19.

Putin, Vladimir. 2022a. "Address of the President of the Russian Federation." Kremlin.ru, February 21.

———. 2022b. "Address of the President of the Russian Federation." Kremlin.ru, February 24.

———. 2021. "On the Historical Unity of Russians and Ukrainians." Kremlin.ru, July 12.

———. 2018. "Presidential Address to the Federal Assembly." Kremlin.ru, March 1.

———. 2014. "Address by the President of the Russian Federation." Kremlin.ru, March 18.

———. 2004. "Address by the President of the Russian Federation." Kremlin.ru, September 4.

———. 2001. "Address by the President of the Russian Federation." Kremlin.ru, September 11.

———. 2000. *First Person: An Astonishingly Frank Self-Portrait by Russia's President Vladimir Putin.* New York: Public Affairs.

———. 1999. "Russia at the Turn of the Millennium." Kremlin.ru, December 31.

Reed, Stanley. 2016. "Russia and Others Join OPEC in Rare Coordinated Push to Cut Oil Output." *New York Times*, December 10.

Remnick, David. 1994. "The Exile Returns." *New Yorker*, February 14 (article dated February 6, 1994).

Reynolds, Nick, and Jack Watling. 2022. "Ukraine through Russia's Eyes." London: Royal United Services Institute, February 25.

Rose, Michael. 2022. "In Moscow, Macron Found a Different, Tougher Putin." Reuters, February 10.

Roth, Andrew. 2023. "Russia Arrests Pro-War Putin Critic Igor Girkin, Reports Say." *Guardian*, July 21.

Rumer, Eugene, and Andrew Weiss. 2021. "Ukraine: Putin's Unfinished Business." Washington, DC: Carnegie Endowment for International Peace, November 12.

Russia Matters. 2024. "Claim (in 2004, 2015 and 2017): The U.S. Government Supported Chechen Separatism." Cambridge, MA: Harvard Kennedy Center.

Russian Federation, Ministry of Foreign Relations. 2021. "Agreement on Measures to Ensure the Security of the Russian Federation and Member States of the North Atlantic Treaty Organization, Draft." December 17.

Seager, Ashley. 2006. "Russia Pays Off Its Soviet-Era Debts to the West." *Guardian*, August 21.

Sestanovich, Stephen. 2020. "The Day after Putin: Russia's Deep State Holds the Key to Succession." *Foreign Affairs*, March 4.

Short, Philip. 2022. *Putin*. New York: Henry Holt.

Solzhenitsyn, Aleksandr. 1991. *Rebuilding Russia: Reflections and Tentative Proposals*. New York: Farrar, Straus and Giroux.

Statista. 2023. "Russia: Estimated Population Size by Federal District." Database. January 1.

Stent, Angela. 2022. "The Putin Doctrine: A Move on Ukraine Has Always Been Part of the Plan." *Foreign Affairs*, January 27.

———. 2019. *Putin's World: Russia against the West and with the Rest*. New York: Twelve Books.

———. 2014. *The Limits of Partnership: U.S.-Russia Relations in the Twenty-First Century*. Princeton, NJ: Princeton University Press.

Talbott, Strobe. 2002. *The Russia Hand: A Memoir of Presidential Diplomacy*. New York: Random House.

Troianovski, Anton, and Valerie Hopkins. 2023. "With Prigozhin's Death, Putin Projects a Message of Power." *New York Times*, August 25.

UNIAN. 2008. "Text of Putin's Speech at NATO Summit (Bucharest April 2, 2008)."

U.S. Department of Justice. 2019. "Report on the Investigation into Russian Interference in the 2016 Presidential Election" (Mueller Report). Washington, DC.

Ware, Robert Bruce. 2005. "Revisiting Russia's Apartment Block Blasts." *Journal of Slavic Military Studies* 18 (4): 599–606.

White House. 2012. "Joint Statement by the President of the United States Barack Obama and President of the Russian Federation Vladimir Putin." Press release, June 18.

———. 2010. "U.S.-Russia Relations 'Reset' Factsheet." Press release, June 24.

Yasmann, Victor. 2008. "Russia Prepares for Lengthy Battle over Ukraine," April 17. In RFE/RL for Russia Report, April 17, 2008 (rferl.org).

Zhegulev, Ilya. 2023. "How Putin Came to Hate Ukraine." *Verstka*, April 25.

Zygar, Mikhail. 2022. "How Putin Lost Interest in the Present." *New York Times*, March 10, 2022.
———. 2016. *All the Kremlin's Men: Inside the Court of Vladimir Putin*. New York: PublicAffairs.

FURTHER READING

Frye, Timothy. 2021. *Weak Strongman: The Limits of Power in Putin's Russia*. Princeton, NJ: Princeton University Press.
Gessen, Keith. 2024. "Could Putin Lose Power? Regime Stability Is a Funny Thing: One Day It Is There, the Next Day—Poof It's Gone." *New Yorker*, July 1.
Gessen, Masha. 2012. *The Man without a Face: The Unlikely Rise of Vladimir Putin*. New York: Riverhead Books.
Giuliano, Elise. 2018. "Who Supported Separatism in Donbas? Ethnicity and Popular Opinion at the Start of the Ukraine Crisis." *Post-Soviet Affairs*, March.
Graham, Thomas. 2019. "Let Russia Be Russia: The Case for a More Pragmatic Approach to Moscow." *Foreign Affairs*, November–December, 134–37.
Hill, Fiona, and Clifford G. Gaddy. 2015. *Mr. Putin: Operative in the Kremlin*. Washington, DC: Brookings Institution Press.
Marten, Kimberly. 2023a. "Inside The Wagner Mercenary Group's Uprising in Russia and Their Former Leader Yevgeny Prigozhin." *Forbes Podcast*, YouTube, June 26.
———. 2023b. "Why the Wagner Group Cannot Be Easily Absorbed by the Russian Military—and What That Means for the West." Russia Matters. Cambridge, MA: Harvard Kennedy School's Belfer Center, September 1.
McFaul, Michael. 2018. *From Cold War to Hot Peace: An American Ambassador in Putin's Russia*. Boston: Houghton Mifflin Harcourt.
Weiss, Andrew, and Brian "Box" Brown. 2022. *Accidental Czar: The Life and Lies of Vladimir Putin*. New York: First Second.
Wezeman, Siemon T. 2020. "Russian Military Spending—FAQs." Stockholm International Peace Research Institute.
Zygar, Mikhail. 2023. *War and Punishment: Putin, Zelensky, and the Path to Russia's Invasion of Ukraine*. New York: Scribner.

Afterword

HARLEY D. BALZER AND STEVEN A. FISHER

The contributors to this book analyze the failures of Vladimir Putin's leadership during the two decades leading up to the February 2022 assault on Ukraine and the implications for Russia's future. Under Putin, Russia has emerged as a weakened, globally less connected, economically uncompetitive, increasingly repressive nation. Authoritarianism, cronyism, and corruption have supplanted the essential forces of change, creativity, and innovation required to transform a Soviet-style system. Putin has consistently demonstrated a readiness to prioritize enriching his cronies and pursuing his dream of a new Russian empire over the well-being of ordinary Russians. His regime, even in decline, continues to cast a menacing presence on the global stage.

Russia under Putin has experienced failure across many dimensions, as detailed in the individual chapters of this book. The interconnections among these diverse failures and their cumulative impact deserve particular emphasis.

Putin's failures necessitate a reevaluation of perspectives that gained popularity during his initial period of apparent success in his first two terms, and of his ostensible geopolitical achievements. Despite weathering the global financial crisis of 2007–2008 and the inevitable fluctuations in hydrocarbon prices since, Russia's economic situation and geopolitical relationships have become far more fraught after February 2022. Increased defense spending is sidelining other economic needs. Closer ties with Iran, China, and North Korea are straining Russia's relations with other Asian countries, including Vietnam and South Korea.

Putin has failed to set Russia's economy on a sustainable trajectory. The economy shows few signs of significant modernization. The heightened military budget is now the primary, if not the sole, driver of economic growth. Putin's state-dominated, resource-dependent, rent-seeking system cannot sustain the self-sufficient military-industrial complex required to achieve his great power ambitions.

After Western export controls were introduced, Russia faced a shortage of key components to produce modern weapons, leading it to rely on China, informal supply chains, and pariah states such as Iran and North Korea. A predatory government discourages outside investment and undermines domestic entrepreneurship. Putin boasts about "parallel imports," ignoring the ways in which those policies preclude developing domestic capacity.

Oligarchs and regime cronies were given broad latitude to build monopolistic empires, with excesses ignored as long as regime priorities were upheld. Putin's counterreforms in response to the EU's sanctions did more damage in Russia than in Europe.[1] These characteristics of Putinomics make Russia's future particularly vulnerable. Economic difficulties have a negative synergistic impact on every aspect of society. That Russia's central bank governor, Elvira Nabiullina, sought to step down, only to have her resignation rejected by President Putin, illustrates the extent of the challenges. She is being called on to perform miracles that she knows cannot solve Russia's problems.

Russia's economic health depends heavily on natural resource prices, which fluctuate. Failure to diversify the economy has resulted in massive reliance on imported intermediate goods, components, and equipment, all of which become more expensive as the value of the ruble declines. Sanctions have necessitated a shift to less formal ways of obtaining crucial imports, adding to price pressures.

In 2024, the Russian federal budget is funding nearly everything, from industry to public goods, social services, welfare, and regional budgets. Corruption continues to impose a tax on nearly all projects, as well as on everyday government services. Ties to the global economy will continue to be restricted. Russia's remaining partners, particularly China and Iran, have their own economic problems. North Korea has persistently been an economic basket case, serving as a cautionary example for Russia if its defense budget continues to swell.

Putin has undermined the federalism enshrined in Russia's 1993 constitution. Regional development is now entirely controlled by Moscow, and few Russian regions are able to exploit their locations or resources to improve economic performance. Profits from businesses are taxed in the cities where firms are headquartered, not where they conduct their operations, exacerbating tremendous regional economic disparities.

Rejoining the international financial community in the 1990s enabled Russia to tap major international financial institutions, particularly the World Bank and the IMF, and to benefit from international assistance programs and foreign investment. Many of the benefits from these opportunities have been squandered. Foreign direct investment (FDI) went overwhelmingly to the natural resources sector. In Putin's virtual economy, this stimulated economic growth only when hydrocarbon prices rose during Putin's first two terms. The model was exhausted after 2008. The Central Bank of Russia performed credibly, but power vertical–aligned corporations supported by a banking sector increasingly under state control crowded out private domestic investment in the real economy.

Western sanctions prevent Russia from accessing international capital markets. Investments from China and developing nations cannot substitute for the scale, caliber, and scope of the Western FDI that has been withdrawn. Secondary sanctions in late 2023 and early 2024 caused many Chinese banks to rethink their role in Russia. The potential to draw on anything beyond Russia's own resources in the near to medium term is highly limited. As a result, Putin has recently begun to talk about supply-side economics for Russia's energy sector. It is unsurprising that Russia's global economic rankings and competitiveness continue to decline.

Russia might be proof that there is no such thing as an energy superpower. Despite possessing vast natural resources, Russia has mismanaged its potential, failed to develop its own technology to increase production, and now has lost access to the foreign equipment and service companies that facilitated developing the more challenging sites.

Russia's budget remains dependent on the price of oil and gas. Despite official rhetoric, the profits from periods of high oil and gas prices were not used to diversify Russia's economy. Some revenues funded the state budget, some went to the stabilization fund, and a substantial share was pocketed by insiders. Many other sectors withered. In 2012, hydrocarbons accounted for nearly half of budget revenues; in 2021 the share was still 45 percent. With the decline in arms sales, the dependency now may be even greater. When the history of Putin's energy policy is written, the failure to develop modern energy industry technology and to use the proceeds from Russia's resource wealth to diversify the economy and climb the technology ladder will rank alongside massive corruption as key reasons for Russia's decline.

Entrepreneurs who became effective managers and learned the value of internationalizing their businesses were replaced by Putin cronies focused on control and rents. Yukos, one of the first Russian companies to become a major player in the global oil and gas market, was destroyed. State-designated "national champions" Gazprom and Rosneft became agents of state policy rather than profit- and efficiency-oriented companies. Notably, in 2023 Gazprom reported significant financial losses for the first time in decades. Nearly every part of Russia's economy became dependent on the price of oil and on imported technology. Yet Putin's administration ignored the impact fluctuating hydrocarbon prices would have on the cost of the imports.

Using Russian energy policy as a foreign policy tool has generated adverse consequences for the economy and in relations with other countries. The carrots (incentives) and sticks (threats) based on hydrocarbons are expensive and blunt instruments. Maintaining control over Russia's oil and gas industries precluded sharing the costs and risks of exploration and development. Low prices for favored partners reduced the revenues available to increase production or fund domestic needs. Threatening to cut off supplies to civilian populations undermined Russia's status as a reliable partner and caused customers to look elsewhere.

Russia's relative but quite real success in agriculture is threatened by climate change and Western sanctions. Russia may be able to feed itself, but it still imports seeds, chemicals, and other crucial inputs. Reduced exports of grain and fertilizer contribute to food shortages on a global scale. The war has imposed new challenges. The global impact on food supplies and prices will inevitably reverberate within Russia itself, and an increasing share of the Russian population will find it more difficult to afford a healthy diet. Agriculture and construction were the sectors experiencing the most serious labor shortages early in the Russia-Ukraine War as some immigrants left and many who remained were conscripted. As the population continues to decline in Russia's Far East, Chinese are increasingly playing a major role in agriculture, purchasing land through Russian partners.

Putin's policies have increasingly undermined any progress made toward the rebirth of civil society, gender rights, and the treatment of Russia's large disabled population. Open political protests in Russia have become impossible.[2] The level of repression directed against Russians who seek to help their neighbors, support people in need, and build cohesive communities is staggering. Yet Russians continue to help each other as their government fails to provide crucial services. In August 2024, the government announced it would provide housing for 2,500 people displaced by Ukraine's military incursion into Kursk oblast.[3] The number of refugees is at least 150,000. Locals have stepped up to help.

Putin's Russia has failed women (including lesbians), gay men, and transgendered people, who collectively constitute more than half of Russia's population. Putin's regime perceives citizen initiatives and diversity as threats. A regime confronting economic, social, and demographic challenges on the scale that Russia does yet neglects public contributions to the economy and society undermines its future, including prosecution of the war in Ukraine.

The same issues are evident in Putin's approach to human capital, including his willingness to accept an astounding exodus of talented Russians from the country. While brain circulation is a common global phenomenon, Russia resembles less-developed countries in being a net loser in the emigration-immigration balance. This is particularly threatening in a country where the education system is less capable of maintaining standards, science and technology capacity is declining, and participation in the global knowledge economy has become severely limited by both foreign rejection and Russia's growing tendency to criminalize international collaboration.

To the extent Russians share Putin's resentment-fueled identity, opposition to the war will remain weak and ineffective. This means that elected officials, Putin's advisers, and the general public will continue to have minimal influence on policy. For Russian society to recognize the realities of the present, its vision of the past must change. This happened to some extent in 1991, 2011–2012, and 2018–2021.[4] There is no guarantee that Russian society would accept the loss of Crimea, but one should not rule out the possibility of change. Putin's approval ratings did begin to diminish as the Ukrainian army advanced into Kursk oblast.[5]

Corruption remains the most pernicious failure infecting the entire Putin system. Russia's corruption problem is a more serious obstacle to development than the hydrocarbon curse as it permeates all aspects of Russian life. Housing, education, scientific activity, and the maternity capital program have all been corrupted. Administrative interference in the legal system created by Putin (a law school graduate) does more to encourage corruption than to combat it. Property rights are unsafe, distorting decisions about investment and business development. That corruption extends to the defense industry and supplies for the military itself highlights one of the most blatant contradictions about the Putin regime. Corruption helps to explain many of Russia's failures on the battlefield. The arrest on corruption charges of a number of high-ranking military officials close to Sergei Shoigu is only the tip of the Russian iceberg.

Russia's War in Ukraine

Russia's war in Ukraine is a defining event that has reshaped the country's relations with the world, amplified domestic challenges, and altered the country's geopolitical standing. Several excellent monographs discuss the war in detail.[6] These analyses are timely and important. Yet focusing on the battlefield or intelligence failures disregards the decay in Russia's economic, social, institutional, and administrative systems that underlies the military setbacks. Golts's chapter on the military, along with other chapters in this book, demonstrates that the failures began earlier and have deep roots in Putin's governance system. Our authors focus on the broader "substructure" failures that precluded the swift victory Putin anticipated in Ukraine. The depth of the problems, exacerbated by sanctions and Russia's mobilization economy, means that Russia will face these same challenges regardless of how the war ends. Excessive state control, increasing militarization, and the wartime economy suggest Russia will experience many of the same problems it encountered when the Soviet Union collapsed.

Russia's military reforms have failed, placing impossible demands on the forces that were deployed in February 2022. The inability to defeat Ukraine was the inevitable outcome. Many of Putin's claims of Russian military prowess have been shown to be more bluster than substance. Russia's corruption-ridden defense industry has lost the capacity to produce equipment that was routine in the Soviet era. Putin's superweapons are years behind schedule, have incurred costs many times greater than originally promised, and exist in small production runs when they exist at all. The one new weapon that has been used in Ukraine, the Kinzhal missile, despite its destructive capabilities, has not proven to be a game changer. Russia's capacity to modernize its armed forces is constrained. The Kremlin must rely on mobilization. Russia's worsening demographic and economic situation, however, makes this increasingly difficult and costly.

Multiple failures in domestic and foreign policy have made Putin's assault on Ukraine a challenge to Russia's future, even if Putin or a successor manages to salvage a less than humiliating outcome. Either Russian intelligence told Putin what he wanted to hear, or he ignored their warnings, or they badly misread the situation. Russia's troops were ignorant of their mission, stupefied by finding themselves fighting in Ukraine, and severely lacking in the supplies and equipment needed for a protracted war. Fearing mobilization, hundreds of thousands of Russians fled the country immediately. Putin allowed them to leave. By September 2022, when a "partial mobilization" was announced, over one million people had left. Only then did the Russian government begin to limit the departure of conscription-age males and some essential personnel.

Putin's failed leadership in the military realm extends beyond the debacle of Russia's disastrous February 2022 invasion of Ukraine. He has been unable to maintain a monopoly on force, a failure dramatically underscored by the Prigozhin military mutiny in June 2023, which exposed cracks in the control over Russia's armed forces. This issue is further compounded by the continued existence of up to fifteen private military organizations operating within Russia. Moreover, the Russian military's failure—or, perhaps more accurately, gross negligence—in safeguarding the nation's borders was laid bare by the Ukrainian armed incursion into Kursk oblast in August 2024. The breach starkly underscores the weaknesses in Russia's defense capabilities under Putin's leadership.

Putin cannot afford to lose his war, yet Russia might be better off if he does. The historical record reminds us that after defeat in the Crimean War, the Russian Empire embarked on the most extended period of reform in the country's history. Similarly, after what was supposed to be a "short, victorious war" against Japan in 1904–1905, Russia's defeat helped bring about the country's most successful democratic revolution. The October Manifesto of 1905 established a legislature, the Duma, that lasted until 1918 despite changes to the electoral law that prevented liberal forces from retaining their initial influence. In August 1914, Russians rallied around Czar Nicholas II. Soldiers went to the front; aristocratic women sewed bandages; everyone waved flags. A year later, the mood had changed. Russia's massive losses in World War I and food shortages at home led to the

February Revolution and the Bolshevik coup in 1917, followed by a long and bloody civil war. Defeat in Afghanistan in 1989 was followed by the demise of the USSR. This legacy makes it vividly clear why Ukraine is an existential issue for Putin.

Far from restoring Russia's superpower status, Putin has made Russia a declining power, though one with a massive nuclear arsenal. The combination is particularly dangerous. Rather than having partners committed to mutually beneficial development projects, Putin prefers purely transactional zero-sum relationships with other autocrats. This means he encounters few questions about human rights or democratic governance. Russian citizens pay the price in reduced living standards, quality of life, and security.

Regardless of the outcome of the war, Putin's failures promise continued debility. Economic difficulties in 2019 prompted a debate in Russian officialdom about the need for a "mobilization" economy. Some argued this would be the only way to overcome sanctions and maintain Russia's capacity to project power in the world. Others warned that it would distort Russia's economy and could potentially result in a repeat of Soviet stagnation. The "partial mobilization" in September 2022 triggered a significant exodus of young people representing not only the educated, tech-savvy generation but many future mothers and fathers who could have helped stem the decline in population growth. That demographic disaster is compounded by the significant loss of Russian lives in Ukraine.

Russia's 2024 federal budget was increasingly geared to defense needs. This created immediate disruptions and long-term challenges in restoring normal economic activity. The Soviet experience of endeavoring to end rationing demonstrates the magnitude of the problems. Each time Stalin's government decreed an end to rationing, Soviet consumers emptied store shelves to protect themselves against renewed rationing, which then became unavoidable.[7] As noted by Gertrude E. Schroeder, in the Brezhnev era, when a significant share of economic actors had found ways to benefit from a suboptimal, state-controlled economy, heroic efforts failed to reform the system.[8] And as Konstantin Simis has illustrated, when the entire system—including food distribution, health care, education, and culture, as well as industry, agriculture, trade, and the police and security services—is corrupt, everyone becomes complicit.[9]

Increased spending on defense requires trade-offs among competing priorities. While defense spending may allow the government to claim growth in GDP and industrial production, these data have little meaning for ordinary Russians. Growth in defense spending in the decade before the war did little to improve Russia's economy but did stimulate greater waste and theft. The budget faces inevitable deficits, while monetary policy and import dependence promise higher inflation. Spending on health, education, and infrastructure will be limited. Regional debt will remain a problem, while regional development continues to be a low priority.

Whether Russia achieves victory, suffers defeat, or comes to a negotiated settlement in Ukraine, the consequences include significant threats. When Russian soldiers returned home from World War I, many supported the Bolshevik Revolution. When Soviet troops came home from Afghanistan, some of these "Afghantsy" became a source of serious social problems involving narcotics use and sales, criminal activity, and violent behavior. Some of the pardoned criminals who survived their agreed-upon period of service in Ukraine are returning to their homes and in a disturbing number of instances are engaging in theft, rape, and murder.[10]

While few members of Putin's team have gone so far as to challenge his decisions directly, the late Yevgeny Prigozhin established a precedent. This may not encourage others to emulate his behavior, but certainly it has induced the regime to become even more obsessed with security. The outcome is tighter control, less initiative, and more instances of people being detained on weak or fabricated evidence.

Foreign Policy

Prior to the 2022 attack on Ukraine, some would have given Putin's foreign policy high marks.[11] Russian military involvement in Georgia, Syria, and Ukraine appeared to be successful without exacting a high cost. The combination of Russia's significant financial reserves and some military reforms (not to mention much-hyped new superweapons) caused some observers, and Putin himself, to believe Russia could achieve his goals. Thus far, this appears to have been a premature judgment.

Many analysts believe that the Ukraine war will eventually conclude with a negotiated settlement. Neither side currently appears capable of achieving a decisive victory. However, Putin has dug in for a prolonged conflict. He expects that Russia's wealth and larger population, combined with fatigue and political twists and turns in Europe and America, will eventually shift the balance in Russia's favor. He has unleashed multiple disinformation campaigns designed to have an impact on elections in Europe and the United States.

Unless facing a total defeat on the battlefield, Russia would, at the very least, aim for a face-saving resolution in which Ukraine would have to relinquish Crimea and the territories currently under Russian control while also renouncing any ambitions to join the EU or NATO. Yet even this relatively successful outcome for Putin would represent a significant defeat for Russia. Previously neutral, Finland and Sweden have now joined NATO. Ukraine has been lost, and Russia is increasingly dependent on China. Russia's influence in the countries of its "near abroad" has significantly weakened. Prospects for immigration from these countries to help offset Russia's demographic decline are far more limited.

Russians and the War

The long-suffering Russian population will continue to bear the costs of Putin's war. Since the heyday of 2000–2008, when a combination of recovery growth and higher prices for Russia's commodities created an economic improvement second only to what Sergei Witte achieved in the last decade of the nineteenth century and early twentieth century, Russian economic growth has been anemic. It is instructive that Witte's achievement was based on foreign investment and a more diversified economy that enabled Russia to withstand its defeat by Japan in 1905. By 1907, Russia's economy was growing again, with far more of the investment coming from domestic sources.[12] It is clear why Finance Minister Alexei Kudrin kept Witte's picture on his office wall. The Russian Empire's economy weakened after 1912, failed during World War I, and crumbled when foreign support ended after the Bolsheviks seized power in October 1917.

Putin himself published the crucial data that Russian natural resource industries would not employ more than about 3 percent of the population.[13] Yet his regime did little to resolve the problem, while his cronies repeatedly appropriated and compromised businesses that could have created well-paid jobs. Kudrin and Gurvich concluded that between 2000 and 2008, Russia reaped $900 billion in resource rents, which helped the economy grow at an average rate of nearly 7 percent per year. Between 2009 and 2013, the energy rents totaled $1.3 trillion, yet the economy grew at less than 1 percent.[14] Putin's model was defunct, yet it has remained the core of his economic policy.

Oil prices declined after 2012. One result was that Russian living standards have declined for more than a decade, with scant prospect for improvement. Accounts of "normal life" in Moscow and St. Petersburg are not matched in the hinterlands. Despite Russia's recent relative success in agriculture, food has consistently been more costly but lower in quality.[15] The government lacks the resources to fund its much-touted national projects.[16] Each time Putin was reelected president, he gave a speech promising the same unrealized improvements he had announced in previous inaugural addresses.

The combination of nationalism and militarism has adversely affected every aspect of Russian society. The entire gamut of personal rights has been sacrificed. Whether it is gender, sexual orientation, disability, ethnicity, or religion, Putin's regime has failed to create a society that embraces the benefits of diversity. That a regime facing serious demographic challenges cannot find ways to tap the rich human potential of its citizens remains a tragedy—it is self-inflicted.

The same self-defeating repression is clear in Putin's failure to draw on the Russian people's genuine interest in contributing to economic and social development. Insistence on control and massive predation have undermined a host of civil society efforts to provide medical care, education, aid for immigrants, services for the indigent and disabled, support for groups facing discrimination, and measures to protect the environment. These all are contributions that would have advanced the regime's purported goals. This psychology was illustrated when staff at the Kurchatov Institute, Russia's leading research and development institution in the field of nuclear energy, spoke about the Soviet-era director, Yevgeny Velikhov. One of Velikhov's favorite expressions was *"nado upravliat', ili unichtozhat'"* (which translates to "it is necessary either to manage something or to destroy it").[17]

Economic consequences include loss of access to global capital markets and the refusal of many nations to risk relying on an undependable Russia for energy supplies. The contrast between Germany and China here is instructive. The Chinese leadership refuses to allow any single energy supplier to become dominant. Gerhard Schröder, on the other hand, was willing to make Gazprom Germany's crucial source. The difference illustrates long-term views: Schröder saw Russia becoming part of Europe (while also benefiting personally); Xi views the relationship as perhaps having a shorter time horizon.

Russia's oligarchs and the *siloviki* are hardly exempt from the consequences of Putin's evolving policies. The bargain, whereby these quite diverse groups could retain their wealth and privileges and enjoy a level of international interaction unheard of in Soviet times in return for loyalty to the regime, is being strained by Putin's war. Billionaires' yachts have been confiscated. Affluent Russians used to luxury ski vacations in the Alps must settle for an increasingly expensive, less glamorous Sochi. Their children are no longer welcome as students in a growing number of countries. Turkey, Indonesia, the UAE, Thailand, and other places in the Middle East and Asia have become alternatives. So has Argentina. Will this wear thin? For how much longer will Russian businessmen remain content with being excluded from opportunities in Europe, America, Japan, and other major markets?

Russia: Down, but Not Necessarily Out

The chapters in this book describe Putin's failures, demonstrating that a weakened and economically deglobalized Russia confronts significant challenges. However, wounded bears can still be dangerous, and Russian tactics have evolved. Russia possesses reserve resources that should not be underestimated: Russia's energy exports to countries in Europe and Asia continue to provide a critical lifeline to its economy; despite significant losses incurred in Ukraine, Russia retains a substantial military force; Russia presents a dangerous cybersecurity threat; and Russia continues to maintain its disruptive presence in international diplomacy.

Since returning to the presidency in 2012, Vladimir Putin has increasingly positioned Russia as a "spoiler" rather than a "contributor" in international affairs. The Ukraine war has made the spoiler role more prominent. Largely owing to Russia's quagmire in Ukraine, Russia continues to search for opportunities to intervene in or disrupt global affairs, resorting to increasingly more desperate measures in its attempts to challenge the Western-led international order. Russia's track record in this regard is mixed. Russia seeks to enlist support in the global south, but its immediate Central Asian neighbors are asserting their independence and increasingly turning toward China and India. Russian peacekeepers did not prevent renewed conflict in Nagorno-Karabakh. Welcoming a distraction from its war in Ukraine, Russia remained silent when Hamas launched its surprise attack on Israel on October 7, 2023. Hamas representatives have been invited to Moscow repeatedly, despite decades of verbal support for Israel and a sizable Russian community living there. Putin has now clearly aligned

Russia with Iran and has found new prospects for profit-driven regime change, Russian style, in Africa.

Putin's efforts to profit from chaos, like his domestic policy failures, are a tragedy for Russians, their neighbors, and the entire world. Russian military forces threaten global food supplies by destroying Ukrainian agriculture and ports. Russia has weaponized the environment, blowing up Ukraine's Kakhovka Dam and militarizing the Zaporizhzhia Nuclear Power Plant. Rhetoric used by Russian leaders normalizes if not glorifies discussion of a nuclear exchange. Putin remains intent on subverting democratic elections in Europe and the United States. Russia has worked with global criminal networks, sometimes deploying criminality in lieu of diplomacy or trade. Russia's much shorter list of economic and technology partners now consists mostly of countries led by autocratic kleptocrats or murderous dictators. A Russia reduced to buying arms from Iran and North Korea creates dangers for itself as well as for others.

Russia currently looks less like a persistent power than like a persistently declining power.[18]

Black Swan?

Black swans are unexpected events, and we should never preclude them.

An optimistic forecast for Ukraine and its supporters would be for some combination of developments within Russia to bring about regime change, resulting in a government that understands the dangers and costs of armed conflict. The causes might include economic difficulties leading to popular protests, splits within the elite, growing regional demands for genuine federalism, ethnic tensions resulting in regional fragmentation, or some segments of the security services determining that their personal futures would be more secure in a regime not based on repressing Russian citizens and decoupling from the West. Democracy requires the simultaneous appearance of popular demand and a portion of the elite deciding that a system offering a mechanism to peacefully gain and lose power without the outcome being permanent is preferable to "winner-take-all" environments.

Durable democratic change, however, requires some form of lustration to exclude supporters of authoritarian systems. Russia achieved authoritarian modernization under Alexander III, thanks to the efforts of Sergei Witte and the continued influence of reform-minded officials from the era of

Alexander II. In 1905, Russia experienced the simultaneous emergence of popular demand and elite supply for democracy, sufficient to create a legislature with some control over the budget. Failure to restrain the monarchy, however, resulted in restoration of autocracy. After the 1991 coup attempt, Boris Yeltsin banned the CPSU (the Communist Party of the Soviet Union)[19] and subsequently split the security services. This was not sufficient. Putin took Russia on a different path.

While we may judge Vladimir Putin's leadership a failure in many important ways, we must acknowledge that authoritarian regimes like Putin's can endure far beyond the point at which pundits proclaim them to be "failed states" or economically unviable. History offers numerous examples of this long tail, including the economically disadvantaged Soviet Union, which survived World War II and went on to challenge the West in the Cold War for nearly fifty years. Other instances include Saddam Hussein's Iraq (1979–2003), Mugabe's Zimbabwe (1980–2017), Castro's Cuba (1959–present), North Korea's Kim family (1948–present), the ongoing Iranian theocracy (1979–present), and the Chávez/Maduro leadership in Venezuela (1999–present). Modern technology may either prolong a regime's existence or, in other cases, hasten its downfall.

Putin will fight to the finish or, more characteristically, until his own end. According to Putin, the state is primary, not its citizens. Putin will mobilize the state, including any entity and any individual, to defend what he perceives to be Russia's national interests (including his own) and sovereignty. He will mobilize any and all national assets in a struggle to preserve what he deems to be Russia's rightful place in the world. He will use methods that break international norms, driven by a wartime mentality claiming Russia is locked in an existential struggle. He will increase repression at home in an attempt to preserve domestic stability. Until he achieves a "new Yalta," where leaders of the "great powers" determine the fate of smaller nations, Putin will act as though he is at war with the West.

Yet the longer Putin stays in power, the deeper Russia will sink into competitive decline. The Russia that emerges from the war will be poorer, more unpredictable, and more isolated in the world. There is no way to gauge whether Russia will follow the path established by Putin, regardless of domestic pressures for a course change or the emergence of new leadership in the Kremlin.

Putin has seriously undermined Russia's prospects. While it may be too early to declare that Russia has forfeited the twenty-first century, under Putin's leadership, Russians will continue to bear a heavy burden. For the rest of the world, Vladimir Putin's chilling declaration that a world without Russia is not a world worth having serves as a stark reminder of the stakes involved.[20]

NOTES

1. A Russian consulting company accredited to evaluate Russian businesses found that global food markets adjusted quite quickly. Far from losing the billions of dollars Putin claimed, the cost to Europe was perhaps $500,000. The cost to Russia has been far greater. National Rating Agency (2020).

2. In late June 2024, the widespread repression against Russians who criticized the war was extended to highly respected theater personnel who staged a play designed as a cautionary tale about Islamic extremism. A well-known playwright and director were detained on the pretext that their production supported terrorism. Hopkins (2024).

3. FilterLabs (2024)

4. Nikolskaya and Dmitriev (2022).

5. FilterLabs (2024).

6. For example, Matthews (2022), Onuch and Hale (2023), and Plokhy (2023).

7. Khlevnyuk and Davies (1999).

8. Schroeder (1979).

9. Simis (1982).

10. Meduza (2023); *Verstka* (2023).

11. The positive assessment of Putin's foreign policy achievements was far from universal. Owen Matthews (2022) quickly assessed Putin's war against Ukraine as "overreach." Thomas Kent (2023) provides a detailed account of Putin consistently deploying similar policies that failed to achieve the intended results. Beginning with Ukraine in Putin's first years in power, Kent emphasizes that NATO expansion resulted from demand by former Soviet satellites and republics rather than any grand plan by the West to diminish Russia. Kent's case studies illustrate the failure of Russian policies in Ukraine, South Africa, Macedonia, and Ecuador and of Russia's efforts to deploy the Sputnik COVID-19 vaccine and Nord Stream 2 pipeline as foreign policy tools. He mentions several other countries where Russian influence has declined, including Sudan, Azerbaijan, and Central Asia.

Analysts are likely to gauge Assad's fall in Syria as a major defeat for Putin. Is a partial victory in Ukraine worth the loss of a key client in the Middle East, undermining Russia's status as a protector of authoritarian allies? Kent notes that South Africa joining the BRICS could provide a basis for more successful results there. Changes over time remind us that assumptions about Russia losing its air and naval bases in Syria, thereby weakening its ability to intervene in the Middle East and Africa, might not be permanent.

12. Von Laue (1969).

13. Balzer (2006).
14. Kudrin and Gurvich (2014).
15. Volchkova and Kuznetsova (2019).
16. Engqvist (2021).
17. Balzer's personal communications with Kurchatov Institute staff on multiple occasions from 1989 to 2018.
18. See Kendall-Taylor and Kofman (2021).
19. Subsequently, a Russian communist party was constituted in February 1993.
20. *RT* (2018).

REFERENCES

Balzer, Harley. 2006. "Vladimir Putin's Academic Writings and Russian Natural Resource Policy." *Problems of Post-Communism* 53 (1): 48–54.

Engqvist, Maria. 2021. "Why Russia's National Projects Went Out in the Cold." RUFS Briefing no. 51. Stockholm: FOI Total Defense Research Institute, April.

FilterLabs. 2024. "Has the Ukrainian Counteroffensive into Kursk Dented Putin's Popularity in Russia?" August 16.

Hopkins, Valerie. 2024. "2 Russian Women Put On a Play. Then the State Came for Them." *New York Times*, June 25.

Kendall-Taylor, Andrea, and Michael Kofman. 2021. "The Myth of Russian Decline: Why Moscow Will Be a Persistent Power." *Foreign Affairs*, November/December.

Kent, Thomas. 2023. *How Russia Loses: Hubris and Miscalculation in Putin's Kremlin*. Washington, DC: Jamestown Foundation.

Khlevnyuk, Oleg, and R. W. Davies. 1999. "The End of Rationing in the Soviet Union, 1934–35." *Europe-Asia Studies* 51 (4): 557–609.

Kudrin, Alexei, and Evsei Gurvich. 2014. "'Novaia model' rosta dlia rossiiskoi ekonomiki" [A new Russian economic growth model]. *Voprosy ekonomiki* 12 (December): 4–36.

Matthews, Owen. 2022. *Overreach: The Inside Story of Putin's War against Ukraine*. London: Mudlark.

Meduza. 2023. "Repeat Offenders: Thousands of Russian Prisoners Joined the Army in Exchange for an Early Release. Many Have Gone Back to Crime upon Their Return." September 8.

National Rating Agency. 2020. "Importozameshchenie ili peremeschenie?" [Import substitution or moving things around?]. Moscow, December.

Nikolskaya, Anastasiya, and Mikhail Dmitriev. 2022. "The End of the Crimean Consensus: How Sustainable Are the New Trends in Russian Public Opinion?" *Russian Politics* 5 (3): 354–74.

Onuch, Olga, and Henry E. Hale. 2023. *The Zelensky Effect*. New York: Oxford University Press.

Plokhy, Serhii. 2023. *The Russo-Ukrainian War: The Return of History*. New York: W. W. Norton.

RT. 2018. "'Why would we want a world without Russia?' Putin on Moscow's Nuclear Doctrine." March 7.

Schroeder, Gertrude E. 1979. "The Soviet Economy on a Treadmill of Reforms." In *The Soviet Economy in a Time of Change*. Washington, DC: U.S. Congress, Joint Economic Committee.

Simis, Konstantin. 1982. *USSR: The Corrupt Society: The Secret World of Soviet Capitalism*. New York: Simon and Schuster.

Verstka. 2023. "Vzialis' za staroe: Pomilovanye zeki iz ChVK 'Vagner' vozrashchaiutsia k prestupnoi deiatelnosti, vlasti stremliatsia skryt fakty novykh prestuplenii" [Up to old tricks: Pardoned prisoners from the Wagner private military group are returning to criminal activity, the authorities are trying to hide the facts about new crimes]. July 5.

Volchkova, N. A., and P. O. Kuznetsova. 2019. "Skol'ko stoiat kontrasanktsii: Analiz blagosostoianiia" [How much do countersanctions cost: A welfare analysis]. *Zhurnal NEA* 43 (3): 173–83.

Von Laue, Theodore H. 1969. *Sergei Witte and the Industrialization of Russia*. New York: Macmillan.

Contributors

HARLEY D. BALZER retired in July 2016 after thirty-three years in the Department of Government, the Walsh School of Foreign Service, and as an associated faculty member in the History Department, Georgetown University. He was founding director of Georgetown's Center for Eurasian, Russian and East European Studies (CERES). In 1982–1983 he was a congressional fellow in the office of Congressman Lee Hamilton, where he helped secure passage of the Soviet–Eastern European Research and Training Act of 1983 (Title VIII). In 1992–1993 he served as executive director and chairman of the board of the International Science Foundation, George Soros's largest program to aid the former Soviet Union.

PETER CLEMENT is a senior research scholar and adjunct professor at Columbia University's School of International and Public Affairs, where he teaches courses on contemporary Russian security policy and intelligence and foreign policy. During a long CIA career, his positions included deputy assistant director of CIA for Europe-Eurasia, deputy director of intelligence for analytic programs, and director of the Office of Russian and Eurasian Analysis. He holds a PhD in Russian history from Michigan State University and has published articles and book chapters on Russia, including a recent *Foreign Affairs Online* article, "Putin's Risk Spiral: The Logic of Escalation in an Unraveling War." He is currently completing a book on the work of CIA analysts and their career trajectories.

ALFRED B. EVANS JR. is professor emeritus in the Department of Political Science, California State University, Fresno. He earned his BA and MA degrees at the University of Texas at Austin and his PhD at the University of Wisconsin, Madison. He is the author of *Soviet Marxism-Leninism: The Decline of an Ideology* and a coeditor of three other books, including *Russian Civil Society: A Critical Assessment*. He has published many book chapters and articles in scholarly journals. His current research focuses on civil society in Russia, with particular emphasis on organizations that carry out public protests.

STEVEN A. FISHER is a career emerging markets finance professional who has worked for thirty-five years with Citibank, including sixteen years in the former Soviet Union in senior leadership positions in Moscow and Kyiv. Fisher's research interests include the political economy of Putin's Russia and the history of Russo-American investment relations. Fisher has spoken regularly at finance and policy forums across the world. He is the author of *Into Russia's Cauldron: An American Vision, Undone* (2021) and is coauthor (with Anders Åslund) of "New Challenges and Dwindling Returns for Russia's National Champions" (Atlantic Council, 2020). He received his MS degree in Foreign Service from Georgetown University and BA degree in Sino-Soviet studies from Cornell University.

ALEKSANDR GOLTS is an analyst at the Swedish Institute of International Affairs. He received an MA degree in journalism from Lomonosov Moscow State University. He was a member of the editorial board of *Krasnaia zvezda* (Red Star) from 1980 to 1996, military editor of *Itogi* weekly magazine from 1996 to 2001, deputy editor in chief of *Ezhenedelnyi zhurnal* (Weekly Journal) from 2001 to 2004, and deputy editor of its website, ej.ru, from 2005 to 2022. He also worked as military analyst for *Novoe vremia* (New Times) magazine. Outside Russia, he was a visiting fellow at the Center for International Security and Cooperation (CISAC), Stanford University, in 2002–2003, a visiting fellow at Uppsala University in 2016 and 2020, and a visiting fellow at the Kennan Institute of the Woodrow Wilson International Center for Scholars in 2018. Golts is the author of *Russian Armed Forces: 11 Lost Years* (Moscow: Zacharov, 2004), *Militarism: The Main Obstacle to Russia's Modernization* (Moscow, 2005), *Military Reform and Militarism in Russia* (Jamestown Foundation, 2019), and *Survive the Cold War* (Moscow: AST, 2021).

AGNIA GRIGAS is a political economist, author, and speaker. She is a senior fellow at the Atlantic Council in Washington, D.C., and a consultant based in Los Angeles. Her three recent books are *The New Geopolitics of Natural Gas* (Harvard University Press, 2017); *Beyond Crimea: The New Russian Empire* (Yale University Press, 2016), which was selected as a *Time* magazine's Top-10 book on Russia; and *The Politics of Energy and Memory between the Baltic States and Russia* (Routledge, 2013). She has lectured at Harvard, Stanford, Yale, Columbia, the University of Pennsylvania, Johns Hopkins, Oxford, the London School of Economics and Political Science, and leading business and security conferences. Her work regularly appears in major economic news publications and outlets, including the *New York Times*, the *Wall Street Journal*, *Forbes*, *Newsweek*, *Financial Times*, Bloomberg, Reuters, *Foreign Affairs*, CNN, and BBC. Grigas earned her doctoral and master's degrees in international relations from the University of Oxford and her BA in economics and political science from Columbia University.

SERGEI GURIEV is professor of economics and dean of the London Business School. In 2004–2013 he was rector of the New Economic School in Moscow. In 2016–2019 he served as chief economist and member of the Executive Committee of the European Bank for Reconstruction and Development (EBRD) and in 2022–2024 as the provost of Sciences Po, Paris. Professor Guriev is a member of the Executive Committee of the International Economic Association and a global member of the Trilateral Commission, a senior member of the Institut Universitaire de France, and an ordinary member of Academia Europaea.

JANET ELISE JOHNSON is professor of political science at Brooklyn College and the Graduate Center, City University of New York, and a specialist in Russia and the region. Her most recent book, *The Routledge Handbook of Gender in Central-Eastern Europe and Eurasia* (coedited with Katalin Fábián and Mara Lazda, 2022), won the 2022 Heldt Prize for the best book in Slavic/East European/Eurasian Women's and Gender Studies from the Association for Women in Slavic Studies. Her previous books are *The Gender of Informal Politics: Russia, Iceland and Twenty-First Century Male Dominance* (Springer, 2018), *Gender Violence in Russia: The Politics of Feminist Intervention* (Indiana University Press, 2009), and *Living Gender after Communism*, coedited with Jean C. Robinson (Indiana University Press, 2007). She publishes in both scholarly journals and general-interest publications such as the *New Yorker*, the *Washington Post*'s *Monkey Cage*, *The Conversation*, and the *Boston Review*. She coordinates a monthly workshop on gender and transformation in Central-Eastern Europe and Eurasia, now affiliated with the CUNY Graduate Center.

AMBASSADOR (RETIRED) ALLAN MUSTARD capped a thirty-eight-year federal career in three foreign affairs agencies as U.S. ambassador to Turkmenistan. He earned honors baccalaureates in Slavic languages and literature and in political science from the University of Washington, a certificate in Russian from Leningrad State University, and a master's degree in agricultural economics from the University of Illinois. He began his Foreign Service career as a Russian-language guide and interpreter for the U.S. International Communication Agency in three cities in the USSR, served twice for a total of seven years at the American embassy in Moscow, and from 1990 to 1995 was responsible for U.S. Department of Agriculture policies and activities in the former Soviet Union.

IVAN PAVLOV is a prominent Russian attorney who stands for freedom of information and government transparency. Pavlov founded the human rights projects Department One and Team 29 and acted as a leader of the Freedom of Information Foundation, a Russian NGO. He has defended Russians accused of treason and espionage, including Ivan Safronov, Grigory Pasko, Oksana Sevastidi, and Svetlana Davydova. Pavlov became the first attorney to be labeled a foreign agent in Russia under the new laws. As a result of his professional endeavors, he faced criminal prosecution, which ultimately compelled him to leave Russia in 2021. Pavlov has played a vital role in raising public awareness regarding modern legislation pertaining to state secrets. His pursuit of justice and government accountability continues to challenge repressive legislation, making a substantial impact in the realm of human rights, both in Russia and internationally. Pavlov received Human Rights Watch's Alison Des Forges Award for Extraordinary Activism in 2018.

MARIA SNEGOVAYA is a senior fellow with the Europe, Russia, and Eurasia Program at the Center for Strategic and International Studies, Georgetown University, and a postdoctoral fellow at Georgetown University's Walsh School of Foreign Service. She earned her PhD from Columbia University. Her research focuses on Russia's domestic and foreign policy, democratic backsliding, and re-autocratization across the post-Soviet space and the tactics used by Russian actors and proxies who circulate disinformation to exploit these dynamics in the region. Her book on this topic, *When Left Moves Right: The Decline of the Left and the Rise of the Populist Right in Postcommunist Europe*, was published by Oxford University Press in 2024. Her research results and analysis have appeared in peer-reviewed policy journals, including *West European Politics*, *Party Politics*, *Journal of Democracy*, and *Post-Soviet Affairs*, and in the *Washington Post*'s *Monkey Cage*. Her research and commentary have appeared in a number of publications and news outlets, including the *New York Times*, the *Wall Street Journal*, Bloomberg, the *Economist*, and *Foreign Policy*.

BRIAN D. TAYLOR is professor of political science and director of the Moynihan Institute of Global Affairs, the Maxwell School of Citizenship and Public Affairs, Syracuse University. Taylor is the author of four books on Russian politics: *Russian Politics: A Very Short Introduction* (Oxford University Press, 2024), *The Code of Putinism* (Oxford University Press, 2018), *State Building in Putin's Russia: Policing and Coercion after Communism* (Cambridge University Press, 2011), and *Politics and the Russian Army: Civil-Military Relations, 1689–2000* (Cambridge University Press, 2003). He received his BA degree from the University of Iowa, an MSc degree from the London School of Economics and Political Science, and a PhD from the Massachusetts Institute of Technology.

GUZEL YUSUPOVA is a sociologist of identity politics and nationalism with expertise in the post-Soviet space. She is a Humboldt Fellow at the Osteuropa-Institut, Freie Universität Berlin. She has held academic appointments in Germany, Canada, the United Kingdom, Sweden, and the Russian Federation. Her research has appeared in the peer-reviewed academic journals *Post-Soviet Affairs*, *Europe-Asia Studies*, *Ethnicities*, *Nations and Nationalism*, and others.

Index

Abashin, Sergei, 288–89
Abkhazia, 412–13
Acemoglu, Daron, 34
Afghanistan, 113, 243, 378, 414, 421, 452–53
agriculture, Russian. *See* Russia, agriculture in
Aho, Esko, 88
Akhmadov, Ilyas, 411, 436n18
al-Assad, Bashar, 418, 421, 428, 431, 459n11
Albright, Madeleine, 409
Alexander III, 457–58
Alfa-Bank, 68
al-Qaeda, 408, 409–11
Altai pipeline, 94
Anti-Ballistic Missile (ABM) Treaty, 409–10, 423
Anti-Corruption Foundation (FBK), 179, 337, 355, 364

anticorruption policies: Putin's reversal of, 27–28
antimonetization movement, 170
antisemitism, 12
apartment bombings, 408, 411, 435n9
Arab Spring, 415–16, 422
Arctic regions 15–16, 83; Arctic LNG, 1–2, 89, 91; energy development in, 89, 98
Argentina, 90, 134, 210, 456
Aristarkhov, Vladimir, 143
Armenia, 63, 207, 209
Ash, Timothy, 52
assimilationist policies, 278, 281, 283–84
Australia: LNG exports and, 89–90, 94
Azarov, Mykola, 414
Azerbaijan, 93, 205, 316, 459

Bahamas, 52
Bailes, Kendall, 215
Balzer, Harley D.: chapter by, 6–7, 193–275
Balzer, Marjorie Mandelstam, 281, 286
banking system, Russian, 65, 68–71, 74; top ten banks, 68
Barbashin, Anton, 171
Bartholomew I, 12
Bashkortostan, 171, 174, 176, 283
Bastrykin, Alexander, 206–07
Belarus, 137, 152, 161n53, 205, 240, 315, 424, 426
Belousov, Andrey, 394, 432
Belton, Catherine, 337
Berlusconi, Silvio, 32, 88
Beslan hostage crisis, 282, 408, 410–11
Biden, Joe, 381, 415, 429
bin Laden, Osama, 408, 410
birth rates in Russia, 194–202, 211, 245, 251n8; birth control, 200–201; pro-natal policies, 198–99, 251n18, 299; variation by region/religion, 202
Black Lives Matter (BLM) movement, 291
Blue Stream pipeline, 82
Bolshevik Revolution, 150, 451–53
Bortnikov, Aleksandr, 334, 338, 341
brain drain, 14, 33, 91, 98, 121, 204, 208–10, 449
brain gain, 210, 253n84
Brandt, Willy, 87
Brazil: annual growth rate of, 72; comparative competitiveness, 50; comparative equity issuance, 63–64; economic development indicators, 56; FDI flows, 55
Brexit, 421–22
Brin, Sergei, 57

British Virgin Islands, 52, 382
Burns, William, 242, 344, 421, 429
Buryatia, 281
Bush, George W., 409–10

Canada, 82, 90, 120; shale oil and, 90
capital flight, 4, 44, 52, 57, 73
Carter, Jimmy, 113; grain embargo, 119
Castro, Fidel, 458
Central African Republic, 428
Central Asia–Center (CAC) gas pipeline, 92
Central Bank of Russia, 36, 45, 50, 52, 65, 72, 429, 447
Chaianov, Aleksandr, 105
Chechnya, 8, 202, 243, 281, 283, 299, 306, 383, 406–10; Beslan hostage crisis and, 282, 408, 410–11; violence against LGBTQ population, 313–14
Chekists, 3, 8–9, 334, 337–39, 342. *See also* siloviki
Chemezov, Sergei, 227
Cherkesov, Viktor, 228, 339
Chernov, Daniil, 155
Chernysheva, Anastasia, 371
China, 94, 234–35, 259n206, 430–31; annual growth rate of, 72; collaborative research and, 224, 235, 256n134, 258n155; comparative equity issuance, 62–64; economic development indicators, 56; emigration from, 205, 242, 288; exports of technology from, 233–37, 242, 446; FDI flows, 55, 76n39; GDP per capita, 24; immigration to, 210; Russian energy exports to, 80, 83, 89–96, 235, 237, 418; Russian sanctions and, 235–36, 427, 447;

share of world GDP, 33–34;
  Ukraine war and, 430–431
Christianity in Russia, 11, 290, 423;
  birth rates and, 202
Clement, Peter: chapter by, 10,
  405–43
climate change, 5, 15–16, 98, 202,
  204, 242, 448
Clinton, Bill, 408–09
Clinton, Hillary, 342, 416; election
  of 2016 and, 421
Cold War, 33, 82, 84, 87, 105–06,
  121, 147, 154, 380, 425, 458
collectivization of agriculture, 5,
  104–06
Collins, James, 408
Commission for the Advancement of
  Women's Status, 305
Control of Corruption Index, 27–28,
  39n12
corporate raiding, 335–36
corruption, 4, 446, 449–50, 452; in
  agricultural sector, 113, 118–119,
  121, 136n44; economic growth
  and; educational system and,
  218–19; FDI and, 49; income
  inequality and, 15; kleptocracy
  and, 9, 258n159, 328, 336–39, 341;
  in military production, 384;
  Morozov story, 255n114; protests
  against, 169; rent-seeking as, 4,
  27, 44, 49–50, 97, 113, 117–19;
  in science and technology,
  225–26, 239–41; siloviki and, 334,
  336–38, 340, 343, 345. *See also*
  anticorruption policies
countersanctions, 211, 214, 237.
  See also Russia, sanctions against
COVID-19 pandemic, 213;
  demographic effect of, 197, 199,
  203–04, 241; economic effects of,
  14, 37; effects of on education, 218;
impact of coronavirus isolation,
  423; protest movements and,
  177–79, 182, 186n54, 186n59
Credit Bank of Moscow, 68
Crimea, 417; NATO expansion and,
  413; Russian annexation of, 5, 31,
  118, 339, 341–42, 347n35, 362, 384,
  390, 417, 419–21, 427–28; Russian
  national identity and, 157. *See also*
  Ukraine, Russian invasion of
  (2014)
Crimean War (1853–1856), 451
Crocus City Hall attack, 288
Cuba, 458
Cyprus, 52
Czelusta, Jesse, 50

Dagestan, 306, 384; apartment
  bombings in, 408, 411, 435n9
Dawisha, Karen, 337
decolonization, 278, 286–87, 292
dedovshchina system, 383
defense spending, 213, 412, 446,
  452–53
demographics, Russian. *See* Russia,
  demographics of
deportation of foreign nationals,
  208
deposit insurance, 25–26
"Discrediting" the Armed Forces
  ("fake news") Law, 369–71
disinformation campaigns, 318,
  438n81, 454
diversity management, 7, 277–80,
  282–84, 292
Donetsk, 379–81, 417, 421, 424
Dronov, Yaroslav Yuryevich
  "Shaman," 157–58
Dubrovka Theater hostage crisis,
  408, 411
Dynasty Foundation, 223
Dzerzhinsky, Felix, 3

East Siberia–Pacific Ocean (ESPO) oil pipeline, 94
Eberstadt, Nicholas, 199
economy, Russian. *See* Russian economy
education in Russia. *See* Russia, education in
Efko, 115
EKN (Sweden), 65
elite continuity, 151–52
emigration from Russia, 37, 195–96, 202, 204–05, 208, 210–11, 218, 449; brain drain, 208–11; of LGBTQ people, 312; as protest, 179–80, 187n69, 199–200
energy sector, Russian. *See* Russia, energy sector of
environmental challenges, 11, 14, 15–16, 18n18, 51; protest movements and, 171–72, 175–76, 184n11, 184n15
equity market, Russian, 44, 62–65; equity issuance breakdown by exchange, 63
Erdoğan, Recep Tayyip, 88
espionage, 360–61, 362. *See also* Treason, Espionage, and State Secrets Law (190-FZ)
Estonia, 16, 87, 315, 316
Ethiopia, 315
ethnic federalism, 280–81
ethnicity in Russia. *See* Russia, ethnicity in
Eurasian Economic Union, 80, 92, 417
Eurasian Women's Forum (GONGO), 318
Eurobond issuance/activity, 59–61
European Bank for Reconstruction and Development (EBRD), 65
Evans, Alfred B. Jr.: chapter by, 6, 169–92; In Memoriam, ix–x

exceptionalism, Russian/Soviet, 144, 146, 148–49, 154, 157
Expansion of MVD Powers Law (424-FZ), 369
Export Development Canada, 65
Export Finance Australia, 65

Federal Guards Service (FSO), 330, 337; tenure of leaders, 331. *See also* siloviki
federalism, 7, 25-26, 280–81, 447, 457
Federal Security Service (FSB), 329–31, 337, 340; control of internet and, 366–67; "professional secrets" and, 367–68; tenure of leaders, 331; Ukraine war and, 341–42, 423–24. *See also* siloviki
Federov, Nikolai, 117
Fedotov, Mikhail, 368
Finland: NATO and, 10, 378, 430, 454
Finnvera (Finland), 65
Fisher, Steven A.: chapter by, 4, 43–78
Flikke, Geir, 176, 184nn11–12
Floyd, George, 291
"Foreign Agents" Law (121-FZ), 308, 314, 355–58, 372n5; individuals declared foreign agents, 356–57
foreign direct investment (FDI), 3–4, 43–56, 71–72, 447; from China, 76n39; cumulative inflow, 45–46; in early twentieth century, 45; effect of sanctions on, 238; endogenous and exogenous factors affecting, 49; geography of, 51; global FDI flows, 55; innovation and, 56–57; inward FDI stock and, 53–54; oil prices and, 50–51; as percentage of GDP, 54; in technology enterprises, 238; unsustainability of, 45, 49–53

Foreign Intelligence Service (SVR), 329–31, 337, 341–42, 368, 382; tenure of leaders, 331. *See also* siloviki
foreign policy of Russia. *See* Russia, foreign policy of
Frolov, Saveliy, 359–60

Gaddafi, Muammar, 415
Gaddy, Clifford, 335, 337
Gagarin, Yuri, 221
Gaidar, Yegor, 150–51
Galeotti, Mark, 343
Ganev, Venelin, 336
Gazprom, 26, 58, 60–61, 73, 80–83, 84, 92, 227, 422, 448; EU and, 86–88; Germany and, 455; LNG sector and, 90; on MOEX, 66; shale oil and, 90
Gazprombank, 68
gender issues in Russia. *See* Russia, gender issues in
Georgia, 10, 93, 205, 209, 315, 384, 453; 2008 Russian war with, 29, 318, 427; NATO and, 412–13; trade with, 113, 118
Gerasimov, Valery, 330, 341, 344, 386, 432
Germany, 105, 224, 233; Russian gas exports to, 82, 84–87, 421–22, 455
Giddens, Anthony, 395
Girkin, Igor, 432
Global Environmental Performance Index (EPI), 16, 18n18
Global financial crisis of 2007–2008, 27–29, 34, 51, 53, 70–71, 428, 445; FDI and, 44
GLONASS system, 239
Goldschmidt, Pinchas, 12
Golts, Aleksandr: chapter by, 9–10, 377–403

Gorbachev, Mikhail, 106, 133n15, 153, 193, 219, 226, 260n220, 412
Gorbunov, Gennady, 118
Gordeev, Aleksei, 117–19, 137n49
Gorodnichenko, Yuriy, 37
Great Patriotic War, 155–56
Greece, 93
Greene, Samuel, 172
Gref, Herman, 25
Grigas, Agnia: chapter by, 4, 79–101
Gudkov, Lev, 146
Gulevich, Olga, 155
Guriev, Sergei, 25, 30; chapter by, 3–4, 23–41

Hamas, 434, 456
Hayat, Arshad, 50
health outcomes in Russia. *See* Russia, health outcomes in
Henry, Laura A., 172, 173, 176
Hill, Fiona, 335
HIV/AIDS, 13, 204, 212
homelessness, 14
Hosking, Geoffrey, 150
human capital, Russian. *See* Russia, human capital of
Hussein, Saddam, 397n5, 458
hyperweapons, 225, 229, 232, 240

Iarovaia, Irina, 252n32
Ickes, Barry, 337
identity. *See* national identity, Russian
Ilyin, Ivan, 425
immigration to Russia, 195–97, 202, 204–11, 253n84, 288–89, 449, 454; agriculture and, 242; effect of sanctions, 205; from former Soviet republics, 279–80, 288–89; immigration laws, 207–08, 288–89; naturalization policies, 7, 288; Ukraine war and, 205–07

import substitution, 7; in agriculture, 103, 114; in science/technology sector, 229–33, 235, 239–41, 430
income inequality, 14–15
India, 50, 53, 55, 56, 63–64, 72, 74, 207; Russian energy exports to, 80, 93, 95; share of world GDP, 33–34
Indonesia, 456
information technology (IT) sector, 238–39
Inozemtsev, Vladislav, 57
International Finance Corporation (IFC), 65
International Monetary Fund (IMF), 14, 36, 419, 447
international syndicated loans, 61
internet, laws regulating, 366–367
Investigative Committee: tenure of leaders, 331
Iran, 10, 38, 222–23, 414, 428, 434, 446, 457; Ukraine war and, 431
Iraq, 316, 378, 397n5, 410, 414, 458
Irisova, Olga, 171
Israel, 205, 431, 456
Italy, 82, 93, 233
Ivan III, 426
Ivanov, Sergei, 339, 341, 409

Japan, 89, 93, 199, 456; Russo-Japanese war, 451, 454
Jewish population of Russia, 11, 12; birth rates and, 202
Johnson, Janet Elise: chapter by, 8, 299–324

Kadyrov, Ramzan, 309
Kanev, Sergei, 337–38
Kara-Murza, Vladimir, 359, 370
Kartapolov, Andrey, 391
Kazakhstan, 25, 27, 80, 82, 92, 113, 205–07, 209, 210, 315–16, 426
Kent, Thomas, 459n11

KGB, 228, 337–38; Putin in, 329–30, 333, 406–07, 434. *See also* Federal Guards Service (FSO)
Khodorkovsky, Mikhail, 26, 336, 364
Kilimnik, Konstantin, 422
Kim family (N. Korea), 458
Kirienko, Sergei, 243
kleptocracy, 9, 328, 336–39, 341, 359
Kneissl, Karin, 88
Kolesnikov, Andrei, 341
Kolker, Dmitry, 225
Kolomytsyn, Anton, 361–62
Kondratev, Nikolai, 105
Konfisakhor, Aleksandr, 178
Kosovo, 315, 407
Kovalchuk, Yuri, 423
Kozyrev, Andrei, 152
Kravtsov, Sergei, 215
Kryshtanovskaya, Ol'ga, 329, 331–32, 335
Kudrin, Alexei, 29, 340, 454
KUKE (Poland), 65
Kulik, Gennady, 133n15
Kursk submarine disaster, 251n11, 408
Kushtau mountain, 171–72, 174, 176, 181, 184n15
Kyrgyzstan, 205, 206, 209, 315

Lakhman, Olga, 370–71
land reform, 25, 108
language reform, 282–83
Lankina, Tomila, 175
Laos, 315
Laruelle, Marlène, 289
Lastochkin, Yuri, 227–28, 258n170
Latvia, 87, 315
Latypova, Leyla, 181
Lavrov, Sergei, 12, 342, 347n35, 411, 425
Law on Extremism (114-FZ), 354–55, 372n2
Law on "Undesirable Organizations" (129-FZ), 363–65

leasing, 232–33
legal code of Russia. *See* Russia, legal code of
Lenin, Vladimir, 151, 327, 334
LGBTQ issues in Russia. *See* Russia, LGBTQ issues in
Liberal Democratic Party (LDPR), 147
Libya, 415–16, 428
life expectancy in Russia, 196–97, 202–04, 211, 213, 241, 246
liquefied natural gas (LNG) industry, 80, 85–90, 94; attempts to increase production, 83, 89–90
Lithuania, 87
livestock production, Russian, 111–12, 130–31
"localizing" of foreign firms, 233
Luhansk, 380, 417, 421, 424
Lut, Oksana, 117, 136n42
Luxembourg, 52
L'vova, Elizaveta, 200
Lysenko, Trofim, 105, 110, 132n6

Macron, Emmanuel, 420, 423
Macrotrends, 196, 244, 246
Magnitsky, Sergei, 259n184
Maidan Revolution of Dignity, 416–17
Makarov, Nikolai, 384
Mäkinen, Sirke, 219, 256n134
Malakhov, Vladimir, 288
Malaysia, 89, 315
Mali, 428
Malinova, Olga, 156
Malofeyev, Konstantin, 318
Manafort, Paul, 422
Mariupol, siege of, 379
Martus, Ellie, 175
Maslov, Anatoly, 225
maternity capital program, 8, 197–99, 202, 299, 307, 310, 320n38, 449
Matveev, Mikhail, 206
MBK Media, 364

"McDonaldization," 116
McGlynn, Jade, 146–47
McKay, John P., 43
media organizations: silencing of, 355–56
Meduza, 178, 356, 365
Medvedchuk, Viktor, 420
Medvedev, Dmitry, 57, 80–81, 156, 229, 330, 347n35, 366, 413–14; Arab Spring and, 415; Putin and, 415, 436n32
Mexico, 53, 55
middle-income trap, 34–35
Mileva, Elitza, 44–45
militarism, 302, 394–97, 399n49, 455
military, Russia. *See* Russian military
Miller, Alexi, 61, 73, 80
minimum tillage, 109–10, 121
Ministry of Defense, 329, 330, 368, 383, 386–88, 390, 391, 394; tenure of leaders, 331. *See also* siloviki
Ministry of Emergency Situations (MChS), 330; tenure of leaders, 331. *See also* siloviki
Ministry of Internal Affairs (MVD), 330–31; expansion of MVD Powers Law (424-FZ), 369; tenure of leaders, 331. *See also* siloviki
Miratorg, 116
Mirzalizade, Idrak, 292
Mizintsev, Mikhail, 386
MOEX Russia Index, 62, 64, 66–67
Moldova, 82, 113, 118, 161n53, 205, 288, 315, 361
Morozov, Pavel (Pavlik), 216, 255n114, 432
mortality rates of Russia, 195–97, 202–03, 211, 213, 241; COVID-19 pandemic and, 203–04
Moscow: apartment building bombings in, 408–09, 411, 435n9; protests in, 170, 183n4

Moskalyov, Alexei, 370
Mugabe, Robert, 458
multiculturalism, 7, 277, 283–86; failed, 7
Muslim population of Russia, 11, 13, 202, 279, 289–90; Chechen war and, 408; demographic trends in, 202, 279; violence against, 290
Mustard, Allan: chapter by, 5, 103–140
Myhre, Marthe, 288

Nabiullina, Elvira, 279–280, 340, 446
Nadezhdin, Boris, 181
Nagorno-Karabakh, 456
Naryshkin, Sergei, 333–34, 338, 342, 382
National Endowment for Democracy, 363
National Guard, 330. *See also* siloviki
national identity, Russian. *See* Russian national identity
naturalization policies, 7, 288
natural resources curse, 4–5, 44, 50–51, 73, 75n10, 97–98
Navalny, Alexei, 171, 173, 179, 355, 364; anticorruption efforts of, 337, 339
Nefedova, Tatiana, 107, 111
Nemtsov, Boris, 171
Nepal, 207
Netesova, Yulia, 175
New Economic Policy (NEP), 25, 28
Nicholas II, 451
Niger, 428
Nikonov, Aleksandr, 120
nongovernmental agencies (NGOs): Foreign Agents Law and, 185n25, 211–12, 314, 355–58; as "undesirable organizations," 363–65, 373n30

Nord Stream 2 pipeline, 81, 84–88, 422
Nord Stream pipeline, 82, 237
Norilsk Nickel, 58, 66
North Atlantic Treaty Organization (NATO), 378, 411–14, 454, 459n11; in Central Asia, 409, 427; Finland and Sweden and, 378, 430, 454; in former Yugoslavia, 407; Putin and, 433–34; Trump and, 422; Ukraine and, 412–13, 417, 420, 427–28, 431; Ukraine war and, 10, 424–25, 430, 435
Northern Distribution Network (NDN), 414
North Korea, 222, 431, 434, 446–47, 457–58; emigration from, 205; Russian military and, 38
Norway, 51, 82, 88
Novatek, 66, 89, 90
Novorossiya, 421, 426

Obama, Barack, 414, 416
OEKB (Austria), 65
OFZ market, 70–71
oil industry, Russian. *See* Russian oil industry
Open Media, 364
Open Russia, 364
Open Society Foundation, 363
Orange Revolution (Ukrainian), 411–12
Orbán, Viktor, 88, 422
Organization for Security and Cooperation in Europe (OSCE), 407, 412
Orthodox Church (Russian), 11–12, 299–300, 308, 314
Orthodox Church (Ukrainian), 12–13
Osin, Evgeny, 155
Ostpolitik, 87
Otkritie FC, 68

Pankov, Nikolay, 386
parallel imports, 229, 232–33, 236
patent issuance, 57–58, 224
Patrushev, Dmitrii, 117
Patrushev, Nikolai, 117, 228, 330–31, 333–34, 338–42, 435n9; Ukraine war and, 341–42
Pavlov, Ivan: chapter by, 9, 353–76
Petrov, Nikolai, 182
Pivovarov, Andrei, 364
Poland, 85, 87, 315
Ponomarev, Lev, 359
Ponomareva, Ekaterina, 243
population of Russia, 194–202; decline in, 196–97; historical data, 244; immigration/emigration, 204–08; population pyramids, 200–201
Poroshenko, Petro, 420
Poupin, Perrine, 176
power ministries. *See* siloviki
Power of Siberia pipeline, 94
Pravozaschita Otkrytki, 364
Presidential Decree No. 273, 365–66
Prigozhin, Yevgeny, 38, 330, 343–44, 386–87, 453; 2023 mutiny by, 329–30, 343, 345, 386–87, 431–32, 434, 438n81, 451; Ukraine war and, 212, 386. *See also* Wagner group
Primakov, Yevgeny, 408
"Professional Secrets" Law (279-FZ), 367–69
Promsvyazbank, 68
protests in Russia. *See* Russia, protests in
Put' Domoi (The Way Home) movement, 180, 309
Putin, Vladimir Vladimirovich, 1, 329, 406, 433–35, 457–59; approval rating, 26, 27, 30; China and, 234; consolidation of power, 2, 7, 26–27, 281–82, 396, 432, 434; corruption and, 337, 212n90, 258n159; demographics of Russia and, 193–95, 197, 251n3; education system and, 220–21; energy industry and, 227–28; fixation on legacy, 421–23; foreign policy to 2021, 427–29; foreign policy since 2022, 430–32, 459n11; foreign policy views of, 406–08, 433; Great Patriotic War and, 155–56; KGB and, 329–30, 333, 406–07, 434; kleptocracy and, 337; Medvedev and, 415, 436n32; NATO expansion and, 411–13, 425; political ideology of, 31, 35; Prigozhin/Wagner mutiny and, 344, 432, 434, 438n81; protests against, 173; "Putinomics," 23, 29, 31–36, 38–39, 138–39; regime change and, 457–58; relationship with U.S. presidents, 408–10, 421–22; response to protests, 172–73, 175, 181–82; Russian energy sector and, 80–81, 88; Russian history and, 425–27, 433; Russian identity and, 144–45, 153–56, 158; Russian legal system and, 353–54, 371; Russian military and, 383–84, 388; self-enrichment of, 339; siloviki and, 329–31, 340, 344–46; Ukraine war and, 144, 341–42, 419, 425, 427, 432; U.S. elections and, 421–22; views on gender and sexuality, 303, 311, 317; wars initiated by, 159n6; Yeltsin and, 329, 345, 406; Zelensky and, 420. *See also* Putinism; "Putinomics"
Putinism: Chekists and, 334; kleptocracy and, 336–37, 341; siloviki and, 332, 334, 340, 345
"Putinomics," 3–4, 29, 31–36, 38–39, 446; pockets of efficiency and, 35–36, 45, 75n5; Ukraine war and, 36–37

Qatar, 88–90, 94–95

racism in Russia, 7, 147, 227, 287, 288, 290–92, 299
Rákosi, Mátyás, 17n1
regional income disparities, 14–16, 447
religion in Russia, 11–13, 455; birth rates and, 202
rent-seeking, 4, 44, 49, 50, 97, 117–19, 446, 454; "rent management system," 337
Renz, Bettina, 332
Renzi, Matteo, 88
Rice, Condoleezza, 412
Ries, Nancy, 149
Rivera, David, 332
Rivera, Sharon Werning, 332
Roberts, Pat, 112
Robertson, Graeme, 170, 172, 183n4, 184n8
Rogov, Kirill, 339
Romania, 226
Rosatom, 90
Rosbank, 68
Rosgvardiya, 330, 334, 344, 379; tenure of leaders, 331
Rosimushchestvo, 73
Rosneft, 26, 45, 73, 81–82, 86, 90, 91, 186, 448; equipment shortages and, 91; LNG sector and, 90; siloviki and, 333; Sino-Russian energy cooperation and, 94–95; and Yukos, 336
Rosselkhozbank, 68
Rosselkhoznadzor, 119
Rostec: siloviki and, 333
Rotenberg, Arkady, 61
ruble finance market, 65
Russia, agriculture in, 5, 103–40, 448, 455; agricultural policies, 117–20; area planted to selected crops, 126–27; attempted renationalization of, 137n49, 137n56; combines and tractors, 105, 110–11, 134nn25–26;
corporate consolidation of, 108–09, 133n21; corruption and, 113, 118–19, 121, 136n44; crop yields, 122–23; decollectivization of, 107–08, 114–17, 121; demand conditions, 112–14; economic impact of, 120; effect of sanctions, 5, 103, 114, 118, 120, 213–14, 448; fertilizer application, 109, 128–29, 137n55; "food sovereignty" and, 113, 119–20; gross production of selected crops, 124–25; immigration and, 242, 448; livestock production, 107, 111–14, 115–16, 128–29, 130–31, 134nn27–30, 135n40; milk production, 111–12, 114, 130–31, 132n8, 135n31, 135n40; oilseed production, 134n23; plant genetics, 110–11; in post-Soviet era, 107–12; Russian economy and, 104, 114, 120, 137n54; scientific research and, 120; in Soviet era, 104–07, 132n6, 135nn31–32; success of, 103–04, 121; Ukraine war and, 120–21; wheat exports, 109–10; workers in, 108–09, 133n21, 178
Russia, demographics of, 6, 178, 195–211, 244–46; birth rates, 194–200, 202, 10–211, 245, 251n8; demographic policies, 195, 197, 200–202, 251n3; deportation of foreign nationals, 208; emigration from Russia, 37, 74, 195–96, 202, 204–05, 208, 210–11, 218, 449; ethnic diversity, 278; immigration to Russia, 195–97, 202, 204–11, 253n84, 288–89, 449, 454; life expectancy, 196–97, 202–04, 211, 213, 241, 246; mortality rates, 195–97, 202–03, 211, 213, 241; of Muslim population, 279, 289–90; population of Russia, 194–202,

244; population pyramids, 200–201; Ukraine war and, 194, 199–200, 202–07, 209–11, 319, 430
Russia, economy of, 38–39, 71–74, 446; 2007–2008 global financial crisis and, 28–29, 34, 44–45, 51, 53, 71, 428; agricultural sector of, 104, 114, 120, 137n54; banking system, 65, 68–71, 74; capital flight and, 4, 44, 52, 57, 73; comparative competitiveness of, 49–50, 68–69; corporate raiding and, 335–36; defense spending and, 213, 412, 446, 452–53; in early twenty-first century, 24–26; economic development indicators, 56; effects of global sanctions, 31, 36, 38, 51, 62, 69, 144, 235, 428–29, 447, 452; energy policy and, 79–98, 227, 228; energy/resource rents, 228, 454; entrepreneurship and, 51–52; equity market and, 62–65; Eurobond issuance/activity and, 59–61; FDI flows (*see* foreign direct investment [FDI]); financial indicators 2000–2024, 47–48; foreign direct investment (FDI), 43–56, 71–72; foreign investment, 26; GNP per capita, 97, 212; growth rate of, 29–30, 72, 209, 243; human capital and, 33, 242–43; import/export data, 250; imports of technology, 228–33, 234–35, 238–39, 242, 250; innovation and, 56–57, 64; international financial institutions and, 447; inward FDI stock and, 53–54; IT sector, 238–39; LNG exports and, 88–90; "localizing" of foreign firms, 233; market capitalization of Russian business, 63–64, 66–67, 73; militarization of, 393–94, 446; "mobilization" economy, 394, 450, 452; nationalization of businesses, 26–27; natural resources curse and, 50–51, 73, 97–98, 446; nontariff barriers and, 52–53; OFZ market, 70–71; pockets of efficiency in, 35–36; "Putinomics" and, 3–4, 31–35; ruble market and, 65, 70; Russian borrowing, 57–62; Russian GDP, 23–25, 29–30, 35, 37, 54; GNP, 212, 213, 216, 242; Russian share of world GDP, 33–34; Russian stock market, 26; siloviki and, 333, 335–336; sovereign debt ratings and, 58, 61–62; Ukraine war and, 31, 36–38, 74, 98, 213, 242–43, 394, 434, 450, 452, 454

Russia, education in, 6–7, 214–21, 241; COVID-19 pandemic and, 218; educational policies, 220–21; ethical problems, 218–19; ethnic diversity and, 284; funding of, 216–17, 223; higher education institutions, 214–17, 248–49, 255n122; higher education rates, 214, 216, 247; science/technology, 221–23; during Soviet era, 216, 220, 255n117, 255n119; technical training, 215, 220; Ukraine war and, 7, 219–20

Russia, energy sector of, 4, 79–98, 447–48; Chinese-Russian energy cooperation, 80, 92–96, 235, 237, 418; decline of, 82–83, 88, 91–92, 96–98; effect of sanctions, 38, 74, 80, 83, 86, 88–90, 93, 95–99, 227, 237, 260n215; energy rents, 228, 454; exports to European markets, 82, 84–88, 92, 421–22, 455–56; exports to non-NATO countries,

82–83, 88–89, 92–96, 418, 456; foreign relations and, 81, 448; LNG and, 80, 85–90; nationalization and, 92, 227; Russian foreign policy and, 84–85, 88, 92; Russian isolation and, 91–93, 97; Russian-Saudi relations and, 419; sanctions against Russia and, 237, 260n215; shale revolution and, 90–91; size of energy reserves, 81–82; state domination of, 97–98; Ukrainian war and, 98

Russia, ethnicity in, 146–47, 277–93; accommodationist strategies, 280–81; assimilationist policies and, 278, 281, 283–84; demographics of, 278; ethnically labeled activities, 286; failed multiculturalism, 7, 277, 283–86; language reform and, 282–83, 285; media narratives about, 278–79, 287; Muslim population and, 279, 289–90; politicization of, 285–86; in popular culture, 291–92; racism and, 7, 147, 287, 288, 290–92, 299; Russian national identity and, 284–85; Russian policies on, 278, 280–81, 283–84; separatist movements, 282; Soviet approaches to, 279–80, 83, 287; Ukraine war and, 286

Russia, foreign policy of, 10, 405–35, 453–54, 459n11; Africa and, 428–34; after 2022, 430–32, 446; Arab Spring and, 415–16; assessing success of, 433–35; China and, 430–31; energy sector and, 84–85, 88, 92; following Ukraine invasion, 430–32; Israel-Hamas conflict and, 456; NATO expansion and, 411–14; prior to Ukraine invasion, 427–29, 453; Putin's views on, 406–08; Russian-Saudi relations, 419; Syria and, 418, 427–28, 453, 459n11; Ukraine war (*see* Ukraine, Russian war with); U.S.-Russia relations, 410–11, 414, 421–23

Russia, gender issues in, 8, 14, 299–300, 302–11, 315–19, 449; contrasted with other nations, 315–16; contrasted with Soviet Union, 302–08; foreign policy and, 318; gender contrasted with sexuality, 300–301; international women's rights and, 302; maternity capital program, 8, 197–99, 202, 299, 307, 310, 320n38, 449; maternity care, 198, 304, 307, 309–10; political participation of women, 302, 304, 308–10, 315–16; political repression of women, 299–300, 308–10; pro-natal policies, 198–99, 251n18, 299; Putin's views on, 317–18; reproductive rights, 304, 307; Ukraine war and, 318; violence against women, 303–04, 306, 309, 315, 318; women's rights issues, 8, 304–10

Russia, health outcomes in, 211–14; birth control and, 200–201; COVID-19 pandemic and, 197, 199, 203–04, 213; disabled/handicapped population, 204, 448; life expectancy, 196–97, 202–04, 211, 213, 241, 246; Russian vaccines, 177–79, 186n54, 213, 254n97; sanctions and, 211; Ukraine war and, 211, 213

Russia, human capital of, 6, 193–250, 449; brain drain, 208–11; demographics, 195–211, 244–46; education, 214–21, 247–49; effect of sanctions, 211; health outcomes, 211–14; immigration and emigration, 204–08; population of Russia, 194–202; Russian economy and, 242–43; science and technology, 221–42, 249–50; Ukraine war and, 242–43, 430

Russia, legal code of, 9, 354–71; Code of Criminal Procedure, 353–54; corruption and, 450; "Discrediting" the Armed Forces ("fake news") Law, 369–71; Expansion of MVD Powers Law (424-FZ), 369; "Foreign Agents" Law (121-FZ), 355–58; internet and, 366–67; Law on Extremism (114-FZ), 354–55; Presidential Decree No. 273, 365–66; "Professional Secrets" Law (279-FZ), 367–69; special operations and, 365; state secrets and, 361–63, 365–66; Treason, Espionage, and State Secrets Law (190-FZ), 358–63; "Work Secrets" Law (172-FZ), 368–69

Russia, LGBTQ issues in, 8, 300–302, 311–19, 449; contrasted with other nations, 316; family law and, 311–13; Foreign Agents Law and, 356; foreign policy and, 318; "gay propaganda" ban, 8, 300, 312–14, 316, 319; gender contrasted with sexuality, 300–301; medical rights and, 312–13; political participation and, 312, 314; Putin's views on, 317–18; same-sex marriage, 316; trans rights and, 312, 314; violence/discrimination against LGBTQ people, 300, 311–15, 318–19; workplace laws and, 312

Russia, military of, 9–10, 382–94, 397, 429; 2014 war with Ukraine (*see* Ukraine, Russian invasion of (2014)); 2022 invasion of Ukraine (*see* Ukraine, Russian war with (2022–present)); annexation of Crimea and, 427; Chechnya and, 408–09; command-and-control system, 385; conscription into, 13–14, 195, 205, 280, 382–84, 390–91, 396, 399n47; culture of, 387–88; defense spending, 213, 412, 446, 452–53; education of, 388–89; effect of sanctions, 38; intervention in Syria, 10, 159n6, 301, 319, 366, 385, 418, 427–29, 453; mass mobilization and, 389–91, 396; militarization of economy, 393–94, 446; military spending, 38, 98; private military companies and, 385–86; Russia as militarist state, 394–97, 399n49, 455; size of, 378, 390, 424; Syria and, 385, 418; use of convicts as soldiers, 212, 225, 254n94, 379, 387; volunteer mobilization and, 391–92; Wagner group and, 386–387; weaponry and equipment, 22, 383, 392–94, 422, 429, 450

Russia, national identity of, 5–6, 143–59, 449; Baltic states and, 149–150; belief in Russian exceptionalism, 144, 146, 148–49, 154, 157; elite continuity and, 151–52; ethnic diversity and, 284–85; inferiority complex and, 154–55; in post-Soviet period, 144–45, 147–48, 149–52, 156, 158–59; Putin and, 153–56, 158; role of war in, 155–58; Russia as great power, 5, 8, 145–48, 154–57, 193, 327–28, 406; Russian nationalism, 455; during Soviet era, 143–50; statism and, 154; Ukraine war and, 5, 144–45, 157–58

Russia, oil industry in, 4, 16, 25–26, 39n17, 81–82, 447–48; effect of falling prices, 95–96, 455; FDI and, 4, 50–51; global sanctions and, 38; human capital and, 194; oil exports, 82, 95–97; as percentage of federal budget, 74n1, 96, 412, 447–48; "Putinomics" and, 31–32; sanctions against Russia and, 237; shale oil and, 90–91; technology of, 228–29. *See also* energy sector, Russian

Russia, protests in, 6, 169–83, 449; antiregime protests, 173, 175, 182; communication technology and, 176–77, 185nn46–47, 186n48; COVID-19 pandemic and, 177–79, 182, 186n54, 186n59; criminalization of, 358–63; demands of protesters, 170–74; demographic composition of protesters, 173–74, 178–79; against electoral fraud, 169–71, 179, 183n4, 415–16; emigration as protest, 179–80, 187n69; environmental issues and, 171–72, 176, 184n11, 184n15; geographic location of, 170, 178, 183n4; involving local issues, 172, 181–82; Law on Extremism and, 354–55; NGOs and, 185n25; official responses to, 182–83, 184n16, 185n24; opportunity structure for, 174–79, 185n35; policy-focused protests, 187n87; repression following, 170, 174–76, 179, 186n62, 359; successful protest movements, 171–72, 177; Ukraine war and, 6, 171, 179–81, 182–83, 187n79

Russia, sanctions against, 38, 96–98, 194, 232, 235–38, 338, 446–47; China and, 234–235; countersanctions, 211, 214, 237, 446, 459n1; effect on agriculture, 5, 103, 114, 118, 120, 211, 214–15, 448; effect on energy industry, 38, 74, 80, 83, 86, 88–90, 93, 95–99, 227, 237, 260n215; effect on military, 38; effect on Russian economy, 31, 36, 51, 62, 69, 144, 235, 428–29, 447, 452; effect on science and technology, 52, 203, 217, 230–40; following Crimea annexation, 338, 363, 418, 427–28; "localization" of businesses, 233; parallel imports and, 229, 232–33, 236; Ukraine wars and, 4, 83, 96–97, 259n184, 428–29, 450

Russia, science and technology in, 221–41, 449; Chinese investment in, 234–35; collaborative research, 224, 235, 256n134, 258n155; corruption in, 225–26, 239–41, 258n159; effect of sanctions, 52, 203, 217, 230–40; funding of, 223, 226; imports of technology, 228–33, 238–39, 242, 250; industrial policy, 232–33; IT sector, 238–239; military technology, 232–33, 238–40, 260n220; patents and, 224; repression of scientists, 224–25; research in, 222–23; scientific publications, 224, 257n147; during Soviet era, 221–22; technological retrogression and, 226–34

"Russia at the Turn of the Millennium" (Putin, 1999), 406

Russian Academy of Agricultural Sciences (RAAS), 120

Russian Energy Strategy for the Period up to 2035 document, 80, 95

Russian Railways, 333

Rutland, Peter, 291

Rybinsk aircraft engine plant, 227–28

Ryzhanov, Viktor, 361–62

Saakashvili, Mikheil, 412
Sadovnichii, Viktor, 230
Safire, William, 332
Safronov, Ivan, 359, 362
Sahadeo, Jeff, 288, 290
Sakhalin-1 and Sakhalin-2 projects, 45, 89, 90
Sakha Republic, 281, 283
Sakharov, Andrei, 222
"salami tactics," 3, 17n1, 223
sanctions against Russia. *See* Russia, sanctions against
Sangin, Manizha, 291–92
Sarmat hypersonic missile, 240
Saudi Arabia, 82, 315, 419, 427
Sberbank, 36, 65, 68, 316
"Scenario 70–80," 30, 66, 71
Scholz, Olaf, 87
Schröder, Gerhard, 86, 88, 422, 455
Schroeder, Gertrude E., 452
science and technology. *See* Russia, science and technology in
Sechin, Igor, 336, 340
separatist movements, 7, 282–83, 413; in Chechnya, 408–11; Ukraine and, 341, 424
September 11 terrorist attacks, 409–11
Serbia, 63, 86, 210, 407
Serdyukov, Anatoly, 9, 384–85, 388–89, 394
Shakhrai, Sergei, 152
shale oil revolution, 4, 81, 83–85, 90–91
Sharafutdinova, Gulnaz, 150, 153, 281–82
Shoigu, Sergei, 280, 330–31, 338, 384, 386, 388–91, 432; mass mobilization and, 390; Ukraine war and, 341, 344, 378
silovarch, 333

siloviki, Russian, 3, 8–9, 327–45, 455–56; Chekism and, 333–34, 339; conflict among, 339–41; corruption and, 334, 336–38, 340, 343, 345; defined, 327, 329–30; hawkishness of, 333; kleptocratic elements of, 336–39; militocracy and, 332; police state and, 334–35; Russian economy and, 333, 335–36; successes of, 328; tenure of leaders, 330–31; Ukraine war and, 341–45, 455–56; use of power by, 334–36
Simis, Konstantin, 452
Simola, Heli, 37
Skolkovo Innovation Center, 57, 229–30
Skrynnik, Elena, 117
Smith, Kathleen, 151
Snegovaya, Maria: chapter by, 5–6, 143–67
Sobchak, Anatoly, 161n60, 406
social media, 13; protest movements and, 176, 177, 185n47, 186n48, 309, 312
Solzhenitsyn, Aleksandr, 258n156, 425–27
Soros, George, 363
Southern Gas Corridor project, 93
South Korea, 33–35, 89, 93, 446
South Ossetia, 412–13
Sovcombank, 68
"sovereign democracy" program, 2, 194
Sovereign Internet Law, 366
Soviet nationalities policy, 7, 17n2, 277, 279–80, 283, 290, 292
Soviet Union, 458; agricultural legacy of, 104–07, 132n4, 132n6, 135nn31–32; economy of, 25, 30, 452, 454; educational approaches, 216, 220, 255n117, 255n119; ethnicity in, 146–47, 279–80, 283, 287, 293; gender policies in,

302–08; influence of on post-Soviet Russia, 150–53, 161n53; military of, 392–93, 396; military sector of, 39, 238; national identity and, 143–50; origin of, 451–52; racism in, 291; repression of LGBTQ population, 311; science and technology in, 221–22, 225–26, 238; Soviet nationalities policy, 7, 17n2, 277, 279–80, 283, 290, 292
"special operations" and Presidential Decree No. 273, 365–66
Sperling, Valerie, 172, 176
"spin dictatorship," 31, 35, 36
Stalin, Joseph, 25, 153, 221–22, 225, 311, 434, 452. *See also* Soviet Union
Starovoitova, Galina, 150–51
state secrets, 361–63, 365–66. *See also* Treason, Espionage, and State Secrets Law (190-FZ)
statism, 154
Stoner, Kathryn, 345
Strategic Offensive Reductions Treaty (SORT), 410
Stroygazmontazh, 61
Sudan, 428
Sullivan, Jake, 381
Sundstrom, Lisa McIntosh, 172, 176
Surovikin, Sergei, 386–87
Suslov, Mikhail, 152
Sweden, 199, 233; NATO and, 10, 378, 430, 454
Switzerland, 233
Syria, 416, 431, 459n11; Russian intervention in, 10, 159n6, 243, 301, 319, 359, 366, 385, 418, 427–29, 453; Wagner Group and, 438n81

Taiwan, 93
Tajikistan, 205
Tarnavsky, Alexander, 365

tax reform, 25, 282
Taylor, Brian D.: chapter by, 8–9, 327–52
technology. *See* Russia, science and technology in
Tertytchnaya, Katerina, 175, 179, 181
Thailand, 210, 456
Tikhonov, Vladimir, 106
Timchenko, Gennady, 338
Tkachev, Aleksandr, 136n42
Topol, Sarah, 207
Toth-Czifra, Andras, 172
transgender issues in Russia. *See* LGBTQ issues in Russia
Transneft, 67, 81, 94; siloviki and, 333
Trapeznikov, Sergei, 222
Treason, Espionage, and State Secrets Law (190-FZ), 358–63
treason, laws against, 358–60
Treisman, Daniel, 26, 333
Trubnikov, Dmitrii, 219
Trubnikova, Ekaterina, 219
Trump, Donald, 318, 342, 21; foreign policy of, 420–21; Putin and, 421–22; Ukraine war and, 434
Tsurkan, Karina, 360–61
Tsyvinski, Aleh, 25, 30
Turkey, 26, 85, 93, 234, 316, 418, 456
Turkmenistan, 92, 94, 316
TurkStream pipeline, 85–86, 93

UEC Saturn, 227–28
Uganda, 315, 316
Ukraine, 416–17, 431–32; Communist Party in, 161n53; emigration from, 205, 288; energy exports to, 85; gender legislation in, 315; Maidan Revolution in, 417; NATO and, 412–413, 420; Novorossiya region of, 421, 426; Orange Revolution in, 411–12; Solzhenitsyn on, 426–27

Ukraine, Russian invasion of (2014), 31, 39n14, 341, 384–85, 417, 421; changes to Russian legal code and, 356, 362; emigration from Russia and, 210; international sanctions and, 338, 418, 428–29; NATO and, 428, 431, 434; Russian food imports and, 114, 118; Russian national identity and, 157, 421; Ukrainian resistance to, 424. *See also* Crimea

Ukraine, Russian war with (2022–present), 39n14, 241, 243, 341–45, 377–82, 397, 424, 429, 431–32, 450–53; convicts as soldiers in, 212, 225, 254n94, 379, 387, 453; decolonization and, 286–87; "Discrediting" the Armed Forces Law and, 369–71; impact on sexuality and gender issues, 301–03, 317–19; environmental crimes, 16; ethnic divisions and, 279, 87; factors leading to, 419–25; faulty intelligence and, 423–24; foreign policy implications of, 430–32; global food supply and, 457; hiring of mercenaries, 195, 207, 243; import substitution and, 233; international sanctions against Russia and, 4, 83, 96–97, 259n184, 428–29, 450; Kursk incursion and, 449, 451; LNG exports and, 85–86, 90; mass mobilization and, 389–91; military strategies employed, 378–82; NATO and, 10, 378, 424–25, 430, 435; potential end of, 434, 453–54; private military companies and, 385–86; protests against, 171, 179–181, 182–83, 187n79; refugees from Kursk oblast and, 449; religious tensions and, 12–13; Russia as "spoiler," 456; Russian agriculture and, 119, 120–21; Russian casualties, 203, 252n42, 392, 434; Russian demographics and, 194, 199–200, 202–07, 209–11, 241, 319, 430, 451; Russian economy and, 4, 31, 36–38, 74, 98, 213, 242–43, 394, 434, 450, 452, 454; Russian education system and, 219–220; Russian energy industry and, 83; Russian health and, 211, 213; Russian military equipment and, 393; Russian military spending and, 15, 98; Russian national identity and, 144–45, 157–58; Russian Orthodox Church and, 11; Russian support for, 159n2; siloviki and, 341–45; Sino-Russian relations and, 430–31, 454; stated goals of, 377–79, 424–25; threat of nuclear weapons, 381–82; Wagner mutiny and, 343, 431–32, 451; war crimes and, 319, 370; Western support of Ukraine and, 380

underdevelopment, 15

United Arab Emirates, 210, 456

United States: Afghanistan war and, 414; agricultural exports, 110, 112–13, 118, 133n15; Chechnya and, 342, 410–11; collaborative research and, 224; energy exports of, 82–83, 88, 90, 96; Foreign Agents Registration Act (FARA) of, 355–56; gender/sexuality issues in, 318; invasion of Iraq, 397n5, 410; post-Soviet Russia and, 107; Russian election interference, 318, 342, 416, 421; shale oil and, 90–91

U.S. Export-Import Bank, 65

U.S.-Russia relations, 408–12, 414, 416
U.S. Russia Foundation, 363
Ustinov, Vladimir, 336
Utkin, Dmitry, 386
Uzbekistan, 92, 205, 207, 316; Ukraine war and, 206–07

Vagts, Arthur, 395
Vavilov, Nikolai, 105
Velikhov, Yevgeny, 455
Veneman, Ann, 118
Venezuela, 39n17, 458
Verkhovsky, Aleksandr, 354
Vietnam, 205, 446
Vinogradov, Mikhail, 208
Vladimir I, 426
Volkov, Denis, 173, 181, 182
volunteer mobilization, 391–92
Vorobyov, Alexei, 362
VTB bank, 65, 67, 68, 71
Vyatkin, Dmitry, 367–68

Wagner group, 96, 334, 379–80, 386–87; 2023 mutiny by, 329–30, 343–45, 330, 386–87, 431–32, 434, 451; Russian military and, 386–87
Watanbe, Kohei, 175
Witte, Sergei, 45, 454, 457–58
"Work Secrets" Law (172-FZ), 367–69
World Bank, 14, 419, 447
World Trade Organization (WTO), 112, 407, 416

World War II, 203, 225, 458; Russian identity and, 155–56
Wright, Gavin, 50

Xi Jinping, 10, 234, 242, 259n206, 418

Yandex, 35–36, 64, 367
Yanukovych, Viktor, 411–12, 414, 417, 421
Yarovaya Law, 366–67
Yashin, Ilya, 370
Yelets–Kremenchuk–Kryvyi Rih pipeline, 86
Yeltsin, Boris, 150–51, 153, 193, 225, 458; Putin and, 329, 345, 406; siloviki and, 330
youth, Russian, 13–14
Yukos, 3, 26, 97, 227, 336, 448
Yushchenko, Viktor, 412, 414
Yusupova, Guzel: chapter by, 7, 277–98

Zakharov, Nikolay, 291
Zaluzhny, Valery, 381, 387, 392
Zamyatin, Konstantin, 280–82, 284
Zelensky, Volodymyr, 381, 420, 424, 429, 443
Zhirinovsky, Vladimir, 147
Zimbabwe, 458
Zimin, Dmitry, 223
Zingales, Luigi, 32
"Z" movements, 13
Zolotov, Viktor, 334
Zygar, Mikhail, 423–24